AMERICA
AND
FRENCH CULTURE

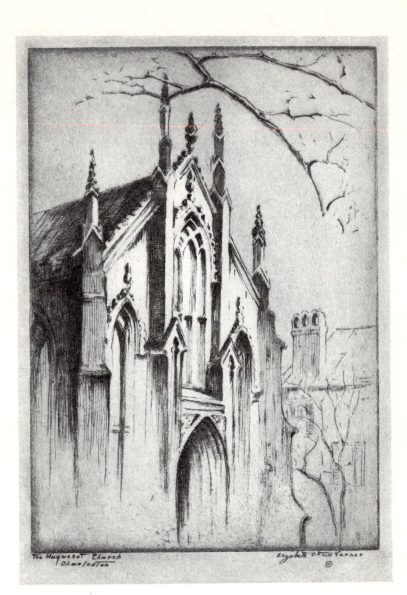

The "Huguenot" Church
Charleston

Elizabeth O'Neill Verner

AMERICA
AND FRENCH CULTURE
1750-1848

By Howard Mumford Jones

Chapel Hill

THE UNIVERSITY OF NORTH CAROLINA PRESS

LONDON: HUMPHREY MILFORD

OXFORD UNIVERSITY PRESS

1927

THE SEEMAN PRESS
DURHAM, N. C.

Printed in the United States of America

REPRINTED AND BOUND BY
NORTH CAROLINA STATE UNIVERSITY PRINT SHOP
RALEIGH, N. C., JULY, 1965—LITHO. USA

TO

GEORGE RALEIGH COFFMAN

Preface

THE PRESENT study is the first of two which I hope to make, the second to be a survey of the American reception of French literature up to 1848. I therefore beg critics of the present book to remember that it is but part of my whole plan. The literary project was my original one, but I found myself unable to estimate the American attitude toward French literature until I had got down to fundamental matters like politics and religion and manners—in short to as many contacts between the two civilizations as I was able to trace with anything like confidence. This volume is therefore but the first half of my task.

The choice of the hundred years from 1750 to 1848 as the central epoch for my purpose is, I think, a sufficiently obvious one. By 1750 the American colonies had passed from infancy into something like maturity; and by 1848 the French influence commenced to wane before the German one.

There are certain grave deficiencies in my book of which no one can be more conscious than I. For one thing I have had to pass over the whole problem of French science in America. I have been unable likewise to do anything satisfactory with Franco-American commerce, a field in which we badly need some detailed studies. Moreover, I have had to generalize in many instances from insufficient data, and I have had to make long, running jumps in various parts of the field—to guess when I wanted to know, and surmise when I would have preferred to prove. But I trust I may have something like the indulgence due to a pioneer volume in the field. It is true that Professor Chinard has been working on Franco-American relations for a number of years—no one can be more grateful for his accomplishments in Jeffersonian problems than I—and Professor Faÿ's brilliant study does for the thirty years it covers something of what I have tried to do for a larger one. And (as the bibliography shows), hundreds of scholars and writers have touched on one aspect or another of the general problem. But no one so far as I know has tried to put the pieces together; that is, no one has tried to see the *general American attitude* toward things French in the hundred years when we were closest to that interesting people. This is what I have tried to do; how imperfectly and, in places, superficially, the reader must judge for himself.

[ix]

However, I shall be satisfied if this book outlines a problem and exemplifies a method. The problem is that of the cultural relationships of the United States with France rather than merely the intellectual contacts of leaders on both sides of the water; and the method is that without which I do not see that the study of comparative literature can succeed. For if comparative literature is, as I think it is, the study of the reception of the ideas propagated by one culture as they are assimilated (or repelled) by another country or culture, I do not see how it is ever to be thorough and true unless it take into account, even inadequately, the sum total of the relationships between two countries, even when these sink to such undignified levels as that of eating and drinking. For it is thus that national attitudes are generated.

The exigencies of academic life in the United States have not permitted me to get at the original material in a great many cases. In the eighteenth century particularly the files of periodicals and magazines are in the East; I, alas! have been a western professor and consequently I have had to rely in this particular on the findings of others. Something of the same is true of letters and correspondence. Library facilities at the University of Texas and the University of North Carolina, though unexpectedly good, have not been inclusive enough for my purposes; nor does the excellent collection of periodicals in the Newberry Library at Chicago contain many eighteenth century publications. But perhaps the deficiencies of my book will be sufficiently obvious without my insisting on them.

I must take this occasion to say an altogether inadequate word of thanks for the help which I have received from many colleagues and friends. Miss Viola Corley, formerly of the University of Texas, kindly placed at my disposal the rich collection of material which she gathered for her master's thesis on the reception of French fiction in America; and when I come to the writing of the second part of this work, a considerable portion of it will be more hers than mine. Professor Frank Graham of the University of North Carolina kindly read the historical portions in manuscript; and Professor Addison Hibbard of the same institution heroically went through the whole manuscript; both have saved me from many errors, and to both gentlemen I am extremely grateful. Professor Vernon Howell of the same university permitted me the use of his interesting library. Professor George Sherburn of the University of Chicago furnished me with lists of books advertised in colonial papers in the British Museum which would not otherwise have been accessible to me. I am indebted to the officials of the Library of Congress, the Avery Library, the Detroit Public Library, and the Library of the University of North Carolina for many courtesies. I owe a debt of gratitude to William Beers of the Howard Memorial Library of New Orleans, the friend of all who are interested in the romantic history of that fascinating city, as well as to Miss Josephine Cerf, in charge of the Schwartz collection when it was in New Orleans. The officials of the Newberry Library were extremely courteous. Professor Yates Snowden of the University of South Carolina showered me with information about the French in that state from an inexhaustible memory. I am indebted to Mary R. Bowman, Bessie J. Zaban, and John Abt of the University of Chicago, and to Miss Clare E. McLure of Chicago, for gathering material for me, as I am to Mr. Leon Radoff of the University of North Carolina. Nor can I close this account without a word of appreciation for the work already done in the field by Professors Faÿ and Chinard, upon whom I have leaned heavily; as well as for the countless studies upon which I have drawn.

Perhaps I should say a word about the index. To list every proper name mentioned in the text would have been both unfeasible and undesirable; I have therefore confined names in the index to three classes; first, important persons and places; second, primary authorities of importance when I have quoted from them; third, a few important secondary authorities, from whom I have quoted. Because of the constant, and, I trust, interesting, documentation in the footnotes, I have usually indexed references both to the text and to the notes. The latter are indicated by "n" after the page number. In preparation of the index I must gratefully acknowledge the patient help of Mr. James Willis Posey of the University of North Carolina.

I can not hope, in handling the thousands of details which go to make up this book, to have escaped error, and I shall be grateful to those who will call my attention to these slips of omission and commission.

The courteous permission of the following authors and publishers to make certain quotations in the following pages from important copyrighted books is gratefully acknowledged as follows:

D. Appleton and Company, New York, publishers of John Bach McMaster's *History of the People of the United States;* Boni and Liveright, publishers of Gustavus Myers' *A History of American Idealism,* and of Lewis Mumford's *Sticks and Stones;* Mr. Philip Alexander Bruce, author of *Social Life of Virginia in the Seventeenth Century;* The Century Company, publishers of Fred Lewis Pattee's *History of American Literature Since 1870;* Dodd, Mead and Company, publishers of James Schouler's *History of the United States,* and of his *Americans of 1776,* and of Woodbridge Riley's *American Philosophy: the Early Schools;* The Harvard University Press, publishers of Kenneth Ballard Murdock's *Increase Mather: the Foremost American Puritan,* and of Wesley Everett Rich's *The History of the United States Post office to the Year 1829;* Henry Holt and Company, publishers of William A. Nitze and E. Preston Dargan's *A History of French Literature,* and of Louis Untermeyer's *New Era in American Poetry;* George W. Jacobs and Company, publishers of Ellis Paxson Oberholtzer's *Jay Cooke: Financier of the Civil War;* Mr. Fiske Kimball, author of *Thomas Jefferson: Architect;* J. B. Lippincott Company, publishers of Anne Hollingsworth Wharton's *Salons Colonial and Republican;* Little, Brown and Company, publishers of Harold D. Eberlein's *The Architecture of Colonial America;* Longmans, Green and Company, publishers of C. H. Lockitt's *The Relations of French and English Society (1763-1793);* The Modern Library, publishers of the Modern Library edition of John Macy's *The Spirit of American Literature;* The Oxford University Press, publishers of William B. Cairns' *History of American Literature;* G. P. Putnam's Sons, publishers of the *Cambridge History of American Literature,* of Meade Minnigerode's *The Fabulous Forties* and of his *Some American Ladies,* and of Samuel H. Wandell and Meade Minnigerode's *Aaron Burr;* Fleming H. Revell Co., publishers of Lucian J. Fosdick's *The French Blood in America;* The Review of Reviews corporation, publishers of the Statesman Edition of the works of Theodore Roosevelt; G. Schirmer, Inc., publishers of Oscar G. Sonneck's *Suum Cuique;* Charles Scribner's Sons, publishers of Henry Adams' *History of the United States (1801-1817),* of George W. Cable's *The Creoles of Louisiana,* of Fiske Kimball's *Domestic Architecture of the American Colonies and of the Early Republic,* and of Barrett Wendell's *A Literary History of America;* The Viking Press,

Inc., publishers of Van Wyck Brooks' *America's Coming of Age,* and Miss Eola Willis, author of *The Charleston Stage in the XVIII Century;* The Yale University Press, publishers of Thomas Goddard Wright's *Literary Culture in Early New England, 1620-1730.*

The permission of the authors of the following books, and of the Columbia University Press, publishers, to make certain quotations is gratefully acknowledged: Elizabeth C. Cook, *Literary Influences in Colonial Newspapers, 1704-1750;* Julia Post Mitchell, *St. Jean de Crèvecoeur;* Ralph Leslie Rusk, *The Literature of the Middle Western Frontier;* Arthur Meier Schlesinger, *The Colonial Merchants and the American Revolution;* Vernon Stauffer, *New England and the Bavarian Illuminati;* Jennette Tandy, *Crackerbox Philosophers in American Humor and Satire;* Alfred H. Upham, *The French Influence on English Literature.*

The quotations from William E. Dodd on pp. 101, 123, 231, 268, 272, 296, 383, 384, 414, and 415 are from *The Cotton Kingdom,* volume 23 of *The Chronicles of America Series,* and are used by permission of the Yale University Press.

The quotations from Amy Lowell's *Tendencies in Modern American Poetry;* Claude Bowers' *Hamilton and Jefferson;* Frederic L. Paxson's *History of the American Frontier, 1763-1893;* and the various volumes of the *American Statesman* Series, are used by permission of, and by special arrangement with, Houghton Mifflin Company.

The quotations from John Spencer Bassett's *A Short History of the United States;* James Bryce's *The American Commonwealth,* second edition, revised; C. E. Merriam's *History of American Political Theories;* A. M. Simons' *Social Forces in American History;* Oscar G. Sonneck's *Miscellaneous Studies in the History of Music;* Henry Osborne Taylor's *Thought and Expression in the Sixteenth Century;* and John Donald Wade's *Augustus Baldwin Longstreet* are used by the kind permission of The MacMillan Company, publishers.

HOWARD MUMFORD JONES.

THE UNIVERSITY OF NORTH CAROLINA,
CHAPEL HILL, NORTH CAROLINA.
September, 1926.

Contents

[xv]

AMERICA
AND
FRENCH CULTURE

I

Introduction

THE PROBLEM OF AMERICAN LITERATURE

In studying the inter-relations of national cultures there are but three methods to employ. One may work from the point of view of the nation which radiates culture, and so interpret any problem of comparative influence in terms of an out-reaching intellectual imperialism.[1] Or one may reverse this attitude, and observing the process as a member of the debtor nation, one may ask why and how the strange flesh of foreign arts and *mores* came to grace the intellectual table of his own nation. In this view a comparative study is a problem in assimilation.[2] Finally, one may choose neutral ground, and either sink such inter-relations into some larger whole, or observe the process as a question of exchange.[3] Any study of the vogue and possible influence of French culture in the United States, if written by an American, must inevitably fall into the second of these categories.

In any event, but particularly in problems of the second order, it is important that the essential inner spirit of the debtor culture shall be thoroughly known. Of course the characteristics of the nation which gives must be grasped with reasonable surety, but it is probably even more important to know the inner life of the culture which receives. In a problem of assimilation the arts and manners of a foreign culture are, from the point of view of the receiving nation, but so many goods in a shop window; the question is not why these particular goods, and no others, are displayed, but why the debtor nation chooses one article from the display and rejects another. Why do particular traits in foreign literatures appeal to a given culture at a given time? How are these strands woven into the warp and woof of

[1] Oliver Elton's *The Augustan Ages* ("Periods of European Literature") is such a study, in which France, or rather the age of Louis XIV, is the conquering power, and the other European countries are cultural provinces.
[2] Cf. Estève, *Bryon et le romantisme français.*
[3] Thus Brandes' *Main Currents of Nineteenth Century Literature* observes the cross-currents of European literature generally over a given epoch; whereas Professor Faÿ's *L'Esprit révolutionnaire en France et aux États-Unis à la fin du xviiie siècle* is a study of the exchange of revolutionary ideas between the two countries.

[3]

the national life of the debtor nation? Questions like these demand a thorough understanding of the strength and the need of the assimilating culture.

For the purpose of this study American culture, particularly American literature, is a debtor culture. But what is the inner spirit, the essence of American culture as it is expressed in literature, the arts, the national life? The answer is not without difficulty. For the sake of simplicity let us confine ourselves to American literature. Now, our national letters are unique in origin and development. Begun as a transplantation of British literature, American literature has so completely changed its quality that, we are informed, current American fiction can not be understood in Great Britain without special information. The same periods which have wrought this divergence have wrought other changes: the ethnographical picture of the American people is no longer one of an overwhelmingly "Anglo-Saxon" civilization, but a composite thing; and there has been evolved from the relatively simple and stable culture of the colonial period the astonishingly complex, rapid and novel civilization of the jazz age. During the process of this change, the American people have produced a literature; that is to say, they have written books, and these books must, to an extent, have satisfied their spiritual needs and expressed their ideals. Therefore they must form an American literature. But when one seeks authoritative utterance by which to define the quality of this literature, one finds no convincing formula at hand.

Commonly, histories of literature are supposed to define the spirit and trace the shaping forces of the literature of which they treat. Thus MM. Nitze and Dargan, setting forth to write a history of French letters, begin by postulating certain traits. "The dominant traits of French literature," they say, "are poise, harmony, reason, sympathy; a sense of structure and a sense of delicacy; a preference for ideas over things, but for active social ideas, not metaphysical ones."[4] *Per contra,* French literature lacks, they say, the variety, the moral emphasis, and the expedient qualities[5] of English literature. And as shaping forces in French literary history these authors have much to say of the classic spirit, of relativity, of realism and romanticism.

[4] Nitze and Dargan, *A History of French Literature,* p. 8.
[5] "We (i.e., people of German tradition) are the children of expediency. We react more readily to impulse or sentiment—to the 'inner fact of things,' as Carlyle used to say—and we distrust logic." *Ibid.,* p. 10.

Now there are many histories of American literature, few or none of which, however, seek to determine what American literature essentially is in terms analagous to those used by MM. Nitze and Dargan. This deficiency is not without meaning for our study.

The average history of American literature is, in effect, a textbook, clear in outline, accurate in statement, and pedagogically usable, presenting in chronological order the main "facts" of American literary history, and incurious as to why these facts are so. In such a book American literary history begins with documents like the writings of Captain John Smith; American literature then "grows" or "develops" by reason of some unexplained inward urge (progress, it is assumed, is the law of American life); produces in convenient order the Revolutionary writers, the Hartford wits, the New England group, the Southern writers, *et hoc omne genus;* and, toward the end, a brilliant spattering of contemporary names concludes the whole.[6] Beyond some reference to the assumed qualities of Puritanism, the hardships of pioneer life, and the characteristics of Brahmin Boston, social reference does not go, although it is recognized that the Civil War is a crucial point in American history, and that in the seventies the West suddenly and without warning appeared as a literary influence. Clearly, there is little to help us in such books.

American scholarship has seen a totally different interpretation of our national life established in related fields. In the last thirty years Professor Turner's classic essay on the significance of the frontier in American history has revolutionized the conception of our national development, beginnings have been made in tracing the economic and social forces at work in the United States, the history of American philosophy has been written in terms of American culture, the development of the "American" language has been sketched, and some attempt has been made at a true history of American art.[7] But these revolutionary con-

---

[6] See, for an excellent example of the type, W. B. Cairns, *A History of American Literature.*

[7] See, besides Turner, Bogart, *The Economic History of the United States;* Simons, *Social Forces in American History;* Weeden, *Economic and Social History of New England;* the various volumes of the *American Nation* series and of the *Chronicles of America* series; Riley's books on American philosophy; Caffin, *The Story of American Painting;* Mumford, *Sticks and Stones* (architecture) and *The Golden Age;* Mencken, *The American Language,* (3rd edition); and the references for chapter one generally. The only three treatises which seem to sense the problem of a history of American letters are John Macy, *The Spirit of American Literature,* suggestive but

cepts have not reached the historians of our letters. For them literary history is still the simple chronological story of books which happened to get themselves written in America. Their documentation is inadequate, their references to an assumed social background are naïve, and, confronted by such a phenomenon as Poe, their shallow classifications break down. In such books literature is a static concept, not a dynamic social agency: writers give birth to writers by the law of sequence, and books are spawned out of books on a sort of biological analogy. It never appears why these particular books, and not others, are written in American society.[8]

No, the tremendous energy of American life must have had more to do with its literature than the histories of that literature discover. American letters are not born in a scholarly vacuum, but out of a maelstrom of forces, and it is to the study of those forces, that one who desires to understand the problem of American letters must turn.

At the heart of any national culture there is usually a conflict, and it is commonly when, for reasons still mysterious, these opposing tendencies are for a time in equilibrium that a great cultural period bursts into flower.[9] American letters are not peculiar. Until one envisages the "case" of our literature in

inadequate; Pattee, *American Literature Since 1870,* which begins too late to understand thoroughly the premises upon which the volume is built; and Hazard, *The Frontier in American Literature,* a brilliant and suggestive book which suffers from the "single-theory" fallacy. Professor Norman Foerster has called attention to the need of a new interpretation of American literature in a provocative essay *New Viewpoints in American Literature* which appeared after my manuscript had been completed. Rusk, *The Literature of the Middle Western Frontier,* is a valuable compilation without attempt at interpretation. Wendell, *A Literary History of America,* much the best of the older books, lacks the newer attitude toward American history. The haphazard and unequal chapters of the *Cambridge History of American Literature* are in painful contrast to the ordered merit of the two historical series named above.

[8] When such writers are called on to explain the comparative dearth of writing of the first rank in the United States, they refer to the "youthfulness" of the nation. Why a nation should be too youthful to produce a literary tradition, and yet mature enough to have given birth to Franklin, Hawthorne, Poe, Emerson, Thoreau, and Whitman within a period, reckoned from birthdate to birthdate, of 113 years (1706-1819), does not appear.

[9] Thus in Russia the problem has been whether Russia shall be the most easterly of western nations or the most westerly of oriental ones. Throughout French literature runs the tendency toward cleavage along the line of classicism vs. the innovating spirit. In English literature the conflicting standards seem to be those of the reason and of the imagination. Other examples will occur to the student. Of course no national literature is to be read wholly in such simplified terms.

terms of conflicting forces, one can not appreciate the nuances of our cultural history or grasp the significance of foreign letters to us.

Thus visualized, American literature begins to classify itself. I shall come presently to the nature of these opposing forces; but if my interpretation be a reasonably true one, it must place the problem of our literature, not with the problems of British or Italian or French literature, but with the problems of Norwegian or German or Russian literature. The difference is this: In the long cultural traditions of France, Great Britain, and Italy, there have been few periods when the cultural terrain of any one of these nations was in danger of conquest by an utterly foreign foe. The question of the relations of these literatures to alien culture has been mainly the problem of determining what part of an alien culture the national tradition chooses to assimilate. But this is not true of literatures which have once yielded to foreign domination. There have been long periods when Norse culture has been, to modern patriotic Norwegians, not Norse, but Danish; and the problem set before Welhaven and Wergeland was how to rid Norway of an alien tradition, and how to create in the vacancy thus made a truly national literature, either by originating a new language (*landsmaal*) and a new tradition, or by a return to the European tradition in a new and independent spirit. Similarly in eighteenth century Germany, when all links with the native artistic past had long been broken, the problem of Gottsched and Lessing was not merely to get rid of the cultural overlordship of France, but also to find ways and means of inventing an essentially new thing that would be German letters. To this day German and Norse literature bear the impress of these struggles.

Now, while the North American terrain has never been conquered by cultural aliens, the basic problem of American letters is more like that of Norse or German literature than it is like that of British or French literature. American literature is a minor literature. Begun as an extension of protestant, Anglo-Saxon culture, the United States has had to originate new modes of expression for a new national spirit, while still remaining in the protestant, Anglo-Saxon tradition, although, in the meantime, the complexion of the people has steadily become less protestant and Anglo-Saxon.[10] It is not merely that since 1783

---

[10] See on this whole point Hilaire Belloc's superficial but suggestive study, *The Contrast;* and Nevins, *American Social History as Recorded by British Travellers,* particularly the various introductions.

we have sought to declare our literary independence of Great
Britain, it is the finding of ways by which we might express our
independence that is the heart of the problem. Clearly, the finding of these modes is definitely related to the question of our
attitude toward a Latin and Catholic tradition like that of
French culture.

But this, it may be said, is nothing new. The contemporary
view is that the problem of American letters is to become
"American." Our writers, it is argued, have failed—with brilliant exceptions—to "come to grips" with the realities of the
national life. Recently, so the theory runs, the contemporary
poets and novelists have sensed this want, so that of late, but
only of late, our literature is truly "American." The assumption
is that to be an "American" author is a simple problem of literary algebra.

This theory has been set forth by a group of brilliant contemporary critics, to whom it may be well to turn for their
formulation of the problem. Thus Mr. John Macy in his striking and informative *The Spirit of American Literature* complains that we have not hitherto dealt with the "realities" of
American life:

American literature is on the whole idealistic, sweet, delicate, nicely
finished. There is little of it which might not have appeared in the
Youth's Companion. The notable exceptions are our most stalwart men
of genius, Thoreau, Whitman, and Mark Twain. Any child can read
American literature, and if it does not make a man of him, it at
least will not lead him into forbidden realms. Indeed, American books
too seldom come to grips with the problems of life, especially the books
cast in artistic forms. The essayists, expounders, and preachers attack
life vigorously and wrestle with the meaning of it. The poets are
thin, moonshiny, meticulous in technique. Novelists are few and feeble,
and dramatists are non-existent.[11]

Wisdom lies in the main with our contemporaries:

Every generation, except the more independent spirits in it, looks
with too Chinese reverence upon its ancestors. Moreover, the passing
generation of American writers, critics and professors, the men who
wrote the prevalent handbooks, are intellectually a poor generation
as compared with their fathers. They have reason to lack confidence in
their contemporaries.

Only in the last quarter of the nineteenth century did the spirit of
realism find itself at home among a people reputed to be sensible and
practical, but really sentimental and foolish and content with a conduct of private and public affairs that fills an intelligent business man
with despair.[12]

[11] Macy, *The Spirit of American Literature,* p. 11.
[12] *Ibid.,* pp. vii, 256.

In this vigorous book Howells is an "excellent, sincere, dreamy clergyman,"[13] and William James and Mark Twain, whose "mind was of universal proportions,"[14] are on the contrary genuinely American.

According to Amy Lowell we have had little really American verse until the arrival of Frost and Sandburg, Robinson and Masters. American poetry sprang mainly from Wordsworth and Byron. Whittier, Bryant, Emerson, Lowell, Longfellow, and Holmes are "English provincial poets in the sense that America was still a literary province of the Mother Country," and even after the Civil War "our poets were largely phonographs to greater English poets dead and gone." The inner spirit of the American tradition is Puritanical, and "Puritanism was always a drastic, soul-searching, joyless religion," although "the people as a whole lived and throve under this threatening horror with the vitality of a race born to endure."[15]

Mr. Louis Untermeyer is equally denunciatory:

Until recently our paintings had filled endless galleries with placid arrangements of Greek nudes, Italian skies, and French theories. Our sculpture was mainly a set of variations of George Washington in a toga and Daniel Webster in baggy, bronze trousers. Our architecture had expressed itself in long rows of English basement houses, placing miniature Egyptian obelisks on top of office buildings and trying to make our libraries, motion-picture "palaces," and terminals look like the Campanile, the Parthenon, and the baths of Caracalla. Our music, up to the last two decades, had been a series of sentimentalized echoes of the least original of Europeans; stale drippings adulterated and sweetened by drawing-room Moodys and Sankeys—while our genuine contributions to music (the negro spirituals, the bold aboriginal dance-rhythms, our despised "popular" tunes with their highly characteristic and energetic rag-time syncopation) had been scorned and neglected. . . . [In poetry] the undoubtedly gifted New England group [did not burn] with a keen and racy originality . . . not one filled his work with the warm, intense, thrilling impact of personality that makes the art of all great writers a human and enduring thing.[16]

Mr. Untermeyer like Miss Lowell finds the cause of our failure in the "peculiar hypocrisy" called Puritanism.

Mr. Van Wyck Brooks is likewise insistent:

What emotions pass through an hereditary American when he calls to mind the worthies who figured in that ubiquitous, long paneled group

---

[13] *Ibid.*, p. 288.
[14] *Ibid.*, p. 274.
[15] Lowell, *Tendencies in Modern American Poetry*, pp. 5-10.
[16] Untermeyer, *The New Era in American Poetry*, pp. 3-5.

of "Our Poets" which occupied once so prominent a place in so many domestic interiors? Our Poets were commonly six in number, kindly, gray-bearded, or otherwise grizzled old men. . . . Nothing could make one feel so like a prodigal son as to look at that picture.

Upon individual examination Brooks finds that none of these poets is truly "American." Lowell's dialect is theatrical and often misrepresentative. Emerson used his "creative skill as an artist . . . to intellectualize and dehumanize everything he touched. Bryant . . . was a chilly and water-color Wordsworth. To Longfellow the world was a German picture-book, never detaching itself from the softly coloured pages. . . . His was an eminently Teutonic nature of the old school, a pale-blue melting nature; and white hair and grand-children still found him with all the confused emotion, the charming sadness, the indefinite high proposals of seventeen."[17]

However these critics may differ among themselves in detail,[18] the excerpts just given make it easy to sum up their general attitude. The New England group is taken as the norm of American literature until recent times. Barring two or three exceptions it is next argued that American literature, particularly the New England group, because it has been imitative of European (English) models, or because it has indulged the pathos of distance, has not expressed, and has not attempted to express, American life. Moreover, the culture drawn from this non-American literature has uncritically encouraged complacency, shallow optimism, and the refusal to regard art as a serious issue in life, a culture attributed to the Puritan middle-class against whom these critics rage. It follows therefore that the business of the contemporary generation is to invent an American literature which *shall* express American life, and, at the same time, serve to break the crust of bourgeois complacency.[19] It is amusing to note, though the inconsistency is not important, that the hortatory attitude, the moral vigor of the program is in kind the hortatory attitude and the moral urge of the New England writers against whom these critics inveigh. That is to say, a crusading spirit, an impatience with the past, and the devotion of literature to the moral task of presenting

[17] Brooks, *America's Coming of Age,* pp. 41-51. See also in this connection his *The Ordeal of Mark Twain.*
[18] For H. L. Mencken's equally slashing attack see *A Book of Prefaces.*
[19] An incidental fallacy is the confusion of "Americanism" with a realistic technique.

the "truth" so that something may be done about it, are characteristics strikingly parallel to those possessed by the very group denounced by the rebels!

Is the theory correct? Or is rebellion against tradition, against the overwhelming force of European precept and example, the "note" of a truly American literature, now as then? Is the choice of native themes and the painting of native character the business of "American" letters?

If it be so, the ground of the criticism is, if not swept away, at least seriously shaken. And as a matter of history, rebellion against puritanism, against middle-class complacency, against European tradition is not a recent development but a normal fact in our literature, and notably so in the work of the American classics against which unthinking criticism is levelled. Random illustration will make this clear.

Thus, a conservative history of American literature declares that Irving's *Knickerbocker's History of New York* "treats flippantly vices which the Puritan felt he could speak of only with abhorrence."[20] Cooper, it is notorious, wrote his first novel because he was utterly disgusted with the fashionable British novel; he was urged to attempt an American theme, and wrote *The Spy;* and he went on to portray in *The Pioneers* the frontier life of his boyhood. All his stories exalt the idea of democracy, we read; "the scenes of all his best stories are laid in America or on board American ships, and his best characters are all Americans."[21] Moreover, he was so disgusted with the one-hundred-percent-ism of his day that he spent half his energies endeavoring to correct the chauvinism of his countrymen. Emerson's disgust with the mob, his praise of the individual is as sharp as Mr. Mencken's. And is this from Poe or from *The American Mercury*?

The fact is, the only remarkable things about Mr. Lord's compositions are their remarkable conceit, ignorance, impudence, platitude, stupidity, and bombast. . . . he has undoubtedly given proof of a very ordinary species of talent. . . .

. . . the epithet funny is perhaps the only one which can be considered as thoroughly applicable to this book. (*The Sacred Mountains* by the Rev. J. T. Headley.)

(Seba Smith's) Powhatan is handsomely bound. Its printing is clear beyond comparison. Its paper is magnificent. . . . Further than

---

[20] Cairns, *A History of American Literature*, p. 165.

[21] *Ibid.*, p. 181; and see the whole discussion of Cooper, pp. 174-183. See also the admirable article by Fred Lewis Pattee on Cooper in *The American Mercury* for March, 1925.

this in the way of commendation no man with both brains and conscience should proceed. In truth, a more absurdly flat affair . . .
was never before paraded to the world with so grotesque an air of
bombast and assumption.[22]

When Bryant moved to New York in 1825 "he established
personal relations with most of the literary men of the city, and
with several of the young enthusiasts who were trying to develop the fine arts in America."[23] Irving, writing the introduction to the British edition of Bryant's poems in 1832, spoke of
the volume as follows:

The descriptive writings of Mr. Bryant are essentially American. They
transport us into the depths of the primeval forest, to the shores of the
lonely lake, the banks of the wild, nameless streams, or the brow of the
rocky upland, rising like a promontory from amid a wide ocean of
foliage, while they shed around us the glories of a climate fierce in its
extremes, but splendid in all its vicissitudes.[24]

Of Lowell's *Democracy and Other Addresses* (1886) and
Political Essays (1888) we read that the author "shows his
appreciation of American short-comings with almost unpleasant
frankness."[25] And if the Yankee poetry of Robert Frost "is
New England,"[26] what shall we say, not merely of this from
Thoreau:

"None is so poor that he need sit on a pumpkin,"[27]
but of this?

I should have felt more nervous about the late comet, if I had thought
the world was ripe. But it is very green yet, if I am not mistaken;
and besides, there is a great deal of coal to use up, which I cannot
bring myself to think was made for nothing.

Or this:

We frequently see persons in the insane hospitals, sent there in consequence of what are called religious mental disturbances. I confess
that I think better of them than of many who hold the same notions,

[22] I have chosen these paragraphs at random from Poe's literary criticism.
Complete Works of Edgar Allan Poe (ed. Harrison), X, 163; XII, 147;
XIII, 203.
[23] Cairns, *op. cit.,* p. 186.
[24] Quoted in Godwin, *Biography of William Cullen Bryant,* I, 271-2.
Irving adds: "Neither, I am convinced, will it be the least of his merits
in your (Samuel Rogers') eyes, that his writings are imbued with the
independent spirit and buoyant aspirations incident to a youthful, a free,
and a rising country," which seems "American" enough!
[25] Cairns, p. 278.
[26] Lowell, *Tendencies in Modern American Poetry,* p. 80.
[27] Quoted in Cairns, p. 240.

and keep their wits and appear to enjoy life very well, outside of the asylums. Any decent person ought to be mad, if he really holds such or such opinions. It is very much to his discredit in every point of view, if he is not.[28]

The last two quotations are from that Brahmin of Brahmins, Oliver Wendell Holmes.

Bryant could not write *A Nocturne in A Deserted Brickyard* —he was happily ignorant of manufacturing districts—and he did not bury his dead by Spoon River, for he preferred the Oregon, but he wrote *To A Waterfowl, Monument Mountain, A Meditation on Rhode Island Coal, The Planting of the Apple-Tree, Robert of Lincoln*—poems as "native" in subject matter as Frost's or Sandburg's or Masters'; and it must strike the impartial observer as slightly humorous that Robinson with *Merlin* and *Ben Jonson Entertains A Man from Stratford* among his principal exhibits should be considered thoroughly "American," while Longfellow, with *Hiawatha, The Courtship of Miles Standish,* and *Paul Revere's Ride* among *his,* is by some denied the honorific epithet. As for Lowell, whatever his dialectic errors, Hosea Bigelow was a part of the national mythology, and it is hardly necessary to argue the case of Whittier— or of Emerson, either, for that matter.

In sum, if the desire for an "American" literature, if sharp criticism of middle-class complacency, if revolt against European domination and protest against a vulgarian democracy are held to be the notes of a truly American letters, there is either something wrong with the criticism expressed by contemporary critics, or the question is not to be settled upon so naive a basis.[29]

But the criticism puts us on the right track. Literature in the United States should, indeed, be "American." But what is it to be "American"? This in turn depends upon the question, who are the Americans? What are their cultural standards, their wants, their ideals? Even a casual inspection of our social history reveals the fact that there is little cultural homogeneity among the Americans in one sense of the word, whatever likenesses James Bryce and other sympathetic observers may have

---

[28] Holmes, *The Autocrat of the Breakfast Table,* pp. 26, 46.
[29] Of course the fallacy is a simple one. It is the unconscious lack of a historical sense; an unconscious attribution to the United States of 1800-1865 of the qualities and characteristics of the machine age, together with the assumption that the Americans of that epoch were yearning for an acrid literature.

found in a broader view; that throughout our national history social forces have been at work which, sometimes hostile to each other, have hindered the creation of a unified and solid culture such as is assumed to be characteristic of the French. American literature, pulled hither and yon by these conflicting tendencies, has represented the ascendancy of now one and now another of these interests. It will be the task of the next chapters to analyze certain of these conflicts; but, since we are not now engaged in re-writing the literary history of America, it will be left to the reader to make such application of the results of our analysis as he may. That such application can be profitably made is evident in the publication of so massive a work as Rusk's *The Literature of the Middle Western Frontier* and in Miss Hazard's *The Frontier in American Literature.* Enriched by the results of such a study, we shall then proceed to the history of the reaction of these various cultural forces to the literature, the products, the ideas, and the politics of France.

II

The Rise of Conflicting Forces

INTRODUCTION: THE SUBJECT OF THE NEXT TWO CHAPTERS

It is evident from the preceding chapter that we can not hope to understand the problem of American culture in relation to a foreign culture until we understand something of the maelstrom of social forces out of which American literature has been born. Who in short are the Americans? The answer is not an easy one, but if among the multiplex of social factors which have gone to the shaping of American history, we can identify two or three important ones, we shall have done much toward an understanding of the main problem of this study, inadequate though our analysis will have to be. Let us then turn to the social history of the Americans, and see them evolve in turn three principal elements which have gone into the shaping of their culture. These elements are (1) *the cosmopolitan spirit;* (2) *the spirit of the frontier;* and (3) *the bourgeois or middle class spirit.* We shall trace the first of these in the New England scholar, the Virginia aristocrat and the merchant prince of Philadelphia and New York; we shall find the second developing in the back country of the seaboard states and afterwards throughout the Mississippi basin and westward to the Pacific; and we shall see the bourgeois morality of the middle class increase with the industrial revolution in the United States. And first, the cosmopolitan spirit: let us look at New England, at Virginia, and certain of the principal seaport towns.

1. THE ORIGINS OF THE COSMOPOLITAN SPIRIT IN THE COLONIES

The American colonies were begun as an extension of mediaeval Europe, whether, as in New England and the Moravian settlements, they were villages with common lands, a religious center for the city-state, and handicraft industries;[1] or

[1] " . . . the settlement of the northern American seaboard prolonged for a little while the social habits and economic institutions which were fast crumbling away in Europe, particularly in England." Mumford, *Sticks and Stones,* pp. 13-14. See in this connection chapter one of Mumford; Earle, *Home Life in Colonial Days;* and Weeden, *Economic and Social History of New England.* The earliest Huguenot settlements partook of this character. See Fosdick, *French Blood in America, passim,* but especially the earlier chapters; and Baird, *The Huguenot Immigration to*

whether, as in the Middle and Southern colonies, there was a social complex of liege lords, patentees, vast estates, indentured servants, and slaves, and a system of entail.[2] In either event the coast towns from the beginning looked eastward; from Europe they imported their learning, their books, their ideas, their social systems; to Europe they went for relief from the tedium of colonial life or for fresh intellectual and mercantile supplies; and thither, if they could, they sent their children to be educated. As a result the Atlantic littoral was until the time of the Revolution less separatist than the interior;[3] out of the coast towns came the great eighteenth century merchant princes of Boston, New York, and Philadelphia; many of the influential Tories; and thither flocked the landed aristocracy of the South, for instance, to Charleston and Williamsburg. So far as might be, the coast cities—Boston, New York, Philadelphia, Annapolis, Charleston, Mobile, New Orleans—liked to prolong the fiction that they were a part of European life.

But a new force entered history—the American frontier.[4] The frontier functioned immediately; it was consolidated, as Turner points out, by Indian opposition, in western Massachusetts, the upper Hudson, the territory just west of Philadelphia, and inland from the early settlements in Virginia, Maryland, the Carolinas; it came into being as soon as the colonists left

America, especially the concluding chapters. As settlement spread westward, environmental conditions forced the frontier settlements into a modified form of the mediaeval community, the chief difference being in the status of religion. See for example the description of the Watauga settlement in Roosevelt, *The Winning of the West* (Statesman édition), I, 201-3, which may be taken as the norm of the frontier settlement.

[2] The classic description of the system as it developed in Virginia is comprised in Bruce's brilliant studies, *Institutional History of Virginia in the Seventeenth Century* (2 vols.) ; *Economic History of Virginia in the Seventeenth Century* (2 vols.) ; and *Social Life of Virginia in the Seventeenth Century.*

[3] Thus Rhode Island, originally the "frontier" for the Massachusetts Bay and Plymouth Colonies and for Connecticut, is distinguished for particularism in Revolution times and during the Critical Period. For a differing analysis of the Massachusetts frontier see, however, the second essay in Turner, *The Significance of the Frontier.* I have unfortunately forgotten who called my attention to the peculiar position of Rhode Island.

[4] Turner, *The Significance of the Frontier in American History;* Paxson, *History of the American Frontier;* Roosevelt, *The Winning of the West* (4 vols.) ; Simons, *Social Forces in American History,* chapter xii; Beard, *Economic Origins of Jeffersonian Democracy;* Bryce, *The American Commonwealth,* II, chap. xiii; de Tocqueville, *Democracy in America;* Nevins, *American Social History as Recorded by British Travellers;* Rusk, *The Literature of the Middle Western Frontier,* I, chap. i; Hazard, *The Frontier in American Literature.*

the sea. By the end of the seventeenth century, the frontier (defined as the edge of the land where the population is two to the square mile)[5] had advanced to the falls line; by 1750 Ohio had been entered, the Scotch-Irish and the Germans had penetrated western Virginia and the Piedmont region of the Carolinas, and the invasion had surged up the Mohawk to the German Flats and into western Pennsylvania. By the era of the Revolution the tide had been dammed by the Alleghenies, except that through water-gap and mountain pass Kentucky and Tennessee had been entered, and the upper waters of the Ohio had been won. By 1820 the frontier line ran along the edge of the Ohio, through southern Indiana and Illinois and along the Mississippi, with brief outcurves in southeastern Missouri and the upper half of Louisiana. Later, the frontier line was to be the Missouri; later still, the Rocky Mountains; eventually the Pacific Coast and Alaska—wherever the edge of the free land lay.[6]

But there is not one, there is a series of frontiers, dissolving into each other with amazing rapidity. The first line of advance is everywhere the explorer, the hunter, the trapper, the fisherman, the scout, the missionary, and the Indian fighter, the videttes of the world's last *Völkerwanderung*. Next come the settlers along the water-courses and the main lines of advance, with their tradition of house-raisings, huskings, quilting-bees, common pasture lands, and the rude beginnings of agriculture. But in time they go, and in their places appear the cowboys and herdsmen, even in the East. These are in the Carolinas and western Virginia along the mountain slopes in 1776, they fight at King's Mountain, and some of them serve under Clark. They push on; in 1830 they are in Illinois; in 1840 they cross the Mississippi; in 1850 they are on the Great Plains, from which—huge, cloudy symbols of a high romance— they disappeared only yesterday. Finally comes the small farmer with serious intent, the permanent town, manufacturing, the small competitive system, that "great amalgamating force in American life."[7] The frontier is gone, but it is the Americans who have killed it.[8] Behind them the European

[5] Turner, p. 3.
[6] Turner, pp. 4-9.
[7] Simons, p. 140. See his chapter xii; Turner, pp. 16-22; and Roosevelt, *passim*.
[8] "It is the Americans themselves who daily quit the spots which gave them birth to acquire extensive domains in a remote country. . . . The

fills in the land, and the industrial system prospers with the middle class.

Meanwhile, behind the frontier the country has changed. At first the familiar hardships of Puritan and Pilgrim and Virginian check the growth of the "plantations."[9] In 1616 there are only 350 people in Virginia. Of 14,000 people sent over by the London Company up to 1624 13,000 died from exposure and disease.[10] In 1681, before the arrival of Penn's settlers, there were only 500 whites on the banks of the Delaware. In 1638 communication with England is possible only by the courtesy of ship captains, who hang up bags in coffeehouses to receive letters, for which they expect a penny apiece, unless it be a double letter, when they will want two pence,[11] and not until 1657 did New Netherlands, more enterprising than her neighbors, move to regulate foreign mail. Indeed, there is no regular packet service to England until 1755.[12] Even in 1789 transportation is barbarous, the postal service quite inadequate;[13] there are only five cities of over 10,000 population—New York, Philadelphia, Boston, Charleston, Baltimore; agriculture is still in its Biblical stage, the soil of the South is being rapidly exhausted, the scientific breeding of

European emigrant always lands, therefore, in a country which is but half full, and where hands are in request; he becomes a workman in easy circumstances; his son goes to seek his fortune in unpeopled regions, and he becomes a rich land-owner." De Tocqueville, *Democracy in America*, I, 314, 315.

[9] The whole subject of population in the American Colonies is exhaustively studied by Franklin B. Dexter, "Estimates of Population in the American Colonies," *Proceedings of the American Antiquarian Society*, October, 1887, pp. 22-50. Unless otherwise stated, the figures in the text are based on Dexter.

[10] Bassett, *A Short History of the United States*, p. 5. "It was computed by one contemporary authority that, during the first thirty years following the earliest settlement of Virginia, not less than five of every six persons landed on its shores soon succumbed to one disease or another, but principally to the debilitating influence of the period of seasoning, at which time the newcomer, accustomed from his birth to the more veiled rays of the English sun and the greater equableness of the English air, was first exposed to a semi-tropical blaze . . . or to those rapid alternations of the atmosphere marking the other parts of the year." Bruce, *Social Life in Virginia in the Seventeenth Century*, p. 16.

[11] Rich, *History of the United States Post Office*, p. 3.

[12] Rich, p. 36.

[13] There were 75 postoffices and 24,000 miles of postroad to serve a population of 3,000,000. Rich, p. 67. Twenty-two of the postoffices were in New England, 19 in the Middle States, and 34 in the South, of which six were in the Carolinas, and one in Georgia. By 1796 the number of postoffices had grown to 503. *A Century of Population Growth*, p. 25.

stock is mainly unknown, while manufacturing is, with few exceptions, still in the household stage.[14]

But we tend to exaggerate the hardships of colonial life. By 1643 there were 16,000 or 17,000 people in Massachusetts, in 1664 there were about 7,000 in New York, in 1685, 7,200 in Pennsylvania, in 1667 "a Maryland clergyman's letter. . . claims at least 20,000 souls for the province," and the number is certainly over 32,000 in 1701, and in Virginia in 1689 there were between 50,000 and 60,000. By 1689 there were over 200,000 people in the colonies;[15] in 1721, half a million. By 1750 the total colonial population of the future United States is 1,370,000.[16] So large a population must develop a leisure class.

2. THE COSMOPOLITAN SPIRIT IN THE RELIGIOUS COLONIES

But before 1750 this leisure class has appeared.[16a] In what may be called the theological colonies, there were men whose wide intellectual interests kept them in touch with things European. For one thing, there are the university men, who were relatively as numerous between 1630 and 1690 in New England as they were in Old England,[17] and who have the

---

[14] Simons, chap. ix.

[15] Bancroft's estimate. Dexter estimates 206,000; Bassett, p. 100, estimates the number 220,000, but does not indicate the basis of his figures.

[16] Simons, p. 56; based on Thwaites's estimate. Dexter's figures agree. See his table on p. 50.

[16a] When Governor William Burnett died in 1729, his effects were advertised to be sold, in the *Boston Weekly News-Letter* for October 2, 1729 (No. 144) as follows: "sundry sorts of Household Goods & Furniture. *viz.* Clocks, Glass-sconces, Tables, Chinaware, Glassware, Pewter, Kitchen Utensils of Copper, Tin, Brass & Iron, a Japan'd Cabinet, Tea Tables, a Scriptore with Glass dors, Bedsteads, Beds and Bedding of sundry sorts, Gilt Leather Screens, Table Linnen, Sadles, Bridles, and other Horse Furniture, Horses for a Coach and Saddle, a Coach, a Chariot, and a Chaise with their Carriages and Harness, Fuzees & Pistols: Two Negro Women, about 12 Years Service of a Malatto Boy: sundry Pictures and Prints, two Water Engines, Glass Bottles, sundry sorts of Liquor in Bottles, a Pipe of old Madera Wine, Sweetmeats & Pickles, and sundry other things." This does not look like grinding hardship.

[17] "It is probable that between the years 1630 and 1690 there were in New England as many graduates of Cambridge and Oxford as could be found in any population of similar size in the mother country. . . . Probably no other community of pioneers so honored study, so reverenced the symbols and instruments of learning." Tyler, *A History of American Literature during the Colonial Period,* I, 98-99. " . . . with Winthrop, or following him in the next ten or fifteen years, were Oxford and Cambridge men to the number of nearly one hundred out of a total population of not more than 25,000." Wright, *Literary Culture in Early New England,* p. 16.

same general interests.[18] One of the first acts of these people is to establish Harvard College with a curriculum of Latin, Greek, Hebrew, theology—useless in conquering the wilderness, invaluable in struggling with the devil—a block of European thought transplanted bodily to America. The education of its graduates is quite as good as those of the English universities.[19] And after a study of literary culture in New England from 1620 to 1730 a careful student concludes that the intercourse between the colonies and Great Britain and Holland (that focus of liberal thought in the seventeenth century) was greater and easier than had been supposed;[19a] he collects lists of libraries and books, shows that the taste for reading is widely diffused, that the demand for European books is constant, that booksellers spring up, that there is a continuing interest in the European mind.[20] What if the libraries are mainly theological? The seventeenth century is the great theological century; out of that century come the liberalizing influences of Calvin, Ramus, Descartes, Gassendi.

Nor is this interest confined to the early, more theological period. There is a constant stream of importations into New England.[21] Even in Plymouth, which was far behind Boston

[18] For example, Increase Mather was keenly interested in contemporary science. See Murdock, *Increase Mather*, pp. 143-148, 167-176, 287-316.

[19] "That the education to be gained at Harvard even in its earliest days was the equivalent of that of Cambridge and Oxford is best shown by the careers of some of its earliest graduates." Wright, pp. 20-21. Of the Harvard graduates before 1656 over a third returned to England. Murdock, p. 58.

[19a] News of Blenheim, *"From the Duke of* Marlborough's *Camp at* Steinhelm, August 17. *N. S.,"* is printed in the *Boston News-Letter* of January 29, 1704/5 (No. 41).

[20] The best single study is Wright, *op. cit.* See his bibliography. An excellent short account is by C. H. Herrick, "The Early New-Englanders: What Did They Read?" in *The Library,* IX, 1-17 (1918). See also Ford, *The Boston Book Market, 1679-1750,* and references; and Cook, *Literary Influences in Colonial Newspapers, 1704-1750.* For representative lists of books in early New England, consult Dexter, "Elder Brewster's Library," *Proceedings of the Massachusetts Historical Society,* second series, V, 37-85; Winsor, *The Prince Library;* Tuttle, "The Libraries of the Mathers," *Proceedings of the American Antiquarian Society,* XX (n.s.), 269-356; Potter, "Catalogue of John Harvard's Library," *Publications of the Colonial Society of Massachusetts,* XXI, Transactions, 1919, pp. 190-230; and "Harvard College Library Duplicates, 1682," *Publications of the Colonial Society of Massachusetts,* XVIII, Transactions, 1915-1916, pp. 407-417.

[21] The evidence shows "that the early settlers did not suffer for books, either old or new, since the good libraries they brought with them were constantly increased by importations." Wright, p. 54.

in culture, books fresh from the press were not unknown.[22]
They have a bookstore in Boston in 1652;[23] in 1663-1690 John
Dunton in his *Life and Errors* enumerates thirteen of them,
"all of high character"; Mr. Brunning, from Holland, is indeed
a "complete Bookseller."[24] A printing press is soon established,[25] a flood of publications pours forth,[26] they too must
participate in the great theological controversies of the age.[27]
Ministers are of course the best customers of the thirteen booksellers,[28] and of some 300 publications printed between the
first setting up of the printing press in New England and the
close of the colonial period, two-thirds are religious.[29] Nevertheless they are a bookish nation, their thirst for reading is
unquenchable. From 1670 to 1700 the flow of books increases;
"it is a mistake to think of (the) booksellers as carrying only
theological or devotional works." In the years 1679-1685
John Usher imported books to the value of £567, which
Wright looks on as merely a minimum figure; one Perry, who
died in 1700, a bookseller, left 6,000 books behind him;[30] by
1702 Cotton Mather has two or three thousand books.[31]

[22] Wright, p. 59, note. English books, it is true, are never quoted for sale
in the newspaper advertisements, according to Cook, before 1730, but one
must remember that newspapers were few and advertising rare. Cook,
Literary Influences in Colonial Newspapers, p. 13. I find in the *Boston
News-Letter* for October 24, 1723 that Samuel Gerrish advertises *"the largest and finest collection of BOOKS that has ever been exposed to Sale in
this Town"*—over 2,000 volumes from London.

[23] Howe, *The Puritan Republic*, p. 175, and reference.

[24] Quoted in Weeden, *Economic and Social History of New England*, I,
302-3. There were even itinerant book-pedlars. "On Thursday last Dyed at
Boston, James Gray, That used to go up and down the Country Selling of
Books, who left some considerable Estate behind him." *Boston News-Letter*,
April 16, 1705. (No. 52).

[25] Cf. Wright, pp. 80-81. There is a study by R. F. Roden, *The Cambridge
Press*, which I have not seen.

[26] See the bibliography of early American publications appended to volume two of Thomas, *History of Printing in America*.

[27] Cf. the discussion of Increase Mather's various and voluminous works
in Murdock, *Increase Mather*. Use the index under *Mather*.

[28] Howe, *The Puritan Republic*, p. 175.

[29] Winsor, "'The Literature of the Colonial Period," *Memorial History of
Boston*, I, 453.

[30] Dexter, "Early Private Libraries in New England," *Proceedings of the
American Antiquarian Society*, XVIII (n.s.), 135-147.

[31] Wright, pp. 111, 114, 119, 123.

They will not stagnate in the new land,[32] European controversies are renewed.[33]

3. THE COSMOPOLITAN SPIRIT IN OTHER RELIGIOUS SECTS

But as the Puritans kept up their interest in the intellectual life of Europe, so, too, did other religious sects. The Moravian settlements maintain their connections, social and intellectual, with the Old World.[34] The French Huguenots are, it is true, in a peculiar position, and dislike the France of Louis XIV.[35] A company of Jews comes from Brazil as early as 1654 to build a synagogue in New York; there are others in Savannah in 1733, in Newport by 1763, in Lancaster in 1776, in Philadelphia in 1780 and again in 1782, in Charleston in 1791: some of them are Portuguese, some of them are French, but the race in general are internationally minded.[36] By 1790 they are found in every state.[37] From Maryland the Roman Catholics send their children for education to the "English" colleges on the continent—Rome, Douay, Louvain, Paris, Seville, Coimbra, St. Omer, Salamanca; and if there are few who

[32] A writer in the *Cambridge History of American Literature,* I, 54, observes that "works of pure literature were as lacking as books of history and political philosophy and science" in early New England. No part of this statement is true, as any one who will take the trouble to consult the library lists already cited can see for himself. On the contrary the New Englanders were much more widely read and much more widely curious than the traditional view allows.

[33] Thus as early as 1727 Isaac Greenwood announces "An Experimental Course of Mechanical Philosophy, wherein the Principles of that Noble Science, with the Discoveries of the incomparable *Sir Isaac Newton* therein" were demonstrated in lectures "in as easy Language as possible," accompanied by "above Three Hundred Curious & Useful *Experiments.*" The course was highly successful. (*Boston Weekly News-Letter,* January 12, 1727 (No. 2); February 23 (No. 8); numbers 27 and 28. In 1734 he lectured on astronomy. *Ibid.,* June 13 and July 11, 1734, No. 1584 and No. 1588.

[34] On the Moravians see Fries, *Records of the Moravians in North Carolina;* Fries, *The Moravians in Georgia;* Bernheim, *History of the German Settlements in North and South Carolina;* and Kuhns, *German and Swiss Settlements of Colonial Pennsylvania.* For a highly unfavorable view of the Moravian policies see Roosevelt, *The Winning of the West* (use index).

[35] For a discussion of the Hugenots, see *post,* chap. iv.

[36] Carroll, *Religious Forces of the United States,* pp. 159-160. Of the Jews in South Carolina, Levasseur has some interesting remarks to make in 1824-25, though he is not always trustworthy. He estimated that there were 1200 Jews in South Carolina, of whom 500 were in Charleston; sixty of them enrolled in the late war. The South Carolina Jews are "more generally of French and Portuguese origin." *Lafayette in America,* II, 62.

[37] See the tables in *A Century of Population Growth.* It is amusing to note that in 1790 there was, according to the table, one lone Hebrew family in North Carolina!

go, they are leaders, the education sinks in.[38] Among Americans so educated are whole generations of the powerful Carroll family,[39] including the future archbishop, John Carroll, Joseph Hathersty, Peter Jenkins, George Knight, Joseph Emmott, Joseph Tyler, Robert Cole, and Joseph Rieve, all abroad at Catholic colleges in 1747.[40] Indeed St. Omer's was "so well known in Virginia and Maryland" that in both colonies good protestants "sent petitions against it to the home government as threatening Protestant supremacy."[41] In the opinion of a Catholic historian the result of this education was to make these young Catholics far superior in the eighteenth century to their Protestant neighbors, who, "educated at home, were narrow and insular in their ideas, ignorant of modern languages, and of all that was going on beyond their county limits, and its fox hunt and races." The Catholics, on the contrary, were "conversant with several languages, with the current literature of Europe, the science of the day, with art and the great galleries where the masterpieces of painting and sculpture could be seen."[42] Let us allow something for sectarian pride, and simply note that out of the religious colony in America comes, curiously enough, the cosmopolitan spirit.[43]

[38] Shea, *History of the Catholic Church in the United States,* II, 29; Hinsdale, *Foreign Influence upon Education in the United States,* I, 594; Guilday, *The Life and Times of John Carroll,* pp. 17-32.

[39] Charles Carroll, who settled in Maryland in 1688, sent his sons, Charles and Daniel abroad; their elder brother Henry was at St. Omers in 1688; Charles attended the Jesuit College at Rheims, the College of Louis-le-Grand in Paris, went in 1753 to Bourges to study civil law, returning to Paris in 1754 where his father visited him in 1757. He returned to America, after visiting England, in 1765. Rowland, *The Life of Charles Carroll of Carrolton,* I, 9-19. At St. Omers Charles met a cousin and other "Marylandians." (*Ibid.,* I, 21.) In the next generation the son went abroad at the age of ten in 1785, his sister Catherine and their cousin Daniel came later; and of the grandchildren, Mary Harper was sent to Poitiers in 1816, and young Charles and young Harper to Paris. (*Ibid.,* II, 101-2, 314-16.) John Carroll, the future archbishop, was at St. Omers in 1747. Guilday, *Life and Times of John Carroll,* pp. 17-22. It is interesting to note that Charles Carroll of Carrolton wrote to his son Daniel in 1786: "You will no doubt endeavor not only to improve yourself in the French language, but also by the acquirement of some of the polish of their manners." Rowland, II, 103.

[40] Shea, II, 29. For a list of John Carroll's fellow-students at Wotten, see Guilday, p. 22.

[41] Guilday, p. 22.

[42] Shea, II, 29.

[43] As late as December, 1782, Samuel Breck, son of the great Boston merchant, was sent on board the frigate *Iris* to begin his journey to the College of Sorèze in Lower Languedoc for his education, a college of the Benedictine monks. *Recollections of Samuel Breck,* pp. 60-65. Again, in 1839 the traveller Combe met in Philadelphia a Protestant gentleman who,

4. THE ARISTOCRATIC ORGANIZATION OF THE SOUTHERN COLONIES

Let us pass from the North to the South, let us pass from one extreme to another. The characteristic notes of Southern colonial society are the aristocratic organization, the large estate, the county unit, and the established church. From the earliest settlement there had been men of superior birth and training, in Virginia, nor throughout the seventeenth century did the emigration of such persons diminish.[44] These persons contributed the social ideals of the new community, where colonials in Virginia, Maryland, and South Carolina, as they became rich, sought to found estates like those of the lower English gentry (the "gentlemen adventurers") and to reproduce their manners, their sports, and their intellectual life.[45] And in addition, the governor and other officers were influential in maintaining the social customs of the mother country.[46]

when a boy, had been sent to a Roman Catholic monastery in Canada for the sake of a thorough education in the French language. Combe, *Notes on America*, II, 32. Such instances, which could be multiplied, indicate the part which Catholic education played in the formation of the cosmopolitan spirit.

[44] See Bruce, *Social Life of Virginia in the Seventeenth Century*, chapters iii-vi. In the "First Supply" of 120 settlers (1608), thirty-three were "gentlemen"; in the "Second Supply," 29 out of 70 were "gentlemen"; in the "Third Supply" there were "a larger number." The proportion of men of high birth in any shipload of emigrants was usually one-fourth or one-fifth. "The different records of the long period from 1624 . . . until the close of the seventeenth century show the continued emigration to Virginia of numerous persons who were connected by ties of blood or marriage with persons of high position in England." P. 51. Another important section sprung from the English merchant class. P. 82.

[45] Bassett, *A Short History of the United States*, p. 137. In confirmation of this view see Bruce, *op. cit.*, chapters viii-xix. The political system was from the beginning organized on a system of ranks and classes, and "there was no period in the history of that social life when it resembled the social life of a community situated on our extreme western frontier, where all social distinctions are merged in a rude social equality" (p. 103). Coats-of-arms were regularly "the most ordinary social badges" (p. 105). So too, the men who "followed a mechanical trade were as careful as the planters" to keep their social distinction. Virginian hospitality originated in the desire "to entertain lavishly as their kinsmen among the country gentlemen of England" were accustomed to entertain; (p. 170, and see chapter xi), and drinking, dancing, the taste for acting, betting, card-playing, horse-racing and to some extent hunting and fishing had similar origins." On hospitality at Westover (the Byrd estate) see Bassett, *Writings of Colonel William Byrd*, the introduction.

[46] See for instance the account of Governor De la Warr's concern for social decorum in Bruce, pp. 103-105; and the reason for Sir William Berkeley's popularity, pp. 81-82.

This aristocracy, living on a land monopoly,[47] on a monopoly of labor and prerogative, sought likewise a monopoly of culture. Despite continual protests,[48] it maintained the only church in America except the Roman Catholic that was wholly under European control.[49] William and Mary College, founded in 1693, was intended to be part of the Anglican Church, and though it was a "free school," it was free only in the sense that it admitted all students who met the intellectual and financial requirements.[50] Williamsburg, near which it was situated, soon became the social capital of the colony; there, an attractive aristocratic society soon developed around the governor and the college, the race-track and the playhouse. But the founding of William and Mary represented no con-

[47] "At his death, Robert Carter, who had been Rector of the College, Speaker of the Burgesses, President of the Council, Acting Governor of Virginia, and Proprietor of the Northern Neck, was described in the *Gentleman's Magazine* of 1732 as the possessor of an estate of 300,000 acres of land, about 1,000 slaves, and ten thousand pounds. Pliny the Younger might well have been proud of such an estate." Mumford, *Sticks and Stones,* p. 55. When the second Byrd died, he owned no less than 179,440 acres of the best land in Virginia. With the exception of one large grant on the Dan and Hico his acquisitions were not extraordinary for the times, as one may see who will read the Council Minutes. He inherited 26,231 acres from his father. See the account of his land acquisition in Bassett, *The Writings of Colonel William Byrd,* pp. lxxxii-lxxxiv. The first grants were for 50 acres per person, but in 1699 the council abandoned the law and ordered that anyone who paid five shillings sterling should have the right to take up 50 acres in lieu of the old "important right." The effect was to throw the land freely on the market. *Ibid.,* pp. ix, x. Bassett thinks that "if the Virginians could have reproduced the English country estate worked by a body of white tenants they would gladly have done it." They did the next best thing, they developed slave-holding estates. *Ibid.,* p. xi.

[48] The Anglican Church supported the movement to make all corporate and proprietary governments dependent on the crown. "Again and again, the dissenting sects in America took alarm as they noted the influence of the Bishop of London in getting America political plums for those who gave promise of being useful allies of the Anglican Church in America." The movement to establish American bishoprics served to alienate the colonists. Consult C. H. Van Tyne, "The Clergy and the American Revolution," *American Historical Review,* XIX, 46-48. See also in this connection Humphrey, *Nationalism and Religion in America, 1774-1789,* especially part II. See also under A. L. Cross in the bibliography. For Virginian religious legislation, see Bruce, *Institutional History of Virginia,* I, chap. xx.

[49] The Anglican Church in America was under the control of the Bishop of London. Under Berkeley a law was passed in Virginia forbidding any other than an Anglican clergyman to conduct religious services. The struggle to maintain this monopoly lasted until about 1760, by which time the influx of Scotch-Irish from Pennsylvania had broken it down. As late as 1765, however, despite the monopoly, there were only five Anglican clergymen in North Carolina. Bassett, *Short History,* p. 152.

[50] Bassett, p. 154. For an account of the founding of William and Mary, see Bruce, *Institutional History of Virginia,* I, chap. xi-xii.

cern for the general education of the masses, and the college itself remained small,[51] the clergyman and the tutor sufficing for the gentry, and the "old field school" for the rest. What did the Virginian gentleman care for schools? He had his private library, though he had little use for learning; what he desired was fashionable polish and the polite vices of cosmopolitan Europe. Accordingly he went abroad himself,[52] or sent his children to be reared in the ways of the world.[53] From the great Colonel William Byrd who was trained in England and Holland, down to Joseph Carrington Cabell, Jefferson's chief aid in founding the University of Virginia, who, "after graduating at William and Mary . . . had gone to Europe for his health, and, having recruited that, had studied in more than one of the leading universities" and had met Pestalozzi in Switzerland,[54] there is a perpetual procession to Europe. In 1661 the Virginia Assembly moved to improve postal service from England; by 1768 a regular packet line had been established from Falmouth to Charleston for the accommodation of passengers, the boats sailing regularly until 1782.[55] The result of this constant intercourse was that Virginia seemed least "American," most like England of all the colonies. The country houses of that colony, built in the Palladian style of grand houses in England,[56] were filled with the comforts and luxuries of Europe. Let Bruce describe them:

The inventories of the estates of the leading citizens show that these colonial residences were furnished and ornamented after the most substantial and attractive patterns which England afforded. There was every variety of bed, protected by hanging mosquito nets, and supplied with the finest linen sheets, and very often with silk counterpanes, whilst the sides were adorned with valances of gold and silver texture.

---

[51] As late as April, 1796, there were only about 30 students. Weld, *Travels,* p. 127. Lord Adam Gordon reports 80 in 1764. "Journal," in Mereness, *Travels in the American Colonies,* p. 403.

[52] Consult Bruce, *Social Life of Virginia,* chap. ix. "Not infrequently as many as eight persons at a single sitting of the county court published their intention of leaving for England, and obtained the license required." Bruce, p. 145.

[53] " . . . not a few families managed to send one representative at least to Europe for study and travel, and that representative was usually the eldest son." Trent, *English Culture in Virginia,* p. 10. Colonel Byrd studied law in the Middle Temple; returned to Virginia in 1698 where he was made a member of the Assembly; returned to England in 1698, where he led a gay life; and came again to America in 1705.

[54] Trent, p. 15.

[55] Rich, *op. cit.,* pp. 5, 36.

[56] Mumford, *Sticks and Stones,* p. 54.

There were couches, which were not infrequently covered with embroidered Russian leather, or Turkey-worked cloth; and chairs ranging in kind from those having the seat made of rushes, or rudely tanned calf skin, to those with the seat and back composed of the costliest Russian leather or cloth elaborately embroidered. In some of the residences, there were as many as twenty-four chairs, bound in the finest Russian leather; in one room alone, no doubt the parlor of Mrs. Elizabeth Digges's home, there were nine chairs covered with Turkey-worked cloth; and eleven with cloth, into which a pattern of arrows had been woven, were found in another apartment.[57]

And there were also books.

Doubtless, in comparison with the New England divine, it may be said that the "Virginian planter thought little and read less,"[58] that since "in Virginia (1610-1700), there were no schools, no printing presses, no literary centers" (a doubtful statement), there were "few people who cared to write books or, apparently, to read them."[59] But it is easy to exaggerate, and the more we press the investigation, the more books turn up, the more we see that the Southern aristocracy kept in contact with European literature, or at least that portion of European literature which interested it.[60] So, from the beginning, they not merely go abroad, they import wines, laces, shoes, fine silver-ware, punchbowls, furniture, books. When they send their tobacco to London, they instruct the factor to send them back a pipe of Madeira and a fixed amount of current literature.[61] In Lower Norfolk County, between 1640 and 1690 we know the names of more than 100 owners of books, we know the very names of the books they read, in English, Latin,

[57] Bruce, *Social Life of Virginia*, p. 160. See the whole chapter, especially pp. 164-6 on clothing and fashion.

[58] Lodge, *George Washington*, I, 23.

[59] *Cambridge History of American Literature*, I, 150. The same writer remarks that "the Southern colonies were not of a literary class, and probably would have written little or nothing under any conditions; in the Southern colonies, and, to a less degree, in the Middle colonies, conditions were distinctly unfavorable to literature." Less than 1,000 lines of verse were produced south of New England in the seventeenth century.

[60] For lists of books in colonial Virginia consult the files of the *William and Mary Historical Quarterly* and *The Virginia Magazine of History and Biography;* Marsden, "A Virginian Minister's Library, 1635," *American Historical Review*, XI, 328-332; Bruce, *Institutional History of Virginia*, I, chaps. xiv-xvi. For North Carolina see S. B. Weeks, "Libraries and Literature of North Carolina," *Annual Report of the American Historical Association*, 1895, pp. 171-270, a courageous attempt to list all the libraries in the state before 1800.

[61] Trent, *op. cit.*, p. 10.

French, Dutch, German, Italian.[62] Colonel John Carter of Lancaster County accumulated between 1675 and 1700 the largest library in the district; Ralph Wormseley of Rosegill in Middlesex County had six and seven hundred books; and the thousand collections for which there are records in the last quarter of the seventeenth century average, it is estimated, twenty books apiece—20,000 in all. New England can hardly do as well.

The lawyers buy lawbooks, the planters, agricultural and surveying texts, the ministers, treatises on theology, but by and large they read the fashionable folly of the day as well—*Astrea,* a "French romance," books from the Cavalier court, and by and by the poems of young Mr. Pope, Defoe, Swift, the works of Voltaire, Smollett, Fielding. As early as 1620 they have a public library—at Henrico—or at least the beginning of one.[63] In England the Rev. Thomas Bray projects a scheme for supplying a library to every Anglican parish in America, and almost completes it, too, nor does he confine his libraries to theological works.[64] Indeed, the whole Atlantic coast is indebted to him. Amid fox-hunting, dancing, gambling, a taste for reading developed. What does it matter if they do not print their own volumes?[65] At least they read; the taste for reading becomes fixed: when the Duc de La Rochefoucauld-Liancourt goes visiting in Virginia in 1796, he tells us that the taste for reading is more common among men of the upper class (la première classe) in Virginia than it is in any other part of America. But, he adds significantly, the common people are perhaps more ignorant than anywhere else.[66]

---

[62] Bruce, *Institutional History of Virginia,* I, 413 ff., gives representative lists.

[63] See B. C. Steiner, "Rev. Thomas Bray and his American Libraries," *American Historical Review,* II, 60. Thomas Burgrave, a minister, left his library, worth 100 marks, to a college there. The college was not built.

[64] Steiner, *op. cit.,* pp. 59-79. He began in 1695; by 1699 he had sent out books to the value of £2400, had begun 30 libraries, and laid the foundation for 70 more. He sent 30 parish libraries to Maryland, over a thousand books to Annapolis, 166 volumes for parish libraries in North Carolina, 870 books for laymen's libraries. One incidental result was the founding of the first law library in North Carolina. Bray's activities, though principally in the south, were not restricted to that region; he sent 221 volumes to Boston in 1698; 77 to Rhode Island in 1700; 211 to New York City, 10 to Albany, 327 to Philadelphia, 30 to Perth Amboy.

[65] As late as 1784 three-fourths of the books in Virginia were of foreign manufacture. McMaster, *History of the People of the United States,* I, 74.

[66] *Voyages,* V, 96-97.

In the main all this learning, this culture, this amusement is for the gentry, not for the poor, scarcely for the middle classes.[67] Whereas New England is educating everybody, of ten colleges founded in the colonies by 1776, only two are Episcopalian; eight of the ten are in the North. Of twenty-four colleges founded by 1800, three are in Virginia, three in Maryland, one in North Carolina; seventeen are in the North.[68] By and by a census will be taken, we will know how many newspapers and periodicals there are, it will be a test of democracy: in 1790 there are 103 of them, but only 24 are in the South, which has no monthly magazine, and only 19 weekly papers.[69] Culture is a monopoly of the established church and the aristocracy. But unfortunately the church is not a proselyting church, and that fact is the beginning of the end. We shall come to this by and by; for the present let us simply note that in the Southern colony the cosmopolitan spirit is present from the earliest times.

5. COSMOPOLITANISM AND THE MERCHANT PRINCES OF THE EIGHTEENTH CENTURY

But though the mediaeval aristocracy in modified form lives long in the South,[70] in the North the theocratic state passes into the commercial province; the seventeenth century, which is religious, fades into the eighteenth, which is commercial; in the northern and middle states, the merchant prince appears.[71] The symbol of the new era is the founding of New Amsterdam as a trading post in 1623; soon the guild system which was established there disappears. "Beginning its life by bargaining in necessities, the trading post ends by making a necessity of bargaining, and it was the impetus from its original commercial habits which determined the characteristics of the abortive city plan that was laid down for Manhattan Island in 1811."[72] In Boston, Newport, New York, Philadelphia, Charleston[73]—and

[67] For an account of elementary education in colonial Virginia see Bruce, *Institutional History*, vol. I, section on education.
[68] See the list in Boone, *Education in the United States*, p. 77.
[69] *A Century of Population Growth*, p. 32.
[70] See *post*, chapters vii and viii.
[71] For an exhaustive study of the rise into power of the mercantile class, see Schlesinger, *The Colonial Merchants and the American Revolution, 1763-1776*, Columbia University Studies in History, Economics and Public Law, LXXVIII.
[72] Mumford, *Sticks and Stones*, pp. 20-21.
[73] Lord Adam Gordon, who was in Charleston in December, 1764, wrote in his Diary on December 8, "There seems in general to be but two Classes

let us add, New Orleans[74]—the trading classes arise;[75] and it
is to regulating their enterprise, to keeping them in their proper
places as colonial merchants, that half the colonial legislation of
the British parliament is directed.[76] For England, too, has a
merchant class, the greatest in the world, Voltaire believes, and
it brooks no brother near the throne.[77] The colonial traders send
out salt-fish, oil, spermaceti candles, whale products, fur, lumber, rum, iron-ore, woolen goods, hats, tobacco, rice, molasses,
naval stores, with or without the sanction of the law;[78] and
with or without the sanction of the law they import fine cloths,
silks, ironware, fine china, cutlery, books, tea, slaves, articles of
luxury.[79] All this trade requires shipping, and the American
merchant marine is born.[80] It requires easier means of com-

of people—the planters who are the proprietors, and the Merchants who
purchase and Ship the produce." "Journal," in Mereness, *Travels in the
American Colonies,* p. 397.
   [74] See *post,* chap. IV, 111-123.
   [75] "Under the stimulus of this ceaseless round of activity, trading communities sprang up in many parts of New England, with Boston and Newport as the chief centers. Ship building leaped into prominence as a leading
industry. . . . New York was the commercial capital of Connecticut and
old East Jersey, just as Philadelphia was the entrepôt of West Jersey and
the Delaware Counties. . . . Throughout New England and the Middle
Provinces, the merchants and their lawyer-allies constituted the dominant
element in colonial society, an ascendency shared in the case of New York
with the landed gentry. The chief trading communities of the commercial
provinces were: Philadelphia, which by 1760 with a population of almost
nineteen thousand had usurped the place of Boston as the greatest emporium of British America; Boston, which ranked second with more than
fifteen thousand population; New York, a city somewhat smaller than
Boston but destined to outstrip her in a few years; and Newport, the fifth
city on the continent with more than seven thousand people. In each center,
wealthy merchant families had come into existence. Who were better or
more favorably known than the Whartons, Pembertons, Willings and Morrises of Philadelphia; the Amorys and Faneuils, the Hancocks and Boyls-
tons of Boston; the Livingstons and Lows, Crugers and Waltons of New
York; the Wartons and Lopezes of Newport, or the Browns,—'Nickey,
Josey, John and Mosey,'—of Providence?" Schlesinger, pp. 27-28.
   [76] *I.e.,* the Navigation Ordnance of 1651, the Navigation Acts of 1660,
1663, 1672, the Molasses Act of 1733, the Stamp Act of 1765, the Town-
shend Acts of 1767, the Tea Tax of 1770. Schlesinger's study traces the
effects of this legislation in British America.
   [77] There is a world of history in Schlesinger's significant remark: "In
their business activities, the merchants showed a capacity for joint undertakings that revealed their kinship with the race that had built up the great
East India Company and the Hudson's Bay Company." Pp. 28-29.
   [78] See Schlesinger, index under smuggling.
   [79] For a study of American commerce see E. R. Johnson and others, *History of Domestic and Foreign Commerce of the United States,* 2 vols.
   [80] Ship-building began in Massachusetts as early as 1631. Edward Randolph reported in 1676 that up to that time 730 vessels had been built in

munication, and the American postoffice takes shape: in 1691 Thomas Neale is given a patent to organize the colonial post, all shipmasters are directed to deliver their letters to the postoffice at New York upon arrival; in 1707 the British postmaster-general takes charge; in 1711 the rate is fixed at a shilling for a "single" letter, New York to London; in 1753 Franklin, having begged for the job two years before his predecessor is dead, before he is even dying, becomes, with one Hunter whom history has forgotten, postmaster-general in the colonies; regular packet lines are established, postage from London to New York is only a penny a single letter— ideas spread more easily.[81] Commerce grows. In 1790 the tonnage of foreign vessels alone in American ports, says one Frenchman, was 264,563 tons.[82]

And commerce familiarizes these sections with the world. They trade with the West Indies, with Africa in 1660, and always with Europe. By and by, after the Revolution, their ships will push beyond the Cape of Good Hope: in 1784 the *Empress of China* is dispatched to Canton; in 1785 Elias Hasket Derby of Salem will send his *Grand Turk* to Mauritius, to India, to China, and soon the merchants of Boston and Philadelphia, New York and Salem, will be bringing home cottons, silks, and teas from India, teas, silks, and porcelains from China, spices from the East Indies—indeed, there were as early

Massachusetts. Fully three-fourths of the commerce of the colonies during the later colonial period was carried in ships of their own construction. *Op. cit.,* I, 72-73.

[81] Rich, pp. 14, 36, 38. British packets sailed regularly from Falmouth to New York until the Cunard steamers came in; the line from Falmouth to Charleston was regularly maintained from 1768 to 1782; French packets from L'Orient to New York ran during the period of the Revolution and up to the French Revolution. Rich, pp. 36, 60. An advertisement in the *State Gazette of North Carolina,* IV, 186, June 30, 1789, announces the "re-establishment" of the packetboats from Bordeaux to Norfolk and New York, sailings scheduled for alternate months. See, however, Johnson, I, 188-9.

[82] La Rochefoucauld-Liancourt, *Voyages,* VII, 333. Some idea of mid-eighteenth century communications with Europe can be gained from the figures preserved by Kalm for the port of Philadelphia, taken from "the gazette of the town:"

Year	Ships Arrived	Sailed
1735	199	212
1740	307	208
1741	292	309
1744	229	271
1745	280	301
1746	273	293

—Kalm, *Travels into North America,* I. 42.

as 1789 fifteen American ships at Canton, of which five hailed from Salem, and in 1790 this same Mr. Derby imported 728,000 pounds of China tea.[83] By the end of the century the furniture in their great houses in Boston and Salem had usually been imported from England, they had much of the celebrated Wedgwood ware, high clocks of English make, and colored engravings by Copley and West.[84] And from the other end of the world China sent over wall-paper; there is in the Metropolitan Museum an American lacquered cabinet, dating from 1700, with Chinese figures in gilded gesso on it; "China" itself replaces pewter and earthenware; and in the gardens of the great manors, even with classical Jefferson at Monticello, pavilions and pagodas are in fashion. Turkish dressing gowns, slippers, and turbans appear in Boston, and in Copley's painting of Nicholas Boylston, in 1767, Turkish ornaments look odd next to a Corinthian pillar.[85]

Cosmopolitan interests increase: twenty-one years before it fell into the hands of the English, New York had, within it or near it, a population speaking eighteen different languages,[86] and the town never loses its international character. Boston in 1765 "is more like an English Old Town than any in America, —the Language and manner of the people, very much resemble the old Country, and all the Neighbouring lands and Villages, carry with them the same Idea."[87] In the same year, it seems to Lord Adam Gordon that "every body in Philadelphia deals more or less in trade,"[88] and they all "live handsomely." A collector gives us the names of more than thirty thousand "immigrants"—German, Swiss, Dutch, French—who come to Pennsylvania between 1727 and 1776.[89] Even in remote Albany of

[83] Johnson, *op. cit.*, 33-34, 98-104, 185-6. When Derby died in 1799, he left an estate of a million dollars or more, and at one time had owned 40 vessels which had traded in the Baltic, the Mediterranean, the West Indies, India, the East Indies, China, and the Philippines. *Ibid.*, I, 186.

[84] McMaster, *History of the People of the United States,* I, 13, 14. A visit to the American wing of the Metropolitan Museum is illuminating in this connection. For a study see Halsey and Cornelius, *A Handbook of the American Wing.*

[85] Mumford, pp. 38-9.

[86] Tyler, *A History of American Literature during the Colonial Period,* II, 206.

[87] "Journal of Lord Adam Gordon," in Mereness, *Travels in the American Colonies,* p. 449.

[88] *Op. cit.,* p. 412.

[89] Rupp, *A Collection of Upwards of Thirty Thousand Names of German, Swiss, Dutch, French and Other Immigrants in Pennsylvania from 1727 to 1776,* etc.

the eighteenth century, Mrs. Grant assures us that "men, who possessed the advantages of early culture and usage of the world, daily arrived on the continent from different parts of Europe,"[90] and some of them, at any rate, go to Albany: Simeon Baldwin does not like the specimen he meets in 1782.[91] By 1790 the country is full of "foreigners"; counting by heads of families there are 78,959 Dutchmen, 17,619 Frenchmen, 176,407 Germans, 10,664 of other nationalities, and of these the majority live in the Northern and Middle states.[92]

The merchants grow rich, develop men like Boylston, Faneuil, Morris, Girard, build great houses, buy land, develop a banking class, a news system, a pushing crowd of lawyers—almost in spite of themselves they are causing the Revolution.[93] Trade requires a solid financial system, the land speculation in the South and West infuriates the back country;[94] after the French and Indians Wars, when times are hard, the back country de-

---

[90] *Memoirs of an American Lady*, I, 121.

[91] "Dined at the Domine Westerlo's; had a very good dinner; but great many disagreeable lattin proverbs. . . . I esteem him as a divine & a man well versed in the Languages, but further than this cannot say that I do.— He is fond of their Eropean (sic) Education & seems to dispise (sic) ours." This was October 5, 1782. *Life and Letters of Simeon Baldwin*, p. 97.

[92] *A Century of Population Growth*, tables.

[93] On the reluctance of the merchant class to declare for independence, see Schlesinger's study. Sumner and de Tocqueville agree that the lawyers mainly engineered the Revolution. "In the generation before the Revolution the intellectual activity of young men, which had previously been expended in theology, began to be directed to the law. As capital increased and property rights became more complicated there was more need for legal training. . . . In truth the range of ideas, among the best classes, about law, history, political science, and political economy, was narrow in the extreme. What the aspiring class of young men who were self-educated, lacked, as compared with the technically 'educated,' was the bits of classical and theological dogmatism which the colleges taught by tradition, and the culture which is obtained by frequenting academical society, however meagre may be the positive instruction given by the institution. . . . They were therefore considered pushing and offensive by the colonial aristocracy of place-holders and established families, who considered that 'the ministry' was the proper place for aspiring cleverness and that it was intrusive when it pushed into civil life. The restiveness of the aspiring class under this repression was one of the great causes of the Revolution. The lawyers became the leaders in the revolt everywhere." Sumner, *Andrew Jackson*, pp. 3-4. De Tocqueville draws a parallel between the place of lawyers in the American Revolution and in the French Revolution. *Democracy in America*, I, chap. xvi. It was the lawyer class which furnished the ideas of the Revolution. "En effet, la résistance des Américains n'était pas strictement politique et économique. Elle était également une crise morale, sentimentale et religieuse." "Et sans ses enfants dissidents la révolution américaine n'eut jamais abouti." Faÿ, *L'Esprit révolutionnaire en France et aux États-unis*, pp. 21, 19.

[94] Simons, *Social Forces in American History*, pp. 58, 66.

mands paper money, but the merchant class will have none of
it. When the Navigation Acts close the West India trade,
specie becomes scarcer, the tension grows, a prime cause of the
revolution was the desire of the debtor class to avoid paying
bills—to the merchants.[95] A stupid parliament infringes upon
the divine rights of trade, lawyers and merchants unite to capitalize back-country unrest—terrified by mob violence, afraid of
the mob they have invoked[96]—but when the Revolution has been
won, when trade has been freed from the mercantile system,
the merchant class and the aristocracy frankly unite to repudi-
ate the democracy they had flattered.[97] The administration of
the first president is truly a republican—and mercantile—court.
For, confronted by Shay's rebellion, the wealthy had staged a
counter-revolution; the proceedings of the constitutional convention are kept secret;[98] of 65 delegates, only 55 were ever

[95] Simons, *op. cit.,* pp. 66-69.

[96] Simons, pp. 73-75. That the merchant class felt it had sown the wind
only to raise the whirlwind is amply shown in Schlesinger, pp. 91-93, 240-262,
279 ff, 432-440, 592-600.

[97] State governments formed during the war (except Pennsylvania) are
bi-cameral, the upper house representing property, the lower, the people,
the bi-cameral system being the only practical modus vivendi between the
class and mass. The provisions of the Ordinance of 1787 indicate that the
Continental Congress was a more popular body than the one which adopted
the Constitution, since a bill of rights is included in the Ordinance, whereas,
with the Federal Constitution, it is added later. Simons, p. 84. The struggle
began early and lasted late as one or two instances will show. (1) In 1760
the wealthy class in Massachusetts, Virginia, and Carolina, at odds with
the small farmer of the interior, referred to the popular party as 'the mob,'
to its leaders as 'demagogues,' while the popular party referred to them
as 'aristocrats' and oppressors of the poor. Bassett, pp. 135-6. (2) The First
Continental Association of 1774 "involved a defeat for the moderates and
the mercantile interests. The radicals . . . achieved several important ends,"
and "the publication of the Continental Association was greeted with a storm
of protest from the moderate press in the leading commercial provinces."
Schlesinger, pp. 432, 435. (3) Despite the terrible poverty of the common
people during the Revolution (Simons, pp. 86-7), the mercantile interests
demanded protective tariffs; and at the conclusion of the struggle, because
of a flood of importations from Great Britain, secured the first protective
tariff, modelled on the Pennsylvania tariff of 1785. Johnson, *History of
Domestic and Foreign Commerce,* I, 135-139; Simons, p. 109. (4) Hamilton's financial program took care of state debts to the extent of $30,000,000,
plus $42,000,000 indebtedness of the Confederation, largely owed to the
monied class, but it repudiated $100,000,000 worth of paper money; this
"repudiation, and subsequent loss by the producing class was one of the
causes of the terrible poverty that prevailed." Simons, p. 113. The establishment of the bank, whose stockholders were largely in the North, is also
to be noted.

[98] The injunction of secrecy was never removed. The last act of the convention was a resolution that its papers should be left with Washington,
subject to the order of the new Congress, if ever formed under the Con-

present at one time or another, only 39 sign the final report, and the new document does not even contain a bill of rights. Of three million people not more than 120,000 can vote, not for the constitution, but for delegates to state conventions to consider the constitution—conventions easier to control; the states are not redistricted, the upper classes are in power and shut out the Westerners. Libby studies the geographical distribution of the vote for these conventions; he finds that frontiersmen, farmers, debtors, people in the country are solidly against it, that the merchants, the money-lenders, the lawyers, the great land-owners, the planters are in its favor.[99] Even then the first ten amendments have to be added as a concession to democratic feeling. But when the new republic is begun the merchant class and the planters are in the saddle, to remain until they are overthrown by the manufacturers or the frontier democrats.

The expression of the ideas of this merchant class is Franklin. Solid, serious men, they demand a solid and serious culture, without frivolity or grace.[100] Let us look at their libraries, their books, their periodicals. For example, in the sea-coast towns during the period of the merchant princes one notes as a characteristic bit of thrifty culture the foundation of "social libraries" as distinguished from the college library of the theocratic state and the private library of the plantation aristocrat.[101]

stitution. March 19, 1796, Washington deposited in the State Department three manuscript volumes. These were not published until October, 1819, together with Additions from Madison's notes. Johnston, *American Political History, 1763-1876* (ed. Woodburn) I, 78.

[99] Simons, pp. 95-98 and references.

[100] After the first half century of New England life, one remarks the advance of the laity in literary activity. Tyler, *A History of American Literature during the Colonial Period,* II, 93. Politics and the Revolution absorbed most of the intellectual force, and the result is that the characteristic literature is overwhelmingly political. Lodge, *Alexander Hamilton,* pp. 67-68. New York produced practically no English verse until the Revolution. *Cambridge History of American Literature,* I, 151. Of the New England of 1800 Adams remarks that classical literature was the main diversion: "Men had not the alternative of listening to political discussions, for stump-speaking was a Southern practice not yet introduced into New England, where such a political canvass would have terrified society with dreams of Jacobin license." *History,* I, 95. Consult Tyler, *The Literary History of the American Revolution,* 2 vols.

[101] The most complete study of libraries in the United States prior to 1850, though very imperfect, is the *Appendix to the Report of the Board of Regents of the Smithsonian Institution,* containing *A Report on the Public Libraries of the United States of America, January 1, 1850.* By Charles C. Jewett. For a brief survey of colonial libraries see Boone, *Education in the United States,* pp. 293-4. There is a chapter on the development of public libraries in Myers' suggestive but unscientific study, *The History of American Idealism.*

From 1656 to 1754 Boston has a public library, founded by Captain Robert Keayne.[102] In 1700 the Sharp Library is given to the town. The Prince Library becomes the property of the Old South Church, and after many vicissitudes is deposited in the Boston Public Library. In 1760 the Social Library of Salem has 800 volumes, including the memoirs of the French Academy, the Royal Society Transactions, the memoirs of the Berlin Academy, and many philosophical works; it is—the characteristic form—a club, or closed corporation. In Newport a literary and philosophical society is organized in 1730, composed of "some of the most respectable men of the town of Newport" under the encouragement of Bishop Berkeley; in 1747 Abraham Redwood gives them £500 sterling for the purchase of books, the society is incorporated, and Henry Collins, "a merchant of Newport, distinguished for his wealth, liberality, and taste" gives them land; a building is erected; a collection of theology, history, arts, and sciences is formed, and "scholars came to it 'from the Carolinas and the West Indies, from New York, and even from Boston.' "[103] In New York, under the government of Lord Bellomont, a "Public Library" is formed in 1700; in 1754 the "New York Society Library." In Philadelphia in 1732 Franklin founds his famous library company, a subscription enterprise with 50 members, an entrance fee of 40 shillings, and annual dues of 10 shillings; thereafter, he says, "reading became fashionable."[104] Then there is the Loganian Library, originally the property of James Logan, the friend and counsellor of William Penn; and the Library of Friends, which dates from 1741, and that of the American Philosophical Society, of 1742. Even in Charleston, the mercantile center of the South, they have a Library Society in 1748. We note two facts about the libraries that arise with the mercantile class; first, that they are associative enterprises, part of that "capacity for joint undertakings that revealed their kinship with the race that had built up the great East India Company and the Hudson's Bay Company";[105] and second, that they are for the aristocracy. The masses felt that they had no share

---

[102] *Publications of the Colonial Society of Massachusetts,* XII, Transactions, 1908-1909, pp. 116-133.
[103] Stockwell, *History of Public Education in Rhode Island;* quoted in Boone, p. 295; *Smithsonian Report, op. cit.,* pp. 48-49.
[104] Quoted in Morse, *Benjamin Franklin,* p. 20.
[105] Schlesinger, pp. 28-29.

in them. We must wait for the lyceum movement before the true public library is begun.[106]

In the main these libraries are filled with solid and useful books. Reading taste in the North—Boston, for instance—is sober and serious, whether gauged by the social library or the possession of books in private homes. In 1784 the puritanical taste is still strong, "the delightful novels of Richardson, of Fielding, of Smollett, and of Sterne found no place on their shelves," says one historian, though the booksellers' lists indicate that his judgment is a little hasty. " 'The Lives of the Martyrs; or, The Dreadful Effects of Popery' stood side by side with Vattel's 'Law of Nations' and Watts's 'Improvement of the Mind.' There might have been seen Young's 'Night Thoughts,' Anson's 'Voyages,' Lucas on 'Happiness,' Rollins's 'Ancient History,' 'The Pilgrim's Progress,' 'The Letters of Junius,' 'The Spectator,' but not the works of the hated author of 'Taxation no Tyranny.' "[107] Before 1790 the Philadelphia presses had printed *Epictetus His Morals, Pamela, Rasselas, Robinson Crusoe, The Sentimental Journey, The Deserted Village, The Vicar of Wakefield, Paradise Lost,* Blackstone's *Commentaries,* Robertson's *Scotland,* Leland's *Ireland,* Chesterfield's *Letters,* Lady Mary Wortley Montagu's *Letters and Pastimes,* Smith's *Wealth of Nations,* an abridgment of the *Lives of the British Poets.* In the ten years from 1790 to 1800 we note the addition of Paley's *Moral Philosophy,* Russell's *Modern Europe,* Aristotle's *Ethics* and *Politics,* Johnson's *Dictionary,* Shakespeare, and the *British Classics* in 38 volumes, and many more.[108] If their own writings are mainly political, these, too, are in the main improving and informative works.

Nor should we forget the ladies. In the Northern colonies in the eighteenth century, the mistress of the house and her daughters were not always encouraged to read. The daughter "learned embroidery and could draw and paint; knew less of novels and more of receipt-books than her descendants; knew little of French, nothing of German, and never went to a play in her

---

[106] Dexter, *History of Education in the United States,* p. 483. McMaster's statement is of interest in this connection. Of the reading of the New England farmer in 1784 he observes that it was "not extended and was, in general, confined to such books as found their way into pedler's packs. The newspaper he rarely saw unless it came wrapped about a bundle. . . ." *History,* I, 19.

[107] McMaster, *History,* I, 14-15.

[108] McMaster, V, 282-3. The student should turn to Evans's *Bibliography.*

life. Many a young damsel passed from girlhood to womanhood without ever looking within the covers of Shakespeare or Sheridan, without ever having attended a dance, and could not tell whether the ace of spades was black or white, or if the king outranked the knave." But there were many exceptions: the daughter of the merchant prince here and there had her favorite novels—Smollett, Fielding, Sterne, *Victoria, Lady Julia Mandeville, Malvern Dale,* and *The Sylph*—although the prejudice against fiction never disappeared.[109] By the end of the century in New York "it has become the fashion . . . to attend lectures on moral philosophy, chemistry, minerology, botany, mechanics, etc., and the ladies in particular have made considerable progress in these studies,"[110] just as the French and British ladies had been doing across the Atlantic. And this mercantile aristocracy had women sufficiently talented and brilliant to charm the young aristocrats of the French army, as we shall see.

If there is little frivolity in this culture, there is a great desire for information, and out of it the colonial newspaper and the colonial magazine are born. In 1741 Franklin experimented with *The General Magazine and Historical Chronicle for all the British Colonies in America,* which lasts six months; in the same year there is also an *American Magazine,* or *Monthly View of the Political State of the British Colonies,* which runs to three numbers.[111] Thereafter they begin to multiply. The newspapers give astonishingly full reports of foreign affairs; indeed, proportionately, their European news is much better than ours,[112] and they are important vehicles for the spread of

---

[109] McMaster, I, 14-15.
[110] Lambert, quoted in Mrs. Lamb, *History of the City of New York,* II, 439.
[111] Ford, *Checklist of American Magazines in the Eighteenth Century;* Smyth, *Philadelphia Magazines and their Contributors, 1741-1850;* Cook, *Literary Influences in Early Colonial Newspapers;* Thomas, *History of Printing in America,* I; North, *History and Present Condition of the Newspaper and Periodical Press of the United States;* Ingram, *A Check List of American Eighteenth Century Newspapers in the Library of Congress;* Beer, *Check List of American Periodicals, 1741-1800.*
[112] It was from a Boston newspaper that the Marquise de la Tour du Pin learned that her father, Colonel Arthur Dillon, had been guillotined in Paris, April 13, 1794, and she adds: 'Indeed all the news from France was printed in the American papers as soon as received.' At General Schuyler's in Albany she learned from the papers of the overthrow of Robespierre. It was from American newspapers that Chateaubriand learned of the flight of the king—news which sent him back to Paris, that Brissot de Warville learned of the arrest of l'Eprémésnil. Fauchet thought the French papers inferior to the American in the department of foreign news. Sherrill, *French Memories of Eighteenth Century America,* pp. 251-2.

ideas. By the time of the battle of Lexington there are 37 newspapers, at the treaty of peace, 43, although few have a continuous existence, and "not one newspaper in the principal cities . . . continued publication during the war."[113] But peace once established, communication growing easier, the newspapers and magazines multiply: in 1790 there are 103 of them, of which—significant fact!—79 are in the Northern and Middle States.[114] By 1810, there are 364 newspapers alone, fifteen of them in foreign languages, and all established since 1775—"no other country could show such figures in that day."[115]

In the commercial provinces, now become states, the magazine began to flourish. In 1792, when the *American Museum, or Repository of Ancient and Modern Fugitive Pieces, Prose or Poetical,* expired, there were but two other magazines in the country (*The Boston Magazine* and *The Columbian Magazine*), but between 1786 and 1792 ten spring up.[116] As we turn their yellowing pages we are impressed by the foreign news, the solid information, the practical quality of these publications, the articles gleaned from British periodicals, French science and speculation, and the classics. Let McMaster describe one of them: "each had a 'Parnassiad' of 'selected poetry,' generally odes to Laura; selections from the writings of Colonel Humphreys and Philip Freneau; epigrams, epitaphs, songs translated from the French, and at times a few lines from Homer. There were 'Political Speculations' . . . There were 'Public Papers' and 'Physical Papers,' giving some 'account of

---

[113] *Cambridge History of American Literature*, II, 173. The important papers were the *Boston Gazette*, the *Connecticut Courant* (Hartford), *The Providence Gazetteer, The Pennsylvania Packet, The Massachusetts Spy, The Independent Chronicle* (Boston), *The New York Journal, The New York Packet, The Newport Mercury, The Maryland Gazette* (Annapolis), *The Pennsylvania Gazette, The Pennsylvania Journal. The Pennsylvania Packet* became the first daily (1784). Suppressed by the British in the principal towns, many papers emigrated to inland villages. Considering the scarcity of paper, and the difficulty of communication, the success of the eighteenth century newspapers is nothing short of astounding.

[114] *A Century of Population Growth*, p. 32.

[115] Schouler, *History*, II, 264.

[116] McMaster, II, 65. It is impossible to secure accurate figures on magazine publication, and even so careful a historian as McMaster falls into error. These ten are, however, *The Boston Magazine, The South Carolina Magazine* (three years), *The American Museum, The Columbian Magazine, The Massachusetts Magazine, The Philadelphia Magazine, The New York Magazine, The Worcester Magazine, Gentlemen and Ladies Town and Country Magazine, The Ladies' Magazine and Repository of Entertaining Knowledge.* It will be observed that nine of the ten are published in the North.

a horse with a living snake in his eye' and 'the true nature and cause of the tails of comets.' There was a chronicle of foreign and domestic news, 'satiricals on old bachelors, old maids, and married men'; reports of law-cases; now and then an 'impartial review' of such a novel as 'Modern Chivalry,' etc."[117] It is all very heavy: "for four or five years of the century Dennie's *Portfolio* contained almost everything of light literature in the United States," and Dennie's *Portfolio* itself refuses to admit Jacobins to its pages, reflects a small literary class, is remarkable for its adhesion to the Tory standards of Burke and Johnson, that arbiter of correct taste.[118] Poor Dennie in his heyday can secure but 1500 subscribers, the *Anthology and Boston Review* in 1805 has only 440,[119] the mercantile class has as much a monopoly on culture in the North as has the aristocrat in the South.[120]

But trade is international;[121] had it been left solely to the

---

[117] McMaster, II, 65-66.
[118] Adams, *History*, IX, 199-201.
[119] Adams, IX, 210.
[120] In 1757 in New York "our schools are of the lowest order—the instructors want instruction, and through a long and shameful neglect of all the arts and sciences, our common speech is extremely corrupt." Smith, *History of New York*, quoted in Tyler, II, 207. Compare the lack of general education facilities in the South. Massachusetts, that center of theological learning and commerce, had to wait for Horace Mann to establish a satisfactory public school system. There was no general educational periodical until the *Academician*, 1818-1819 (New York). *The American Journal of Education*, 1826-1830, "aimed at the cultured classes." The foundation of a modern school system is usually dated from Mann's *Seventh Annual Report*, 1844. Cf. *Cambridge History of American Literature*, vol. III, bk. iii, chap. xxiii.
[121] "The enterprising merchants of Salem are hoping to appropriate a large share of the whale fishery; and their ships are penetrating the northern ice. They are favourite customers in the Russian ports, and are familiar with the Swedish and Norwegian coasts. They have nearly as much commerce with Bremen as with Liverpool. They speak of Fayal and the other Azores as if they were close at hand. The fruits of the Mediterranean countries are on every table. They have a large acquaintance at Cairo. They know Napoleon's grave at St. Helena, and have wild tales to tell of Mosambique and Madagascar, and store of ivory to show from thence. They speak of the power of the king of Muscat, and are sensible of the riches of the south-east coast of Arabia. It entered some wise person's head, a few seasons ago, to export ice to India. . . . The young ladies of America have rare shells from Ceylon in their cabinets; and their drawing-rooms are decked with Chinese copies of English prints. I was amused with two: the scene of Hero swooning in the church from 'Much Ado About Nothing'; and Shakespeare between Tragedy and Comedy. The faces of Comedy and Beatrice from the hands of Chinese! . . . . They have hopes of Van Diemen's Land, think well of Singapore, and acknowledge great expectations from New Zealand. Any body will give you anecdotes from

merchants there might have been no war in 1812.[122] War interferes with commerce, and the mercantile spirit is solid and shrewd. And so, among these princes of commerce, practical, worldly-wise, curious, wealthy—here, too, in its way the cosmopolitan spirit is born. "I think," wrote de Tocqueville, who visited us in the afternoon of mercantile power, "that in no country in the civilized world is less attention paid to philosophy than in the United States."[123] But politics, the practical science of regulating government and trade, takes its place.[124] A practical interest! "The inhabitants of that country (America) look upon what are properly styled literary pursuits with a kind of disapprobation. . . . The spirit of the Americans is averse to general ideas; and it does not seek theoretical discoveries." "In America, the inventions of Europe are adopted with sagacity; they are perfected, and adapted with admirable skill to the wants of the country. Manufacturers exist, but the science of manufacturing is not cultivated; and they have good workmen, but very few inventors."[125] Is not this the spirit of Poor Richard, who so perfectly expresses the eighteenth century? And yet—there is that Chinese cabinet, "dating from 1700," in the Metropolitan Museum!

Canton, and descriptions of the Society and Sandwich Islands. . . . The 'famous Salem Museum' contains curiosities from this trade." Martineau, *Society in America*, II, 67-69. (1837)

[122] ". . . commerce found its interest in submission (to the British blockade) . . . on the whole the British frigates and admiralty courts created comparatively little scandal by injustice, while they served as a protection from the piratical privateers of Spain and France . . . the profits of neutrality soothed the offended merchant, and the blockade of New York was already a fixed practice (1806). Had the British commanders been satisfied with a moderate exercise of their power, the United States would probably have allowed the habit of neutral blockade to grow into a belligerent right by prescription." Adams, *History*, III, 92-93.

[123] II, 484.

[124] American literature from 1760 to 1789 is "predominantly political in content, style, and purpose. The Revolutionary leaders . . . were concerned chiefly with such weighty matters as the nature of the British constitution, the formulation of colonial rights, and the elaboration of schemes of government and administration. . . ." The sources of this literature are the classical education of the age, the moulding power of closely reasoned theological and legal treatises on which ministers and lawyers fed, and the subtle, pervasive influence of the English Bible. (*Cambridge History of American Literature*, I, 124.) In 1775-1781 this literature runs low, when the case had been fully stated and hostilities were on; but it flares up again from 1781 to 1789 with peace and the demands of trade for stable government. *Ibid.*, I, 143, 145.

[125] de Tocqueville, I, 266, 339.

III

The Rise of Conflicting Forces
(*continued*)

1. THE RISE OF THE FRONTIER SPIRIT; DEFINITION
OF ITS QUALITIES

WE HAVE seen how in the seaboard regions the cosmopolitan spirit develops; the theologians and their spiritual descendants look to Europe for guidance in theology and philosophy and ethics; the aristocracy, for polite letters and the arts, for fashionable follies and the tradition of good manners; the mercantile classes, for information about continental politics and diplomacy, economics, revolutions and wars, and the balance of trade. Meanwhile, in the back country, a new spirit arises: it is the spirit of the frontier.

Always pushing west, the Americans yet move in waves; when times are good along the coastal plain the wave subsides; when times are bad, the flow increases. The great western drift of our people began almost at the moment they became Americans, and ceased to be merely British colonists:[1] it is the Critical Period of American history. Again, from the outbreak of the French Revolution down to 1800 Kentucky and Tennessee fill up, states that profit little by the prosperity of the East; then in 1803 the movement is checked. But when the Embargo Act goes into effect, immigration pours into Ohio until the War of 1812 halts it for a time. From 1815 to 1818 the flow is phenomenal, largely at the expense of the East, which receives little emigration from Europe: it is the Napoleonic period.[2] This vigorous, active West, continually increasing, comes in

---

[1] Roosevelt, *The Winning of the West*, I, 324; and see chap. i ("The Indian Wars, 1784-1787"), III.

[2] See McMaster, IV, chap. xxxii. From 1790 to 1820 immigration from Europe was only about 250,000, an average of less than 8,500 a year. *A Century of Population Growth*, p. 85. In 1817 the figures for ten ports, according to Gall, a careful observer, are 22,240. *Meine Auswanderungen*, II, 547. The figures for 1831 are 23,000; for 1837, 78,000; for 1839, 52,000 (the panic of 1837 made the United States less attractive). McMaster, VII, 221. From 1820 to 1850 there were 2,455,815 immigrants, an average of almost 82,000 per year, or ten times the average for the previous years. *A Century of Population Growth*, p. 85. It is easily seen that from 1790 to 1820 the West increased at the expense of the East. Some of the New England states actually declined in population.

time to develop a culture of its own: we shall call it the frontier spirit. What are its qualities?[3]

On the frontier, says Turner, is formed from twenty different nations that composite nationality which is America, for here the complexities of European culture are reduced to their elements; what is useless is rejected, what is needed, survives, takes new form, and develops. Sheer distance decreases the dependence of these people upon Europe for supplies; a middleman class, the merchants of the East, arises to supply their wants, and in time becomes likewise less European. The frontier develops a political program: a demand for free land, internal improvements, free navigation of the Mississippi, paper currency, a tariff; and out of such demands come the Louisiana purchase, the state banks, state currency, and the "American system" of Clay.[4] Indeed, the middle states, as the frontier flows across them, become the typically American states; they are by and by to be called the Valley of Democracy, and Gopher Prairie and Zenith lie across the boundaries of the century. In the meantime the doctrinaire democracy of Jefferson becomes the national republicanism of Monroe, the militant individualism of Jackson—a new and distinct entity enters American life.

In the first place, environment makes the frontiersman an

---

[3] Consult Turner, *The Frontier in American History;* Roosevelt; Paxson. For a brief résumé of the psychological and racial characteristics of the frontier see Roosevelt, *Life of Thomas Hart Benton,* chap. i. There is an excellent picture of frontier life in Georgia in the 1820's in Wade, *Augustus Baldwin Longstreet,* chap. iii. Consult also Murat, *A Moral and Political Sketch of the United States,* letter three, for a sketch of the frontier in the thirties; and for an unfavorable view, Mrs. Trollope, *The Domestic Manners of the Americans,* especially on the Mississippi country. Of course the various travellers listed in the bibliography have a good deal to add, most of it unfavorable.

[4] From Clay's speech on the tariff of 1824: "What is the cause of this widespreading distress, of this deep depression which we behold stamped on the public countenance? It is to be found in the fact that during almost the whole existence of the Government we have shaped our industry, our navigation, and our commerce in reference to an extraordinary war in Europe and to foreign markets which no longer exist; in the fact that we have depended too much upon foreign sources of supply and excited too little the native; in the fact that while we have cultivated with assiduous care our foreign resources, we have suffered those at home to wither in a state of neglect and abandonment. . . . Let us create also a home market to give further scope to the consumption of American industry" and "adopt a genuine American policy." The appellation outweighed argument, and the bill passed. McMasters, V, 235-6. Murat (*op. cit.,* pp. 342-3) notes that communism and the American system are the two extremes of thought.

intense individualist.[5] This intense individualism[6] passes into social life.[7] Paradoxically, the tendency of that life is anti-social: "it produces antipathy to control, and particularly to any direct control. The tax-gatherer is viewed as a representative of oppression."[8] Their military and political leaders can hardly hold them in; the race is "a race of hereditary rebels,"[9] physically large and strong, mentally alert, socially rebellious,— the state of Franklin, for instance, is their creation,[10] and Burr thought he would find them pliable.[11] Clark and other Western men, in defiance of Washington's proclamations, offered their services to Genêt.[12] Self-confidence, equality, and the demand for autonomy constitute their political theory; "a belief in natural rights found ready lodgment in the minds of residents along the frontier";[13] restless and ready for experiment, they support everything from unlimited manhood suffrage to the initiative, referendum, and recall. They believe in themselves; their minds are characterized by coarseness and strength, acute-

[5] Roosevelt, *The Winning of the West,* I, 154; III, 102-4.

[6] "Many of the Americans of the West were born in the woods, and they mix the ideas and customs of savage life with the civilization of their parents. Their passions are more intense; their religious morality less authoritative; and their convictions less secure. The inhabitants exercise no sort of control over their fellow-citizens, for they are scarcely acquainted with each other. The nations of the west display, to a certain extent, the inexperience and the rude habits of a people in its infancy; for although they are composed of old elements, their assemblage is of recent date." De Tocqueville, I, 347.

[7] "The whole character of the westward movement, the methods of warfare, of settlement, and government, were determined by the extreme and defiant individualism of the backwoodsmen, their inborn independence and self-reliance, and their intensely democratic spirit. The West was won and settled by a number of groups of men, all acting independently of one another, but with a common object and at about the same time." Roosevelt, III, 61. (Cf. the account of the battle of King's Mountain for a typical instance, II, 296 ff.) Their "little communities were extremely independent in feeling, not only of the Federal Government, but of their parent States, and even of one another." *Ibid.,* III, 65. "In the strongly marked frontier character no traits were more pronounced than the dislike of crowding and the tendency to roam to and fro, hither and thither, always with a westward trend." *Ibid.,* IV, 270.

[8] Turner, p. 30.

[9] Simons, p. 141.

[10] Cf. the account in Roosevelt of the State of Franklin, III, 242 ff.; and of the separatist movements which preceded its formation, III, 176 ff.

[11] See Wandell and Minnigerode, *Aaron Burr,* vol. II, parts vi-viii.

[12] Paxson, p. 107.

[13] Paxson, p. 100. "The man who within his own lifetime has been the whole process of social evolution going on under his eyes is not a believer in the unchangeableness of social institutions." Simons, p. 141.

ness and acquisitiveness; they are practical and inventive; they have a grasp of material things, are completely blind to the artistic;[14] they develop in their thinking a restless nervous energy in contrast to the phlegm of the colonists. They are buoyant and exuberant,[15] they possess an exhilaration springing from the freedom of the great spaces they inhabit. The frontiersman has "little patience with finely drawn distinctions or scruples of method";[16] his sense of business honor in state affairs is lax, whatever his personal integrity. In such a society leadership develops on the ancient basis of a man's personal sway over his followers: Clay, Jackson, Harrison, Lincoln—these are their leaders, no less than Sevier, Boone, and Davy Crockett—and the spoils system they bring in is astonishingly like the giving of rings in Beowulf. Here, if ever, "society became atomic"; it is the individual who counts.[17]

This democracy breeds also equality; and if the anarchic individualism of the frontier exalted the American, its equality depressed him.

[14] Writing of frontier Georgia in the 1820's Wade remarks that the people had had no opportunity of knowing art. There were nomadic portrait painters, and "some magazines that carried with endless boasts on the part of their editors, some atrocious colored pictures of Georgia scenery." Much later the Greek Slave was brought to Augusta to be exhibited. "It was glowingly admired by the editor of one paper, and by the male population, one can suppose, in general. What the ladies thought of it must, since the ladies were required to view the masterpiece at a soirée for 'ladies only,' remain forever a secret. That good Georgian, Major Jones, found the statuary adorning the Capitol at Washington a little more pornographic than he could well endure." Wade, *Augustus Baldwin Longstreet*, p. 68.
[15] Cf. the chapter on "The Laughter of the West" in Pattee, *A History of American Literature Since 1870*. Nichols, in *Forty Years of American Life*, I, 286-8, collects the following instances of exuberant frontier humor. "A Western man sleeps so sound, it would take an earthquake to wake him. He is in danger pretty considerable much, because somebody was down on him, like the whole Missouri on a sand-bar. He is a gone 'coon.' He is down on all cussed varmints, gets into an everlasting fix, and holds that the longest pole knocks down the persimmons. A story smells rather tall. Stranger, he says, in bar hunts I am numerous. He says a pathetic story sunk into his feelings like a snagged boat into the Mississippi. He tells of a person as cross as a bar with two cubs and a sore tail. He laughs like a hyena over a dead nigger. He walks through a fence like a falling tree through a cobweb. He goes the whole hog. He raises right smart of corn and lives where there is a smart chance of bars. Bust me wide open, he says, if I didn't bulge into the creek in the twinkling of a bedpost, I was so thunderin' savagerous. . . . The story of land so rich that a squash vine in its rapid growth, overtook a drove of pigs, was a western exaggeration." The American chapters of *Martin Chuzzlewit* are not greatly exaggerated, it would seem.
[16] Turner, p. 212.
[17] My indebtedness to Turner in the above paragraph is obvious.

It is a nice question whether the equalitarian or the individualizing forces were the weightier. The one condition that the pioneer could not get away from was the oppressive similarity of his life with that of his neighbours. He had a tendency to suffer from whatever affected them. . . . He resented the equality, but shrank from standing out as different. He was keenly resentful of anything that seemed like coercion, but saw nothing inconsistent in being intolerant of the habits or opinions of others.[18]

We trace this levelling tendency everywhere in the West. After the Revolution the Kentuckians grew to dislike thoroughly the Church of England and welcomed the Baptist in its place: "the rough democracy of the border welcomed a sect which was itself essentially democratic," and "where their preachers obtained foothold, it was made a matter of reproach to the Presbyterian clergymen that they had been educated in early life for the ministry for a profession."[19] In the Holston settlements men were predominantly Calvinists: "of the great recognized creeds it was the most republican in its tendencies, and so the best suited to the backwoodsmen."[20] Their political institutions are in their infancy pure republicanism: read, for instance, the outline of the Watauga constitution as given by Roosevelt,[21] and this democratic tendency clings to the state constitutions of the Western states as opposed to the Eastern. On the one hand they are greatly tolerant, even of creeds (like the Anglican and the Roman Catholic) which in theory they despise; where all are alike, individual eccentricity may develop when it carries with it no power for controlling others. But equally they despise those who attempt to rise above the common level: "the typical frontiersman felt a stolid pride in his disdain for intellectual attainment. The few who possessed unusual culture were generally forced, if they wished to gain the confidence of their neighbors, to adapt themselves as rapidly as possible to the more primitive environment. Louis Philippe, obliged to act as mediator in a backwoods tavern brawl, learned the spirit of Western democracy."[22]

So from these opposite and inevitable traits opposite and necessary results arise. On the one hand there is a proud

[18] Paxson, p. 251.
[19] Roosevelt, II, 3, 4.
[20] Roosevelt, II, 276.
[21] III, 22 ff., 41 ff.
[22] Rusk, *The Literature of the Middle Western Frontier*, I, 75-76. See the whole passage.

belief in a manifest American destiny; on the other, an abnormal sensitiveness to criticism. Both were nourished by the isolation of the frontier regions,[23] their lack of communication with the East and with Europe. Thus thrust upon its own resources, ignorant and distrustful of the culture of the East, the West came to believe in progress as the fated destiny of America.

The pioneer created progress, progress meant expansion, expansion meant one-hundred-per-cent Americanism, a superb arrogance, a conscious sense of superiority to the effete kingdoms of Europe. Listen to young James Buchanan delivering his Fourth-of-July oration before the Washington Society of Lancaster in 1815:

Foreign influence has been, in every age, the curse of Republics. Her jaundiced eye sees all things in false colors. The thick atmosphere of prejudice, by which she is forever surrounded, excludes from her sight the light of reason; while she worships the nations which she favors for their very crimes, she curses the enemies of that nation, even their virtues. In every age she has marched before the enemies of her country, "proclaiming peace, when there was no peace," and lulling its defenders into fatal security, whilst the iron hand of despotism has been aiming a death-blow at their liberties. . . . We are separated from the nations of Europe by an immense ocean. We are still more disconnected from them by a different form of government, and by the enjoyment of true liberty. Why, then, should we injure ourselves by taking part in the ambitious contests of foreign despots and kings?[24]

[23] "In spite of the constant Westward drift of a great body of population, the means of communication, though always improving, were primitive enough throughout the pioneer period to have a considerable influence in checking the spread of intelligence and preventing close intellectual contact with the outside world." Rusk, I, 23. Kentucky and Ohio were not free from the Indian menace until the end of the eighteenth century, and even then, as the War of 1812 and the Black Hawk War were to prove, the middle West was not safe. The first steamboat, the *New Orleans,* made the voyage from Pittsburg down the Ohio and the Mississippi in 1811; in 1817 the first steamer ascended the river from St. Louis. There was no steamship on Lake Erie until 1818, when *Walk-in-the-Water* began its run from Detroit to Buffalo, and no daily line of vessels until 1830. As late as 1840 there were only a few short railroad lines in the West. Mails to and from the West from 1800 to 1840 were the cause of constant complaint. In the early years of this period the government dispatched the mail once or twice a week over the western routes; there were long delays; and it frequently took one or two months for a letter or newspaper to reach Kentucky and Ohio from the East. In 1810 the time from Lexington to Philadelphia for the mail was two weeks. Rusk, I, 23-28.

[24] Quoted in Curtis, *James Buchanan,* I, 13. Compare Emerson's paragraph on monarchs who "look with apprehension" on America. *Journals, 1820-1824,* pp. 246-7. For his fear of the frontier elements, see pp. 247-8.

Why, indeed? A thousand orators ask the same question. It was, in its way, a magnificent dream: Europe in the seventeenth century had led many to draw an ideal picture of a people happy without the vices of civilization,[25] an Arcadian land of Indians, more temperate, more rational (*raisonable*) than Europeans;[26] the eighteenth had seen the creation of a republic such as Montesquieu and Rousseau had pictured, and now the Americans, conscious of carrying out the desire of the world, of conducting a unique social laboratory, were not unnaturally proud of their place in the sun: Miss Martineau saw them "as a great embryo poet."[27] To deny the superiority of the Americans is to deny the creed of the frontier.[28]

But it is not always poetical to boast. Public opinion in the United States, says Chevalier in 1834, is "intolerant towards foreign nations; the American democracy in particular, bred up in the belief that the nations of Europe groan ignobly under the yoke of absolute despots, looks upon them with a mixture of pity and contempt."[29] Traveller after traveller comments upon this chauvinism[30]—an egotism that irritates for once the philosophic calm of de Tocqueville:

[25] Consult Chinard, *L'Exotisme américain dans la littérature française au xvie siècle.*
[26] Chinard, p. 242. Communistic experiments begin with Rapp's colony in 1804-5, and are practical expressions of this dream. See McMaster, X, chap. xliii.
[27] "For the last fifty years no pains have been spared to convince the inhabitants of the United States that they constitute the only religious, enlightened, and free people. They perceive that, for the present, their own democratic institutions succeed, while those of other countries fail; hence they conceive an overweening opinion of their superiority, and they are not very remote from believing themselves to belong to a distinct race of mankind." De Tocqueville, II, 433.
[28] A single instance will serve for many, this being of western Georgia. "Richard Henry Wilde, in addition to being a good lawyer, and a successful politician, had got into his head a decided love of pure literature; but Longstreet probably could not endorse this sort of love any too much. In the first place it was inspired by poets like Collins and Gray, to whom Mr. Pope, he held, was manifestly superior; was inspired, too, by Italian poets of mediaeval times, by persons who believed, in spiritual matters even, as well as in temporal, in the principle of autocratic authority. In the second place, it was understood that Mr. Wilde considered the possibility of going to Europe and spending years, if necessary, in an effort to write a life of those long-dead papists—this in a time when the spirit of man was struggling to arise from the long stupor in which the very autocracy which Wilde found so attractive had for so long held it." Wade, *Augustus Baldwin Longstreet,* p. 75. See also the quotation from Miller's *Bench and Bar* on p. 190.
[29] Chevalier, *United States,* p. 188.
[30] Consult Mesick, *The English Traveller in America, 1785-1835;* and Nevins, *American Social History as Recorded by British Travellers,* for brief surveys. See also chap. xiv, 496-500 below.

Nothing is more embarrassing in the ordinary intercourse of life than this irritating patriotism of the Americans. . . . America is . . . a free country, in which, lest anybody should be hurt by your remarks, you are not allowed to speak freely of private individuals, or of the State, of the citizens or of the authorities, or, in short, of anything at all, except it be of the climate and the soil; and even then Americans will be found ready to defend either the one or the other, as if they had been contrived by the inhabitants of the country.[31]

But if the frontier spirit is proud, arrogant, and boastful, it is likewise sensitive to a fault. Duelling long survived, because of the intense sensitiveness bred by lonely lives and social equality,[32] and the same sensitiveness, arising from concealed fear of inferiority, may be traced in many ways. So good a historian as Henry Adams assures us that the dislike of diplomacy manifested from the early days of the republic "was a relic of the old colonial status when America had been dependent on Europe,—a prejudice rising chiefly from an uneasy sense of social disadvantage."[33] "Members of this great republic," wrote the great Lyell in 1848, "are sensitive and touchy about their country," and he gives passage after passage to prove that it is so.[34] The spirit spreads—even to Boston: "the Bostonians" are "most sensitive to any illiberal remarks about their country," even though they pride themselves on their English ways —or because of it, Captain Marryat does not know which.[35] "You class us," said a politician to Lyell, "with the South American republics; your ambassadors to us come from Brazil, and Mexico, and consider it a step in their advancement to go from the United States to Spain or some second-rate German court."[36] On board the *Andrew Jackson* another American complains to him of the absence from English newspapers of any discussion of the Oregon question: it is an affront to the country.[37] Buckingham, who agrees with Captain Marryat that the Bostonians are proud of their British ancestry, agrees also that "as a singular contrast to this, there is perhaps no city in the Union, where the jealousy of the English is greater, or

[31] *Democracy in America,* I, 249.
[32] Paxson, p. 251.
[33] Adams, *History,* IV, 467.
[34] Lyell, *A Second Visit to the United States of America,* I, 131. The first volume of this work is filled with illustrative incidents.
[35] Marryat, *Diary in America,* I, 87.
[36] Lyell, *op. cit.,* I, 226.
[37] *Ibid.,* II, 170. Compare the political discussions in *Martin Chuzzlewit.*

where the people feel more reluctance to admit the superiority of the English to themselves in any matter of art, science, literature, skill, language, character or manners."[38] And if this be the attitude toward foreign criticism, it is equally the attitude towards things at home. A jealousy of riches, a distrust of the desire of the wealthy to live in genteel fashion—Sir Charles Lyell, de Tocqueville, Lord Bryce, all comment upon this levelling influence, making for the monotony of American life.[39]

This alternation of arrogance and sensitiveness produces in turn its profound spiritual effects upon the culture of the regions over which the frontier moves. Of the civilization which has been left behind much is shed, but of what remains the frontier is tenacious to a degree. Religion, morality, education,—these great fundamental facts, reduced to their lowest denominator, exert a conservative tendency upon the wild and luxuriant exuberance of the backwoods. Almost the first act of the settlers is to found schools;[40] learning is prized; "many a backwoods woman by thrift and industry, by the sale of her butter and cheese, and the calves from her cows, enabled her husband to give his sons good schooling, and perhaps to provide for some favored member of the family the opportunity to secure a really first-class education."[41] And by and by they secure textbooks, sometimes writing them and printing them in rude print-shops along the Ohio and in Kentucky, textbooks that teach a moral and social conservatism surprising in communities of this character—one-sided, prejudiced, blind to the artistic and the imaginative; it is practical morality, practical knowl-

---

[38] Buckingham, *America,* III, 422. For American resentment of British criticism see McMaster, V, chap. xlviii and Spiller, *The American in England,* chap. ix. The student will find an evaluation of the different travel books in Mesick, *The English Traveller in America,* and Nevins, *op. cit.* In general I have cited their books with a good deal of caution. "Where so good a judge (as Dwight) professed ignorance, other observers were likely to mislead; and Frenchmen like Liancourt, Englishmen like Wild, or Germans like Bülow, were almost equally worthless authorities on a subject which none understood, *i.e.,* national habits of life and thought." Adams, *History,* I, 41.

[39] Lyell tells a story of a candidate for office in Alabama who canvassed great distances on foot, though he could afford a horse, as he did not wish to antagonize the poorer voters. Lyell, *op. cit.,* II, 62. "I know no country in which there is so little true independence of mind and freedom of discussion as in America. . . . In America the majority raises very formidable barriers to the liberty of opinion." De Tocqueville, I, 280, 281. In Bryce's *American Commonwealth,* consult the chapter on "The Uniformity of American Life."

[40] Roosevelt, III, 102.

[41] *Ibid.,* I, 196.

edge that avail. The early school readers are "emphatic in the glorification of moral, religious, and purely practical concerns, and aiding thus on one side of cultural growth, they failed almost completely to stir the imagination, and they scarcely suggested the possibility of enjoyment in music and the fine arts or in literature freed of too immediate didactic purposes. Thus, while these vastly influential educational classics helped destroy much of the crudity of the older frontier civilization, they may also be held largely responsible for withholding from later generations of Westerners an appreciation of some of the finer elements of culture."[42] Their religion is instinct with the stubborn, protestant spirit; theirs is the Old Testament spirit, which adds to their belief in a divine call to clear the land of Frenchmen, Britishers, and savages;[43] they have the simple, patriarchal virtues;[44] but they are at the same time credulous, superstitious, hostile to Episcopalianism, to the Roman Catholic; theirs is the fundamentalism of the non-conformist conscience. They affect to jeer at book-learning, but when they themselves come to compose books, they affect the style of the cultured world, or rather a style that the world of letters has already discarded; their dreary epics, their verbose and "literary" novels, stilted dramas, and artificial satires are impossible to read; but such is their innate conservatism that they do not turn to pulsating life around them for their themes, or, if they do, they bury all reality under barbarous imitations of popular English classics,[45] and the simple, eloquent pages of their diaries and journals to which today we turn with interest are not for them literature at all. The stilted diction of Johnson, the artificial grandeurs of Byronism, the pompous emotionalism of Chateaubriand come oddly from these lips: it is like a child dressing up in the garments of kings. They are too humble, too servile to the East.

But the frontier is a paradox. It accepts, and it repels, effete civilization. It hastens to found newspapers, and prides itself on its bad grammar. It imitates Byron, and it insists on local

---

[42] Rusk, *Literature of the Middle Western Frontier*, I, 269. For descriptions of particular books, such as James Hall's *The Western Reader*, 1833, see I, pp. 265 ff.

[43] Read the highly interesting passage in Roosevelt, II, 197-8, as to the effect of the Old Testament upon the frontier attitude toward the Indians.

[44] Roosevelt, I, 156, 194-5; II, 2.

[45] The best study is of course Rusk, *The Literature of the Middle Western Frontier*. Consult also Venable, *The Beginnings of Literary Culture in the Ohio Valley*.

literature. It is extremely sceptical, and it is rich in religious conservatism. It is a law unto itself, and it is highly moral, demanding didactic fiction and improving verse. It is cynical to the last degree, and dotes on sentimentalism in its poetry, in its simple music, in its crude and pathetic art. It wants to stand alone, and it looks back wistfully to the old home. And so we note that together with this conservative acceptance of outworn literary standards, the frontier is likewise *sui generis,* and arrogantly self-sufficient.

There arises the desire that America shall be for the Americans, a contempt for things of culture, a feeling that to be interested in European art is to pose, to be unpatriotic. Thus it is that frontier oratory exhibits "the freedom of the Westerner . . . to say what he thought on any subject, either within or without the province of his knowledge, and to defy all critical dicta" with "unrestrained superlatives and extravagantly florid diction" designed to "represent a race of vigorous men who were the possessors of a new and vast country destined to become the commercial, political, and cultural center of the world."[46] Thus it is that Major Jack Downing emerges from the Maine woods to inaugurate the racy line of cracker-box philosophers,[47] that after Natty Bumppo, Davy Crockett takes his part in the national mythology, Arkansas becomes humorous, and mis-spelling is a characteristic of American humor—a slap at the correctness of the East. "After Crockett," we read, "it became almost necessary that a Western candidate for the presidency should claim a suitably wild nickname, or at least some of the personal characteristics of the frontiersman."[48] The wild man of the West in the person of Artemus Ward, Walt Whitman, Joaquin Miller, or Mark Twain by and by becomes for London the standard American figure.[49] Eventually the frontier, uneducated, shrewd, superficially irreverent, utterly independent and honest, will in the person of Mark Twain sit in immortal judgment upon the glories and the shams of Europe: *Innocents Abroad* is the frontier confronting the eastern world, but it is not written until the sixties.

[46] Rusk, I, 205.
[47] Consult Tandy, *Crackerbox Philosophers,* chap. ii.
[48] Tandy, p. 69. Old Rough and Ready, The Railsplitter, The Log Cabin Campaign, The Mill Boy of the Slashes. See chap. iv.
[49] Consult Pattee, *A History of American Literature Since 1870,* chap. ii.

But before we take our leave of the frontier spirit, let that admirable observer, de Tocqueville, define the paradox of its qualities:

If it be your intention to confer a certain elevation upon the human mind, and to teach it to regard the things of this world with generous feelings, to inspire men with a scorn of mere temporal advantage, to give birth to living convictions, and to keep alive the spirit of honourable devotedness; if you hold it to be a good thing to refine the habits, to embellish the manners, to cultivate the arts of a nation, and to promote the love of poetry, of beauty, and of renown; if you would constitute a people not unfitted to act with power upon all other nations, nor unprepared for those high enterprises which, whatever be the result of its efforts, will leave a name forever famous in time—if you believe such to be the principal object of society, you must avoid the government of democracy. . . .
But if you hold it to be expedient to divert the moral and intellectual activity of man to the production of comfort and to the acquirement of the necessaries of life; if a clear understanding be more profitable to man than genius; if your object be not to stimulate the virtues of heroism, but to create habits of peace; if you had rather witness vices than crimes, and are content with fewer noble deeds, provided offences be diminished in the same proportion; if, instead of living in the midst of a brilliant state of society, you are contented to have prosperity around you; if, in short, you are of the opinion that the principal object of a Government is to . . . insure the greatest degree of enjoyment and the least degree of misery to each of the individuals who compose it . . . you can have no surer means of satisfying them than by equalizing the conditions of men, and establishing democratic institutions.[50]

"Equalizing the conditions of men, and establishing democratic institutions!" This was the ultimate work of the frontier.

2. THE RISE OF THE MIDDLE CLASS SPIRIT; DEFINITION OF ITS QUALITIES

But the cultural conflict in America is not merely between the cosmopolitan spirit and the spirit of the frontier. Each of these bifurcates, as it were: the merchant prince of the seacoast, the theocratic state, give birth to the bourgeoisie; and as the frontier is settled, as small towns spring up, the middle class arises. The inciting cause? As life becomes stabilized, manufacture becomes possible: we have an industrial revolution in America. The seventeenth century yields to the eighteenth; the eighteenth to the nineteenth; and in the nineteenth century, the spirit of the middle class is dominant.[51]

[50] *Democracy in America*, I, 269-70.
[51] Although the middle class is clearly the most important single element in the cultural history of the nineteenth century, no single study has been consecrated to tracing the development of an American bourgeoisie.

The merchant is an aristocrat in all but birth, but the small trader, the established small farmer, the members of the evangelical churches, the inhabitants of the villages and towns are, though involved in the eighteenth century commercial system, as different in spirit and interest from the lordly mercantile aristocracy of the sea-coast as they are from the rough, tumultuous democracy of the frontier. Under Washington the merchants and the planters are in power; but the merchants must have articles to sell, and, moreover, as the frontier rolls westward, it is increasingly difficult to secure from Europe the articles it desires. Consequently, as new sources of raw material develop in the United States, the merchants, to their own political undoing, call into being the manufacturing classes. Hamilton's financial policy may almost be said to have created American manufactures; he sought to create a class which would be dependent upon a strong central government.[52] The merchants and the manufacturers are for a time allied against the planters, the South loses, the North gains; but the merchants at the opening of the nineteenth century[53] are, nevertheless, driven from power.[54] For one thing they make themselves unpopular; they try to suppress the expression of sympathy with the French Revolution; and they are contemptuous of the "mob." But, what is more important, when European products are shut off by the Napoleonic wars, domestic manufactures thrive,[55] and a new force enters the nation. "This new and vigorous industrial interest, pulsating with power, present and potential, contributed strongly to the overthrow of Hamiltonian Federalism and the installation of Jeffersonian individualism. . . . It was not the old planters of the sea-board that placed Jefferson in the presidential chair. On the contrary, these were more generally Federalist in their sympathies. They were united

[52] On the scarcity of manufacturing during the Revolution see Bogart, *An Economic History of the United States,* chap. x. There is a convenient excerpt from Hamilton's famous Report on Manufactures (1791), pp. 151-2. "The moderately protective tariff and the land policy, combined with a most intense public sentiment in favor of domestic products amounting to a boycott on foreign products where the domestic was attainable, led to a rapid development of manufactures." Simons, *op. cit.,* p. 117.

[53] Bogart selects the year 1808 as a convenient date for distinguishing the industrial independence of the United States. P. 159.

[54] For a typical instance consult Fox's brilliant study, *The Decline of Aristocracy in the Politics of New York.*

[55] The census of 1810 returned the manufactures of the country as $198,-613,474. Bogart, p. 160. In 1789 Tench Coxe estimated the total value of American manufactures as about $50,000,000. *Ibid.,* p. 152.

by many ties of the past, if not of the present, with the New England merchants."[56] If it was not the planters, then the new upland cotton raisers, the back country farmers, western interests, and the manufacturers accomplished the feat.[57]

As the War of 1812 has been called a second war of independence, an independence reflected in the increased feeling of nationalism which shows in all departments of life,[58] so it may be said also to mark a national independence in industry. The result was eventually the industrial transformation of the country, the emergence of the machine-owning capitalist class. Shipowners put their capital into manufactures, always stimulated by war; societies were formed to encourage industry; premiums, bounties, tax exemptions were offered to foster it; strenuous efforts were made to entice foreign artisans to the United States.[59] But an industrial system is not possible without a credit system; to achieve credit, one must be socially reputable, responsible, able to meet one's obligations, have money, be thrifty,—be in short a pillar of the community. Respectability becomes the standard of society, and respectability is the symbol of the middle class.

Respectability, it is true, is nothing new. It is marked in New

---

[56] Simons, pp. 124-5.

[57] Simons, *ibid.* Cf. Fox, chap. viii, "Property or People," a discussion of the various elements and views in the New York Constitutional Convention of 1821.

[58] "For the first time in their history the people of the United States learned in June, 1807 [date of the Chesapeake-Leonard affair] the feeling of a true national emotion . . . the outrage committed on the 'Chesapeake' stung through hide-bound prejudices, and made democrat and aristocrat writhe alike." The Orders in Council of November 11, 1807, "gave an impulse so energetic to the history of the United States, they worked effectually to drive American into a new path." Adams, IV, 27, 79. "The war gave a severe shock to the Anglican sympathies of society, and peace seemed to widen the breach between European and American tastes. Interest in Europe languished after Napoleon's overthrow. France ceased to affect American opinion." *Ibid.,* IX, 221. This study will show that the last statement is mistaken.

[59] Bogart, chap. xi; Simons, pp. 147-8. In 1811 there were 87 mills operating 80,000 spindles, using 2,880,000 pounds of yarn, and employing 4,000 employees; in 1815, there were 500,000 spindles using 27,000,000 pounds of raw cotton, with 76,000 employees. The iron industry lacked only 3,000 tons of supplying the whole country. Pittsburgh came into being, the number of patents increased, and *Niles Weekly Register,* founded in 1811, became the organ of class interests, the defender of protective tariffs. Pennsylvania became the center of political power, the "keystone state." In 1787 Tench Coxe estimated that less than one-eighth of the population was engaged in manufactures, fisheries, navigation, and trade; the census of 1820 gave 13.7 per cent of the working population as engaged in manufacturing and mechanic arts alone.

England from the beginning. It is part of eighteenth century consciousness; and in the eighteenth century one can see in America the emergence of that new class of society, the bourgeoisie.[60] The United States is still a part of Europe—that Europe which saw the emergence of the middle class in France, in Great Britain, in Germany, to political and social power. Wherever there is trade, there tends to develop a middle class. In Europe this class evolves a literature of its own in praise of the family virtues, of morality, of thrift, prudence, a saving and economical life—sentimental comedy, bourgeois tragedy, the moralistic fiction of Richardson and Marmontel, of Marivaux and Goldsmith, and all this is, to greater or less degree, transported to America. In the eighteenth century the middle class in the colonies shares therefore in the cosmopolitan spirit, for it is a part of the trading spirit. But a middle class dependent upon small scale industry develops mainly in the nineteenth century; unlike its predecessor in the eighteenth century, it is strongly nationalistic in spirit—it keeps England separated from the continent, it creates a Louis Philippe who is not king of France, but King of the French, and it is this same middle class, nationalistic, moral, respectable, that develops in nineteenth century America between the end of the eighteenth century and the coming of large-scale industry after the Civil War.

And this class has its own cultural ideals. In economics it supports the laissez-faire system of Smith,[61] the utilitarianism of Bentham, the cautious liberalism of Burke and Macaulay and Mill. The British classical economists were followed in the

[60] Here are two typical instances of New England morality. Samuel Peters writes in his *General History of Connecticut* (1781) that "the women of Connecticut are strictly virtuous. . . . They are not permitted to read plays; cannot converse about whiste, quadrille, or operas; but will talk freely upon the subjects of history, geography and the mathematics." (Stedman and Hutchinson, III, 214.) Or again, Timothy Dwight boasts in 1796 that when the managers of the Theater in Boston applied "for leave to occupy the upper story of this building (the new market in Salem) as a theatre," "after consulting each other on the proposal," the proprietors "informed him, that they would sooner set it on fire." He is glad that there was not a single four-wheeled pleasure carriage in the town. *Travels,* I, 448.

[61] There is greatly needed a series of studies tracing the vogue of these writers in America. For the general indebtedness of American political economy to the British classical school see Professor E. R. A. Seligman's account in the *Cambridge History of American Literature,* chap. xxiv. Smith was reprinted in 1789, 1811, and 1818, but this does not measure the extent of his influence. For the influence of Adam Smith on Franklin, who passed on the torch, see Thomas D. Eliot, "The Relations between Adam Smith and Benjamin Franklin before 1776," *Political Science Quarterly,* XXXIX, March, 1924, pp. 67-96.

United States; and one notes that the doctrine of laissez-faire was re-enforced by an interest in the common-sense philosophy of Reid and the Scottish school,[62] as it shows its power in the American repudiation of the communistic doctrines of Saint-Simon and Fourier.[63] In fact, the complaint of humanitarians and of those interested in the conservation of national resources, whether material or human, is precisely against the overwhelming adoption of the laissez-faire philosophy of the nineteenth century.[64]

In morals they build on all the Poor Richard virtues. Inheritors of the great sentimental tradition of the eighteenth century, that is to say, of improving fiction, didactic poem without art or grace, and ameliorative essay, they add to this tradition in the nineteenth century a peculiar flavor of their own, the spirit

[62] First introduced at Princeton in 1768 by President Witherspoon, but not influential until later. See Riley, *American Thought from Puritanism to Pragmatism.*

[63] "That the mass of our countrymen had ever heard of Charles Fourier and his scheme of social reform prior to 1840 may well be doubted." Mc-Master, VII, 142. Emerson's essay on the Chardon Street Convention illumines the general American attitude.

[64] American industrial conditions were on a par with those in England. One notes that Matthew Carey, in his *Essays on Political Economy,* pp. 458-9, is enthusiastic over the employment of girls in New England factories at $1.50 a week. Women and children in 1836 went to work at half-past four in the morning, were given a half hour for breakfast, three-quarters of an hour for dinner, and were required to work as long as they could see. The working class was helpless in the grip of a middle-class. "The governor of Massachusetts was required to be 'a Christian worth £1000,'" and "the governor of Georgia must be the possessor of 500 acres of land and £4000." Voting was indirect, and jailing for debt still practiced. Lack of interest in the laborer is noted in the fact that "educational facilities were at their lowest ebb in 1814-18." Dexter, *History of Education in the United States,* pp. 97-8. De Witt Clinton, whose influence is fundamental in forming the educational system of New York State, was enthusiastic for the Lancasterian system; as he said in his address of 1809, "it arrives at its object with the least possible trouble and expense. Its distinguished characters are economy, facility and expedition, and its peculiar improvements are cheapness, activity, order and emulation." ("Least possible trouble . . . economy . . . cheapness!") See Fitzpatrick, *The Educational Views and Influence of De Witt Clinton,* p. 150, a very significant study. Fox remarks with grim humor that "it was a proud day when, in 1824, the *Commercial Advertiser* could announce that Mr. Ayres of Ithaca who manufactured imitation Leghorn hats, would soon employ 'one hundred females, some of whom are not more than eight years of age.'" Fox, *The Decline of Aristocracy,* p. 319. The laborer's only escape was to pioneer life.

Marks of protest against the system begin to appear in 1827, with the publication of *The Journeyman Mechanic's Advocate,* the first labor paper in the world (Cf. *Cambridge History of American Literature,* IV, 436); *The Mechanic's Free Press* (1828-31); and *The Workingmen's Advocate* (1829-36). Consult Simons, chap. xvii.

of the Pharisee: they thank God that they are not as other men are, especially Frenchmen.[65] In sum, to the sentimental morality of the eighteenth century, the nineteenth century adds the moral reaction away from the French Revolution, which the middle class views with the eyes of Burke. They abhor Tom Paine and Jefferson, the deism taught at Harvard and Yale, believed in Virginia and Philadelphia; they fear the materialism of Cadwallader Colden, Joseph Buchanan, Priestley, Thomas Cooper, Benjamin Rush, Condorcet, and the French *idéologues*.[66] When Jefferson was elected there was a religious revival in Kentucky; and the Federalists said that there was deep meaning in "such an outbreak of religious zeal immediately on the election of Thomas Jefferson, a man who worshipped at no altar and acknowledged no creed."[67]

And morality is so difficult to maintain! Dancing, for instance, must be put down lest it lead to evil, and besides, it wastes time.[68] Novel-reading must be stopped, for "novels not

[65] Among a hundred instances, let us select one. William Jay of New York to James Fenimore-Cooper, 5 January, 1827: "I was much amused with the lively picture you give me of french Society. It entirely agrees with the opinion I had previously formed of it. There is I presume no city in which all the arts that minister to sensual gratification are carried to greater perfection than in Paris; nor is there I suspect any city in which there is less real substantial happiness enjoyed. Vice and luxury lead to universal selfishness, and selfishness, by sacrificing the interests and happiness of others to individual gratication, mars and interrupts the general welfare. I was lately shocked to find from some official documents, that of all who are annually born in Paris one fourth are deserted by their parents, and of all who die, one tenth end their days in a hospital. What a frightful picture of vice and wretchedness do these facts exhibit! In vain will the nation seek in the triumphs of its arms, and the splendor of its arts and sciences, a compensation for this extinction of natural affection, and this wide spread destitution and suffering. May our republican simplicity and religious habits never be exchanged for the magnificence, heartlessness and wretchedness of France." *Correspondence of James Fenimore-Cooper*, I, 112-3.

[66] "Rousseau, Voltaire, Diderot, &c., were read by the old federals, but now (1832) they seem known more as naughty words than as great names." Mrs. Trollope, *Domestic Manners of the Americans*, pp. 281-2.

[67] McMaster, II, 583. For a choice collection of conservative estimates of Jefferson see chapter i in Fox, *The Decline of Aristocracy*.

[68] For instance, Gérard, the French Minister to America in 1778, wrote Vergennes that Congress, at the instigation of the Presbyterian delegates, passed a resolution renewing their request that the several states forbid dancing and theatrical representations, but "the very day this resolution was published there were held theatricals, acted by army officers and whig citizens. The next day the governor of Philadelphia gave a ball to a numerous company!" Quoted in Sherrill, *French Memories of Eighteenth Century America*, p. 36. However, dancing did not fare so well in New England. For instance, in the winter of 1781-2, there was a dancing school held in

only pollute the imaginations of young women, but also give
them false ideas of life, which too often make them act im-
properly, owing to the romantic turn of thinking they imbibe
from their favourite studies."[69] This quotation is from an
eighteenth century periodical; one learns in 1801 that novels are
"one great engine in the hands of the fiends of darkness,"[70]
that they are written by "the insidious propagaters of infidelity"; in 1817 that "the perusal of novels is calculated to do
mischief. It is, in the first place, a useless and criminal waste
of time; and it is fitted in the second place to unhinge good
habits and dissipate all sober reflection."[71] Novels, we read in
1822, "add fuel to the flames of passion," and this, alas!
"enervates the mind; it generates a sickliness of fancy; and it
renders the ordinary affairs of life insipid." Besides, it wastes
time.[72] Moreover, "a 'novel-reading female' expects attention
from her husband, which the cares of the business will not permit him to pay"[73]—business before all! And this evangelical

New Haven. Simeon Baldwin's diary records the event: March 7: "A great
Noise about the Dancing School. Meets of Select Men & Civil Authy . . ."
March 12: "Great dissatisfaction about the School of polite manners, called
the Dancing School." March 29, 1782, Simeon Baldwin to Isaacs: "Our
Dancing School . . . has become the subject of Paper wars, Political De-
bates & Tea table Chittchat. . . ." April 11: "Violent Proceedgs about danc-
ing Master—to leave To to-morrow." Baldwin, *Life and Letters of Simeon
Baldwin*, pp. 77-78.

[69] *Columbian Magazine*, third series, II, October, 1792, pp. 225-6.

[70] *Philadelphia Repository and Weekly Register*, I, 238, Saturday, June 6,
1801. However, the next month the first instalment of *Edward Walmen*,
an original novel by "a young gentleman of Philadelphia" occupies the front
page of the magazine! (July 4, 1801).

[71] *The Analectic Magazine*, IX, 31, January, 1817. See also Dwight,
Travels, I, 516, (1821); and John E. Edwards, "Novel Reading," *The
Ladies Repository*, III, 115-7, January, 1843 for the ecclesiastical point
of view.

[72] *Portfolio*, I, 280 ff. "Let any person calculate the number of actual
hours expended in a large family, where, perhaps, 30 or more of these volumes have been perused by 5 or 6 individuals, and let him multiply this
into the aggregate of the national reading." P. 283.

[73] *The Analectic Magazine*, IX, 238, September, 1817. Novels "always
nourish, and often give birth to, that sickly train of feelings commonly
known by the name of sentiment . . . a weak woman is left open to the
flatteries of an idler, who has time to throw them away upon petty services,
delicate attentions, sentiment, and sensibility." Even Scott came under the
ban. ". . . we cannot but think that such splendid powers of imagination
and intellect were bestowed by Providence for some higher purpose than
novel writing; we cannot but fear that 39 volumes of mere tales, without any
good or useful object in view, will form a sorry item in the final account
of a human being thus gifted, and responsible for the application of his
time, his faculties, and his opportunity of glorifying God, and benefitting
mankind." The *Portfolio*, I (n. s.), 241, September, 1822.

attitude spreads westward. Nothing gives the flavor of it like this extract from *The Ladies' Repository,* published under the editorship of the Rev. L. L. Hamline in Cincinnati in the forties:

As we were sailing down the river a few days since, several passengers, among whom were a Presbyterian and two Methodist clergymen, discussed the subject of novel reading. One and another uttered their views, till at last it was averred by a member of the company that "novel-reading is the crying sin of the church—that it is a fearful curse to society—that it generates more evil than intemperance ever did, and that a reformation is needed in this particular as much as in the use of alcoholic drinks." Some seemed startled at this; and apparently to moderate the zeal of the speaker, one mentioned that a very respectable and devout clergyman had a few days previously recommended to his daughter the perusal of the *Scottish Chiefs* and *Thadeus* (sic) *of Warsaw,* as very proper books for young ladies. If the company present were surprised at the *morals* of a minister who could recommend novels for the entertainment of the young, they were certainly no less surprised at his taste in recommending *such* novels as those here mentioned.

We cannot conceive who this servant of Jesus is, nor where he was educated, nor by what model he formed his morals or his literary taste. Is he a Methodist? Has he read his Discipline? . . . Had he just descended from the pulpit or come out of his closet, when he recommended to the young daughters of his friend, the "Scottish Chiefs" and "Thadeus of Warsaw?" . . . We should have thought no worse of him if he had counseled a child of ours to procure a pack of cards, and spend a few hours daily at games of whist. Indeed, we believe the latter is an innocent employment compared with the perusal of such books as the above. Whist would be a waste of time, but the reading would be this, and somewhat more. It would be insinuating poisons into the affections, and corrupting the whole heart. (*The Ladies' Repository,* III, 32, January, 1843).

As for the theater, that is the home of Satan himself. For instance, that excellent clergyman, the Rev. Henry Boehm, travelling companion to Bishop Asbury, "went to the theater in Philadelphia [about 1800]. I had heard much of the theater, and I wanted to see what it was. I got along very well until mimic thunder and lightning was brought in to illustrate the play. When I saw and heard this I was shocked. It seemed to me so irreverent and presumptuous that I thought the Almighty in his displeasure would send real thunder and lightning to terrify those imitators. . . . I prayed, and promised God, if he would only spare me to get out of the house and return safely home, I would never enter such a place again. That was my first and last visit to the theater."[74] The scruples of such persons, translated into municipal regulation, long hindered the development of the American theater,[75] the opera, the ballet.[76] The divine Fanny Elssler, who, more than anyone else, broke down the prejudice against stage dancing in America, is afraid that "a free use of her limbs" in the cracovienne may be offensive, and Boston gravely debates whether it may properly attend her exhibition—Boston, where they call the "theater" a "Museum."[77] Then again, there is painting and statuary—so often portraying the nude. Whatever is to be done about it? Art is a good thing—there are Shakespeare and Raphael—but still—! So one makes an uneasy compromise. A painting depicting Adam and Eve, naked, is permitted only because it is a "sacred subject"; in Philadelphia the ladies roam the halls of the statuary room by pairs and flee at the sound of a male footstep; corsets can not be named in polite company; and when A. K. Stewart exhibits them in his show windows, letters denouncing the immorality of his exhibit come in, and he withdraws the offending garments.[78] The robust morality of Franklin dwindles into a word that sums up an attitude,—such things are "indelicate."

But on the other hand, if morality is erected as a fence against aestheticism, it is not so intended against didacticism. Art that is didactic, improving, godly—that is the desire of the epoch. It is the age of Maria Edgeworth, Mrs. Hemans, Pierpont's *Airs from Palestine,* and the gentle lyricism of Longfellow. The novel may be wicked, especially when it is written by George Sand, Hugo, Dumas, or Sue; but when it is written by Madame Genlis, or Miss Burney, "the language is good, and

[74] *Reminiscences of Rev. Henry Boehm,* p. 15.
[75] See Hornblow, *History of the Theater in America,* vol. I, for a history of the struggle with middle-class morality.
[76] "Me han dicho, que el gusto de los Américanos no está decidido en favor de la ópera." Ramon de la Sagra, *Cinco Meses en los Estados-Unidos.* "They do not dislike the ballet, but they have no enthusiasm for its extravagances." Mackay, *Western World,* I, 144. (Of Philadelphia in 1846.) Hornblow remarks that 1798 is the ending of the experimental period in American theatrical history (opening of the Park Theatre in New York); but he points out that the centres of theatrical interest are New York, Charleston, Philadelphia, Annapolis, Baltimore, Boston, Newport, Richmond—that is to say, coast cities where the cosmopolitan spirit is strong. *Op. cit.,* I, 244, 245.
[77] See the chapter entitled "The Divine Fanny" in Minnigerode, *The Fabulous Forties.*
[78] See, among other places, A. B. Hart, *Slavery and Abolition,* chap. i, and the various chapters of social comment in McMaster for this period.

the sentiments . . . are excellent."[79] Not all novels are bad, profligate novels are rare, and "good" novels are numerous, says one writer in 1804, who argues that "a just and powerful picture of human life in which the connection between vice and misery, and between felicity and virtue is vividly portrayed, is the most solid and useful reading that a moral and social being . . . can read."[80] In 1820 another critic lays down the law that before novels "aspire to a higher need, they must zealously inculcate the precepts and the practice of virtue: and, so far from being satisfied with standing on the defensive when morality is attacked, they must be ever ready to run all hazards in behalf of its ordinances. . . . They must show as well by argument as by example, that if the very first inroad of vice be not strenuously resisted, transgression will so produce transgression, that the difficulty of reformation will increase with each succeeding minute. . . ."[81] And to the end of the epoch this narrow utilitarianism is the fundamental principle of aesthetics. The family, morality, God, and business—these are the four corners of the middle class.[82]

To the support of this concern for conduct there comes a great protestant religious revival. In the post-Napoleonic period, indeed, there is a world-wide religious revival; in the United States, it is evangelical, bourgeois, and anti-Catholic. In the first quarter of the century the evangelical churches grow by leaps and bounds.[83] They send out missionaries to convert the god-

[79] The quotation is from the *Philadelphia Repository and Weekly Register*, Saturday, June 27, 1801, p. 261, an article by "J," who suggests a national board of censorship, to be appointed by the president.

[80] *Literary Magazine and American Register*, I, 6, 403, March, 1804. This was Charles B. Brown's magazine. See also III, 16, January 1, 1805; and *The Portfolio*, V, 10, January 12, 1805.

[81] *The Portfolio*, X, 244, September, 1820. For further "defences" see *North American Review*, July, 1827, p. 184; *The Hesperian*, I, 299, August, 1838; *Arthur's Ladies' Magazine*, II, 90, August, 1844; *Southern Literary Messenger*, VIII, January, 1842, article "Modern Fiction" by E. D.

[82] Betsy Patterson Bonaparte to Lady Morgan, writing from Baltimore in 1824: You have "no idea of the mode of existence inflicted on us. The men are all merchants; and commerce, although it may fill the purse, clogs the brain. Beyond their counting-houses they possess not a single idea; they never visit except when they wish to marry. The women are all occupied in *les détails de ménage* and nursing children; these are useful occupations, but do not render people agreeable to their neighbors." Didier, *Life and Letters of Madame Bonaparte*, p. 159.

[83] Bacon, *A History of American Christianity;* Buckley, *A History of the Methodists in the United States;* Carroll, *The Religious Forces of the United States;* Newman, *A History of the Baptist Churches in the United States;* Thompson, *A History of the Presbyterian Churches in the United States;* Williston, *A History of the Congregational Churches in the United States;* Humphrey, *Nationalism and Religion in America.*

less frontier,[84] and from Princeton they combat the deism of the cosmopolitan eighteenth century. There is a whole literature of religion, religious magazines, religious newspapers, religious books—sermons, essays, hortatory volumes of all sorts, books for the young.[85] The blue laws are re-enforced; travellers can not journey on Sunday; there is a protest against moving the mails on the Sabbath—but they move, for business must be done, even by the godly.[86] The patriarchal society of the Old Testament becomes for many the ideal society; a kind of religious primitivism re-enforces family morality.[87] When de Tocqueville visits an American bookstore, he finds that the characteristic books on the shelves are elementary treatises, the Bible, religious works, and political pamphlets.[88] In Georgia the Methodists and Baptists in control of the legislature refuse to rebuild the state university because it had been a Presbyterian institution;[89] in Milledgeville in 1827 people are converted at the rate of twenty-five a day and in Athens, Greensboro, Washington, (a town noted for "wealth, hospitality, refinement, scepticism and wickedness,") revival meetings are held.[90] What is true of Georgia is true elsewhere, but we can not give space to everything; by 1830, in the opinion of James Gordon Bennett, who, being a newspaper man, is a bit cynical, "there was a curious mixture of reform, zealotry, fanaticism, and absurdity abroad."[91] The forties see a reaction from this excessive zeal.[92]

It is the age dominated by the spirit of Samuel Smiles—the age of self-help. The middle-class believes in education—of a sort. Even the cosmopolitan Jefferson yields to the movement

---

[84] See chaps. xi-xii below.
[85] See the chapter on juvenile literature in *The Cambridge History of American Literature.*
[86] Rich, pp. 105-6.
[87] Longstreet and Calhoun agreed that the ideal society was patriarchal. See the quotation from Calhoun in Wade, *Augustus Baldwin Longstreet,* p. 60.
[88] de Tocqueville, II, 539.
[89] Wade, p. 103.
[90] Wade, *op. cit.* See his chapter iv in this connection.
[91] Pray, *Memoirs of James Gordon Bennett and His Times,* p. 113.
[92] Minnigerode, *The Fabulous Forties,* indicates the change. Yet Godley (*Letters from America,* II, 64) found the theatre "little patronized" in New England in 1844. After the play he went to an evening party, which lasted to half-past eleven—"very dissipated for Boston!"

and talks for a while like a Babbitt;[93] the object of education is to get on in the world. Educational literature in this country begins with Franklin, and Franklin is wholly of a practical temper.[94] For a time education, so far as the middle class is concerned, is at a standstill: from 1776 through the War of 1812, "the schools, which are, after all, the barometer of social and economic success, were running down" in the East.[95] Then the middle class invented the academy, and imported the Lancasterian system.[96] The Latin grammar school is gone;[97] social control is no longer in the hands of those who believe in the eighteenth century tradition—wherefore the academy, serious, moral, shallow, guaranteed to impart respectability, takes its place. By 1850 there are 6,095 academies, 12,260 teachers, 263,096 pupils, an annual income of $5,831,179.[98] After the

[93] "But why send an American youth to Europe for education? What are the objects of useful American education? Classical knowledge, modern languages, chiefly French, Spanish, and Italian, mathematics, natural philosophy, natural history, civil history, and ethics. . . . It is true that the habit of speaking the modern languages cannot be so well acquired in America; but every other article can be as well acquired at William and Mary College as at any place in Europe . . . the medical class of students, therefore, is the only one which need come to Europe. Let us view the disadvantages of sending a youth to Europe. To enumerate them would require a volume. . . . If he goes to Europe he learns drinking, horse-racing and boxing. These are the peculiarities of English education. The following circumstances are common to education in that and the other countries of Europe." He enumerates luxury and dissipation and "contempt for the simplicity of his own country"; the youth will be fascinated by aristocracy, by foreign friendships, female intrigue, voluptuousness; he will despise ordinary dress and acts, and will write and speak his native tongue like a foreigner. "It appears to me, then, that an American coming to Europe for education, loses in his knowledge, in his morals, in his health, in his habits, and in his happiness." Jefferson to J. Banister. Quoted in Forman, *Life and Writings of Thomas Jefferson*, pp. 196-7.

[94] *Cambridge History of American Literature*, III, 397.

[95] Dexter, *History of Education in the United States*, p. 101; Fitzpatrick, *The Educational Views and Influence of De Witt Clinton*, part I, "Conditions in New York State, 1783-1805."

[96] See Dexter and Fitzpatrick on the Lancasterian movement.

[97] "At the close of the Revolution scarcely a Latin grammar school worthy of the name existed anywhere in New England." Grizzell, *Origin and Development of the High School in New England before 1865*, p. 29.

[98] Dexter, p. 96. Representative figures are given (p. 94) for certain states:

State	1800	1801-20	1821-40	1841-60
Maine	5	20	31	34
New Hampshire	10	18	59	23
Vermont	10	24	22	10
Massachusetts	17	19	78	40
New York	19	33	176	183
Maryland	5	24	40	23
North Carolina	30	113	43	
Georgia	6	14		

academy comes the high school, the development of which begins in the period 1821-1865. The high school is a public school, whereas the academies are private, but the distinguishing feature of the high school is that it has none of the Latin curriculum of the older kind[99]—Latin, somehow, does not prove useful in business. During the thirties and forties 67 colleges and universities are founded and still exist; 24 were nonsectarian, but it is when we examine the others that we know the period, for 12 are Methodist; ten are Baptist; the Presbyterians, Lutherans and Friends each have three; the Reformed Presbyterians, two; the Disciples, the United Presbyterians, and the United Brethren, one each; the Catholics, seven to the Protestants' 36. By 1850 there were 11 theological seminaries, 135 colleges. It is the age of the moral, Christian, middle-class home;[100] children must be brought up under godly influences—then they will get on in the world. Something is even to be said for educating women.[101]

The middle class is ambitious. Business and the desire for social prestige combine to make attractive the means of disseminating and receiving information which the merchant princes, the aristocrats, and the scholars had employed. By 1810 there are 366 newspapers in the country, 27 of them being daily papers. Politics are still their principal staple,[102] but with the coming of the railroad and the telegraph, politics becomes less important, and it is news that counts, that illumines these

---

[99] Grizzell, p. 287.

[100] McMaster, VII, 161. Yet out of a population of over seventeen millions, nearly six hundred thousand white men and women over twenty years of age could not write, and there were but 16,000 students in 173 universities and colleges, 164,000 students in 3200 academies and grammar schools, 1,854,000 school children in 47,000 primary and common schools in 1840. The true public school had not come. Schools were still bad in the 1840's. McMaster, VII, 75, 157.

[101] Answering Albert Picket and others in regard to the advisability of establishing a "female college" and the proper course of study to be pursued, Madison does not doubt the capacity of the female mind for "studies of the highest order," and thinks the experiment worth trying. (1821) *Letters and Other Writing of James Madison,* III, 232.

[102] "The number of periodical and occasional publications which appear in the United States actually surpasses belief. . . . The characteristics of the American journalist consist in an open and coarse appeal to the passions of the populace; and he habitually abandons the principles of political science to assail the characters of individuals, to track them into private life, and disclose all their weaknesses and errors." De Tocqueville, I, 191, 192. The middle classes, however, viewed such tactics with disfavor, and received James Gordon Bennett, the father of modern journalism, with uneasiness and disapprobation. See Pray, *op. cit.*

dull horizons. The magazines do not pay very much, but "the newspapers became the means of support of innumerable authors" in the 1830's.[103] None came out on Sunday. But every town has its paper, which, so far as may be, caters to the taste of its readers, and gives them the satisfaction of feeling that they, too, know something about Europe.[104] Chevalier found the papers "chiefly mere advertising sheets," a significant fact, since this is a business age. "They do not," he continues, "direct public opinion, they follow it."[105] But they do give news. In 1810 foreign intelligence came from 19 to 29 days late from Europe.[106] In 1818, writing from his settlement in Illinois, Birkbeck says that "we receive the Philadelphia daily papers once a week, about a month after they are published; in these we read extracts from the English journals of the month preceeding; so we take up the news as you forget it; and what happened three months ago in Europe is just now on the carpet here," but this is on the frontier.[107] Boardman describes the New York papers of 1833: "European news is copiously reported, and is as eagerly read; but no namby-pamby trash of fashionable movements, routes, and dinners, finds its way into the columns of American papers, such absurdities being justly held up to ridicule."[108] By 1838 the tone of Cincinnati papers is such that a careful observer writes: "the journals here seem to be conducted in a more fair and generous spirit, and with more of moderation in tone and spirit, than is general throughout the United States; and . . . such of the editors as I had an opportunity of seeing personally, were superior in mind and manners to the great mass of those filling this situation in other places." Cincinnati has become a business city. At the end of our epoch Lyell, having "purchased newspapers at random in northern, middle, southern, and western states, came to the conclusion that the press of the United States is quite as re-

---

[103] *Cambridge History of American Literature,* II, 185.

[104] "Towns once content to read such Packets and Courants as came by the postboy, (by 1792) boasted of Mirrors and Oracles of their own." By the new postal law, newspapers were mailable, but not magazines. McMaster, II, 63-66.

[105] Chevalier, *United States,* p. 452, note 8.

[106] Schouler, *History,* II, 264.

[107] Birkbeck, *Letters from Illinois,* p. 20. Foreign news reached Cincinnati six weeks late in 1817. Fearon, *Sketches of America,* p. 230. See in this connection Rusk, *op. cit.,* I, 147.

[108] Boardman, *America and the Americans,* p. 77.

spectable as our (British) own. . . . ." A large portion of almost every paper is given over to literary extracts, novels, tales, travels, and "often more serious works." Some of them are especially devoted to particular religious sects, and nearly all of these are against war with England. He notes both temperance and anti-slavery papers.[109] The middle class wants solid, sensible information.[110]

One way to acquire this information is to have a public library: it is a cheap means of self-help, and under proper moral guidance[111] will do good. The typical libraries of the eighteenth century are college and university libraries, and occasional lending libraries; the public library as such is overwhelmingly the creation of the middle class in the first half of the nineteenth century.[112] Typical is the creation of the Mechanics' Library, the Apprentices' Library, the Library of the Young Men's Insti-

---

[109] Lyell, *Travels in the United States, Second Visit*, II, 41.

[110] The first penny newspaper appeared in 1833—the *New York Sun*. The cheap press comes in with the rise of a more complex industrial civilization. See Schouler, *History*, IV, 356-8. The Atlantic Cable was laid in 1845-7. *Ibid.*, V, 402-4. In July 1850 the Liverpool steamer off Halifax was boarded by an Associated Press reporter, and the news wired to New York *via* Portland. *Ibid.*, V, 216. Yet as late as 1845 postage to England and France was 24 cents a half-ounze, plus inland postage. McMaster, VII, 101.

[111] The Social Library of New Haven, formed as a voluntary association in 1808, was incorporated in 1810. "One of the articles of its constitution was that 'no Novels, Romances, Tales or Plays' should be admitted into the library, unless by vote of two thirds of the members, at a legal meeting. A catalogue of its books in 1815 shows that only Coelebs in Search of a Wife, Don Quixote, Miss Edgeworth's popular Tales, and Tales of Fashionable Life, Forester's American Tales, Gil Blas, Johnson's Rasselas, Marmontel's Moral Tales, Percival's Tales, and the Vicar of Wakefield ran this gauntlet successfully." Baldwin, *Life and Letters of Simeon Baldwin*, p. 319.

Lyell, remarking in 1848 on the great number of lending libraries in the United States, says that "the best English poets and novelists are almost always to be met with in each collection and works of biography, history, travel, natural history, and science. The selection is carefully made with reference to what the people will read and not what men of higher education and station think they ought to read." *Travels in the United States, Second Visit*, I, 154.

[112] See table below, and consult the Smithsonian Report there cited.

TABULAR VIEW OF THE FOUNDING OF
LIBRARIES IN THE U. S.

(Based on the Appendix to the Report of the Board of Regents of the Smithsonian Institution, containing *A Report on the Public Libraries of the United States of America, January 1, 1850.*)

The following tables include only those libraries, the date of the founding of which was definitely given in the report. No date is given in 101 instances. C—College, Academy, High School, or University Library;

tute—every considerable town has one or more of these useful associations for getting on in the world.[113]

G—General Library, including Mechanics Institutes, and the like; S—Special Library (Historical, Agriculture, Medical, Legal, and what not).

	1770-1779			1780-1789			1790-1799			1800-1809			1810-1819			1820-1829			1830-1839			1840-1850		
	C	G	S	C	G	S	C	G	S	C	G	S	C	G	S	C	G	S	C	G	S	C	G	S
Maine	0	0	0	0	0	0	0	0	0	1	0	0	1	0	0	1	1	1	1	0	1	0	1	0
N. H.	0	0	0	2	1	0	1	2	0	1	0	0	1	2	0	1	2	1	1	1	0	2	0	0
Vermont ..	0	0	0	0	0	0	0	0	0	2	0	0	0	0	0	0	0	0	0	0	1	1	0	0
Mass.	0	0	0	0	0	1	1	1	2	1	1	1	0	1	1	3	3	2	1	1	2	2	3	2
R. I.	0	0	0	0	0	0	0	0	0	0	0	0	0	0	0	0	2	1	1	0	0	0	0	0
Conn.	0	0	0	0	0	0	0	0	0	0	0	0	0	1	0	1	0	1	2	1	0	0	0	0
N. Y.	0	0	0	0	0	0	1	0	1	0	1	1	5	0	2	4	5	0	3	8	3	2	1	0
N. J.	0	0	0	0	0	0	0	0	0	1	0	0	1	0	0	1	0	0	0	0	0	1	1	1
Penn.	0	1	0	1	0	0	0	1	0	1	1	1	2	2	2	4	3	2	4	2	0	3	1	0
Del.	0	0	0	0	0	0	0	0	0	0	0	0	0	1	0	0	0	0	1	0	1	0	0	0
Maryland	0	0	0	2	0	0	0	1	0	1	0	0	0	0	0	0	0	1	0	1	0	1	4	1
D. C.	0	0	0	0	0	1	1	0	1	0	1	0	1	0	0	1	0	0	0	0	1	0	0	3
Virginia .	1	0	0	1	0	0	1	0	0	1	0	0	0	2	0	2	0	1	2	0	1	4	3	0
N. C.	0	0	0	0	0	0	1	0	0	1	0	0	0	0	0	0	0	0	0	0	0	0	0	0
S. C.	0	0	0	1	0	0	0	0	0	1	0	0	0	0	0	1	1	0	2	0	0	1	0	0
Georgia ..	0	0	0	0	0	0	0	0	0	0	0	0	0	0	0	0	0	0	6	0	1	0	1	0
Alabama ..	0	0	0	0	0	0	0	0	0	0	0	0	0	0	0	0	0	0	1	1	0	1	1	0
Florida ...	0	0	0	0	0	0	0	0	0	0	0	0	0	0	0	0	0	0	0	0	0	0	0	2
Miss.	0	0	0	0	0	0	0	0	0	0	0	0	0	0	0	0	0	0	1	0	1	1	0	0
La.	0	0	0	0	0	0	0	0	0	0	0	0	0	0	0	0	0	0	1	0	0	1	0	0
Arkansas .	0	0	0	0	0	0	0	0	0	0	0	0	0	0	0	0	0	0	0	0	0	0	0	0
Texas ...	0	0	1	0	0	0	0	0	0	0	0	0	0	0	0	0	0	0	0	0	1	1	0	0
Tenn.	0	0	0	0	0	0	0	0	0	0	0	0	1	0	0	2	0	0	2	0	0	3	0	0
Kentucky .	0	0	0	0	0	0	1	0	0	0	0	0	0	0	0	3	0	0	2	0	2	1	0	0
Ohio	0	0	0	0	0	0	0	0	0	1	0	0	1	0	1	3	2	0	4	2	1	6	1	0
Indiana ..	0	0	0	0	0	0	0	0	0	0	1	0	1	0	0	1	0	1	1	0	0	1	0	0
Illinois ..	0	0	0	0	0	0	0	0	0	0	0	0	0	0	0	1	0	0	2	0	1	1	1	0
Missouri ..	0	0	0	0	0	0	0	0	0	0	0	0	0	0	0	1	0	1	0	0	0	2	1	2
Michigan .	0	0	0	0	0	0	0	0	0	0	0	0	0	0	0	0	0	0	1	1	1	1	0	0
Iowa	0	0	0	0	0	0	0	0	0	0	0	0	0	0	0	0	0	0	0	0	1	0	0	1
Wisconsin	0	0	0	0	0	0	0	0	0	0	0	0	0	0	0	0	0	0	0	0	1	0	0	1
Minnesota	0	0	0	0	0	0	0	0	0	0	0	0	0	0	0	0	0	0	0	0	0	0	1	2
	1	1	1	7	1	2	7	5	4	12	5	3	14	9	5	29	19	13	39	18	20	36	0	15

Total number of libraries in 1850... 10,640*
Total number of libraries having 50,000 books or more............... 4**
Total number of libraries having 20,000-50,000 books................. 11
Total number of libraries having 10,000-20,000 books................. 38
Total number of libraries having 5,000-10,000 books.................. 75
Total number of state libraries (includes federal)................... 38
Total number of social libraries.................................... 98
Total number of college libraries.................................. 119
Total number of students' libraries in colleges.................... 134
Total number of libraries in professional schools and academies.... 222
Total number of libraries belonging to learned societies........... 33

* This number is delusive, since all but 644 of these libraries were district school libraries.

** These were Harvard, the Philadelphia and Loganian Libraries, the Library of Congress, and the Boston Athenaeum.

The whole report is admittedly imperfect, but it is the only data available.

[113] In 1840 there were five circulating libraries in Boston alone; *viz.*, the Mercantile, the Apprentices', the Columbian, the Literary Society, and the Athenaeum. Bernard in 1825 reported 20,000 volumes in the latter. *Travels*, I, 42; and see Buckingham, *America*, III, 316-9, for the state of Boston

What kind of reading is fostered by this morality, these libraries, these associations for moral improvement? In 1825 Bernhard visited a bookseller in Geneva, New York; he finds that the ancient classics and religious books have the readiest sale, although medical books, law books, and fiction are sold. In Albany the bookstores "seem to be well furnished"; and he even finds a travelling bookstore on one of the boats in the Erie Canal; a Mr. Wilcox established it, who went back and forth several times a year, doing a considerable business in the ancient authors, in religious and medical works, in law books, and a few novels. In Philadelphia the stock of books for sale by Messrs. Carey, Lea, and Carey, the publishers of the respectable Cooper, "appeared to be well assorted."[114] In Dayton, Ohio, in 1838, Buckingham reports that "the book-trade is said to be the dullest of all here,"[115] but for the same period the trustworthy Grund has preserved a list of American publications, exclusive of pamphlets, periodicals, and new editions: figures are not very exciting, but let us look at these, compiled from the *American Booksellers' Advertiser:*

TABLE OF AMERICAN PUBLICATIONS 1835[116]

Description	American	Foreign Reprint	Total
Almanacs	10	0	10
Arts and Sciences	15	8	23
Biography	19	11	30
Education	60	15	75
Ethics and Politics	5	3	8
History	4	8	12
Juvenile	22	17	39
Law	9	3	12
Medicine and Surgery	6	5	11
Novels and Tales	31	33	64
Poetry	7	12	19
Religious and Domestic Duties	15	15	30
Statistics and Commerce	9	2	11
Travel	12	11	23
Theology	20	22	42
Miscellaneous	24	10	34
	268	175	443

libraries in 1838. Bristed is contemptuous. *Resources of the United States,* p. 311 (1818). Bernhard admired the Philadelphia libraries (1825). *Travels* I, 147. Candler disparages them, and find nothing to admire in libraries at Albany, Richmond, or New York. *Summary View of America,* pp. 104-5. (1822-23).

[114] Bernhard, *Travels,* I, 70, 59, 139.
[115] Buckingham, *America: Eastern and Western States,* II, 420.
[116] Grund, *The Americans* (Boston edition), p. 98.

Out of 443 works, but 83 are devoted to belles lettres (64 are novels and tales, 19 are poetry), and the remainder, 360 works, are all solid and improving volumes: 72 are devoted to religion (religious and domestic duties, 30; theology 42), 75 to education, 39 to juvenile reading, all of it, we may be sure, hortatory and moral. The middle class is improving its mind, taking over the ideas of the merchant princes, the aristocracy, and the scholars—to such an extent, indeed, that Michigan, settled largely from New York and the New England states, by 1850 "had . . . more libraries, more newspapers and periodicals, more public schools, less white illiterates, than had Arkansas or Missouri."[117]

Their literary taste, though zealously fostered in this fashion, is perhaps not very sound. There is something admirable in the solid political literature of the mercantile princes, in the erudition of the scholars, but this culture is second-hand, artificial, and insincere. In 1810, says a competent historian, our "culture . . . was squeamish, affected, finical, full of classical pretensions, the toad-eater of the rich and patronizing to the poor, inane, wholly out of sympathy with American democracy and imitative of English authors," and "to many educated minds science seemed inseparable from scepticism."[118] To another the age is the "puerile age of our literature" and "was justly denounced as such by Poe,"[119] nor does it change for the better until the decade ending in 1850. It is a selfish culture; it will not encourage native authors, nor yet pay adequately, sometimes not at all, for the works of foreign ones—it prefers to buy cheap books.[120] It will not support an international copyright

[117] McMaster, VII, 199. Michigan and Arkansas were admitted to the union in 1836; Missouri, in 1820.
[118] Schouler, *History*, II, 259. See McMaster, V, chap. xlvii, for an excellent discussion of the early bourgeois period.
[119] McMaster, VII, 94.
[120] A three volume novel, published in London at a guinea and a half, sold to 1500 copies, has been issued in New York in 24 hours after its arrival in a sixpenny or shilling pamphlet, in an edition of 20,000 copies. Nichols, *Forty Years of American Life*, I, 340.
From 1789 to 1816 there was no tariff on books. The Acts of May 22, 1824, and February 11, 1825, laid a charge of four cents a volume on all books printed before 1775 and on all books in a modern foreign language; the Act of September 11, 1841, changed this to a duty of 20%. The latter act put a duty on all other books, bound, of 30c a pound; this was changed August 30, 1842. Hereafter the schedules grow more complex. The essential part of the act of 1842 is that books printed more than five years before importation or more than one year, if not reprinted in the United States, were charged 15c a pound. The Act of July 30, 1846, laid a flat rate on

act. When Dickens visited America in 1842, he found American publishers hostile to international copyright, and American authors as a class shy of meddling. "These were times when the business of cheap American reprints in this country was to an excess most unusual, and newspapers and broadsides served up British literature by the column in fine print and dingy paper. This compelled the chief publishing houses to ransack their dusty plates and reissue old books in cheap form. With Shakespeares, family libraries, dictionaries, novels, and miscellanies, a huge mass of pirated matter, the market was soon overstocked; but the popular taste for good literature was expanded."[121] The middle class was not out of pocket thereby.

It is shrewd business, culture at half price. In the late twenties "it was unusual for American families to visit Europe,"[122] but books of travels, which one can read in his armchair, will be educative and less alarming.[123] We talk much about Europe, but we do not really know very much about European thought, even though we send parties of business men abroad.[124] For instance, here is Jared Sparks complaining in the *North American Review* for March, 1817, that Italian literature has been neglected;[125] however, we will do better by and by: Byron and Madame de Staël having called our attention to its merits.[126] Despite our interest in Manzoni, we shall wait on the safe guidance of Longfellow before making any very profound investigations—Longfellow, and

books and periodicals. See *Special Report on the Customs-Tariff Legislation of the United States,* Appendix A. The general effect is obviously to keep out books printed abroad, and to encourage American reprints, on which no royalty is paid.

[121] Schouler, *History,* IV, 421-2.

[122] Susan Cooper's reminiscences in *Correspondence of James Fenimore-Cooper,* I, 52. Her mother, the wife of the novelist, was greatly alarmed when the novelist broached the idea that the whole family go to France.

[123] The head of Harper Brothers told John L. Stephens that "travels sell about the best of anything we get hold of. They don't always go off with a rush, like a novel by a celebrated author, but they sell longer, and in the end, pay better." Nichols, *Forty Years of American Life,* I, 343.

[124] "About the year 1818-19 American importers, chiefly Boston men, visited Europe, and studied the factory systems of Holland, France, and England. They conceived the plan of turning the water power of New England to good account, and by the year 1820 had introduced calico printers from the old country." Pray, *Memoirs of James Gordon Bennett and His Times,* p. 93.

[125] IV, 309.

[126] Consult J. Marsh, "Italian Literature," *North American Review,* XV, 94 ff., July, 1822.

Lowell.[127] As for Spanish literature, despite an occasional article, we must wait the publication of Ticknor's *History* in 1849,[128] though we all know *Don Quixote*. As for German, the country is "nearly as unknown as China, until Madame de Staël published her famous work in 1814. Even young George Ticknor, incited by its accounts of German university education, could find neither a good teacher, nor a dictionary, nor a German book in the shops or public libraries of the city or at the college in Cambridge."[129] In fact, George Ticknor, writing of Boston in 1808-1811, complains that even British publications reach us slowly, and new books from the continent, scarcely at all.[130] But that is during the Napoleonic period. Afterwards there is, as we shall see, a flood of travel books to tell us of the wonders of the Old World, while we remain snug and patriotic in the New.

But we are not going to pay too much for any book. In 1800 when the great mass of popular literature is still of British origin, standard works cost too much, and "works that cost more than five dollars, works in two, three, or four volumes, or such as were likely to have a large sale, were generally reprinted, at less cost."[131] Sharp practice grows. When culture is expensive the middle class does not want to pay for it;[132] it is the cheap reprint that will serve—let the author go starve. In

---

[127] On Manzoni see George Greene, *North American Review*, LI, 333 ff., October 1840. On the general interest in Italian, H. T. Tuckerman, *Southern Literary Messenger*, XV, 587 ff., September, 1849.

[128] Consult Longfellow, "Spanish Literature and Language," *North American Review*, XXXVI, 316 ff., April, 1833. For reviews of Ticknor, see *North American Review*, LXX, 1 ff., January, 1850; *Southern Quarterly Review*, XVIII, 85, 273, September and November, 1850; *Littel's Living Age*, XXV, 12 ff., April 6, 1850 (reprint from the *Spectator*) ; ibid., XVII, 427, March 30, 1850 (reprint from the *Times*).

[129] Adams, *History*, I, 94, and see *Cambridge History of American Literature*, IV, 453 ff. Goodnight places the birth of interest in German at 1817 when Everett and Ticknor returned from Göttingen. They were followed by A. H. Everett, George Bancroft, G. H. Calvert, and J. G. Coggswell. In 1823 Dr. Charles Follen was appointed instructor in German at Harvard; in 1831 a chair of German languages and literature was established. Interest rose in the 30's under the influence of Carlyle and the *Dial;* and was increased after 1848. Consult Goodnight, *German Literature in the United States Prior to 1846;* Hinsdale, *Notes on the History of Foreign Influence upon Education in the United States;* Handschin, *The Teaching of Modern Languages in the United States.*

[130] Godwin, *Biography of William Cullen Bryant,* p. 60, note 1.

[131] McMaster, V, 280.

[132] "The value of books imported from Europe during the year 1829-1830," says Hamilton (it is true, a hostile observer), "for public institutions, amounted only to 10,829 dollars." *Men and Manners in America,* I, 369, note.

1832 or 1833, 274 literary works of native growth and 206 works reprinted from foreign sources were published in America, says Abdy; the former in 306 volumes for $375.47, the latter in 303 volumes for $216.99. This averages a little less than a dollar and a quarter a volume for the home product, and less than seventy-five cents for the foreigner. The European works, moreover, appear in smaller type.[133] Lyell reports in 1848 that novels priced at 31 shillings in England are sold at sixpence here, and that Harpers, who were then notorious for this kind of piracy, sold 2,000,000 volumes in 1845. In 1849 some 20,000 copies of Macaulay's *History* were sold in the United States:[134] it is a cheap and improving work. Somehow, there is a Yankee sharpness about the business which does not please foreign observers. And then there is the lyceum movement which has been often described; a movement which divides the field with the libraries after 1825,[135] but the history of the lyceum movement, especially in its connection with literary men and orators, is known to every student of American letters, and we must hurry on.

3. THE SIGNIFICANCE OF THE FINDINGS OF THE LAST TWO CHAPTERS

The cosmopolitan spirit, the spirit of the frontier, the middle class spirit—these are, we have said, fundamental in American culture. There are of course other forces at work, but these are at any rate basic, living elements in American culture, elements that lend meaning and dignity to the attempt at achieving a national art, an aesthetic independence. Doubtless many will not like to see the old terms disappear—Puritanism, for instance,

---

[133] Abdy, *Journal,* II, 330, note.

[134] Lyell, *Travels in the United States, Second Visit,* II, 252. He tells of the father of a family "of the humblest class" reading to his wife and four or five children one of the best modern (British) novels, for which he paid 25c. The same man might buy in two or three successive numbers of a penny newspaper entire reprints of Dickens or Bulwer. *Ibid.,* I, 152-3. In 1842 Bulwer's *Disowned, Devereux,* and *Paul Clifford* were published at 25 cents each. *The Magnolia,* I, 321, November, 1842. A railway newsboy offered Lyell "a novel by Paul de Kock, the Bulwer of France, for 25 cents —all the go!—more popular than the *Wandering Jew.*" Lyell, *op. cit.,* II, 41.

[135] Godley found the Boston lyceum "most fashionable," the amusement consisting of "lectures delivered by literary men upon all sorts of subjects." The lyceum, he remarks, answers the purpose of "affording amusement to those who object to the theatre" by offering "a little pleasing excitement of partly intellectual and partly sensual (!) kind." The ladies often attended two or three in an evening, and it seemed to him that the "lecture mania" had been carried too far. *Letters from America* (1844), II, 49.

which our formula, inadequate as all formulae are that deal with
the human spirit, does not, it is true, wholly account for. But
what is Puritanism? If Edward's famous sermon on sinners in
the hands of an angry God expresses the Puritan spirit, then
Longfellow's *Christus* is not Puritan; and if Cotton Mather's
trembling walk with God is the essence of Puritanism, then
Beecher's *Norwood* is not the expression of the Puritan spirit.
And if Puritanism be in its essentials religious mysticism,
then religious mysticism, which knows no national boundaries
and has no country save Heaven, is part of the cosmopolitan
spirit; it is that same mysticism which finds expression in
Jansenism, in quietism, in the Moravian Brotherhood, in all
of Europe from Sweden to Italy.   Primarily, it would seem,
Puritanism is not *sui generis* and unique; it shares in the vague
religious disquietude of the seventeenth century in which it
took shape; and when it crystallized in the code of conduct that
many now dislike, it is because it expresses the middle-class
attitude toward life. Puritanism is altogether an unsatisfactory
term.

At any rate, we have arrived at an analysis of the American
spirit as it is expressed up to 1848. After that epoch, in the
era of city building, we should have to add a fourth great
factor to a situation steadily growing more complicated: what
we might call the urban spirit, that spirit which calls American
realism into being. For beneath the American adoption of
European fashions in culture, there is always some basic need;
as, for instance, in the case of romanticism. We have our romantic movement in America, but it is curious and interesting
to see what parts of the European system of romanticism we
adopt, and what parts we reject. For instance, we take over the
moral urge, the lofty idealism of German metaphysics, but we
reject the anarchic immorality of *Lucinde;* we take over the
sublime abstractions of Rousseau and the religious vagueness
of Lamartine and Chateaubriand, but we shudder before
George Sand and Victor Hugo; we take over the individualism
of Byron and the categorical imperative of Kant and Carlyle,
and reject the "atheism" of Shelley and the godlessness of Godwin and Tom Paine. The middle class is in the saddle in the
East, that cautious middle class with its safe aspirations toward
culture, its solid, unshakable belief in conventional morality and
a personal God.

We might go further. The intellectual curiosity of the cosmopolitan spirit is expressed, for instance, in those who live in

the realm of ideas like Poe, no less than in those who live in the world of Europe, like Lowell. The independent spirit of the frontier comes to fruition in Whitman and Mark Twain and Emerson. The solid qualities of the bourgeosie dominate the American novel and the New England poets. And in addition there is the vast and complicated hinterland of literature where the national life is equally expressed: the novels that nobody reads nowadays save specialists, the poems that are forgotten, the crusades that have crumbled, the campaigns that are dead beyond resuscitation, and it is here, in the vast wash of conflicting forces, rather than in the famous figures, that the battle of American culture is fought. What indeed *is* American culture? We do not yet know, for it is yet taking shape. Clearly it is to be sought for, not merely in literary works, but in the total expression of our national life. We, it may be, are too close to the phenomenon to see it. But let us close this chapter by setting down the characteristics which Bryce, observing with candid eyes the whole course of our intellectual history, has said are peculiarly our own. They are ten in all:

1. A desire to be abreast of the best thought and work of the world everywhere, to have every form of literature and art adequately represented, and excellent of its kind, so that America shall be felt to hold her own among the nations.

2. A fondness for bold and striking effects, a preference for large generalizations and theories which have an air of completeness.

3. An absence among the multitude of refined taste, and disposition to be attracted rather by general brilliance than by delicacy of workmanship; a want of mellowness and inadequate perception of the difference between first-rate work in a quiet style and mere flatness.

4. Little respect for canons or traditions, accompanied by the notion that new conditions must necessarily produce new ideas.

5. An undervaluing of special knowledge or experience, except perhaps in the sphere of applied science and commerce, an idea that an able man can do one thing pretty much as well as another.

6. An admiration for literary or scientific eminence, an enthusiasm for anything that can be called genius with an over-readiness to discover it.

7. A love of intellectual novelties.

8. An intellectual impatience, and desire for quick and patent results.

9. An over-valuing of the judgments of the multitude, a disposition to judge by "success" work which has not been produced for the sake of success.

10. A tendency to mistake bigness for greatness.[136]

---

[136] Bryce, *American Commonwealth*, II, 630-631. Cf. also the list of traits which Nevins puts together from the British travel books in *American Social History as Recorded by British Travellers*, pp. 3-26.

Do we not see in this philosophic accounting the results of the historical struggle among the cosmopolitan spirit, the frontier spirit, the middle class spirit, all of which we have analyzed, and of the urban spirit, which lies beyond the boundary of our period?

IV

French Migration to America

INTRODUCTION

W<small>E HAVE</small> traced in previous chapters three of the basic elements which by the year 1848 had gone to the making of American culture. Were we engaged in studying that culture, it would now be in place to show how the cosmopolitan spirit, the frontier spirit, and the bourgeois spirit find their expression in the arts and literature of the United States. But our purpose is other: we must rather show what elements in a foreign culture, namely, that of the French, in proportion as their civilization was known and understood in America, were liked or disliked by our countrymen. In studying this problem, our first interest is naturally to discover what contacts existed between Latin and Catholic France and Protestant and Anglo-Saxon America. One such contact is obviously the presence in the New World of varying thousands of Frenchmen—immigrants, explorers, scientists, travellers, visionaries, propagandists, noblemen, commoners, refugees—all the diverse elements which sought in the New World refuge from persecution, opportunity for building a new Jerusalem, a laboratory for social study, a field for exploration, an ally or an enemy in politics and war. Let us then turn to the general question of determining how many and what sorts of Frenchmen were known to Americans in the epoch we are traversing.

It must be admitted that no exact answer to the question is possible. For large periods in that epoch no immigration figures are obtainable; and even when they are to be had, they tell us little or nothing of the character or quality of the French they number. Obviously there were many hundred French people who must have made some impression upon their neighbors, the records of whose journeys and settlements have entirely disappeared. Obviously also, where records are to be obtained, they do not always tell us what ideas, what attitude toward life these immigrants or travellers brought with them, nor whether the expression of such attitudes pleased or irritated their American neighbors and acquaintances. We shall have to be content with such waifs and strays of information as our imperfect search may assemble; and perhaps, if we can not estimate exactly the numbers and qualities of particular groups of Frenchmen in the United States, we can at least indicate tendencies. Let us accordingly divide our general topic under its separate heads, and sketch in outline the successive movements of the French toward America. We shall speak first of the explorers on the Atlantic coast, the Gulf of Mexico, and in the Mississippi Valley; then of the great wave of Huguenot migration at the turn of the seventeenth century; thirdly of certain special groups in the mid-eighteenth century such as the French Swiss, the Acadians, and the Walloons, of such miscellaneous bits of information of the movements of Frenchmen before 1775 as do not readily group themselves elsewhere. Next, we shall speak of the settlement of the region around New Orleans. Resuming our groupings with the Revolution, let us speak of the presence of Frenchmen in this country from the outbreak of the American Revolution to the outbreak of the French Revolution; then of the émigrés driven here from Santo Domingo and France by the French Revolution; then of the Napoleonic group; and finally, let us group together all those who came here when France was governed by the Bourbons or by Louis Philippe, not omitting, however, the French settlers in the West. Perhaps no part of our survey will be exhaustive, since to make it so would require the labors of a lifetime, but the composite picture, we may hope, will not be untrue to the facts.

1. FRENCH EXPLORERS AND THEIR INFLUENCE

The French government exhibited little interest in the exploration and conquest of the New World until the ministry of Colbert[1] and the earlier years of Louis XIV. Cartier sighted the shores of Newfoundland in May, 1534; but after his final voyage of 1541-1542 some sixty years passed by in which France made no serious effort to found a colony in the New World. Champlain and De Monts made a futile attempt at settlement on the Acadian coast in 1604 (at St. Croix); Quebec was firmly established in 1608; and by 1609 Champlain had pushed into what is now New York and fought his fatal battle with the Iroquois near Ticonderoga. In 1615 Champlain pushed west to Georgian Bay, where a Récollet

---

[1] On the general history of French exploration in the New World, William Bennett Munro's *Crusaders of New France* in the *Chronicles of America Series* is an admirable little volume.

father had already anticipated him, and had seen Lake Ontario, and the exploration of the central part of the American continent had begun.

The principal events in the history of French exploration, famous in the pages of Parkman, are part of our general education, and require little discussion here. La Salle began his great expeditions in 1669; by December, 1680, he had reached the confluence of the Illinois with the Mississippi; in 1682 he had reached the mouth of the Mississippi; and in his wake—sometimes even before him—came the motley crew of Jesuits,[2] Récollets, *voyageurs*, noblemen and adventurers, who give color to the early years of western history. In 1684 he set sail for the Gulf where, on the sands of Matagorda Bay, he founded his short-lived colony; with his assassination in 1687 a great and heroic figure passed away. By 1700 French fur-traders had achieved "a strangle-hold" upon "all the vital arteries" of the western country.[3] By that time also Fort Frontenac, Detroit, Niagara, Sault Ste. Marie, Michilimackinac, Green Bay, Fort St. Antoine, Fort St. Nicholas, Fort St. Croix, Fort Perrot, Fort St. Louis and many other outposts testified to the power of the Grand Monarque. Indeed, the only waterway in control of the English was the Hudson. The West was definitely French.

Today all this is vanished. *Coureur-de-bois* and explorer, Jesuit and Récollet have gone to join their Indian comrades in whatever happy hunting ground is appointed for them, leaving behind only a legend and a name. It may seem therefore idle to devote even these brief paragraphs to them. But it is precisely because they have passed into a legend and a name that they must be reckoned with in estimating the American attitude toward French culture. They wrote few books as such, and the songs of the *coureur-de-bois* form no part of American folk-lore.[4] But they contributed toward making the composite American picture of the French character. On the one hand the romantic appeal of their strange adventures among Indians

---

[2] Four Jesuit priests came to Quebec in 1625. Their numbers did not increase until 1633, when the epoch of their great explorations and sufferings began. There is a convenient brief discussion in Monroe, chapter vii.
[3] Monroe, p. 159.
[4] Rusk was able to collect but two fragments. See his *Literature of the Middle Western Frontier*, I, 304. On books by early explorers, see I, 80 ff. There is an excellent collection of Canadian folk songs selected and translated by J. Murray Gibbon, New York, 1927, based on Gagnon's *Chansons Populaires du Canada*.

in the unknown forests has furnished a theme of endless appeal to the American novelist and romancer, and even to the American historian: the French in the wilderness, with their bravery, their gaiety, their politeness, their astuteness, have figured in countless novels wherein they are regular stage properties of romance. On the other hand, because of an historical and geographical accident, the alliance of the Frenchman with the cruelties of Indian warfare has darkened the picture. To the frontier, especially, the French, the Catholic,[4a] the devil, and the Indian were alike children of Belial to be hated and destroyed.[5] In Cooper's *The Last of the Mohicans* the French and the hostile Indians are villains in the tale—one remembers how much of the Leatherstocking tales comes out of tradition familiar to Cooper—a fact which we may take as symbolic of an attitude.[6] Consequently the hostility of the frontier spirit toward things French under the Bourbons becomes fundamental in the American attitude; it is significant that the sympathetic reception of the French Huguenots is true of the coast towns, comparatively remote from the dangers of border war-

---

[4a] Governor Shute told the Massachusetts General Assembly that he had sent a whole detachment to catch "Monsieur *Rallee,* the French Jesuit, residing among the *Norridgewock* Indians," who was stirring up the savages with the aid of the Canadian government. "Rallee" escaped, but his papers were captured and sent to England. *Boston News-Letter,* No. 946, March 19, 1722.

[5] Besides the Deerfield massacre directed by Hertel de Rouville, and various thrilling capture-and-escape narratives, consider the bitterness engendered by such "news" as these items from the *Boston News-Letter*: "*Northampton,* May 13 (1704). A Company of Indians and French between day break and Sun-rising, about 60 Set upon a Garrison-House of *Benj. Jones's,* about two Miles from the body of the Town, and set fire to it ere they were aware of it; kill'd and carryed Captive about 30 Persons." (No. 5, May 22, 1704).

May 29, 1704 (No. 6): Men from Martinique "also said the French had taken one *Pease of Rhode-Island,* who stoutly resisted the Privateer, kill'd one of them, and wounded several; however being two (sic) strong for him, they boarded him, & he cry'd quarter, yet notwithstanding because of his Noble Courage they barbarously kill'd him."

May 14, 1705 (No. 56): "Monsieur Supercosse took a Child, and barbarously cut its throat, and sent it by a Souldier with a Message to the Garrison (at St. John's, Newfoundland), That if they did not Surrender to him, he would so serve all therein, and the Prisoners that he had taken; upon which Capt. *Moody* bid the Messenger be gone else he would shoot him."

See also Neal's *History of New-England,* II:56-57; 80-84; 94-95; 175 ff., for similar tales.

[6] Of course, after the British acquired the Western posts, this hostility was transferred to them. One notes that Harrison becomes the "Hair-Buyer" in Clark's campaign on the Wabash.

fare, just as it is significant that, the Bourbons once away, and the danger from the French likewise removed, the West became enthusiastic for the French Revolution, and bitterly hostile to Spaniard and Briton alike.

If the French explorer and *coureur-de-bois,* Jesuit missionary and military officer, have become a legend, they have likewise left behind them their names. Detroit, Des Moines, Dubuque, Duluth, Eau Claire, Joliet, La Crosse, Prairie du Chien, Racine, Saint Joseph, Saint Louis, Saint Paul, Vincennes—such names on the roll of American cities recall the early French.[7] Through the Middle West and the Far West geographical designations recall the days of the early explorers, whether the name be that of some pioneer trader or whether it be descriptive.[8] Sometimes,

[7] On French place names in the United States consult Gannett, *The Origin of Certain Place Names in the United States;* Appendix B to Rosengarten, *French Colonists and Exiles;* John C. Branner, "Some Old French Place Names in the State of Arkansas," *Modern Language Notes,* XIV, 65-79, February, 1899; Louis N. Feipel, "American Place Names," in *American Speech,* 1, 78-91, November, 1925; Mencken, *The American Language,* chap. x. The whole subject of American place names and their implications has scarcely been studied.

[8] Thus Barraque, Arkansas; Bottineau (county and town), N.D.; Cadillac, Michigan; Celeron Island (Detroit river); Champlain, New York; Charlevoix (county and village), Michigan; Choteau (county and township), Montana; Depue (village and creek), Illinois; De Smet, Idaho; De Smet, South Dakota; Dubois (county), Indiana; Dupage (river and county), Illinois; Duquesne (borough in Allegheny county), Pennsylvania; Fontanelle, Iowa; Fontanelle (creek), Wyoming; Fort Pierre, S. D. (for Pierre Choteau); Gervais, Oregon; Isle Lamotte, Vermont; Jeromeville, Ohio; Julien (township in Dubuque county), Iowa (for Julien Dubuque); Julesberg, Colorado (for Jules Bernard); Labaddie, Missouri; LaClede (township), Illinois; Laclede (county and town), Missouri; La Harpe (township and city), Illinois; Laporte (borough), Pennsylvania; Laramie (village and river), Ohio; Laramie (county, city, mountain), Wyoming; Laramie (river); Lasalle (county and city), Illinois; Lasalle, New York; Lasalle (county), Texas; Le Claire, Iowa; Lesueur (county and borough), Minnesota; Marquette, Kansas; Marquette (county, city, and river), Michigan; Marquette, Wisconsin; Montour (county, ridge, borough), Pennsylvania; Nicollet (county and village), Minnesota; Obion (county and river), Tennessee; Pere Marquette, Michigan; Pierre, S.D. (Pierre Choteau); Roubedeau (river and pass), Nebraska; Saint Joseph, Missouri (for Joseph Robidoux); Sauvie (island in Columbia River: for Jean Baptiste Sauvé); Tonti (township and village), Illinois; and various other places recall the names of early French explorers, officers, missionaries, and settlers. I have chosen these names at random from Gannett: it will be noticed that the overwhelming majority are in the Mississippi River basin.

Descriptive place names are equally common, and extremely interesting. Thus Auxvasse, Missouri, is named from the mud which seemed to characterize it (vase); Belpré, Ohio, is a "beautiful prairie"; Bois Brule (township and creek in Missouri) is said to be named from burned timber found there; Bois d'Arc, Missouri, from the wood good for bow-making; the Bois de Sioux river in North Dakota is obvious; Boise (county, city, and river), Idaho, points to an early condition of the place (boisé—"wooded"); Bonne-

indeed the name is twisted and turned almost beyond recogni-
terre, Missouri, is so named because French settlers found lead in the earth
there; Bonpas (creek and town) in Illinois are named from the prairie
good to walk on; Bouquet River in New York is named either from
flowers on its bank or from the French "bacquet," a trough; the Bourbeuse
River in Missouri is the "miry" river; Butte, Montana, is descriptive, whereas
Butte des Morts, Wisconsin, is named from a hill nearby where the Indians
buried their dead. Cache la Poudre Creek in Colorado is obvious, as is
Cache county, village, stream, and valley in Utah, and Cacheville, California.
The Cannon River in Minnesota recalls the French, "rivière aux canots,"
whereas the Cannonball River in North Dakota is named from the real
article, "le boulet." Champaign, Illinois, is obvious. Cloquet, Minnesota, is
named from the sound of the windmills (?). Coeur d'Alene, Idaho, recalls a
French translation of an Indian tribal name; the Coquille River in Oregon
is named for shells on its banks; Grève Coeur, Missouri, recalls the heart-
break of early exploration; Cuivre River, Missouri, is obvious; and numerous "dalles" are named from the French word signifying either slab or
trough—there is dispute as to the real meaning. Des Moines, Iowa, has a
curious history. It may be a French form of an Indian word, "moingana,"
road; named by the French, "rivière des moins." Then, as it became associated with a convent of Trappist monks, popular etymology established the
present spelling.

The Des Plaines River in Illinois is named from maple trees (plaine).
Eau Claire, Eau Galle, and Eau Pleine are obvious; the Ecorse River in
Michigan gets its name from birchbark; and the Flambeau River and lakes
in Wisconsin recall torchlight fishing. Fond du Lac again, is obvious, as is
Fontaine-qui-bouille, a creek in Colorado. Framboise Island in the Missouri
is so called because of its raspberries. The French Broad in North Carolina
is probably named from the French occupation, as is French Camp, Missis-
sippi, and Frenchman Bay in Maine, a name which itself may be French.
Grand Isle, Vermont, recalls an island in Lake Champlain now known as
South Hero, whereas Grand Ronde valley in Oregon is named from its
circular shape. Lake Great Butte des Morts, Wisconsin, was named by the
French, as was Grosse Isle, Michigan, and Grossepoint in the same state.
Guyandot, West Virginia, is French for Wyandot. Lake Huron, like Lake
Superior, is French (hure); the Isle au Chene in Lake Superior is obvious,
like Isle au Haut off the coast of Maine. Lac qui Parle in Minnesota is said
to be so named from the echoes. Lac Traverse in Minnesota means, apparently, "across the lake."

Lacygne, Kansas, however pronounced, was once French, and L'Anguille,
a stream and township in Arkansas, is named from the eel. Leboeuf, a
township in Erie county, Pennsylvania, recalls the buffalo; Malade, Iowa,
some illness; Malheur River in Oregon, a misfortune; and Marais, Missouri,
a swamp. The Marais des Cygnes River still flows through Kansas, and so
does Marmiton Creek (or river) in Missouri. Mauvaises Terres, North
Dakota, is near the "bad lands," and Millelacs, Minnesota, is the center of
innumerable lakes. The Nez Perce River, in Yellowstone Park, and the
county and town in Idaho, recall the Nez Percé, or "nose-pierced" Indians,
as Papillion, Nebraska, remembers something more poetical. Nor should the
Pend Oreille lake in Idaho be overlooked. The Pomme de Terre River is in
Missouri. Portage is a common name in the Middle West, in itself, or in
combinations, such as Portage des Sioux, Missouri. There are various kinds
of "prairies"—du Chien, du Rocher, du Sac, for example, but only one
Presque Isle in Maine, though there is a county in Michigan by the name.
The Roche a Gris (Roche Gris) River runs in Wisconsin; whether through
gray rock or not I do not know, but the Roche Moutonnée and the Roche
Percée streams are to be noted, one in Colorado, and one in Missouri.

tion,[9] but nevertheless it recalls its origin wherever local history

Roseau county, lake, and river in Minnesota are named from coarse grass; Sable (sand) is a not uncommon place name; and various "saints" recall the piety of early explorers, settlers, and missionaries: Saint Anne, Illinois; Saint Anthony Falls, Minnesota; Saint Charles, Missouri; Saint Claire, Michigan; Saint Cloud, Minnesota—probably from the French town—Saint Croix, Maine, several Saint Francis's or Saint Francois, Saint Genevieve, Missouri; Saint Ignace and Saint Joseph (Michigan); Saint Lawrence (gulf), Saint Louise (river in Minnesota named by Verendrye in 1749), Saint Mary, Saint Marys, Saint Peters, Saint Regis, Saint Paul, and Sault Sainte Marie. Trempealeau, Wisconsin, is a French translation of the Indian epithet, "mountain with its feet in the water." Vermont may be "vert mont."

[9] Feipel (*op. cit.*) thinks that Dutch and French place names were more frequently corrupted than English and Spanish ones. Names given by the French pioneers are sometimes turned directly into English. Thus: the "bad lands" are the French "mauvaises terres;" The Big Blue, or Bluewater, Creek in Missouri is from "rivière de l'eau bleue," the Big Gravois in the same state is the big "rubbish" (part translated, part not), and the Big Muddy Creek is from "grande rivière vaseuse." So, too, the Bigwood River in Idaho is apparently from "boisé." The Cannon and Cannonball Rivers have been mentioned. (See previous note.) Cow Island in the Missouri is from "ile de vache." Crown Point, New York, may be from "point au chevelure": scalping parties departed from that place. The Fever River in Illinois has an interesting history: originally "la rivière de fève" (river of the bean), folk etymology turned the "fève" into "fèvre"—whence "fever." The Grass River in New York was originally the "fertile" river—"la rivière grasse." Green Bay, Wisconsin, may be (1) a translation of the French name; or (2) a perversion of "la grande baie." The Knife River was originally the "couteau" (North Dakota). Lake of the Woods, Minnesota, was named "lac des bois." The Mine River was once "la rivière à la mine" (Missouri). The Purgatory River in Colorado is a direct translation from its French name, and so is the Wolf River in Kansas. This process of direct translation seems to be more characteristic of bodies of water than of towns.

Often the English name is a result of an attempt at phonetic spelling, sometimes with weird results. The Babruly Creek in Missouri is from "bois brulé." Baraboo, Wisconsin, was named from Jean Baribault (?). One etymology for Benzie county, Michigan, is from "aux becs scies," which seems a little far-fetched. Bureau, Illinois, is an interesting case of spelling a French name falsely; it seems to have been named for one Pierre de Beuro. The Franceway Creek in Arkansas was originally the François, just as the Great Sinabar Creek in Missouri was once the "chenal au barre." Labette county, Kansas, *may be* "the beet," but there is no doubt that L'Agles River in Arkansas is a mis-spelling of "Aigles" and that Lagrue River in the same state was once "la grue." But the two prize names in Arkansas are Low Freight Creek (l'eau froide) and Smackover Creek (chemin couvert). In the same region Loose Creek (Osage County, Missouri), was once L'Ours; Marine Saline township is from "marais saline," the Badcaw was once the Badeau (?), the Badock River was once the "bois d'arc," Bouff was once "boeuf," Caddo was once "les caddaux" (Indians), the Cash River was once the "cache," the Cossatot the "casse tête," the De Gray the "de grès," the Des Arc the "des arcs," the Devoe the "de veau," Eleven Points was once "levé pont," Lufra was once "l'eau froide," Mason, "maison," Maumelle "mamelle," the Meter River the "bayou miterre," and the Tchemanahaut the "chemin à haut" or "à l'eau." Even the Ozarks have been derived from "aux arcs" or "aux akansas" or "arkansas." Movestar Creek in Illinois was once "mauvaise terre." Odebolt, Iowa, was formerly Odebeau; Ozan,

is remembered or taught in the school. One must remember that the Americans of 1800-1848 were as sensitive to the romantic appeal of their history as later Americans;[10] this romantic appeal has some basis in these French place names, whereby the brave story of early exploration and travel was, as well as by other matters, kept alive.

2. THE HUGUENOT MIGRATION

The next great surge of the French toward the New World is the Huguenot migration, following shortly upon the Revocation of the Edict of Nantes in 1685, a movement concerning which we have a good deal of specific information,[11] both as to the numbers concerned and the quality of the immigrants. It is also the movement which has been most considerably studied, so that, although there are many embarrassing gaps in our information, we are yet able to give a more continuous picture of the Huguenot migration than we can of certain other waves of influence.[12]

The Huguenot migration to America divides into two general epochs; the period from 1555 when Admiral Coligny

Arkansas, was once the "prairie d'âne" or "aux ânes," Point Remove was formerly "remous," Rickreal, Oregon, may have something to do with "la creole," Salisaw, Oklahoma was once the "bayou salaison," Schroon, New York, has been derived from "Scharon," and Galley Rock, Arkansas from "galets."

[10] Cf. Bassett's discussion of American historians, 1783-1850, chap. xvii, Vol. II, *Cambridge History of American Literature.* The Vincennes Historical and Antiquarian Society was founded as early as 1808. Rusk I, 236.

[11] The best single study is Chinard, *Les réfugiés huguenots en Amérique.* Consult also Fosdick, *French Blood in America;* Poole, *History of the Huguenots of the Dispersion;* Baird, *History of the Huguenot Emigration to America* (excellent) ; Rosengarten, *French Colonists and Exiles.*

[12] A confusing fact, however, is both the change of names by the Huguenots themselves, and the corruption of French names by the Americans. Often, to escape detection, the Huguenot, fleeing from France into Switzerland, Holland, or Great Britain, mis-spelled his name. See, for some astonishing samples, Smith, *Colonial Days and Ways,* pp. 155-6. Here is a representative list from Rosengarten, *French Colonists and Exiles,* pp. 60-61 : in Pennsylvania the Le Beaus became Lebos; the Bésores, Bashores or Baysores ; Jacques becomes Jacob ; De Saussier, Sausser ; Monier, Money ; Grosjean, Groshong ; Souplis, Suplee ; Perot, Berrot ; Doutel, Dutill ; Votturin, Woodring ; Moreau, Morrow ; St. Gris, Sangree ; Lamothe, Lamotte ; Cassart, Cassatt ; Dreyvault, Dravo ; Fortineau, Fortney ; Boucquet, Buckey, and so on. Not all of these are Huguenots, but the list illustrates the difficulty of historians and genealogists. Lieber (*The Stranger in America,* II, 89) found a family in Salem, Masachusetts, named Blumpay, a name which proved to be a corruption of Blancpied. A more astonishing transformation is that of a German named Feuerstein, who "settled in the West when the French prevailed in that portion of the country" ; his name was changed to Pierre à Fusil, and this in turn was anglicised to Peter Gun!

dreamed of establishing a Protestant France in the New World, to the Revocation of the Edict of Nantes in 1685; and the period from 1685 to about 1750, by which year not only had emigration for some years been negligible, but the Huguenots themselves (except in certain localities) had ceased to be aliens as the maturing second generation merged into colonial life.

Lured by the dream of a golden age in the strange New World, one finds French Protestant leaders attempting to establish colonies for the faithful in Brazil in 1555-58; in South Carolina and Florida in 1562-65; in Port-Royal (Annapolis) in 1604;[13] in the Antilles in 1611; and at Mount Desert in 1613; but no one of these enterprises—and most perished—had much influence so far as determining the future of the Huguenots in the British colonies is concerned.[14] We must look rather to the dispersion of the Huguenots into Germany, Holland, and England for our first traces of an emigration destined to furnish America with some of its ablest citizens.[15] It was in the Low Countries that the Puritans, leaving England, came into contact with the Huguenots and Walloons; and among the passengers on the *Mayflower* there were French and Walloons.[16] In 1622 a small body petitioned for the right to settle in Massachusetts,—the exact number is not known.[17] There was no large emigration to Massachusetts for twenty years thereafter. Salem, however, received a number from the Channel Islands where there were some fifty Huguenot ministers. Again in 1682 there are traces of a few fugitives who came to Boston.[18] Among these earlier comers John Touton de la Rochelle, a physician, and Philippe l'Anglois, called Philip English, were most important, the latter distinguishing himself as a

[13] Canada was closed to the Huguenots in 1633. The crowded and complicated history of the Acadian enterprise is sketched in Chinard, *Les réfugiés huguenots*, pp. 9-18, and given at length in Baird, I, chap. i.

[14] For a clear and admirable account of the significance of these enterprises consult Chinard, *op. cit.*, chap. i; and see also the introduction; and his *L'Exotisme américain dans la littérature française au XVIe siècle;* and *L'Amérique et le rêve exotique dans la littérature française au XVIIe et au XVIIIe siècle.*

[15] Weiss, *History of the French Protestant Refugees* is a full account; a brief manual, giving the essential facts, is Poole, *History of the Huguenots of the Dispersion.*

[16] William Mullins (Molines), his wife, and two children, Joseph and Priscilla; their servant, Robert Carter (Cartier?), and possibly George Sowle (Soulé? Sole?) Cf. Chinard, *Les réfugiés huguenots,* pp. 27-28. Also Samuel Terry and Philip Delanoy.

[17] Baird, *History of the Huguenot Emigration to America,* II, 190-1.

[18] Baird, *op. cit.,* II, 194-5.

merchant, building "England's great house" which stood till 1833, and getting himself accused of witchcraft; he was one of the earliest important merchants of Salem, and all in all an amazing person.[19] But it can not be said that this small group exercised any dominant influence upon the development of Massachusetts culture;[20] about all that can be safely said is, as Chinard points out, that, from the absence of complaint, we may safely assume that they gave no scandal and fitted into the general scheme of things.

Of early New York (New Amsterdam) we may speak more confidently.[21] In 1623 the *Niew Nederlandt* sailed for the New World with a company of 30 families, Walloons and Huguenots being among them,[22] and these families scattered into Connecticut, Delaware, and New York: eighteen of them settled at Albany, but, although there was French blood in these families, because of the scarcity of records of the New Amsterdam colony for the first fifteen years of its existence, we know little about them.   Certain it is that the first child born in Manhattan was Jean Vigné (1614). By 1628 there were settlements of Walloons and French on the shores and islands of Manhattan.   In New Harlem, laid out in 1658, of 32 males in 1661, nearly one-half were French or Walloon.   The redoubtable Stuyvesant married a French Protestant, Judith Bayard, and from 1657 to 1663 small bodies of French Protestants came to the new colony from Holland—mainly from the north of France.[23] The first doctor of New Amsterdam, La Montagne, was French; and so was the first schoolmaster, who came in 1637; and as a result of the continued migration, by 1656 it was found necessary to issue all government and

---

[19] Baird, II, 1902-3; Chinard, *op. cit.*, pp. 30-3.

[20] The Rev. Adin Ballou (1803-1890), a great Unitarian light, was descended, it is interesting to note, from Maturin Ballou, who came to Providence Plantations in 1646—a Norman-French Huguenot, it is believed. *Autobiography of Adin Ballou,* pp. 1, 3.

[21] Baird, I, chap. ii; Chinard, chap. iii.

[22] Chinard conjectures that among these were some of those who signed the petition to the Virginia Company for permission to settle, which request was refused. See him, pp. 37-41. A facsimile of this petition is given in Baird, I. The request was refused because the Virginians' "stock is so utterly exhausted" that they "are not able to give them any help" and because of the desire of the prospective colonists to live in "one gross and entire body." Baird, I, 164.

[23] Baird, I, 169-185; Chinard, chap. iii. See the genealogy of the (Walloon) de Peyster family in Allaben, *John Watts de Puyster,* I, chap. i, for an illustration of the Walloon intermixture.

town proclamations in French and Dutch.[24] In 1652 Isaac Bedloe (Bethlo) had come from Picardy to give his name to Bedloe's Island; and a little later Toussaint Briell, François Grion la Capelle, Jean Casjou, Claude Barbier, and Antoine Jeroe settled at Buswick, Long Island. From 1656 to 1657 the immigration increased: thus on December 25, 1656, 167 colonists in three ships sailed for New Amsterdam; were shipwrecked near Fire Island Inlet; and finally settled in Delaware, though some remained on Manhattan. In the next few years others settled on Staten Island—Waldenses in all probability. Shortly they desired to have a church.[25] When in 1664 New Amsterdam became New York, French names were signed to the protest sent to Holland against the conquest.[26] In 1660 a Dutch ship brought over a group of expatriates from the Palatinate who at first settled at Esopus (Kingston), whence in 1663 they were driven by the Indians; but though the Dutch government sent out a punitive expedition, many were uneasy and founded New Paltz in 1677. There were at least eleven Huguenots among the original settlers at New Paltz; and the first schoolmaster was Jean Cottin who was given a house to live in, in 1689. Indeed, the place was so French that the church records from 1683 to 1702 are in that language.[27] Unlike other groups the New Paltz settlers seem to have kept to themselves; at least their historian finds little intermarriage with the surrounding Dutch until the third generation; and the church service was carried on for fifty years in French.[28] In general these Huguenot settlers were artisans and farmers; and since they were often more Flemish than French, and in view of their relative poverty, Chinard is quite right in cautioning us against taking their influence upon the New World too seriously. Nevertheless, in contrast to the New England settlers, the New York group is distinguished for keeping its culture and its language untouched for a long period by surrounding culture. Perhaps the relative ease of their communication with the Huguenots in the West Indies may account for this interesting phenomenon.

The newcomers made possible, and leaders of the church in Europe began, a definite propaganda of emigration which

[24] Fosdick, p. 216.
[25] See the selection from Drisius' report in Chinard, p. 54.
[26] Chinard, p. 55.
[27] Baird, I, 189-199; Lefevre, *History of New Paltz*, pp. 20-23, 37-43.
[28] Lefevre, pp. 44-45, 134, 136. The church was founded in 1683.

increased as the restrictions upon Protestants in France increased in severity.[29] Nevertheless, these slight settlements, together with some scattering attempts in the South,[30] would not of themselves have drawn a great increase in immigration, had not the Revocation of the Edict of Nantes made further residence in France impossible for the conscientious. But immediately before the Revocation a series of steps undertaken by the French government, of which the most important are the abolishing of Protestant schools (1664-1685), the decree of 1681 permitting the conversion of Huguenot children to Catholicism at the mature age of seven (kidnapping was often undertaken as a means of "conversion"), the closing of Protestant churches (1662-1685), and the *Dragonnades* (1681) increased alike the sufferings of the victims and the number of emigrants. The edict permitting the "conversion" of Protestant children roused even Charles II to action, and on July 28, 1681, a royal proclamation offered letters of denization to fleeing Protestants, promised naturalization if they desired it, and commanded the civil and military officers to give them passports and assistance; also collections were commanded to provide relief for the destitute.[31] The flame of sympathy spread to the New World: one finds the Reverend Increase Mather printing in 1682 *The Church a Subject of Persecution,* in which, after detailing the sufferings of the Huguenots, Mather characteristically argues that the sins of the Second Church were strong, and that God might well send a persecution to chasten them.[32] A correspondence developed between the British Isles, the French, and the representatives of the governing classes in Boston, the general result of which was to permit the Protestants to settle in New England. Thereafter one notes an increased emigration to those colonies, the refugees coming from France, England, Holland, the Palatinate, and other havens of refuge.[33] Let us study the movement from 1685 on.

[29] On the nature and extent of this propaganda see Chinard's admirable chapter (iv), *op. cit.*

[30] In 1610 a group of French were prepared to plant vines in De la Warr's colony; de Sancé tried to colonize a group in Virginia in 1629; but the colony scattered. Fosdick, *op. cit.,* pp. 345, 359. Fosdick points out that French names have survived in Norfolk County. See also Chinard, pp. 187-9. Baird (I, 165 note) promises, but does not give, an account.

[31] Baird, I, 238-255.

[32] Murdock, *Increase Mather,* pp. 136-7.

[33] The official account of the London relief committee, according to Poole, in December, 1687, reports that 13,500 refugees have been helped in London

New England first. In the year 1686 fifteen French families arrived from Saint Christopher—this was in August, and they followed upon twelve poor refugees come in 1682. Five weeks later, that is to say in September, a small ship-load disembarked at Salem. Thereafter every month brought its small contingent until it seems to the historian of the movement that Palfrey's original estimate of 150 families is too low.[34] Some of those who disembarked in New England, it is true, did not stay, going to South Carolina, New York and Delaware; and not all remained in Massachusetts. But among those who remained in the future Old Bay State were men of power and families of influence—Gabriel Bernon, for example, their chief business man,[35] the Boudoin (Bowdoin), Cazneau, Sigourney, Faneuil, Freneau and Allaire families; and presently there was founded a completely Huguenot settlement at Oxford, or New Oxford, on the Manexit or French River under the leadership of the said Bernon in 1687.[36] There, where each farmer had his 150 acres of land, church services were held in French, and there, despite varying troubles, they continued to remain until after the Deerfield massacre of 1704.[37] In the meantime the French in Boston itself had increased to the point where it was possible to found a French church (1685) which retained its identity until 1748.[38] Despite suspicion and jealousy, the French in Boston seem to have got on very well with their British neighbors; "they brought," says their historian, "a buoyancy and a cheerfulness, that must have been contagious, even amidst the pervading austerity. They brought a love for the beautiful, that showed itself in the culture of flowers,"

---

in 1687, and 2000 at the seaports, all artificers and laborers except 143 ministers. The principal occupations were those of making beaver hats, furriers, lacemaking, fine linen, sailcloth, glassmaking, and paper making. Poole, *History of the Huguenots of the Dispersion,* pp. 81-94. Some of these occupations were transferred to the colonies.

[34] Fosdick sets the New England migration at between 4000 and 5000, (p. 209).

[35] See the account in Chinard, pp. 84 ff. A good deal of help was extended the French. Fosdick, p. 133.

[36] Bernon himself had his house in Boston.

[37] On the troubled history of New Oxford consult Chinard, pp. 86-93. *The Boston News-Letter* for March 13, 1709, contains a notice to French Protestants, "sometimes Inhabitants of the said Village in *Oxford,* that have for several years past left and deserted their places there" to file notice of their intention to return when they "shall have such Lott & Right in the said Village as other *English* Inhabitants."

[38] Baird, II, 221-245. The members joined English churches in that year.

and he speaks of the strength of their religious convictions, and their love of liberty.[39] And one need not expatiate upon the place of the Faneuil, Bowdoin, Sigourney, Revere, and Dupuy families in New England history.[40]

In Connecticut there were fewer Huguenots, though at Melford and Hartford Baird traces the influences of small groups.[41] In Rhode Island, however, near East Greenwich, some forty or fifty families were settled in 1686; unfortunately for American hospitality their right to the ownership of land was challenged by the greed of neighboring farmers, and after five years the settlement was broken up.[42] If, as one turns the pages of Farmer's *Genealogical Register of the First Settlers of New England,* one finds few French names, if the total immigration into New England was small, one must yet note that judged by history, the work of pastors like Pierre Daillé and Lemercier, of merchants like the Faneuils, Bernon, and Philip English, are part and parcel of New England colonial life; and the tact of the first named in smoothing out points of difference, the fact that French families moved with comparative ease in New England circles, kept in the view of the Puritan some other picture of the French than that they were abominable Papists or inciters of the savages.[43]

In New York, meanwhile, little groups of Huguenots drifted steadily in. By 1688 two hundred Huguenot families had found a home in New York, or about one-quarter of the

[39] Baird, II, 253. There are, indeed, many evidences that the French had the cordial regard of their Puritan neighbors. Fosdick, p. 159. *The Boston News-Letter* for September 1, 1707, prints a summary of the address to Queen Anne from the French churches in London. The members "account themselves so happy in Living under her Majesties gentle government."

[40] Andrew Faneuil, who died in 1738, received a great public funeral. Peter Faneuil (died 1743) became the wealthiest merchant in Boston. James Bowdoin, once governor of Massachusetts, was one of the founders, and the first president, of the American Academy of Arts and Letters, to which he left his library. His son James was minister to Spain in 1804. R. H. Dana was one of the founders of the North American Review, and his son, R. H. Dana, Jr., wrote *Two Years Before the Mast.* Fosdick properly remarks in view of such records as these that the Huguenots were "a hotbed of talent." (p. 209).

[41] Baird, II, chap. xiv.

[42] Baird, II, chap. xiii; Chinard, pp. 102-111. Stephen Decatur's paternal grandfather, a native of La Rochelle, went to the West Indies, and later joined a small French colony in Newport, R. I., about 1750. Mackenzie, *Life of Stephen Decatur,* p. 8.

[43] However, the Huguenots were under suspicion during the French and Indian Wars.

population.[44] As early as 1659 there were enough Huguenots to make possible the founding of a French church, and this congregation, heterogeneous though it was,[45] under the vigorous leadership of M. Pierre Peiret after 1687, built a house of worship whither at first the faithful from New Rochelle and other surrounding settlements came to worship. The congregation suffered varying fortune. In the anonymous *History of North America,* published in 1776, we find a fair statement of the case: "The French Church, by the contentions of 1724,[46] and the disuse of the language, is now reduced to an inconsiderable handful. The building is of stone, nearly a square, plain both within and without. It is fenced from the street, has a steeple and a bell, the latter of which was the gift of Sir Henry Ashurst of London."[47] From 1776 to 1796 the church closed its doors, during which interval most of its members either joined, or attended, Trinity Church. In 1796 the church was re-opened, using the Episcopal liturgy, with M. Albert, a Swiss, for pastor; and in 1804 the church was consecrated by the Episcopal bishop of New York as "The French Church of the Holy Spirit," and as such it became a fashionable place of worship. Writing in 1833 in his *Journal* Abdy informs us that "the service is regularly performed by the minister in the French language; and many attend for the sole purpose of studying the idiom of a fashionable tongue."[48] Until the present day the French Church has been one of the enduring monuments of the Huguenots in New York, and one of the centers of influence for French culture.

How many French Huguenots came to New York City it

[44] Fosdick, *French Blood in America,* p. 224.

[45] "Le nombre même des réfugiés, leurs provenances diverses, étaient des obstacles considérables à leur accord. Venus d'Angleterre, du pays de Vaud, de Saint-Christophe et des Antilles, de toutes les provinces françaises et s'ajoutant aux Huguenots déjà établis dans la colonie depuis longtemps, ils formaient en groupe assez hétérogène qu'il était presque impossible de réunir dans une même congrégation." Chinard, p. 151. On the personnel of the French Huguenots in New York, consult Baird, II, *passim.*

[46] Described in Chinard, pp. 151 ff.

[47] *A History of North America,* p. 101. Birket (*Some Cursory Remarks,* p. 45) remarks in 1750-51 that the young people are abandoning the French Church, "which now has but a small congregation."

[48] Abdy's *Journal,* I, 341. Cf. the description in Buckingham, *America: Eastern and Western States,* I, 8, written 1842, when the building was burned (September 22). It was rebuilt.

is impossible to estimate exactly;[49] but the most remarkable monument of the migration after 1685 was the growth of New Rochelle. Settlement seems to have begun in 1688 or 1689.[50] Under the leadership of David Bonrepos, who later went as minister to the settlement on Staten Island, this interesting colony began its long and useful life. In 1694 or 1695 more than twenty French families lived at New Rochelle,[51] who were compelled to go the long way to New York to attend service. Shortly (1701?) they had a congregation of their own, which in 1709 accepted the Episcopal ritual. In 1710 official permission was given to construct a church, at which date there were 67 male and 137 female Christians in the village. Although after 1713 English became the official language of New Rochelle, and although the Rev. Daniel Bondet (Boudet?) preached "very intelligibly" in English as well as French,[52] New Rochelle was long a training place both in French and in manners for the surrounding British. By 1727 the population had grown to 400.[53] After the death of the Rev. Michael Houdin, the last French preacher, in 1766, an Englishman, the Rev. Mr. Seabury, had charge of the congregation, which the American Revolution was to scatter;[54]

[49] Some estimate may be made from John Miller's *Description of the Province and City of New York . . . in the Year 1695,* in which he writes: "The number of inhabitants in this province are about three thousand families, whereof almost one-half are naturally Dutch, a great part English, and the rest French. . . . As to their religion, they are very much divided; few of them intelligent and sincere, but the most part ignorant and conceited, fickle and regardless. As to their wealth and disposition thereto, the Dutch are rich and sparing; the English neither very rich, nor too great husbands; the French are poor, and therefore forced to be penurious. As to their way of trade and dealing, they are all generally cunning and crafty, but many of them not so just to their word as they should be." Quoted in Stedman and Hutchinson, II, 209. When the smallpox swept the town in 1731, the burial figures indicate the proportion of races. Of 478 whites who died from Aug. 25 to Nov. 25, 229 were Church of England members, 212 were Dutch, 15 were buried at the French church, 16 were Presbyterians, there were two each of the Quakers, Baptists, and Jews, and one Lutheran. *Boston Weekly News-Letter,* November 25, 1731 (No. 1452).

[50] Cf. Chinard, chap. iv; Baird, II; Fosdick, *French Blood in America,* pp. 231 ff.; Stapleton, *Memorials of the Huguenots in America, passim,* Waldron, *The Huguenots of Westchester, passim.*

[51] Cf. the description of the Huguenots going to church in Smith, *Colonial Days and Ways,* pp. 143 ff.

[52] Waldron, *op. cit.,* pp. 33-41, describes the pastors of the church.

[53] Letter of the Rev. Pierre Stouppe (d. 1760), pastor, cited by Waldron, p. 34. There was some intermixture of Dutch, however. Cf. Chinard, pp. 173-4, note.

[54] Waldron, p. 41.

and by 1829 "the manners of the mother country," for which New Rochelle was famed, seemed in the opinion of one observer, to "have entirely left them," although he remarks that the names of the people are still very generally French—Petit, Badeau, Bonet, Gallaudet, Renaud, Le Compte, Le Fevre, etc.[55] But in the meantime the settlement at New Rochelle was accomplishing its task of spreading a knowledge of French and of gentle manners.[56]

The Huguenots at New Paltz clung even more stubbornly to their French inheritance.[57] As late as 1750 the church members in New Paltz protested that they were still an independent "French Reformed Church," and although services were no longer said in French the church continued independent until the Revolution. In no part of the United States, says Chinard, has the memory of the Huguenots remained more lively or more actual than in this village which bears, in origin and appearance, a German name.[58] And we may remark with the genealogist that "in Ulster and Dutchess counties many of their (the Huguenots') descendants still reside."[59] And there were other settlements on the upper Hudson.[60]

In Pennsylvania likewise there were Huguenot settlements.[61] Prior to the grant of Pennsylvania to Penn in 1681, Pennsylvania and Delaware contained some Huguenots, the most of them in Delaware, where the principal migration seems to have occurred in 1654-64,[62] though there was a steady migration thereafter. However that may be, one notes such names as Edmond du Castle, John de la Vall and Andrew Droz

---

[55] Stuart, *Three Years in North America*, II, 13.
[56] Cf. Fosdick, pp. 233-5, 413-4; Smith, *Colonial Days and Ways*, pp. 163-166.
[57] See Le Fevre, *History of New Paltz*.
[58] Chinard, p. 184.
[59] Rupp, *Names of Immigrants in Pennsylvania*, p. 6. See the list of names in Appendix XIII, pp. 463-4. For instance, Cooper, the novelist, bought a farm near Scarsdale, N. Y., called Angevine from the name of the Huguenot tenant who preceded him; and the Cooper children were nursed by Katie Arnault, a young girl from a Huguenot family. An old Frenchwoman made Susan Cooper a little French cap; and near by lived the Flandreau, Comel, and Bonnet families. *Correspondence of James Fenimore-Cooper*, I, 28, 35.
[60] On the connection between French and Dutch in Albany, see Mrs. Grant, *Memoirs of an American Lady*.
[61] Rupp, *op. cit.*; Stapleton, *Memorials of the Huguenots in America, with Special Reference to their Emigration to Pennsylvania;* Chinard, pp. 185-6.
[62] Fosdick, pp. 290-1; Stapleton, pp. 42-43. For a list of Huguenot settlers in Delaware from 1686-1700 see him, pp. 43-44.

among the original citizens of Philadelphia—Droz, a vine-dresser, had a plantation of 200 acres on the Schuylkill. Gabriel Rappe and Nicholas Reboteau were naturalized in Philadelphia in 1683; Elias Boudinot, who came to New York in 1686, had a son who later removed to Philadelphia; Andros Souplis (Suplee) came there in 1684; and thereafter the migration to Philadelphia seems to have increased. The country around Philadelphia proved attractive to the French farmers. One notes, for instance, that Madame Ferree and the Rev. Joshua Kocherthal headed a party which, landing in New York in 1709, secured land in Lancaster County, Pennslyvania, in 1710; that the Schuylkill Valley drew others; and that the little town of Oley attracted Isaac de Turk (Turque?) in 1712. Germantown, founded in 1683, included a number of Huguenot families; the Perkiomen and lower Schuylkill country included Palatines, Alsatians, and Huguenots who came from Europe and from New York—such families as the Boyer (Bayer, Beyer), Pechin, Purviance, Trego (Tricot, Trico), and Delliker (de la Cour) families being enumerated by their historians. Bucks, Monroe, and Lehigh Counties have their Huguenot infusion; at the Minisink Flats near the Delaware Water Gap there were Huguenots from Esopus; so, too, the Lehigh Valley and the Conestoga Valley drew their quota. In the meantime such important families as the Duché, Benezet, Roberdeau, and Garrigues, in addition to those already noted, were settling in Philadelphia.[63] Alsace and Lorraine furnished a large contingent in this migration which was steady from 1700 to 1754 at least.

If we move South, we may note the rather abortive attempt of the Labadists to found a colony near the Bohemia River in 1683.[63a] In Virginia we have already observed an unsuccessful attempt on the part of the French to found a colony. In 1619-21 it was desired to secure some French vine-growers—one of the persistent dreams of colonizers in the New World was that the vine could be cultivated anywhere from Maine to

---

[63] The above data are from Stapleton. He lists 535 different family names, pp. 149-157, mostly in New York, New Jersey, and Pennsylvania. Some are, it is true, duplicates, owing to the habit of phonetic spelling, but if we suppose this to be true of 35 names, there yet remain 500 different names in this one volume alone. For further lists see Fosdick, chap. i, part III. On Benezet see Benjamin Rush's account quoted in Stedman and Hutchinson. III, 369-70; and that of Chastellux, *Voyages*, I, 240 ff.
[63a] Described in James, *The Labadist Colony in Maryland*.

Florida—and it appears that eight had come.[64] The attempt of de Sancé to establish a settlement has been touched upon; all traces of it have disappeared. Until the Revocation there were but few who came,[65] but in the last decade of the seventeenth century the British government actively encouraged the emigration of the Huguenots to Southern colonies. In 1690, according to Poole, William III sent out the colonists of French extraction who settled on the James River, 20 miles from Richmond, where they planted the "Monacan" settlement.[66] "In the year 1699, there went over about three hundred of these, and the year following about two hundred more, and so on, till there arrived in all between seven and eight hundred Men, Women, and Children, who had fled from *France* on account of their religion," says an early Virginian historian.[67] There in 1702 they tried vine-growing;[68] and there they received help from the governor and the assembly and from the great Colonel Byrd,[69] although, because of internal dissensions, some of the colonists remained in Jamestown and others scattered into Norfolk County. According to Poole these original immigrations were increased by the addition of 600 families.[70] One of the first acts of the Manakin settlers was to establish a church, which, though no longer French, lasted until 1857.[71] From these centers the Huguenots seem also to have dispersed over Virginia.[72] Later, a group of Huguenots, dissatisfied with conditions in Manakintown,[73]

[64] Chinard, p. 188.
[65] An examination of Greer's *Early Virginia Immigrants*, covering the first part of the seventeenth century, reveals that the overwhelming majority are British names.
[66] Poole, *op. cit.*, p. 98.
[67] Beverley, *The History of Virginia*, pp. 244-45.
[68] "I heard a Gentleman, who had tasted it, give it (their claret) great Commendation." *Ibid.*, p. 245.
[69] Chinard, pp. 191-2, cites a document setting forth Byrd's services to the refugees which is apparently not in the edition of Beverley used by me.
[70] Poole, *op. cit.*, p. 97. Baird, a better authority, estimates 700. II, 177.
[71] Fosdick, p. 354.
[72] See the lists of towns, counties and names in Fosdick, pp. 355-62. John Marshall married (1783) Mary Willis Ambler, daughter of the treasurer of Virginia and a descendant of the La Roche Jacquelines of France. Magruder, *John Marshall*, p. 48. Moncure D. Conway's ancestors were French in origin, his great-great-grandfather, John Moncure, who died in 1765, being the first to come to Virginia. *Autobiography of Moncure Daniel Conway*, I, 7.
[73] The reason for their dissatisfaction was because they failed to take up enough land; and the English surveyed around their allotments and hemmed them in. Lawson, *History of North Carolina*, p. 66.

removed to the Trent River in North Carolina, taking their pastor, one Rybourg, with them. This was in 1707, and in North Carolina they intended to take up the cultivation of the vine.[74] One of them discovered a coal mine while hunting, but the English surveyed it away from him; the group as a whole made good flax, hemp, linen cloth and thread, which they traded with their neighbors.[75]

But the chief Huguenot group in the South (aside from some stray settlers in Florida and Georgia) was in South Carolina. Here, as in New Rochelle and New Paltz, the group long retained its peculiar individuality.[76] In 1670 Richard Batin, Jacques Jours, and Richard Deyos came to Charleston;[77] in 1680 the English frigate, *The Richmond*, brought over 45 Huguenots at the command of Charles II.[78] The great flood here, as elsewhere, came with the Revocation,[79] but mi-

[74] See Lawson's remarks, pp. 65-6.
[75] See in addition to Lawson, Williamson, *The History of North Carolina*, I, 178-9. Descendants of this colony still live in the state.
[76] The chief source of information is the *Transactions of the Huguenot Society of South Carolina*.
[77] Henry A. M. Smith, "The Orange Quarter and the First French Settlers in South Carolina," *South Carolina Historical and Genealogical Magazine*, XVIII, no. 3, argues that the traditional statement, made by McCrady and others, that lots were granted to Richard Batin, Jacques Jours, Richard Deyos in 1670; in 1677 to Jean Batton; and in 1678 to Jean Bazant and Richard Gaillard, Huguenots all, is in error. He argues (pp. 101-104) that with the exception of Gaillard or Gilliard, all these were English or Irish. He seems to overlook the possibility that these settlers may have come first to England or Ireland and thence to the New World, and may be nonetheless Huguenots or of Huguenot descent.
[78] The traditional view that the King dispatched *two* vessels in 1679 seems to be wrong. See Smith, *op. cit.* No list of the French arriving on the *Richmond* is extant. Smith points out that the chief sources for the names of French settlers are the land grants, the records of which are admittedly imperfect, stray references in contemporaneous writings, and the Ravenel or St. Julien list of about 1696 (in the *Transactions of the Huguenot Society of South Carolina* for 1897, pp. 49-52). These give a total of 154 heads of families, with about 28 duplicates, making 126 in all. In addition to these the Act of the Provincial Assembly of March 10, 1696-7 for naturalizing aliens, gives 63 names of which 56, according to Smith, are French. See on the *Richmond*, the *Transactions* for 1905 (no. 12), pp. 22-24.
[79] Robert Wilson, "The Huguenot Influence in Colonial South Carolina," (*Transactions* for 1897, no. 4, pp. 26-38) sets the number of French protestants by March 1698-9 as 6,000. Smith, who desires to minimize the number, argues that "the entire French settlement in South Carolina bore numerically a very small proportion to the entire population," (*op. cit.*, p. 122)—something like 10% of the total white population in 1698-9. As the white population was about 5,500, ten per cent would give 550 Frenchmen. He argues that in two-thirds of the state the French population was negligible, an argument which does not seem quite relevant, for it hardly seems likely that 550 is sufficient foundation for that grip on the eastern

gration into South Carolina from the northern colonies was not uncommon; and a feature of the movement was that many had been naturalized in London as British subjects—a fact which did not prevent a certain amount of trouble and opposition. From 1680 to 1696 the movement was steady; and in 1687, on land given by Ralph Izard, there was begun the erection of the famous French church of Charleston.[80] Aside from Charleston there were six separate establishments of Huguenots within the colony: Goose Creek, Orange Quarter,[81] French Santee, Saint John's Berkeley, Purysburg, and New Bordeaux. The great bulk of the settlement was on the Santee and Cooper rivers. Of Charleston itself Lawson wrote in 1700:

Since the first Planters abundance of French and others have gone over, and raised themselves to considerable Fortunes. . . . Their cohabiting in a Town has drawn to them ingenious People of most Sciences, whereby they have Tutors amongst them that educate their Youth a-la-mode.

He observes also that there is "likewise a French Church in Town of the Reform'd Religion."[82] This same church[83] had as its first pastor a descendant of Prioli, doge of Venice in 1618, one Elias Prioleau.[84] In Charleston entire streets were

branch of the Cooper River which, says Smith, the French maintained until the Civil War. Smith's article is an excellent case of special pleading, but if Wilson's figure is too high, Smith's seems to me too low. The difference arises in the problem of what constitutes the French Huguenot migration; i.e., Smith has in mind the migration coming immediately from France, or almost immediately by way of England. Wilson, however, points out that Huguenots migrating to England and Flanders, as early as 1585, sent representatives to South Carolina who were thoroughly Anglicised. Should they be counted or not? And should people like them be counted? Truth probably lies in *media viae*.

[80] This is the traditional view. The indefatigable Smith argues, however, that there was no church edifice in Charleston until 1701. *Op cit.,* p. 118.

[81] The view that the first settlers in the Orange Quarter came on the *Richmond* is combated by Smith, who gives a list of the settlers in that region (p. 114), none of whom—some twenty families in all—came, he says, on that vessel. However, we do not have a list of those coming on the *Richmond*. Services in the Orange Quarter were apparently first held in a private house, and a church was not erected until about 1703. Smith, p. 121.

[82] *History of North Carolina*, "Introduction," p. xiv.

[83] It used Durel's translation of the book of common prayer—a fact which shows how close was the Huguenot to the Anglican faith. The church was burned in 1740 and again in 1796. In 1808 the communicants were few in number. Ramsay, *History of South Carolina*, II, 38-39.

[84] On the Prioleau family see *Transactions*, 1899, no. 6, pp. 5-37.

built by the Huguenots,[85] who were noted for their manufacture of silk and wool. There were three other churches built—
the Santee church, the Orange Quarter church, and one at
St. John's Berkeley, all of which were eventually merged with
the Anglican. In these (but not in the Charleston church) the
use of French was abandoned by 1750.[86] In Charleston, however, as in New York, fashion helped to keep the French
church alive.[87]

The South Carolina movement is characterized by its long
continuance. In 1761 an act was passed by the colonial assembly encouraging foreign protestants to settle in the colony
and offering bounties, as a result of which some 600 came in
1763-64. On May 28, 1762, an Order in Council refers to
the petition of 114 French protestants, mostly bred to agriculture, who desired to settle in the British Colonies, and a
letter from the Lords of Trade to Governor Boone suggest
that a tract of 20,000 acres on the Savannah River be set
aside for them. This group, which eventually amounted to
212 settlers, under the leadership of their pastor, the Reverend
Jean Louis Gibert, laid out New Bordeaux, the Assembly
meeting in special session April 19-23, 1764 to grant £500
sterling towards settling them. This amount proving insufficient, £200 more was advanced August 3, when the settlement was actually taking place. At New Bordeaux the manufacture of silk became an industry.[88] Farming, however, was
still important, as the following quotation from Lawson will
show:

[85] The earliest settlers were of course agriculturalists.
[86] Primer, "The Huguenot Element in Charleston's Pronunciation," *Publications of the Modern Language Association,* IV (old series), p. 220.
Primer points out that the larger proportion of the Huguenots came from
towns and villages of the Loire and the Gironde, and that La Rochelle and
the Isle of Ré sent relatively small quotas, though all parts of France and
Yverdon in Switzerland were represented. P. 215.
[87] Charleston Huguenot families include the Bayard, Bonneau, Benoit,
Bocquet, Bacot, Chevalier, Corde, Chastaquier, Duprè, Deslisles, Dubose,
Dubois, Dutarque, de la Coursillière, Dubouxdieu, Fayssaux, Gaillard,
Gendron, Horry, Guignard, Huger, Legaré, Lauren, Lausac, Marion,
Mazycq, Manigault, Mallichamp, Neuville, Péronneau, Porcher, Peyre,
Ravenel, Saint Julien, and Trevezant families. On some of these families
there are special studies. See note 92 below.
[88] The facts are from Snowden, "The French Protestants of the Abbe-
ville District, South Carolina, 1761-1765," *Collections of the South Carolina
Historical Society,* II, 75-103. See also Ramsay, *History of South Carolina,*
I, 19-20. Snowden gives a list of the names and also of the occupations of
these immigrants, who were laborers, farmers, *vignerons,* carpenters, and
perruqiers!

[He found] seventy Families living on this (Santee) River, who live as Decently and Happily, as any Planters in these Southward parts of America. The French, being a temperate Industrious People, some of them bringing very little of Effects, yet by their endeavors and Mutual Assistance amongst themselves (which is highly to be Commended) have outstrip't our English, who brought with them Larger Fortunes, tho' as it seems less endeavor to manage their Talent to the best Advantage.

He "lay all night at Mons. Eugee's" (Huger's); at noon he came up to "several French Plantations," and found the French "very officious" in helping his party over the creeks. All the Huguenots were "clean and decent in their apparel." They dined with Mons. L. Jandro, where there were "some French ladies" lately come from England, and Mons. "L'Grand," a "worthy Norman." A French doctor sent his servant to guide them to "Mons. Galian's the elder" who lived "in a very curious contriv'd House, built of Brick and Stone, which is gotten near that Place"—36 miles from Charleston by land and 100 by water.[89]

Comment has often been made upon the extraordinary influence of this Huguenot group upon the life of South Carolina. There was at first, it is true, some inter-racial friction. Because of the antipathy of the English in 1693 the French settlers were uneasy that there was no provincial law to secure their estates to their heirs, for they feared that upon their death their lands would escheat to the proprietors of the colony, and their children would be beggars. Under Governor Archdale this sense of hostility so increased that he found their total exclusion from all connexion with the legislature necessary and issued writs to two counties only, so that only English members (eighteen in all) were chosen. Upon his retirement the colonial council voted an address to the proprietors to the effect that

. . . they had no contending factions nor clashing interests among the people, excepting what respects the french refugees; who were unhappy at their not being allowed all the privileges and liberties of english subjects, particularly those of sitting in assembly and voting at the election of its members, which could not be granted them with-

[89] Lawson, *History of North Carolina*, pp. 5-7. He speaks also of their ship-building on the Santee where were "vast Ciprus-Trees, of which the French make Canoes, that will carry fifty or sizty barrels," which have "two Masts and Bermudas Sails" and were used for coastwise navigation between the French settlement and "Charles Town." P. 3.

out losing the affections of the english settlers and involving the colony in civil broils.[90]

But by 1686 feeling against the French began to abate as they "proved to be honest, reliable folk"; and in that year the General Assembly passed "an Act for Making Aliens Free," by which all those Huguenots who had not been naturalized in England, could be so naturalized upon petition.[91] Even before this time some of the French Protestants had served in the assembly, and in part of the country were the French more thoroughly imbued with Anglo-Saxon ideas.[92] Griswold expresses a common sentiment when he writes that "in casting

[90] Ramsay, *History of South Carolina*, I, 49-50. The true basis of English jealousy is shown by the history of Craven County where the French, admittedly an orderly, industrious and religious people, bought land and succeeded. The English thereupon became jealous and looked upon them as aliens, legally entitled to no privileges. The proprietors, in view of the stand of the royal government, took the part of the refugees as they were in honor bound to do, and instructed Governor Ludwell as early as 1692 to allow them the rights and privileges of the English. However, Archdale, as we have seen, refused to allow the county to elect a single representative to the legislature in the ensuing election. *Ibid.*, I, 43-44.

[91] Salley, *Narratives of Early Carolina*, p. 239, note; Ramsay, *History of South Carolina*, I, 50-51.

[92] As early as 1692 six out of 20 members of the Commons were French Protestants. Salley, p. 238. Salley, by the way, estimates (p. 246) the number of Huguenots at the time of their coming as 3% or 4% of the population. As marking the rise to influence of the Huguenots, certain facts are of interest. Thus Henry Le Noble was proprietary deputy and a member of the Governor's Council in 1702. The elder Le Surrurier was a wealthy merchant prince, and James Le Surrurier was Commissioner of the church in 1704. Peter St. Julien was one of twelve counsellors who supported Governor Johnson in 1719. Isaac Mazyck, another merchant prince, arrived in 1686 with interest in a cargo of goods to £1000, and shortly became one of the largest landowners in the province. He died in 1835. Stephen Godin was likewise an important merchant. René Ravenel and Philip Gendron were commissioners under the Church Act in 1706. Wilson, "The Huguenot Influence in Colonial South Carolina," *Transactions* for 1897, no. 4, pp. 26-38. For the Manigault family (came in 1685) see *Transactions* for 1897, no. 4, pp. 48-84. *The Ravenel Records*, compiled by Henry E. Ravenel, give a good deal of information about that important family, the founder of which was of the French noblesse; the first important "American" Ravenel, René, mentioned above, married Charlotte de St. Julien at Pomkinhill Plantation, October 24, 1687. Regarding the Legaré family there is a dispute as to whether it was first established in Massachusetts in 1691 (Baird, II, 111-112), or in South Carolina. The first Carolinian of this family was Solomon Legaré, who fled to Bristol in 1685, married an Englishwoman, and came to Charleston in 1686. He became one of the largest landowners in Charleston, leaving his nine children in comfortable circumstances. Fludd, *Biographical Sketches of the Huguenot Solomon Legaré*. Daniel Trevezant, who died in 1726, one of the merchant princes of the time, is said to have brought plenty of money with him, and at his death left a plantation and slaves to his heir. See on this family Trevezant, *The Trevezant Family in the United States*.

his eyes over the names belonging to this colony, one is struck with the large number evidently French," and he adds that they were all patriots in the Revolution.[93] As evidencing the influence of the group on South Carolina, it is to be noted that the Huguenot Society of that state, said to be the largest in the world, numbers 2,000 members, most of them descendants of the early settlers.[94] In the eighteenth century the French were hospitable and helpful to travellers and explorers;[95] and already a tradition of hospitality and intellectual achievement was well established. Professor Dodd describes the place of the French in South Carolina during the opening years of the eighteenth century in the following paragraph:

An important racial element was contributed to the life of South Carolina by the French Huguenots of high intellectual endowment and even literary culture whose ancestors had driven in family coaches and had read good books for three generations. Unsurpassed in commercial pursuits, they heaped up fortunes which made their names known on both sides of the Atlantic during the Revolution and the decades which followed the adoption of the Federal Constitution. But aristocratic groups seldom maintain themselves. The Huguenots were fast merging into the planter-lawyer class, and when cotton became king in the South, their quaint accent was about all that remained to mark them as a race apart.[96]

But it was this merging process which helped to contribute to the life of the state. Certain it is that during the last half of our period we have a succession of tributes to the hospitality and courtesy of the French in Charleston. Thus in 1825 when Lafayette visited the city, he was greeted by a corps of troops whose uniform was "exactly that worn by the Paris Guards at the period of our (French) glorious revolution"; the benevolent society[97] joined in the procession in his honor; and in Charleston he met Mr. Bollman and Mr. Huger who had tried to rescue him from Austrian dungeons, the latter a descendant

[93] Griswold, *Republican Court*, p. 65.
[94] Willis, *The Charleston Stage*, p. 233.
[95] Thus when Colonel Chicken went to negotiate with the Cherokee Indians in 1725 we find him entertained at the house of Mr. Peter St. Julien, near Dorchester, June 17, 1725. "Colonel Chicken's Journal to the Cherokees, 1725," in Mereness, *Travels in the American Colonies*, p. 97. Instances could be multiplied, but consult Michaux's *Journal* for examples of hospitality extended to him at the close of the century.
[96] Dodd, *The Cotton Kingdom*, p. 17.
[97] The Huguenots founded a society to aid widows and orphans in 1736. Rosengarten, *French Colonists and Exiles*, p. 93.

of that Huger whose name, sometimes spelled "Eugee" we have met before.[98] When Agassiz and Pourtalès, his assistant, went to Charleston in the winter of 1846-7 "the broad and generous hospitality of the planters attracted him much, and Agassiz and Pourtalès were both glad to meet gentlemen, coming from their common stock of French and Swiss Protestants, like de Saussure, Ravenel, and others, or Dr. Fabre, an old Swabe student of the University of Tübingen."[99] And writing in 1850, Frederika Bremer describes her visit to the House of Mr. Poinsett, "a French gentilhomme in his whole exterior and demeanor" who "unites the refinement and natural courtesy of the Frenchman, with the truthful simplicity and straightforwardness which I so much like in the true American"; and the same lady observes that there are many families descended from the Huguenots, and though "language, manners, (?) memories have become obliterated under the influence of the legislative, amalgamating race of the New World, . . . yet, nevertheless, somewhat of the French mode, of the French tone of mind, exists still in the life and temperament of the Southern people."[100] And one need not labor the point that a racial stock which has contributed Francis Marion, Henry Laurens, the Manigault and Ravenel families, Washington Allston and Bishop Capers to the life of the state, has been a powerful influence in shaping that commonwealth.[101]

Such, imperfectly sketched, was the Huguenot migration to this country. "Originating in a forced flight, the movement continues to present to the imagination the appearance of a dispersion, hasty and incoherent," writes Baird, but "it will be found, on further inquiry, that the emigration was an intelligent one."[102] Unfortunately the very conditions of the emigration make it impossible to estimate with anything like accuracy the numbers concerned. It may well be doubted whether the total migration exceeded 15,000 souls.[103] What matters more

[98] Levasseur, *Lafayette in America*, II, 54-5.
[99] Marcou, *Life, Letters and Works of Louis Agassiz*, I, 292.
[100] Bremer, *Homes in the New World*, I, 287 ff., 382.
[101] Ramsay, *History of South Carolina*, I, 8-9; Flagg, *Life and Letters of Washington Allston*, p. 2; Wightman, *Life of William Capers*, p. 12.
[102] Baird, *op. cit.*, II, 188.
[103] Any statement is mainly guess-work. However, it is estimated that the Huguenot population of South Carolina when the period of migration closed amounted to no more than 3% of the population. This state admittedly had

is the quality of the immigrants; and it is safe to assume that no single body of aliens (i.e., non-English-speaking people) have contributed more to American life. The late Henry Cabot Lodge, from a study of names contained in *Appleton's Encyclopedia of American Biography,* found that among the men who before 1789 were of sufficient distinction to be named in that work, there were 589 of Huguenot descent, and that this group holds fourth place in his list.[104] Indeed, it is interesting to note those leaders of the American Revolution who were of Huguenot descent. The Rev. Jacob Duché opened the first Continental Congress with prayer. John Jay, Henry Laurens, and Elias Boudinot were at various times presidents of that body. When the Treaty of Paris was signed, Jay and Laurens attached their signatures; and the third, as president of Congress, signed the congressional ratification of the treaty. The first treasurer of the United States, Michael Hilligas, was a Huguenot, and so was Boudinot, the director of the Mint in 1795. Marion and Pickens and the Huger brothers were soldiers of fame; and Manigault, as a financier, was hardly less important than Morris. John Sevier, the Le Conte family, Paul Revere, the Ravenel's, the Dana's, the Tourgee's, the Soulé's, the Delano's, the Sigourney's, the Trevezant's, the Lamar's, the Crittenden's—all are important in American development,[105] not to speak of the merchant families whose names we have listed elsewhere. To attempt to write the history of the Huguenot families now, is not, however, our purpose; let us go on to other French elements in the United States.

a large Huguenot population. In 1721, by which time the movement had ceased, Dexter, as we have seen, estimates 500,000 population for the colonies. Many states had only a scattering Huguenot population; and even if we estimate 3% for the whole country, we shall have only 15,000, a figure which includes a large natural increase. It would be tedious to list the various emigration lists, which may be found in Baird, and which are admittedly imperfect, but in all, 15,000 does not appear too small, and the chances are rather that it is too high.

[104] Lodge, "The Distribution of Ability in the United States," *Century Magazine,* XLII, 687-694, September, 1891. "If we add the French and the French Huguenots together, we find that the people of French blood exceed absolutely, in the ability produced, all the other races represented in Appleton's Encyclopedia of American Biography, except the English and Scotch-Irish, and show a percentage in proportion to their total original immigration much higher than that of any other race." Lodge does not, however, attempt to estimate the total original immigration.

[105] I have summarized this list from Stapleton, *Memorials of the Huguenots in America,* chap. xvi. For Crittenden, see Coleman, *Life of John J. Crittenden,* I, 13. For the Trevezant family, see Trevezant, *op. cit.*

3. SWISS, ALSATIAN, AND WALLOON IMMIGRANTS IN THE EIGHTEENTH CENTURY; THE ACADIANS.

Among the strains blending with the Huguenots we have already noted the Swiss, the Alsatians and the Walloons. We do not have information which enables us to distinguish sharply among such divergent stocks, nor perhaps is it necessary that we should; yet we would ignore an important element in the French migrations did we fail to note, however inadequately, certain aspects of these groups.

There seems to have been a definite propaganda in the course of the eighteenth century among certain cantons in Switzerland, including the French-speaking ones, to induce migration to the land of religious liberty and primeval promise.[106] This movement was in the main directed towards Pennsylvania and the Carolinas. The important town of New Bern, North Carolina, the name of which betrays its character, was founded in 1710. In 1732 John Peter Pury of Neuchâtel, after visiting South Carolina, went to England, arranged a contract with the authorities, and induced 170 Swiss to come to America. They were followed a little later by 200 more. The governor of South Carolina allotted them 40,000 acres on the northeast side of the Savannah river, and there was founded the town of Purysburg.[107] The Rev. Mr. Bignion, a Swiss minister, was ordained by the Bishop of London to care for the spiritual welfare of the settlers, but the change of climate was felt, many died, and more became discontented, blaming Pury for their lot. Nevertheless the settlement survived.[108] In the meantime others came, and by 1734 the settlement had increased to 600.[109] In 1712 Swiss settlements were

---

[106] See Faust, "Swiss Emigration to the American Colonies in the Eighteenth Century," *American Historical Review*, XXII, 21-44.

[107] The "Proposals by Mr. Peter Purry, of Newfchatel, for Encouragement of such Swiss Protestants as should agree to accompany him to Carolina, to settle a New Colony, and also, a Description of the Province of South Carolina drawn up at Charles-Town, in September, 1731," are printed by R. R. Carroll, in the *Historical Collections of South Carolina*, II. Those who go as servants must be carpenters, vine planters, husbandmen, or labourers, and ought to take with them three or four good shirts and a suit of clothes. They were expected to sign a contract for three years, and were to receive as wages 100 livres or 50 crowns Neuchâtel. Others should have at least 50 crowns. The article also describes the proposed plan of Purysburg, which is located in a country of rich soil. A good deal of emphasis is placed upon the possibilities of vine cultivating.

[108] Ramsay, *History of South Carolina*, I, 107-8; Faust, p. 21.

[109] Rupp, *Names of Immigrants in Pennsylvania*, pp. 14-15.

formed in Lancaster County, Pennsylvania—a mixed French and German population; thence, after 1716, settlers and immigrants commenced to work westward into the present counties of Montgomery and Berks.[110] The high tide of this eighteenth century migration seems to have been between 1734 and 1744.[111] The situation indeed became alarming. The historian of the movement shows that in these years 2300 left the canton of Zürich; from Bern, probably 3000; from Basel, 1500; Aargau, Shaffhausen, Graubünden, Solothurn each furnished 2500; and there were in all some 12,000 Swiss who came to the United States in these years alone.[112] Naturally the canton governments did what they could to check this drain on their resources. Faust nevertheless estimates the total migration of the Swiss to the New World in the eighteenth century as amounting to 20,000 or 25,000; and believes that the total to 1910 is 250,000. During the Revolutionary years and the Napoleonic régime there were but a few hundreds who came over; in 1828 there were 1500; in 1834, 1400.[113]

Melish, writing in 1810, tells of a Swiss settlement on the Ohio across from Kentucky, the inhabitants of which had settled there about 1800 where they were attempting the cultivation of the vine; 56 persons in the settlement, he says; and they were manufacturing claret and madeira, the former rich but acid. However, they had sold 2400 gallons at $1.50 the previous year.[114] Gall, arriving in 1819, came over with a shipload of Swiss emigrants who settled, he says, mainly in Pennsylvania and Virginia, and who didn't like the country.[115] Vevay, in Indiana, became quite a notable settlement: indeed, I take Melish's description to refer to this place. When, for instance, Lafayette was in Cincinnati in 1825, he was visited by a delegation of French Swiss from that town; they had come to America from the Canton de Vaud and were making wine, and they possessed a small company of artillery in neat

---

[110] Rupp, pp. 8, 10.
[111] Faust, p. 27; Ramsay, however, speaks of a steady migration to the Savannah river from 1730 to 1750. I, 11.
[112] Faust, p. 43.
[113] These are representative figures from Faust, p. 44.
[114] Melish, *Travels,* p. 371. We ought to note perhaps a colony described by Fauchet—some five or six hundred artisans and "capitalists" from Geneva, driven from their own country, who had united in 1795 to erect an establishment on the North River in New York. Sherrill, *French Memories,* pp. 295-6.
[115] Gall, *Meine Auswanderungen,* II, 63.

and elegant uniform. Most of them had served in the French army.[116] The anonymous author of *The Americans as They Are,* who visited the place in 1827, describes the settlement as follows:

Vevay, in Indiana, became a settlement twenty years ago, by Swiss emigrants, who obtained a grant of land, equal to 200 acres for each family, under the condition of cultivating the vine; they accordingly settled here, and laid out vineyards. The original settlers may have amounted to thirty; others joined them afterwards, and in this manner was founded the country town of New Switzerland in Indiana, which consists almost exclusively of these French and Swiss settlers.

He found, however, that the vines had deteriorated and the town was declining.[117]

The Swiss who came to America seem to have been mainly from the French and German cantons, the majority from the latter. Usually they were farmers, with some admixture of artisans. They do not seem to have radiated any such cultural influence as did the Huguenots at New Rochelle or Charleston; but they made good citizens, and, being for the most part Protestants, did not arouse the antipapal feeling which interfered between the French and the Americans. Perhaps it could be shown that insofar as they were Calvinists, they helped to increase the vogue of their peculiar doctrines in the United States, but in view of the tremendous pressure already brought to bear in favor of Calvin by Huguenot and Puritan, we may well believe that their coming made little material difference.

Among the groups related to the French migration, we should also include the Alsatians, but unfortunately I have not been able to secure anything but the most random references to their coming. Doubtless many came from Alsace who are included in other groups. Of the Jerseys in 1781 Robin observes that "les habitans, Alsaciens & Hollandois d'extraction pour la plupart, portent, dans leur air aisé, gai, prévenant, l'empreinte de l'heureuse contrée qu'ils habitent."[118] In 1802 the younger Michaux, traveling in western Pennsylvania, passed *"Probe's Furnace,"* two miles from West Liberty Town, where an Alsatian Frenchman had established a foundry. He

fabricates caldrons of yellow copper of different sizes. The largest will contain two hundred pints; they are sent to Kentucky and Ten-

---

[116] Levasseur, *Lafayette in America,* II, 196-8.
[117] *The Americans as They Are,* pp. 31-32.
[118] Robin, *Nouveau Voyage,* p. 81.

nessee, and employed in the preparation of salt by evaporation. Others, of a much smaller size, are intended for domestic use.[119]

In 1837 Grund remarked that a large number of the inhabitants of Old Bavaria and of the French province of Alsace are annually wandering to the United States and "so inviting are the letters of those who are already settled, to their friends and relations in Europe, that some of the German governments have already been obliged to make provisions to arrest the depopulation."[120] So far as these Alsatians were French, there seems no need of distinguishing them from the general group of French immigrants.

Besides the Huguenots, Swiss, and Alsatians, a fourth special group is the Acadians, whose unhappy history has long been debated among the historians.[121] Into the vexed question of the history and ethics of the situation it is not here necessary to go further than to state two facts; first, that the Acadians were by no means blameless in their neutrality; and second, that neither the warfare nor the diplomacy of the eighteenth century found any fault with the idea of deportation itself, however the methods might have been ameliorated. The English government could not afford to have 9,000 Frenchmen near Louisburg under the influence of French agents such as Le Loutre, and accordingly, at the direction of Governor Shirley and Colonel Charles Lawrence, it was determined to remove and scatter the whole body of Acadians among the British colonies to the south. The movement went on through the summer, fall and winter of 1755; and the total number of deportations seems to have been something over 6,000. Inasmuch as the colonies, or rather Massachusetts, agreed to furnish transports and supplies, the deportation was a matter of special attention in America; and coming as it did in the midst of a protracted struggle with the French, it is not surprising to learn that the Acadians were hated and shunned in the seaboard towns. The evidence collected in Winsor shows that they were distributed from Boston south; in New England, despite some opposition, subscriptions were taken up in

---

[119] Michaux, *Travels,* p. 58.

[120] Grund, *The Americans,* II, 55.

[121] The history of the deportation is given in Parkman, *Montcalm and Wolfe,* I; and in Winsor, *Narrative and Critical History of America,* V, 452-464. See also Johnston, *In Acadia*; and the references in Winsor.

their behalf.[122] Few seem to have gone to New York. In
Philadelphia Governor Morris refused to aid them, and feeling was bitter.[123] Nevertheless they were aided by the French
Huguenots and by private benevolence. In Maryland they
insisted upon being treated as prisoners of war; "they have
almost eat us up," wrote Daniel Dulany in 1755,[124] and they
were not popular. In 1781 Robin found their quarter in Baltimore the most poorly built and most poverty-stricken in the
city; but they kept the French language and simple manners,
and had their own church, wherein they asked Robin to offi-
ciate.[125] Into Virginia were sent a group of 1,140 to the alarm
of the government; and "the legislatures directed their reship-
ment to England at a cost of £5,000."[126] In the Carolinas they
were not wanted. About 1500[127] were sent to Charleston of
whom, says Ramsay, some rose to distinction, but most of them
in a short time after the peace left the country. He describes
them as hardworking and industrious.[128] About 400 went to
Georgia.[129] Most of these groups, however, are unimportant
when compared with the movement of the Acadians out of the
British colonies to Louisiana.[130] Precisely how many came,

[122] From 1755 to 1769 the charge of supporting the French neutrals entered
more or less into the burdens of the New England towns among which
they were scattered. Winsor, V, 461. See the excerpt from Hutchinson's
History of Massachusetts in Stedman and Hutchinson, III, 58-61 for a
contemporary view.

[123] Cf. Scharf and Westcott, *History of Philadelphia*, I, 248-50; II, 1369.
455 exiles came to that city. Cf. also Winsor, V, 462.

[124] Winsor, V, 462.

[125] Robin, *Nouveau Voyage*, pp. 98-101. Schoepf notices their presence.
Travels in the Confederation, I, 331.

[126] Winsor, V, 463.

[127] Yates Snowden in an article in *The Carolinian*, XVIII, 74-81, December, 1905, says that 1,020 Acadians were landed in Charleston in November,
1756, some of whom attempted to escape. A contemporary *Charleston
Gazette* announces that some of them had attempted to rob the John Williams plantation, and there was considerable consternation. On 19 May 1758
an act was passed to provide for their support for three months, under
which £2,794.02.08 was expended. The "Cajians" scattered generally over
the colony.

[128] Ramsay, *History of South Carolina*, I, 15.

[129] Winsor, V, 463.

[130] February 28, 1765, Foucault wrote the French minister that 193 Acadians had come to New Orleans from Santo Domingo; on May 4, 80 more
have come; and in the month of May, 48 more. On November 16, 1766, 216
arrived from Halifax. On April 30, 1765, Aubrey reports that it has cost
15,500 livres to care for them and that 200 have recently arrived. Fortier,
History of Louisiana, I, 152-3. On the "Cajian" district in Louisiana see
the map in Cable, *The Creoles of Louisiana;* on the life of the Cajians consult Johnston, *In Acadia*.

whether from the future United States or from the West Indies is not definitely known; by the 1880's the Cajian population of Louisana was estimated at 50,000.[131] They retain in Louisiana today many of the primitive ways of their forefathers, speak their own peculiar kind of French, originally Norman but with an infiltration of English and Creole *patois*. While important writers and politicians have come from the group, they have not been distinguished by ambition as a whole.

After the original deportation of 1755, it must not be supposed that Acadia was depopulated. Some fled to the future state of Maine rather than go on board the British transports, where today many villages contain their descendants.[132] Others were removed at intervals from 1756 to 1762, and the lot of these later fugitives seems to have been more unhappy than that of their predecessors.[133] To offset these numerical gains, it must be remembered that upon the conclusion of peace in 1763 some wandered back to Acadia and others to France.[134] Probably the total number of Acadians thus exiled to the British colonies did not exceed 10,000, and may have been nearer 8,000.[135] Because of their very neutrality and because they were Catholics, their reception by the Americans was marked by greater ill-feeling than in the case of the Huguenots. Everywhere, however, except in Louisiana and perhaps Maine, they seem to have been absorbed into the surrounding population, and except as they were industrious, frugal, obstinate, and simple, and as they increased the Catholic population, they do not seem greatly to have affected American life. One must of course note that they were the occasion of Longfellow's *Evangeline,* a production largely responsible for the haze of romantic melancholy in which the whole movement has been

---

[131] Winsor, V, 463.
[132] Winsor, V, 463 and references.
[133] Winsor, V, 462.
[134] Winsor notes that among the Parkman papers in the Massachusetts Historical Society there is one dated London, 1763, which says there are 866 in England, 2,000 in France, and 10,000 in the English colonies. Another French paper estimates the number in France at from 3,000 to 3,500. V, 463.
[135] How difficult it is really to trace the movement one may learn when he reads in Fortier, *History of Louisiana,* II, 110, that as late as 1785 "there was a considerable accession to the population by the arrival of a number of Acadian families, who came over at the expense of the King of France and were settled on both sides of the river near Plaquemines, at Terre aux Boeufs, on Bayou Lafourche, and in the Attakapas and Opelousas."

shrouded. Perhaps no single group of French immigrants contributed more to American culture than did the Acadians in furnishing the occasion for this universally known poem.

We must not imagine that in enumerating the explorers, the Huguenots, the Swiss, the Alsatians, and the Acadians, we have exhausted the number of French immigrants to the future United States before the American Revolution. Leaving aside Louisiana, to which we shall presently come, we must remember that outside of any formal movement there were drifting Frenchmen of all sorts from Europe, from Canada, from the West Indies, who sought in the New World oblivion or opportunity.[135a] These it is impossible to enumerate, though here and there we catch glimpses of them. For example Lawson reported (about 1700) that there had been in New York harbor "a French Man of War, who had on Board Men and Necessaries to make a Colony, and was intended for the Mississippi River, there to settle"—probably a group intended for Louisiana.[136] Doubtless when Governor Spotswood of Virginia wrote to the Rev. Francis Fountain (Fontaine), the descendant of Jean de la Fontaine, in 1716 offering him a position at William and Mary, we have but one example of others, could we find them, of the employment of French teachers and tutors from the old world.[137] "Here is abundance of Transient French Merch[ts]," wrote Birket, visiting Newport in 1750 and 1751, "which are concerned with the people in trade to Cape Briton, Cape Francois, &c."[138] There must have been other French travellers besides the anonymous author of the "Journal of a French Traveller in the Colonies, 1765,"[139] who landed at Beaufort March 15, 1765, and travelled into Virginia—a government agent probably, in view of his interest in tar, pitch, and turpentine. Frenchmen, whether Huguenots or no, taught at Harvard and Princeton and the future University of Pennsylvania;[140] notably after the conclusion of the Seven Years War,

---

[135a] Entries for runaway French servants occur in the colonial papers. See, for an example, an advertisement for James Larrance, 25 or 26, who "speaks not a word of English" in the *Boston News-Letter* for August 26, 1717.

[136] Lawson, *History of North Carolina*, "Introduction," p. xiii.

[137] Fountain became professor of Oriental languages in 1729. "The Official Letters of Alexander Spotswood," *Collections of the Virginia Historical Society*, II (n.s.), pp. 166-167.

[138] Birket, *Some Cursory Remarks*, p. 30.

[139] *American Historical Review*, XXVI, 726-747; XXVII, 70-90.

[140] On the teaching of French, see chap. vi.

the abundance of French dancing masters, French wig-makers, French fencing-teachers, French musicians, and the like, testifies to a thin but steady migration.[141] But the absence of immigration statistics and the paucity of travellers' reports makes it impossible to estimate the numbers of these emigrants who belonged to no particular movement. The general picture that one gets of the seaport towns is that each contained its quota, large or small, of French inhabitants; and that to the New World, where all might come (except as barred by the regulations of His Britannic Majesty), soldiers of fortune and refugees continued to flock, especially after the conclusion of peace. This migration, so far as one can judge it, seems to have been directed in the main to the cities; farming was more especially the occupation of Swiss and Huguenot, of Alsatian and Acadian.[142] But we have in the meantime neglected to trace the history of Louisiana, which was in the New World, but not yet a part of the United States. Let us turn to this task; and then endeavor to arrive at some picture of the French migration of 1775 and thereafter.

4. THE SETTLEMENT OF NEW ORLEANS AND ITS ENVIRONS

The settlement of Louisiana, so far as the southern borders of that once vast territory are concerned, was begun when Iberville, one of the most remarkable men in the history of French colonization, founded his fort at Biloxi, Mississippi, in 1699.[143] On January 16, 1702, Bienville and Sèrigny commenced to work on a fort on the Mobile River (Fort Louis), around which on August 31, 1704, there were clustered 180 men bearing arms; 27 French families; a number of slaves, and four ecclesiastics.[144] A census of August 1, 1706, gives the names of 82 heads of families. New Orleans (named for Philip of Orleans, Regent of France) was founded in February,

[141] For details consult chapters vii and ix. There was even a hermit near Albany, who "did not seem to inspire much veneration among the Albanians." Mrs. Grant, *Memoirs of an American Lady,* I, 49.
[142] Of course there were often large groups of these in the cities as well.
[143] Fortier, *History of Louisiana,* I and II, founded upon the earlier work of Gayarré and Martin and upon the documents in the possession of the State Historical Museum, is reliable; the remaining volumes are inferior. For the history of New Orleans consult Rightor, *Standard History of New Orleans;* and Kendall, *History of New Orleans* (3 volumes), which supersedes it. The publications of the Louisiana State Historical Society contain much valuable material.
[144] The intendant's report of that date. Fortier, I, 51-52, 52-53.

1718, by Bienville, only after Biloxi and Mobile had proved unsatisfactory. The original settlement numbered fifty persons. By 1721 the colony had grown to 6000 persons, including 600 negroes.[145] A year later the Duchesse de Lesdiguières received a letter from Charlevoix, dated January 10, 1722, describing the city; the 800 fine houses reputed in France to constitute the city are in reality only 100 huts, but the city is fated to be great.[146] By 1726 there are in Louisiana 1952 masters, 276 hired men and servants, 1540 negro slaves, 229 Indian slaves; by 1731 there are 5000 whites and 2000 negroes.[147] Meantime New Orleans had begun to take on its peculiar character.

For to the governing classes in that historic city, New Orleans was to be a bit of Paris transferred, as well as might be, to the New World. Fashionable life and fashionable vices were taken over. By 1722 it was necessary for the king to issue an ordinance against gambling; by 1728 Sister Madeleine Hachard, of the Ursuline Nuns, was writing home about the magnificent dresses of the ladies, and there was sung on the streets a song which said that New Orleans was like Paris.[148] These same Ursuline Nuns were to educate generations of New Orleans ladies in elegant and fashionable manners; for in the meantime, Louis XV, anxious for the moral well-being of his colony had sent over the *filles à casette* to marry and give sons to Louisiana. The quarrels of the Old World were transferred to the New; the Jesuits came in 1724, were expelled in 1763, and returned only with the cession of the colony to Spain in 1768.[149] Under Governor de Vaudreuil the characteristic Creole life was beginning to develop:

In the lofty halls and spacious drawing-rooms of these homes—frequently, too, in the heart of the town, in the houses of the humblest exterior, their low, single-story wooden or brick walls rising from a ground but partly drained even of its storm water, infested with reptile life and frequently overflowed—was beginning to be shown a splen-

[145] The census of Louisiana, taken under Bienville, is published in the *Publications of the Louisiana State Historical Society*, V, 79-103. In New Orleans and "lieux circonvoisins" there were 293 men, 140 women, 96 children, 155 French domestics; 514 negro slaves, 51 Indian slaves; 231 "bestes à corne" and 28 horses. This was in May, 1722.
[146] Quoted in Fortier, I, 73-74.
[147] See the various censuses in Fortier, I, 101; 118.
[148] Fortier, I, 86, 105.
[149] Kendall, *History of New Orleans,* II, 698 ff., gives the religious history of the city.

dor of dress and personal adornment hardly in harmony with the rude
simplicity of apartments and furniture, and scarcely to be expected
in a town of unpaved, unlighted, and often impassable streets, surrounded by swamps and morasses on one of the wildest of American
frontiers.
Slaves—not always or generally the dull, ill-featured Congo or fierce
Banbara, imported for the plantations, but comely Yaloff and Man-
dingo boys and girls, the shapelier for their scanty dress—waited on
every caprice, whether good or ill, and dropped themselves down in the
corridors and on the verandas for stolen naps among the dogs, and
whips, and saddles, in such odd moments of day or night as found
their masters and mistresses tired of being served . . . black domestic
service made it easy for the Creoles to emulate the ostentatious living
of the colonial officials.[150]

Meanwhile official corruption had set in, public morals were
debased, idleness and intemperance spread, and religion and
education made little headway. Yet nevertheless the charm of
this civilization, unique in the history of the world, was already beginning to be felt. Around the city and up the river
were the plantations with their low airy houses, and in the
town where now the French quarter stands, cavalier and great
lady pretended that Versailles was not so very far away.[151]
In 1724 the Marigny family was establishing itself in New
Orleans; in 1718 the "Sieurs de Gentilly" (Mathurin and
Pierre Dreux) had come and were about to select their famous
plantation, now become Gentilly Terrace in New Orleans; in
1732 Jean Joseph Delfau de Pontalba arrived in the new
colony; by the same period the Villeré's, the family of d'Arens-
bourg, of de la Chaise, of Chauvin (Lafrénière), of Huchet
de Kernion, de Livaudais, Soniat du Fossat had struck roots
in the soil; afterwards arrived Jean Etienne de Boré and others
famous in Louisiana history.[152]
    Meanwhile there came a shock and a rebellion. Astonished
Creoles learned in 1764 that the colony had been sold or

---

[150] Cable, *The Creoles of Louisiana,* pp. 45-46.
    [151] On the origins of Creole social life, see besides Cable, Miss King's
invaluable study, *Creole Families of New Orleans.* "There was apparently
little 'roughing it' during these early days of the city's life. . . . They
brought with them for their new homes an outfit of furniture, linen and
glass; and for themselves silks, satins, laces and jewelry." They found waiting them servants, rich foods, their own language, the good manners of
France, and "a society that, although gay, was kept within the bounds of
the proper and discreet by the rigid maintenance of the etiquette of society
in Paris, and the strict enforcement of French laws for preserving the
purity of blood and family prestige." King, pp. 7-8.
    [152] Consult King.

granted to Spain; in 1766 Don Antonio de Ulloa and two companies of Spanish infantry landed to take possession of a territory vaster than Spain and France together; there followed the ill-fated insurrection of Lafrénière; and in 1769 Count O'Reilly, an Irishman in Spanish service, and 24 ships arrived —Don Alexandro O'Reilly who was not interested in rebellions except to crush them and before whose cold and calculating intelligence Creole ebullience was treason. Shortly there was shooting of prisoners and a change of government. Under Unzaga and Galvez and Mirò and Carondelet and Gayoso de Lemos, Spaniards of temperament varying from the energetic Galvez to the indulgent Unzaga, New Orleans enjoyed the dubious blessings of Spanish rule.

But the town did not change—much. It is April 1, 1788, and Governor Mirò is penning a letter to the Council of the Indies on the state of things in Louisiana. He writes that "the introduction of the Spanish language in the province was a difficult work, and one requiring a long time, as had been the case in all countries where a change of domination has taken place." He is discouraged at the prospect; so far all that has been accomplished is that the proceedings of the courts of justice are in Spanish; the books of the merchants (except Spaniards) are kept in French and therefore persons desiring to make their sons merchants, persons who do not own plantations, give their children instruction in French.[153] Eight years later Bishop Peñalver—in the meantime New Orleans, attached to the see of Santiago de Cuba, has in 1781 become part of the Bishopric of St. Christopher of Havana, and was in 1793 erected into an independent see[154]—Bishop Peñalver, we say, who has now been here the best part of a year writes home of certain difficulties experienced by these same Ursuline nuns: "Excellent results are obtained from the Convent of the Ursulines," says the worthy bishop, "in which a good many girls are educated; but their inclinations are so decidedly French, that they have even refused to admit among them Spanish women who wished to become nuns, so long as these applicants should remain ignorant of the French idiom, and they have shed many tears on account of their being obliged to read in Spanish books their spiritual exercises, and to comply with the other duties of their community in the manner prescribed

[153] Fortier, II, 117.
[154] Kendall, *op. cit.*, II, 698.

to them."[155] The worthy bishop judged rightly: the Ursulines were to remain French until the present day. The population grows: Mirò, taking the census of West Louisiana in 1787, finds 1587 souls; and the whole population of the province in 1785 is 32,115, or double what it was under the disillusioned O'Reilly.[156] Three years later—Mirò is an inveterate census-taker,—there are 19,445 white persons living in Louisiana, and the total number of souls in the province is 42,611.[157] And the heart of this region is New Orleans, and New Orleans remains persistently French—or rather, Creole.[158]

It is true, there are some changes. Merchants from New York, Philadelphia, and Boston, had established themselves in New Orleans; one Pollock becomes in 1776-8 the avowed agent of the American government, and a fateful Yankee immigration was beginning to filter in. In 1779 His Most Catholic Majesty of Spain declared war on his royal brother of Britain; and Creoles and Acadians, somewhat to their bewilderment, found themselves attacking British forts at Baton Rouge and Manchac, and in May, 1781, Pensacola astonishingly surrendered to the energetic Galvez and Mirò of the census-taking proclivities—the former being one who "ruled . . . with great credit, as well as splendor, and died suddenly, in his thirty-eighth year, from the fatigues of a hunt."[159] In 1779 there was a hurricane which demolished many houses, and in 1788 there was a fire which destroyed 856 houses—half the town, and another in 1794 that burned down 212 stores and buildings. The modern French quarter in New Orleans is therefore not French, for when the town was re-built after

---

[155] Fortier, II, 165.

[156] New Orleans, 4980; from Balize to the city, 2100; at Terre aux Boeufs, 576; on Bayous St. John and Gentilly, 678; Tchoupitoulas, 7046; parish of St. Charles, 1903; St. John the Baptist, 1300; St. James, 1332; Lafourche, 646; Lafourche intérieur, 352; Iberville, 673; Pointe Coupée, 1521; Opelousas, 1211; Attakapas, 1070; New Iberia, 125; Quachita, 207; Rapides, 88; Avoyelles, 287; Natchitoches, 756; Arkansas, 196; St. Gènevière, 694; St. Louis, 897; Manchac, 77; Galveston (*not* Texas!), 242; Baton Rouge, 270; Natchez, 1550; Mobile, 746; Pensacola, 592. This included Acadians and some Germans besides Creoles, Spaniards and some English; Negro and Indian slaves. Fortier, II, 110. The total number of whites was probably only 15,000.

[157] Fortier, II, 119. New Orleans had increased to 5338.

[158] A Creole is properly a member of the French-speaking portion of the ruling class in Louisiana, whether of Spanish or French descent or both. He is never an Acadian, who is a "Cajian." Cf. Cable, pp. 41-42.

[159] Cable, p. 92; on Louisiana in the American Revolution, consult Fortier, Volume II.

these repeated calamities, the standard type of architecture was mainly Spanish-American—"adobe or brick walls, arcades, inner courts, ponderous doors and windows, heavy iron bolts and gratings (for houses began to be worth breaking into), balconies, portes-cochères, and white and yellow lime-washed stucco, soon stained a hundred colors by sun and rain."[160] The Pontalbas presently intermarried with the Spaniards; the Gayarré's with the French; the Bouligny family, originally Italian, had French connections before any branch of it came to the Crescent City; Don Andres Almonaster y Roxas took to wife Louise de la Rone—he was sixty, she was sixteen—indeed, half the families in Miss King's book represent French and Spanish intermarriage, and Creole culture received the modifying influences of Castile. Nevertheless it remained basically French; and when the Revolutionary troubles broke out in Santo Domingo, French planters fled to New Orleans, just as monarchist émigrés were to do then and later. With this influx of French monarchists, New Orleans entered upon a new phase of its cultural history; social thought, little interested in moribund Spain, discovered with keen interest that the city was French; and throughout the rest of our period the interest of the average Creole was much keener in the affairs of Europe than it was in the affairs of the United States. Napoleon and Louis Philippe and the Chamber of Deputies occupied him; he had only a secondary interest in Webster, Jackson, and the debates in the Senate.[161]

When in 1803 the Louisiana Purchase brought New Orleans into the domain of the United States, its peculiar life was already well established. In 1794 the *Moniteur de la Louisiane* was established, the first French newspaper to be published, and the first in a succession of similar enterprises.[162] The school for boys established by Father Cecil, a Capuchin, in 1724, had disappeared; but the Ursuline Nuns were continuing their useful work. Many scions of the wealthy planters

---

[160] Cable, p. 103. The careful observer in the French quarter today can tell which houses are purely French. The picture facing page 10 in Miss King's book gives some idea of the houses of purely French construction, of which few now remain.

[161] For a discussion of this émigré movement, see chapter v.

[162] The earliest number known to be extant is number 26, dated Monday, August 25, 1794; it contains European news of April. The paper was markedly anti-Jacobin, and was published by L. Duclot. Fortier, II, 154-6. For a list of French newspapers published in New Orleans, see Belisle, *Histoire e la Presse Franco-Américain,,* pp. 380-1.

were being sent to France or Canada for an education.[163]
Thus it was that French tradition was maintained. The
Masons had established their lodges, which were strengthened
by the émigrés, and were a focus of political agitation.[164]
Bishop Peñalver laid down his office in 1802; thereafter the
Catholic Church passed through a variety of government until
Dubourg became bishop September 24, 1815,[165] but the influence of the church was profound, and the church was mainly
officered by French priests. Artists like A. D. Lansot were
occasionally to be found,[166] and in the wooden theater, to be
condemned as unsafe in December, 1803, comedies were being
played.[167] Duels were being fought by the hot-headed under
the famous oaks,[168] and on the sugar plantations, thanks to the
inventiveness of Étienne de Boré, sugar was being made commercially successful,[169] and all the magnificence, the hospitality,
the politeness could be paid for.

When Louisiana was sold to the United States, a great
change was wrought in the cultural history of New Orleans.
Hitherto the city had presented the spectacle of a unity of
Latin culture, but with the coming of the Americans a new,
and not altogether happy, chapter was written in the life of the
Crescent City: the story of the long struggle between the
American and Latin factions for control. The Spaniard had
amalgamated with the Frenchman, but the American would
not. Consequently the history of the city from 1803 to 1848
is best understood in terms of a cultural conflict. On the one
hand the fact that New Orleans was at the mouth of the river
brought to it all the flotsam and jetsam of the Mississippi

---

[163] See the chapter on "Education" by John R. Ficklen in Rightor, *Standard History of New Orleans.*

[164] The Masons came in the latter part of the eighteenth century, and were hostile to Spain and friendly to France. They do not seem to have grown until the arrival of the refugees. French lodges were established in 1793-4 and 1798; and in 1801 and 1804. The Grand Lodge for the state was formed in 1812. See chapter xiii on Secret Orders, by Walter Parker, in Rightor.

[165] Kendall, *op. cit.,* II, 698-701.

[166] Consult Cline, *Art and Artists in New Orleans.*

[167] See Price, "Le Spectacle de la Rue St. Pierre," *Louisiana Historical Quarterly,* I, 215-223.

[168] See Augustin, "The Old Duelling Grounds of New Orleans," *Art and Letters* (New Orleans), pp. 123-34.

[169] See the account of Boré's discovery (1794) in Fortier, I, 133; II, 158 ff. Cane was introduced by the Jesuits in 1751. Joseph Dubreuil established the first large plantation in 1758, and a ship-load of inferior sugar was sent to France in 1765.

Valley, attracted thither by the open immorality of the town. On the other hand the fact that it was a seaport town made it, as its commercial importance increased, another international dêpot; half the language of the occident could be heard on its wharves.[170] And meanwhile Yankees and pioneer business men were moving in, seeking to modernize the city, seeking to stir the Creole from his slothful ways.[171] The Creole seldom fought back—the episode of Marigny is one case when he did—but he had a talent for stubbornness, he had behind him the traditions of a century, and he either held his own (that is, kept his culture intact), or withdrew in good order, so that to this day the French Quarter is alien and picturesque among American cities. Let us note certain aspects of this cultural struggle.

American occupation began under unfortunate auspices. On March 26, 1803, the Creoles learned with some consternation but with growing enthusiasm that they were once more subject to their beloved France; and on Monday, December 20, 1803, they found themselves citizens of the United States, a country much more unknown than France, from which they had been separated for almost forty years.[172] Is it any wonder that they wept?[173] Or that at the Sunday ball on January 8, 1804, there was a small battle between those who wished to dance a French quadrille and those who wished to dance an

[170] See Pavie, *Souvenirs Atlantiques,* II, chap. xxxiv, for the polyglot nature of the "quais."
[171] For a typical Yankee's story consult Kerman, George C. H., "Samuel Jarvis Peters—The Man Who Made New Orleans of Today and Became a National Personality," *Publications of the Louisiana Historical Society,* VII, 62-96. Peters' autobiography is included in the article. Peters, born in Canada, 30 July, 1801, came to New Orleans, penniless, in 1822, at a time when "that city was looked upon as a vast grave yard, and ... none who went from New England ever returned." He had learned French in New York, an accomplishment which increased his popularity in New Orleans where he established the house of Peters and Millard. In 1829 he was elected a member of the City Council, and began his great system of financial reform and modernization of the town—modern wharves, a railroad, water-works, etc. He was also one of the founders of the public school system. His autobiography (see pp. 70-78) shows clearly the racial friction he encountered.
[172] When Louisiana was colonized it was under the personal rule of Louis XIV. In 1712 it was given over to Crozat; in 1717, to the Compagnie de l'Occident; in 1731, to the personal rule of Louis XV. In 1762 it was ceded to Spain, and in 1801, back to France, although the transaction was not definitely known until the arrival of Laussat in March, 1803. When one realizes these various changes of government, he begins to visualize the stubbornness with which Creole culture endured.
[173] See the account of the transfer and the accompanying ceremony in Fortier, II, 286-8, with its excerpts from Laussat's *Memoirs.*

English one?[174] According to the first United States census, there were 8,056 people in New Orleans, and the Americans were in the minority.[175] "The French, Spanish, and Americans here keep very separate society," wrote John F. Watson in his diary in 1804. "The Americans congregate much together, and the French, except in business, keep much aloof," but he adds that he enters both groups freely and finds them very friendly and agreeable.[176] And the ladies found a certain difficulty in getting acquainted: "ladies in this country never visit strangers first. All expect to be visited by the ladies newly arrived. Our ladies (American) will not yield to this seemingly awkward position, and therefore they pass without native society."[177] Such was the awkward situation which the

[174] Two quadrilles were formed at the same time, and an American threatened a musician with his cane, whereupon there was tumult. Claiborne, the governor, who did not speak French, was embarrassed, but managed to calm the American army surgeon. The French quadrille began, when it was interrupted by an English one, and thereupon some one exclaimed, "If the women have a single drop of French blood in their veins, they will not dance." The women left the room. A similar incident occurred January 22, including the arrest of one Gauthier by the police—or so the people thought —while Wilkinson and his staff sang Hail Columbia, and the French poured forth their feelings in Enfants de la Patrie, Peuple Français, Peuple de Frères. Harmony was restored only at a banquet of reconciliation. See the account in Laussat's *Memoirs,* quoted in Fortier, II, 288-291.

[175] See the figures in Fortier, II, 302. Claiborne wrote the Secretary of State May 18, 1809, that there were in 1806 26,069 whites in Louisiana Territory, of which 13,000 were natives, mostly of French descent; 3,500 were "Americans" and 9,500 were Europeans (French, Spanish, English, German, and Irish). He estimates the immigration from 1806 to 1809 at three or four thousand, of which two-thirds were Americans. Perez, "French Refugees to New Orleans in 1809," *Publications of the Southern History Association,* IX, 296.

[176] Watson was struck by the difference in architecture and activity between New Orleans and Philadelphia. "The chief of the houses are of brick and plastered over smoothly with white mortar; few of them are above one story, unless they are public edifices; all are more decorated with ornamental work than any I have before seen. One-story houses, however, have their ground floor part so high as to make good storehouses. Almost all of them have galleries around them." Cf. Fortier, III, 27. See also John F. Watson, "Notitia of Incidents at New Orleans in 1804 and 1805," *The American Pioneer,* II; 227-237. (May, 1843).

[177] *Ibid.,* III, 28. But he found them attractive—these Creoles. "The ladies are beautiful in person, gestures, and action; all are brunettes; few are blue-eyed or light-haired; none have color in their cheeks, but none look unhealthy. Young ladies do not dare to ride out or appear abroad with young gentlemen; but ladies frequently ride abroad in a chair *(volante)*; managing the horse themselves. Their *volante* carriages are very ugly. Often they drive mules, and sometimes horses and mules are driven three or four abreast. They usually drive in gallops; no trotting is seen. Ladies all dress their own hair without curls or ornaments. Girls are never forward or garrulous in conversation; they are all retire and madest in their department,

Americans acquired.[178]

The town was already a metropolis of 10,000, and as yet the American merchants were in a minority. There were 1,200 or 1,400 dwellings and stores, and more outhouses than either —say, 4,000 roofs in all. In 1802, 265 vessels, amounting to 31,241 tons registery, had sailed from the harbor loaded; the exports amount to $2,000,000, the imports to $2,500,000— cotton, sugar, molasses, rice, peltries, indigo, lumber, flour, beef, pork, tobacco, corn, butter, hams, meal, lard, beans, hides, staves, cordage, besides a smuggling trade via the pirates of Barataria, and secret commerce in slaves.

The Creole was on every side—handsome, proud, illiterate, elegant in manner, slow, a seeker of office and military commission, ruling society with fierce exclusiveness, looking upon toil as the slave's proper badge, lending money now at twelve and now at twenty-four per cent., and taking but a secondary and unsympathetic part in the commercial life from which was springing the future greatness of his town . . . ill-equipped and uncommercial, the Creole was fortunate to secure even a third or fourth mercantile rank in the city of his birth. But he had one stronghold. He owned the urban and suburban real estate, and presently took high station as the seller of lots and as a *rentier*.

Presently the Faubourg St. Mary was to fill up.[179] In 1802 M. Lafon announced through the columns of the *Moniteur* that he thought of building a theater. "It appears to me," he said, "superfluous to set forth the utility of comedy."[180] Miniature painters, tutors, booksellers, came in—for the benefit of the upper classes, who were interested in Europe.[181] Presently

and very mild and amiable. I have never seen a presumptuous, talkative rattlecup or hoyden here. The ladies appear seldom abroad before the evening; then they sit at their doors or walk on the levee." He remarks also that "gentlemen cannot visit young ladies often unless they declare themselves as intended suitors." III, 31, 28. See his description of masquerades and "sherri-varries," of the carnival of January, 1805, and of Holy Week. III, 29.

[178] Records on file at the Custom House show how unencouraging conditions were. The customs-duties were not paid, and smuggling was fashionable. Jefferson instituted a policy of conciliation; there are some hundreds of letters from Albert Gallatin to Hare Browse Trist, then collector of the port of New Orleans, unremittingly recommending a conciliatory policy. Good results appeared under Jefferson's second administration. See "Grace King's Scrap Book, Ye Olden Time," *Louisiana Historical Quarterly,* III, 125-127.

[179] Cable, pp. 137-9.

[180] See Fortier, II, 218, 219-25.

[181] For typical connections of a New Orleans family with the old world, see the letter on the Montegut family in the *Louisiana Historical Quarterly,* I, 95-98. Consult King, especially with respect to the Marigny and Pontalba families.

they had a regular theater—opera—ballet.[182] French children, educated in the Old World, brought back news of French affairs —politics and romanticism predominating; it was already a little strange, a little foreign, for New Orleans is *sui generis* in history. They even talked about a university—the College of Orleans, created in 1805, which sank in a sea of troubles, though it was supposed to represent French influence, as the College of Louisiana was supposed to represent English (American) influence.[183] But the Creole cared little for schooling, and had to wait on energetic "Americans" like John McDonogh to force education on him.

Between 1804 and 1810 New Orleans doubled its population, and no more motley city was to be found on the American continent. Claiborne wrote of these years that "England has her partisans; Ferdinand the Seventh, some faithful subjects; Bonaparte, his admirers; and there is a fourth description of men, commonly called *Burrites,* who would join any standard which would promise rapine and plunder."[184] The patient Claiborne and the amazing Wilkinson conducted themselves in their various peculiar fashions in the farce-tragedy of Burr's conspiracy,[185] which did not serve to increase good feeling. Street brawls and fine manners, gambling hells and gilded ballrooms, quadroon "ladies" and pirates, Napoleonic officers and exiled Bourbon noblemen, half-castes, Spaniards, Kentuckians, prostitutes, soldiers, great ladies, Negroes, Indians—these were some of the concomitant portions of the most bewildering city on the continent—a city set off from the rest of the world by a thousand miles of savage river, surrounded by swamps, threatened with inundations, swept by pestilence, and finally beseiged by the British. In December, 1815, Andrew Jackson, whose horse, eternally rearing on a stone base, stands forever on the old Place d'Armes, fought and won the

---

[182] There is no proof that opera was given before 1806, but it seems likely. Some seventy operas were produced from 1806 to 1811, usually in the Théâtre St. Pierre (Spectacle de la Rue St. Pierre). There were, for instance, operatic or theatrical performances each month of the year 1807. Price, "Le Spectacle de la Rue St. Pierre," *Louisiana Historical Quarterly,* I, 215-223.

[183] Breaux, "Some Early Colleges and Schools of Louisiana," *Publications of the Louisiana Historical Society,* VII, 136-142. See also Fortier, III, 191-4.

[184] Quoted in Cable, pp. 158-9.

[185] Consult the second volume of Wandell and Minnigerode, *Aaron Burr;* and Roosevelt, *The Winning of the West,* Volume IV, for opposing views of this episode.

battle of New Orleans. That Packenham should have won the battle is somehow typical—the city always blunders through. Is it any wonder that travellers do not know what to make of the place?

The anonymous author of *The Americans as They Are* reports in 1817 that swarms of needy Yankees and Kentuckians have alienated the Creoles. A good Briton, he says that "the little respect paid to the Sabbath is a relic of the French Revolution and of Buonaparte, for whom the French and the creoles of Louisiana have an unlimited respect, imitating him as poor minds generally do, as far as they are able, in his bad qualities, his contempt of venerable customs, and his egotism, and leaving his great deeds and the noble traits in his character to the imitation of others."[186] Darby sees nothing wrong in this: "Much distortion of opinion has existed, and is, not yet eradicated in the other parts of the United States," he says in 1816, "respecting public morals and manners in New Orleans. Divested of preconceived ideas on the subject, an observing man will find little to condemn in New Orleans, more than in other commercial cities, and will find that noble distinction of all active communities, acuteness of conception, urbanity of manners, and polished exterior. There are few places where human life can be enjoyed with more pleasure or employed to more pecuniary profit."[187] Pleasure and pecuniary profit! The Americans come swarming in.[188] Traveller after traveller tries to describe the town.[189] Most of them shudder and admire.

[186] Pp. 169-70, 148. Montulé (*Voyage to North America in 1817*, pp. 50-56) found the Hotel Trimoulet swarming with Bonapartists.

[187] Darby, *Geographical Description of Louisiana*, quoted in Fortier, III, 185.

[188] As illustrating the conflict of testimony, we have on the one hand the famous story of Madame Lalaurie, who was driven out of the city because of her cruelty to her slaves; and on the other hand, the statement of the author of *The Americans as They Are*, pp. 132-3, that the Anglo-Americans treat their slaves better than do the French, who treat them like beasts and who expect the slave to repay in profit in three years what it cost to purchase him. The free blacks, he says, are worse. Slaves were governed by the famous Black Code. By the by, when Bryant went abroad in 1884, Madame Lalaurie was among the passengers; and when she attended the Havre theater, she was hissed. Godwin, *Biography of William Cullen Bryant*, I, chap. xvi.

[189] See Bernhard, *Travels*, II, passim (1826); Hodgson, *Letters from North America*, I, letter ix (1820); Levasseur, *Lafayette in America*, II, chaps. vii and viii (1825); Latrobe's *Journal*, pp. 159-245 (1818-19); Hamilton, *Men and Manners in America*, II, chap. v (1833); Power, *Impressions of America*, II, 168-182, 227-77 (1835); Mackay, *Western World*, II, 293-4 (1846-7); Lyell, *Travels in the United States, Second Visit*, II, 90 ff. (1847-8), for representative opinions.

What does that matter to Creole, Bonapartist, or émigé? Between 1830 and 1840 the population grew to 100,000. The city must become the most important commercial center in the United States—has it not the whole vast Mississippi valley to draw on? Cotton—is it not king? The center of the stage was held by the plantation owner, finely described by Cable:

The brow and cheek of this man were darkened by outdoor exposure, but they were not weather-beaten. His shapely bronzed hand was no harder or rougher than was due to the use of the bridle-rein and the gunstock. His eye was the eye of a steed; his neck—the same. His hair was a little luxuriant. His speech was positive, his manner was military, his sentiments were antique, his clothing was of broadcloth, his boots were neat, and his hat was soft, broad, and slouched a little to show its fineness. Such in his best aspect was the Mississippi River planter. When sugar was his crop and Creole French his native tongue, his polish would sometimes be finer still, with a finish got in Paris, and his hotel would be the St. Louis.

He was growing to be a great power. The enormous agricultural resources of Louisiana, Mississippi, Arkansas, and Tennessee were his. The money-lender gyrated around him with sweet smiles and open purse. He was mortgaged to the eyes, and still commanded a credit that courted and importuned him. He caused an immense increase of trade. His extravagant wants and the needs of his armies of slaves kept the city drained of its capital almost or quite the whole year round. . . . Millions of capital that would have yielded slower but immensely better final results in other channels went into the planters' paper based on the value of slaves and of lands whose value depended on slave labor,— a species of wealth unexchangeable in the great world of commerce, fictitious as paper money, and even more illusory.[190]

Perhaps the economics of this selection is doubtful, but the picture is not. "French influence," writes Professor Dodd, "contributed much that was valuable to the plantation system."[191] New Orleans in 1848 was the Paris of that system, the most European city in America, where music, literature, art, manners, and vice and business flourished. We shall find no more important cultural center in our investigations.

[190] Cable, pp. 227-8.
[191] *The Cotton Kingdom*, p. 19

V

French Migration to America
(*continued*)

1. FRENCH TRAVELLERS AND EMIGRANTS IN THE PERIOD OF THE AMERICAN REVOLUTION AND SUBSEQUENT YEARS

NATURALLY enough during the periods of war against Louis XIV and Louis XV, French emigration to the British colonies was small. It seems clear, however, that upon the conclusion of the peace in 1763, numerous French soldiers of fortune, hair-dressers, dancing masters, adventurers, and ne'er-do-wells came to the New World, many of them settling in centers like Philadelphia, Charleston, Annapolis, and the like, where, in our discussion of French influence upon American manners and American art, we shall trace their occupations.[1] We shall not therefore repeat here what is said there. It is to be noted, however, that until about 1770 the American attitude toward Frenchmen was still a grudging one, except in those cosmopolitan circles which affected Old World culture.[2] Let us now describe the next important influx of French into this country, namely that which followed upon the American Revolution. The characteristic note of this movement is that it was a purely temporary one; few remained to settle in the new republic as the Huguenots, the Acadians, the émigrés and the Royalist and Bonapartist exiles settled there.

The first effect of the American Revolution was to draw from France and Santo Domingo various adventurers who saw in the war a chance for advancement or gain, and who did little to increase the good opinion of Americans concerning Frenchmen.[3] Opinon, it is true, was not unanimous concerning their bad qualities. Thus a British agent (?) wrote of Washington's army in 1779 that it "contains many French low characters, who behave with great Impudence (?illegible) to the Farmers."[4] On the other hand, it was the opinion of M. de

---

[1] See chapters vii and ix.
[2] See chapters iv and xiv, *passim*.
[3] See chapter xiv, section III, *passim*, for the character of some of these adventurers and the embarrassment caused by them.
[4] Stevens' *Facsimiles*, No. 123. A letter in the handwriting of William Smith(?) sent to the Earl of Carlisle.

Fleury (16 November, 1779) that in New Hampshire, "they have seen a few Frenchmen, and like them better. Their gratitude towards the nation has not been lessened by the imprudence of individuals." However, in Boston the "French are liked more than they are esteemed. . . . They judge us to be like pedlers, very honest thieves. They are English as regards Frenchmen, but Americans towards the English."[5] Lafayette observed that "le plus grand nombre de ceux qui se présentèrent [to serve in the American army] furent refusés et revinrent en France, à quelques exceptions près, porter leurs préjugés contre les Américains. Il paraît que quelques-uns de ceux qui restèrent écriverent dans le même sens."[6] We should not, of course, confound with these, various French observers sent over by Choiseul or Vergennes, who seem to have made pleasant impressions on the Americans.[7]

But one of the reasons for the approbation with which Deane and Franklin viewed the coming of Lafayette to America was that it might destroy the unfavorable impression made by French volunteers hitherto,[8] and it must be confessed that the character of the group which came with the gallant Marquis was very different from that of the needy adventurers who had hitherto tried to squeeze money out of Congress.[9] To remove certain difficulties which had arisen in the handling of the Beaumarchais enterprise, M. Conrad-Alex-

[5] Stevens' *Facsimiles*, No. 1616. Mons. de Fleury, "Summary of the political and military conditions of America."
[6] *Mémoires de Lafayette*, I, 98.
[7] See chapter xiv, pp. 515-17. One or two random references to French agents in 1777 are not without interest. Dr. Bancroft(?) to Paul Wentworth, May, 1777: "There is a French Agent in America who Corresponds in Cypher directly with the Kings elder Brother—several of his Letters written from New England to Monsieur have passed through our hands." Stevens' *Facsimiles*, No. 151. Again, John Adams writes his wife from Philadelphia 13 April, 1777, describing the destruction of the ship Morris, of Nantes, and says that two French gentlemen got on shore who were said to have brought dispatches from France to Congress. *Letters of John Adams*, I, 213.
[8] Faÿ, p. 59.
[9] Kalb, Conway, de Gouvion, Duportail, Laradière, Laumoy, Ternant, La Colombe, La Rouërie, Geniat, Fleury, Mauduit-Duplessis, Touzard, L'Enfant, Steuben, Kozciusko, Pulaski are listed by Lafayette as coming with him or as serving in 1777-78 in the army. *Mémoires*, I, 95-98. There should also be included MM. de Kermoran (1776), de Boisbertrand (1776), de Coudray (1777), and de la Rouërie (1777), unless Lafayette's La Rouërie is the same. The Americans were not altogether blameless. Congress sent M. de la Rouërie a brevet appointing him officer, and then tried to send one to his valet de chambre! *Mémoires du Comte de Moré*, p. 87.

andre Gérard was sent as Minister in 1778,[10] who made a pleasant impression. M. le Comte de Moré arrived in 1777, being most romantically shipwrecked on the American coast; he later joined Lafayette, returned to France in 1779, and came back to America in 1791.[11] And one should not forget the Reverend Francis Louis Chartier de Lotbinière of the Order of Malta who was commissioned chaplain of the Catholic "Congress' Own" regiment and who served in the advance on Canada.[12] Clearly, these were men of a different stripe.

The coming of Rochambeau deepened the favorable impression.[13] These gallant officers, these well-drilled and well-disciplined soldiers deepened the American respect for France. The officers in particular were received as guests and admired by the ladies.[14] In Boston they were dined and wined by merchant princes like Samuel Breck;[15] and in Newport there were illuminations, fireworks, bell-ringings.[16] If they could not speak English, they tried Latin;[17] and bought dictionaries and grammars in order to learn our language.[18] Lauzun was impressed with the virtue of the Americans; he left Newport with regret, where he had become one of the family of Mme. Hunter and two charming girls, who were sisters to him—apparently he did not make love to them as he did to every other woman he met. Leaving Newport for Lebanon was like going to Siberia. He does not always agree with Rochambeau, but on the other hand when the great march to Virginia took place, what acclamations in Philadelphia! What joy when

---

[10] *Mémoires du Comte de Moré*, p. 85.
[11] See his *Mémoires*. On the early French officers (before Rochambeau) see in this connection, Balch, *The French in America during the War of Independence*, pp. 81-82.
[12] Humphrey, *Nationalism and Religion*, pp. 126-7.
[13] See the *Journal of Claude Blanchard; Narrative of the Prince de Broglie; Mémoires du Duc de Lauzun;* Lafayette's *Mémoires;* Chotteau, *Les Français en Amérique;* Merlant, *Soldiers and Sailors of France in the American War for Independence;* Sherrill, *French Memories of Eighteenth Century America.*
[14] Faÿ, p. 122. See, for example, de Broglie's *Mémoires*, pp. 233-4, 306, 374-5, 376-7.
[15] See *Recollections of Samuel Breck, passim.*
[16] Chotteau, p. 179. Rochambeau received a deputation of Indian chiefs with great suavity, p. 222. For a list of the principal officers, see him, pp. 166-168.
[17] As Blanchard did. *Journal*, pp. 47-48, 56.
[18] Blanchard, p. 51. See the account of Blanchard's visit to Boston with Chevalier de Luz and M. de Capellis, pp. 49-51. They were well received, and the French consul, M. de Volnois, was popular.

Washington learned that de Grasse was actually in the Chesapeake! And though he was glad to return to France to continue his suit with Mme. de Caigny and where he was received "de la manière la plus touchante," he was delighted to re-visit the Hunters, even though he had almost died in America.[19] Then there was de Broglie, who had begun with dreams of monarchy, but who, after conveying 2,500,000 livres to Philadelphia, visited Philadelphia society with Lauzun, and almost choked himself drinking tea because he did not know enough to put his spoon across his cup. He finds Mrs. Gouverneur Morris delightful; on his journey to the army he meets only "pleasant thoughts and agreeable subjects"—a "genuine hospitality"; Miss Champlain in Newport was "dressed and coiffée with taste," which, alas, most of the American ladies were not; besides she "spoke and understood our language." As for the Hunter girls, they are charming, and for Polly Lawton, the Quakeress, they must give a ball—for her and all the other enchantresses in Newport, "that charming place regretted by the whole army."[20] What the common soldiers were doing, does not appear; perhaps we had better not ask. And when warfare died away, Rochambeau encouraged his preux chevaliers to ride over the country—philosophic Chastellux, Lauzun the ladies' man, the Comte de Damas, the Vicomte de Noailles, the Comte de Charlus, the Comte de Broglie.[21] The Comte de Moré thinks it was a mistake to let them: they acquired revolutionary ideas.[22] When the army departed, there was universal regret; nothing had done more to cement American friendship than the character and qualities of the French officers. They did not know it, but many of them were to return as émigrés, some of them to die. For example Tom Paine brought his Parisian host, Bonneville, to the United States—his son became an American officer of distinction, the Bonneville of Washington Irving's volume;[23] and de la Gardette of the Soissonais regiment settled here.[24] Nor were the

[19] *Mémoires*, pp. 142-156.
[20] *Narrative of the Prince de Broglie*, pp. 181-5, 231-4, 306-9.
[21] Faÿ, p. 82; Chotteau, pp. 362-3; Chastellux, *Voyages.*
[22] *Mémoires*, p. 105.
[23] An earlier de Bonneville, an engineer in the French War of 1756-1763, had published a book on America in 1771, according to Rosengarten, p. 66. I have not seen it.
[24] Rosengarten, pp. 69-71, gives a list of Revolutionary officers who returned as *émigrés.*

French naval officers less charming, although, naturally, one saw less of them. When a squadron put in at Boston, New York, or Philadelphia, the officers were agreeably entertained.[25] All in all the 32,000 sailors and the 12,000 soldiers did much for Franco-American understanding.[26]

The entente continued after the war, but there were occasional little rifts within the lute. The American Philosophical Society voted to include a number of distinguished Frenchmen among its members.[27] Target, La Rochefoucauld-Liancourt, Condorcet, and others were made honorary citizens of New Haven, Connecticut,[28] in 1784. The Order of the Cincinnati, founded May 10, 1783, was officially sanctioned by Louis XVI in December. The King became a patron, and important French members were Lafayette, Rochambeau, de Grasse, Chastellux, Dumas, de Noailles, Collot, Deux Ponts, Lauzun, Charles Alexandre and Théodore de Lameth, Bougainville, Ségur, Broglie, Custine, Ferson, Blanchard, du Bourg, Bozon de Périgord, Closen, Pontgibaud, Ternant, Gérard and Luzerne.[29] The order came under a good deal of criticism, it is true, because it was manipulated—or so ran the charge— by Hamilton,[30] but on the whole it made for friendship. Thus, when Washington came to Boston in 1788, Ponteves, de Traversay, and the Chevalier de Braye participated as members of the Cincinnati in the reception tendered him[31] and in Charleston the order was "highly esteemed."[32] Aside from

[25] Thus the French naval officers were entertained in 1787, 1788, and 1789 in Boston, and had been so entertained at varying times in other ports. *Recollections of Samuel Breck*, pp. 123-5. In 1789 Governor Hancock invited the admiral and the officers to dine; also Washington; and an awkward social situation developed over the question of precedence between the General and the Governor, pp. 127-30. Hancock had ignored the Comte de Moustier, the French minister, who, when he was in Boston, confined his attentions to the Breck family, pp. 131-2.

[26] Thirty-two thousand six hundred and nine officers and sailors; 697 officers and 11,983 soldiers. Merlant, p. 204.

[27] See chapter xi, p. 404 (note) for the list.

[28] Faÿ, p. 139; La Rochefoucauld-Liancourt, *Voyages*, III, 244.

[29] Sherrill, *French Memories, passim.*

[30] Cf. Bowers, p. 48. F. M. Bayard found Virginia favorable for his revolutionary theories in 1791, but complained that primitive virtues were being corrupted by luxury and by the Order of the Cincinnati. See his *Voyage dans l'intérieur des États-Unis.*

[31] Griswold, *Republican Court*, p. 190.

[32] Ravenel, *Charleston: the Place and the People*, pp. 358-363. The chief complaint against the order was that it was undemocratic, in being an order at all, and in comprising only officers. As marking the close association of

the Cincinnati Crèvecoeur, Clavière and Brissot de Warville tried to establish a Société Gallo-Américaine in January, 1787,[33] which was later merged into the Society of the Friends of the Blacks, also a Gallo-American affair, organized in February, 1788, and totalling three hundred members, including Mirabeau, Lafayette, La Rochefoucauld-Liancourt, Sieyès, Grégoire, Volney, William Short, and Crèvecoeur.[34] Many Frenchmen planned to migrate to the New World between 1784 and 1788 to found there a perfect society—people like Lanthenas, Roland, Bernardin de St. Pierre and Lezay Marnésia: the chief results of the dream were the books of Brissot de Warville, and the famous Scioto project.[35] Aside from the social success of the French ministers,[36] perhaps the most striking episode of the eighties was Lafayette's visit to America. Landing in August, 1784, he visited Mount Vernon, New York, Albany, New England, Philadelphia, returning in December to France. Everywhere (except in New York, which was having trouble with the Tories)[37] he was received with mounting enthusiasm. In Boston:

A general ringing of the bells of Boston call'd us from table & announced the Approach of the *Marquiss La Fayete*—the main street was crowed (sic) with spectators, who were all anxious to repeat the applause of their country & renew the Honours due to so distinguished & heroic son of Liberty—the Company of Cadetts preceded on foot— Then the Marquiss & Gen. Knox between two other Gent of distinction—the Consul La Tombe & several french & American Officers followed in carriages or on horses—with many Gent of the Town—I stood near the stump of the liberty Tree—once so famous—as soon as the Marquiss came near the spot almost sacred to Liberty—he was welcom'd by three general cheers—sounds which carried with them the Gratitude of those who uttered them. a numerous crowd followed him

French and Americans in the society, one notes that Major L'Enfant designed the badge of the order; that the chief French officers were presented with complimentary medals; and that the Comte de Grasse, in the name of the French navy, sent a medal of gold, enamel, and diamonds to Washington, which is still extant.

[33] The constitution is at Harvard in a volume called American Land Companies. Twelve members were to live in Paris, 24 in the provinces, and an equal number in the United States. The equality of all members was provided for. The society met for three months, but does not seem to have proved successful. The general object was to improve knowledge and commerce by providing a central depot of ideas. Mitchell, *St. Jean de Crèvecoeur,* pp. 154-9.

[34] *Ibid.*

[35] Faÿ, pp. 156 ff.

[36] For which see chapter vii, *passim.*

[37] McMaster, I, 216-219.

to his lodgings in State street—received his thanks—from the walk over the door—repeated the huzza's & dispersed—I really felt emotions which were peculiarly animating, let the cause be what it would—[38]

The reception was everywhere repeated. "Wherever he passes," wrote Madison, "he receives the most flattering tokens of sincere affection from all ranks."[39]

One can accumulate bits of evidence about other Frenchmen during the period, which are instructive and illuminating. In Philadelphia Dr. Chovet, in his 79th year, although not a professor, said Schoepf, has lectured on anatomy and is particularly known for his beautiful wax-work collection designed to illustrate the parts of the human body.[40] In 1786, says Watson, my former partner in France, M. Cossoul, came to America and "I journeyed south with him."[41] In Philadelphia Dr. Le Mayeur offered to "transplant teeth," something of a novelty in those days,[42] and in Philadelphia Benezet[43] and Peter du Ponceau were names to conjure with.[44] Chastellux had made his celebrated journey through America in 1781 and 1782,[45] and La Rochefoucauld-Liancourt and, later, Volney were to come. In 1788 Madison says he has been called upon by "a M. St. Trise," a former French cavalry officer, who sends his compliments to Jefferson.[46] Nor should we forget that during this period Crèvecoeur was doing everything he could to strengthen the friendship of the two nations.[47]

In the South we glean a great deal of information from

---

[38] Baldwin, *Life and Letters of Simeon Baldwin*, pp. 228. The Marquis was taken by the elder Breck to see a dignified town-meeting in Faneuil Hall, but the sequel proved unfortunate. *Recollections of Samuel Breck*, pp. 39-40.

[39] *Letters*, I, 101. Madison met him in Baltimore and talked to him about the navigation of the Mississippi.

[40] *Travels in the Confederation*, I, 84.

[41] *Men and Times of the Revolution*, p. 283.

[42] Scharf and Westcott, *History of Philadelphia*, II, 885.

[43] Benezet is described by Chastellux, *Voyages*, I, 240 ff.; and see Stedman and Hutchinson, III, 369-70.

[44] Brissot de Warville, *Travels*, letter xix, letter xxiv; Combe, *Notes on America*, II, 37-40 (1839). Ramon de la Sagra met "el respetable Mr. Duponceau" in "Filadelfia" in 1835. *Cinco Meses en los Estados-Unidos*, p. 182.

[45] He called at Monticello where he shared Jefferson's enthusiasm for Ossian. *Voyages*, II, 34 ff.

[46] *Letters*, I, 446.

[47] See Julia St. Mitchell; and Chinard, *Les amitiés américaines de Madame d'Houdetot*.

the diary of the elder Michaux.[48] Born at Satory near Versailles, March 7, 1746, the son of a great traveller, André Michaux came to New York in 1785, ostensibly to obtain American plants and trees for France, but also as an agent of the French government. He spent two years in that vicinity, founding a nursery and making short botanical excursions into New Jersey, Pennsylvania, and Maryland, and sending home after one year twelve boxes of seed, 5000 seedling trees, and some live partridges. In 1787 he went to Charleston, which became his headquarters, and there he started his famous garden.[49] After travelling widely, he secured financial aid from the American Philosophical Society for a trip west of Missouri, but the French minister sent him to Missouri instead.[50] He returned to France in 1796. He tells us in his diary (28 May, 1787) that he visited Col. Le Roy Hammond, three miles from Augusta, S. C.: the Colonel's two nieces were at home and were "très aimables" and "cette mansion me parut très distinguée à tous égard par les bonnes manières, la richesse et l'élégance." Two days later he was received by "Mr. Pece" who "nous reçut avec beaucoup de civilités parque[sic] no[us] étions français." June 3, 1787, he visited New Bordeaux, a very scattered colony, so that "je n'en visitay [sic] qu'un seul." But "les français de cet établissement sont généralement estimés pa. la probité et les bonnes moeurs." June 9 he met Mr. Martin, a Frenchman. Nov. 24, 1788, he consulted a French physician at Washington, some 46 miles from Augusta. Five days later he visited M. Terundet, who was "très considéré." December 22 he slept at Captain Baudet's, near Charleston.[51] We shall have more to say of him presently.

It is true there were various complaints, ranging from flute playing[52] to sharp business practice[53] alleged against the

---

[48] Published in *Proceedings of the American Philosophical Society*, XXVI, pp. 8-145, under the editorship of C. S. Sargent.

[49] Described by W. C. Coker, "The Garden of André Michaux," *Journal of the Elisha Mitchell Scientific Society*, XXVII, 65-72. There is some dispute as to whether the garden was begun in 1786 or 1787.

[50] He may have suggested the Lewis and Clark expedition to Jefferson.

[51] "Diary," pp. 2-7, 14, 15, 16, 17, 44, 49.

[52] The Abbé Robin tells of a Frenchman lodged with him who played the flute on Sunday. The people were aroused and "alloit se porter à des excès" (who can translate so thoroughly French a phrase?), but the host had instructed him not to violate the Connecticut code. *Nouveau Voyage*, p. 11.

[53] The French complained that the Americans cheated them. Brissot de Warville, *Travels*, I, 129.

French. "There are at present (1788)," wrote Brissot, "very few French merchants in Philadelphia. The failure of those who first came discouraged the others, and has put the Americans on their guard." Such men "measured Philadelphia on the scale of Paris." Some Frenchmen, alas! "paraded themselves here publicly with their mistresses, who displayed those light and wanton airs which they had practised at Paris. . . . Contempt was the consequence; want of credit followed the contempt; and what is a merchant without credit?"[54] What, indeed? Doubtless Savary de Valcoulon, in coming to the United States to prosecute claims against Virginia for advances made by his house in Lyons during the war,[55] did not make himself popular. And yet the general picture that one forms of the period is one of peculiar concord—a period in which the ideas and manners of the French were extraordinarily influential in shaping American ways.[56]

2. THE MOVEMENT OF FRENCH EMIGRES FROM FRANCE
AND THE WEST INDIES

The most picturesque group of French emigrants to America, and, with the Huguenots, the group whose movements have been most studied, is that composed of the émigré nobles who fled to this country to escape the Revolution in France or in Santo Domingo.[57] The movement of events in France is too familiar to require recital here, but the insurrection in Santo Domingo is not so well known, and must be briefly reviewed in order to understand a peculiar phase of this emigration.[58]

The population of French Santo Domingo in 1788 consisted of three classes: whites, mulattoes, and negro slaves. Government was entirely in the hands of a Governor-General

---

[54] *Ibid.*, pp. 275-7. For a running account of Frenchmen in the United States in 1788, see him, Vol. I.
[55] Stevens, *Albert Gallatin*, p. 19.
[56] See chap. vii.
[57] See Faÿ, especially chaps. iv and v; Rosengarten, *French Colonists and Exiles;* Baldensperger, *Le mouvement des idées dans l'émigration française;* Carré, "Les émigrés français en Amérique, 1789-93," *La Revue de Paris,* May, 1898, pp. 311-340; Sherrill, *French Memories of Eighteenth Century America,* and the special treatises cited *passim* in this section.
[58] See Hazard, *Santo Domingo, Past and Present;* Edwards, *The History, Civil and Commercial, of the British Colonies in the West Indies,* IV; the anonymous *History of the Island of St. Domingo;* Herrick, *Audubon the Naturalist,* I, chap. iii.

and his subordinate officials; and the mulattoes were rigidly excluded from all political and social standing except that they were required to perform military service at their own expense. The complicated story of the troubles in the French province are best understood if it is seen that from 1789 to 1795 there were three revolutions in the island; that of the whites, that of the mulattoes, and that of the negroes. Upon the news of the summoning of the National Assembly the Creoles formed a general assembly and three provincial assemblies for the three divisions of the province (north, south, and west), from which there were elected eighteen representatives to the National Assembly in Paris, which, however, declined to receive all but six of them. In Paris, meantime, the mulattoes, with the sympathy of the Société des Amis des Noirs, presented a petition to the National Assembly, asking for full civil and political rights for the mulattoes in Santo Domingo, to which the President of the Assembly responded sympathetically. But in 1790 the National Assembly dispatched to Santo Domingo a decree to the effect that it "has never meant to comprehend the interior government of the colonies in the constitution which they had framed for the mother country,"[59] a death-blow to the hopes of the mulattoes; and the whites accordingly refused to yield civic and social rights to them. The angry mulattoes rallied to the Governor (Peynier) in the hope of securing their desires; in May, 1790, the General Assembly of French Santo Domingo published a constitution for the island which the governor refused to recognize, and in an effort to suppress the recalcitrant Assembly, resorted to force. In the midst of this confusion the mulattoes rose under James Ogé, but were defeated, and Ogé himself was executed. Peynier was replaced by Blanchelande, who could not rely on the troops to support him; Colonel Mauduit, who had been loyal to the governor, was infamously murdered by his own soldiers; and at this juncture (1791) there came from France the decree that the colonial assemblies should admit to membership people of color born of free parents. The whites refused to recognize the decree. The slaves, meanwhile, under the leadership of Jean François, a mulatto, and Boukmann, a slave, revolted and marched on the town of Cape François, carrying as their banner the body of a white infant on a spearhead, and spread-

---

[59] Edwards, IV, 26-7. The French Assembly was fearful that the creoles would declare their independence of France.

ing destruction in their wake. The alarmed assembly now voted to admit the operation of the decree of 1791; but unfortunately, the French National Assembly, perturbed at the news from Santo Domingo, voted the repeal of the decree in question, and the mulattoes, persuaded of the bad faith of the whites, joined with the negroes in a general rebellion and massacre. In the meantime the whites themselves remained divided into two parties; and by March, 1792, the combined blacks and mulattoes were in possession of the island; nor, despite occasional temporary success, did the French ever succeed in regaining its possession. To relate the events of subsequent years, including the British attempt at a conquest of the province, would be to recapitulate a tedious story of treachery, stupidity, and massacre. The whites fled from the island, the emigration beginning with the revolt of the negroes in 1791; and by the year of the British attempt on Santo Domingo in 1793, nine-tenths of the white inhabitants had fled.[60] The number who came to the United States can not be exactly known; it was probably not lower than 10,000, and may have been as high as 20,000.[61] Most of them were royalist in sympathy. These, added to the number of émigrés who came from France or by way of England, made up the group of royalist refugees which has been variously estimated as from 10,000 to 25,000 in number.[62] The creoles from Santo Domingo mainly took refuge in the central and southern states; the emigrants from the Continent went mainly to the northern and central states.[63]

Before discussing this emigration in detail, a word should be said regarding the general character of the emigration. From the nature of the case the émigrés belonged to the aristocracy, and brought with them their aristocratic prepossessions. Accordingly they did not, like the Huguenots or the Acadians, make farmers or villagers, nor were they used to toil; and the conditions of life in the United States forbade the re-establishment of that salon life they had abandoned.[64] Few of them felt at home in America; and Baldensperger points

[60] Edwards, IV, 147. He estimates the number of white French who joined the British in the attempt at pacification at 2,000. P. 148.
[61] The anonymous *History of Santo Domingo* (p. 96) estimates 10,000.
[62] Baldensperger, I, 105; Chinard, *Volney et l'Amérique*, p. 28.
[63] Faÿ, p. 205.
[64] Cf. Baldensperger, I, 156-8.

out that they mingled more easily with the Europeans in this country than with the natives, a statement that is, with some exceptions, true. On the other hand, many accepted the necessity to work, gallantly and with grace; it is possible that "a vague melancholy" was left on their spirits which may have had great influence in spreading romanticism in America as it did in France after their return.[65] They were, moreover, more varied as a group than seems at first possible.

Ils étaient de toute provenance et représentaient toutes les opinions possibles, anciens officiers de l'armée de Rochambeau, revenues dans le pays pour lequel ils avaient combattu, avec l'intention de faire valoir leurs titres à la reconnaissance des Américains, colons de Saint-Domingue, habitués au delicieux far-niente des Iles et qui avaient fui devant la révolte des noirs, modérés de la Gironde, Jacobins qui avaient fini par redouter la Terreur; tout ce monde bizarre vivait une vie pleine de regrets stériles, de querelles politiques, de polémiques forcenées, imprimant des pamphlets royalistes ou jacobins, cherchant à intéresser les Américains à leur cause et réduits pour trouver leur morceau de pain quotidien, à solliciter un repas chez de riches Américains qu'ils affectaient entre eux de mépriser, ou de donner les leçons de français ou de danse.[66]

The very revolutionists were disgusted with the practice of equality as it was discovered in America.[67] And yet there were many who, like Dupont de Nemours, Michaux, Volney, La Rochefoucauld-Liancourt and Collot, rendered real services to the new republic. On the whole they were generously treated by the Americans,[68] and many sought to repay in gratitude what they had received. And as a group "they brought to us the ideas and manners of a splendid though wrecked civilization, and strange experiences, fruitful of wise suggestion; to our forming society they offered examples of courtly usages; and to the children of our wealthier families, in several instances, princes and nobles for teachers and associates."[69]

On the whole New England was less affected by this emigration than other geographical units. In Boston, it is true, there was Nancrède, who may have been an officer in Rochambeau's army, who was a professor at Harvard in 1787, and who married Hannah Dixey in 1788. He wrote his *L'Abeille Française* for the Harvard students in 1792, a docu-

---

[65] Consult Baldensperger, I, chap. i.
[66] Chinard, *Volney et l'Amérique*, p. 28.
[67] Faÿ, p. 269. Moreau de Saint-Méry is a case in point.
[68] Cf. La Rouchefoucauld-Liancourt, *Voyages*, VIII, 147-9.
[69] Griswold, *Republican Court*, p. 322.

ment full of the cloudy sentimentalism of Rousseau; and in
Marlborough street he founded a bookstore from which appeared a *Télémaque,* a translation of Saint-Pierre, one of *Paul
and Virginia,* one of Condorcet, and so on.[70] Later he was to
move to Philadelphia. In Boston mesmerism was introduced
by M. Poyen, a French Creole, from one of the West India
islands[71] and the town had its usual complement of dancing
masters, entertainers, and restauranteurs.[72] But there was not
sufficient interest in things French for Nancrède to continue
his *Courrier de Boston* for more than seven months;[73] and
though the town was visited by various wandering Frenchmen, though the Catholic church there flourished, one does
not perceive at this distance any such local colony as distinguished Philadelphia, New York or Charleston.

Scattered over New England there were, it is true, various
Frenchmen. Dr. Peter Bryant, father of the poet, was a pupil
of Leprilète, a refugee from Santo Domingo, educated in
Paris, who settled in Norton, Massachusetts, where he married
a farmer's daughter and acquired an extensive reputation as
a surgeon.[74] In Hartford La Rochefoucauld-Liancourt, over-
hearing two men talking French, found that they were both
from Martinique and that they had both bought farms; he
stopped and had a long conversation with them.[75] In Ston-
ington he found the French were highly esteemed;[76] and it
is curious to know that Brissot thought that New England
inns were superior to French taverns in 1792.[77]

In the case of New York, however, the tale is more specific.
The state subscribed $11,624 in 1793 to aid the Creoles in New
York; and the legislature later contributed $11,215 for the
same purpose, for which the state is enthusiastically praised
by La Rochefoucauld-Liancourt.[78] The city of New York had

[70] Schinz, "Un 'Rousseauiste' en Amérique," *Modern Language Notes,*
XXXV, 10-18.
[71] Nichols, *Forty Years of American Life,* II, 19.
[72] See chapter ix.
[73] Belisle, *Histoire de la Presse Franco-Américaine,* pp. 355-9.
[74] Godwin, *Biography of William Cullen Bryant,* I, 2. He dressed with
"great elegance and precision, wearing ruffles at his wrists," and seems to
have viewed his wife's diet with some disfavor.
[75] *Voyages,* III, 210-2.
[76] *Ibid.,* V, 134.
[77] McMaster, II, 564.
[78] Who observes, however, that many of the recipients of this bounty
later returned to France, VII, 141-2.

a veritable colony of Frenchmen. Chastellux met "le Baron de Montesquieu . . . petit-fils de l'auteur de l'Esprit des loix" in New York or near it in 1780 or 1781.[79] When Saint-Méry was there in May, 1794, he visited Guerlain, who gave him a job as a shipping clerk which he despised; Goynard; Talleyrand and Beaumetz, who came in June; Dauzar, a surgeon from Santo Domingo; Devarenne; Cazenove and the Baron de la Roche (German) with whom he went into partnership. Saint-Méry was taken to see the "hospice" for the French; and attended a concert at the house of Desèze of Santo Domingo, and dined with Bayard.[80] New York society included Brillat-Savarin who came in 1793 and spent three years; he taught French, he played in theater orchestras; and he taught Julien to cook eggs with cheese. His favorite lounging place was Little's Tavern, where the turtle soup was good; and it was in New York that he met the Vicomte de Massue and M. Fehr of Marsailles, whom he treated to Welch-rabbit.[81] Louis Philippe and his two brothers, the Duc de Montpensier and the Comte de Beaujolais spent the winter of 1798-9 in the city where Copley "once attended a dinner given by Louis Philippe at his modest lodgings where one half of the guests were seated upon the side of the bed for want of room to place chairs elsewhere."[82] When the Park theater was built in 1798 the plans were furnished by Marc Isambard Brunel, a French engineer émigré;[83] and it was in New York that Elkanah Watson remet general Moreau.[84] In New York Auguste Louis de Singeron, one of the officers who defended the Tuileries from the mob, after vainly trying to teach French, became a pastry cook; and it was there that Admiral Pierre de Landais, who had fought with John Paul Jones, miraculously lived for forty

[79] Chastellux, *Voyages,* I, 375.
[80] *Voyages aux États-unis,* pp. 137-143. Guerlain had come from Milliflore du Havre and had been educated in England. Pp. 140-141.
[81] *Magazine of American History,* III, 262; VI, 61. Rosengarten, pp. 103-5. The famous epicure travelled into Connecticut; he was a guest of Barlow in Hartford in October, 1794, and in the same town he gave a dinner to his American friends, with wings of partridges en papillote, gray squirrels cooked in Madeira, and roast turkey. *Labuntur anni!*
[82] Mrs. Lamb, *History of the City of New York,* II, 447. They were aided by Gouverneur Morris. See Allison, *The Curious Legend of Louis Philippe in Kentucky,* for Louis Philippe's western adventures.
[83] Hornblow, *History of the Theatre in America,* I, 247.
[84] In 1780. *Men and Times of the Revolution,* p. 124.

years on $105 per annum.[85] And there it was that La Rochefou-
cauld-Liancourt met M. Olive who was a merchant and had a
country house, but who could not forget France.[86]

There were various groups of exiles over the state. West
Point in 1796 was commanded by M. de Rochefontaine, formerly in the Revolutionary war and once a French officer.[87]
Near Freehold lived M. Rovère, former maréchal des logis des
gardes du corps, possessing a little farm in 1796 which he had
sold his watches and jewels to buy; he was sixty years old
when Liancourt visited him, he lived on milk and potatoes
and worked from dawn to dusk.[88] Near the west end of Lake
Oneida, on a small island, lived a "respectable Frenchman"
who had voluntarily sequestered himself from the world with
his dog, his guns, and his library.[89] Near the Genesee river
lived M. de Boui from Santo-Domingo, who had become a
misanthrope; at Tonnawanta (Tonnawanda) La Rochefoucauld-Liancourt visited Poudrit "qui est aussi bon claquedent
que bon coureur"; and at Rotterdam he learned from M. de
Vatine that M. Desjardins had bought 500,000 acres along the
Black river in "Hongrybay," in company with two other Frenchmen, one of whom, M. Faroux, an architect, had been drowned.
The said Desjardins lived in Albany.[90] And at Albany there was
a colony comparable to the one in New York City. There La
Rochefoucauld-Liancourt found M. and Madame de Gouvernet; she was pretty and had saved her husband in Paris, and
now (1795) they were living in Albany with a young man who
had fled with them, quite ignored by the inhabitants. In the
northern suburbs of Albany (known as the Colonie) there lived
M. Le Couteulx, formerly of Paris, whose residence was the
rendezvous of the French inhabitants; they included the Comte
Latour Dupin, and his wife (who had saved two trunks of
fine towels and nothing else from the wreckage), M. Phar-
oux, a very learned man, Desjardins, and at times Volney

---

[85] Lamprey, "French Exiles in New York," *Americana*, V, 702-3. The
admiral, meeting his bitterest enemy late in life, "spat on the pavement"—
"Consider that your face!"
[86] *Voyages*, VII, 146-7. This was in 1797.
[87] La Rochefoucauld-Liancourt, V. 295. Lafayette met MM. Berard,
du Commun, and Gimbrède, instructors at West Point, in 1824; they "appeared to enjoy much esteem in the establishment." Levasseur, *La Fayette
in America*, I, 104.
[88] *Ibid.*, V, 265.
[89] Watson, *Men and Times of the Revolution*. This was in 1791. P. 343.
[90] La Rochefoucauld-Liancourt, *Voyages*, I, 269-274, 294; II, 260-1.

and Talleyrand.[91] Feeling between the Americans and the French was not of the best.[92]

The great center for the French émigrés was, however, Philadelphia. To run through the *Mémoires* of Saint-Méry is to catch some glimpse of this society, which Saint-Méry at one time estimated as amounting to a colony of 25,000.[93] Saint-Méry met there L'Ami, Milhet, Sureau, Prieur, Mde. Seur; Aubert and his family; and a crowd of unfortunate friends from the French colonies, in addition to Longuemarre and Marcel who came to the United States with him in May, 1794. On May 22 he met Beaumetz and Talleyrand—Beaumetz who had been president of the provincial council of Artois and a deputy of the National Assembly, and who had fled from the Terror to England and thence to America, where he became a partner of Talleyrand in a land enterprise in Maine and a commercial enterprise to India. Balcon, de Noailles, Talon, and La Colombe, aide-de-camp to Lafayette in the American Revolution, must be added to the group, as well as Louis Narbonne, Cadignan, and Terrier. Olive de St. Malo lodged with M. Dessoti Destourelles; and the de Leysser family was there in September, for the son died of yellow fever in that month. Descombatz became clerk to Saint-Méry in October; Pillet, another one of Lafayette's aides came in November; La Rochefoucauld-Liancourt, the elder Terrier, Mlle. Boudier and Geanty he met later. A man calling himself the Comte de Beaufort escaped from Lyons and arrived in February, 1795. On March 2 Saint-Méry dined with Martial la Roque; and on June 3, he went to a ball where M. le Comte le jeune Bousquet of Lyons assembled many of the French. On June 15 he has seen Adet and Mozart, formerly l'avocat au Conseil de Paris; and a little later, M. l'Abbé Mangin. In September he dined with General Collot, just back from

---

[91] *Men and Times of the Revolution,* pp. 387-8; La Rochefoucauld-Liancourt, *Voyages,* II, 316-9.

[92] "Ils (the Governets) vivent seuls avec un jeune homme qui les a suivis dans leur fuite de France, et qui partage leurs travaux et leur société. Le ville d'Albany leur est de peu de ressource sous ce dernier rapport. L'ignorance où la plupart des personnes de la première classe de la ville sont de l'exitence de Mad. de Gouvernet dans leur voisinage, et l'indifférence, avec laquelle l'y voient ceux qui sont plus à portée de connaître son mérite et celui de son mari, feraient seules le procès à l'hospitalité des habitans d'Albany." *Voyages,* II, 318. Watson remarks that Desjardins was violently anti-American.

[93] *Voyages aux États-unis,* p. 286. The estimate is too high.

Guadaloupe; and that same month he took for masterworker in his printshop one La Granage, a Parisian. Gatereau began the publication of *Le Courrier de la France et de ses Colonies* in October. In January, 1796, he notes that Liancourt and de Grandprey were elected members of the philosophical society; and in January, 1797, M. Foncin, an engineer, arrived from Cayenne. In June he dined with Gallet, formerly councillor of the superior council of Cayenne. The same month M. Robineau de Bugon, son of the former Procureur-Général of the Conseil du Cap visited him; and he mentions Mde. Tully, Lapaquérie, M. Bruneau, young Lafayette, Rozier (French consul at New York), Mourgues, Rouvray, Mde. Beausan and the Homassel family in 1797-98.[94] The center of this society was Saint-Méry's bookshop, which Volney visited in October, 1795.[95] There it was that the Vicomte de Noailles, Talleyrand, Demeunier, Payen de Boisneuf, Talon, and others foregathered until the yellow fever scattered their group,[96] and thither it was that Louis Philippe and his two brothers sometimes came. Cobbett taught them English[97] and some of them taught the Americans French.[98] In the boarding-house kept by the Frenchman Francis on Fourth street the Vice-President (Adams) and members of Congress lived, as Thomas Twining attests.[99] And this society, poverty-stricken and brilliant, mixed with the Hamiltons, the Binghams, the Morrises, the Wolcotts, for they all agreed that democracy did not mean mob-rule, and that the nice conduct of a clouded cane was part of the necessary business of a statesman.[100] And to the whims of this society catered the French pastry-cook, the gentleman dancing master and the teacher of fencing and deportment.

[94] *Voyages aux États-unis, passim.*
[95] Chinard, *Volney et l'Amérique*, p. 28.
[96] Cf. Chinard, *Volney et l'Amérique*, p. 29; *Recollections of Samuel Breck*, pp. 193-4, 246-8, 197 ff. And see Michaux, "Diary," pp. 68-91.
[97] Cf. Cole, *Life of William Cobbett*, pp. 53-4, 63, 234. Cobbett tells an anecdote of "a Frenchman, who went to a Protestant church with me for the first time in Philadelphia. He saw everybody comfortably seated in pews whilst a couple of stoves were keeping the place as warm as a slack oven: 'Pardi!' he exclaimed, 'On sert Dieu bien à son aise, ici!'"
[98] *Ibid.*, p. 345.
[99] *Travels in America 100 Years Ago*, pp. 33-34.
[100] Cf. chap. vii; Bowers, chap. vi; Faÿ, pp. 270-271; Twining, pp. 30, 136; Talleyrand, *Memoirs*, I, 169-187; Scharf & Westcott, *History of Philadelphia*, II, 918-22, 963-4; Montulé, *A Voyage to North America*, pp. 6-7.

A good many Frenchmen settled in Pennsylvania. At Springmill near Philadelphia, La Rochefoucauld-Liancourt visited the farm of Legaux (an assumed name), who had been an avocat in Metz and a person of importance in Guadeloupe, and whose reputation in Philadelphia was none too good. At Potsgrove he met a Frenchman named Gerbier, the nephew of a celebrated Parisian avocat, who had been in Santo Domingo. At Whitehorst, four miles from Potsgrove, the inn was kept by a Lorraine German who had married an American girl, the daughter of a man from Avignon and a woman of Franche Comté. At Middletown, 27 miles from Lancaster, he met three Frenchman, one a jeweler and clockmaker, and one a doctor; the third remains anonymous to the muse of history. At Harrisburg there was a French doctor from Martinique who toasted Lafayette in good Madeira.[101] In August, 1793, Michaux interviewed some Frenchmen in Pittsburg, one of whom—Louisière—had been concerned in a plot to deliver Havre to the English-Spanish fleet.[102] The younger Michaux, travelling the same way in 1802, remained in Pittsburg ten days, "during which," he writes

I frequently saw the Chevalier Dubac, formerly a French officer, who, being compelled by the occurrences of the revolution to quit France, had at first, fixed his abode at Scioto, but soon afterwards changed his residence and settled at Pittsburgh, where he is engaged in commerce. His knowledge of the western country is very correct.[103]

And forty years later de Tocqueville met in a remote district of Pennsylvania a Frenchman who had begun as an ardent demagogue and who now defended property rights and quoted the evangelists in support of his views.[104] But the most singular settlement in Pennsylvania was Asylum, to which we must turn.

Asylum, on the right bank of the Susquehannah near Wilkesbarre in Luzerne county, was begun as a land speculation by MM. Talon and de Noailles. Thither they proposed to move a colony of Santo Domingan creoles who, they reasoned, would make good farmers. Talon moved out to the tract in 1793 where he built a log house, leaving de Noailles

[101] *Voyages*, I, 17-22, 35-37, 38, 87, 94, 95.
[102] Michaux, "Diary," p. 93.
[103] Michaux, *Travels*, pp. 88-89. Michaux went down the Ohio and the Mississippi to New Orleans.
[104] *Democracy in America*, I, 320-321.

(who succeeded in involving Morris and Nicholson in the enterprise) to watch over the Philadelphia interests of the scheme. By 1795, when La Rochefoucauld-Liancourt visited the place, thirty houses had been built, inhabited by creoles, some émigrés from France, and a few French laborers and Americans. M. de Montulé was in charge of clearing the land, and the list of families is quite impressive: M. de Blacons, former deputy of Dauphiné who had married a de Maulde; their partner, M. Colin, formerly M. l'abbé de Sévigny of Toul; the said Montulé; Mde. de Sybert his "cousine"; M. de Bec-de Lièvre, a former canon; the MM. de la Roue, soldiers; M. Beaulieu, an infantry captain who had served in the United States; M. Bayard, late of Santo Domingo and a doctor; M. de Noailles; M. d'Andelot, an infantry officer from Franche-Comté; M. du Petit-Thouars, a naval officer with a romantic past; M. Norès, a student "de la Saint-Chappelle" who was now felling trees; M. Reting, an Irishman; M. Renaud, a rich merchant of Santo Domingo; M. Carler, formerly a canon of Quercy; M. Brevost, a bourgeois of Paris; Madame d'Autrepont, the widow of an intendant of Paris and her sons.[105] Potash, sugar, molasses, and vinegar were manufactured. One house was reserved for the king and queen of France should they escape. The colony lasted some ten years, when some departed for France and some for New Orleans. The settlement must have been quaint and interesting, for the houses had chimneys, doors, staircases, window-glass, shutters, piazzas, summer-houses—all unknown luxuries; and there were little French shops on the public square, a small chapel, and a theater and bakery. For a while a weekly express was maintained to Philadelphia, and accounts of the success of the enterprise later drew other Frenchmen to the Susquehannah. But the king and queen never came, and the settlement vanished.[106]

There were émigrés in New Jersey and Delaware besides. At Newark Liancourt found "une assez grande quantité de familles échapées" from the West Indies,[107] settling near Princeton and buying farms at Cedar Grove and Cherry Valley. They are described by a historian as "men of character and intelligence. Some of them belonged to noble families, and had possessed great wealth and high position," and curiously

---

[105] *Voyages*, I, 151-162; Rosengarten, pp. 69-73.
[106] Rosengarten, *French Colonists and Exiles*, pp. 99 ff.; *Voyages* as before.
[107] *Voyages*, III, 263.

enough, many were Huguenots, and some were liberal Catholics. Elizabethtown had its quota; and as a group they had Thomas P. Johnson, a lawyer who understood French, as their counsel.[108] Newark had likewise its French academy.[109] At Wilmington, Delaware, in 1797, La Rochefoucauld-Liancourt found about forty families from Santo Domingo, who had all saved something from the wreck; when a subscription list was opened for the more unfortunate among them, the generosity was abused until the administration of the fund was put in the hands of M. Thousard. Some were too proud to accept charity; and members of the group were sufficiently cultured to enlist the interest of General Dickinson of Pennsylvania.[110] Nor must we forget Dupont de Nemours, who, after many adventurings, died in Delaware in 1817, the friend of Jefferson and the projector of new schemes of education. And it may be pertinent to remark that when Priest was travelling in Delaware in 1794, he observed that Fort Mifflin had remained in a state of ruin "till last year when a french engineer was engaged to put it again into a state of defence," which he did in very modern style.[111]

In Maryland there were likewise groups of French émigrés. "Since the war," wrote Weld in 1795, "a great many French have arrived both from France and from West India Islands" and have settled in Baltimore.[112] The town gave a great deal of aid to the refugees, and the Maryland legislature subscribed as well.[113] The Santo-Domingans went in for gardening[114] as well as for art[115] and the usual accomplishments. Volney and Talleyrand were among those who visited, or

---

[108] Hageman, *Princeton and Its Institutions,* I, 191-205. The families included the Vienney, L'Homme, Jourdan, Jacob Pothier, Legay, St. Louis, Bona, Teisseire, Chiplon, La Rue, Joubert, Husage, Charles Ancellein and Tulane families. Obviously some of these are relics of the Huguenot migration of the seventeenth century. The last named had been treasurer of the civil government of Guadeloupe. Peter A. Malon, an émigré Jesuit priest, seems to have ministered to their spiritual wants, together with the Rev. Anthony Schmit.

[109] Saint-Méry, p. 125.

[110] *Voyages,* VI, 36-7.

[111] Priest, *Travels,* p. 75.

[112] *Travels,* p. 47.

[113] La Rochefoucauld-Liancourt, *Voyages,* VI, 178.

[114] Saint-Méry, *Voyages,* p. 89.

[115] Cf. Dunlap, *History of the Arts of Design,* III, 173-4. See also Baldwin, *Life and Letters of Simeon Baldwin,* p. 351.

planned to visit Baltimore, as Twining reports,[116] and Mr. and Mrs. Law entertained the French at Georgetown. At Ellicot's-mill, near Baltimore, La Rochefoucauld-Liancourt met three Frenchmen, including Thomas, former French consul in the city and his doctor, and certain difficulties arose in finding beds.[117] An interesting feature of the Baltimore migration was the incoming of French Catholic priests, to which we shall turn in a moment.

In Virginia Norfolk became a center of refuge, where the inhabitants "showed a constant affection for the French."[118] Saint-Méry in 1794 found the town crowded with unfortunate émigrés, of whom he mentions M. Longuemare, M. Marcet, M. Brière, M. Goynard, the captain of a French packet, the Baudrey family, Denard and his mother-in-law, Bousseant, M. Crousilles, and others. Mass was said for the refugees by an Irish priest. One gathers that these French were not so badly off as other groups.[119] La Rochefoucauld-Liancourt gives a long account of one Plumard de Rieux, near Bird-ordinary in Virginia, whose house had recently burned, and who was from Nantes.[120] In Petersburg in 1795 he found a Mr. Campbell who had married Mademoiselle de la Porte, niece of M. de Tubeuf, who, after three years in the back country, had been assassinated by two Irishmen.[121] And as late as 1824, at the reception for Lafayette in Richmond, there were a group of Frenchmen present, many of whom had come from Santo Domingo, or whose fathers were émigrés.[122] Doubtless other references may be found, but enough has been shown to indicate that the French in Virginia constituted a numerous group at the end of the eighteenth century.

There were some in North Carolina as well, but we must not stop for everything; let us turn our attention to Charleston, the center of French influence in the two Carolinas. The city was, as we have seen, a center of Huguenot life; and through-

---

[116] *Travels in America 100 Years Ago*, pp. 121-2, 105.

[117] *Voyages*, V, 115-6.

[118] Saint-Méry, *Voyages aux États-unis*, p. 56.

[119] *Voyages aux États-unis*, pp. 38-61. He speaks of "l'affluence des français" at Norfolk and says expenses were not high. Levasseur in 1824 found "a considerable number of French families who emigrated from St. Domingo in 1824." *Lafayette in America*, I, 192.

[120] *Voyages*, V, 11-13.

[121] *Ibid.*, IV, 340.

[122] Levasseur, I, 194.

out the eighteenth century it had been a place to which Frenchmen naturally came,[123] so that by the time of the French Revolution, the French had already exercised a considerable cultural influence.[124] From Santo Domingo came several hundred refugees, most of whom lived in or near the city.[125]
Concerning their general character and life we learn a good
deal from La Rochefoucauld-Liancourt:

Charleston is, as I have said, filled with French, the colonists from St.
Domingo and privateers (corsaires). Some of the colonists have
brought fortunes with them, and these are not entirely dissipated.
Many have not saved anything, or have nothing more, and live on the
product of the renting-out of some of their negroes whom they brought
with them. The opinions, or rather the political dialect, of the colonials
and of the privateers are very different; but love of play levels everything, and around the French gaming tables with which Charleston is
filled assemble alike the mad aristocrats (les aristocrates forcenés)
and the sans-culottes. They say that the stakes are high. French dema-
goguery has long prevailed in Charles-town, where for many years a
Jacobin club has been established, of which M. Harper, now a great
federalist, was a zealous member. Mangourit, the consul, predecessor
of the actual consul, was an assiduous member as well; but neither his
quality as agent of the French nation nor that as president of the club
prevented a French sailor from denouncing him to the club on the
suspicion of lack of patriotism (incivisme), or from hearing his own
exclusion from the society being pronounced, an exclusion which the
eloquence of an American perruquier, however, retarded and finally
prevented. Since the new French constitution, this club has submitted
to the same interdiction as those of France. At the moment of its
destruction it was composed only of Frenchmen, all the Americans,
including the perruquier who defended consul Mangourit, having
deserted it.[126]

Politics were warm in a town crowded with every conceivable
variety of opinion. The French were favorably received, how-

[123] For instance, in the *South Carolina Gazette,* February 14, 1774, there
is an advertisement that Mr. Valton's Concert of Vocal and Instrumental
Musick will be performed. In Josiah Quincy's *Journal,* there is the entry:
"One Abercrombie, a Frenchman just arrived, played the first violin and
a solo incomparably better than anyone I ever heard. He cannot speak
a word of English, and has a salary of five hundred guineas a year from
the Cecilia Society." Quoted in Willis, *The Charleston Stage,* p. 65. Again,
Schoepf notes that a French dancing master was the promoter of a dancing hall which later burned. (1783-4.) *Travels in the Confederation,* II,
168.
[124] See the charming book by Mrs. Ravenel, *Charleston: the Place and the
People.*
[125] Ramsay, *History of South Carolina,* I, 22.
[126] *Voyages,* IV, 70-71.

ever,[127] and soon had their place in society.[128] The numbers included bakers, pastry-cooks, dress-makers, hairdressers, and clearstarchers[129] as well as botanists[130] and physicians.[131] There was soon established a French theater which lasted from April to September of 1794, when it was partially merged with an American theater,[132] and there was an attempt in 1784 at a French newspaper.[133] If there were rows by seamen,[134] absurd Revolutionary clubs, and a warm reception for Genêt, yet the good temper of the émigrés, of whom a greater number seem to have been more permanent acquisitions than was the case among the Philadelphia group, led to a complete fusion between the French and the Americans.

We may pass rapidly over Georgia,[135] to dwell for a moment on the situation in New Orleans, shortly to become American. For this city, thanks to official regulations, we have very definite figures.[136] Some 4000 are said to have taken

[127] "The French refugees filled many posts of honor in Charleston's educational system, and Mme. Talvande's French Academy for Demoiselles was famous throughout the South." Willis, *The Charleston Stage*, p. 235. The French refugees from Santo Domingo "were soon taking an active part in the city's life, and many of them being accomplished, became teachers of the Arts and Sciences, and gave lessons in music, painting and the languages, and immediately some of the men took places in the Orchestras of the two theatres." McCrady, quoted in Willis, pp. 234-5.
[128] The city gave $12,500, and the state government, $1,750 in aid. Ravenel, p. 365. There were besides various benefit performances. Willis, p. 234. Edward Rutledge distinguished himself for his benevolence to the refugees. La Rochefoucauld-Liancourt, IV, 234-5.
[129] Ravenel, p. 366.
[130] La Rochefoucauld-Liancourt traveled with M. de Beauvois, very passionate for botany, a man of respectable and sweet character, IV, 91-2. Michaux's garden, just out of Charleston, interested him, although Michaux had been in America a great many years, IV, 80-81.
[131] Among the exiles was Doctor Polony, whose "knowledge of almost all the sciences makes him a remarkable man in any country in the world. He belongs to a great number of learned societies in Europe. The many journeys which he has made in all parts of North and South America, his profound knowledge and his good sense (bon esprit) have enabled him to enrich the academy of sciences with a great number of new and useful observations. In natural history and chemistry he was particularly esteemed by M. de Buffon, and this proves no less his active application to the sciences." *Ibid.*, IV, 71-2. The Duke also found in Charleston an old college friend, M. de la Chapelle, who was living in extreme poverty.
[132] See chap. x of Willis, and chap. xi below.
[133] Willis, p. 233-4.
[134] *Ibid.*, pp. 206-7.
[135] "The population had just been augmented by the arrival of a number of French colonists, refugees from late massacres in the West Indies" in 1791-2-3. Wade, *Augustus Baldwin Longstreet*, p. 15.
[136] Cf. Perez, "French Refugees in New Orleans in 1809," *Publications of the Southern History Association*, IX, 293-310.

refuge in New Orleans in 1791[137] including a troupe of actors, the first in Louisiana.[138] But a larger emigration was in store. More than 27,000 people had fled from Santo Domingo to Cuba in 1803, most of whom were agriculturalists. As a result of the French invasion of Spain in 1808, it was proclaimed on April 11, 1809, that they must leave Cuba, and the Governor requested the American vessels in the harbor to transport them to the United States. They were taken to New Orleans; 55 shiploads, it is said, were landed from May to August, a total of 6,060 emigrants, including 1,887 whites, 2060 free blacks, and 2113 slaves. In addition some 1484 came in August. The care of them proved to be a serious problem. "I regret," wrote Claiborne to the Secretary of State, "to see a space in our society filled with a foreign population, which I had hoped would have been occupied by native citizens of the United States," but he eased the regulation against them, and in August he wrote: "I have not had one complaint lodged with me against any of them since the first arrivals to this date. Their conduct generally breathes respect for our Laws; and their industry and activity (are) astonishing indeed." He says that two-thirds of the males possess some trade (he enumerates cabinet makers, turners, cakers (caulkers), glaziers, and upholsterers), and says that some are in the hospital; and Claiborne was eventually compelled to warn new-comers that, because of the crowded conditions in the city, they could not bring in their slaves.[139] To the same city came Louis Philippe and his brothers in 1798 where they were entertained by the great creole families, and there were others. When, however, the British counted on the help of the refugees against Americans in the War of 1812, it was found that their sentiments had become pro-American; and even the French pirates like Lafitte and Dominique Yon fought against Packenham.[140]

We must note also the great Scioto project in the West. Speculation in American real estate had gone hand in hand with dreams of a perfect society in the primitive wilderness.[141]

[137] See *Publications of the Louisiana Historical Society*, VII, 137.
[138] Fortier, *History of Louisiana*, II, 146.
[139] The correspondence is in Perez, *op. cit.*
[140] Rosengarten, pp. 50-51; Fortier, II, 171-2. See the article on Major Auguste Davezac, the friend of Livingston and Jackson, in the *Democratic Review*, XVI, 109-111 (February, 1845).
[141] Faÿ, pp. 178 ff; Rosengarten, pp. 106-120.

Some of these speculations involved vast tracts of land. Gouverneur Morris, while abroad, was active in speculation; in 1789 he broached the project to be located on the St. Lawrence river to his French friends; and in 1790 he wrote Robert Morris that frequent applications were being made to him for advice in the purchase of American lands and advised the opening of a Parisian land office. When Donatien and Le Ray de Chaumont came to settle the problem of certain loans to the colonies, they bought large tracts of land in northern New York.[142] We shall return to this project in discussing the Bonapartist exiles. More famous, however, is the Scioto project, which had its remoter origin in the same years. Into the intricate and dubious details of the origin of the company, there is not space to go.[143] M. du Val d'Eprésmesnil, a councillor of the parlement of Paris and a member of the National Assembly, was the principal organizer of the project, which involved the purchase of a tract of land in Ohio through Barlow, Duer, Cutler, and Playfair, an Englishman, members of the Ohio Company. The Americans sold, not a title, but a pre-emption to the land, the difference not being made known to the French emigrants at the time. A prospectus was issued, and although there were rumors that the land was valueless, d'Eprésmesnil "bought" a thousand acres in 1790 with his wife; and a little later, 10,000 acres, which he did not live to see.[144] A *Compagnie du Scioto* was formed of some 24 members.[145] Into the scene came then the curious figure of Lezay-Marnésia, a dreaming deputy of the National Assembly, author of a pamphlet, now extremely rare, *Lettres écrites des rives de l'Ohio*, which was seized by the police. Lezay-Marnésia sought an environment in which his peculiar moral, religious, and social

[142] Thirty thousand acres in Franklin County, 73,000 in St. Lawrence County, 143,500 in Jefferson County, 100,000 in Lewis County. Rosengarten, pp. 16-8.

[143] Consult Carré, *Les émigrés français en Amérique, 1789-93;* Belote, *The Scioto Speculation;* E. C. Dawes, "The Scioto Purchase of 1787," *Magazine of American History,* XXII, 470-482; Volney, *View of the Soil and Climate of the United States,* pp. 322-330; S. P. Hildreth, "History of an Early Voyage on the Ohio and Mississippi Rivers," *The American Pioneer,* I, 94-95 (March, 1842) ; and the letter from Waldurard Mentelle, *ibid.,* II, 182-187 (April, 1843).

[144] He was held back by laws against emigrating, got as far as Havre, where he was arrested, returned to Paris, and was executed in 1794. Carré, p. 312.

[145] There seem to have been two companies, but we may omit the more intricate details.

theories could be worked out; he was the enthusiast of the movement.[146] An excited discussion over the project began in France, and all sorts of people expressed their views, a common idea being that the colonists were charlatans, visionaries or dupes. However that may be, Marnésia and Malartie left Havre on 26 May, 1790, aboard an English ship with 119 passengers, of whom thirty were "people of distinction," the rest being laborers, farmers and the like, and landed at Alexandria, Maryland, after 67 days on the ocean. While the general project seems to have had the approval of many prominent Americans, the emigrants, who eventually numbered in all some six hundred, discovered when they removed to the new Eden, first, that the land was not theirs and second, that it was not the Paradise they had dreamed of. The Chevalier du Bac arrived in October, sent by d'Eprésmesnil as a kind of supervisor, but the city of refuge did not materialize. Finding their titles vague, some removed to Chemingo on the Tyogo River, where the land proved too rocky; and then into Pennsylvania where, between Wysall and Wyalusing on the Susquehannah they founded Frenchtown.[147] Others took advantage of a grant of land made in their behalf by Congress in 1795, of 24,000 acres opposite the mouth of the Little Sandusky, to settle on the "French grant."[148] Others, utterly weary, sold their rights and went to the Mississippi or to Louisiana.[149] The town, Gallipolis,[150] and Gallia county remained the chief memorials of this oddly fated enterprise, the significance of which lies rather in the mood in which it was conceived than in any practical influence on American life—that mood of dreamy idealism which was a common French attitude of mind where the New World was concerned.

[146] He asked the colonists for "billets de confession" which they often forged; he preferred "femmes grosses" for colonists; he insisted that d'Eprésmesnil should be the model legislature for the colony, a role that d'Eprésmesnil was not loath to assume. He later wrote: "Il faut à mon coeur un espace plus libre. J'ai besoin de consolations. Je tiendrai toutes mes promesses. Aucun des soins qu'exigera le bonheur de la colonie naissante ne sera negligé; et si la Providence me laisse assez de jours, ou permet qu'on me succède avec les mêmes vues, j'espère que mon établissement produira d'heureux fruits, non seulement pour l'Amérique septentrionale, mais encore pour l'humanité entière." Carré, p. 317.

[147] Hall, *Travels in Canada and the United States.* Most of these returned to France, except the Le Fevre family.

[148] McMaster, II, 149-151.

[149] Schulz, *Travels,* I, 170-173. See also Michaux, "Diary," p. 94. Michaux found various other émigrés scattered over the West, pp. 102-7.

[150] See Ashe's *Travels,* Letters XVIII and XX.

Nor can we leave this aspect of French migration without some reference to the effect upon the Catholic Church in America.[151] Some 46,000 priests refused to take the Oath of the Clergy prescribed by the Revolutionary government in 1790, and many of these fled to the United States. In the period immediately following the episcopate of Carroll (died 1815) the six episcopal sees in the United States were ruled by French ecclesiastics who had fled from the chaotic upheaval of their own land during Carroll's time.[152] Five priests and two seminarists were on the boat that brought Chateaubriand to Baltimore; there they established a Sulpitian seminary in 1791; in 1792 eight more came; from 1793 to 1798 some twenty-nine more.[153] The first Catholic priest came to Charleston about 1786, but ground for a building—St. Mary's—was not purchased until 1789. By 1790 there were 200 Roman Catholics; by 1791, there were 400 or 500. In this year a legislative act incorporated the church as the Roman Catholic Church of Charleston; and in 1793 the ministry of Father Gallagher did much to allay bitterness.[154] The whole émigré movement necessarily did much to build up and extend the influence of the Catholic Church in the United States.[155]

Another element of the emigration which should be remembered is the group of travellers and observers which came from it. Possibly André Michaux, botanist and agent for the French government, does not belong with the émigré group; but although his mission was ostensibly scientific, he seems to have been also a political agent for the French Republic. General Collot undertook a voyage down the Ohio and Missisippi at the behest of Adet who desired to have a military survey of the valley. This was undertaken in 1796; Collot got himself arrested by Carondelet in New Orleans, who did not, however, retain him long, for Collot went to Philadelphia and then to France, where he died in 1805, but not before

[151] See chap. x, below.
[152] Guilday, *The Life and Times of John Carroll, Archbishop of Baltimore,* p. 417.
[153] Rosengarten, pp. 99-100; de Courcy and Shea, *History of the Catholic Church in the United States,* pp. 65-68. Many of these later went to Canada.
[154] Hopkins, Thomas F., D. D., "St. Mary's Church, Charleston, S. C.," in the *Year Book* (1897) *City of Charleston,* pp. 427-502. A schism existed, 1815-1821 because the congregation, and not the priest, owned the church.
[155] De Courcy and Shea, chapters vi, xxiii, xxxix in particular.

publishing his *Voyage down the Ohio and the Mississippi* in two volumes.[156] Greatest among the literary exiles was Chateaubriand, over the authencity of whose *Travels in America and Italy* a controversy has raged.[157] His book is certainly a compound of borrowing from Bartram, Carver and Imlay, and he did not make all the journeys that he said he made, but there seems to be no reason for doubting that he was in the United States; that, for instance, he came to Baltimore and that his letter was received by Washington and probably that he travelled over part of the route he describes. Saint-Méry, whose *Voyages* we have had occasion to quote, travelled from Virginia at least as far as New York, and in Philadelphia opened a bookstore and printing press which became a center of French influence. Opinion varies regarding the quality of his observations.[158] Most philosophical of travellers was La Rochefoucauld-Liancourt, who visited all parts of the United States except the West and the lower South, who visited all the leading men, and whose book was, until de Tocqueville, the best French book on the United States. Most influential of travellers in the sequel was Louis Philippe who, with his brothers, explored most of the country, including the West,[159] and who drew from his experiences an affection for the country which was to serve us well in the quarrel over the spoliations claims under Jackson. Volney, who enjoyed a reputation for wisdom before he was attacked by Priestley as an atheist, seems to have been received with various degrees of hostility and warmth; in the opinion of Professor Chinard, his work on the United States is a remarkably modern document.[160] Besides these there were other

[156] Cruzat, "General Collot's Arrest in New Orleans," *Louisiana Historical Quarterly,* I, 303-20.

[157] See Armstrong, "Chauteabriand's America, Arrival in America and First Impressions," *Publications of the Modern Language Association* (new series) XV, 345-70; Chinard, "Notes sur le Voyage de Chateaubriand en Amérique," *University of California Publications in Modern Philology,* IV, 269-349.

[158] On his publications see *Voyages,* pp. xx-xxi, on his itinerary, pp. xix-xx. His last days were embittered by the hostile feeling which gave shape to the Alien Bill, under which de Méry was in a sense proscribed (p. xxvii), but it seems a little harsh to speak of his book as a "chef-d'oeuvre of wounded fatuity and shortsightedness." Faÿ, p. 269.

[159] On various anecdotes on Louis Philippe in the West see Latrobe, *The Rambler in North America,* II, 105-8; Buckingham, *America, Eastern and Western States,* II, 184; Willis, *Pencillings by the Way,* p. 134.

[160] See Chinard, *Volney et l'Amérique.* For various anecdotes concerning Volney's reception see Faux, *Memorable Days in America,* p. 457; Buck-

travellers like Étienne Marchant, an early writer on Alaska, Baudry des Louzières, Milfort, Bossu, Berquin-Duvallon, Perrin du Lac and Captain Bourgeois, not to speak of François André Michaux, son of the Michaux already mentioned,[161] as well as J. E. Bonnet and Mandrillon, whose work comes a little earlier. And perhaps one should not forget (though they did not write books) itinerant musicians like Gehot and Victor Pelissier.[162]

3. ROYALIST REFUGEES IN AMERICA

Under the Napoleonic regime a group of royalist exiles found their way to America. Hyde de Neuville, future ambassador to the United States, was here from 1807 to 1814, during which time he corresponded with various royalists. His friends included the Crugers, the Wilkes, the Churches, the Simonds, the Roulets and the Moreaus, most of whom were also exiles from the Emperor. After two years in a French prison his brother joined him in New York, and later became Dr. Neuville of that city. In 1816 Hyde de Neuville was made French minister to the United States.[163] It is, however, difficult to distinguish this group from the general émigré group we have been describing.[164]

4. BONAPARTIST EXILES IN AMERICA

Of greater importance were the Bonapartist exiles in America. A royal ordinance of 24 July, 1815,[165] stipulated

ingham, *America, Eastern and Western States,* II, 414-5. He completed his travels just when animosity against France was growing. "They fancied that I was engaged in a conspiracy (me, a single solitary Frenchman) to throw Louisiana into the hands of the directory." *View of the Soil and Climate of the United States,* p. vii.

[161] Sherrill, *French Memories,* pp. 7-24.

[162] Sonneck, *Miscellaneous Studies,* pp. 54-55.

[163] Rosengarten, pp. 176-9. On Victor Moreau, "whose clemency demands the fairest page in the annals of mankind" in John Davis's opinion, see Kellogg, *Life and Works of John Davis,* pp. 95-7.

[164] For instance, who were the French whom Melish found in Pittsburg in 1810? *Travels,* p. 317.

[165] However, other Bonapartists had come before the arrival of the group described. In *Hall's Wilmington Gazette* for November 15, 1798, for instance, there is a paragraph copied from the *Gazette of the United States* which runs: "Our readers will doubtless recollect to have seen frequent mention of Surrurier, as commander of a sub-horde of the plunderers of Italy, under Buonaparte. As every miscreant who has ever held communication with our infernal enemy ought, at this time to be noted, and narrowly watched; it is thought proper thus publicly to mention that he has recently arrived in this country."

that a given list of generals and officers who had betrayed the king were to be arrested and tried before councils of war in various parts of France.[166] A second list was prepared of those who were to quit Paris in three days and retire to the provinces in places indicated by the minister of police until the Chamber should decide their fate—trial or exile.[167] On December 6, 1815, Richelieu presented the Chamber with a project of amnesty which the Chamber would not accept,[168] and during 1816, to escape persecution, many fled to the United States, how many is not definitely known. Certain prominent exiles deserve to be listed. Joseph Bonaparte came with the sons of General Murat, the ex-King of Naples; the two Lallemands (Charles and Henri), after adventurous careers, arrived in 1817; General Rigaud escaped to the United States after being condemned to death; Lefebvre-Desnouettes, whom even Hyde de Neuville praised, left for the New World shortly after Waterloo; Grouchy came to live in Philadelphia, but returned to France in 1819; and Bertrand, General Vandamme, Le Comte Réal, Regnault de Saint-Jean d'Angély, Garnier de Saintes and Lakanal are important figures in this movement.[169] Regarding the movements of the group our information is not too definite. In 1815, through du Ponceau, Joseph Bonaparte acquired 150,-000 acres in New York as a refuge for Napoleon, should he ever escape, and a site for a manufacturing establishment. Le Ray Chaumont built a large house at Le Rayville, ten miles east of Watertown, where he entertained many notables; and in 1815 Joseph Bonaparte came to look over the land. In 1828 Joseph built a hunting lodge and, dressed in a green hunting suit, he could be seen driving over the forest roads in his coach and six or riding in his six-oared gondola on the Black river.[170] But he did not make it his permanent abode.

---

[166] Philips, *Les Réfugiés Bonapartistes,* p. 12. This list included the two Lallemands, Lefebvre-Desnouettes, Grouchy, and Clausel, all of whom escaped to the United States.

[167] This list included Réal, Dirat, Reynault, Garnier de Saintes, and de Cluis, all of whom went to the United States. Philips, pp. 12-15.

[168] Philips, *op. cit.*; Moreton Macdonald, *A History of France,* III, chap. xxxv.

[169] Philips, pp. 19-34, traces the careers of these various people. See Rosengarten, pp. 159 ff; Reeves, "The Napoleonic Exiles in America," *The Johns Hopkins University Studies in History and Political Science,* XXIII, Nos. 9-10.

[170] Rosengarten, pp. 108-112. Joseph Bonaparte sold his land to La Farge in 1835.

After considering the purchase of Hunter's Island near Long Island,[171] he purchased his famous estate near Bordentown,[172] from whence he made occasional visits to Philadelphia, and where, among his art treasures, he entertained, in addition to the Napoleonic exiles already named, Combes, de Girardin, Latapie, Miot de Mélito, Quinet, the two sons of Fouché, Eugene Ney, duc de Montebello, Lafayette, and his own relatives, Charles and Jerome.[173] Jerome, who had married Elizabeth Patterson of Baltimore in 1803, did not return to America, although his son, Jerome Napoleon Bonaparte, became an American citizen,[174] and the founder of the American Bonapartes. Charles Lucien Bonaparte, who made notable contributions to science, was in America for some years with Jerome, but returned to Italy in 1828: he was instrumental in bringing Agassiz to this country in 1846 and at one time planned to come to the United States with him.[175]

To return, however, to the tracts of land in western New York, one finds that Le Ray Chaumont sold various parcels of it to Caullaincourt, Réal, Grouchy, de Furneaux, and (possibly) to Madame de Staël.[176] But the New York exiles were overshadowed in political importance by the famous attempt of the Vine and Olive Society to cultivate land in Alabama.[177]

This group it was which aroused the suspicions of Hyde de Neuville. Indeed some vague plan for rescuing Napoleon seems to have existed among them.[178] The facts of the coloni-

---

[171] Stuart, *Three Years in North America*, II, 19.
[172] Often described. See chapter viii, p. 271, footnotes; and add *A Subaltern's Furlough*, I, 124; Levasseur, *Lafayette in America*, II, 251; Darusmont, *Views of the Society and Manners in America*, letter, viii; Montulé, *A Journey to North America in 1817*, p. 5; Buckingham, *America, Eastern and Western States*, I, 456; and Power, *Impressions of America*, I, 338.
[173] Philips, p. 55. See the obituary notice of Joseph Bonaparte in the *Proceedings of the American Philosophical Society for 1840*. There is a study, *Joseph Bonaparte en Amérique* (Paris, 1893) by G. Bertlin, which I have not seen.
[174] Didier, *Life and Letters of Madame Bonaparte*, pp. 5-10; Bernhard, *Travels in North America*, I, 38.
[175] Herrick, *Audubon the Naturalist*, I, 329; Agassiz, *Louis Agassiz*, I, 355.
[176] This group tried to cultivate vines and mulberries in Jefferson county, New York. Rosengarten, pp. 108-112.
[177] "Much is expected from the exertions of a French colony lately settled in the Alabama territory, whose principal object is the culture of the vine." *Blowe's Immigrants' Directory* (1820), p. 89.
[178] See Philips, pp. 35-49; Reeves, *op. cit.*; Pickett, *History of Alabama*, chapter xlv; Haines, *The State of Alabama*, pp. 23-24; Rosengarten, pp. 159 ff.

zation project are these: After some attempts at founding a colony in Pennsylvania, Parmentier obtained land in Alabama in 1817;[179] and thither in 1818 a group of enthusiasts made their way. Near St. Stephens on the Tombigbee they built Demopolis and attempted to cultivate the vine and olive.[180] Twice, however, owing to uncertain surveys, they were compelled to move their town. The group was a distinguished one, including as it did Lefebvre-Desnouettes, Peniers, Nicholas Raoul, Cluis, and Simon Chaudron, editor of *L'Abeille Américaine*.[181] This colony, together with the one in Texas, frightened Hyde de Neuville into believing that a Napoleonic invasion of Mexico was in the offing with Joseph Bonaparte as Emperor.

But, in the midst of all their trials and vissitudes [says a contemporary account], the French refugees were happy. Immured in the depths of the Tombigby forest, where for several years want pressed them on all sides—cut off from their friends in France—surrounded by the Choctaws on one side, and the unprincipled squatters and land-thieves on the other—assailed by the venom of insects and prostrating fevers —nevertheless, their native gaiety prevailed. Being in the habit of much social intercourse, their evenings were spent in conversation, music and dancing. The larger portion were well educated, while all had seen much of the world, and such materials were ample to afford an elevated society. Sometimes their distant friends sent them rich wines and other luxuries, and upon such occasions parties were given, and the foreign delicacies brought back many interesting associations. Well cultivated gardens, and the abundance of wild game, rendered the common living of the French quite respectable. The female circle was highly interested. They had brought with them their books, guitars,

---

[179] Congress authorized a sale of 90,000 acres of public land on a credit of fourteen years, leaving it optional with the French what part of the public domain they would choose. They chose Alabama because the climate was reported to resemble that of France and because the soil was suitable for vineyards. Haines, p. 23.

[180] When Mrs. Anne Royall was in Knoxville she met a traveller in 1825 or 1826 who told her of the settlement of the French in Demopolis, and described their awkward method of clearing the ground for a vineyard. A falling tree had killed two and crippled several. He reported that they were not only ignorant, but given to all manner of vice, and that they had no way of earning a living except by peddling. *Sketches*, pp. 25-26. Rumor painted full of tongues seems responsible for this extraordinary paragraph! Bernhard, whose observations are, unlike Mrs. Royall's, reliable, says that after the failure of the vine-and-olive idea, some began to cultivate cotton, and others disposed of their land profitably and went to various parts of the country as dancing and fencing masters, shopkeepers, or croupiers at hazard tables in Mobile and New Orleans. At the time of his visit (1826) there were but five French people living at Demopolis. *Travels*, II, 34-5.

[181] Raoul had commanded Napoleon's advance guard on his return to Paris. Peniers had been a member of the National Assembly. Haines, p. 24.

silks, parasols and ribbons, and the village, in which most of them dwelt, resembled, at night, a miniature French town. And then, further in the forest, others lived, the imprints of whose beautiful Parisian shoes on the wild prairie, occasionally arrested the glance of a solitary traveller. And then, again, when the old imperial heroes talked of their emperor, their hearts were warmed with sympathy, their eyes kindled with enthusiasm, and tears stole down their furrowed cheeks.[182]

Alas, the colony melted away, like all the others.

A second attempt was made to found a city of refuge in Texas. This was particularly under the leadership of General Rigaud and the two Lallemands. In 1818 the expedition, numbering eventually some 300 or 400, set sail for Galveston, equipped, it must be confessed, more like a plundering expedition than like an agricultural one, and after being welcomed by Jean Lafitte, landed at Galveston. General Charles Lallemand arrived with the remainder in March, when the united companies moved from Galveston to a place on the Trinity River which they christened the Champ d'Asile. General Lallemand issued a political proclamation,[183] which aroused some enthusiasm in France, where it was republished in *La Minerve,* the anti-government organ. A subscription of 100,000 francs was raised to support the colony, in honor of which Béranger composed a song, but the fund never reached Lallemand. The military discipline imposed by Lallemand and the terrors of the climate and of frontier life proved too impossible, and a retreat was ordered to Galveston. Some joined D'Auvray who planned to wrest Texas from Spain; others drifted to New Orleans or Philadelphia. Once again, the French had proved unsuccessful in establishing a colony.[184]

In addition to such centers as these, Bonapartist exiles were scattered over the country. Bryant, for instance, had French

---

[182] From conversations with contemporaries in Pickett, pp. 623-33. Cf. Philips, pp. 80-96.

[183] Reeves, pp. 85-86. *The Analectic Magazine* prints an account, translated from the *Minerve Français* for September, 1818, and protests against French usurpation. XIII, 58-63 (Jan. 1819).

[184] Reeves, chapters vi and vii. At Cahawba, Alabama, in 1825 Lafayette met at a public dinner some Frenchmen who "had been driven from France by political events. They recounted to us how they had once belonged to the unfortunate colony of Champ d'Asile. They now live in a small town which they have founded in the state of Alabama, and which they have named Gallipolis. Everything led me to suppose that they are not in a very prosperous state. I suspect their European prejudices, and their ignorance of commerce and agriculture, will prevent them, for a long time, from becoming powerful rivals of the Americans." Levasseur, *Lafayette in America,* II, 93.

lessons from an officer of Napoleon's army who lived in Great Barrington, Massachusetts (1824), and with whom he corresponded in French.[185] When Fearon went to visit Cobbett on his Long Island farm in 1817, he met there a "French gentleman" who "had been in the suite of Napoleon" and who "whistled and sang with a thoughtless gaiety peculiarly French" and talked to him about Napoleon.[186] Mrs. Anne Royall, journeying by coach from Washington to Baltimore in 1824, discovered that one of the passengers was a "very lively" Frenchman who was a friend, and perhaps an officer of Bonaparte, wore a threadbare coat, and possessed a highly improved and polished mind.[187] Hodgson found at Charles Carroll's a French count with a budget of news (July, 1820), as well as a "little lapdog, which Lord Wellington gave to Madam Jerome Bonaparte."[188] In Pennsylvania, besides the Philadelphia group, there were various scattered Bonapartists. For instance, Howitt, crossing the Delaware into Pennsylvania at Milford in 1819, "met with a French emigrant, ignorant of the English language, who had arrived four months ago; he had brought with him watches and shoes," and he "spoke with enthusiasm of Napoleon."[189] Stuart, visiting Frankford, picked him some interesting anecdotes of Waterloo in that village.[190] General Bernard cut an important figure in the annals of New York and Washington.[191] In North Carolina Peter Ney was long thought to be Maréchal Ney, and men now living remember Captain Martino of Hillsboro, an old soldier of Napoleon.[192] Achille Murat married a Mrs. Gray of Virginia and

---

[185] Godwin, *Biography of William Cullen Bryant*, I, 205. He later boarded in New York with M. Evrard and his family, who tried to convert him to Catholicism, pp. 214 ff.

[186] *Sketches of America*, p. 65. He met Genêt who was living in retirement at Albany (p. 129), describes Joseph Bonaparte's home (pp. 132-3), and in Philadelphia saw "Talleyrand's oath of allegiance to the United States in his own hand-writing." (P. 154.)

[187] His stories seem to have had the *esprit gaulois*. See *Sketches*, pp. 183-4.

[188] *Letters from North America*, I, 326-7.

[189] *Letters from the United States*, p. 22.

[190] *Three Years in North America*, II, 37.

[191] See Murat, *A Moral and Political Sketch of the United States of America*, p. 260; Darusmont, *Views of Society and Manners in America*, pp. 40-43; Ouseley, *Remarks on the . . . United States*, p. 103; Philips, pp. 73-79.

[192] Ney was the image of the marshal, except for the absence of a silver plate in his skull. Both the above facts were kindly communicated to me by Major Kane of Chapel Hill. On the Ney legend see Weston, *Historic Doubts as to the Execution of Marshal Ney*.

bought a plantation near Tallahassee, Florida, where he was visited by Emerson, who liked him;[193] and he wrote an original and interesting book on his adopted country.[194] In New Orleans, the Napoleon fever raged. As early as 1784 Pontalba submitted a memoir on Louisiana to Napoleon. In the battle of New Orleans, General Humbert, who had lost Napoleon's favor, commanded under Jackson, went in 1816 to fight for Mexican independence, and returned to die in 1823. General Moreau, Latour of the French Polytechnic School, and Lefebvre all aided in the battle. Lakanal added another chapter to his stormy career in education, serving as principal of the College of New Orleans, retiring thence to a farm on Mobile Bay, and returning to France in 1837.[195] When Montulé visited New Orleans in April, 1817, he went to the Hotel Trimoulet, where Lefebvre, Bernard and "Lallemant" were lodging, and where he found a society of thirty persons, twenty of whom had quitted France for political reasons; they "spoke freely of politics and government"—that is to say, there were stormy discussions of the kind exiles indulge in.[196] The Napoleon mania would not be daunted. A residence was built for the Emperor (it is still pointed out) at Chartres and St. Louis streets by Nicholas Girod, in the hope that he might escape from St. Helena. Indeed, his escape was planned; the ship *Seraphine* was built and equipped to rescue him. Under command of Captain Bossier and Dominique Yon, the expedition set sail but it returned when it was signalled by a French merchantman that Napoleon had died May 5, 1821.[197] Antommarchi brought his death mask instead, (some doubt has been cast on its authenticity) which may still be seen in the Cabildo, for the town is full of Napoleonic relics. America was still a refuge for Europe in the first half of the nineteenth century.

[193] *Journals of Emerson, 1824-32*, pp. 182-3; Didier, *Life and Letters of Madame Bonaparte*, p. 110 note.

[194] *The Moral and Political Sketch of the United States.* The first letter gives a general view of the union; the second discusses the origin and history of parties; the third, the frontier; the fourth, slavery; the fifth, religion; the sixth, justice; the seventh, the laws; the eighth, the army and navy and Indians; the ninth, finance; the tenth, manners, fine arts and literature. London edition, 1833.

[195] Rosengarten, pp. 43-44. Lakanal had once settled near Vevay, Indiana.

[196] Montulé, *Voyage to North America in 1817*, pp. 49-50. He went hunting with M. Laurent and with General de Laure, and left New Orleans in May, pp. 51-56.

[197] Cline, *Art and Artists in New Orleans* p. 4.

5. THE FRENCH IN THE MISSISSIPPI BASIN NORTH OF NEW ORLEANS

The Americans passing westward came into contact with a French culture unique and old in the great Mississippi basin, which they absorbed or destroyed. The first permanent settlement in the Mississippi valley had been the founding of the Jesuit mission at Kaskaskia in 1684. Tonti came to Illinois with twenty Canadian settlers in 1700, and Cadillac sent a hundred French to settle Detroit in 1701. Vincennes seems to have been settled as early as 1735. Alabama was opened to French settlers in 1736. By 1768 there were 600 white French in Kaskaskia, 300 in Cahokia, 300 in Vincenness, 600 in Detroit, most of the inhabitants being Picards or Normans. By 1750 five French villages had an estimated population of 1100 whites and 300 blacks; by 1784 there were 400 French families in the Illinois country, 400 at Vincennes, and 400 at Kaskaskia and Cahokia. By 1787 there were 520 French at Vincennes, 121 at Kaskaskia, 239 at Cahokia, 11 at St. Philippe, 78 at Prairie du Rocher, making, with the stragglers, 1040 French on the Wabash and in the Illinois country as against 240 Americans.[198] Burr, in his careful figures in *America's Race Heritage,* estimates that there were 40,000 French in the Northwest Territory and Vermont in 1790, 15,000 in the Illinois country and the Western posts, and 14,000 in Louisiana and West Florida, a total of 69,000 French outside the territory of the thirteen original states.[199] Necessarily, the great bulk of these did not live in the characteristic old-world communities like Detroit or Kaskaskia, which the British had left undisturbed.

Three generations of life in the wilderness had rendered these settlements unique. Communal villages, the portion of the common set aside was divided into strips of one arpent in front by forty in depth, which were then allotted to members of the village; the farms which were privately owned ran back in long strips from a narrow front along some stream. The people were tillers of the soil, blacksmiths, carpenters, hunters, and traders, not especially industrious and thrifty, satisfied with crude implements and much ignorance. The form of government was patriarchal, the commandant of the fort being the little father of the community, and they never did understand American ways. "The little villages in which they dwelt were

[198] Rosengarten, pp. 13-28, based on Roosevelt.
[199] Pp. 252-258.

pretty places, with wide shaded streets. The houses lay far apart, often a couple of hundred feet from one another. They were built of heavy hewn timbers; those of the better sort were furnished with broad verandas, and contained large, low-ceilinged rooms, the high mantel-pieces and the moldings of the doors and windows being made of curiously carved wood. Each village was defended by a palisaded fort and blockhouses, and was occasionally surrounded by a high wooden stockade."[200] Such was the organization of every French village in the vast basin of the Mississippi north of New Orleans. Such was the civilization utterly incapable of withstanding the rude shock of Clark and his frontiersmen in 1778-9, or the oncoming of the pioneer Americans.[201]

Imlay estimated in 1797 that the inhabitants of the Ohio country did not, including French, amount to five thousand in 1797,[202] and Volney calculated that of these 2,500 were of French origin.[203] Other Frenchmen came in, however. Sometime before May, 1803, a young Frenchman named Francis Dacosta (the name itself is Portuguese) bought a farm at Mill Grove, Pennsylvania, and later tried lead-mining there. J. J. Audubon came to Mill Grove, and by 1806, Ferdinand Rozier had come out with him, the son of his father's partner. Together they closed the Mill Grove enterprise and moved on to the Ohio, and eventually the Mississippi.[204] The inhabitants of Pittsburg, wrote Stuart in 1830, are "a mixture of all nations—Germans, Irish, English, Scotch, French, etc."[205] Pavie found a man there who had accompanied Lafayette, in 1832, as well as various other Frenchmen.[206] Ashe met in Cincinnati in 1806 "some French emigrants (who) took up their

[200] Roosevelt, I, chap. ii.
[201] "Throughout the West, communities of Frenchmen, living under such conditions as those which have been described, retained, it is true, an almost inalienable social charm, but soon lost nearly every trace of the mental alertness characteristic of their race. They seem to have taken little interest in the political and civic affairs with which their neighbors of English stock busied themselves." Rusk, *Literature of the Middle Western Frontier*, I, 9. Their poverty is shown by the nickname "Paincourt" for St. Louis, and "Vide Poche" for Carondelet. *Ibid.*, I, 8.
[202] *Topographical Description*, pp. 497-502. Patrick Kennedy's *Journal*.
[203] Chinard, *Volney et l'Amérique*, p. 48.
[204] Herrick, *Audubon the Naturalist*, I, 113; chap. viii; and see the index under Rozier.
[205] *Three Years in North America*, II, 512.
[206] *Souvenirs Atlantiques*, II, 35.

abode in Cincinnati, and their publicity consists in their introduction of the dance, music, billiards, and the fabric of liquors, sweetmeats and savory patties."[207] Michaux, in 1802, found a Frenchman at Marietta who had established a "plantation" above the town on the banks of the great Muskingum.[208] In Chillicothe Montulé met "Mr. Belage," who was interested in mounds, in 1817.[209] The inhabitants of Cincinnati in 1827 were, according to the author of *The Americans as They are,* chiefly American born, with some admixture of German, French, and Irish, in consequence of which "freedom of thought prevails in a high degree, and toleration is exercised without limitation."[210]

Louisville, Kentucky, was something of a French center, but rather because of emigration than because it was an early settlement. Twenty-four Catholic families came there in 1785 from Maryland. In 1793 Bishop Carroll sent M. Badin of New Orleans as their spiritual director; and in 1797-99 a group of French priests, exiles, came from France. As a result of this interest, an episcopal see was established at Bardstown, Kentucky, where the French Trappists later built a convent, and Bourbon County, Paris, Versailles, Louisville, all owe their names to this, and similar migration.[211] By 1817-18 Shippingport had become a small center. Cobbett stopped there "at the house of Mr. Berthoud, a very respectable French gentleman" for two nights and a day;[212] and Montulé describes the immense flour mill which belonged to the celebrated Tarascon brothers, exporters to New Orleans, who welcomed Rafinesque to Kentucky.[213] In Louisville itself the café Napoleon was a center for the French of Kentucky.[214] These are, however, on the fringes of the original French settlement.

Volney, who went down the Ohio to Louisville and thence

[207] *Travels,* II, 178.
[208] Michaux, *Travels,* 113.
[209] *Voyage to North America in 1817,* pp. 82-83.
[210] Pp. 5, 9. Perhaps the passenger list of a keelboat on the Ohio in 1827 may be indicative of the character of the population. There were 10 ladies, 11 gentlemen, including three planters from Louisiana and Mississippi, three merchants, of whom one was a Frenchman, a lawyer from Tennessee, and two doctors. The Frenchman found fault with everything but the dinner. Pp. 54-55.
[211] Rosengarten, pp. 97-98.
[212] Cobbett's *Year's Residence,* Part III, 467. Berthoud was the brother-in-law of Audubon. Herrick, *Audubon the Naturalist,* I, 303.
[213] Montulé, *Voyage to North America in 1817,* p. 78; Herrick, *op. cit.,* I; 291.
[214] Pavie, *Souvenirs Atlantiques* (1832), II, 72.

to Vincennes, Cahokia, and the other French towns, including
"St. Lewis," in 1796-7, found the civilization in a state of
decay, the French ignorant, and filled with "apathy, indolence,
and poverty." The Americans were rapidly supplanting them;
the French, he thought, could not bear competition with the
less impetuous, more patient and dogged American stock.[215]
Melish in 1810 found the settlements backward; "it is only
of late that any material progress has been made."[216] Cahokia
in 1819 is described as "a miserable dirty little hole." "The pig
pens in Pennsylvania are generally as clean and much better
built than the miserable huts occupied by these lazy people,"
and yet they had their balls.[217] On the Wabash Faux found
"two lonely families of naked-legged French settlers," and at
Vincennes there was only a Catholic church, so that Sunday
was "only a day of frolic and recreation."[218] On Lafayette's
arrival in Kaskaskia in 1825 the French inhabitants were
amazed to hear of the fall of Napoleon's empire; they thought
that Napoleon was a great general of the Bourbons.[219] Obviously the general picture is one of decline. Kaskaskia which had
7000 inhabitants, says Stuart, has now only a thousand.[220]
And yet in gaiety and good manners these settlements must
have contributed their quota to a developing life around them.
"Indiana is full of adventurers" in 1827, numbers of whom
are French, and as late as 1842 Vincennes was "still said to
be characterized by French architecture and French manners."[221]

[215] Volney, *View of the Soil and Climate*, pp. 331-351. His view is confirmed by Michaux, "Diary," pp. 122-23. The French habitants are "les
plus parasseux et les plus ignorants de tous les hommes," live like savages,
and do not even wear "britches," being content with a piece of cloth between the thighs.
[216] *Travels*, p. 383. Schoepf, however, reports that two French commissioners were in Richmond in 1783-4 from the Wabash country, and remarks: "From the dress and behavior of these gentlemen, as well as from
other information, good-living and luxury seem to prevail in a high degree
in those distant and little known regions." *Travels in the Confederation*,
II, 70. See also II, 326-7.
[217] R. L. Mason, *Narrative*, pp. 56-61. The French are "light-hearted and
dirty."
[218] *Memorable Days in America*, pp. 301-2, 214.
[219] Levasseur, *Lafayette in America*, II, 147-8. The Mesnard family were
important people. II, 157-62.
[220] *Three Years in North America*, II, 338. See also Buckingham, *America,
Eastern and Western States*, III, 208, and *Blowe's Emigrants' Directory*,
pp. 537-578, *passim*.
[221] *The Americans As They Are*, p. 36; Buckingham, *op cit.*, III, 56.

In Michigan the impression was deeper. Little change was wrought by British lordship, and even as late as 1898 a French speaking colony lingered on in Monroe County.[222] Americans did not arrive in any number in Detroit until 1805; though by 1834 they outnumbered the French five to one, in 1814 and 1817, the majority of the inhabitants were French.[223] Detroit therefore long remained the center of French influence in the North West; it was long a "French" settlement, and as late as 1810 a petition was presented requesting that the laws be published in both languages.[224] At the very close of our period Benwell thought it was "peopled principally by French and Dutch, who appeared to be in low circumstances and who follow the usual town occupations"; the town he thought "essentially Gaelic (Gallic) in appearance."[225] So characteristically French an organization as the moral and benevolent society was organized as late as 1818.[226] And in Wisconsin in 1845 there were said to be five thousand French Catholics.[227]

In Missouri the tale was much the same. St. Louis was founded in 1764 by Auguste Choteau and Laclede,[228] and became a typically French community of the old type,[229] as did St. Genevieve[230] and St. Charles.[231] Life here was influenced by creole civilization in Louisiana to a great degree.[232] Even

[222] Brandon, "A French Colony in Michigan," *Modern Language Notes*, XIII, 242-7.
[223] Rusk, I, 36.
[224] McLaughlin, *Life of Lewis Cass*, pp. 6, 15-30.
[225] *An Englishman's Travels in America*, p. 65.
[226] The charter is in the Burton collection of the Detroit Public Library which kindly furnished me a copy. It has been published in incomplete form.
[227] *The American Protestant Magazine*, I, 92.
[228] Fortier, *History of Louisiana*, II, 308.
[229] See Beckwith, *Creoles of St. Louis,* on the French families. The Chouteaus intermarried with the Bourbon and Napoleonic nobility. Schulz (*Travels,* II, 41) describes the town in 1807.
[230] See Ashe's *Travels,* III, 116-120.
[231] Melish, *Travels,* p. 387.
[232] See Atwater, *Remarks made on a Tour to Prairie du Chien,* pp. 48-53. Billon, *Annals of St. Louis in the Early Days,* speaks of the persistence of French traits, even under Spanish rule: "During the thirty-four years of Spanish authority succeeding the first six years of French rule, the place continued to be French in every essential but the partial use of Spanish in a few official documents; the intercourse of the people with each other and their governors, their commerce, trade habits, customs, manners, amusements, marriages, funerals, services in church, parish registers, everything, was French; the governors and the officers all spoke French, it was a *sine qua non* in their appointment; the few Spaniards that

as late as the twenties and thirties these towns retained something of their old-world atmosphere, and the French fur-traders became in fact the aristocracy of the future cities,[233] but the Americans, coming in about 1825 in larger numbers than before,[234] overwhelmed the creole civilization. Natchez had a small French and German population in 1817.[235] Arkansas in the same period enjoyed a dubious reputation.[236] In the coast cities of Florida and Alabama traces of creole culture persisted to the time of the Civil War.[237] But, over the whole territory, the observation of one traveller in 1827 prevails: the French "now assume by degrees the American manners and language. Many of them are wealthy store-keepers, merchants, and farmers; but for the most part, however, a light-footed kind of people, who, from their fathers, have inherited frivolity, and from their mothers, Indian women, uncleanliness."[238] The rich families were of course more like the Louisiana creoles.

6. THE CHARACTER OF FRENCH EMIGRATION, 1815 TO 1848

Aside from the special groups already discussed it is difficult to be exact about the character or quantity of French mi-

settled in the country soon became Frenchmen and all married French wives; no Frenchman became a Spaniard; two or three of the governors were Frenchmen by birth; the wives of Governors Piernas and Trudeau were French. With the exception of the Spanish officials and soldiers, not more than a dozen Spaniards came to the place during the domination of Spain; Governor de Lassus was born in France, and Trudeau was of French stock, and nearly all the papers in the archives were in the French language. The country was only Spanish by possession, but practically French in all else." Quoted in Fortier, II, 312.

[233] See *The Americans as They Are*, p. 94; Buckingham, *America, Eastern and Western States*, III, 94; Stuart, *Three Years in North America*, II, 339, 342-358; Shirreff, *A Tour Through North America*, pp. 261-4; Levasseur, *op. cit.*, II, 136-142; Montulé, *op. cit.*, p. 73; Latrobe, *The Rambler in North America*, I, letter xi, for various accounts.

[234] Rusk, I, 35, 36; *Blowe's Emigrants' Directory*, pp. 680-686.

[235] Montulé, p. 63.

[236] Arkansas was "a refuge for poor adventurers, foreigners, French Soldiers, German redemptioners, with a few respectable families." Men of fortune preferred Mississippi or Louisiana. *The Americans as They Are*, p. 227. See also Stuart, *Three Years in North America*, II, 302.

[237] Bernhard (*Travels*, II, 39) reports of Mobile in 1826 that the creole families had dispersed, leaving only the lower elements behind. A new generation of moneyseekers was coming in, and French and Spanish were spoken only in the substrata of society. At a social gathering in Pensacola there were several creole ladies who spoke bad French, but who looked well and dressed with taste, and who "supported" an "animated" conversation. II, 49.

[238] *The Americans as They Are*, pp. 84-85.

gration from 1815 to 1848. There are, it is true, at the very end of this period two particular movements of immigration which can be studied. One is the ill-fated Icarian settlement in Texas—another communistic failure, the inhabitants of which, some 500 in number, eventually moved to Nauvoo, Illinois, after that town was vacated by the Mormons.[239] The second is the movement of Canadian French into New England, particularly after the rebellion of 1837-9. By 1838 there was a sufficient colony of Canadian French in Burlington, Vermont, for Ludger Duvernay to found a paper, *Le Patriote*. Some of the rebels went farther west—to Kankakee, where Chiniquy, "fameux apostat" took refuge, to Chiraco, Bourbonnais, Saint Paul, Prairie du Chien, Faribault, and Detroit. But the bulk of the Canadian-French migration had to wait upon the railroads and the Civil War, and falls outside of our limits.[240]

Beginning in 1820 we have, it is true, definite figures on the immigration from France and Corsica during the rest of the period—figures it is well to present:

1820— 371	1829— 582	1838— 3675	1847—20040
1821— 370	1830—1174	1839— 7198	1848— 7743
1822— 351	1831—2038	1840— 7419	
1823— 460	1832—5361*	1841— 5006	
1824— 377	1833—4682	1842— 4505	
1825— 515	1834—2989	1843— 3346**	
1826— 545	1835—2696	1844— 3155	
1827—1280	1836—4443	1845— 7663	
1828—2843	1837—5974	1846—10583	

* Fifteen months.
** Three months.

These statistics are not very impressive, especially when it is remembered that the total immigration in 1820 was 7,691; in 1830, 7,217; in 1840, 80,125, and in 1848, 218,025.[241] Moreover, one wants to know more about the distribution of these newcomers. There are, it is true, certain rather unsatisfactory bits of evidence. From *Blowe's Emigrants' Directory* (1820) one can make a rough survey of the distribution of the French over the United States. New York state receives "some" emigrants from France. Philadelphia has a "French benevolent

[239] Studied in Prudhommeaux, *Icarie et son Fondateur Etienne Cabet*.
[240] Belisle, *Histoire de la Presse Franco-Américaine*, pp. 1-11. Buckingham found M. Bouchette, a Canadian rebel, "following the example of the exiled Louis Philippe," and giving lessons in French, Italian, and drawing in Portland, Maine, in 1842. *America, Eastern and Western States*. I, 212.
[12] Wright, p. 105.

society," and the inhabitants are English, Irish, Scotch, Germans, French, and American-born citizens. Pittsburg has "principally Americans; a good many Irish, some English, Scotch, French, Dutch, and Swiss, and a few Welsh and Italians." In Baltimore "the English, Irish, Scotch, and French greatly predominate." To our knowledge of Charleston, Gallipolis, Cahokia, Prairie du Rochers, and New Orleans Blowe adds little. However, in Illinois "the French have made wine"; he lists various settlements in Louisiana with their proportion of French; he remarks that below New Orleans the population is entirely French or descendants of Frenchmen; and in Missouri Territory he lists the French settlements, as he does for Michigan.[242] Again the state prison in Massachusetts in 1825 contained 13 Englishmen, 17 Irishmen, eight Scots, two Canadians, three West Indians, two Swedes, two Italians, a Portuguese, a German, and four Frenchmen.[243] Of 125 inmates in the New York House of Refuge in 1831, 61 were Americans, 32 Irish, 15 English, two German, and eight French.[244] Of 485 prisoners in the penitentiary at Columbus, Ohio, in 1838 (an interest in penitentiaries had been aroused by the panopticon, de Tocqueville's visit, and the humane societies), 64 were foreigners; of these 42 were from the British Isles, 11 from Canada, three from the West Indies, three from France, three from Poland, one from Switzerland, one from Hungary.[245] About 1844 Godley was told that there were 22,000 Frenchmen in New York, a figure which he doubted, "though there are certainly a great many."[246] Figures like these may mean anything or nothing. I give them for what they are worth.

Certain it is that the character of the immigration changed. Many discovered that America was not the land of primitivism and promise they had supposed.[247] Hence, the idealist and the idéologues stayed at home. The majority of the Frenchmen who

[242] Pp. 385, 414, 417, 423, 446, 492, 537, 576, 578, 642, 645, 680-686, 696.
[243] Bernhard, *Travels,* I, 40.
[244] Abdy's *Journal,* I, 65.
[245] Buckingham, *America, Eastern and Western States,* II, 307.
[246] *Letters from America,* II, 24.
[247] On landing in New York in July, 1819, Gall fell in with a Frenchman, who with 104 of his countrymen, had come from Havre four weeks before. These and eleven others were returning. They complained of having been cheated. Gall observes: "Sein hartes Urtheil über die Amerikaner im Allgemeinen war, dass sie alle schlechten Eigenschaften der Britten in sich vereinigten, ohne nur eine einzige ihrer Tugenden zu besetzen." *Meine Auswanderungen,* II, 13.

came to America after 1820, says Orth, were factory workers and professional people who remained in the cities.[248] Certainly one could not say of the émigré movement what Latrobe said of the French emigrants aboard the vessel he took passage on from Havre to New York, namely, that they were "Jews and sharpers if they were not maligned,"[249] a statement which means probably little except that the French were simply immigrants, lumped with other immigrants by travellers like Mackay and Benwell,[250] and no longer a vivid cultural entity.

Sometimes, however, we catch glimpses of this otherwise undistinguished migration which are vivid, human, amusing, or what not. Power, visiting Marblehead, Massachusetts, in 1834, says that it looks like a French fishing town in Normandy, and attributes this appearance to the fact that it is said to have been originally settled by a colony of fishers from Guernsey, whose descendants still retained many customs of the islands, and some words of the patois there in use.[251] Lafayette visited with pleasure the famous Deaf and Dumb Institute at Hartford in 1824, supervised by M. Clerc (Leclerc?), a pupil of the Abbé Sicard, whom "the love of liberty and of humanity had led to (this) country."[252] Agassiz brought a small scientific group with him to East Boston in 1847 for work in marine biology—the Comte François de Pourtalès, Desor, Jacques Burkhardt, Charles Girard, A. Sonrel, and by and by Charles Louis Philippe Christinat of the Canton de Vaud, a political exile[253]— a group which met various misadventures.

If we leave New England for New York we may accumulate a good deal of information. When Lafayette landed at Castle Garden in 1824 more than 200 French residents under the presidency of M. Monneron met him,[254] and the festivities

---

[248] *Our Foreigners*, p. 252.
[249] *Rambler in North America*, I, 17.
[250] Mackay, *Western World*, I, 5; Benwell, *An Englishman's Travels in America*, p. 68.
[251] *Impressions of America*, II, 4-5.
[252] Levasseur, *Lafayette in America*, I, 80.
[253] Marcou, *Life, Letters and Works of Louis Agassiz*, I, 294; E. C. Agassiz, *Louis Agassiz*, II, 442-3. The proclamation of the French Republic in 1848 brought about disturbances in Neuchâtel (Agassiz' canton), which ceased to be dependent upon the Prussian monarchy, so that Agassiz lost his position in the royal service. The new scientific school at Harvard thereupon secured his services in the chair of natural history at $1500 a year. Agassiz, *Louis Agassiz*, II, 456-7.
[254] Levasseur, *op. cit.*, I, 14.

were magnificent.[255] Even Mrs. Anne Royall, who was never pleased with anything, praised "Mr. Barraree," proprietor of the Chatham Garden Theatre, who, it seems, "deserves much credit for his liberality in patronizing the genius of his native country," who was a Frenchman by birth, and a "gentleman of amiable disposition, and generosity of heart."[256] Probably he gave her a pass—she was in the habit of asking for them. At any rate James Gordon Bennett remembered how in 1825, at the production of *Il Barbiere di Seviglia,* "the old French and Italian gentlemen in the pit almost melted into tears—and the venerable Da Ponte, sitting in the centre, with his head uncovered," enjoyed "the glory and the delight of the scene."[257] Two years later Captain Hall described the New Orleans theater troupe, "with all their lap-dogs, black servants, helmets, swords and draperies" about to embark for the South and chattering French, Spanish, German, Italian, and English.[258] Indeed, Stuart wrote in 1828 that "one hears the French and Spanish languages almost in every street," so great was the number of foreigners in New York.[259] One of them, a Frenchman, visited Cooper, a "great dandy," who had written several books; Susan Cooper remembered his dining there and how he sat opposite one of those mantelpiece long mirrors admiring himself—not that he did not admire Natty Bumppo and Chingachgook.[260] In their younger years the Cooper children had a French governess and a French tutor,[261] as did John Watts de Peyster in 1829 or 1830—one Arnoux or Arnaud, who was a "nice man," but "like most Frenchmen I have met did not get along pleasantly in his own family."[262] In the thirties Lieber[263]

---

[255] There was a ball, of course. A tall spar was raised in the center of the ball room; a vast awning of sail-cloth covered the whole, which was concealed by flags that gave a soft, airy finish—all flooded by lights. The national anthem hailed Lafayette's arrival. "The brilliant throngs and gay dancers over the floor fell into line like a charm, forming a lane, through which the old man passed, giving and receiving warm and affectionate salutations at every step to the small marquee in the midst, prepared for the 'Guest of the Nation.' He was like a father among his children." (Cooper's description). Phillips, *James Fenimore Cooper,* pp. 114-5.

[256] *Sketches,* pp. 267-8.

[257] Pray, *Memoirs of James Gordon Bennett and His Times,* p. 63.

[258] *Travels in North America,* II, 209-210.

[259] *Three Years in North America,* I, 25.

[260] *Correspondence of James Fenimore-Cooper,* I, 58.

[261] *Ibid.,* I, 54-5.

[262] Allaben, *John Watts de Peyster,* I, 108.

[263] *The Stranger in America,* I, 207.

confirms Hall's description of the polyglot character of the New York wharves, where one could hear English, German, French, Spanish, and Italian. Exotic it must have been: one poor Frenchman shocked his fellow passengers on Abdy's boat by getting a light from a negro; and another was pelted by brickbats on the streets for speaking civilly to a negress.[264] Some were wealthy: Harriet Martineau tells of a French merchant, who in the great fire of December, 1835, bought a horse and cart with which he saved goods to the amount of $100,-000;[265] some were intellectual, like de Tocqueville, who in his visit from May, 1831 to February, 1832, managed to see everybody of importance;[266] and all were hospitable—at least to Frenchmen—as Pavie tells us, who left this city, "moitié européene," with reluctance.[267]

"Up State," Saratoga was a fashionable rallying point where Frenchmen sometimes came. There were foreigners who could not speak a word of English at the American spa in 1828;[268] Pavie met "trois joyeux Parisiens" at Saratoga in 1833 or so, who woke him up one morning by singing French songs;[269] and three years later Caroline Gilman reported that "a lovely demi-French family" was the life of the place.[270] At Kingston (Aesopus) Stuart's landlady was a Frenchwoman (1829).[271] When John Eyre was going through the Erie Canal "a poor Frenchman, (I think he was,) to save me [from a low bridge] pulled me backwards as I was sitting on a stool."[272] Montulé says that a French baker, one Despares, established at Buffalo, had realized a small fortune in 1817;[273] however, in 1835 at Niagara Ramon de la Sagra was afflicted with a Frenchman from Montreal, a barrel-maker, who told him a long tale of woe about business depressions.[274] Perhaps one ought to remember the French gentleman of Coke's description who was in Buffalo in 1832, and "exclaimed on seeing an

[264] Abdy's *Journal,* I, 301-2. This was in 1833.
[265] *Society in America,* II, 73.
[266] See *Democracy in America,* I, vii.
[267] *Souvenirs Atlantiques,* I, 260, 235.
[268] Mrs. Anne Royall, *The Black Book,* I, 46.
[269] *Souvenirs Atlantiques,* I, 219.
[270] *The Poetry of Travelling in the United States,* pp. 84-88.
[271] *Three Years in North America,* II, 6.
[272] Eyre, *The Christian Spectator,* p. 35.
[273] *Voyage to North America,* pp. 89-95.
[274] *Cinco Meses en los Estados-Unidos,* pp. 264-5.

Indian squaw, raised his hands in astonishment" and cried, "Oh! la malheureuse! la malheureuse!"[275]

In Philadelphia the American Philosophical Society continued to elect Frenchmen, resident or otherwise, to its membership—Lesueur the naturalist in 1817; Desmarest, Blainville and Latreille (all of Paris) in 1819; Joseph and Lucien Bonaparte in 1829; Louis Philippe in 1831. In 1833 the members subscribed for a statue of Cuvier, and in that same year Nicollet of Paris, a "French professor employed by the general government of the United States to make a survey of the North-west Territory,"[276] (this was in 1840 or 1841), made a report. Other worthies elected to the Society included Larrey the famous surgeon, Roux de Rochelle, Guizot, de Tocqueville, Poussin the French minister, Bouchet, Michel Chevalier, Cauchey, Brown-Sequard, Durand, Elie de Beaumont, and so on down through Pasteur to Poincaré.[277] It was in Philadelphia that Coke met Chabert, the fire king, exceedingly doleful because he had lost $1500 the previous day;[278] and there Caroline Gilman had the doubtful privilege of looking into the room of an insane Frenchman whose sole comfort was reading and writing, and who thrust his writings upon her.[279] As for western Pennsylvania, it was continually traversed by random itinerant Frenchmen, of whom we catch occasional glimpses. Melish's stage picked up "a sort of Frenchman, *bound the Lord knows whither*" at Chambersburg in August, 1810, and the Frenchman's antics on the trip down the Ohio which they took together seems to have confirmed the Briton in his detestation of the race.[280] Or again the more sympathetic Power presents vividly one of these small itinerant groups. Travelling in western Pennsylvania in 1834 he met a French pair, the woman a little creature dressed in an old-fashioned flowered gown with sleeves to the elbows, met by black mittens of faded silk, and a very small close bonnet of the same colour. She had small brass buckles in her shoes; a cane, like those borne by running footmen, in one hand, and upon the other arm a small basket, rolled

---

[275] *A Subaltern's Furlough,* II, 27.

[276] Buckingham, *America, Eastern and Western States,* III, 138. See also Lyell, *Travels in North America,* I, 198.

[277] Rosengarten, pp. 195-6. Ramon de la Sagra interviewed Chevalier. *Op. cit.,* p. 136.

[278] In 1833. *A Subaltern's Furlough,* I, 59.

[279] *Poetry of Travelling,* p. 35.

[280] Melish, *Travels,* p. 300. See chapters lxxi-lxxviii *passim.*

up in which lay a tabby cat, to which she talked in broken French and English. The man was tall and bent, had a soldier-like air, white hair combed back and gathered in a thick club, a greatcoat and a broad-leaved hat. They were attending a single horse wagon up Laurel Hill. Power addressed the cat in French (O tactful Irishman!) and the pair were delighted. She was an ancient Parisienne, with all the graceful volubility of a well-bred Frenchwoman; they had had a romantic escape from France, and were seeking to establish themselves in the New World.[281]

In Baltimore Harriet Martineau was told of a Frenchman who, talking of his poultry-yard, informed a friend that he had "fifty head of hen."[282] In Washington French servants and French ministers played their various parts. In the middle West there presently appeared two amazing and romantic figures— Constantine Rafinesque and J. J. Audubon. Rafinesque, poet, pedant, and scientist, of whom Thomas Peirce wrote bitterly,

> Bolanus, happy in a skull
> Of proof, impenetrably dull,

was for a time professor of biology at Transylvania University, but he quarreled with his colleagues and went East after seven years—an incredible figure, publishing French verse, books on antiquities, a monograph of the Fluviatile Bivalve Shells of the River Ohio, an Ichthyologia Ohiensis—an enormous bibliography.[283] Audubon, whose origins and whose life were alike romantic, came to America as we have seen in 1803; returned to France; came again in 1806, and led a colorful life as an ornithologist, merchant, travelling painter, and dancing master, encouraged by a faithful wife, and bitterly denounced as a charlatan; wandering over New York, Kentucky, Missouri, Ohio, and Louisiana; going to England in 1826 and beginning

---

[281] *Impressions of America,* I, 301-6. This was near Pittsburg.
[282] *Society in America,* I, 239.
[283] The most available account of Rafinesque is in Rusk. Use the index. Audubon describes Rafinesque in 1818 as follows: "A long, loose coat of yellow nankeen, much the worse for the many rubs it had got in its time, and stained all over with the juice of plants, hung loosely about him like a sac. A waistcoat of the same, with enormous pockets, and buttoned up to the chin, reached below over a pair of tight pantaloons, the lower parts of which were buttoned down to the ankles. His beard was as long as I have known mine to be during my peregrinations, and his lank black hair hung loosely over his shoulders. His forehead was . . . broad and prominent. . . . His words impressed with an assurance of rigid truth. . . ." Herrick, *Audubon the Naturalist,* I, 286; and see him also chap. xix.

publication of the famous *Birds of America;* returning to America in 1831 and again in 1836 and 1839, where he died in 1851.[284] Indeed, the West seemed to attract philosophers; at New Harmony, Indiana, the Duke of Saxe-Weimer was "much annoyed" by an elderly Frenchwoman who tormented him with her philosophical views.[285]

Of the South we hear less. Levasseur had the pleasure of conversing with the professors of the college at Columbia, South Carolina, three of whom spoke French with great facility, and who had "long resided in Paris." The wife of one of them was a native of Paris and had been in the country only three months: there is a touch of pathos in Levasseur's remark that she greeted Lafayette with particular enthusiasm.[286] Bernhard was likewise impressed: he met only two professors, it is true, but one of them spoke French and German, and the other had studied in France and England; and at the governor's ball he met M. Herbemont, formerly a professor, whom he classifies as an "interesting Frenchman."[287] In Savannah, Georgia, Lafayette was received by a deputation of French and their descendants (on Sunday, too!) headed by Petit de Villers, who made the inevitable speech; and at Milledgeville he found that the mayor, Mr. Jaillet, was of French origin.[288] And of far-off Florida the *American Monthly Review* complains in 1837 that the forming of two companies of French and German volunteers on the Florida service is "the most arrogant exercise of irresponsible power" that "the present unprincipaled administration (that of Van Buren) has yet attempted."[289]

[284] See Herrick's fascinating biography, *Audubon the Naturalist.*
[285] Stuart, *Three Years in North America,* II, 441.
[286] *Lafayette in America,* II, 51-52.
[287] *Travels,* I, 209.
[288] Levasseur, II, 67, 77.
[289] November, 1837, pp. 503-4.

VI

The French Language in America

INTRODUCTION: GENERAL CONSIDERATIONS ON LANGUAGE
BARRIERS AND ON THE FRENCH INFLUENCE ON
AMERICAN SPEECH

DIFFERENCE in language is obviously a barrier to the diffusion of culture across national boundary lines; when one does not understand another's speech, one grows impatient with his ideas. Between France and America this barrier has always existed, but it has nevertheless among certain groups and at certain times broken down. Clearly, some approximate knowledge of the extent to which French was read and understood by the Americans, together with some indication of the social levels at which international intercourse was possible, is essential to our general task. To state exactly how many Americans spoke and read French at any given time is impossible, just as it is impossible to state how many French immigrants coming to this country spoke and read English, but we must nevertheless do the best we can; and if we can not always speak with exactness, we can at least indicate tendencies.

Two or three preliminary matters must first be got out of the way. Certain colonies of French have settled in the territory of the United States: in Louisiana; along the Wabash, the Ohio, and the Mississippi; in Michigan; in Maine; and in certain of the larger centers such as Charleston, New York, and Philadelphia. In general it is to be noted that the influence of English upon the French spoken in these speech-colonies has been greater than the reciprocal influence of the French upon the surrounding English; and except where formal teaching was done, as at New Rochelle and Charleston, this latter influence has done nothing to make French a better known language in the United States.[1] It is rather to the social prestige of

[1] The question of the influence of French upon American English may be studied in Mencken, *The American Language,* pp. 410-413 and references; Fortier, "The French Language in Louisiana and the Negro-French Dialect," *Transactions and Proceedings of the Modern Language Association,* I, 40-44; "The Acadians of Louisiana and Their Dialect," *Publications of the Modern Language Association* (old series) VI, 64-94; "French Literature in Louisiana," *Transactions and Proceedings of the Modern Language Association,* II, 31-60; and "The French Literature of Louisiana

French that we must look for the reasons why Americans took the trouble to learn it.

For if the ignorance of the Americans is a barrier against the diffusion of French influence, the barrier is, so to speak, lower during our period than one would expect. The first British settlements date from the period of the Tudors; they grew under the Stuarts; and expanded under the house of Orange and under the House of Hanover. It is a remarkable fact that during this period in England French possessed an increasing prestige as a language—the language of diplomacy, of the arts, of science, of philosophy. To the average Englishman from the days of Henry VIII to the days of Victoria, German was an unknown tongue, and Italian or Spanish an accidental possession. But no gentleman was completely a gentleman who did not know French. "In the reign of Elizabeth," writes a close student of French-English literary relationships, "as well as that of the . . . Stuarts ample evidence attests the wide knowledge of the French language, particularly among the educated classes of England, and likewise the familiarity of these people with French literature."[2] With the accession and marriage of Charles I (to Henrietta Maria), "when French *préciosité* and French Platonizing, despite national protest, gained a considerable hold upon English court society," there came a fresh wave of French impulse.[3] The military and diplomatic triumphs of Louis XIV added to the prestige of French; and in the eighteenth century the French language attained an eminence which made it preeminently the international language, supplanting

in 1887 and 1888," *Modern Language Notes,* IV, 97-101, 228-233; and in the same publication for 1889-1890, V, 165-169, 349-352. In "Some Specimens of a Canadian-French Dialect Spoken in Maine," *Publications of the Modern Language Association,* IV, 210-218 (old series), Edward S. Sheldon describes a dialect island, the consideration of which falls outside this study. Edgar E. Brandon in *Modern Language Notes,* XIII, 242-8, describes a similar speech colony in Michigan which descends from the eighteenth century. An important study is Sylvester Primer, "The Huguenot Element in Charleston's Pronunciation," *Publications of the Modern Language Association* (old series), IV, 214-244, which attributes the origin of certain characteristic elements in Charleston pronunciation to French influence—almost the sole example of a direct influence upon American speech that has been recorded. Branner's "Some Old French Place Names in the State of Arkansas," *Modern Language Notes,* XIV, 75-80, records among other matters a list of degenerate phonetic spellings of names which indicates how little French was understood in a region originally dominated by them. Doubtless investigation would dredge up more facts but, in general, speech contacts between the French and the Americans have oftener modified French than they English.

[2] Upham, *French Influence on English Literature,* pp. 6-11, 24.
[3] *Ibid.,* p. 24.

even Latin. It is incredible that the cosmopolitan society of America whose origin and growth we have traced, should remain unaffected by the doctrine that a knowledge of French was a part of a genteel education no less than of a scientific or scholarly one; and in fact, such it not the case. A reading knowledge of French was not uncommon among the colonists from the earliest times, and at least among the cosmopolitan group this knowledge was never lost. Let us therefore turn to an examination of the evidence: we shall have to make a mosaic of a hundred little references, and perhaps we shall be a little dull, but the facts are necessary to our study.

1. EVIDENCE FOR THE KNOWLEDGE OF FRENCH IN AMERICA, 1620-1700

Aside from what has been said elsewhere regarding instruction in French by the Huguenots,[4] the evidence for assuming some knowledge of the language among the colonists of the seventeenth century rests largely upon the possession by them of books in the French language. Books were scarce and costly; and it is unlikely that a New England scholar or a Virginia gentleman would acquire a book in a language he could not read. Moreover, with reference to New England, it is to be noted that the center of Protestant theology was Calvinistic Geneva; and although much of the theological literature was in Latin, the fact that Calvin and his disciples wrote in French tended to make French the secondary modern foreign language among the Puritan divines. To avoid the duplication of detail, the actual titles of French books in their libraries are listed and discussed elsewhere;[5] but it is clear from the evidence that the Puritan fathers often read in French. In the period from 1620 to 1670 Wright lists Miles Standish, John Harvard, Governor Thomas Dudley, John Winthrop, Jr., Thomas Grocer, Nathaniel Morton, and Anne Bradstreet as, either by the possession of French books, or by their correspondence or literary citations, exhibiting some knowledge of French.[6] John Winthrop, Jr., on March 28, 1648-9, wrote a friend asking him to procure "Vigi-

---

[4] The Huguenots of course had libraries. Pierre Daillé left all his French and Latin books to the French church in Boston in 1715, for example; Le Mercier, his successor as pastor, wrote two volumes on Geneva and on "Detraction"; Peter Faneuil bought books abroad; and in the seventeenth century James Rawlings was the "French Schoolmaster in Boston." Fosdick, pp. 164, 165, 176, 190.

[5] See chap. x. The convenient summary of New England booklists is Wright, *Literary Culture in Early New England.*

[6] Wright, pp. 25-71.

neere des Cyphres" (*Traités des chiffres* by Blaise de Vigenère)
"wch you know is to be had in Paris," and indisputably the
book must have been read in French,[7] when, or if, it was procured. This same Winthrop, dying in 1676, left behind him a
library of 300 titles, including an unusual number of books in
the modern languages;[8] and as showing some interest in modern
language instruction, it is to be noted that John Harvard's
library possessed Minsheu's *Guide to the Tongues*.[9] The inventory of Thomas Dudley of Suffolk, who died in 1653, credits
him with 50 books, among them eight French books, which presumably he or some one connected with him could read.[10]
Thomas Grocer died in Boston in 1664 in the possession of
"Six Sermons de la Reconciliation de l'homme avec Dieu," a
book printed by Gilbert Primrose at Sedan in 1624,[11] and presumably took his knowledge of French with him to the grave.
From facts like these it is at least a fair inference that French
was not unknown in early New England.

In the thirty years from 1670 to 1700 the evidence for some
knowledge of French in the same region increases. Samuel
Sewall, Harvard 1671, criticises the translation of the English
Bible and compares it to a French translation; of John 10:16,
for instance, he observes that the English "flock" is in French,
un seul tropeau.[12] Cotton Mather possessed enough knowledge
of the language to write at least one tract in French; and in
the *Magnalia* he quotes from Ronsard's commentary on Du
Bartas (*Magnalia*, II:28) and from Rabelais (*Magnalia*, II:
645). The same estimable divine has a number of references to
other French works which, in the opinion of Wright, he could
not have read in translation.[13] The references to French litera-

---

[7] Wright, pp. 45-46.
[8] Dexter, "Early Private Libraries in New England," *Publications of the
American Antiquarian Society* (new series), XVIII, 139.
[9] Dexter, *op. cit.*, p. 140. Upham (*op. cit.*) gives a list of English texts
of the French language published between 1566 and 1656, taken from the
Stationers' Register (pp. 9-11). Unfortunately I am not able to say how
many of these early language books emigrated to New England.
[10] Herrick, "The Early New-Englanders: What Did They Read?" *The
Library*, IX, 4.
[11] Ford, *The Boston Book Market, 1679-1700*, p. 74.
[12] Wright, p. 105.
[13] Wright, pp. 111, 147, 242-254. Cotton Mather knew Hebrew, Latin,
Greek, French, Spanish, and one Indian tongue, and composed or published works in most of these languages. Cf. Tyler, cited below, II, 78. Mr.
Kenneth B. Murdock kindly called my attention to Cotton Mather's re-

ture in Increase Mather are, however, chiefly to Latin works.[14] William Bradford knew Dutch, French, Latin, and Greek.[15] In the Prince library there were a good many French books, including a "Royal Dictionary," English and French, published in London in 1699; F. Chéneau's French grammar, London, 1685; a "Compleat Frenchmaster"; and apparently another later edition of the same book (11th edition, London, 1733).[16] A knowledge of French was sufficiently widespread in New England to permit the printing of a pamphlet in French by Samuel Green; the book was written by Ezechiel Carré, "cy deuant ministre de la Rochechalois en France, à present ministre de l'eglise française de Boston en La Nouvelle Angleterre," and is directed against the Jesuits.[17] Apparently some influence was being felt from the Huguenots in Boston and New England generally: at any rate, "N. Walter" of Boston knew enough French to translate into English a sermon by this same Ezechiel Carré, *The Charitable Samaritan,* published by the said Green in 1689.[18] With a French church in Boston, a French work being translated in a Boston print shop, and another translated by a Boston man, French, it is evident, takes on the character of a living language in New England. We must remember the little groups of Huguenot settlers scattered over these colonies in the epoch.

In New York, meanwhile, a knowledge of French was steadily spreading, due largely to the influence of the Huguenots. All the town proclamations were in French and Dutch

marks on the desirability of the study of French in his *Manuductio ad Ministerium,* 1726.

[14] Wright, pp. 237-42. His list, however, covers but a part of Mather's references. Increase Mather possessed a copy of Paul Pellison's history of the French Academy, one of Lazare Rivière's *Practise of Physick,* and the *Philosophical Conferences of the Virtuosi of France.* These were in English. Murdock, *Increase Mather,* pp. 125; 75-6; 175.

[15] Cf. Tyler, *History of American Literature (1607-1676),* I, 118, note 1.

[16] Winsor, *The Prince Library.* Prince died in 1758.

[17] Item 504 in Evans' Bibliography: "Echantillon. De la doctrine que les Jesuites enseignent aus sauvages du nouveaux monde, pour les convertir, tirée de leurs propres manuscrits trouvés ces jours passés en Albanie proche de Nieuyorke. Examinée par Ezechiel Carre (*sic*)," etc.

[18] Item 464 in Evans. "The Charitable Samaritan. A Sermon on the Tenth Chapter of Luke, ver. 30-35, pronounced in the French church at Boston. . . . Translated into English by N. Walter. Boston. Printed by Samuel Green. 1689." There is a copy in the New York Public Library. (N. Walter is Nehemiah Walter the well known divine connected with the Mather family. See Murdock, *op. cit.,* 318.)

by the year 1656,[19] and the first schoolmaster, Dr. La Montagne, who came in 1637, was a Frenchman.[20] By 1698 Governor Bellomont was writing to the Board of Trade that "I must acquaint your lordships that the French here are very factious and their numbers considerable. At the last election they ran in with the Jacobite party, and have been so insolent as to boast they had turned the scale and could balance the interests as they pleased."[21] Insolence or no, French became a living tongue in New York: from 1648 to 1658 the public documents were in French, Dutch, and English; and by 1688 one quarter of the population were French.[22] Shortly the French church became a fashionable place in which to learn correct accent, and to this educational agency one must add the schools at New Rochelle, where in 1690 there was no one who knew enough English to serve as justice of the peace, and whither English boys were sent to live and learn French.[23] That the instruction was good may be inferred from the story of one of the teachers told by Smith. Daniel L'Estrange of Orleans, France, who matriculated as a student of philosophy in the Academy of Geneva in 1672 (the only place where a Huguenot could be educated), was afterwards an officer in the royal guard and subsequently in that of James II. Upon the Revocation of the Edict of Nantes he fled to America (his wife going a different route and the children yet another), settled in New Rochelle and later in New York, where this polished officer taught French and the classic tongues to the Americans.[24] With the increase in the number of French-speaking people in New York and its vicinity, it became possible and profitable to publish works in French: for instance, *Le Trésor des consolations divines et humaines ou traité dans le quel le Chretien peur (peut?) apprendre à vaincre et à surmonter les afflictions et les misères de cette vie. A New-York chez Guillaume Bradford, al'enseigne de la Bible, 1696.*[25]

[19] Fosdick, *French Blood in America*, p. 216.
[20] *Ibid.*, p. 215.
[21] Quoted in Fosdick, p. 224.
[22] *Ibid.*, p. 224. In 1661 half the inhabitants of Harlem were French Huguenots.
[23] *Ibid.*, pp. 231-246. The settlement was begun in 1689, though some came earlier. John Jay, Washington Irving, and General Philip Schuyler are among those who learned French at New Rochelle where in the grammar school, "French was then spoken generally."
[24] Smith, *Colonial Days and Ways*, pp. 130-8.
[25] Item 775 in Evans. It is a work in 98 pages. It was printed for a Mr. Pintard in fulfillment of a vow, according to Hildeburne, *Printers and Printing in New York*, pp. 5-6.

Meanwhile we are neglecting the South. In Maryland, as we have seen, the connections between the Catholics and Catholic France were close, and the scions of the wealthy were frequently sent to the Jesuit colleges in the Old World where they learned French.[26] In seventeenth century Virginia we can trace here and there a reading knowledge of French. Thus when John Kemp of Lower Norfolk county died in 1648 he left behind him "Mr. Calvin's Institutions," but in what language does not appear. The inventory of Captain William Moseley, however, dated November 10, 1671, is more explicit: it includes "a pcell of Books Some french, duch, Latten & English." In York county, Lieutenant-Colonel Thomas Ludlow, dying, left in 1660 "one little chest wth some French bookes in it." Mathey Hubard (Huberd), also of York county, who died seven years later, left behind him "Astrea a french Romance q^{to}," which may have been English, and also a "french Accident q^{to}," which certainly points to an interest in French. In 1690 Colonel John Carter of Lancaster county left Howell's *French and English Dictionary* behind him, as well as two volumes of French "chirurgery" and a volume of "Spanish and French Dialogues."[27] And in this period was begun the collecting of the superb library of the Byrd family, shelf upon shelf of which was French.[28] Obviously some of the Virginia gentry read French.

Perhaps none of this knowledge is either widespread or profound. When Jasper Danckaerts, a Dutch scholar, visited Harvard in 1680, he could not speak English fluently, but he "understood Dutch or French well, which they (the students) did not."[29] When, however, one remembers that for every list of books which has come down to us, six or eight other lists have perished; when one recalls that of all human accomplishments in the seventeenth century, a knowledge of French is not the likeliest one to be recorded; when one argues from these scanty records back to the proportion of those for whom no records exist, it is safe to assert that a reading knowledge of French was not uncommon in America in the seventeenth

[26] Hinsdale, *Foreign Influence Upon Education in the United States*, I, 594.

[27] From the lists of inventories compiled by E. W. James, "Libraries in Colonial Virginia," *William and Mary College Quarterly Historical Magazine*, II, 175; III, 43, 44, 181; VIII, 18.

[28] See the list in the appendix to Bassett, *The Writings of Colonel William Byrd of Westover, in Virginia, Esquire.*

[29] Wright, *Literary Culture*, p. 101.

century. Other languages there were—Dutch, Swedish, Spanish, Walloon; Latin was still the great learned tongue, and Greek and Hebrew were known to all theologians, but French was more likely to be generally known than any other foreign language except, perhaps, Latin. It is something to build on, this seventeenth century knowledge of French.

2. THE SAME FOR 1700-1750

The period from 1700 to 1750 is not distinguished by any great growth of an interest in the French language. The era is marked, it is true, by the adoption of French into the curriculum of Harvard and of certain smaller colleges; there are French dancing masters, who frequently taught French as well; and there are the usual indications of the possession of French books by the colonists. But at Harvard the teacher of French was dismissed;[30] and the best that can be said of the period from our point of view is that the knowledge of French did not, in all probability, decline. On the other hand it did not increase with the growth of the colonies, perhaps because so much of the time was devoted to warring against the French.[31] Foreign languages do not grow in popularity during war, especially when they are spoken by an enemy bitterly hated and feared.

The formal teaching of French in America begins with the Catholic missionaries who, as early as 1608, if Handschin is to be believed, were instructing the Maine Indians in the Gallic tongue.[32] No results, of course, flowed from this casual instruction; however, it may be noted that in the future Northwest Territory and in the vast regions of Louisiana, Sulpitian and Jesuit priests were here and there engaged from 1700 to 1750 in the more or less formal teaching of French in the wilderness. Formal French instruction in New Orleans was offered to girls in 1727, with the coming of the Ursuline nuns.[33] In Alabama, where the French held sway after 1702, conditions were much the same as in Louisiana—that is to say, there were occasional private teachers and schools. It is need-

---

[30] See Quincy, *History of Harvard University*, I, 574-6. This was in 1735.
[31] 1701-1713, Queen Anne's War; 1745-1748, King George's War; 1754-1763, French and Indian War.
[32] Handschin, *The Teaching of Modern Languages in the United States*, p. 9; Dexter, *History of Education in the United States*, chap. viii.
[33] Handschin, p. 10; Fortier, *History of Louisiana*, I, 105. Handschin estimates 400 children in French schools in Louisiana up to 1788 as a normal number.

less to remark, of course, that French was the language of daily life in both Mobile and New Orleans, as in the Louisiana territory.[34] And if we turn to the British colonies, although the general statement may be hazarded that "French was taught early in private schools in the colonies,"[35] but few references appear for the first half of the century, barring what we know of centers like New Rochelle and Charleston. These were the years when Franklin was learning French, Italian, and Spanish in Philadelphia.[36]

In New England, however, we note that French books are still being bought and presumably read. Samuel Sewall ordered from England in 1705 Crompton's *L'Authoritie et Jurisdiction des Courts* and Horn's *Miroir des Justices;* and six years later, all of Calvin's commentaries. An advertisement in the *Boston News-Letter* for February 6, 1715/16, announces the sale of books in Latin, English, and French at the Crown Coffee-House in Boston: Wright quotes it in his volume. Among the 700 volumes sent to Yale from England there were certainly some French books, just as John Harvard's library contained a number of similar books.[37] The Mather books, as descending to Samuel Mather in 1745, certainly include volumes in French,[38] and there is in the Harvard Divinity School a French Bible given the French church in Boston by Queen Anne.[39] Huguenots like Peter Faneuil were accustomed to import books in French,[40] and all in all there was enough in-

[34] John B. Trudeau, the only schoolmaster in St. Louis under the Spanish rule, continued to teach his little French school until 1825 or so. Fortier, II, 315.

[35] Handschin, p. 13.

[36] Morse, *Benjamin Franklin,* p. 35.

[37] Wright, *Literary Culture,* pp. 174-175, 177 and note, 179, 265-272. Other booksellers' advertisements may include French books. Thus on May 14, 1716, "a Valuable Collection of Books & Pamphlets . . . in several Languages" is to be sold. (*Boston News-Letter,* No. 630). Aug. 27, 1716 "A Collection of Choice Books, Ancient and Modern in several Languages" is offered. *Ibid.,* No. 647. June 9, 1718, "A Collection of very valuable Books in most Languages" is to be sold. *Ibid.,* No. 738. January 15, 1729, "A Collection of very valuable BOOKS, English, French, Latin, &c" is offered. *Boston Weekly News-Letter,* No. 107. Similar advertisements appear on November 5, 1730, July 8, 1731, December 16, 1731, etc.

[38] Tuttle, "Libraries of the Mathers," *Proceedings of the American Antiquarian Society,* XX, 301-310.

[39] *Ibid.*

[40] Weeden, *Economic and Social Life of New England,* II, 628. Peter Faneuil imported a book of Common Prayer "in French for my own use" about 1739. Apparently this was to replace one stolen and advertised for in the *Boston Weekly News-Letter* of September 23, 1731.

terest in the language to call for some manuals of instruction—
for instance, Blair's *Some Short and Easy Rules Teaching the
True Pronunciation of French,* published in Boston in 1720.[41]
French tutors begin to advertise in the papers by 1719.[41a]
One finds also that the printing of books in French at Boston is
not uncommon.[42] Such straws indicate that if French was not
spreading, it was at least not retrograding. Even the servants
occasionally knew French.[43]

In New York likewise William Bradford possessed types
and secured printers who could set French books.[43a] In Philadelphia there was enough interest in French to call for advertisements of French school books in the *Pennsylvania Gazette,*[44]
and in the various catalogues of imported books in Evans'
Bibliography for this epoch, we should find, I think, a number
in the French language. In Pennsylvania Rabelais was being
advertised for sale in 1738-9, and Voltaire was included in
Franklin's first library catalog.[44a]

In the South, meanwhile, there are traces of a knowledge of
French. When Richard Hickman of Williamsburg died, for
example, he left behind him a "Law french dictionary,"
"Hurdes ffrench Dictionary, French Litturgy, and Boyers
French Dictionary," not to speak of a copy of *Télémaque.*
Ralph Wormeley of Middlesex county owned "a ffrench &
English Dxionary," a "ffrench gramer," an "easy Compendium
ffrench gramer," "a Dialogue of ffrench English & Latin," and

[41] Item 2096 in Evans.
[41a] See the *Boston News-Letter* for November 2, 1719; February 2, 1727;
March 12, 1730, etc. One man offers "Writing, Cyphering, Latin, French,
Geography" and Latin and French conversation.
[42] Item 1493 in Evans: *A. B. C. des Chrétiens.* Boston. Printed by B.
Green (?), 1711; item 1498: John Hill, *De par Son Excellence M. Jean
Hill, Général & Commandant en chef les troupes de sa Majesté Britan-
nique en Amérique.* A Boston: chez B. Green. 1711 (Broadside folio); and
two translations of Cotton Mather's sermons, *Le Vrai Patron des Saines
Paroles* (Boston, 1704) and *Voix du Ciel à la France* (Boston, 1724). One
notes the propaganda character of these printings.
[43] "A short thick Indian girl, named Grace, age about 17 years" who
"speaks English, Dutch and French" is advertised after by "Master Nicholas
Jamain of New York Merchant" in the *Boston News-Letter,* No. 148,
February 17, 1706.
[43a] He printed in 1696 *Le Trésor des consolations divines et humaines,* as
we have seen. (Evans, item 775.)
[44] Evans, item 3249, notes "A French School Book" advertised as being
for sale in that magazine April 16, 1730. The book is to be printed by
Franklin and Meredith and is by Thomas Ball.
[44a] Cook, *op. cit.,* pp. 105-6; 113.

a "sure guide to the french tongue," not to speak of numerous pieces of French literature. Richard Lee of Westmoreland county (died 1715) had a "ffrench Dictionary," "Mangers ffrench Grammar," a "ffrench schoolmaster," and the "Gold mine of the french tongue," besides numerous works in French. Robert Carter's library contained *La Méchanique des Langues,* a French "spelling Dichonary," and numerous French works. Dr. David Black of Prince George county died possessed of a French dictionary and other works.[45] Obviously, a good many Virginians read French. Doubtless there were tutors of French unknown to history; in his *Reminiscences,* for instance, Wheeler quotes the will of a North Carolinian, dated 1735, which provides for the education of the testator's children in French among other things; "perhaps," the document suggests, "some Frenchman on the Pee Dee might be engaged."[46] Certain it is that Charleston was a center for the acquirement of the French tongue, where French books were printed by Louis Timothée,[47] and where Timothée's *Gazette* carried advertisements of "the most modern books in English and French."[48] French verse was also appearing in the *Gazette* in the forties. It is safe to say that in any of the larger cultural centers of America no French document from 1700 to 1750 need have gone untranslated if there was need to put it into English.

3. THE SAME FOR 1750-1770

What progress, if any, was made in the acquiring of French in America in the years 1750 to 1770? We may say, first of all, that there is no reason to suppose any lower percentage among the Americans who could read or understand French than in the previous years; and we may add, in the second place, that the period is marked by an increase in the amount of formal instruction in the French language.

[45] James, "Libraries in Colonial Virginia," *William and Mary College Quarterly Historical Magazine,* III, 250-251; II, 171-174, 248-250; XI, 23, 26; VIII, 149.
[46] Weeks, *Libraries and Literature in North Carolina in the Eighteenth Century,* p. 176.
[47] Louis Timothée (Timothy), the son of a Huguenot refugee, was employed by Franklin and by the Philadelphia Library Company; he removed to Charleston in 1733; published the first permanent newspaper in 1734, and founded a family of printers. Thomas, *History of Printing,* I, 341-3. For books printed by the Timothee family consult Evans.
[48] Edward Wigg is importing French books in 1732; Whitemarsh in 1732-3; Crokatt and Seaman on September 18, 1736, have just imported "a curious collection of" English and French books. Cook, *Literary Influences on Colonial Newspapers,* pp. 249-256.

Thus, following the debâcle of Langloisserie at Harvard, Mr. Curtis, on avowing himself to be a protestant, was permitted to teach French in 1769. At the future University of Pennsylvania in 1754 Professor William Creamer became the first faculty member to teach French and German, continuing until 1775; Professor Creamer's position originated from Franklin's idea of teaching French at the Academy of Philadelphia (founded in 1749) as an extra-mural or private study. In the same university Paul Fooks commenced to teach French and Spanish in 1766.[49] Paul Fooks, by the by, did legal work in three languages.[50] In the same city Elizabeth Murphy offered instruction in French from seven to nine in the morning, so that the children might go to school—a fact in itself significant as to the spread of French.[51] Meanwhile, of course, the *petits maîtres* were regularly offering to teach French as well as dancing and fencing. In 1750 Franklin drew up a scheme for the university in which French had a prominent part.[52] At Princeton President Witherspoon introduced French into the curriculum in 1768.[53] At Yale in 1770 Louis Delille of the University of Bordeaux gave lessons in French and history; later he went to Harvard.[54] At New Rochelle, as of yore, French was being regularly taught; for example, Gouverneur Morris learned there "to speak and write this language almost as well as he could write English."[55] Robert Livingston "spoke and wrote the English, French, and Dutch languages with fluency and clearness" apparently as the result of similar instruction.[56] In Maryland rich planters were learning French abroad.[57] In Virginia, in 1752, at the age of nine Thomas

[49] See the convenient table in Handschin; and for the particular facts, see him, p. 13.
[50] Scharf and Westcott, *History of Philadelphia*, II, 887. They give the date when Fooks began as 1768.
[51] *Ibid.*,
[52] Faÿ, p. 26, citing Franklin's *Writings*, III, 24-28; IV, 419-423.
[53] Hageman, *Princeton and Its Institutions*, II, 260-2. He gave 300 volumes to the library, some of them French. Maclean, *History of the College of New Jersey*, I, 388.
[54] *Diary of Ezra Stiles*, I, 388.
[55] Roosevelt, *Gouverneur Morris*, p. 3.
[56] Smith, *Colonial Days & Ways*, p. 193.
[57] See letters from Charles Carroll to Charles Carroll of Carrollton advising the latter to study French (1754-59), French manners, and good society abroad. *Unpublished Letters of Charles Carroll of Carrollton*, pp. 20-35.

Jefferson was placed under the care of the Rev. William Douglas, a Scot, who taught him the beginnings of Latin, Greek, French, and mathematics; at 14 the future president went to a school kept by the Rev. James Maury, a Huguenot, and when he left William and Mary it was with "a sound knowledge of French, Greek, Latin, and the higher mathematics, good health, and an open inquisitive mind."[58] The school founded by this same James Maury or Marye, by the way, grew into the Fredericksburg Classical and Mathematical Academy, the principal educational institution of northern Virginia in its day, and Washington attended Maury's school.[59] Even in backward Southern colonies like Georgia and North Carolina there was an increasing number of French books and presumably of people to read them.[60]

While the formal instruction in French was thus increasing in these twenty years, the importation of French books was likewise increasing. The more books, the greater the desire to read them; and the greater the knowledge of French, the greater the demand for French books. When now it is remembered that these two decades were years of growing uneasiness regarding the political situation and that after Hobbes and Locke, the scepter of eminence in political speculation had passed to Montesquieu, some reason for the growing prestige of the French language appears. In the next place, following 1750, there was an increase in the number of French *petits maîtres,* particularly in such intellectual capitals as Philadelphia and Charleston, and in addition to its intellectual prestige, a social prestige came to attach itself to French: French is no longer the language of the theological student, of the diplomat, of the merchant alone, it is the language of the salon, of

---

[58] Forman, *Life and Writings of Thomas Jefferson,* pp. 3-4, 5. On Jefferson as a translator of French cf. Chinard, *Jefferson et les Idéologues* and *Volney et l'Amérique.* As a youth Jefferson read Greek, Latin, and English classics, and "to some extent also in French and Italian." Morse, *Thomas Jefferson,* p. 6.

[59] M. D. Conway, *Autobiography,* I, 35.

[60] "This province (Georgia) was scarcely settled thirty years before it had three fine libraries in the city of Savannah, the fourth at Ebenezer, and a fifth 96 3/4 miles from the sea, upon the stream of Savannah. In these libraries could be had books written in the Chaldaic, Hebrew, Arabic, Siriac, Coptic, Malabar, Greek, Latin, French, German, Dutch, and Spanish, besides the English: viz., in thirteen languages." From a ms. in Harvard Library; quoted in *Report on Public Libraries, House Miscellaneous Documents No. 50, 31st Congress, 1st Session,* p. 158. For North Carolina turn to the lists of books in colonial libraries in Weeks, *Libraries and Literature of North Carolina in the Eighteenth Century.*

the novel, of the memoir-writers. We may rightfully attribute to these twenty years the beginning of the social prestige which French as a language has since possessed in America.

4. THE SAME FOR 1770-1800

On the other hand, among the Huguenot settlers French as a language was slowly dying out. Roosevelt has summarized the situation with respect to New York, where "many nationalities were being blended into one. The descendants of the old Dutch inhabitants were still more numerous than those of any other one race, while the French Huguenots, who, being of the same Calvinistic faith, were closely mixed with them, and had been in the land nearly as long, were also plentiful." But the process of assimilation "was going on almost as rapidly a hundred years ago as it is at present (1888). A young Dutchman or Huguenot felt it necessary . . . to learn English . . . during the century that elapsed between the final British conquest of the colony and the Revolution, the New Yorkers . . . had become in the main welded into one people."[61] Similar changes were being wrought in other Huguenot centers. One means of disseminating a knowledge of French was slowly disappearing. As a result, in the 1770's, many Americans who should have had some knowledge of French were ignorant of the language.

De Moré, who first came to this country in the autumn of 1777, found it necessary to have an interpreter in Virginia, and comments on the ignorance of French in New England;[62] he himself did not speak English at this time. John Adams, appointed commissioner to France in 1778, knew no French when he sailed.[63] Silas Deane, sent to France by the Continental Congress in 1776, "could not even speak French."[64] When the

---

[61] Roosevelt, *Gouverneur Morris,* pp. 9, 12, 13.

[62] *Mémoires,* pp. 55, 56 ff.

[63] Morse, *Life of John Adams,* p. 149. However, he soon learned. Marking the spirit of the time is this paragraph from Adams' letter to his wife from Philadelphia, 18 February, 1776: "I wish I understood French as well as you. I would have gone to Canada, if I had. I feel the want of education every day, particularly of that language. I pray, my dear, that you would not suffer your sons or your daughter ever to feel a similar pain. It is in your power to teach them French, and I, every day, see more and more, that it will become a necessary accomplishment of an American gentleman or lady. Pray write me in your next the name of the author of your thick French grammar, which gives you the pronunciation of the French words in English letters. . . ." *Letters,* I, 86-7.

[64] Morse, *Benjamin Franklin,* p. 220; Faÿ, p. 58.

French fleet visited Boston in 1778, the "lack of a knowledge of French was a matter of regret with every gentleman in the town," and the earlier intercourse was through Latin, Dr. Cooper acting as an interpreter, and the elder Breck and Governor Hancock tried to learn the language, but in vain.[65] When Lieutenant Anburey visited Colonel Bland, a Virginia gentleman living near Charlottesville, in May, 1779, Bland, desirous to convince the British officer that he knew French, commanded his negro servant in great anger, "Donney moi—donney moi" —and, after great hesitation— "donney moi mon scabbard."[66] Watson tells an amusing story of a French officer "in three-cornered cocked hat, laced coat, a long queue tied close to his head, with a ribbon in a large double bow, his hair powdered, and a long sword dangling at his side," trying to make a Charleston negro understand his French, and finally dashing after the frightened Ethiopian with drawn sword.[67] Even in Charleston, it appears, not every one spoke French.

But on the other hand the growing *rapprochement,* intellectual and political, between France and the rebellious colonies, brought French to the fore. Handschin speaks, quite properly, of the growing tendency to follow French guidance in establishing educational institutions during the Revolutionary and post-Revolutionary periods,[68] and naturally French played some part in the curriculum. After 1770 it is the opinion of Faÿ, a careful student, that there is a widespread growth in the teaching and reading of French; and after examining a great many colonial booklists he thinks that a quarter of the books imported into New York were French and that the proportion in other cities was smaller, but seldom less than an eighth.[69] Let us gather together some stray facts regarding the knowledge of French in this country during the years from 1770 to 1780.

Schouler describes a private school for young ladies in Boston conducted "by a lady" where French, English, and needlework were principal branches; and observes that French and dancing were commonly provided as "extras" in those schools. Both represented accomplishments that, in the opinion of a

[65] *Recollections of Samuel Breck,* pp. 47-48. The three Breck children learned to speak French fluently. Breck could not talk to the French naval officers at the dinner he gave them.
[66] Anburey's *Travels,* II, 230.
[67] Watson, *Men and Times of the Revolution,* p. 57.
[68] Handschin, p. 15; and see chap. xiii below.
[69] Faÿ, p. 26; and see the the long note on p. 43.

French refugee of 1776, "are now becoming more necessary as the means how to behave in fine company."[70] Faÿ observes that books by de Pauw and Raynal were read and criticised in America almost immediately upon publication; and of the South Carolina papers in 1770 and after, he notes that articles in French were often printed.[71] Robert Bolling, of Chellow in the county of Buckingham, who died a few years before the Revolution, "wrote," says the *Columbian Magazine,* "elegant poetry in Latin, French, and Italian."[72] In 1774, Rev. Mr. Tétard, he who married "Hector St. John" and Mehitabel Tippet in 1769,[73] the pastor of the French church in New York, advertises a French pension; two years before M. Giraut, protestant of Poitou, was teaching French at a night school in the same city.[74] M. de Saint Pry offers to teach French and dancing in New York in 1775; John Haumaid was "répétiteur de français" for students at King's College in this epoch; and in 1774 three Italians were teaching dancing, music, and French in the same city.[75] In Boston, M. de Viart, the fencing master, may have taught French; and M. Régnier certainly did.[76] Textbooks begin to increase also. As early as 1757 there is advertised *A Direct Guide to the French Language* to be published in Philadelphia, which may or may not have been published.[77] In 1779 Styner and Cist in Philadelphia brought out *A Grammar of the French Tongue, Grounded on . . . the French Academy,* a reprint of the second London edition,[78] a book so popular as to reach its ninth edition in 1794.[79] In Philadelphia Francis Daymon was writing a syntax of French verbs in the seventies.[80] *The Columbian Magazine* for April, 1791, notices a "curious explanation of the words ordeal and theft" translated from a modern French Dictionary. In the next decade, as we shall see, elementary textbooks multiplied. Certain it is that a

[70] Schouler, *Americans of 1776,* pp. 212-3.
[71] Faÿ, p. 27, and references.
[72] *Columbian Magazine,* II, 212, April, 1788.
[73] Mitchell, *St. Jean de Crèvecoeur,* p. 39.
[74] Faÿ, p. 26.
[75] *Ibid.,* and references.
[76] *Ibid.*
[77] Item 8011 in Evans. Prefontaine, Peter Papin de, *A Direct Guide to the French Language.* Philadelphia: B. Franklin & D. Hall (?), 1757. The proposal to print is found in the *Pennsylvania Gazette* for October 28, 1756.
[78] Item 16461 in Evans.
[79] Cf. item 27493 in Evans.
[80] Faÿ, p. 26.

good deal of propaganda material is in French; some of it translated by Pierre Eugène du Simitière, and some of it from unknown pens, and the existence of this material points to the ability of the colonists to write the language.[81] And in Faÿ's *Bibliographie Critique des ouvrages français relatifs aux États-unis (1770-1800)*, one will find a number of works in French printed in the United States; one may therefore legitimately argue that there were printers and publishers competent in the French language.

In fact, by 1776 the Americans were already representing a medley of tongues. It is estimated that one-fifth of the colonists in 1775 spoke a foreign language.[82] It is not therefore surprising in the seventies to find a competent knowledge of spoken French among the American leaders. The young French officers, for example, were fond of Hamilton, among other reasons, because of his perfect command of their language, an accomplishment which his biographer, it is true, esteems "a very rare accomplishment in the colonies."[83] Peter du Ponceau in Philadelphia of course spoke French; so did President Witherspoon of Princeton, with whom Chastellux had a long conversation; and at Colonel Cox's home, Lafayette and Rochambeau had the pleasure of conversing in their own language with Mrs. Cox's French aunts, the Demoiselles Chevalier.[84] At Yale, Ezra Stiles, inaugurated president in 1778, having taught French to his son, [85] argued in a Latin address for the study of languages.[86] These are at least significant straws.

But the decade of the seventies was only preparatory to the great increase in an interest in French in the eighties and nineties. The eighties are marked by the foundation of a French newspaper press, an increase in the teaching of French,

---

[81] Most of this propaganda material is addressed to the French inhabitants of Canada and the Illinois country. Cf. Evans, items 12421, 13740, 14302, 14543, 14575, 15123, 15190 for typical instances. Some of this material is printed by William Bradford, and some of it by Fleury Mesplet, both of Philadelphia. In addition to Simitière, Daymon apparently helped to prepare broadsides and army manuals in French.

[82] Schouler, *Americans of 1776,* p. 308 and note. Schouler lists the immigrants in relative order as coming from France, Sweden, Holland, and Germany.

[83] Lodge, *Life of Alexander Hamilton*, p. 25.

[84] Schouler, *Americans of 1776,* p. 226; Wharton, *Salons Colonial & Republican*, p. 100.

[85] Stiles, *Diary*, I, 409.

[86] *Cambridge History of American Literature*, IV, 446.

and an increase in the number of publications in French, as well as translations from the French, published by American printers. Let us begin with some general observations.

"It is asserted," says Handschin, "by an eighteenth century writer that French was taught in New England academies," as, for instance: Dummer Academy, founded 1763, incorporated, 1782; Phillips Exeter, founded 1778, incorporated 1780; the Academy of Leicester, incorporated in 1784; the academy at Hingham, founded in 1784; the academy at Marblehead, 1790; the academy at Hallowell, Maine, 1791.[87] The reciprocal influences between France and the United States in the period immediately following the American Revolution, involving as they did "frequent social and general intercourse," "growing and mutually profitable commercial interests" and "the necessary and ruling diplomatic relations resulting" from these, were such in the opinion of a historian of American education, "that the study of the French language naturally followed."[88] Since the affiliations of the South were more foreign and less provincial than those of the North (except in the educational institutions), they "earlier introduced the study of the European tongues, especially the French," in the opinion of the same writer.[89] French, remarks Faÿ, came in in all the cities, even those occupied by the British, and he cites a number of advertisements from Baltimore, Boston, New York, Philadelphia, and Richmond papers to prove that this is so.[90] French was both fashionable and important.

We have a great deal of evidence as to the introduction of French into institutions of learning in the eighties, the years in which a "marked interest in the introduction of the modern

[87] Handschin, *op. cit.* The writer in question is C. D. Ebeling, *Erdbeschreibung und Geschichte bon Amerika,* Hamburg, 1793, pp. 302 ff. I have not seen the book.
[88] Boone, *Education in the United States,* pp. 170-1. Boone adds also the "incipient republican impulse, and a waxing protestant spirit" as factors making "an alliance with the new European thought and literature both easy and important."
[89] *Ibid.*
[90] One of the most amusing is the advertisement of M. Brival de La Borderie in the *Pennsylvania Ledger,* Januray 21, 1778, and reprinted, which is addressed especially to the ladies:
"Sexe aimable, daignez lui prêter votre égide,
Recevez-moi pour caution,
Sous les ailes d'un pareil guide
On ne craint jamais le faucon."
Faÿ, pp. 83-4, and references.

languages in American colleges was manifested."[91] Under the influence of Jefferson, William and Mary established in 1779-80 the first professorship of modern languages in America. In 1780 French became a regular subject of instruction at Harvard;[91a] and in 1782 could be substituted for freshman and sophomore Hebrew. In 1784 Columbia University appointed its first French professor, as such; and in the same year Brown University (the College of Rhode Island) solicited the aid of Louis XVI in securing and maintaining a professor of French.[92] As for Yale, Silas Deane wrote from Paris to President Stiles, suggesting the creation of a chair in French and of a French library; affluent Frenchmen, he said, would assist, but Stiles did not dare accept the offer, and nothing came of it.[93] Yet at Cokesbury College (Abingdon, Maryland), the first Methodist Episcopal college in America, "the course of study embraced the various English branches, the Latin and Greek languages, together with Hebrew, German, and French"; the college opened its doors December 8, 1787.[94] And in Massachusetts, a provision was inserted into the constitution providing for the teaching of the beaux arts, and, on the French example, an Academy of Arts and Sciences was founded in Boston in which, eventually, there was instruction in French.[95] Quesnay, about the same time, was proposing a French Academy of Arts and Sciences of the United States of America, to be located at Richmond, with branches in Baltimore, Philadelphia, and New York, and with European affiliations—an unrealized dream, however, except as it played its part in shaping the curriculum of Jefferson's pet University of Virginia.[96] Meanwhile (the impulse originating in Virginia), radical Kentucky was introducing French into its new academies, of which some thirty (including seminaries) were established from 1783 to 1798.

[91] Handschin, p. 17.
[91a] Gallatin had 70 students in French. Stevens, *Albert Gallatin,* p. 18.
[92] The king never received the memorial sent him. Handschin, pp. 17-18; Hinsdale, *Foreign Influence Upon Education in the United States,* I, 599-603. On Columbia see *A History of Columbia University,* p. 61, 63-4. The Rev. John P. Tétard was elected professor at a salary of £100 per annum. For further references see Faÿ, pp. 84-5.
[93] *Diary of Ezra Stiles,* II, 296-7, 300-301.
[94] Strickland, *The Pioneer Bishop,* p. 166. It burned in 1796.
[95] Handschin, p. 16; Faÿ, p. 85, citing the *Works and Writings of John Adams,* IV, 259-60.
[96] This scheme is discussed in chap. xiii. For a brief outline of it see Handschin, pp. 15-16.

Transylvania Seminary, established at Danville in 1785, and moved to Lexington in 1788, included French in its curriculum,[97] and generally speaking, of all the modern languages French alone received any considerable attention on the western frontier,[98] where the clergy had less influence.[99] Again, in North Carolina, still something of a frontier state, one finds that French is coming in.[100] In addition to these influences, one must note that the growing intimacy between French and American scientific bodies like the American Philosophical Society, drew attention to the values of French as an aid to science. Students of the law, because of the immense prestige of Montesquieu, and because of their desire to liberate America from British law, were interested in French.[101] When the Harvard Medical School was established the French consul was present;[102] the king sent books to Pennsylvania and William and Mary;[103] the Parisian Academy of Sciences sent its publications to Harvard; and through the agency of Crèvecoeur as French consul the *Journal de médicine, chirurgie et pharmacie militaire* was widely distributed to scientific societies and doctors in the North.[104] It is perhaps not too much say that by 1783 French, as a key to scientific information, held the posi-

[97] Cf. Handschin, p. 14.
[98] Mary Estelle Delcamp, according to Rusk, in her MS., *The Early Life of Lexington Before the Year 1820*, now in the Lexington Public Library, includes five French schools in her list for Lexington from 1787 to 1820. *Literature of the Middle Western Frontier*, I, 52 and note.
[99] Cf. Faÿ, pp. 13-14.
[100] Thus Henry Pattillo advertises in the *State Gazette of North Carolina*, January 24-31, 1789, that at the Williamsburgh Seminary in Granville County, English, French, Latin, Greek and other branches will be taught; and in the same paper, October 8, 1789, the Reverend Samuel McDougall of Halifax, will open an academy and has teachers and assistants in English, Latin, Greek, and French (for boys).
[101] Faÿ, pp. 13-4. They usually had learned French, if they were rich, in some private school.
[102] Faÿ, pp. 140-1 and references.
[103] To the college of Philadelphia, where many of the books still remain; those at William and Mary were left in a damp cellar and later burned. Cf. Mitchell, *St. Jean de Crèvecoeur*, p. 146; "The Library of the College of William and Mary," *William and Mary College Quarterly Historical Magazine*, xix, 49.
[104] Faÿ, pp. 140-1, and references; Mitchell, *St. Jean de Crèvecoeur*, pp. 109-110. Mitchell lists doctors in Providence, Connecticut, Trenton, Boston, and Cambridge who asked for the journal and who, therefore, read French; in fact, the demand became so heavy that Crèvecoeur could not meet it and resolved to have Dr. Joseph Brown of New York translate and publish the journal by subscription. On other French scientific magazines thus distributed see Faÿ.

tion occupied by German after the founding of Johns Hopkins less than a century later.

French was more than ever *à la mode*. Faÿ goes through the contemporary newspapers in 1785 and collects the advertisements: the teachers of French increase in all the towns: in Philadelphia there are five, two devoted to the ladies; in New York, three; in Baltimore, eight, in Annapolis, one, in Boston, two or three, and any number in the South which is closer to the West Indies.[105] It becomes fashionable to subscribe for a French newspaper, such as the *Courrier de Boston*, 1789, which, edited by Joseph de Nancrède, ran to 26 numbers.[106] It becomes fashionable for professors, merchants, modists, and exporters of French wine to advertise in the French language.[107] And to meet this demand books commence to multiply.

For instance, F. Bailey of Philadelphia found it profitable to issue in 1870 a "broadside" containing C. Carré's *A Table of French Verbs . . . together with remarks on their particular irregularities. Inscribed to the American Philosophical Society*.[108] This was followed in 1784 by *Fables choisis, à l'usage des enfants et des autres personnes qui commencent à apprendre la langue française, avec un index alphabétique de tous les mots traduits en Anglois*—an early example of a reading book with a vocabulary, and reprinted.[109] Perrin's *Grammar of the French Tongue* (1779) has been noted; it was followed by his *Practice of the French Pronunciation* in 1780, and some *Instructive and Entertaining Exercises* in writing French in 1781.[110] Of even more consequence was John Mary's *A New French & English Grammar*, 1784, the first to be

[105] Faÿ, p. 140, and newspapers cited. At Charlestown and Winchester (Virginia) the schools were to unite in 1796; they wanted a Frenchman to teach French. La Rochefoucauld-Liancourt, *Voyages*, V. 79.

[106] In Philadelphia in July (?), 1784, Boinod and Gaillard printed a prospectus of *Le Courrier de l'Amérique*, of which, however, no copies are known to be extant. (Evans, item 18424.) For Nancrède's paper see Evans, item 21773; and for *L'Abeille Française*, item 24566. On the latter see Schinz, "Un Rousseauiste en Amérique," *Modern Language Notes*, XXXV, 10-18. On the Franco-American press see Belisle, *Histoire de la Presse Franco-Américaine*, and North, *The Newspaper and Periodical Press*, pp. 128-9.

[107] Cf. Faÿ, p. 139.

[108] Evans, item 16730. Carré published in 1794 from the press of S. and J. Adams in Wilmington a "Tableau de son & accens de la langue Anglaise" for the benefit of French émigrés. Evans, 26743.

[109] First printed by Charles Cist, Philadelphia, in 1784. Reprinted in 1793. Evans, items 18393 and 25273.

[110] Philadelphia (Cist) publications. Evans, 16461, 16946, 17308.

written by an American.[111] Finally one notes the publication of that favorite book, *Télémaque* "avec des notes et des remarques" in Philadelphia in 1784.[112] The demand has created the supply. French is indeed so popular that Brissot de Warville suggests all Americans drop English, the tongue of the tyrant, and learn French, the tongue of the generous ally.[113]

In view of all this instruction, how well is French understood? No question is more difficult to decide. Since the émigrés of the eighties and the nineties were not, on the whole, wealthy, there must have been a native reading public sufficient to make profitable the publication of the numerous books and pamphlets of propaganda which issued from the Philadelphia, New York, and Charleston printers.[114] It seems evident also that the French travellers of the eighties and the nineties had less difficulty in making themselves understood than, for instance, did Moré in the seventies, but this may in part be due to their knowledge of English. Brissot de Warville, whose testimony is open to suspicion, pictures a Frenchman complaining because the Philadelphia women do not speak French,[115] but in view of other testimony this does not seem to have been universally the case. Miss Vining, for instance, who at 25 was the belle of Philadelphia in 1783, spoke French fluently and with elegance, a fact which "made her a general favorite with the French officers" who wrote to Paris about her, and excited the curiosity of Marie Antoinette.[116] Colonel Bland, the congressional delegate from "Caroline" spoke French: he had learned it in the West Indies,[117] and when, on Brissot's own testimony, even a negro doctor knew the language,[118] we must conclude that some spoke it and many read it, at least in the metropolitan centers. Philadelphia, New York, Boston, Charles-

---

[111] Evans, 18575. Mary was French instructor at the "University of Cambridge"—i.e., Harvard.

[112] Evans, 18466. Boinod and Gaillard, Philadelphia, 1784.

[113] Quoted in Sherrill, *French Memories, 236-7.* Chastellux thought Hebrew would do better.

[114] The list is too long to quote here, but consult Evans' *Bibliography,* vols. VIII and IX, *passim.*

[115] Quoted in Griswold, *Republican Court,* p. 85, but I have not been able to find the passage.

[116] Griswold, *op. cit.* She corresponded with many distinguished men, and Lafayette was attached to her.

[117] Chastellux, *Voyages,* I, 188.

[118] James Derham, who "speaks French with facility and has some knowledge of Spanish." Brissot de Warville, *Travels,* I, 243.

ton, Annapolis, Baltimore—these are, in a sense, European outposts in the process of becoming Americanized; in each of these cities there is a colony of French exiles; in each there is a group of cosmopolitan Americans—diplomats, merchants, salon leaders, to whom French is at once a necessary accomplishment and a necessary ornament. It is probable that at no period in American history was French more generally understood than in the last fifteen years of the eighteenth century. But let us go on to the last decade of the century.

So far as formal instruction is concerned, two opposite tendencies are manifested in the nineties: a natural growth in the amount of instruction offered, and a reaction against all things French due to the excesses of the revolutionists and the conservative religious movement in the United States. It is true that "the love and knowledge of the French language and literature continued to grow, the instruction spreading also to the public high schools and, sporadically, to the elementary schools as well," but it is equally true, in the words of the same author, that "this influence was destined to decline."[119] In the conservative reaction away from the French Revolution may be seen one of the chief causes for this decline; and the conservative reaction commences to grow after 1793. On the other hand the number of émigrés for a while increased, and for them to teach French was frequently the simplest and easiest means of earning a livelihood. For a while the balance of forces was about even. Two magazine articles, published in 1790, typify the opposite views that were taken of the desirability of extending a knowledge of French in America. Benjamin Rush, in *Thoughts upon Female Education,* published in May, has little patience with the learning of French:

I beg leave further to bear testimony against the practice of making the French language a part of female education in America. In Britain where company and pleasure are the principal business of ladies; where the nursery and the kitchen form no part of their care, and where a daily intercourse is maintained with French-men and other foreigners who speak the French language, a knowledge of it is necessary. But the case is widely different in this country. . . . It certainly comports more with female delicacy as well as with the natural politeness of the French nation, to make it necessary for French-men to learn to speak our language in order to converse with our ladies, than for our ladies to learn their language, in order to converse with them.

Let it not be said in defence of a knowledge of the French language, that many elegant books are written in it. Those of them that are truly

[119] Handschin, p. 16.

valuable are translated; but, if this were not the case, the English language certainly contains many more books of real utility & useful information than can be read without neglecting other duties, by the daughter, or wife of an American citizen.[120]

The argument is familiar, but it is deftly side-stepped by John Swanwick in his *Thoughts on Education, addressed to the Visitors of the Young Ladies' Academy, in Philadelphia,* in the same magazine for October:

As to the study of the French language, it is true, at present it does not appear so necessary in America as in Europe; but when we reflect that education is the preparation we make for the journey of life, and that it is hard to say where this may lead, or upon what shore it may cast us. (*sic*) It seems very adviseable for those who can afford time and expence (*sic*), to make themselves acquainted with a language which, by common consent, is now become that of the world. . . . Our intercourse with Europe must be expected to be extended, especially with that part of it to whose illustrious exertions in our defence, in the late struggle for freedom, we are so greatly indebted for peace, liberty, and safety.[121]

Even in language, it is evident, political animosities were felt.

On the whole, during the greater part of the nineties French either held its own or positively increased.[121a] In 1792 Williams College accepted French for entrance as a substitute for the classics. In 1793 William and Mary required it for entrance, as did the University of North Carolina from its opening in 1795. In the same year Williams established its first professorship—one in French, and in 1799 Transylvania University created a tutorship in that language.[122] At Union College, New York, French in 1797 could be substituted for Greek in certain cases.[123] In 1790 the Boarding School in Bethlehem (Pennsylvania) for the Education of Young Misses announces the arrival of a lady from Europe versed in French, five Span-

---

[120] *Columbian Magazine,* IV, 288-89. A less determined, but nonetheless hostile stand is taken in an article published in *Ibid.,* I, September, 1787, p. 644.

[121] *Columbian Magazine,* V, 229 (September and October, 1790). A writer in the (Philadelphia) *American Museum,* V, June, 1789, 525-535, violently attacks Greek and Latin in favor of French and German.

[121a] A catalog of Moreau de St. Méry and Co.'s book store for 1795, examined by Bradsher, shows 920 entries for French books alone. *Cambridge History of American Literature,* IV, 536.

[122] Handschin, pp. 18-19.

[123] *Ibid.* French was taught in the preparatory school of the University of North Carolina. Cf. Battle, *History of the University of North Carolina,* I, 50.

ish dollars per annum being the charge for instruction;[124] and Handschin finds that it was the general practice for private schools in Boston to teach Latin, English, and French, and that the same thing is true of young ladies' schools, north and south.[125] Testifying to the interest in French in Boston is the printing of Nancrède's *L'Abeille Francaise,* 1792, composed especially for students at Harvard; John Hancock, John Q. Adams, James Lowell, Rev. Joseph Willard, D.D., Rev. Thaddeus M. Harris, Dr. John Warren, MM. Coolidge, Parkman, Sargent, and Thayer, and Elisa Ticknor are among the subscribers.[126] This same Nancrède published in 1797 an edition of *Télémaque* revised and corrected by himself, and dedicated to young America of both sexes.[127] In 1793 Chambaud's *Fables* was reprinted at Philadelphia, as we have seen; and the next year Perrin brought out his *Elements of French Conversation,* his *French Grammar* in that same year reaching its ninth edition.[128] If Americans did not know French, it was not for want of textbooks.

The nineties are marked also by an efflorescence of French newspapers, which, though their main circulation was among the émigrés, must have done something toward spreading the language, especially since many of them were printed in both French and English.[129] *Le Courrier de l'Amérique* has already

---

[124] Handschin, p. 13.

[125] Ibid., pp. 13-14. Saint-Méry (*Voyages,* p. 125), for example, notes that French, the classic languages, and English, are taught at Newark Academy in 1794. He describes "pensions pour les enfans" at New Utrecht directed by M. Tot, where day scholars and boarding pupils were taught Latin, Greek, French, and mathematics, and he doesn't like the idea. Pp. 187-8. Again in the *North Carolina Gazette* (Newbern) for April 30, 1796, M. Reverchon informs the citizens of Newbern that he will open a school for the purpose of intsructing young gentlemen and ladies in the principles of the French language; the advertisement is several times reprinted. Once more, La Rochefoucauld-Liancourt reports that at Nazareth Academy (Moravian), ten miles from Bethlehem, French was taught, but that the instructors were poor and scarcely read it well. Most of the pupils, he says, come from the West Indies, where the Moravians had missionaries. *Voyages,* VII, 43-44.

[126] Evans, item 24566. Published by the press of Belknap and Young. And see Schinz, *op. cit.* The selections in *L'Abeille* are highly Rousseauistic.

[127] Schinz, p. 17.

[128] Evans, items 27492 and 27493. Inasmuch as Evans is still incomplete it is difficult to know what French texts were published after 1794.

[129] As marking the prevalence of the French language in Philadelphia, it is interesting to note that when Colonel de la Balme wished to advertise employment for the destitute at his workshops twenty-eight miles from Philadelphia, he printed his broadside in French, German, and English, three parallel columns. This is as early as 1778. Evans, item 15861.

been noticed, and so, too, has the *Courier de Boston*. In 1792-3 the Abbé Louis de Rousvelet edited *Le Courier Politique de l'univers*, published in Boston by the press of J. Bumstead, a short-lived enterprise. This was succeeded by the *Courrier politique de le France et de ses colonies*, a tri-weekly, published in Philadelphia in 1793-4 and running to at least 45 numbers. In the same years and in the same city appeared the *Journal des révolutions*, a continuation of a Santo Domingo paper; and in 1793 there is some trace of a *Journal politique et littéraire de Philadelphia*.[130] In 1794 a bi-lingual paper, *The American Star, or, Historical, Political, Critical & Moral Journal*, edited by C. C. Tanguy de la Boissière, was published in Philadelphia, and survived to its fortieth issue. Of more consequence was the *Courrier Français* (April 15-December, 1794, and continuing down to 1798), published by Pierre Parent, and of some significance as being a daily paper in French. In the same city in 1794 there was issued from October, 1794 to January, 1796, a bi-lingual paper, *The Level of Europe & North America*, edited by Peter Eyron, LL.D.[131] These papers are all short-lived, but their very existence must have helped to spread a knowledge of French. Nor did the publications of book and pamphlet in that language cease.[132]

If one runs through John Davis's *Travels in America, 1798-1802* or the *Diary* of André Michaux (1787-1796),[133] he will have a fair survey which will offer some hint of the amount of French spoken in America outside the larger centers, and on the whole, the number who knew the language is larger than one might expect. According to Griswold, but upon what authority I do not know, it is said that when Freneau was appointed "translator of the French language for the state department" in 1791, "the place is said to have been a sine-

---

[130] *Le Radoteur*, September-December, 1793, was issued from same office as the *Courrier politique*, but little is known of it. Evans, 26051.

[131] See Evans, items 18424, 21773, 25351, 25352, 25673, 25674, 26051, 26561, 26822, 27218.

[132] See Evans, especially volume IX, index under French language. As marking the profitableness of printing in French, it is to be noted that M. Mozard, formerly printer in Port-au-Prince, came to Boston in 1790, bringing a small press and several fonts of neat types made in Paris with him. He was afterwards consul for the French Republic, and later sold his types to John Mycall, who took them to Harvard, Worcester County, and afterwards to Cambridgeport. Thomas, *History of Printing*, I, 10-11, note. At no time, however, did the publication of books in French equal the publication of the books in German.

[133] *Proceedings of the American Philosophical Society*, XXVI, 8-145.

cure, as other clerks in the office were familiar with the French language,"[134] a fact which seems to point to a considerable diffusion of the tongue. A French traveller quoted in Sherrill, observes that New Rochelle is "inhabited only by Frenchmen, who speak the purest French in the United States, and indeed but little else; children are sent there to learn it, and everybody there speaks it, even the negroes,"[135] so that we must not imagine that the older centers of diffusion had lost their influence. And even as late as 1798 Latrobe, writing to Ferdinand Fairfax, is outlining a scheme of education which includes the teaching of French and English, as well as Greek and Latin, in American academies.[136] Nevertheless the growing irritation between the two countries, culminating in the publication of the X.Y.Z. correspondence and the naval war of 1798-1800 meant that French was no longer popular.[137] It is probably too much to say with Faÿ that all the ground gained from 1774 to 1795 was lost for twenty years, but it is significant that after 1797 the advertisements of French masters disappear from the newspapers, except in the West.[138] And as showing the signs of the times, it is interesting to note the increasing number of manuals of English for Frenchmen published in the nineties: the French, instead of teaching their own language, were learning English.[139]

The eighteenth century saw French extending its hold. It became the language of diplomacy and social intercourse; powerful political and commercial interests favored its popu-

---

[134] Griswold, *Republican Court,* p. 288.

[135] *French Memories,* p. 177. Count de Revel, examining General Nelson's Virginia home, reported in this epoch that "if you wished diversion you found at your hand very good English and French books." *Ibid.,* p. 190.

[136] *Journal of Latrobe,* p. 75.

[137] The political disturbance is possibly responsible for the "revolt" against French at Harvard. When he was there in 1796 and later, young Washington Allston "drew one picture representing his French class seated around a table, except one boy reciting, the French master holding a pig in his hands and directing the boy to pronounce 'oui' just like the noise made by the little brute." Flagg, *Life and Letters of Washington Allston,* p. 34.

[138] Faÿ, pp. 302-3.

[139] Pierre Siret, *Elements de la langue Anglaise,* Philadelphia, 1792; C. Carré, *Tableau de son & accents de la langue Anglaise,* Wilmington, 1794; *La nomenclature Anglaise* (list of English verbs), Philadelphia, 1794; Peyton, *Les éléments de la langue Angloise,* Philadelphia, 1794; Siret, new edition, Philadelphia, 1794. Evans, items 24289, 26743, 27418, 27498, 27705. Cobbett, whose first occupation in America was teaching English to the émigrés, mainly in Philadelphia, published his *Le Tuteur Anglais* in 1795, but used it in manuscript long before. He earned £330 teaching English. Cole, *Life of William Cobbett,* pp. 53-54.

larity; and certainly among the upper classes there was a marked tendency to learn French. Came then at the very close of the century a marked conservative movement, and the language, among all things else that were French, necessarily suffered. Nevertheless, the damage done was not felt until after the opening years of the nineteenth century. Let us therefore extend our inquiry into the last 48 years covered by this investigation.

5. THE SAME FOR 1800-1848

Of the nineteenth century certain general facts may be observed. In the first fifteen years of that century intercourse with France was at all times precarious, and not infrequently stopped; and, because of the Revolution in Santo Domingo, intercourse with the West Indies was no longer productive of an interest in things French. In the next place a profound disgust with the excesses of the Revolution and with the tyranny of Napoleon characterized the attitude of the American people. Again, the religious reaction was in full power; and the French language was necessarily associated with writers and doctrines held to be atheistic, anarchic, and dangerous. Lastly, the French press, until the establishment of the *Courrier des États-unis* in New York in 1828, seems to have died out.[140] These matters were not favorable to the spread of a knowledge of the language. And we must remember also that the French in this country were gradually dropping their native tongue.

On the other hand, to offset these factors, there were certain positive considerations. The social prestige of French as a language, though it might suffer an eclipse, could not be destroyed. Again, after the Louisiana purchase of 1803, Americans, and particularly certain merchants and planters, came increasingly into contact with such centers of French culture as New Orleans[140a] and Mobile. In the next place, the settlement of the Northwest Territory meant a new contact with French culture—a dying culture, it is true, yet one sufficiently vital

---

[140] The *Gazette Française* of 1825 seems to have reached only four issues. Belisle, *Histoire de la Presse Franco-Américaine*, pp. 16 ff. However, see pp. 213-14, below.

[140a] Thus when Judah P. Benjamin went into business in New Orleans, he was acute enough to recognize the advantage of a thorough familiarity with French; so he sought pupils who needed coaching in English, and traded his services for French lessons. As marking the inter-racial mixture, one notes that he married a Creole Catholic, Natalie St. Martin. Butler, *Judah P. Benjamin*, pp. 33; 35-6.

to keep alive a few struggling newspapers and printing presses. And, what is perhaps even more important, the desire of the middle classes (beginning to emerge in this period into social importance) for all that had made brilliant the life of the cosmopolitan upper groups, naturally led to the spread of French among schools and academies patronized by this group, even though French was being discontinued in Eastern universities.

French made, it is true, certain gains among educational institutions from 1800 to 1815. Thus, in 1801 it was ordered that no student at the University of North Carolina should be graduated without Greek or French.[141] In 1800 when the University of Georgia was organized—on paper, at any rate— it was ordered that "French might be substituted for Greek or Latin if the tutor was able to teach it," and in 1806 the trustees elect M. Petit de Clairville professor of French at $400 per annum.[142] The regulations issued in 1804 for South Carolina College permit the election of French in the sophomore and junior years, and after the opening of the college in January, 1805, the board resolved to ask the legislature for a full-time professor of French. M. Herbemont was elected French tutor 23 April, 1807, and at the first commencement, December, 1807, there was a French declamation.[143] At Dartmouth, in 1811, the study of French and Oriental languages was recommended to the students.[144] In Louisiana, meanwhile, the legislature created the College of Orleans in 1805, which began its rather stormy career under the presidency of Jules d'Avezac of Santo Domingo: the college naturally taught French.[145] But Harvard dropped instruction in French about the beginning of the century; and so did Yale, Brown, and Columbia; and Handschin is probably right in saying of the Eastern institutions that "after a period of trial, of greater or less duration, nearly every institution seems to have reached the conclusion that the new subjects (modern languages) were not

[141] Handschin, p. 19.
[142] Hull, *A Historical Sketch of the University of Georgia*, pp. 10, 20. At the same time that the trustees paid the French "professor" $400, they hired a "tutor" (who happened to be an American) at $800.
[143] Handschin, p. 19, says that French was *required* in the sophomore and junior years, but this seems not to have been the case. See Laborde, *History of South Carolina College*, pp. 30, 39-40, 43. Herbemont resigned his position November 25, 1817. A professorship of French was then created at $1200. P. 90. Bernhard met Herbemont in 1825, *Travels*, I, 209.
[144] Smith, *The History of Dartmouth College*, p. 84.
[145] Cf. Breaux, "Some Early Colleges and Schools of Louisiana," *Publications of the Louisiana Historical Society*, VII, 136-142.

successful."[146] Bad teaching, the objections of traditional classicists, and above all a fear that the morals of the young might be warped by such texts as Nancrède's *L'Abeille* are the causes for this attitude.[147]

In the West, of course, as in Louisiana, French was being taught.[148] In Louisiana territory the parish academies taught French, especially after 1811.[149] Michigan, a territory which "had the stamp of French nationality markedly until the middle of the nineteenth century," had its French Catholic schools in the eighteenth century; curiously enough, however, the Ladies' Seminary established in Detroit in 1804 seems to have had no provision for French instruction.[150] Rich French youths were sent to Quebec and Montreal to learn French. And in American newspapers published in the West a considerable amount of space, says Rusk, was often given to articles or advertisements in the French language; for instance, *The Michigan Essay,* a short-lived paper printed in Detroit in 1809, contained about a column of French and advertised books in that language.[151] Books in French were actually printed at Detroit in 1809.[152]

---

[146] Handschin, p. 19.

[147] Handschin lists only three French textbooks for the period 1800-1815, *A New Grammar of the French Language, Originally Compiled for the Use of the American Military Academy by a French Gentleman,* New York, 1804 (194 pp.); Phillips, *A Key to French Pronunciation and French Idiom,* Baltimore, 1812; and *Syllabaire François, or a French Spelling-Book, also an Introduction to French Grammar by Way of Question and Answer. By Mr. Porney* (Pyron du Martre), New York, 1815. (Handschin, pp. 104-5.) Dufief in Philadelphia, who called himself "professor of French literature and bookseller," published in 1810 a three-volume *Pronouncing Dictionary of French and English,* and also *Nature Displayed; or, A New and Infallible Method of Acquiring a Language in the Shortest Time Possible. Deduced from an Analysis of the Human Mind,* which by 1884, had reached twenty-one editions. (See also Kellogg, *Life and Works of John Davis,* p. 84.) In 1806 there appeared in Philadelphia a rival publication, *Nature Explained,* by one D'Arlic, intended to teach French by an opposite method. Scharf and Westcott, *History of Philadelphia,* II, 1145. We must wait the completion of the Evans *Bibliography* before we know how many French textbooks were published by 1820.

[148] The West in general was less affected by the conservative reaction than the East; hence the desire of Eastern protestants to found academies and colleges as missionary enterprises to convert the radicals.

[149] Handschin, pp. 9-10.

[150] Handschin, p. 12.

[151] Rusk, *The Literature of the Middle Western Frontier,* I, 10-11. At St. Louis in 1810 a prospectus was issued for a French paper to be called the *Gazette de la Louisiane,* but Rusk finds no evidence that it ever came to birth.

[152] James Miller, who printed the *Michigan Essay,* published in 1809, *L'ame penitente ou le nouveau pensez-y-bien.* In 1810 Coxshaw of Detroit

Generally speaking, however, this Western influence was not great.

French of course was not suppressed and did not disappear. John Davis contributed essays in French to the (London) *European Magazine* and the *London Monthly Magazine* in 1800, sending the manuscripts from America.[153] John Quincy Adams read French, and after his presidency solaced himself by reading in the tongue he had earlier acquired.[154] Bryant learned the rudiments of Latin and French from his father some time before 1811, and later took lessons in French and fencing from a Napoleonic officer living in Great Barrington.[155] If German was unknown, "a few Bostonians could read and even speak French," and it was owing to this fact that Madame de Staël opened the eyes of many to the culture of Germany.[156] In Philadelphia the "omniscient Dr. Samuel Latham Mitchill" had three Indian songs translated into French and out of French into English.[157] Richard Alsop, one of the Hartford Wits, translated from the French and the Italian languages.[158] Theodosia Burr Allston sought and found French lodgings in New York in 1809; and reports to her father from South Carolina that her boy "reads and speaks French with facility."[159] Burr, meantime, was making a great collection of French books to bring home to his daughter and her son; he himself, of course, spoke and read French easily.[160] In Virginia, Francis Gilmer

published *Neuvaine à l'honneur de St. François Xavier,* and in 1811, *Les ornements de la mémoire; ou les traits brilliants des poètes françois les plus célèbres.* In 1812 Théophile Mettez printed three books at Detroit with French and English on opposite pages, one by Berquin. For these books, and for a discussion of the bibliographical problem involved see Rusk, pp. 11-12. The Constitution of the French Moral and Benevolent Society of Detroit, to which my attention was called by Rusk's book, and a copy of which was kindly furnished me by the librarian of the Burton Collection of the Detroit Public Library (the printed bulletin is incomplete), seems to indicate a laudable interest in French letters on the part of its members. See *Blowe's Emigrants' Directory,* p. 697.

[153] Kellogg, *Life and Works of John Davis,* p. 65. He set up a "private French and Latin academy" in May, 1805. *Ibid.,* pp. 93-94, and see pp. 83-5. He also translated Berquin-Duvallon's *Travels in Louisiana,* and *The Life and Campaigns of Victor Moreau. Ibid.,* pp. 96-7.

[154] Morse, *John Quincy Adams,* p. 223.

[155] Godwin, *Biography of William Cullen Bryant,* I, 85, 205.

[156] Adams, *History,* I, 94.

[157] *Cambridge History of American Literature,* IV, 445.

[158] *Ibid.,* IV, 446.

[159] Davis, *The Private Journal of Aaron Burr,* I, 129, 244, 284.

[160] Davis, *The Private Journal of Aaron Burr, passim.* He had a good deal

corresponded with Dupont de Nemours in French, deciphering the Frenchman's letters, it is true, with some difficulty.[161] And it is needless to remark that the "Virginia dynasty" all read French, and that Jefferson was something of a French scholar. But to multiply instances were wearisome; the great mass of Americans were not interested in French, and in view of the ignorance involved, its was Melish's opinion in 1806 that, in place of the French exciting an anti-British prejudice, the difference in language meant that "there really is little whereon to ground a free interchange of sentiments and friendship" between French immigrants and Americans,[162] a sentiment repeated by other travellers. It is undeniable that French was on the decline between 1800 and 1815.

With the conclusion of the Napoleonic wars, however, conditions changed. America no longer had anything to fear from either France or Great Britain. The opening of the sea-lanes made communications with France again feasible, and with the improved means of transport, an increasing number of Americans went to Paris. On the other hand, the older generation of politicians and patriots were dying out: they have their last stand with John Quincy Adams in 1825; with Jackson in 1829 they are mainly gone, taking with them the animosities of a world that is to their descendants merely a tale in a history book. The old prejudices against French disappeared; and with the increasing prestige of the middle-class, a knowledge of French became more and more the mark of social accomplishment.

Thus of New York boarding schools in 1817 Fearon remarks: "The dead languages, music, surveying, drawing, dancing, and French are taught at the superior schools: the latter is rather generally understood, and in some measure necessary, French families being more frequently met with here than in England."[163] Of America generally in 1822-3 Candler says that "reading, writing, arithmetic, grammar, and geography, with a smattering of French, and a few lessons in music and

of difficulty in getting French dictionaries to suit him. Cf. I, 436, 439, 447; II, 209, 210, 219. This may mean that no good dictionaries were available in America, but I doubt it; it is rather a bit of Burr's fastidious and dictatorial temperament.

[161] Trent, *English Culture in Virginia*, pp. 40-41.
[162] Melish, *Travels*, pp. 155-56.
[163] Fearon, *Sketches of America*, p. 39. French, geography, and philosophy cost $60 each per annum; arithmetic, reading, and writing, $40; and Greek, Latin, and mathematics, $80.

dancing, are all that even with the wealthiest are commonly necessary for their daughters."[164] In 1845 enough persons knew French in New York to make Mrs. Tiffany's excruciating mispronunciations in Mrs. Mowatt's *Fashion* popular; indeed, by that date, the habit of using elegant French phrases in books by polite writers is wide-spread—witness the volumes of N. P. Willis. In Boston in the winter of 1846-7, Agassiz delivered a series of lectures on "les glaciers et l'époque glaciaire" in French; the subscription list was large, the ladies outnumbering the gentlemen, and according to his own account it was the best course of lectures he ever delivered.[165] Perhaps no one of these passages will bear much weight; but taken together, they are significant. A knowledge of French had once more become socially a desideratum.

Probably this knowledge was superficial. "In quoting from books in French and other foreign languages," wrote Candler in 1822-23, "a translation is given instead of the original. French and Latin are supposed to be so generally understood in England, as to render a translation unnecessary; but I believe that at least half, and probably three-fourths of the readers of our reviews, are unacquainted with either. The same I doubt not is the case in America." And he notices an absence of French phrases in the *North American Review.*[166] Mrs. Trollope a little later comments on the "incorrectness of the press" which she finds "very great; . . . they make strange work in the reprints of French and Italian."[167] Doubtless the captain of the Plymouth militia company who accepted the flag "in the name of this corpse" was not sole and singular in his blunder in 1838,[168] for American education was at a low ebb in the twenties and the thirties. Indeed, there is something grotesquely pathetic in the directions of that queer genius, Constantine Rafinesque, when printing his original French verse in *The Western Review and Miscellaneous Magazine* in Lexing-

---

[164] Candler, *Summary View of America,* p. 71.
[165] Marcou, *Life, Letters and Works of Louis Agassiz,* I, 291.
[166] Candler, *Summary View of America,* pp. 355-6.
[167] *Domestic Manners of the Americans,* pp. 293-4. She says the editors do not do much better with Latin, and do not often meddle with Greek.
[168] "Not a muscle of any countenance betrayed the slightest perception of the error in pronunciation; for in America it is common to give all French words used in the language, such as *route, tour,* etc., the pronunciation which their orthography would warrant if they were English." Buckingham, *America,* III, 535.

ton, that the "reader must supply the accents."[169] Probably not one reader in fifty could do it.

Nevertheless, after a period of hesitation from 1815 to 1830, the teaching of French began once more to prosper. Among the older schools, Harvard, which had dropped the teaching of French at the opening of the century, was given the Smith Professorship of Belles Lettres in 1816, and in the same year Francis Sales was made assistant in French.[170] Ticknor began active work in 1819; in 1825-27, when the "elective plan" was introduced, the modern languages were given a larger place in the curriculum, and in 1847-8 French was required in the freshman and sophomore years.[171] At the University of Pennsylvania J. F. Grillet was instructor in French from 1823 to 1829; and A. de Valville from 1829 to 1844. At Columbia French was taught from 1828 to 1839 by the Rev. Antoine Verren; and from 1839 to 1856 by Felix G. Berteau, both being professors in the faculty; and in 1836 a grammatical knowledge of French was required for entrance.[172] When Amherst opened in 1821 no French was offered, but three years later French appears in the catalogue, together with German, and a second course paralleling the classical course, established in 1825 or 1826, permits the substitution of French and Spanish for the ancient languages.[173] This "course," however, was abolished in 1829, and French became one of the regular studies.[174] At Princeton from 1806 to 1830 instruction was offered by a succession of persons; and in 1829 the alumni tried to endow a chair in the modern languages; thereafter French seems to have been regularly taught. When James B. Angell attended Brown in 1845-9, the librarian, Charles C. Jewett, had charge of sophomore

[169] Rusk, *Literature of the Middle Western Frontier*, I, 165-7, discusses this queerly cosmopolitan publication.
[170] Ticknor, in accepting the professorship (he was elected in July, 1816) stipulated that the salary from 1815 to 1816 should be spent on purchasing suitable books for the library. Quincy, *History of Harvard University*, II, 324.
[171] For this and the general data about the colleges and universities, consult Handschin, *passim*, unless otherwise specified.
[172] At Washington Institute, on Thirteenth Street in New York, there was a tutor in French. Allaben, *John Watts de Peyster*, I. 108.
[173] Tyler, *A History of Amherst College*, pp. 31-32, 43, 64. The first French professor, a native Frenchman, proved incompetent and was dismissed (pp. 66-67), but the demand for the modern languages was never heavy.
[174] Tyler, *op. cit.*, p. 67.

French; when he went to the Smithsonian Institute, his place was taken by George E. Greene, whose life had been mainly spent in Europe: in 1848 Greene spent most of the class hour discussing the European revolutions.[175]

At Dickinson College Claudius Berard taught French, Spanish, Italian, and German from 1814 to 1816; then followed a vacant period; then a professorship in the modern languages in 1826 or 1826. At Bowdoin in 1820 French was taught by a native Frenchman; in 1825-54 there existed a professorship in junior and senior French, the incumbents of which seem to have possessed the purest Anglo-Saxon names. From 1825 to 1832 French was optional at Yale; in 1834 it seems to have received a kind of re-instatement; but no professorship was created until 1864. Rutgers had a professor of French in 1841. By 1832 there were professors of French at Middlebury College, the University of the City of New York, Wesleyan University, Hartford College, Columbian College (Washington, D. C.), and Geneva College (N. Y.).

In the South the University of Virginia established a professorship of modern languages in 1825. Dr. George Blaettermann, whose name betrays his nationality, filled the position till 1840, teaching French and German.[176] However, at the University of North Carolina French was dropped from the curriculum in 1818, nor was it reinstated until 1875, the cause being the fear of infidelity. At South Carolina College, Mr. Michaelowitz was teaching Hebrew, Arabic, and the modern languages in 1829 at the munificent salary of $600 a year;[177] before his incumbency the history of French in the institution had been varying.[178] At the University of Georgia Professor James Jackson taught chemistry and French (the combination is significant) in 1823; about 1830 William Lehman of Germany became professor of modern languages, remaining until 1841.[179] When Longstreet became president of Emory College

---

[175] Angell, *Reminiscences*, p. 24.

[176] Patton's remark (*Jefferson, Cabell, and the University of Virginia,* p. 97) that Blaettermann's appointment came at a time when no American university "had done more for a modern language than to license an occasional French dancing-master to give lessons in his native tongue" is hardly warranted.

[177] Laborde, *History of the South Carolina College,* p. 150.

[178] There was an instructor from 1804-6; "Professor" Paul H. Perrault taught from 1806 to 1811; there was a tutorship from 1807 to 1818; and a vacancy from 1819 to 1828. The figures are Handschin's.

[179] Hull, *A Historical Sketch of the University of Georgia,* pp. 41-42, 50-51. Dr. Moses Waddell, president of the institution during the 1820's, is said to have been an excellent French scholar. Cf. Wade, *Augustus Baldwin Longstreet,* pp. 25 ff.

in the same state in the forties, he added Professor Haderman to the faculty as professor of modern languages, but although Haderman's standing as graduate of Leipsic and Paris was loudly proclaimed, the man and the subject were both dropped.[180]

In the West also the popularity of French was growing.[181] French was taught during the brilliant days of Transylvania University.[182] French was recognized as a subject in the University of Michigan in 1817. The discipline was introduced at Vincennes University in 1810; and at Miami in the years 1827-30 R. W. Schenck taught French. After 1835 the subject was discontinued, but in 1841 it was resumed. And in Louisiana French was a regular subject of instruction in the various higher educational institutions established by the legislature.[183]

But perhaps of more significance is the introduction of French into the secondary schools, public and private. In New England "after 1830 it became typical to offer instruction in this subject even if only as an incidental study to which was attached a special fee."[184] In the private seminaries and academies it was offered as a social accomplishment; the practice spread from the East to the West and from the academies to the newly organized high schools.[185] Certain of these secondary

---

[180] Wade, *op. cit.*, p. 260.

[181] Before taking up the Western schools, we ought to observe that French was regularly taught at West Point. Cf. Bernhard, *Travels*, I, 111-113; and Captain Hall, *Travels in North America*, I, 88. The cadets were required to read French but not to speak it.

[182] On Western schools cf. Rusk, I, 51-67. Lafayette was addressed in French in Lexington in 1825. Levasseur, *Lafayette in America*, II, 187.

[183] Cf. Fortier, *History of Louisiana*, III, *passim*.

[184] Handschin, p. 13; Grizzell, *Origin and Development of the High School in New England Before 1865*, p. 289. Of twenty-four high schools in 1818 one offered French; of eight in 1827, none; of three in 1836-7, one; of six in 1840-49, three. The figures are from the specimen curricula given, pp. 289-295, and indicate that French was spreading.

[185] Thus Godley observes that there is a large attendance of boys and girls in the private schools of Boston, and that they are taught Latin, Greek, French and certain other subjects. *Letters from America*, II, 93. He notes that French is taught in the Philadelphia high school, II, 154. (This is in the forties.) At the very end of our period Lyell gives the curriculum of the Boston Latin School; it includes French, mathematics and "other branches preparatory to a mercantile career," besides the conventional curriculum. *Travels in the United States, Second Visit*, I, 149. Handschin lists certain northern high schools in the order of their adoption of French as follows: English High School, Boston, 1832; the high school of the College of the City of New York, 1838; the Central High School, Philadelphia, 1839; Newburyport Female High School, 1845; the Sandusky High School, 1846; the Massillon (Ohio) High School, 1848. See him, p. 26.

schools, indeed, were famous for their teachers, who were often native Frenchmen; one such is the Cates Classical School in Charleston, where French was taught from 1820 on; another was Carré and Sanderson's Seminary in Philadelphia (French taught after 1816). Handschin remarks that certain schools in North Carolina "were celebrated as being equal to the best in America, and were attended by young ladies from various Southern States"; he finds 1000 pupils in the compass of forty miles in North Carolina in 1816, and in these schools French became standard.[186]

French spread, as I have said, to the Western academies. Thus in 1826 it was already being taught in the Cincinnati Female College, The Female Boarding School, and the Cincinnati Female School.[187] As early as 1808 Dr. Scott was teaching French in his private school at Vincennes, Indiana. The Lancaster Institute for Young Ladies (to return to Ohio) offered French in 1838. So did the Hillsboro Female Seminary in 1839. So did the Norwalk Academy in the same year for $5.00 a quarter, and the Female Seminary of Norwalk in 1840 at $8.00. In the Twinsburg Institute (Twinsburg, Ohio), you could in 1843 study both German and French, a combination rather rare. From these schools, writes the historian of the subject, "the study spread until we find it in most of the better academies, especially those for girls in Ohio," and it was mostly taught by women.[188] At the Academy of the Sacred Heart in St. Louis in 1818 French was taught, as it was generally in the Catholic institutions in the old Louisiana territory.[189] In fact, French spread so generally over the country as a subject for study that by 1838 it was even being taught to the blind.[190]

Another method of testing the growth of an interest in French after Waterloo is to observe what books were published

---

[186] Handschin, p. 14. I find in the *North-Carolina Standard,* 26 December 1834, an advertisement for the Warrenton Female School (Mrs. Harriet J. Allen) : board and tuition per session, $50; music, $20; French, $7.50.

[187] The data in the above paragraph are from Handschin unless otherwise specified.

[188] It was usually (together with music and dancing) an optional subject, and required a special fee, on the British model. See the conversation of Alice and the Mock Turtle.

[189] It is interesting to note that the Louisiana legislature in 1846 passed a bill to purchase one hundred copies of Gayarré's *History* in French for the use of the public schools. Fortier, *History,* III, 240.

[190] Fact. Combe visited the Institution for the Blind in New York City, and reports that "the pupils shewed great intelligence in reading both in English and French." *Notes on America,* I, 61.

dealing with the acquirement of this particular foreign language. Thus I find in 1816 a magazine notice of *Jean et Jeannette, ou les petits aventuriers Parisiens,* "by one of the most interesting romance writers of France," a book which will educate the young in the language.[191] In 1817 Peter A. Chazotte published in Philadelphia a philologico-pedagogic treatise with an enormous title,[192] which he followed in 1819 with the *Metaphysics and Philology of Languages.*[193] Carré brought out *A new and expeditious method for learning the French language, exemplified by an interlinear translation,* etc. in 1822 (Philadelphia); and N. M. Hentz published in the same year *A Manual of French phrases and French conversations adapted to Wanostrocht's grammar* at Boston the same year. This same writer's *A classical French reader* (Boston, 1825) was, I believe, widely used; the same year saw Poppleton's *New elements of conversation in English and French,* etc. Boston, 1825. We are, however, omitting Texier de la Pommeraye's *Abridgment of a French and English Grammar,* Philadelphia, 1822, which he followed in 1826 with a *Lecteur Français Amusant et Instructif.* [194]

So much for the twenties. It seems odd in view of the number of language books available, that Longfellow was compelled to prepare his own texts upon his return from Europe in 1829, but so he did[195]—*The Elements of French Grammar,*

[191] *Analectic Magazine,* VIII, 276, September, 1816.
[192] *An essay on the best method of teaching foreign languages, as applied with extraordinary success to the French language; with a table displaying the philosophy of the relative personal pronouns, and rendering their use and syntax perfectly easy at first sight. To which is prefixed a discourse on the formation and progress of language.*
[193] Scharf and Westcott, *History of Philadelphia,* II, 1145.
[194] For the above cf. Handschin, pp. 104-5; and Scharf and Westcott, *op. cit.* Hentz proposed to issue a collection of French plays with notes in 1826. *North American Review,* XXII (April, 1826), 475. *A Nouveau Dictionnaire Français-Espagnol et Espagnol-Français* by Don Domingo Gian Trapany and A. de Rossilly was published in New York in 1826. *North American Review,* XXIII, October, 1826, p. 496.
[195] Higginson, *Henry Wadsworth Longfellow,* pp. 56-57. C. N. G. Dufief's *Nature displayed in her mode of teaching the French language* had reached a sixth edition in 1825; M. l'Abbé Bossut's *The French Phrase Book, or Key to French Conversation,* Boston, 1826; Levizac's *Theoretical and Practical Grammar of the French Tongue,* revised by Stephen Pasquier (4th American edition) New York, 1826; ditto, a new edition, 1827; *Le Lecteur Français de la Jeunesse,* Northampton, Mass., 1827; *The French Genders taught in six tables ... By the Master of a Grammar School,* Boston, 1827; Bossut's *Explanatory and Pronouncing French Word-Book,* Boston, 1827; an edition of *Télémaque* by A. Bolmar, Philadelphia, 1828 are all listed in the *North American Review* in the given years, and were presumably available.

translated from Lhomond (Portland, 1830); *French Exercises,* from Wanostrocht (Portland, 1830), a *Cours de Langue Française,* published in Boston in 1832, and—this indicates the spread of French—a *Syllabus de la Grammaire Italienne . . . à l'usage de ceux qui possédent la Langue Française* (Boston, 1832).[196] William B. Fowle, principal of the Monitorial School in Boston, wrote *The First French Class Book* (Boston, 1832), which the *American Monthly Review* has no hesitation in recommending.[197] In 1832 the same magazine noticed *La Bagatelle; intended to introduce very young children to some knowledge of the French language* (n. d., n. p.); and in 1833, Ticknor's *Lecture on the Best Methods of Teaching the Living Languages.*[198] In 1834 there appeared in New York Manesca's *A Philological Recorder, adapted for the oral system of teaching living languages*; in 1837 there was published in Boston an anonymous *Conversational Phrases and Dialogues for French and English;* and in the same year appeared one of the most popular of the French textbooks, Bugard's *Practical Translator.*[199] In 1838 there were published *A New French Manual,* by A. Pestiaux, "professor of the French language in the city of New York,"[200] a *Progressive French Grammar and Exercises,* published in Philadelphia; a *New French Manual,* by Gabriel Luzenne (New York) and a *Treatise on French Poetry; or Explanation of the Rules of French Prosody . . .* by François Turner of Yale University.[201] The following year the *North American* notices the *Fables de la Fontaine avec des Notes Historiques, Mythologiques, et Grammaticales, à l'usage des Collèges et des Écoles. Par F. Sales, Maître de*

[196] From the Longfellow bibliography in the *Cambridge History of American Literature.* Longfellow contributed an article to the *North American Review* in April, 1831, on the "Origin and Progress of the French Language," and one to the same magazine in October, 1840, on "The French Language in England." Incidentally, the Lhomond grammar (in French) is listed in the *North American Review* as published in Boston, XXII (July, 1826), p. 240.

[197] *American Monthly Review,* April, 1832, pp. 413-4. The reviewer does not, however, find all the selections equally interesting. Florian's stories do not engage strongly the attention of the pupil; *Télémaque* is "a heavy undertaking," but the *Ami des enfans* of Berquin is "excellent."

[198] Boston, 1833. *American Monthly Review,* October, 1832, pp. 346-8 and May, 1833, pp. 373-377.

[199] This is the second edition, Boston, 1837. I have not traced the first. Reviewed in the *North American,* October, 1838, p. 505.

[200] Cf. Handschin, pp. 104-5.

[201] Reviewed in the *North American Review,* XLVII (October, 1838), 505; and July, p. 264; *New York Review,* III (October, 1838) 479.

Français et d'Espagnol à l'université de Harvard.[202] Thereafter the number of texts steadily increases, but to go on were
tedious; let us consign them to a footnote,[203] and content ourselves with the fact.

[202] XLVIII (January, 1839), p. 316. Additional language texts in the
thirties, as listed by the *North American Review* include: *Easy Lessons
in Learning French, Boston* (XXXVI, April, 1833, 545); *Principles of
General Grammar . . .* from the French of A. J. S. de Lacy, by D. Fos-
dick, Jr., Andover (XXXVIII, April, 1834, 540); *French Dialogues and
Phrases . . .* by A. G. Callot, Philadelphia (XLI, October, 1835, 523);
George Folsom, *A New French and English Pronouncing Dictionary,* n. p.,
(Do.); *L'Abeille pour les enfans,* Philadelphia, (XLI, July, 1835, 257);
Levizac's French Grammar improved and enlarged by A. Balmar, Philadelphia, and C. de Behr's *New and Simple Method of Teaching the French
Grammar,* New York (XL, April, 1835, 538); J. Mouls, *The Art of Speak-
ing the French Language in a Short Time,* New York, (XLIII, October,
1836, 546); a new edition of Levizac, New York (XLII, April, 1836, 551),
etc., etc.

[203] Thus *The North American Review* notices the *Parisian Linguist; or,
an Easy Method of Acquiring a Perfect Pronunciation of the Language
Without a French Master. Intended for Academies and Schools in the
United States and for American Travellers in Europe. By an American
Resident in Paris.* Boston, in October, 1841 (LIII, 537); and the *Christian
Examiner* (XXXI—3d series, XIII—November, 1841, pp. 275-6) takes cognizance of it also. The *Boston Quarterly Review* (V, 256, April, 1842)
thinks that J. A. Weisse's *Key to the French Language,* Boston, 1842, is
admirable for "its completeness and cheapness." (See also the *North American,* LV, 278, July, 1842). The *Democratic Review* for March, 1844 (XIV,
326) and *The Evergreen* for November, 1846 (III, 351) devote some space
to Sarah E. Seaman's *A New System of French Grammar,* based on Nöel
and Chapsal, and revised by C. P. Boardman (New York, 1843). The
North American lists Laporte's *French Grammar* in January, 1844 (LVIII,
258) among the new books, and the Seaman volume in April, 1844 (LVIII,
519). In the same number (p. 517) the reviewer finds *A New and Complete
French and English, and an English and French Dictionary, on the basis
of the Royal Dictionary. Compiled by Professors Fleming and Tibbins* and
"prepared with additions by J. Dobson" (Philadelphia) something that
satisfies a long-felt need for an accurate and complete work of this kind.
On p. 520 Ullman's *French Made Easy* is listed. In *The Evergreen* for
July, 1846 (III, 223-4) there is a review of Gabriel Surenne's *Standard
Pronouncing Dictionary of the French and English Languages* (New York),
and of Ollendorff's *New Method of Learning to Read, Write and Speak
the French Language;* both are recommended. The *Democratic Review* for
August, 1847, notices, *Morceaux Choisis des Auteurs Modernes à l'usage
de la Jeunesse* by F. M. Rowan. New York (Cf. *Literary World,* July 17,
1847, I, 568, and *Graham's Magazine,* September, 1847, XXXI, 156). The
book includes extracts from Balzac, Dumas, Janin, Lamartine, Michelet,
Sismondi, Tocqueville, Thiers, and others. See also the *American Whig
Review,* August, 1847, VI, 220. Of M. de Fivas's *Elementary French
Reader,* the *Democratic Review* observes with due obeisance to custom that
"no student should be without it." (January, 1847, XX, 90.) The same magazine (April, 1847, XX, 379) opines that Callot's *New French Reader*
"supplies a great want" since it includes material from French drama.
The *American Whig Review* passes a favorable judgment on Pinney's
The Oratorical French Teacher (Hartford and New York, 1847), finding
the conversational method a sound one, but I am unable to say whether

Meanwhile we must not forget that other means of spreading a knowledge of French had not failed. French newspapers had by no means disappeared: the *Courrier des États-unis* was only beginning its long and honorable career, and there were others.[204] In New Orleans, in particular, French newspapers flourished: of the ten papers in New Orleans in 1810, one, a tri-weekly, was in French; one, a daily, was in English and French; three were weeklies in English and French, and the rest were minor sheets. In 1810 was founded *Le Propagateur Catholique* which in 1880 was still alive. *L'Abeille,* which is *par excellence* the French newspaper of New Orleans, began publication in 1827. And in New Orleans, of course, there was a considerable business done in publishing French books.[205] Men in the diplomatic service and in public life not infrequently knew French.[206] Men in the army knew French as well.[207] Nor did the

Pinney's *The Practical French Teacher,* noticed by the *North American* in April, 1847 (LXIV, 524) is the same book or not; at any rate, the same periodical notices the fourth edition of the second in January, 1848 (LXVI, 258). *De Bow's Commercial Review* for March, 1848 (V, 299-300) lists four elementary language books, including Rowan and Callot, and the *North American* names three by Laporte of Harvard in October, 1847. The *Democratic Review* for November, 1848 (XXIII, 375), lists Girard's *An Elementary Practical Book for Learning the French Language.* This list could, I think, be extended, but enough has been cited to indicate the efflorescence of French textbooks in the thirties and forties.

[204] The *Detroit Gazette,* 1817, lasted only four months. The *Gazette Française,* 1825, lived out four issues. *Le Patriote* (Burlington, Vermont), 1838, a propaganda paper, survived two months. *L'Ami de la Jeunesse* (Detroit, 1843), lived four months. But after the Canadian insurrection there is a marked increase in French newspapers in the United States. Belisle, *Historie de la Presse Franco-Américaine,* pp. 27, 17.

[205] See Du Menil, *Literature of the Louisiana Territory;* Fortier, "French Literature in Louisiana," *Transactions and Proceedings of the Modern Language Association,* II, 31-60; and the bibliography of the subject in volume IV of the *Cambridge History of American Literature.* For early French books published in the West see Rusk, *Literature of the Middle Western Frontier,* II, 42ff. (bibliography) ; and I, 11-12.

[206] Thus Buchanan, Minister to Russia 1832-3, writes Jackson October 1/13, 1832, from St. Petersburg that he has already made considerable advances in his knowledge of French; and at the end of the month he informs Mrs. Slaymaker that he has begun to speak it. Yet as late as December, 1832, he is still distrustful of his command of the language. Curtis, *James Buchanan,* I, 151, 156, 163, 170. His successor, George Miffin Dallas, knew French very well; at any rate he has read Lamartine's *Voyage en Orient,* for in his *Diary* he compares a description in Lamartine with life in Russia. *Diary,* p. 31. James Fenimore Cooper had his family learn French before he went abroad with them as consul at Lyons. They had a governess from New Rochelle and a French teacher (the same Manesca who wrought the elementary book noted above) from Santo Domingo. *Correspondence of James Fenimore-Cooper.* I, 54-5. Spencer Fullerton Baird, the second secretary of the Smithsonian Institute.

practice of private tutoring in the language cease with the last great wave of émigrés.[208] Every Frenchmen in the United States listed in the previous two chapters of this study, was a potential, and many a one was an actual, teacher of French.[209] It is sufficient to observe that in the period from 1815 to 1848, after some ten or fifteen years of wavering, the study of French in the United States continually increased;[210] and no American in the urban centers need have gone without a knowledge of the tongue if he wished to acquire it, and few in the rural communities, provided they were near one of the innumerable academies in which French, after some fashion, was not uncommonly taught.

was studying earnestly at French and German in 1842-3. Dall, *Spencer Fullerton Baird*, p. 94. Rufus Choate read regularly in the French classics. Brown, *Life of Rufus Choate*, pp. 99, 101, 102, 142, 144, 145. Instances could, I think, be indefinitely multiplied.

[207] Levasseur, seated next to Major General M'Comb of the Engineers at Monroe's dinner in honor of Lafayette was charmed to find that the American "speaks French with perfect facility." *Lafayette in America*, I, 169. This was in 1824. I do not know where else to introduce a story too good to lose. The American military system was strongly influenced by French practice, even to words of command. When General Gaines, who hated General Scott, "was asked what he thought of General Scott's plan of retaining the French words of command in his 'System of Tactics,' he responded, 'I a— think, sir, that—a—the—a English language is a— sufficiently copious—to express—a—all the ideas that—a General Scott will —a—ever have." Mrs. Davis, *Jefferson Davis*, I, 210-2.

[208] Thus when young James Gordon Bennett first came to New York he thought of opening "a permanent commercial school" and the prospectus announces that, if required, French and Spanish will be taught "by natives of these countries." Pray, *Memoirs of James Gordon Bennett and His Times*, p. 50. *The Magnolia*, I, September, 1842, 200, remarks that "for new books—English, German, Italian and Spanish—we commend the reader to the collection of Samuel Hart Sen.," at Charleston. *Debow's Commercial Review*, IV, December, 1847, pp. 559-60, carries an account of M. Vattemare's activity in the international exchange of books, for which Congress voted $500. These items indicate the effectiveness of such tutoring.

[209] French tutors show up in unexpected places. H. M. Brackenridge, son of the author of *Modern Chivalry*, born at Fort Pitt, was as a child sent to St. Genevieve that he might learn the language. He then spent a year in Gallipolis, and a dozen years after his first journey, he lived again in St. Genevieve. Rusk, I, 124.

[210] "The impulse after 1850 toward the study of the modern languages and literatures was due rather to the immigration which had been set up by the European troubles of 1848, and which brought many cultivated Germans and Frenchmen to the United States. Hindered by our own political disturbances during the fifties and sixties, and helped by the 'scientific' and utilitarian opposition to the classics, it reached self-consciousness and scholarship in the seventies, with the foundation of the Johns Hopkins University (1876). . . . " *Cambridge History of American Literature*, IV, 459.

6. SUMMARY AND SIGNIFICANCE OF THE CHAPTER

What now have we learned? That the great mass of the American people ever learned enough French to read or speak it does not appear. But among the cultivated classes from the earliest times there were those who were familiar with the language; and it is from these leaders that ideas and attitudes descended to the rank and file in the United States. Insofar, therefore, as the leaders were able to know French literature and French ideas at first hand, they were able to give a version of French life to their followers more nearly correct than would otherwise have been possible. But even among leading Americans, unfortunately, there were many throughout our whole period with no command of the tongues. On the other hand the command of French by social and intellectual leaders gave that language a peculiar prestige; German, for example, a language in which in the eighteenth century more books were actually printed in the United States than were books in French, never possessed this social glamor, and did not develop in the United States until after the emigrations of 1848 and the rise of the modern German universities; Italian, which lacked both emigrants to speak it, and prestige to make it desirable, was but little known—Spanish, except on the borders, still less so. The most important fact gleaned from our study is the social prestige which French acquired.

If we glance back over the periods traversed, we shall see that in the seventeenth century, so far as Anglo-Saxons are concerned, French was mainly the possession of the New England scholar and the Southern gentry. In the same century, however, the Huguenots began their great work of teaching their mother-tongue, a work that is among the chief influences in the spread of French in New York and Charleston and in smaller centers. Gradually the Huguenots became Americanized and gave up French, though never in our period did they wholly lose it. Meanwhile, from 1700 to 1750, because of the wars, French failed to increase among the Americans, if it did not positively decline. From 1750 to 1770 a renewed emigration from France developed in the larger centers the habit of employing private tutors in French. Then in the years 1770 to 1797 French as a language reached its height, so far as the eighteenth century is concerned: politics, war, social glamor, science, all combined to make a knowledge of French desirable. But the controversy over the Revolution ideas, the differences between the two countries, especially from 1797 to 1800, raised up a counter-spirit; afterwards, when the British navy closed the seas, and our only source of information about France was London, the prestige of French steadily declined, so that from 1800 to 1815 the teaching of French in the United States fell off. Incidentally we may observe that the return of many émigrés to their own country may have reduced the opportunities for competent instruction. From 1815 to 1830 is mainly a period of uncertainty, due to the shifting basis of social life in America; however, college and university instruction tended to increase. When by 1830 the bourgeois spirit was largely in possession of the chief centers, when it became increasingly common to make the trip to Paris, but above all, when the successful middle-class, desirous of aping the cosmopolitan groups, wished to acquire a French accent along with a French costume, we observe a remarkable spread of French teaching through the collegiate institutions and through such thoroughly middle-class schools as the academy and the high school. Incidentally, we have observed that the passing of the animosities of the Revolutionary and Napoleonic periods removed a barrier to the diffusion of French. But, by the very nature of the interest in French, the study of the language was never very thorough. With the loss of influence from the émigré and Huguenot groups, we must observe also in the nineteenth century the opening of contacts with modern Louisiana, and the vast Western country where French had acquired a hold, particularly at St. Louis and in Michigan. Incident to our whole discussion is, of course, the obvious fact that geographical accident has removed us far from France. Since this is true, the remarkable fact is not that so few Americans knew French; the remarkable fact is its wide diffusion in a Protestant, Anglo-Saxon culture.

VII

French Manners in America

1. THE SOCIAL QUALITY OF FRENCH CULTURE; THE LEVELS AT
   WHICH IT REACHED THE AMERICANS

Fᴿᴱɴᴄʜ culture is essentially social, or so its apologists would
have us believe. It is not primarily individualistic or mystic,
but on the contrary finds its best expression in the midst of
highly sensitized social groups—groups which permit ideas to
flow freely. The cénacle, the salon, the court, the poetic school—
how instinctively one recalls the great periods of French art in
terms of some form of social expression, some literary and
artistic group! And so it is that French culture, particularly
in manners and what one may call the minor arts, has spread
most easily over the frontiers of France when there have been
groups in other lands specially prepared, as it were, to receive a
social impress: the court of Catherine the Great, for example,
the courts of the German princes in the eighteenth century, or
the court of the Stuarts, set apart after the Puritan regime from
the rest of England, and prepared by its long sojourn abroad,
to become "French." It is, indeed, in the eighteenth, most social
of centuries, that French manners conquered the western world.
Can they have penetrated America? Let us see.

But we must first determine where to look. We have divided
the cultural forces of American life during our period into
three—the frontier, the middle-class, and the cosmopolitan
spirit. It is too much to expect that all three of these will have
been impregnated by French manners. Barring random traces
of influence, we must, to begin with, omit the frontier from
this portion of our inquiry. For the spirit of the frontier,
though it is not anti-social (witness the husking-bee, the dance,
the house-raising, and the revival), is essentially un-social—un-
social, that is, in the sense which implies social relations that are
a kind of culture to be consciously pursued. The manners of
the frontier are not necessarily "un-cosmopolitan" in one
sense; the frontier itself is hospitable to many and various types
of people; there, as to the foreign legion, all the world may
come without question. But the intricate social backgrounds
of a dozen nationalities are on the frontier broken and reduced
to their elements; and whatever the distant sources of the

communal activities of the frontier may be, the culture thus created is *sui generis* and suspicious of all social attitudes not its own. Whatever elements *coureur de bois* and missionary, the French settlement and the French trapper may have contributed to the folk-ways of the frontier (for instance, in the community dance), it is not here that we shall look for any very profound influence upon American manners of Gallic modes and customs.

Nor, despite the curiosity of the middle-class about the life of Europe, should we look among the bourgeoisie for such influence, save for one or two important considerations. The first of these considerations is the law of imitation which leads each stratum of the social pyramid by a kind of instinct to imitate the stratum immediately above it—think what their superiors think, do what they do, admire what they admire (all within limits) ; and thus it is that French manners being once established as desirable at the apex of the pyramid, French manners, diluted to the ideals of the middle-class, become worthy of imitation in the central region of its slopes. That is to say, the *nouveaux riches,* in proportion as they imitate the F. F. V., may be paying unconscious tribute to the court of Louis XIV.

And in the second place, the practical spirit of the middle-class, avid of all that will help it get on, may adopt from French modes of life, either directly or at second hand, such matters as it finds useful, no less than those which are ornamental; and this may be the case particularly in those small arts which lie on the borderland between manners and things aesthetic: cooking, for instance, dress-making, and what not. The insularity of the bourgeois spirit is not the insularity of the frontier spirit; it is rather a relative insularity. Hence it will ignore what does not feed its peculiar appetites, but it will reach out for what it desires. What it desires, above all, is that, retaining the solid satisfaction of middle-class existence, it shall amalgamate with these something of the glittering uselessness of upper-class life; that it shall enjoy the satisfactions of virtue and also the pleasures of vice.

It is evident therefore that to determine the influence of French manners upon American manners, we are driven back upon the leisure class, which is the social expression of the cosmopolitan spirit. If we establish proof that the leisure class has adopted French ways, we may reasonably assume without further argument that much of these adaptations will percolate down to the aspiring bourgeoisie. Let us turn accordingly to a survey of the leisure class in America in its relation to French manners during the period covered by this study.

2. THE FRANCO-BRITISH ORIGINS OF THE MANNERS OF THE COLONIAL LEISURE CLASS

No leisure class could appear in the American colonies until economic development had gone far enough to maintain that class, nor does it appear that a truly indigenous American leisure class of any size can be found in the colonies until well toward the close of the seventeenth century. We may put aside the gentleman adventurers of the early experiments of the London Company and others in the South as resulting in no enduring social history, save a tradition of fine manners; and if the statement that no leisure class developed in America until about 1700 seems to ignore what we have said elsewhere regarding the great planters, the royal governors, and the proprietors in the Middle and Southern colonies in the seventeenth century, it is yet true enough in the sense we are now speaking. These various elements formed a leisure class imposed from above, or rather, from without. One may take as symbolic of the situation Locke's famous constitution for Carolina with its three ranks of landed proprietors; the constitution was never enforced because it did not fit American needs, but it points to the fact that the upper classes were thought of as temporarily living in exile, out of England and in America, and as being in fact a transplanted portion of English nobility and gentry. So it is that the visiting royal governors and proprietors—men like Ashley, Ablemarle, Carteret, and Craven of the Carolina company, or the Calverts in Maryland, or Lord De La Ware, or the various governors of Virginia, New York, and Massachusetts, thought of themselves as exiled on business in America.[1] With this attitude they infected the resident planters, merchants, and gentry. The connections of the great colonial families were overwhelmingly British; to England, when they could, they gladly returned;[2] and it was not until a second and

---

[1] "The habits, life, customs, computations, etc., of the Virginians are much the same as about London, which they esteem their home." Hugh Jones, *The Present State of Virginia* (1724). Quoted in Stedman and Hutchinson, II, 279. Jones further argues that Britons acquire mistaken sentiments of Virginia because they listen to sailors' talk.

[2] Barring those in religious exile. During the Commonwealth in England, however, movement back and forth between New England and the mother

third generation of great landed proprietors had struck roots
in the soil, it was not until the Boston and Philadelphia merchants had begun their great business of developing American
commerce, that a truly indigenous leisure class developed.

Men thus deracinated may, before 1660, for our purposes,
be ignored. But with the Restoration one notes that the tendency of Charles II to give away grants in America to his
favorites inevitably meant a greater contact between the colonists and the British leisure class, and this during a period of
steady colonial development. Now in this epoch polite England
looked with reverence upon the social customs of France; and
the Chevalier de Grammont was the *arbiter elegantiarum* of a
court half-French, the manners of which, as reflected in Hamilton's *Memoirs,* are those of Versailles. It was therefore inevitable from 1660 on, that as the basis of the colonial leisure
class slowly shifted from Great Britain to America, French
manners[3] should filter into the colonies, particularly in the
South. In consequence, such matters as gallantry and punctilio,
an exaggerated respect for women and a swaggering disdain
for one's inferiors, an interest in the play-house and the gaming
table,[4] the elaborate dueling system, and the decorous—or in-

country is an important social factor. See Murdock, *Increase Mather,*
especially the early chapters; and for the close relations between Great
Britain and the Puritan colonies under William III, see Murdock, chaps.
xiv-xvi.

[3] The anonymous French traveller of 1765 arrived at Williamsburg, and
records in his diary under date of April 25 that "on our arrival we had
great Difficulty to get lodgings but thanks to mr sprowl I got a room at
mrs. vaubes's tavern, where all the best people resorted. I soon got ac-
qainted with several of them, but particularly with Colonel Burd, sir
peton skiper, Capt. Russel, Capt. le foré, and others, which I soon was
like to have had reason to repent, for they are all professed gamesters,
Especially Colonel Burd, who is never happy but when he has the box
and Dices in hand. this Gentleman from a man of the greatest property of
any in america has reduced himself to that Degree by gameing, that few
or nobody will Credit him for Ever so small a sum of money." "Journal of
a French Traveller in the Colonies," *American Historical Review,* XXVI,
741-2.

[4] Complaint was soon made in New England. Benjamin Tompson's
New England's Crisis (dated about 1675) complains of the inroads which
European fashions have made upon the ways of the good old times:

> "Deep-skirted doublets, puritanic capes
>
> . . . .
>
> Was comlier wear, our wiser fathers thought,
> Than the cast fashions from all Europe brought."

He complains also about the importation of French wines. The good old
days were days

> "Ere wines from France and Muscadoe to,
> Without the which the drink will scarcely do."

Quoted in Stedman and Hutchinson, II, 33-35.

decorous—taking of wine, a finicky regard for dress, elaborate verbal ceremony—all, in short, that distinguishes the second Lord Baltimore from Captain John Smith, all that distinguishes the Cavalier gentleman from the Elizabethan freebooter, became the code of manners by which the Southern gentry lived, and which was fundamental to the code of manners of the Old South. But the basis is French.[5] Williamsburg became a colonial court in imitation of the court of the Stuarts, which was in turn an imitation of the court of the Bourbons.[6] The Americans began by receiving their French culture at second hand, and upon this second-hand model Virginian social life was formed.[7] In the South the contagion was not resisted, whatever the political situation might be: Bacon's Rebellion was not directed against aristocratic manners. In the North, especially in Massachusetts, the appointment of the king's friends to the governorships alienated colonial feeling—the gap between nobleman and puritan was too great to be bridged.[8]

Thus it was, however remotely, that French influence served to soften the manners of the early colonials. But direct contacts were to be had, and it is to the Huguenot settlers in America that one looks more immediately in this earlier period for the training of the leisure class in gentle manners. New

[5] For example, the *Virginia Gazette* for November 18-25, 1737, carries the following advertisement:

> November 25, 1737
> This is to give Notice, that this day the subscriber has opened his School at the College, where all Gentlemens Sons may be taught Dancing, according to the newest *French* manner, on Fridays and Saturdays once in Three Weeks, by
> *William Dering, Dancing-Master*

The paper was published at Williamsburg.

[6] Consult Bruce, *Institutional History of Virginia in the Seventeenth Century*; and *Social Life of Virginia in the Seventeeth Century*; and Bassett, *Writings of Colonel William Byrd,* the introduction.

[7] It is symbolical that in 1675 the management of colonial affairs in London was in the hands of the *Lords* of trade. Not until 1768 was there a secretary of state for colonial affairs. The phrase marks the shift from an aristocratic and arbitrary management to a mercantile management. Bassett, *Short History,* p. 77.

[8] A prime example is Andros, appointed by James II. "The new regime also gave offense by celebrating Christmas, by requiring persons taking an oath to kiss the Bible instead of holding up the hand, by ordering that school teachers should have licenses from the governor, and by requiring the shops to close on the anniversary of the death of Charles I. All these offenses, however, were surpassed by the extreme zeal with which the governor ordered and celebrated public thanksgivings for the birth of a son to their Catholic majesties in 1688." Bassett, *ibid.,* p. 95.

York and Charleston may serve as two typical centers of such influence. Thus in New York the French played an important role in giving shape to colonial "society." Huguenot immigration increased after the Revocation of the Edict of Nantes and continued to 1700 or thereabouts; and the immigrants were of notable character. "Socially," says Fosdick, "they were a most effective factor, tempering the tone of society, and in large measure creating it. That so many of the streets of the city, as Des Brosses, Lispenard, etc., were named after the French citizens, shows that they were men of note in the business and public life of the time. The intermingling of the French and Dutch produced a strong and charming type of character in which the best traits of both races appear."[9] An important social element was the French club, established largely by the Bayard family; another was the French Huguenot church, founded in 1659, whither the polite resorted to polish their French—here, or at New Rochelle. Such families as the de Lanceys, the de Forests, the Montgomerys, the Freneaus, the Vassars, the Gallandets, and the Ganos, gave social tone to society, and distinction to urban life.[10] Of even more consequence for social training were the Huguenot colonies at New Rochelle and New Paltz. New Rochelle in particular served as a school for the sons and daughters of the nobility and gentry. John Jay, Washington Irving, and General Philip Schuyler[11] are representative instances of Huguenot training.

[9] Fosdick, *French Blood in America*, pp. 222-223.

[10] List culled from Fosdick, p. 287. Writing of the eighteenth century, Mrs. Grant says that to the "polished society" of New York City, "the accession of many families of French huguenots, rather above the middling rank, contributed not a little: those conscientious exiles had more knowledge and piety than any other class of the inhabitants; their religion seemed indeed endeared to them, by what they had suffered for adhering to it. Their number and wealth was such, as enabled them to build not only a street, but a very respectable church in the new city. In this place worship continued to be celebrated in the French language within my recollection, though the original congregation was by that time much blended in the mass of general society." *Memoirs of an American Lady*, I, 42. Lists of family names may be found in Baird and Rosengarten.

[11] Mrs. Grant apparently was not sure that the general had been at New Rochelle. She says that he was a man of "excellent understanding, which had received more culture than was usual in that country. But whether he had returned to Europe, for the purpose of acquiring knowledge in the public seminaries there, or had been instructed by any of the French protestants, who were sometimes retained in the principal families for such purposes, I do not exactly know; but am led rather to suppose the latter, from the connexion which always subsisted between that class of people and the Schuyler family." *Op. cit.*, I, 151.

New Rochelle became a resort "not only for the acquirement of the French language, but on account of the hospitality and politeness of its inhabitants."[12] The citizens were, indeed, "men of birth and breeding and of good estate in France—of a far higher average culture than the English and Dutch of New York."[13] On week days in New Rochelle there were tableaux and little comedies," and "dancing was the expected amusement in most households at every evening gathering, and these took place as often as possible." The boarding and day schools of the French Protestants, thus eagerly patronized, taught language (English and French),[14] and all the genteel accomplishments. There the young lady learned to play and sing, and received instruction in the arts (the painting of flower-pieces and water-colors was thought genteel), and in embroideries; and there the young gentleman learned to make his bow. Gentle manners were the special forte of these schools; "how to avoid awkwardness of movement or carriage; how to bear themselves gracefully erect; how to enter a drawing-room with a grave and gracious inclination," and so on.[15] Similar instruction was to be obtained at Charleston,[16] at Philadelphia, at Boston, at various centers where there were French Huguenots, a French dancing master, a French musician.

Even in staid New England French fashions, though frowned upon, had their vogue. In the *Boston News-Letter* for Feb. 23-Mar. 2, 1712, this interesting advertisement appears:

"At the House of Mr. George Brownwell in Wings-Lane Boston is taught Writing, Cyphering, Dancing, Treble Violin, Flute, Spinnet, &c. Also English and French Quilting, Imbroidery, Florishing, Plain Work, Marking in several sorts of Stiches, and several other works, where Scholars may board."

In September of the same year Mr. Richard Bill was selling at auction at the house of Richard Pullen a cargo of imported goods, including "Allamods French and English." In February 1713 Mr. Stephen Labbe, "Vendue Master," announces that he will sell on March 4 "sundry European goods," mostly dress

---

[12] Fosdick, p. 235.
[13] *Ibid.*
[14] An English master was engaged for the former subject.
[15] Smith, *Colonial Days and Ways*, pp. 160-166; Fosdick, pp. 413-4.
[16] On Charleston see Mrs. Ravenel's *Charleston* and Rosengarten, pp. 93-94; and chap. iv, 101 ff. above. For Charleston in the late eighteenth century see Fraser, *Reminiscences of Charleston*, especially pp. 51-64.

goods, and including "Choice French Linings." In July, 1721, Governor Samuel Shute, addressing the General Court, scolded the house severely for adjourning without his knowledge, since he had important matters to communicate, namely

"to persuade you to take some Effectual Measures to prevent the Plague coming amongst us, there being nothing so likely to bring it in, as the French Silks and Stuffs which are constantly brought into this province."

The Governor instructed the printer of the *Boston News-Letter* to say that the fault did not lie in the customs officers, "who have done their utmost Indeavours in preventing such illegal Practices, and stopping such Clandestine Trade," but "the many Harbours of this Province" favored the smuggling of French goods. In June, 1728, we read that there are

"To be Sold by Jonathan *Barnard* at his Shop over against the Town House in Corn Hill, *Boston*, Fine Mecklyn Laces and Edgings, fine Cambricks, best sort Dutch black Padisoys, best Dutch black Mantua Italian black & colour'd Mantua's Rich French Allamode, India fl(o)w'red Damasks, stript & plain India Sattens, Venetian flow'red Damasks fine Chints both white & coloured. Men and Womens silk Stockings, low priz'd Table Cloaths, and a variety of English Goods."

If such excerpts give us some glimpse at the fashions in clothing, we learn from a contributor to the *News-Letter* for Nov. 16-23, 1732, what the older heads thought of these new-fangled ways. The writer sternly denounces "Mr. *Pelham's* Dancing School," which as entertainment is a "formidable. . . . Monster in this part of the World," "a Licentious and Expensive diversion." The new generation cries out "for Musick, Balls and Assemblies like Children for their Bells and Rattles;" it is well known, he says, "how our Extravagance in Apparel, and Luxury at our Tables, are hastening the ruin of our country," along with "Dress and Dancing."[16a]

The Huguenots meanwhile helped to teach the colonists how to live. Bringing them the arts, the accomplishments, the graces of the most polished civilization in the world, together with a gaiety and good humor in strong contrast to the New England or the Pennsylvania temperament, the Huguenot ameliorated the condition of colonial life, softened the hard edges of existence. The French at New Rochelle were, according to tradition, the first to utilize the remnants of worn-out garments by cutting them into strips and weaving them into carpets; they brought in

[16a] *Boston News-Letter*, nos. 463, 439, 514, 913; *Boston Weekly News-Letter*, nos. 76, 1504.

better spinning wheels; better grafts and roots from the fruit-growing and wine-making districts of France; they imported hangings, mirrors, china, and furniture; and whereas the English and Dutch dyed linen yarn and wove it into ugly stripes and checks for bed and window curtains, the French used white linen or dainty colors, usually in one shade, with light designs. Their homes, in fact, were more attractive and dainty, their skill in dress and color, with needle and bobbin, more commendable, and withal, they were thrifty—admirable models for the growing leisure class.[17]

3. FRANCO-BRITISH INFLUENCES ON THE DEVELOPMENT OF THIS CLASS

For a leisure class, modelling itself upon France and England, was developing. "Reverence for European institutions and traditions—a formal reverence at least—stamped these colonies from the outset; and class distinctions were everywhere accepted as part of the established order of things."[18] Patricians took the lead everywhere; even in smaller towns and rural neighborhoods each household knew and kept its place.[19] Read Schouler's description of the stately funeral of Lord Botetourt in Williamsburg;[20] the date, it is true, is 1770, but such customs have been long established. Or consider the colonial belles and beaux described in Sale's *Old Time Belles and Cavaliers*: Pocahontas taken into English court society; Robert Carter, who, dying in 1772, left 10,000 pounds sterling, 1000 slaves, 300,000 acres of land, and who visited England more than once; William Byrd II, born in 1674, the friend of the Duke of Argyle, the heir of over 25,000 acres, husband of the daughter of Governor Parke of the Leeward Islands, who remained abroad until 1726, whose daughter, Evelyn, was a reigning belle at court; the Fairfaxes—Thomas, for example, who came to Belvoir, near Mount Vernon, fresh from the most brilliant drawing rooms of London, and who became the eighth Lord Fairfax—it is a true aristocracy, a true leisure class. In Maryland the Catholic planters educate their sons in France or England; in Charleston "it is the fashion to Send home all their Children for education, and if it

---

[17] Fosdick, pp. 410-411; Smith, pp. 7-8.
[18] Schouler, *Americans of 1776*, p. 7.
[19] *Ibid.*, p. 307.
[20] *Ibid.*, pp. 45-46.

was not owing to the nature of their Estates in this Province, which they keep all in their own hands, and require the immediate overlooking of the Proprietor, I am of opinion the most opulent planters, would prefer a home (i.e., British) life. It is in general believed, that they are more attached to the Mother Country, than those Provinces which lie more to the Northward."[21]

The Virginia Tuckahoe wore fine clothes, drove in a stylish coach with livery, was fond of fine horses and fair women; the South Carolina planter took his fashions from London or Paris—and so did the colonists everywhere when they could afford it, and sometimes when they could not. Look at the colonial portraits—the costumes are rich, elaborate, imitative of Europe; there are gorgeous gowns, silks, satins, brocades: Schouler, enumerating the importations, constructs a poem in clothes.[22] And these aristocrats, thus richly arrayed, moved easily through complex social ceremonies. Even Massachusetts and Connecticut were "great exemplars of ceremonial etiquette" and long continued so. At Harvard and Yale students were arranged in class lists according to their family consequence late into the nineteenth century.[23] Ceremonial forms and ex-

---

[21] "Journal of Lord Adam Gordon," in Mereness, *Travels in the American Colonies,* pp. 397-8. The noble lord is writing of the sixties. A single instance is the cousin of Washington Allston, the painter, affianced to young Neville or Neuville, who was sent to complete her studies in England and to make a tour of Europe in the third quarter of the century. Flagg, *Life and Letters of Washington Allston,* p. 3. Instances could be indefinitely multiplied. For instance, Dr. Pringle of "Charles-town," who had completed his medical education in Europe, visited by La Rochefoucauld-Liancourt in 1796. *Voyages,* IV, 111-2.

[22] He mentions "imported brocades, lute-strings, taffeties, sarsanet, poplin, serges, shalloons, silks and satins; they adorned themselves with garnet or pearl necklaces, breast-flowers, aigrets, ruffles, Brussels lace, and handkerchiefs superfine; silk gloves and mits, satin shoes and silk hose gave delicate protection; muffs, furs, and tippets were donned in winter. They sported jaunty riding hats of white and black beaver, with feathers, or warded off rough weather with quilted bonnets from London. Cambrics, lawns and muslin served for summer wear. Dress and undress caps had becoming ribbons; their lawns were spotted or flowered; their handkerchiefs flower-bordered or checked." There were staffs and buckram and hoops, gilt and silver lace, and cocked hats. "In fact, the fashionable of both sexes gave, in this age, at home or abroad, absurd attention to the minutiae of wigs, perukes, and hairdressing generally." *Americans of 1776,* pp. 86-9.

[23] "Even our Revolutionary Press indulged the prevalent taste of pompously announcing great public characters; thus, in 1776, 'arrived in Boston from Philadelphia, that most worthy and patriotic gentleman, the Hon. Samuel Adams, Esqu., a member of that august and united body, the right honorable the Continental Congress.'" Schouler, *op. cit.,* p. 9.

pressions used at Westminster were familiar here; one reads that "His Excellency the Governor" in Massachusetts Bay, "was pleased to prorogue the great and general court or assembly of the province." Tittle-tattle from London touching the peers and persons of quality filled the colonial press, the names denoted by a dash between consonants, and the colonial capitals were occasionally "gratified" by the sight of peers of the realm, when stateliness increased.[24] Such a society supported the select dancing assembly at the provincial capital. Jefferson used to recall with delight winter balls at the Raleigh Tavern at Williamsburg, which he used to attend as a student at William and Mary. As far back as 1765, Schouler tells us, we read of a ball given at Boston, in which the British army and navy officers were prominent—a brilliant social affair. In 1774 at the close of the colonial epoch, this is balanced by a public dance given by the Virginia gentry in honor of St. Tammany; "from all such gatherings mechanics and the tradespeople were excluded."[25] And a certain section of colonial literature faithfully reflects this formal and elegant leisure class:

American literature, while colonial conditions lasted, imitated with subservience the style then prevalent in the mother country, which was sentimental and stilted. Elegance of phrase was affected for trivial thoughts, jewels not worth the setting; fine description, fine writing, vapid reflections, supposed to be suggested by scenes of nature viewed commonly at second-hand—these characterized the literary effusions of London magazines, which our colonial printer transferred to his own columns to fill up vacant space and render homage to culture. . . . (The productions include) the lounger's dawdling essay to be gallant or satirical; ambling verses, the result of an idle hour; amorous sonnets, signed Theodosius or Corydon, full of compliment to some fair lady whose name is veiled in the vowels and discerned through the consonants. "Genteel is my Damon" in 1765 is the product of a great lady.[26]

No one who has read in the colonial newspapers can fail to recognize the accuracy of Schouler's paragraph.

The colonial leisure class, which, beginning in the last quarter of the seventeenth century, thus expands until it colors our whole picture of colonial life,[27]—where did it learn its

[24] *Ibid.*, pp. 8-9.
[25] Schouler, *op. cit.*, p. 106.
[26] Condensed from Schouler, *op. cit.*, p. 130.
[27] As instanced in such novels of colonial life as *To Have and To Hold* by Mary Johnston; Ford's *Janice Meredith;* James Boyd's *Drums;* Mitchell's *Hugh Wynne, Free Quaker;* and the opening chapters of Winston Churchill's *The Crossing.*

manners? In the beginning, as we have indicated, from the Stuart court and from the Huguenots; and then, as the Stuarts went the way of all kings, as the Huguenots were amalgamated with the general population, from British society, from Paris, from itinerant Frenchmen. The colonial gentry, returning to England, found that high society regularly embarked on the Grand Tour,[28] that Paris was the capital of the fashionable world, that distinguished Frenchmen—literary men, scientists, nobles, diplomats—were visiting England,[29] that the visits were returned. Consider the names given below, a list that could be extended: an international cult, a cosmopolitan society is being created on both sides the Channel:

ENGLISH VISITORS OF NOTE IN FRANCE, 1763-1770[30]

1763. Duchess of Hamilton, Duke and Duchess of Ancaster, Hon. C. Cadogan, Mrs. Mack, Lord Coventry, Lord Holland, Lord Holderness, General Clarke, Gibbon, Mrs. Montagu, Horne, Lord Palmerston, Wilkes.

1764. Earl of March, George Selwyn, Barré, Wedderburn, Garrick.

1765. Lady Holland, Lady Louisa Conolly, Lady Sarah Bunbury, Lascelles, Lord W. Gordon, Walpole, Lord Ossory, Crawford, Grandey, Garrick, Horne, Duke of Richmond, Wilkes, Sterne, Foote, Sir Gilbert Elliot, Duke of Beaufort, James Barry.

1766. Sir C. and Lady Bunbury, Duke of Northumberland, Mrs. Greville, Mr. Jenkinson (afterwards Earl of Liverpool), Sterne, Lord and Lady G. Lennox, Mr. and Mrs. Fitzroy, Lord Carlisle, Selwyn, Miss Lloyd, Adam Smith, Col. Gordon, Charles James Fox, Stephen Fox, Lord and Lady Fife.

1767. Lord Fitzwilliam, Duke of York, Walpole, Selwyn, Lord March, Lord and Lady G. Lennox, Lady Sarah Bunbury, Lady M. Coke, Lord Palmerston, William Pars (the draughtsman), Mr. Wood (Under-secretary of State), Lord Algernon Percy, Lord Carlisle, Pringle, Franklin.

1768. C. Churchill, Lord Cranbrassbill, Lord Carlisle, Lady Pembroke, H. St. John, Sir John Dalrymple, General Irwin.

[28] Consult Meade, *The Grand Tour in the Eighteenth Century.*
[29] Professor Faÿ informs me that it cost but three francs to cross the English channel at the close of the seventeenth century. Travel increased notably after the death of Louis XIV. The popularity, both in France and England, of Voltaire's *Lettres Philosophiques* (1734), and of Montesquieu's *Esprit des Lois* (1748), increased the Anglomania in France, and an interest in France in Great Britain. The Anglomania in polite French circles, particularly after 1760, has often been remarked, including, as it did, not only an interest in English literature, English ideas, and English politics, but one in English horses and styles. The correspondence of Horace Walpole with Madame du Deffand should be consulted.
[30] Lockitt, *The Relations of French and English Society (1763-1793)*, pp. 123-125. The whole monograph is illuminating.

1769. C. J. Fox, Crawford, General Irwin, Mrs. Cholmondeley, Lord Holland, Lord and Lady Dacre, Walpole, Duke and Duchess of Richmond, Lady Orford, Mrs. Hart, Mr. Stuart.
1770. Dr. Burney, Lady Mary Coke, Sir H. Clinton, Lord Edward Bentinck, Duchess of Northumberland.

FRENCH VISITORS OF DISTINCTION IN ENGLAND, 1763-1770

1763. Camus, Condamine, de la Lande, M. d'Uson, M. de Fleury, Mme. de Boufflers, Duc de Nivernois.
1764. Helvétius, M. Elie de Beaumont.
1765. M. de Lauraguais, Comte de Caraman.
1766. M. de Lauraguais, M. de Lillebonne, Duc de Croÿ, Duc de Havre, M. de Fitzjames.
1767. Duc de Lauzun, Duc de Fronsac.
1768. Chevalier de Chastellux.
1769. Baron d'Holbach.

Even when war threatens these close bonds are not broken: Stormont, the British ambassador in Paris in 1776-1778, "was a very likable and popular young man,"[31] and after the French Alliance is formed they do not arrest Admiral Rodney who is in Paris, they politely offer him his sword and let him depart,[32] so close are the intellectual and social bonds between the two countries. Turn to the various pictures of colonial society that have been made—to Sale's *Old Time Belles and Cavaliers,* or to Wharton's *Salons Colonial and Republican;* it is to this society of Frenchmen and Gallicized Britons that we must look for the American notion of a salon, it is to this group that colonial travellers and envoys—men like Franklin, Deane, Lee, Adams, and the rest—are introduced, whether in London or in Paris. For instance, there is "M. Powell" whom Chastellux met in Philadelphia: "M. Powell" had journeyed to Europe, whence he brought back "le goût des beaux-arts"; his house "est ornée d'estampes précieuses et de bonnes copies de plusieurs tableaux d'Italie."[33] There is the unfortunate Blennerhasset: Irish by birth, he had lived in France, returned to Ireland, and then (1796) come to America "with a library" and a "philosophical

[31] Faÿ, *L'Ésprit Révolutionnaire en France et aux États-unis à la fin du xviiie siècle,* p. 47.
[32] Faÿ, p. 73. "On espérait une guerre brève, et l'on pensait que l'Angleterre accepterait des arrangements pour céder avec bonne grâce. Ni le ministre, ni l'opinion publique n'éprouvaient de haine contre elle. On était heureux de lui donner une leçon, mais on admirait sa civilization et on la savait nécessaire pour l'équilibre de l'Europe. On peut dire que les rapports ne cessèrent jamais d'être courtois ou même qu'ils furent plus courtois après le début des hostilités qu'auparavant." P. 73.
[33] Chastellux, *Voyages,* I, 173.

apparatus."[34] There is Elkanah Watson, whose memoirs tell us a good deal about society in the eighteenth century, who travelled extensively in France, Holland, and Great Britain, mingled with the best society, was introduced by Franklin to polite circles in Paris, and became the friend and correspondent of Franklin, John Adams, Livingston, Philip Schuyler, and others.[35] But why multiply instances? Let us note that for those who did not go to Paris or London, there remained republican Geneva, whither resorted Francis Kinloch, William Smith (later representative from South Carolina and once a special envoy to France), the two Penns, Bache, the grandson of Franklin, Colonel "Lawrens," son of the former president of Congress, sent there for his education,[36] and Albert Gallatin, himself a Swiss.[37]

But we are running a little ahead of our story. What did the American leisure class draw from this Gallo-British social group in the Old World? Mr. Lockitt gives us a picture of this international group in London in the last half of the eighteenth century: the French are imitating English—and American—dress, admiring English furniture, importing the habit of inoculation, riding in British cabs, drinking English beer. "The fashion of subdued and negligent attire, that in their zeal for English forms they have borrowed from their neighbors, has been returned with interest, till Walpole meets in London the 'hats and valences, the folds above the chins of the ladies, the dirty shirts and shaggy hair of the young men who have levelled nobility.' "[38] The introduction of gambling for high stakes in the days of Charles II into England has been followed by the reciprocal vogue of English whist in France: in both French and English society thereafter "reckless gambling proved most infectious."[39] The French admire horse-racing; wherefore the English are flattered and race the more.[40] In French society the vogue of English clubs has worked to multiply salons; and French club and French salon in turn react upon the social life of London: lodges of Rosicrucians and Masons are formed,

[34] McMaster, III, 57.
[35] Watson, *Men and Times of the Revolution*, pp. 95-269.
[36] Chastellux, *Voyages*, I, 160; Faÿ, p. 42, note.
[37] Stevens, *Life of Gallatin*, p. 4.
[38] Lockitt, *op. cit.*, pp. 40-45.
[39] *Ibid.*, p. 46.
[40] *Ibid.*, pp. 48-49.

bringing with them a taste for philosophy and mysticism.[41]
Dueling is once more in vogue, and in France suicide becomes
fashionable; there is a craze for amateur acting; fashionable
immorality is re-enforced on either side of the water by the
example of the complementary capital; and sentimental deism
sometimes assists, and sometimes reforms, depravity.[42]

When now we turn to colonial Virginia, that most aristocratic of colonies, we find a pale reflection of all this "high
life." Travellers inform us that while the management of the
plantation is left in the hands of the overseer, the owner
lounges at his ease, drinks, goes to the races, fights duels,
enters the House of Burgesses (and later on the legislature
or congress), supports the playhouse, goes abroad. The oldest
and best French wines are imported, theaters are built; troupes
of actors come to amuse this society, to the scandal of New
England. At the horse races the "cock-fighting parsons"[43]
appear and bet on the horses.[44] Williamsburg becomes the
"focus of Virginian deism";[45] the infection spreads. Weld,
travelling in Virginia in 1796, found "very little regard paid
by the people in general to Sunday. Indeed, throughout the
lower parts of Virginia, that is, between the mountains and
the sea, the people have scarcely any sense of religion, and
in the country parts the churches are all falling into decay."[46]
Indeed, the Anglican church is satisfied to have "established
their churches in Charleston, Savannah, and other towns," to
have "set up chapels of ease in the outlying parishes,"[47] religion being a little old-fashioned in such a community. By
and by fashionable imported deism disestablishes the fashionable church: ungrateful Jefferson, learning from Dr. William
Small, professor of mathematics at William and Mary, his
first lessons in agnosticism,[48] votes in the Virginia Convention
of 1775-6 to separate church and state.[49] The private lives of

[41] *Ibid.*, pp. 49-53, 60-64.
[42] *Ibid.*, pp. 53-54, 65-58, 29, 34-35, 84-89, Saurin's *L'ennuyeux Anglo-
mane* was written to satirize the French Anglomania, Faÿ, pp. 6; 40 (note).
[43] Bassett, p. 152.
[44] Dodd, *The Cotton Kingdom*, p. 15. His graphic picture is of a later
date than colonial times, but the foundations of this order go back to the
period we are discussing.
[45] Adams, *Life of John Randolph*, p. 9.
[46] Weld, *Travels*, p. 133.
[47] Dodd, p. 14.
[48] Forman, *Life and Writings of Thomas Jefferson*, p. 4-5.
[49] *Ibid.*, p. 15.

Alexander Hamilton, Colonel Aaron Burr, and certain other founders of the republic are not all that one could wish: can it be that fashionable immorality abroad has set the example? And as for Masonic Lodges, Illuminati, Committees of Correspondence, political clubs, and the like, have gallicized London and anglicized Paris by any chance helped to form them?

Certain it is that Americans are received in London most cordially by the Rockingham Whigs, that new school of Whigs which "revives in all their freshness the principles that men had long learnt to identify with Whiggism, friendship to liberty, hostility to prerogative, love of toleration"; and the close connection in England between the Rockingham Whigs and French society must be something more than a coincidence. Lord Shelburne talks to Franklin on the means of promoting the happiness of mankind; something of that kind had been said by Montesquieu. Toryism is the same in all three countries: the Whigs, like Lafayette, Montesquieu, Diderot, and Raynal, dream of liberating the blacks; and the advanced party in France take the Whigs as their models. The closest ties of intimacy knit Shelburne, Barré, Conway, Richmond, Fox and other members of the Government of 1782 with the aristocracy and philosophers of France, an intimacy that has been growing over many years. Shelburne, Barré and Wilkes dine with Holbach; Shelburne is intimate with Morellet and Mirabeau, visits the principal salons; and Paine wrote Washington that he believed Shelburne would make a good minister for England from the point of view of America and a better agreement with France. Burke visited France; there he was courted by all the literary lights. Fox visited Necker and Mme. Geoffrin, mixed with the liberal nobility and so did the Duke of Richmond, Walpole, Wilkes, General Conway, Fitzpatrick—all the friends of America, and those men to whom the American representatives in London turned.[50] Where there is so much intellectual sympathy, the pattern of social intercourse must likewise be modified, and American travellers and representatives, mingling in France or England with this society which receives them so sympathetically, bring back a profound sympathy for this Franco-British mode of life.

But the Americans do not have to wait upon the returned traveller to learn the manners of polite society. Besides the

[50] I have summarized Lockitt's discussion, pp. 77-80.

schools of deportment such as those at New Rochelle, they might learn the nice conduct of a clouded cane from itinerant Frenchmen in almost any of the sea-board towns. Notably after the conclusion of the Seven Years War is there a marked increase in the colonial interest in the arts of the dancer, the dueller, the peruke-maker, and the teacher of deportment. Of the number of French dancing masters in America before the Revolution some indication has already been given; let us simply recall here that dancing schools were set up in Philadelphia, in New York, in Boston, in all the large colonial towns, and from thence "the agile dancing-master invaded at intervals the more quiet communities, to instruct people in the graces of fashion."[51] Needless to say, these dancing masters were usually French, teaching not only the minuet, but all the polite accomplishments. "It was not uncommon for one to teach French or music besides, to give lessons in fencing with the small sword or in playing upon the violin or guitar. . . . A dancing-master from Paris was the French instructor at Harvard College. French women, too, helped to fill the conjugal purse in such pursuits; and one fencing-master's wife, fresh from Paris advertised to take in fine washing, starched lawns, muslins, and laces, and proffered, moreover, to teach young ladies either the French tongue or elegant embroidery."[52] And if these statements seem too general, let us turn to a particular city; let us examine the huge volumes of Scharf and Westcott's *History of Philadelphia*. In that city, the first dancing master, it is true, bears an English name: John Walsh, in 1761, had his place of business in Videll's Alley. But thereafter the French names multiply. In 1763 John Baptiste Tyrol advertises (this is in August) that he has toured Europe and that he would teach as soon as the weather cooled. Signor Sodi on Chestnut Street about the same year taught "all the new French dances"; namely rigadoons, paspies, and so on. In 1768 Fay, with his Italian rival, Tioli, taught dancing and fencing. In 1763 John de Florette, "fencing-master at the Prince of Orange, in Second Street," taught the broadsword, backsword, spaderoon, and dagger. In 1768 Louis Duchateau, "the French peruke-maker and hair-cutter at Mr. Lortie's" advertises "frizets for the ladies." In 1760 "M. du Cimitiere," a Genevan painter, came to Philadelphia, where he remained for nearly

[51] Schouler, *Americans of 1776*, p. 106.
[52] *Ibid.*, p. 107.

thirty years, interested in miniatures and natural history; his likenesses were engraved "in Paris, for sale."[53] By the 1770's the French were in the possession of all the little fashionable arts in Philadelphia, saving perhaps, music,[54] and the same situation was duplicated in all the larger centers.[55] In Philadelphia by 1771—last tribute of all!—men were wearing roquelaures, of oiled linen, a French invention: umbrellas had not yet come in.[56] The *haut ton*, as Mrs. Mowatt's heroine was to say in *Fashion* (1845), "scrupulously followed the foreign fashions" in colonial society, and the foreign fashions were directly or indirectly, French.

4. THE AMERICAN LEISURE CLASS AND FRENCH MANNERS IN THE LAST QUARTER OF THE EIGHTEENTH CENTURY.

At the outbreak of the Revolution American society is ordered in ranks and classes, to the mingled chagrin[57] and pleasure of the gallant French officers who came to aid in the struggle. A doctrinaire interpretation of the United States in terms of democratic primitivism had prepared these enthusiasts for Spartan frugality. Was not America the land of the Quaker? Of the noble savage? Of the republican successors of Brutus, Harmodius, and Aristogeiton? A land where all the women were virtuous and all the men were chaste?[58] The home of virtue proved on inspection to be filled with delightful houses, lovely and intelligent ladies, sufficient wealth, politeness, and excellent things to eat.[59] Into this cosmopolitan society they fitted with little sense of strangeness, and their

[53] Griswold, *Republican Court,* p. 352.
[54] Mrs. Ball in 1730 advertised "French playing on the spinet and dancing taught." The remaining names in Scharf and Westcott are also English until very late in the century. *History of Philadelphia,* II, 962.
[55] Scharf and Westcott, II, 879, 886, 879-80, 885.
[56] Scharf and Westcott, II, 889.
[57] Frenchmen were astonished at the American love of luxury. They came from a land possessing an inbred frugality and were shocked by the worldly tone of America.
[58] Cf. Faÿ, chap. i; Chinard, *Jefferson et les idéologues françaises; and* see Bulow's remarks to Brillat-Savarin, *Physiologie du Goût,* pp. 78-79.
[59] Complaint of American extravagance and frivolity was not confined to French theorists. See Mrs. Mercy Warren's poem, "Woman's Trifling Needs," from *Poems, Dramatic and Miscellaneous,* quoted in Stedman and Hutchinson, in which that spirited lady ridicules the desire of her sex for finery during the revolution, and enumerates the various articles of attire. However, she remarks also,
"Can the stern patriot Clara's suit deny?
'Tis Beauty asks, and Reason must comply."

memoirs give us the most vivid picture of American society
at the close of the eighteenth century.[60] They show us how in
Philadelphia, Charleston, Boston, Newport, Providence, Hartford, New Haven, Albany, Baltimore, New York, something
like a salon class had already developed, a class to whose further
progress they were to lend unconscious aid. "Come, miss, have
a care what you are doing," shouted the Master of Ceremonies
to a damsel who was permitting a bit of gossip to interrupt
her turn in a contra-dance, "Do you think you are here for
your own pleasure?" This was in Philadelphia in 1781; it is
with this anecdote that Sherrill opens his book.[61] Society is
something to be seriously pursued. Let us look for a while at
this society, north and south.

"I must acknowledge," wrote Schoepf in 1783, "that those
among the Philadelphians who have visited foreign countries
are incomparably more engaging and polite than those who
hold courtesy to be reserve; those who have travelled have
learned by experience how obliging even the smallest attention
is to a stranger, and they practice what elsewhere has pleased
them."[62] Going abroad constituted a principal item in the education of that society.

Thus John Wentworth of New England, sent to Europe
in 1765, made a social hit in London; George Digges of
Maryland, when in that same city, was known as the handsome
American and became something of a macaroni, and upon
his return to his home at Warburton, across from Mount
Vernon, he entertained Major L'Enfant. Alice de Lancy, of
Huguenot blood, who spent her girlhood in the society of New
York City, married Ralph Izard, and went to South Carolina
with her husband, was perhaps the first to introduce silk-worm
culture into that state; and after 1769 we find the Izards
going abroad to educate their children. Mrs. Izard incidentally
becomes a queen of fashion. Benjamin, Count Rumford, lost
to America, it is true, married the daughter of Lavoisier;
later on, John Adams, without incongruity, wrote to offer him
the command of West Point and a position as Inspector-
General of the Army, both of which honors he declined. John
McPherson of Pennsylvania went to England in 1772 to learn

---

[60] Conveniently summarized in Sherrill's *French Memories of Eighteenth
Century America.*
[61] *Ibid.,* p. 31.
[62] Schoepf, *Travels in the Confederation,* I, 97.

law—he was killed early in the Revolution. Sarah Livingston, who became Mrs. John Jay, was the acknowledged leader of a certain section of Parisian society in 1782; upon her return to America she became a leader of American society, second only to Mrs. Washington. Lady Kitty Duer, at her military wedding in New York, received gifts from the Earl of Shelburne, the Duchess of Gordon, and other titled friends of her father, Lord Stirling. Nor can one forget the unfortunate Peggy Shippen, who became Mrs. Benedict Arnold; or the more fortunate Anne Willing, who became Mrs. William Bingham, who was at the court of Louis XVI with her husband in 1784, whose Philadelphia home, modelled on Manchester House, became one of the leading social centers of America.[63] There is Samuel Breck of the delightful memoirs, sent by his father in 1782 to France, where he became known as "le petit Bostonian," who toured France, turned Roman Catholic and then turned back again, got to know Jefferson and Crèvecoeur, Brissot de Warville and de Valady, and who returned just before the French Revolution on one of the packets which the French government had established for the American trade, the passenger list including John Paul Jones, Joseph Norris of Philadelphia, Mr. and Mrs. Rucker, (a New York merchant), Miss Betsy Ramsay, Mr. Mumford of Richmond, and Mr. Holker, the son of the French consul at Philadelphia, not to speak of a nameless French-Canadian marquis, and Mademoiselle de Beaumanoir who took his berth away from him.[64] There was Louis Littlepage who went with Jay to the Spanish court, travelled extensively in Europe, and who, after the dismemberment of Poland, returned to Fredericksburg, Virginia.[65] But we can not list them all: not even doctors like Dr. Kuhn, who, having begun his medical education when Philadelphia was a British province, finished his education in the schools of Europe "under the most able and distinguished teachers of the day, including Linnaeus," and who held the chair of Theory and Practice of Physic in the medical school at Philadelphia at the end of the eighteenth century.[66] However, we

[63] Sale, *Old Time Belles and Cavaliers*, pp. 99-171.
[64] She later married a M. de la Forest in New York. *Recollections of Samuel Breck*, chap. II. Breck made a second European tour in 1791. Pp. 162-75. See also Mitchell, *St. Jean de Crèvecoeur*, pp. 262-3.
[65] He participated in the siege of Gibraltar, became unofficial prime minister of Poland, and officially the Polish ambassador to Russia. Watson, *Men and Times of the Revolution*, pp. 131-2.
[66] *Autobiography of Charles Caldwell, M.D.*, p. 121.

must not neglect the cosmopolitan Adams family. Mrs. J. Q. Adams was originally Louisa Catherine Johnson, daughter of Joshua Johnson of Maryland, who, becoming a merchant in London, removed to Nantes when the Revolution broke out, as agent of the Maryland colony. She was married July 26, 1797,[67] to J. Q. Adams, who had gone with his father in February, 1778, to Paris; hardly was he well established in school there when they returned, but within three months they were back again in France. He went to school in Paris, Amsterdam, Leyden; at fourteen became private secretary to Francis Dana, the American envoy to Russia; returned after six months to Paris, where Adams, Franklin, and Jefferson, were negotiating the Treaty of Peace, and arrived in America in 1785—a truly cosmopolitan product.[68] And as for the great figures of American diplomacy—Franklin, Deane, Jefferson, Lee, the two Adams's —they oscillated perpetually between Europe and the United States. A society dominated by persons of this quality can not be called provincial except in the geographical sense of the word. Is it necessary to labor the point that in this epoch the various European capitals were paying homage to the manners of France?

But let us narrow the picture. For instance, let us confine ourselves to Philadelphia society during the epoch of the Revolution and after,—Philadelphia where Lambert Cadwalader formed a company for service during the Revolution characteristically known as the Silk Stocking Company.[69] Here, indeed, a true salon life on Franco-British models may be found. There is, for example, Elizabeth Graeme, the daughter of Dr. Thomas Graeme, the leading physician of Philadelphia in the 1760's. Her mother was the step-daughter of Sir William Keith, the Governor of Pennsylvania, a lady who made verses and transmitted the talent to her daughter. Miss Graeme translated *Télémaque* into English verse—the manuscript is preserved. In 1764, at the age of 25, Miss Graeme went to England for a year under the tutorial care of the Reverend Richard Peters of Philadelphia; in London she moved easily in the most polished society of the day; she received from a British relative what may be the first bookplate in America; she met Laurence Sterne, she went to the races, she was, in short, a belle. Upon

---

[67] Adams, *Charles Francis Adams*, pp. 1-2.
[68] Morse, *John Quincy Adams*, pp. 4-17.
[69] Sale, p. 88.

her mother's death she returned to Philadelphia where she held in her father's house, on Chestnut Street above Sixth, a kind of salon. Her Saturday evenings attracted all the genius of the colonies; and genius, going there, found a woman of wide knowledge—they were, said Dr. Benjamin Rush, evenings of an "Attic kind," and he describes a typical one.[70] She conducted a rimed correspondence as "Laura" with Nathaniel Evans, after the modish fashion of that day; she married—unhappily—a young gentleman from Scotland; and then, as Mrs. Hugh Ferguson she resumed her evenings. There were more literary and scientific men in Philadelphia than elsewhere, and they all flocked to her—all the members of the City Dancing Assembly—Francis Hopkinson, James Wilson (the advocate), John Beveridge (the Latin scholar), Dr. Francis Alison, Mrs. William Blumstead, Mrs. Joseph Shippen, Mrs. Charles Willing, Sarah Evans—in short, the whole Anglican set.[71] Does this seem petty and provincial? The polished French noblemen do not find it so.[72]

The Revolution dimmed but it did not long eclipse the glory of this social prestige. While the British held the city, the Tory belles were in ascendant, but upon the return of the Americans the Whig ladies drove them out: the split threatened to disrupt society—it was like Paris in the War of the Fronde.[73] But, the war over, the new government established,

[70] Wharton, *Salons Colonial and Republican,* pp. 20-22.
[71] *Ibid.,* pp. 11-35.
[72] Thus Bayard comments upon the social attainments of American ladies: "they would have been considered remarkable even at the witty and brillant French court." Most of the French travelers (Félix de Beaujour alone complains that we talked exclusively of money) admired the conversational gifts of this society. Brissot, Mandrillon, and Chastellux are loud in their praise of conversation in Boston; and Chastellux of conversation in Philadelphia. Volney found us silent, a taciturnity to which he attributed our business success. Again, Adet, writing his government February 23, 1796, says: "Yesterday evening they gave the President a ball, the subscription for which was, as is customary, opened a few days before. All that luxury, flattery, idolatry could imagine was there combined. There were only lacking Body Guards and the red and blue ribbons of decorations to enable one to imagine himself at the Court of a King. Courtiers were certainly not lacking." The bias is obvious, but the facts are plain. See Sherrill, *op. cit.,* pp. 33, 43-46, 146.
[73] The French minister, Gérard, was obliged to give up the idea of a ball for the king's birthday, August 24, 1778, because "they wished to establish an absolute line of separation between the Whigs and Tories, especially between the ladies." Sherrill, p. 36. The breach was not formally healed until the Duc de Lauzun gave his famous ball in honor of the birth of the Dauphin (Washington celebrated the event with a state dinner, and there were fireworks and dancing at West Point), which Washington and

society resumed it sway; and class distinctions were once more rigorously insisted on.[74] And the leisure class resumed its brilliant reign.[75] Shall we survey the several centers that drew to themselves the brilliant leaders of a brilliant city?

There was, as we have seen, Mrs. Hugh Ferguson. There was John Tracy, the merchant prince, who entertained Chastellux and M. de Vaudreuil. There was Mrs. Robert Morris, a great social light. There was Mrs. Samuel Meredith, with whom Chastellux conversed about literature, poetry, romance, and the history of France—a true salon conversation. At Dr. Shippen's Chastellux found the *conversazione* were held on the Italian model. Mrs. Samuel Powell is, he writes, "well-read and intelligent; but what distinguishes her most is her taste for conversation, and the truly European use that she knows how to make of her understanding and information." Let us glance at Mr. and Mrs. William Bingham, returned from London and Paris, who become the center of a brilliant social group. Mr. Wansey, the traveller, dined with them: "the house and garden in the best English style," he writes, "the drawing-room chairs from Seldon's, in London, the carpet one of Moore's most expensive patterns, and the paper in French taste, after the style of the Vatican in Rome," all "very handsome and

Rochambeau attended. So did everybody else of consequence. Lauzun borrowed thirty cooks from the French army to prepare the feast. Wharton, *op. cit.*, pp. 118 ff.

[74] "The inhabitants of Philadelphia," wrote Bayard in 1797, "like all citizens of the United States, are classified by their fortunes. The first class is composed of carriage folk. Almost all these gentry, whatever their origin, have their coats of arms painted upon their carriage doors. The son of a deported thief has liveried servants just like everybody else. Nobility having been abolished by the Constitution alone, it is not astonishing that so many individuals pretend to be descended from ancient English families. This fad has become a sort of mania in mercantile cities. The second class is composed of merchants, lawyers, and business men without carriages, and doctors who pay their visits on foot. In a third class are found people who exercise the mechanical arts. Ladies who possess carriages never so far forget themselves as to receive in their homes those of the third class." Sherrill, *op. cit.*, p. 47.

[75] For that matter it was never seriously interrupted. Gérard reported to his government that the Americans were unwilling to allow Congress to interfere with dancing. When Northern delegates pressed a resolution to forbid dancing and theatrical performances, the very day the resolution was published, there were theatricals given by army officers and whig citizens, and the day after, the governor of Philadelphia gave a ball to a numerous company. Gérard to Vergennes, Sherrill, p. 36. John Adams wrote his wife from Philadelphia, August 12, 1776, announcing the arrival of a French Vessel with limes and adding that "trade, we see, even now, in the midst of summer, is not totally interrupted by all the efforts of our enemies." *Letters of John Adams*, I, 147. French goods continued to be imported.

effective," an opinion that other travellers confirm.[76] Thither
went Mr. Willing, president of the Bank of the United States
(Mrs. Bingham's father), Monsieur Cailot, the exiled governor
of Guadeloupe, and the Vicomte de Noailles. There could be
seen Jefferson, Jay, Oliver Wolcott and his wife, Mr. and Mrs.
Joseph Hopkinson, the Madisons, the Duc de Rochefoucauld-
Liancourt, Talleyrand, Volney, Samuel Breck, the merchant,
Mr. and Mrs. John Adams, Lord Erskine, Martinez de Yrujo,
the Spanish ambassador, who took an American wife, Barbé-
Marbois, Louis-Philippe—a truly cosmopolitan society, over
which Mrs. Bingham presided—she who had returned, as Mrs.
Adams acidly remarked, to give laws to Philadelphia women
in fashion and elegance. And thither went also many of the
exiles from Santo Domingo—the Sigoignes, the Tesseires, the
Monges, the de la Roches, the Gillous, the Clapiers, and others,
French families of education and refinement.[77]

There were Quaker salons as well. For instance, there was
Mrs. George Logan, whose country-place, Stenton, on the
Germantown Road, was frequented by a brilliant group. Thither
resorted statesmen and literary men—Washington, the Chevalier Ternant, Jefferson, Genêt, Kosciusko, Mr. John Vaughan,
Major Pierce Butler, Dupont de Nemours, John Randolph of
Roanoke, Peter du Ponceau, the learned Abbé Correa de Serra,
Dr. Caspar Wistar, for whom the wistaria was named, and
whose immortality it has been to have the name of the plant
misspelled.[78] If this was the Quaker end of town, Third Street
was the "court end." The Willings, the Powells, the Byrds,
the Vauxes, the Chews, the Hopkinsons, the McCalls, the
Bordleys, and the McKeans had their houses on Third Street
or near it. What the social life was, is pictured in Chastellux,
Brissot de Warville, in the travels of Henry Wansey, and the
prodigious work of La Rochefoucauld-Liancourt, and the memoirs and letters of Mrs. John Warder and Thomas Twining.
Mrs. Warder, for instance, describes entertainments at the

---

[76] For instance, Schoepf. "In the matter of interior decorations the English style is imitated here as throughout America. The furniture, tables,
bureaus, bedsteads &c, are commonly of mahogany, at least in the best
houses. Carpets, Scottish and Turkish, are much used . . . stairs and rooms
are laid with them. The houses are seldom without paper tapestries, the
vestibule being especially so treated." *Travels in the Confederation*, I, 60.
On the importation of French wall paper see Halsey and Cornelius, *A
Handbook of the American Wing*, pp. 176, 234, 248, 253.
[77] Wharton, *Salons Colonial and Republican*, pp. 118-161.
[78] *Ibid.*, pp. 118-172.

house of Samuel Pleasant, tells of her experience with the John Cliffords, with "Billy" Morris, George Emlen, James Pemberton, Mr. Miers, and Sally Fisher—mainly Quakers these, but all witty and wise. Richard Penn became the first president of the Jockey Club, and married at Christ Church Miss Polly Masters: as the distinction between Tory and Whig society broke down, so the distinction between Quaker and Anglican faded. At Colonel Cox's they talk French; at James Wilson's they dine. Speaking of an evening at the Wolcott's, Judge Francis Hopkinson said: "When I mention such names as Ellsworth, Ames, Griswold, Goodrich, Tracy, you may imagine what a rich intellectual society it was." There were balls on the president's birthday, which Isaac Weld describes. Mrs. Adams thought the theater equal to most of the theaters out of France. Jefferson said that social life in Philadelphia was more stimulating than elsewhere—why should he not? He numbered among his friends the Rev. William White, Dr. Ashbell Green (both chaplains of Congress), Dr. Abercrombie, Dr. Blackwell, Dr. William Smith (Provost of the College of Pennsylvania), Dr. Benjamin Rush, Dr. Wistar, John Vaughan, William Bartram the botanist, David Rittenhouse the astronomer, Benjamin Smith Barton, Dr. Priestley, and many more. The close of the eighteenth century is a brilliant period in cosmopolitan society at Philadelphia.[79]

It would be tedious to rehearse the tale for other cities; perhaps an indication or two will suffice. "The Bostonians," wrote the austere Brissot, "unite simplicity of morals with that French politeness and delicacy of manners which render virtue more amiable."[80] When New York was the capital, Washington's first concern was for decorum: Mrs. Washington's drawing-rooms were a kind of state salon where John Adams, Jay, Hamilton, Madison, Jefferson, Edmund Randolph, Livingston, James Iredell, Charles Carroll of Carrolton, William Bradford (the attorney general), Morris, Benjamin Huntington of Connecticut, Rufus King, William King, Henry Knox, and others mingled.[81] The Virginians lived in Maiden Lane; Sir John Temple and his wife (he was the British consul-general) had an "elegant establishment"; Mrs. John Jay, Lady Kitty Duer,

[79] Consult Wharton, pp. 70-117.
[80] Brissot de Warville, *Travels*, I, 71. "I found everywhere that hospitality, that affability, that friendship for the French, which M. (Chastellux) has so much exalted." P. 75. See Sherrill, pp. 153-4.
[81] Consult volume I of Wandell and Minnigerode, *Aaron Burr*.

Mrs. Ralph Izard, Mrs. James Beekman, Mrs. George Clinton, Mrs John Bayard, Mrs. Hamilton (Betsy Schuyler), and others were queens of wit and fashion, Among the titled ladies of the administration were Lady Mary Watts, Lady Catherine Duer, Lady Temple, Lady Christiana Griffin (wife of the president of Congress), and Lady Stirling.[82] The tone was set by Mrs. Jay, "admirably fitted through her long residence in the Spanish and French capitals" for entertaining "distinguished arrivals from various parts of the United States, and from Europe." In such a society the French representatives— Otto, afterwards Comte de Masloy, who married twice in New York; the Marquis de Moustier (he came in 1787 with his sister, Madame de Brehan)—played important roles.[83] Fashions were continental;[84] and members of the fashionable group were necessarily its arbiters.

Of Virginia we learn in 1783-4 that "the entire commerce . . . was for long almost altogether in the hands of European houses who have maintained their ware-houses and factors here,"[85] and by this commerce fashionable society was nourished and clothed. La Rochefoucauld-Liancourt visited in 1797 the farm of Dr. Warton, a mile from Washington; the doctor (afterwards an Anglican clergyman) had been educated by the Jesuits at Saint-Omer and spoke French well.[85a] Society had its great ladies; some of them even ruled politics. For instance, there is Mrs. David Bell (Judith Cary), who, when the Virginia Convention was passing laws for the government of the state, wrote to her brother, Colonel Archibald Cary, and to other leading members of the Convention, in favor of abolishing primogeniture and of disestablishing the Church, Anglican and aristocrat though she was.

Of Charleston after the war Schoepf tells us that "notwithstanding the material injury suffered by South Carolina during the war, recovery is more rapid than in any other of the states; commerce is almost as flourishing. . . . It is gen-

---

[82] Wharton, pp. 35-69.

[83] Mrs. Lamb, *History of the City of New York*, II, 301-3. On Mrs. Jay see Pellew, *John Jay*, pp. 218-9.

[84] "You will find here (New York) the English fashions." Brissot de Warville, quoted in Griswold, *Republican Court*, p. 87. "The Count de Rochambeau observed at the close of the war that the wives of our merchants and bankers were 'clad to the tip of the French fashions, of which they were remarkably fond.'" *Ibid.*, p. 267.

[85] Schoepf, *Travels in the Confederation*, II, 59.

[85a] *Voyages*, VI, 27-28.

erally admitted, and is a matter of surprise to every incoming European that at Charleston finer manners and a more tasteful mode of life are unmistakably prevalent."[86] Crèvecoeur and others confirm his opinion. La Rochefoucauld-Liancourt, who, it is true, preferred the society of the Philadelphia ladies, wrote nevertheless that "la plupart des riches habitans de la Caroline du Sud, ayant été élevé en Europe, en ont apporté plus de goût, et des connaissances plus analogues à nos moeurs, que les habitans des provinces du Nord, ce qui doit leur donner généralement sur ceux-ci de l'avantage en société."[87] Charleston, says Crèvecoeur, is to North America what Lima is to South America: the magnificent pleasure capital of the continent.[88]

Such was the leisure class in the final quarter of the eighteenth cenutry, that is to say, from the outbreak of the Revolution to the presidency of Jefferson. It is precisely one of those self-consious social groups upon which French manners exercise their charms; and it is owing to the accidents of history that this period is the period when French affairs were closest to well-informed Americans. The alienation from England, the French Alliance, the going abroad of Americans like Silas Deane, Franklin, Jefferson, Jay, and the Adams's, the coming to America of French representatives, of French army officers and volunteers, who came directly into contact with this leisure class,

---

[86] *Travels in the Confederation,* II, 203. Charleston was the first port of call for west-bound ships sailing by way of the Azores to avoid the Gulf Stream and the easterly trade winds of the North Atlantic. Cf. Sherrill, pp. 143 ff.

[87] *Voyages,* IV, 13.

[88] Quoted in Sherrill, p. 152. "An European upon his arrival must be greatly surprised when he sees the elegance of their houses, their sumptuous furniture, as well as the magnificence of their tables—can he believe himself in a country whose establishment is so recent! The inhabitants are the gayest in America; it is known as the centre of our beau monde, and is always filled with the richest planters of the province who resort hither in quest of wealth and pleasure. The round of gaiety and the expenditures upon these citizens' tables are much superior to what you would imagine." *Ibid.,* pp. 151-2.

"Perhaps no other city of America exhibits, in proportion, so much splendor and style, as Charleston. The rich planters of the State live in almost Asiatic luxury, and usually, before the Revolution, educated their sons in Europe." Watson, *Men and Times of the Revolution,* p. 68.

"The planters and merchants are rich, and wellbred; the people are showy, and expensive in their dress and way of living; so that everything conspires to make this (Charleston) the liveliest, the pleasantest, and the politest place, as it is one of the richest, too, in all America." Smyth, *Tour in the United States,* II, 83.

the outbreak of the Revolution in France and the West Indies, which drove cultured émigrés to America by the thousands— these were the direct contacts by which French manners were assimilated in America. Even the resumption of relations, diplomatic and social with Great Britain, served to Frenchify Americans, for this is the period when the Gallomania of British high society was at its height. Let us trace out some of these social contacts and then consider the state of society in the remaining period of our epoch.

VIII

French Manners in America

(continued)

1. THE FRENCH IN AMERICAN SOCIETY DURING THE AMERICAN REVOLUTION

W<small>E</small> HAVE seen how successive waves of Frenchmen came to the United States in the last quarter of the eighteenth century, and we have traced the development of that brilliant society in the New World which was at once so cosmopolitan and so charming. If, from the Seven Years War to the outbreak of the Revolution, the contacts between French and American manners in this country were mainly by way of the dancing master, this condition changed abruptly upon the outbreak of the Revolution. Barring one or two secret representatives here and there, the character of the first-comers was not, it is true, calculated to ingratiate the Americans.[1] It is not surprising to learn from a memoir by a wandering French officer who landed in Charleston and planned to join Lafayette that "when we said we were French officers, led solely by the desire for glory, and to defend their liberty, we were pointed to in scorn by the populace, and treated as adventurers, even by Frenchmen, who were very numerous in Charleston." The anonymous writer—it may have been the Chevalier du Buysson—continues, and explains the cause of this extraordinary treatment:

Most of these Frenchmen are officers deeply in debt, several discharged from their corps. The French colonies have many such. The governors clear them as well as they can of all worthless fellows who arrive from France, by giving them letters of recommendation to the Anglo-American Generals. The earlier ones were very well received, but their conduct having shewn what they were, people have no longer any faith in letters of recommendation, and in America very little is

[1] "La plupart des premiers Français venus en Amérique, au bruit de la révolution, étoient des hommes perdus de dettes & de réputation, qui s'annonçoient avec des titres & des noms faux, obtenoient des grades distingués dans l'armée Américaine, recevoient des avances considérables, & disparoissoient ensuite. La simplicité des Américains, leur peu d'expérience rendirent ces supercheries faciles. Plusieurs même de ces aventuriers y ont commis des crimes dignes des derniers supplices. Les premiers merchandises que les Bostoniens reçurent aussi de France, ont encore généralement contribué à les entretenir dans ces idées peu favorables de notre bonne foi & de notre industrie ; actuellement même celles qui en viennent, se vendent, par cette raison, à un prix bien inférieur à celles de l'Angleterre de la même espèce." Robin, *Nouveau Voyage*, pp. 26-27.

thought of those who bring them. . . . . The populace of Charleston, as well as that of all this part of the continent detest the French, and call them adventurers.[2]

"A l'arrivée de M. le Comte d'Estain (sic)," wrote the Abbé Robin, "le peuple fut très-étonné de ne pas voir des hommes si frêles & si difformes; il crut qu'on les avoit exprès choisis pour lui donner une idée plus avantageuse de la Nation: quelques figures enluminées, dont la toilette étoit un peu soignée, les persuaderent que nous faisions l'usage du rouge."[3]

But as America drew closer and closer to the French Alliance, and particularly upon the arrival of Lafayette, the tone of national sentiment changed. The letters of Mr. and Mrs. John Adams are eloquent of this revolution. Honest John writes home to Abigail under the date of June 3, 1778 that

Their (the French) arts and manners, taste and language, are more respected in Europe than those of any other nation. Luxury, dissipation and effeminacy are pretty nearly of the same degree of excess here, and in every other part of Europe. The great cardinal virtue of temperance, however, I believe, flourishes here more than in any other part of Europe.

On February 9, 1779, he observes:

This much I can say with perfect sincerity, that I have found nothing to disgust me, or in any manner disturb me, in the French nation. My evils here arise altogether from Americans.[4]

In 1780 he is describing with great detail the architecture and gardens of Versailles and Paris.[5] Incidentally he has learned to admire the ladies,[6] and by and by his opinions were to change,[7] but for two years he could see no fault in the French.

[2] *Memoir by one of the French Officers who Accompanied the Marquis de Lafayette to America,* etc. . . . Despatched from Philadelphia, 12 September, 1777. Archives des Affaires Étrangères, États-unis, IV, no. 152, folio, 425. In Steven's *Facsimiles,* no. 754.

[3] Robin, *op. cit.,* p.27.

[4] *Letters,* II, 24, 43.

[5] *Ibid.,* II, 66-70.

[6] "To tell you the truth, I admire the ladies here. Don't be jealous. They are handsome, and very well educated. Their accomplishments are exceedingly brilliant, and their knowledge of letters and arts exceeds that of the English ladies, I believe." II, 22-23.

[7] "There is every thing here that can inform the understanding or refine the taste, and indeed, one would think, that could purify the heart. Yet it must be remembered, there is every thing here, too, which can seduce, betray, deceive, deprave, corrupt and debauch it." He fears that "the siren song of sloth" may appeal to his children. II, 70.

In America, meanwhile, Lafayette was carrying all before him. Of the word *Marquis,* the term by which Lafayette was generally known, Robin observes: "déjà le mot de *Marquis,* qui tant de fois a servi chez nous à caractériser la légèreté & la frivolité, est devenu pour les Américains un signe chéri qui excite leur admiration & leur reconnoissance."[8] American newspapers commenced to publish articles protesting against the British usages of society as not sufficiently refined: thus, a writer in the *American Museum* for August, 1788, hopes that we will "abolish many disgusting, embarrassing, destructive English customs" now that "our infant country is happily extricated from the British yoke," and substitute those of the French, who do not drink people's health at table and who do not get drunk— "disguised with liquor," as he says. Among the French every man drinks out of his own glass, not all out of "one vessel"; and the French do not take pretentious leave of the company, but "walk softly away without saying a word." Let the Americans learn these traits[9]—which, indeed, large numbers of Americans seriously incline to do. In 1777 Washington wrote to Congress that it would be necessary to receive La Fayette well because of his high social station, and "dans ses papiers il y a une liste des gentilshommes les plus distingués de l'armée française qu'il avait demandé à La Fayette de lui dresser en 1780."[10] If the French possessed an evil reputation for gallantry, if they seemed to be a nation "légère, présomptueuse, bruyante, fastueuse,"[11] the soberness of the conduct of the French at Newport, the frugality of their officers, and their politeness and charm soon increased the favorable opinion which the gallant Marquis had helped to form.[12] The French officers, touched with the glamor of war, did more than the diplomats to engender a wave of enthusiasm of the French; they were, says their historian, "plus propres à toucher l'âme d'un peuple généreux et jeune";

[8] Robin, *op. cit.,* p. 72. This is confirmed by Brillat-Savarin, *Physiologie du Goût,* p. 77.

[9] *American Museum,* IV, August, 1788, pp. 121-2. "Comparison between certain French and American customs" by "a sentimental traveller," who writes from "Nantz," March 20, 1781. This is probably by Elkanah Watson. Faÿ collects earlier evidences of similar articles from the *Massachusetts Spy* in 1781. *Op. cit.,* 83 and note. See also Chastellux, *Voyage,* I, 276. The *State Gazette of North Carolina* (16 January, 1789) prints extracts from Sherlock's *Letters* on the grace and charm of the French and on their desire to please. IV, 184.

[10] Faÿ, p. 83; *Writings of Washington,* VI, 160-1.

[11] Robin, *op. cit.,* pp. 31-32, 30.

[12] Robin, *ibid.*

almost all of them were brave and gave proof of their constancy.[13] Immediately "tous les milieux mondaines, riches et commerçants s'ouvrirent aux officiers français. C'étaient aussi les milieux intellectuels. On peut deviner que cette fusion ne fut pas sans influer sur la vie spirituel des États-unis. D'autant plus qu'en même temps se répondaient dans tous les ports des marchands français. A vrai dire ils étaient mal adaptés aux États-unis. Quelques-uns d'entre eux réussirent pourtant. Ceux qui échouaient restaient dans les villes et se faisaient professeurs. Il y eut encore quelques officiers sans ressource qui firent le même."[14] And as Rochambeau, for instance, encouraged his officers to travel widely in order to keep them well informed,[15] the consequence was that all parts of this cosmpolitan society came to know them.

Whole groups of distinguished Frenchmen came to America: soldiers like Rochambeau, Chastellux, du Bourg, Colsen, Blanchard, Deux-ponts, Ségur, de Noailles, and the marquis de la Rouërie, who, in place of becoming a Trappist monk, came to the United States, raised a corps of cavalry, grumbled at Congress, but nonetheless fought bravely;[16] philosophers like Robin, Brissot de Warville, Dupont de Nemours, Bayard, Beaujour; travellers like Marchand, Milfort, Bossu, Bourgeois; diplomatic agents like Luzerne, Genêt, Rayneval, Moustier, Ternant; curiosity seekers like the Comte de Moré, whose memoirs are invaluable.[17] After these men came the exiles like Chateaubriand, Talleyrand, the Marquis de la Tour du Pin, La Rochefoucauld-Liancourt, Volney, Louis Philippe. From the seventy-odd memoirs on America written by these men it is possible to see that most of them were received by the best society, it is possible to reconstruct a picture of the times. And when, in addition, one recalls the work of Franklin, Jefferson, Jay, the Adams's, Paine, Priestley and others in explaining

---

[13] Faÿ, pp. 81-83, and references.

[14] Faÿ, p. 83. "Il y avait ces six milles soldats, les meilleurs de l'armée française, dont la belle taille, la discipline, le courage séduirent tous les coeurs. Certes, on les admiraient, on s'étonnait de les voir si différénts de ce que les Anglais avaient dit, si polis, si modérés, si stricts à éviter tout pillage." *Ibid*, p. 82.

[15] Sherrill, p. 205; *Mémoires du Comte de Moré*, p. 105.

[16] Cf. Faÿ, p. 82.

[17] Faÿ, pp. 269-70. For bibliographies of the travel books written by Frenchmen at the end of the eighteenth century, see the list in Sherrill; and cf. Faÿ, *Bibliographie Critique des Ouvrages Français relatifs aux États-Unis (1770-1800)*.

French ways to America, it is easy to understand how this Gallic fervor made its impression upon American manners. Nothing escapes these French writers—our love of dancing, our visits of ceremony, the nascent love for music in America; card playing and conversation; the general love of luxury in contrast to frugal France; the purity of our speech and manners; our love of French fashion and elegant dress; our strange and innocent customs in courtship and marriage, and our annoying habit of drinking each other's health; the cleanliness of our kitchens, our habit of smoking, our adaptability, our curiosity, our climate, our energy, our longevity, our tallness, our habits in the country, in travelling, in the cities, the high social standing of our inn-keepers and their uncivilized habit of putting two men in a bed; our general literacy and the co-education of our children; our colleges and newspapers; our keen interest in politics; our puritan Sabbath and our religious tolerance; the state of the learned professions, of manufacturers, of trade, of our merchant marine, our army, our navy. Nothing is left out. It is evident that they must have penetrated deeply into American life; that since they were our allies, we must have admired and imitated them. Let us accordingly select certain illuminating episodes from this period and see what they have to say regarding our aptitude in imitating French ways in the period from 1778 to 1789.

The Marquis de Lafayette is popular, even in New England.[18] In Connecticut in 1781, says Robin, "les coiffures de toutes les femmes, excepté celles de Quakers, y sont élevées, volumineuses, garnies de nos (French) gazes."[19] In Boston hair dressing follows the French mode, but is necessarily some years behind. The ladies do not use powder, but wash with "l'eau de savon," and "les plus recherchées commencent cependant à adopter la manière Européenne"—they have less ease than the French ladies, but more nobility.[20] In the same fair city "les officiers de notre marine ont été reçus par-tout, non seulement comme des alliés, mais comme des frères; ils ont été admis à la plus grande familiarité par les dames de Boston, sans qu'une seule indiscretion."[21] When Simeon Baldwin called

[18] Faÿ, p. 83, and references.
[19] Robin, *op. cit.,* p. 38.
[20] Robin, p. 14. They play music agreeably, but their singing is monotonous. "Narrative of the Prince de Broglie," *Magazine of American History,* I, 379.
[21] Chastellux, *Voyages,* II, 225-6. See on New England also de Broglie's *Mémoires,* pp. 306, 374-377. De Broglie met "genuine hospitality" everywhere.

on de la Tombe, the French consul in Boston in 1784, he and his companions were invited to dine with him on their return, and indeed, they took a glass of wine with him, found him agreeable, polite and attentive, had "a little agreeable chit-chat," and were again asked to dine.[22] The same Simeon has a sister Mary who writes him from Connecticut, December 3, 1780:

> I think you have doubtless heard that there is a number of the french troops stationed at Lebanon they seem to be the chief topick of discourse   I think now in town & I hear since I come home that the Duke is going to have a grand Ball next friday at Lathrops so as to get acquainted with our Norwich Ladys   I suppose he has had one at Windham   What will be the event of these things I cant say but he Who governs all things will no doubt order all things for the best.[23]

This appeal to Deity looks a little alarming, but then, this is New England. Meanwhile, or rather a little later, the Marquis de Chastellux and the Marquis de Vaudreuil were drinking tea at Mrs. Bowdoin's in Boston, having supper with twenty "select people of the city"; next day, meeting thirty persons at Mr. Breck's, including Mrs. Tudor "who knew French perfectly," and Mrs. Morton, who spoke French and, what is more, wrote poetry, attending the Tuesday evening club.[24] Of course, these Frenchmen smile a little, too; for instance, the Comte de Moré, on his way to join Lafayette's army in 1777, stopped overnight at a New England house; his host said he would be very glad to have a Frenchman in the house, since now he would have somebody to shave him;[25] and Moré says that a Frenchman having forgotten his boots, they were exhibited "comme une merveille" in a museum in New York.[26] The gentry knew better, however, even in New England.[27] I "hardly

[22] Baldwin, *Life and Letters of Simeon Baldwin*, pp. 220, 226.
[23] *Ibid.*, pp. 5-6. Breck's father gave a grand fête in honor of the birth of the Dauphin. Drink was distributed from hogsheads, and the whole town was made welcome to the house and gardens at Winter and Common streets in Boston. P. 38.
[24] Griswold, *Republican Court*, p. 9.
[25] *Mémoires du comte de Moré*, p. 68. Moré explains that this ignorance is due to the rareness and difficulty of their communication with Europe during the war, since Boston and Philadelphia are in the hands of the British, and one is almost as remote (arriéré) on the seacoast as in the interior. P. 69.
[26] *Ibid.*, p. 69.
[27] As marking the close social relations between the French and the Americans, the Vicomte Pontèves, the Marquis de Traversay, the Chevalier de Braye, and the Marquis de Galissomere, all members of the Order of the Cincinnati, participated in the reception tendered Washington in Boston in 1788 when the president visited the French naval vessels. Griswold, *Republican Court*, p. 190.

expected to find French fashions in the midst of American forests," said Robin, but in Connecticut he found "active taste for dress—I might even say . . . much luxury amid customs so simple and pure that they resembled those of the ancient patriarchs."[28]

In New York, during most of the war in the hands of the British, the vogue of French fashion increased with the inauguration of Washington, and the social popularity of the French ministers. M. de Marbois, M. Louis Otto, M. Gérard, the Duc de Luzerne,—they are all such charming men! Even the Marquis de Moustier is charming, who, coming in 1787, began most unfortunately with complaints on the score of etiquette, but who later "contributed much to the gayety and happiness of New York society."[28a] And they gave such wonderful balls! For instance, one recalls the fête given in New York in 1783 by the Duc de Lauzun, which amused the city for weeks, so that hundreds went to see the great building which M. le Duc erected for the dancing room—a structure sixty feet wide, the roof supported by pillars festooned and painted. A corps of hair-dressers worked overtime; "many ladies were obliged to have their heads dressed between four and six o'clock in the morning" and sat bolt upright until seven in the evening when the party began. At eight-thirty there was dancing, at nine, fire-works to amuse the ten thousand spectators, for whose benefit the magnificent duke kindly broke down part of the wall that they might see; at twelve, supper was served in three large tents; at three o'clock, the affair closed— Washington, we hope, went home earlier![29] By the side of this magnificence Moustier's ball in honor of the president some five years later (May 14, 1788) rather fades, and yet it had its features: one young lady wrote, "I heard the Marchioness declare she had exhausted every resource to produce an entertainment worthy of France." There were present cotillion dancers "in complete military costumes," the dancers, four and four, in French and American uniforms—Elias Boudinot

---

[28] Quoted in Sherrill, p. 60.
[28a] Griswold, *Republican Court*, pp. 82-83 Crèvecoeur complains in 1783 that the increased extravagance of New Yorkers is due to the example of the ambassadors and the large number of foreigners, as well as to the taste which Americans brought back from abroad. Mitchell, *St. Jean de Crèvecoeur*, p 265.
[29] See the contemporary description by Dr. Benjamin Rush in Griswold, *Republican Court*, p. 21; and the letter in the *Columbian Magazine*, I, 26-263 (February, 1787).

describes it.[30] Touching concord! which the next few years were rudely to interrupt. In the meantime the craze spread: "assemblies" opened with a Passe-Pie and ended with the Sarabande à l'Espagnole—it is the French way.[31] At the ball accompanying Washington's inauguration in New York "a sufficient number of fans had been made for the purpose in Paris, the ivory frames of which displayed, as they were opened . . . an extremely well executed medallion portrait of Washington, in profile," and a page gave one "with the compliments of the managers" to each lady as every couple passed the receiver of tickets.[32]

In Philadelphia the French nobility made a special appeal.[33] In the suburbs, at a place called Lebanon, a Frenchman dispensed tea, coffee, bottled mead, cakes, fruits, and comfits to "orderly genteel, and reputable people" as early as 1770,[34] which apparently was fashionable. In July, 1778, there was a grand banquet in honor of M. Gérard, the French ambassador; and on August 23 "everybody" called on him in honor of the birthday of Louis XVI; and the polite ambassador gave a dinner on August 25.[35] A little later the Marquis de Marbois, the French chargé d'affaires, who was a great favorite in Philadelphia society, married Miss Moore of that city.[36] And, speaking mainly with reference to Philadelphia, the French memoir writers tell us how the women followed French fashions. The Baron Closen, for example, is of the opinion that American women are pretty, that they have good style, and dress excellently in the French manner. General Rochambeau declares that the women have taken up the French fashions, and are deeply interested in them. Moreau de St.

[30] See the description in Griswold, pp. 157-8.
[31] New York Packet, January 5, 1784. Quoted in McMaster, I, 66, note.
[32] Griswold, p. 156. See the description of the dinner given in honor of the French ambassador (Luzerne) in November, 1783, by Governor Clinton, when there were present "more than one hundred gentlemen, besides the Commander-in-Chief, with his general officers in the city" and state officials. Ibid., p. 2.
[33] See the description of social activities centering about the French in Scharf and Westcott, History of Philadelphia, I, chap. xviii (part III), too long to transcribe here.
[34] Schouler, Americans of 1776, p. 119, note.
[35] Scharf and Westcott, History of Philadelphia, II, 899.
[36] Griswold, Republican Court, pp. 81-82, note. He wrote a History of Louisiana, and a book on the treason of Benedict Arnold, and later held important offices under Napoleon, having an influential voice in the negotiations for the Louisiana purchase.

Méry tells the same story, but adds that they scorn veils and laces, and do not go in for artificial flowers. The Prince de Broglie, an ungallant but truthful historian, remarks that the ladies of Philadelphia, although magnificent enough in their costumes, generally do not wear them with much taste, and though in arranging their hair, they follow the French mode, they have less lightness of touch; they have good figures, he says, but lack grace and make their curtsies badly.[37] Even the French *petit maître* could not teach everything! "Every year," says the laborious Schoepf, "dressed dolls are brought from Europe, which, silent, give the law of the mode." The men are naturally less touched by French fashion than the women. "Only a few young gentlemen," he writes, "especially those of the army, approximate to the French cut, but they by no means give themselves to . . . ostentatious frippery," and to the prudent German, taste in male attire is mainly English.[38] But then, French fashion is the English vogue just now. The infection spreads even to remoter districts: in 1788 Anburey, an officer in Burgoyne's army, sourly observes in Lancaster, then the most considerable inland town in America, a lot of "French frippery," which, he says, the inhabitants will not purchase.[39] The world looks yellow, we must remember, to the defeated.

The French modes, however, continue to be fascinating. Chastellux says they are everywhere, and describes a lady who was eager to lead a crusade in their favor, for she "has taste as delicate as her health." "Excessively enthusiastic over fashions," he continues, "she only awaits the end of this trifling revolution now taking place to initiate an even more important one in the customs of her nation."[40] In New York in 1788 Francis Durand at 15 Queen Street was advertising as "imported in French packets" cotton and silk fabrics, umbrellas of different sizes, men's black and white hose, black "modes", white and colored kid gloves.[40a] In Annapolis in 1781 the

[37] For characteristic quotations see Sherrill, pp. 60-62.
[38] Schoepf, *Travels in the Confederation,* I, 100. On the rage for English dress in France at the close of the eighteenth century see Lockitt, *op. cit.,* pp. 40-45.
[39] Anburey, *Travels,* II, 176.
[40] See the passage in Sherrill, pp. 60-62.
[40a] Mitchell, *St. Jean de Crèvecoeur,* p. 211. For Crèvecoeur's attempts to institute a bureau of information on French imports, and to increase commerce between the two countries, see chaps. XI-XII.

feminine luxury surpassed the provincial luxury of France; and a French hair-dresser, a man of importance, received 1000 crowns a year from a single lady.[41] Indeed, the hair-dressers become so important that they are addressed in verse; as for instance in a poem by "S," an "Ode to Faelix (*sic*) Brunot," which appeared in 1787:

> Brunot's fingers touch the hairs,
> Each look untoward disappears,
>   And smooth the toupees lie.
>
>   .   .   .   .   .   .
>
> Then young and old, black, brown and grey,
> Females and males, swart, grave and gay,
>   To Brunot's shop repair:
> There ye shall each, with pleasure find
> He'll cut and trim you to your mind,
>   And dress you to a hair.[42]

Are your teeth troubling you? One Le Mayeur, who called himself a doctor, made the fashion of transplanting teeth fashionable in New York and Philadelphia in 1784.[43] Do you wish to look in the mirror? Buy a French mirror, with the Father of his country, who purchased two of the French minister.[44] Do you long to dance? "Cotillions came in . . . with the French refugees from the West Indies"[45]—even before, as we have seen. Do you wish to be amused? Montgolfier and Blanchard are to make ballooning a fad: "great numbers of balloons were constructed, and many ascents made," following their exhibitions: it is a parallel to Franklin's conquest of the lightning, this conquest of the air.[46] In fact, the French are *à la mode*: even in Charleston, where our anonymous French officer was not well received at first, good society made amends and he and his companions were "fêted everywhere. . . . We have," he writes, "spent eight days in fêtes and galas,"[47] following Lafayette's arrival. But let us go on to other matters.

---

[41] Robin, *Nouveau Voyage*, p. 104.
[42] *Columbian Magazine*, I, 505 (June, 1787). There are eight six-line stanzas in the poem.
[43] McMaster, I, 65-6.
[44] Griswold, *Republican Court*, p. 244.
[45] *Ibid.*, p. 47.
[46] McMaster, I, 223, note. Blanchard had a "run" in Philadelphia in 1792-3.
[47] Stevens' *Facsimiles*, no. 754. On July 2, 1785, the *South Carolina Gazette* prints in its London letter the information that Beaumarchais' new play has given rise to a head-dress in Paris, "and, as folly travels faster than wit, the fashion had reached London where the Comedy is yet un-

2. THE ÉMIGRÉ MOVEMENT AND AMERICAN SOCIETY

With the outbreak of the French Revolution, as we have seen, a new group of Frenchmen came to America from France, from England, from the West Indies—men who represented in many cases the pink of French society. The centers of influence in social matters of these exiles were Boston, New York, Philadelphia, and Charleston; New Orleans also, but New Orleans is not yet, so to speak, in the American scene. Under the impetus thus given to fashionable society, dancing masters increase their numbers, social entertainment takes on new colors; and if the Revolution alienated one large portion of society, it increased the enthusiasm of the Gallomaniacs, whose social performances assume a political tinge: certain French manners,—or shall we say mannerisms?—became the platform of a political group.[48]

The *petits-maîtres* begin, as I have said, to multiply: their arts are the refuge of many a needy exile. For instance, B. Quesnet, an artist of merit, became dancing master to Hallam's company, and set up a dancing school in 1800, dying in 1819. In 1800 William Francis taught "the last new minuet" straight from the "Grand Opera House, Paris." M. Sicard, a famous dancing master from 1790 to 1812, retired with a com-

known. It is called 'La Plume de Figaro' and is much worn by the belles of fashion. The Werter bonnet is much the rage—the *Charlotified* wearer assumes the pensive air of Werter's favorite girl, and seems conscious that they have equal power to inspire love and kill men." Willis, *The Charleston Stage*, p. 94. It is in these devious ways that the influence of fashion is felt. The general entrepôt of the French merchants was London, and at this period the connection between Charleston and London was close, as I have elsewhere indicated. Faÿ, *op. cit.*, p. 6.

[48] See the discussion of this problem in chapter xv. For the present, it is sufficient to glimpse the political animosity of the time in such a passage as this from John Adams' letters: "Our countrymen are about to abandon the good old, grave, solid manners of Englishmen, their ancestors, and adopt all the apery, levity, and frivolity, of the French. *Ça ira.*" *Letters,* II, 124 (From Philadelphia, January 21, 1793). John has changed his tune since 1778. Mrs. Adams was not much better pleased when she was in France in 1784-85. She writes Lucy Cranch that she was disappointed in Paris, gives a most amusing description of Madame Helvétius, and adds that "I hope . . . to find amongst the French ladies manners more consistent with my ideas of decency, or I shall be a mere recluse." After she met the Marquise de Lafayette, she confided to Mrs. Cranch that "there is not a lady in our country, who would have gone abroad to dine so little dressed." However, by January 20, 1875, she has grown reconciled to many things, and writes Mrs. Storer that, though she can not bring herself to visit French ladies first (which is the custom), their dress and manners are light, airy, and genteel. She even finds the "dancing on the stage" "a great amusement," and the dancers' "dresses are beautifully fanciful." Shades of Increase Mather! *Letters,* II, 56, 61, 69-70, 76, 77.

petence and (for dancing must go on) his assistant, succeeded him. All this is in Philadelphia: the year 1800 there is prolific in dancing masters, as, for example, M. Auguste Auriol, late of Paris, who taught till 1809, returned to Paris, and again taught in Philadelphia from 1810 to 1818; Ignace Frasier ("Monsieur Ignace"), a French officer in the American army, who opened a dancing academy by 1802, achieved a prodigious success and died in 1825; and M. Eperail, who tried vainly to introduce masquerade balls in 1808.[49] In Boston Washington Allston "played the fop" at a charity ball for the benefit of a run-down French dancing-master in 1796 or later;[50] and in the same intellectual city in 1796, a Frenchman, an "habile écuyer," constructed "un cirque pour ses exercises." He and his troupe drew crowds of spectators, and though on Monday, September 5, the roof collapsed, nobody was hurt, which was gratifying.[51] In New York in 1793 M. Desdoity was advertising "a parcel of hats and some Plaster of Paris" and on other occasions an "elegant assortment" of dry-goods, a piano-forte, hair, window-glasses, sail duck, and brandy.[51a] Even the Iroquois had their French dancing-master, M. Violet, as Chateaubriand tells us, and there seems no reason to believe that the poet is not telling the truth.[52]

In Philadelphia in 1797 many of the shops, in the opinion of La Rochefoucauld-Liancourt, were as well furnished as those of Paris or of London, and the state of society impresses him as being positively brilliant. "Voila," he exclaims, "le véritable état de la société à Philadelphia: grands dîners, grand thés, pour les arrivons d'Europe, Anglais, Français, étrangers de tous pays, de toute classe, de tout caractère: philosophe, prêtre, homme de lettres, prince, arracheur de dents, homme d'esprit ou idiot." If the traveller is a prospective land-purchaser the festivities are prolonged. "J'ai vu des bals, au jour de naissance du Président, où des ornamens de la salle, l'élégance et la variété des parures rappelaient l'Europe."[53] In or near Philadelphia, partaking of this brilliant life, were such persons as M. Duportail, who bought a little farm near Philadelphia; le

---

[49] Scharf and Westcott, *History of Philadelphia,* II, 962-963.
[50] Flagg, *Life and Letters of Washington Allston,* p. 28.
[51] La Rochefoucauld-Liancourt, *Voyages,* V, 196-7.
[51a] Mitchell, *op. cit.,* pp. 211-2.
[52] See Chinard, *Notes sur le voyage de Chateaubriand en Amérique,* pp. 284-5.
[53] *Voyages,* VI, 323, 330.

Comte de Moré, come to collect some money due him; M. Moreau de Saint-Méry, who was running a stationer's shop; Antoine-Omer Talon, Volney, Talleyrand, the vicomte de Noailles (who insisted that a Philadelphia notary give him his full name and titles such as vicomte, chevalier de Saint-Louis, chevalier de Malte, for which he was criticized in the public press and, one suspects, adored by the *jeunes filles*) ; and by and by Louis-Philippe and his brothers.[54] Besides these "un grand nombre de Français de tout sexe, de tout rang, de toutes opinions, se trouvaient ainsi rassemblés depuis Philadelphie jusqu'à New York."[55] One of them, by the way, a former member of the royal body-guard, bought an elephant, exhibited it, and made 40,000 francs."[55] Markno, the former "cuisinier" of the chevalier de Capellis, was the center of émigré life, and had the reputation of being an excellent pâtissier, and one much patronized by the gentry.[57] Talleyrand was not, it is true, popular; persons who escort negro women through the streets as their mistresses, are not likely to be;[58] but on the whole, the émigrés were socially in good repute[59] in Philadelphia.

We must pass over many other interesting items;[60] but as

---

[54] *Mémoires du comte de Moré*, pp. 146-7, 148-9, 153, 163.

[55] *Ibid.*, p. 165.

[56] *Ibid.*

[57] *Ibid.*, p. 163. Others in this group were Colombe, a former aide-de-camp of Lafayette (*Ibid.*, p. 170) ; Demeusnier, Théophile de Cazenove, Beaumetz, Nancrède and Boislandry. Faÿ, *op. cit.*, pp. 269-70. Another center was the book-store of Moreau de Saint-Méry, whose memoirs are, says Faÿ, a chef-d'oeuvre of wounded fatuity and shortsightedness. The fact that the American upper classes did not especially concern themselves with him is probably due to his character rather than to his poverty. In remarking that the group of intelligent men, patriots and sincere revolutionists in Philadelphia, were unwise in being so violent and ill-natured in their attitude toward Americans, Faÿ seems to me to have been misled by a too great dependence upon Saint-Méry's *Memoirs*. Faÿ, p. 269.

[58] Fact. Cf. de Moré, pp. 155-6. Talleyrand does not mention this interesting incident in his *Memoirs*. For his own description of his Philadelphia existence, see his *Memoirs*, I, 169-187. He had come to Philadelphia fresh from intimacy in London with the Marquis of Hastings, Richard Price, Priestley, Canning, Samuel Romilly, Robert Smith, Pierre Dumont, Bentham, Lord Henry Petty, and Fox, and in America was chiefly interested in Robert Morris and Hamilton.

[59] On the social activities of the émigrés, cf. Scharf and Westcott, *History of Philadelphia*, II, 918-22, 963-4.

[60] For instance, writing of Newark in 1794, Saint-Méry tells us that Mde. Capron, whose husband, a native of Lille in Flanders, is a player on the bass, is employed by the orchestra of the Philadelphia Company; and that many little girls and young demoiselles come to Newark for social training. For $136 (a year?) they learn French, English, writing, geography, design, and embroidery of all kinds. Saint-Méry, *Voyages aux États-*

we have glanced at Philadelphia, the social capital of the North, let us glance at Charleston, the social capital of the South, in the last decade of the eighteenth century. "The inhabitants of Charles-town," says La Rochefoucauld-Liancourt, "are obliging and polite," and receive strangers cordially and frankly,[61] even when the politeness is ill repaid. Here, too, one finds dancing-masters and hair-dressers[62] and here, too, French modes are popular. For instance, a quotation from *The Columbia Herald* announces the Parisian fashions of 1795-6; Miss Willis has included it in her valuable book:

The Greek dress among the females is already out of fashion; they now wear a kind of chemise-robe with a girdle which is worn very high. Though the dress of both sexes is very simple, it is nevertheless extremely expensive because of the many particular ornaments belonging thereto.

For Evening-Dress, the hair in small curls, and the hind-hair in ringlets. Bandeaux of silver tissue, and colours interwined in the hair and two white ostrich feathers at the side or in front are also worn.

For Morning-Dress: Brunswick Chemise of fine India muslin, scalloped and embroidered at the bottom. Long sleeves, sash of white satin

unis, p. 125. Again, as marking the vogue of French hair-dressers, it is amusing to read the indignant advertisement of John Harford, "Ladies and Gentlemens' Hair-Dresser," in the *North-Carolina Journal*, October 10, 1792, who is from neither London nor Paris, but a downright Hibernian, and proud of the fact. Or again, Latrobe comments on the fact that in Virginia, country-houses are given French names; Colonel Skipwith's house in Cumberland County, for example, is "Horsdumon," and Richard Randolph's is "Bizarre." *The Journal of Latrobe*, pp. 10-11.

[61] The whole passage is of interest: "Les habitans de Charles-town sont obligeans, polis, et reçoivent les étrangers avec empressement et franchise: ils ont été d'une bienfaisance, d'une hospitalité remarquable pour les Français échappées des iles: argent, secours, linge, logement, soins de toute nature leur ont été prodigués avec une générosité affectueuse, simple et soutenue. Il est pénible de devoir ajouter que la conduit des obligés n'a pas toujours été digne de ce de ces bienfaiteurs; que l'inconséquence trop commune du peuple colon, a tiré un profit peu utile de l'assistance qu'ils ont reçue, et a pour ainsi dire forcé les habitans de Charles-town de changer de conduite, quoique beaucoup de secours soient encore continués. On trouve par-tout les Français qui disent du mal des Américains, qui les détestent, et aussi souvent on trouve des Américains qui les ont obligés avec loyauté, et qui ne s'en sont lassés que par de trop bonnes raisons." *Voyages*, IV, 11.

[62] "Among the celebrated French Dancing Masters, who all had 'Long Rooms,' was Pierre Tastet, whose 'Long Room' was entered through Rope Lane which formed an eastern entrance to old Concert Hall. . . ." "Hair Powder and Cosmetics" were advertised by Louis Martin, Peruke-Maker and Hair-dresser from Paris. "One of Charleston's little hair-dressers, Dubard by name, who was a violent sansculotte, and who had been in France at the height of the Revolution, 'entertained' his customers with his impressions upon viewing the guillotining of Marie Antoinette, whilst frizzing their hair and manipulating the powder-puff." Willis, *The Charleston Stage*, pp. 235, 297, 236.

ribband, and large muslin handkerchief around the neck. Jonquil gloves and yellow shoes. The hair in light curls and Gipsy straw bonnet, with a wreath of flowers around the middle.[63]

It is thus that the Empire dress comes to Charleston; the Carolinians, who "jusqu'ici dans l'usage d'envoyer leurs enfans aux collèges des États du Nord, ou à ceux d'Angleterre,"[64] where French fashions are in vogue, are struck by it. Indeed, in 1793, feathered head-dresses (following Paris styles) were so much the rage that the *Gazette* on March 21, carries a "Theatrical Request to the Ladies" to lay aside their head-dresses so that the gentlemen who attend them may have a glance at the stage.[65] Perhaps Mrs. Izard, who is "instructed, amiable, polite, and obliging" and who has travelled in Europe and now lives in Charleston,[66] has helped to make them the vogue. However, all is not peace; and a correspondent in the *City Gazette* for October 18, 1794, suggests that the municipality appoint a Master of Ceremonies, as they have done in Boston, to settle all kinds of social disputes, especially over the possession of stage boxes, for one unfortunate misunderstanding has resulted in a duel.[67] Charleston, which had already been profoundly impressed by the Huguenots, was made even more French by the émigrés; in "social forms French culture yet lingers in South Carolina and notably in Charleston," as it does, for that matter, to some extent, in Virginia and the Carolinas.[68]

3. FRENCH MANNERS IN AMERICA IN THE DAYS OF JEFFERSON

Let us take our stand a little later, just at the turn of the century, as Adams is going out and Jefferson is coming in, and once more survey society. This is the society in which Abigail Adams moved: she who was 13 when her father was appointed joint commissioner to France, who went with him to London where she became the belle of St. James's, and where she married W. S. Smith of the American legation. Dolly Madison was beginning the impressive social career which was to be

---

[63] Quoted in Willis, *The Charleston Stage*, pp. 297-8.
[64] La Rochefoucauld-Liancourt, *Voyages*, IV, 61.
[65] Willis, *op. cit.*, pp. 166-7.
[66] La Rochefoucauld-Liancourt, *op. cit.*, IV, 72-74. The Duke was much impressed by the Izards.
[67] Willis, p. 261.
[68] See R. A. Hinsdale, *Foreign Influence Upon Education in the United States*, I, 598.

capped by eight years in the White House, in which republican palace she counted "the greatest political and social dignitaries of England and America and France among her guests." Indeed, it is alleged that she was so popular that she was responsible for her husband's second term—this is politics in the grand manner with a vengeance! Mrs. Thomas Mann Randolph, Jefferson's daughter, was a social light, as indeed, she deserved to be, considering her painful education: on any typical day of her girlhood, she studied music from eight to ten; from ten to one she danced one day and "drew" another; from one to two, said her father, "draw the day you dance and write a letter the next day"; from three to four she devoted herself to French; from four to five, music; and, until bed time, she worked at her English or else she wrote letters. Such, at any rate, was her father's schedule in those iron days when society was a vocation and not an amusement. She had joined her father in Paris when she was fifteen, she had been educated at a convent at Parthemont, she had moved in the best circles of French society—naturally, she adorned American social circles. This was also the era when Sally McKean married the Marquis d'Yrujo, with all the fashionable world to see; when Theodosia Burr, beautiful and unfortunate, was trained by her father to read Greek, Latin, and French, and took charge of his household when she was fourteen, entertaining Jerome Bonaparte, Louis Philippe, Talleyrand and others, and marrying Joseph Allston of South Carolina; when Betsy Patterson married Jerome Bonaparte, she whom the great Napoleon so disliked though he rather admired her caustic wit—she returned to America, staying from 1805 to 1815, was bored to death, went back to Paris, came home again in 1834—a brilliant social career with an obscure ending.[69]

Davis's *Travels in America from 1798 to 1802* gives a lively, if sometimes inaccurate, picture of the period. He begins by repudiating the "frantic crew of deists" though he dedicates his book to Thomas Jefferson. In New York he fell in with M. H. Caritat, a French book-seller, for whom he translated *Buonaparte's Campaign in Italy* which was published "amidst the acclamations of the Democrats, and the revilings of the Federalists." He was patronized by Burr: "Miss Theodosia Burr speaks French and Italian with facility." "Martel, a

[69] Sale, *Old Time Belles and Cavaliers*, pp. 178 ff; Wandell and Minnegerode, *Aaron Burr* (see index under Theodosia); Didier, *The Life and Letters of Madame Bonaparte*.

Frenchman," he continues, "has dedicated a volume of his productions to Miss Burr, with the horatian epithet of 'dulce decus.' " He went to Philadelphia just before the outbreak of yellow fever: "None but *French* people were to be found seeking pleasure in society," he says, which seems to indicate, at any rate, that the French were "in society." He stayed at a French hotel kept by M. Pecquet, where at suppers there were "a dozen French ladies and gentlemen, who could not utter a word of English." He took "pacquet" for Charleston September 22, 1798; Monsieur Lartique was aboard, "an old French gentlemen from St. Domingo," and they were considerably afraid of being captured by French privateers. When he reached Charleston he set up as a tutor in Latin and French. He admired L'Enfant's plan for Washington, in which city he met "a lively young Frenchman" who made an epigram. When he returned to Philadelphia his "love for the Gallic idiom" led him "to the shop of Mr. *Dufief,* a *French* bookseller, in *North Fourth Street,"* with whom he dined, who had an unsaleable bust of Voltaire over his door, and who taught French. He reports that near Occoquan, Virginia, at Clearmount, lived "a French gentleman of the name of *Gerardine,* whose reputation for the *Belles Lettres,* induced me to write him from my solitude"; and in Chester, Pennsylvania, he supped with Monsieur Pichon, "the French ambassador."[70] Of Philadelphia manners he observes generally: "It is to Mademoiselle *de Florian* (the daughter of his lodging-house keeper) and a few other of her countrymen that the young ladies of *Philadelphia* owe their present graceful mien. The revolution in France produced a revolution in the walk of the *Philadelphia* damsels. . . . When the revolution drove so many of the *Gallic* damsels to the banks of the *Delaware,* the *American* girls blushed at their own awkwardness; and each strove to copy that swimming air, that *nonchalance,* that ease and apparent unconsciousness of being observed, which characterized the *French* young ladies as they passed through the streets."[71] Davis was an adventurer and a good deal of a scoundrel; if in a book not devoted to anything but his own literary adventures, he yet casually notes so many Frenchmen as these, one gets some glimpse into the profound effect upon American manners of these exiles.

[70] Davis, *Travels in America,* pp. 3, 19-21, 25, 39-40, 47-49, 169, 174, 205-6, 238, 311.
[71] *Ibid.,* pp. 322-3.

In New York about this time families of "colonial taste" turned up their noses at everything French, and yet they had to confess that "the light French manners" were making inroads upon those derived from provincial England.[72] "The saying in the upper classes was that courtly manners went out with the Federalist party." The rival milliners were English and French, Mrs. Toole and Madame Bouchard; and alas for "courtly manners!"—the "dashing belles of the town appeared to prefer the latter." French hair-dressers cut and trimmed after the Titus and Brutus fashion for the men, and intermixed gauze, muslin, and jewels in ladies' head-dresses; powder, wigs, knee-buckles, and small-clothes were getting unfashionable,[73] and although the old beaux kept constant to silk waistcoats and the snuffbox, the young men played billiards, offered cigars, and wore black uniforms at evening parties—social distinctions were beginning to crumble. French refugees taught the waltz, the stately minuet being tabooed at parties where old ladies, in stiff buckram and brocades, "felt scandalized at the exhibition of low-cut dresses and French draperies." We have passed fully into the period of the Empire, by way of the Consulate.[74] "Madame Bonaparte," wrote Mrs. William Seaton, the friend of Dolly Madison, "is a model of fashion, and many of our belles strive to imitate her," though they could not match her back and shoulders.[75]

---

[72] For a picture of the conservative gentry of New York during this epoch consult Fox, *The Decline of Aristocracy in the Politics of New York,* chaps. i and ii.

[73] The French Revolution abolished silk stockings. Mrs. Lamb, *History of the City of New York,* II, 550.

[74] Schouler, *History of the United States,* II, 274.

[75] Wharton, *Salons Colonial and Republican,* p. 204. Nothing is more amusing than the letter which the sedate Simeon Baldwin wrote his wife from Washington on January 12, 1805: "Young Bonaparte & his wife were here last week. I did not have an opportunity to inspect her charms but her dress at a Ball which she attended has been the general topic of conversation in all circles—Having married a Parissian (*sic*) she assumed the mode of dress in which it is said the Ladies of Paris are clothed—if that may be called clothing which leaves half of the body naked & the shape of the rest perfectly visible—Several of the Gent^n who saw her say they could put all the cloaths she had on in their vest pockett—& it is said she did not appear at all abashed when the inquisitive Eyes of the young Galants led them to chat with her tete a tete (*sic*).—Tho' her taste & appearance was condemned by those who saw her, yet such fashions are astonishingly bewitching & will gradually progress, & we may well reflect on what we shall be when fashion shall remove all barriers from the chastity of women." Baldwin, *Life and Letters of Simeon Baldwin,* p. 345. At her marriage "all the clothes worn by the bride might have been put in my pocket." Didier, *op. cit.,* pp. 5-10, describes the wedding.

Many, like Simeon Baldwin, condemned the French mania of fashionable society—as many were to do in subsequent decades. To the ears of fashionable society in 1801

no music was pleasing which did not form part of some French opera, and was not to be heard at a concert in a tea-garden or a public ball. French manners had corrupted them. Since the fall of the Bastile, it was said complainingly, every Republican must dress like a Frenchman, and every Federalist like a subject of King George. If you happen to oppose the administration, you must go regularly to the shop of M. Sansculotte, before whose door is a flaring liberty-pole, painted tricolor and surmounted with a red cap of liberty, and have your hair cut à la Brutus; your pantaloons must fit tight to the leg and come down to your yellow top-boots or, better yet, your shoes. If you persist in wearing breeches and silk stockings and square-toed boots, then you are an old fogy, or a Federalist, which is the same thing, and must inscribe your brass buttons, "Long live the President."
The folly of the French dress was a source of never-ending amusement. Dress became every season more and more hideous, more and more uncomfortable, more and more devoid of good sense and good taste. . . . The pantaloons of a beau went up to his arm-pits; to get into them was a morning's work, and, when in, to sit down was impossible. His hat was too small to contain his handkerchief, and was not expected to stay on his head. His hair was brushed from the crown of his head toward his forehead. . . . About his neck was a spotted linen handkerchief; the skirts of his green coat were cut away to a mathematical point behind; his favorite drink was brandy, and his favorite talk of the last French play. . . . Women were thought worse than the men.[76]

"The ladies in New York" in this same epoch, according to a foreign observer quoted by Mrs. Lamb, "in general seem more partial to the various and dashing drapery of the Parisian belles than to the elegant and becoming attire of our London beauties, who"—it is a Briton who speaks—"improve upon the French fashions."[77]
Indeed, the fever was hard to resist. When Jefferson (in Washington) endeavored to do away with the levee, Washington society swept down upon him in wrath: etiquette must

---

[76] McMaster, *History*, II, 543-4.
[77] According to the same observer the dress of the gentleman "corresponds in every respect with the English costume." One sees what he goes forth to see. Mrs. Lamb, *History of the City of New York*, II, 440. Conservative Boston was less a slave to the prevailing Gallomania. The typical entertainment among conservative circles there was "the state dinner—not the light feminine triviality which France introduced into an amusement-loving world, but the serious dinner of Sir Robert Walpole and Lord North, where gout and plethora waited behind the chairs; an effort of animal endurance." Adams, *History*, I, 92.

be preserved.[78] When the French ambassador came to call on a New Year's day, fashionable society rubbed its eyes at a "rolling ball of burnished gold, carried with swiftness through the air by two gilt wings." The coach was the ball, two gorgeous footmen with chapeaux bras, gilt braided skirts, and splendid swords, were the wings, and the contents were the French representative.[79] At the very White House, under this regime of republican simplicity, there were eleven servants—a French cook, a French steward,[80] and an Irish coachman among them. The table, according to Bacon's memory of it (he was steward at Monticello), was full almost every day with congressmen, foreigners and people of all kinds.[81] A little later "Mr. G. Flower" visited Monticello, and later told Faux that Jefferson "lives splendidly in French style, on top of the beautiful mountain Monticello," where he was wasting his estate—which was true enough, but French styles were not responsible.[82] In far-off St. Louis Schulz reports that the ladies were celebrated for the taste and splendour of their dress, which was—naturally enough—French;[83] and in Kentucky, Ohio, and Tennessee—the "western country"—Michaux found that "silk goods, such as taffeties, silk stockings, etc., brandy and millstones, notwithstanding their great weight, and the distance from the seaports" were brought from France.[84] Ashe describes the social tone of Saint Genevieve in 1806 as thoroughly French,[85] and for that matter, the incoming Americans found the manners of Versailles at all the decaying French towns in the upper Mississippi basin.

Melish admired General Moreau's house at Morrisville, Pennsylvania, in 1806[86]—a social rendezvous for friends of the general. At Princeton, New Jersey, in the same year, he attended a ball, and did not like the showy dresses of the women, nor the dance, a French cotillion, in which, it seemed to him,

[78] See the amusing account of this battle in Wharton, *Salons Colonial and Republican,* pp. 175-209.
[79] *Ibid.,* pp. 194-5.
[80] This was Petit. As secretary of state in Philadelphia, Jefferson kept five horses, Petit, his daughter's maid, and four or five men servants. Wharton, p. 109.
[81] Wharton, p. 190.
[82] Faux, *Memorable Days in America,* p. 277.
[83] Schulz, *Travels,* II, 41.
[84] Michaux, *Travels,* p. 156.
[85] Ashe, *Travels,* III, 116-120.
[86] Melish, *Travels,* p. 115.

they "sprawled and sprauchled."[87] In Philadelphia the number of French entertainers steadily increased in the opening years of the last century,[88] but to go on were tedious. In sum, the trail of French taste was over the fashions, the amusements, the entertainments of the upper classes under Jefferson; and its effect was felt in American life, whether it results in imitation of French fashion, or in a violent reaction against inflooding degeneracy.

4. THE IMPORTATION OF FRENCH FASHIONS

By 1806 the importing house of Laurence Huron in Philadelphia was doing a regular business in fashionable attire; and so, too, was the rival establishment of Benjamin Bakewell in New York, which purchased gloves and laces in Rochelle.[89] Imports rose from $23,000,000 in 1700 to $113,041,000 in 1815; the trade with the French, Dutch, Danish, and Spanish West Indies was highly prosperous until 1807, when trade was restricted, and the French Islands were captured by the British; in 1818 the imports jumped to $121,750,000; and then, in the years of trade recession, 1819-1830, "France alone, of the commercial countries which shipped large quantities of foreign goods to America, continued to increase the volume of her shipments."[90] It is needless to remark that manufactured goods

[87] *Ibid.*, p. 111.
[88] Scharf and Westcott, *History of Philadelphia*, II, 956 ff.
[89] Herrick, *Audubon the Naturalist*, I, 153. J. J. Audubon to Francis Rozier of Nantes, from New York, May 30, 1807: "I can now inform you of their sale, which is also advantageous, although the principal part was fine and of very great price. The gloves in prices of 23 28 D, are what is needed for this market here, and especially if they are of any other color than yellow or bottle green they are less apt to soil; further, they conceal defects more, and find in consequence more purchasers. The laces are better, although there was a heavy duty. You should know that here the extravagance of the women equals or rather quite balances the circumspection of the men, so that all articles for women should be beautiful, that is to say, conspicuous." *Ibid.*, I, 164.
[90] Johnson, *History of Domestic and Foreign Commerce of the United States*, II, 20, 24, 32, 37. Beaujour, Appendix, *Aperçu des États-unis* gives the imports of the United States in 1802-3-4 from Great Britain as $35,970,-000; from Russia, Prussia, and Germany, $7,094,000; from Holland, France, Spain and Italy, $25,475,000; some scattering items I omit. The total is $75,316,000. The Tariff Act of August, 1790, legalized a ten per cent discount on imports in American vessels, a provision reaffirmed May, 1792. An Act of June, 1794, imposed a ten per cent increase in the duties on imports in foreign vessels, a policy reaffirmed in 1795, 1797, 1800, and 1804, as well as in 1812 and 1813. In 1815 the ten per cent discrimination was repealed in cases of direct trade with nations granting reciprocal privileges, but the Act of April, 1816, reaffirmed the ten per cent increase

and luxuries were important items in this French trade. If we introduce these figures, the fact is significant: in the period from 1810 to 1830 the grand manner, socially speaking, gave way in the North with the increase in population, the increased importance of the middle class, and the tendency—a temporary one—towards an equable distribution of wealth.[91] The Southern aristocracy suffered a temporary setback, but only a temporary one, and it turned, as we shall see, to one old center (Charleston) and to one new one (New Orleans) for the tradition of its social heritage.[92] But by and large, we pass from the age of Jefferson to the age of Jackson: stately ceremony and an aristocracy of birth and breeding slowly fade in this transition epoch; and the leisure class of the nascent industrial era, that is to say, the wealthy *bourgeoisie,* climbs to the vacant throne. Moreover, the increasing industrialism of American life leaves less room for mere manners. It is likewise an era of a marked moral reaction: the glitter of the Empire was felt to be immoral, the fall of Napoleon was a mighty lesson which justified the ways of God with man. An intense nationalistic spirit combatted, as never before, the prestige of foreign influence. Yet the precedent had been established; the aristocracy of the republican court had established for all time in the United States the dictatorship of Paris fashions as well as the tradition that for light amusement, France and Frenchmen are your only leaders. Accordingly, we must look, not to the dying salon class, but to the general diffusion of French fashions throughout the country to ascertain how the French influenced us: French manners become less and less important, French dresses become more and more consequential.

except where otherwise provided by treaty or law. In May, 1822, tonnage discrimination against the French was suspended upon the completion of suitable arrangements by the President, and in March, 1823, was so suspended. *Ibid.,* II, 349. The general effect of this legislation was to increase the amount of imports carried in American vessels.

[91] "In the twenty years immediately following the War of 1812 forces were evolving, institutions arising and changing, centers of social gravity shifting, and deep basic movements of various sorts taking place that have had the most lasting effects upon the whole structure of American life." The Virginia dynasty was being impoverished and losing both political and industrial power (see p. 55 ff.), the old New England ruling class was being disrupted, and power was being slowly transferred to the Middle and Western states. Simons, *Social Forces in American History,* pp. 151, 153-7.

[92] For a picture of Southern culture before the war see Dodd, *op. cit.,* and Wade, *Augustus Baldwin Longstreet.*

At the turn of the century and thereafter, for some twenty years, social records are scarcer than they are for the previous decades. The Napoleonic struggles and the War of 1812 necessarily cut off the New World from the Old. Moreover, that eager curiosity regarding the new social experiment represented by the United States was, if not eclipsed, at least dulled by the kaleidoscopic turn of events in Europe; and while America was still regarded as a land of promise, it was to the Napoleonic exiles rather a refuge than a social laboratory.[93] The Napoleonic soldiers were handier with the sabre than they were with the pen; they left behind them no such body of memoirs as that written by the Revolutionary officers or the émigrés; and for one reason and another, British travellers were scarcer in the twenty years from 1800 to 1820 than in any subsequent twenty years of the nineteenth century. Travel accounts exist, however, and throw some light on the dearth of enthusiasm for French ways. Thus there appeared in the *American Review of History and Politics* for 1811 a series of "Letters on France and England," the author of which had resided in France, finding that literature there was at a low ebb, that Napoleon was an elaborate fraud and a gigantic genius, that diffuseness, affectation, superficiality were characteristic of the time. The *Analectic Review* for December, 1815, carries a notice of a *Journal of Events in Paris* for 1815 by an American, published in Philadelphia. John Scott's *A Visit to Paris* led the reviewer in 1816 to think that French profligacy had been overdone, it is true, but the *Analectic Magazine* felt in 1817 that the French were "trifling upon serious subjects and serious upon trifling ones." M. M. Noah published his *Travels in England, Spain, France, and the Barbary States* in New York in 1819, but he was too much concerned with his removal from the consulate at Tunis (on the ground that he was not a Christian) to illumine French society. From the South, meanwhile, there appeared *Letters from Geneva and France,* written during a residence of between two or three years in those countries, and "addressed to a lady in Virginia, by her father" (Boston, 1819); and such stray travelers as Mr. Freers of Abingdon, Virginia, visited by Hodgson in 1820, and Francis Gilmer, who went abroad in 1824 to look up professors for the University of Virginia, kept up some intercourse with France.[93a] The lists are not rich. Let us, however, do what we

[93] See the letter from Lakanal to Jefferson, 1816, in Reeves, *The Napoleonic Exiles in America,* pp. 31-32.
[93a] *American Review of History and Politics,* I, 110-165; II, 297-354; III, 161-220; *Analectic Review,* VI, December, 1815, 522; *North American*

can to picture the diffusion of French fashions in the North from 1810 to 1830[94]

Thus Francis Hall in 1816 grumbles that "accident gave French fashions a double advantage in America"; the ladies, he says, "think they import Parisian graces with Parisian bonnets," that they "unite French grace with English modesty," though the splenetic Hall denies that they have any grace at all.[95] American ladies, he observes, "dance cotillions because they fancy they excel in French dances, and despise the country dances for the same reason," and at Albany, in the Museum, they have the bad taste to enjoy French waxworks with a ghastly semblance of life.[96] In the same epoch the *American Monthly Magazine and Critical Review* proves its patriotism by printing an excerpt from the *European Magazine* satirizing the prevalence of "Frenchiness" in British fashionable society, particularly the use of French phrases; may America, the implication is, be saved from such![97] But alas, that same year, Montulé, who was visiting New York, lodged in a French boarding house, and was writing of the "vast influx of strangers" which "gives to New York that lively air which characterizes several cities of Europe." He admired the fashionable elegance of the females, and recorded in his notebook that although the duties on French merchandise were enormous, yet "our merchants have not yet found that there is anything too beautiful or too expensive for the American market."[98] Of M. Hyde de Neuville, the Bourbon representative in the United States, Faux says that he was "full of Bourbon importance and French vivacity,"[99] that he gave "petits soupers every Saturday evening during the winter and extolled Louis *le desiré*"—this is about 1819. Fashionable Washington of course attended.[100]

Review, II, March, 1816, 399-432; *Analectic Magazine*, IX, February, 1817, 131-140; *American Monthly Magazine and Critical Review*, March, 1819, 341-355; April, 1819, 431-438; *North American Review*, XI, July, 1820, 19-31; Hodgson, *Letters from North America*, I, 293; Trent, *English Culture in Virginia*, pp. 44-45.

[94] One minor mode of the diffusion of French culture was by marriage North and South. "Wealthy young men of the East went to the homes of the planters for their wives, and ambitious young slaveholders in the cotton belt married in Philadelphia, New York, and Boston." Dodd gives a list of representative names. Dodd, *The Cotton Kingdom*, p. 41.

[95] Hall, *Travels in Canada and the United States*, p. 180.

[96] *Ibid.*, pp. 26, 12.

[97] December, 1817, pp. 153-4.

[98] *Voyage to North America . . . in 1817*, pp. 1-4.

[99] He utterly lacked a sense of humor. See Reeves, *op. cit.*, chap. iv.

[100] Faux, *Memorable Days in America*, pp. 367-77. De Neuville had long been a resident of the United States. Faux admits that he was "benevolent" but that he "now represents a cypher." It is a Briton who speaks.

In 1820 Hodgson finds that the women of the merchants, the lawyers, the upper farmers, etc., are indebted to "the short passages from Europe" for fashions from London and Paris, and to the accommodating tariff—with the passing of the gentry, it is clear, the middle classes, as we prophesied, are taking on French fashion. The young ladies in New York he found to be "fond of French style."[101] *Blowe's Emigrants' Directory* that same year remarks on the cheapness of French and India silks in Philadelphia; and of Louisiana declares that the people of the state are in "their manners pretty much the same as the French."[102] In 1822 and 1823 Candler visited America; he found that the American women "copy the French fashions rather more than the English, and seem to unite the elegance of each,"[103] which is nice, if true. The next year (1824) was election year: "ready-made vests were imported from France, each wrought up with its picture that the customer might select a Jackson, an Adams, or a Clay one"—it must have been curious.[104] That opinionated person, Mrs. Anne Royall, after describing the articles in the Salem Museum, informs us that the cosmopolitan spirit is there very much alive: "you find few gentlemen in Salem, who have not visited almost every part of the world, and who do not possess more general knowledge than those of any other town in the Union."[105] Perhaps it is infiltration of the Salem spirit that leads young ladies in Litchfield to embroider heraldic designs out of Edmondson's *Complete Body of Heraldry* in 1815.[106] Of Boston, however, we have no doubts. "Many of the ladies," remarks the superb Mrs. Royall, "have visited France and Italy, from which they haved culled the choicest specimens of the fine arts, particularly the latter. Garlands, flowers, fruit in the finest alabaster, embodying every grace of form and ingenuity, to a degree beyond the power of the most luxuriant fancy to conceive."[107] Somehow, the total effect does seem a little overpowering.

In New York in 1824, Levasseur, Lafayette's secretary during the memorable visit of the aged warrior to America, observed that "the women here adopt the French fashion in

---

[101] Hodgson, *Letters from North America,* II, 29, 109.
[102] Pp. 413, 645.
[103] Candler, *Summary View of America,* p. 69.
[104] Schouler, *History,* III, 312.
[105] Mrs. Anne Royall, *Sketches,* p. 363.
[106] See Wade, *Augustus Baldwin Longstreet,* p. 41.
[107] Mrs. Anne Royall, *Sketches,* p. 339.

their dress," but, he adds, amusingly enough, they "are entirely American in their manners; that is to say, they devote almost their whole life to the management of their household and the education of their children."[108] When one considers the implications of this statement, it is no wonder that our conception of French domestic life has always been a little mixed. At any rate, that Levasseur was right about the fashions is shown by the testimony of Frances Wright. Of New York, in 1819, she says: "The fashions here are copied from the French; but I am told by those that are knowing in such matters, that they are not very changeable . . . the dances are also French, chiefly quadrilles."[109]

The twenties in America were observed by one particularly cosmopolitan and keen-eyed traveller, Bernhard, Duke of Saxe-Weimar, who had an eye for foreign ways in the midst of our democracy. Society he found "uncommonly fine and lively, especially when ladies are not present"—*O mores Teutonices!* "So much care is bestowed upon the education of the female sex that would in other countries be considered superfluous,"[110] he says, that young ladies learn Latin and Greek, speak of other things besides fashions and tea-table subjects; and he describes a gathering without dancing, music or cards, which was "quite in the European style" and "lively and agreeable." "M. Artiguenave, formerly of the Théâtre Française," was present, a professor now, at Cambridge University, if you please. "Many of these people," he laboriously records, "have travelled in Europe, sometimes accompanied by their ladies," and the "generality of houses offer something attractive in the fine arts." In Montreal, of all places, he was entertained by the Binghams, of whom we have read; at Albany he was the guest of the Livingstons, and there he was invited to a ball "which was animated," "the ladies elegantly attired," and dancing "nothing but French contra dances, for the American ladies have so much modesty they object to waltzing."[111] In the New England Museum he found wax works, stuffed animals, portraits, French caricatures, and a good model of the Bastille. In Washington

---

[108] Levasseur, *Lafayette in America*, I, 120. Lafayette's reception in New York is described in Phillips, *James Fenimore Cooper*, pp. 114-5.

[109] Darusmont, *Views of Society and Manners in America*, p. 37. In 1812 in New York "old-school fashions had by no means become obsolete," however. Mrs. Lamb, *op. cit.*, II, 550.

[110] See Timothy Dwight's protest against the fashionable education of young ladies in the North, *Travels*, I, letter XLVIII.

[111] The point of this observation is that the waltz is of German origin.

the Baron Marueil gave a dinner in honor of the French king's
name-day at which the numerous French legation, Consul-
General Durand de St. André, vice-consul Thierry, de Brasson,
and others were present, including the Duke, and at the ball
given by the Baron, the "ladies were very elegantly dressed
and danced very well. They danced mostly French quadrilles,
but always with the same figure."[112] We shall come in a moment
to what he says about the South.

Philadelphia was of course the center of contact between
French and American ways in the North. Walking on Chestnut Street in 1819, Frances Wright met a knot of young men.
"No lounger there, no gay Parisian beau, fresh from the fencing master, could have worn waists more slender, or looked
more like fashion's nondescripts," she observes of these young
Americans.[113] A decade later Basil Hall tells us that "the ladies
in America obtain their fashions direct from Paris. I speak now
of the great cities on the sea-coast, where the communication
with Europe is easy and frequent,"[114] and Philadelphia was not
only a great sea-coast city, but a focal point for the French
émigrés, Revolutionary, Napoleonic, and, by and by, Bourbon.
There it was that Mrs. Royall met Mrs. Lallemand, widow
of General Lallemand, and brother to Lallemand of New York,
both devoted followers of Napoleon;[115] as Mrs. Lallemand's
uncle was Stephen Girard, she was in an excellent social standing.[116] Nearby, at Bordentown, was the palace-like home of
Joseph Bonaparte, full of art treasures, a true cosmopolitan
center, where he entertained Lafayette, Clauzel, Lallemand,
Desnouettes, Henry Clay, Daniel Webster, J. Q. Adams, Win-
field Scott, Commodore R. F. Stockton, and their ladies.[117] All
the travellers gaze curiously at the home of ex-royalty, and
some of them get inside. "The rooms," writes Howitt, "are
literally crowded with the best specimens of the fine arts," and
the same traveller speaks of Joseph's "ready adaptation of the
customs of the Americans."[118] The Comte de Survilliers "by

[112] Bernhard, *Travels,* I, 50, 97, 134, 38, 171, 180.
[113] Darusmont, *Views of Society and Manners in America,* p. 128.
[114] Hall, *Travels in North America,* I, 156.
[115] See Reeves, *The Napoleonic Exiles in America, passim.*
[116] Mrs. Anne Royall, *The Black Book,* I, 318.
[117] For a full description of the Bordentown mansion see F. B. Lee,
"Residence of Joseph Bonaparte in New Jersey," in *American Historical
Magazine,* I, 178 ff. Joseph Bonaparte was known as the Comte de Survilliers. He came to America in 1817, and died in Italy in 1844.
[118] E. Howitt, *Letters from the United States,* p. 99. For other notices
of Joseph Bonaparte see Gall, *Meine Auswanderungen,* II, 86-89 (long

his simplicity and benevolence of character, has succeeded in winning golden opinions from all classes of Americans," writes Hamilton, who tells us how he mingles a good deal with Philadelphia society.[119] When Cooper, the novelist, dined with him in 1839, he had a capital dinner off the Imperial plates, which were of gold with the eagle embossed on them, and it was curious to hear him say "when I was King of Naples," or "that happened when I was King of Spain."[120] Naturally, Philadelphia society was flattered to entertain royalty, even though royalty had "a hand like a spit," and in fairness it should be said that Joseph's services to American art and science were great.

While society was thus becoming more democratic in the North, it appears that the aristocratic caste in the South was retaining and solidifying its position. Educated in the University of Virginia, or in Europe, the plantation owners took up their winter residence in the nearest cities, in order to see the elder Booth, who made his American debut in Petersburg in 1821, or to hear *The Barber of Seville* in New Orleans, or to sit to De Veaux and Fraser for their portraits in Charleston.[121] "Like wealthy men of all ages, they cultivated the arts in an amateurish fashion; they loved to sit for artists for their portraits, and they liked to read good books, or at any rate put them on the shelves of their libraries."[122] They even form clubs to encourage literature, but alas, they do "not read enough contemporary books to recognize the merit of one of their own writers when he appeared,"[123] and though New Orleans was the first city in America seriously to support opera, the love of the Old South for music, sculpture, and painting was that of the dilettante.[124] But manners became a fine art in themselves; manners inherited from the court of Charles II and Louis XIV,

description of the estate in 1819) ; Faux, *Memorable Days in America*, p. 155 (brief notices, 1819) ; Boardman, *America and the Americans* (1833), pp. 268-9; Wied-Neuwied, *Voyages*, I, 37-39 (1832) ; Stuart, *Three Years in North America*, I, 386 (1828) ; Combe, *Notes on America*, I, 291-2 (1838), besides other references cited in this paragraph.

[119] Hamilton, *Men and Manners in America*, I, 390-2. The apartment wherein Hamilton saw him being warm, "the ex-king took out his pocket handkerchief and deliberately mopped his bald discrowned head with a hand that belonged rather to a spit than to a sceptre."

[120] Cooper to his son Paul, March 30, 1839. *Correspondence*, I, 388.

[121] Dodd, *The Cotton Kingdom*, p. 96.

[122] *Ibid.*

[123] *Ibid.*, p. 85.

[124] *Ibid.*, p. 82.

and kept alive and important in such centers of French influence as Charleston, Mobile, and New Orleans. Charleston is an old story; in Mobile Hodgson found "an old Spanish town, with mingled traces of the manners and language of the French and Spaniards."[125] but the new element in the situation is New Orleans.

Before 1803 New Orleans exerted little influence upon American manners, but with the purchase of Louisiana, the Americans commenced to flock in, engendering a feeling of resentment among the creole population when they were "too Yankee" in their ways.[126] Jackson's unfortunate treatment of the creoles after the Battle of New Orleans did little to allay this sense of resentment.[127] But if the creoles resented the pushing Yankees, they exerted themselves to be hospitable until hospitality ceased to be a virtue;[128] and the gap between the creole aristocrat and the Southern planter was less great. Plantation life, in point of fact, was worked out in the essential details which characterize the Old South, by creole planters even before it had been worked out in the upper South.[129] At any rate, the Crescent City became one of the centers of social culture of the Old South during the first quarter of the nineteenth century.[130] There it was that the duelling oaks implied the

[125] Hodgson, *Letters from North America*, I, 152. This is in 1820. In Pensacola in 1826 Bernhard reports that he was present at a party where there were several creole ladies who spoke what seemed to him bad French, but who looked well and dressed with taste. Conversation was the only amusement, but it was "animated and well supported." *Travels*, II, 49.

[126] "The population of New-Orleans is rapidly increasing by emigrations from all the other States in the Union, and from almost every country in Europe." Bristed, *Resources of the United States* (1818), p. 19.

[127] Fortier, *History of Louisiana*, III, 150 ff, gives a brief account.

[128] Kentuckians, calling at creole plantations in Mississippi and Louisiana, according to one observer, got drunk, called the creoles dogs, and knocked them down in their own houses. "These people are the horror of all creoles, who, when they wish to describe the highest degree of barbarity, designate it by the name of Kentuckian." The term "Kentuckian" or "Yankee" came to mean any Northerner. See *The Americans as They Are*, pp. 142-3.

[129] Cf. Pontalba's Journal in King, *Creole Families of New Orleans*, pp. 85-112, for glimpses of old Louisiana plantation life ca. 1795.

[130] See Ashe, *Travels*, III, 229-277, for New Orleans life in 1806; *The Journal of Latrobe*, pp. 159-245, for the period, 1818-19; Hodgson, *Letters from North America*, I, Letter IX (1820) ; Power, *Impressions of America*, II, 168-182, 227-277 (1835) ; Nichols, *Forty Years of American Life*, I, chap. xvi, for characteristic accounts. Bernhard, *Travels*, II, 55 ff., describes New Orleans life in 1826-27 in great detail. The most charming account of creole culture is probably Grace King, *Creole Families of New Orleans*, a work written out of an exhaustive knowledge of the subject.

strict observance of the code.[131] There it was that life was lived in the grand manner by French families dating back to the days of Louis XIV, who had houses on St. Charles, Royal, or Toulouse street, owned plantations on the river, or offices on Canal Street, and attended French opera in the evening, and who shared with the Southerner a common detestation of the Yankee.[132] Their wealth, like that of the Southern planter to the north of them, was invested in slaves or sugar or cotton; their quaint old coaches were seen along the Strand or the Esplanade; and their children took dancing lessons with French masters who taught both old and young what was good form in France. There it was that gambling was king,[133] and cooking an art, and that dances retained the flavor of old-world elegance. Let us select as illustrative of this vanished civilization, neither French nor American, neither European nor Spanish-American, and yet dominantly Latin, the description of a single ball— that given by the Marquis de Casa Calvo, who entertained Laussat, the Napoleonic commissioner, at an entertainment costing 15,000 francs. C. C. Robin describes it:

The Louisiana ladies appeared there with a magnificence that was astonishing in such a colony, and that magnificence could be compared with what is most brilliant in our principal towns in France. The stature of the ladies, generally tall, and their fair complexion, which

For the earlier period (i.e., just before the American purchase), see Fortier, *History of Louisiana*, II. Kendall, *History of New Orleans*, is useful. I quote from *L'Ami des Lois et Journal du Soir* some of the French importations advertised for sale in 1817: un nouvel assortiment de Fusils de Chasse, un assortiment de Rubans, Satins à dente de scie, et tissus couleurs de choix; cache peignes et faussesqueues en cheveux à la derniere mode; droguets de soie à petits picos (?) couleur de choix, première qualité; soie à coudre, première qualité de Lyon assortie; plumes d'Autriche en panache de trois; duvets de cigne en panache de cinq; marmites d'un à huit points; crêpe noir, etc., etc. Issues for January, 1817. This list is as illuminating as the travel-books.

[131] See John Augustin, "The Oaks: The Old Duelling Grounds of New Orleans" in the anonymous *Art and Letters*, pp. 123-134, at the Howard Memorial Library, which includes an account of the duelling code and a history of some of the famous duels.

[132] Cf. Dodd, *The Cotton Kingdom*, pp. 17-18. I have employed his language in a good many places in the above paragraph. Consult King as before. On the Pontalba family see in addition, Fortier, II, chap. viii; and on Julien Poydras, see him, II, 66 ff.

[133] For instance, as early as December 15, 1722, a royal decree forbade all persons of whatever condition to play bassette, pharaon, lasquenet, hoca, quinquenove, beriby, dice, and other games of chance, because of the quarrels, odious usury, and debauchery which have arisen, under penalty of five hundred livres fine for the first offense. The decree is summarized in Fortier, I, 86.

was set off to advantage by their light dresses, gave a fairy-like appearance to these festivities. The last one, especially, astonished me by its magnificence. After the tea, the concert, the dances, the guests descended at midnight into a hall where, on a table of sixty to eighty covers, rose from the midst of rocks the temple of Good Faith, surrounded with columns and surmounted by a dove; underneath was the statue of the allegorical goddess. But further, outside of that hall, the brilliance of the lights attracted the guests under an immense gallery closed by awnings. Forty to fifty dishes, served in different styles, were offered to the choice of four or five hundred guests who were assembled in little groups.[134]

At Laussat's dinner, which followed this, the last dancer left the house at eight o'clock in the morning.[135]

By the 1820's the culture of New Orleans seems to have been increasingly influential in the Lower South. The Mardi Gras, begun in 1827,[136] was a colorful part of the city life, the more colorful because it was then unique. Traveller after traveller describes the life of the city: let us, to illustrate it, select some of the descriptions of Bernhard, who was there in 1826. There were, he says, subscription balls twice a week at the French theater, to which none but the best society was admitted. The first of these which he attended was not crowded, the "generality of the ladies present were very pretty and had a very genteel French air." He found their dress "extremely elegant and after the latest Paris fashion." They danced excellently, "did great honor to their French teachers" indeed, as well they might, since their principal education was dancing and music. The gentlemen he found "less elegant." He left early, going to the quadroon balls for greater amusement, leaving he says, a large number of ladies behind, who were forced to form "tapestry."[137] He also attended the masked ball, held every

[134] Quoted in Fortier, II, 240-241.
[135] See the account in Fortier, II, 282-3.
[136] The first Mardi Gras is said to have been organized by Louisianians returned from Paris, and was originally merely a street procession of maskers. It grew in popularity, and began to be closed with a grand concluding ball. Bernard Marigny in 1833 did much for the festival. It is to be noted, however, that the open-air pageant was introduced into New Orleans from Mobile about 1837; it was adopted in Mobile as early as 1831. Cf. Kendall, *History of New Orleans,* II, chapter on the Mardi Gras.
[137] Bernhard, *Travels,* II, 59. The quadroon ball is a feature of New Orleans life often described. Bernhard remarks that many wealthy fathers sent their quadroon daughters to France to escape the prejudice of people in the United States; in France the quadroon ladies have opportunity to form a "legitimate establishment." He says that only quadroon ladies were admitted, and that the quadroon men were shut out by the white men. *Ibid.,* II, 62.

evening during the carnival at the French theater, where the
dances were cotillions and waltzes. The dresses of the ladies
present he found "very elegant," but he understood that most
of those dancing did not belong to the best society.[138] At the
subscription ball on Washington's birthday in 1826 he reports
that the attendance fell off, not for the ostensible reason (lack
of prosperity), but because the creoles did not regard the Americans as their countrymen.[139] That, however, creole ways helped
to influence social conventions in the South, particularly with
reference to the gallant attitude toward women, duelling, gambling, and the like is scarcely to be doubted.

In the same epoch the Americans, pushing westward, came
into contact with French manners in the Middle West. The
towns on the Wabash had long since lost any very definite
French character, but St. Louis, at least, was a minor focus of
French influence. The author of *The Americans as They Are*
reported, it is true, that the creoles were fast losing their national characteristics[140] but of St. Louis he writes that it "is a
sort of New Orleans on a smaller scale; in both places are to be
found a number of coffee-houses and dancing rooms. The
French are seen engaged in the same amusements and passions
that formerly characterized the creoles of Louisiana," except
that their reputation for honesty was not good. From this fault
the creoles are free, "owing to the greater respectability of their
visitors and settlers, from Europe and from the north. . . ."[141]
Atwater, who visited St. Louis in 1829, found the inhabitants
"of as mixed a character, as almost any town in the Union presents," but he admired the Choteau, Menard and Vallis families
as exceptional among the French for industry, and liked their
manners.[142] Certain it is that when Jay Cooke was in St.
Louis in 1836, he learned both French and dancing, and he can
not have been sole and singular in these studies.[143] His description of the town is lively and amusing:

[138] *Ibid.*, II, 55.
[139] See his account, II, 72.
[140] *The Americans as They Are*, p. 84.
[141] *Ibid.*, p. 94. Louisville in this epoch had the only billiard table between
Philadelphia and St. Louis, and there "luxury is carried to a higher pitch"
than in any other town west of the Alleghanies. *The Americans as They
Are*, p. 47 (1827).
[142] *Remarks Made on a Tour to Prairie du Chien*, pp. 48-49, 53.
[143] "While in St. Louis (1836) I attended a writing school . . . also attended on other winter evenings a French dancing school where I learned
to waltz and took lessons in the French language so that I could converse
quite freely with the ladies who came to the store." Oberholtzer, *Jay Cooke,
Financier of the Civil War*, I, 34.

Pitt, I have fine times. I go to the dancing school twice a week. . . .
Picture to yourself your brother Jay in a spacious ball-room with a
beautiful French brunette by his side, skipping along and having fine
times, and dressed in a fine brown coat (four inches shorter than
usual) with white silk vest, black cassimere pants, white silk stockings, fine pumps, white handkerchief and gloves, hair dressed and all
erect, talking Parley Voo with the beautiful creatures.

[The population] consists of part French (almost Savages), Spaniards, Italians, Mexicans, Polish (all noblemen!!!), Indians, a set of
gambling Southerners, and a few skinflint Yankees. There is but few
respectable persons in St. Louis. . . . The old French people and the
Spaniards look more like cut-throats than men.[144]

This is amusing enough, but it does not appear that the French
in St. Louis exerted much influence in forming western
manners.[145]

5. FRENCH FASHIONS AND MANNERS, 1830-1848

The last twenty years of our epoch, that is to say, the years
from 1830 to 1848, are ruled, socially speaking, by that amazing
spirit of artifice and false glamor, the full fine flowers of which
are Mrs. Mowatt and N. P. Willis. It was as though American
society, having been truly cosmopolitan under Washington and
Adams, having, as it were, been swamped by the eruption of the
West under Jackson, was determined to regain its ground, and
set as its goal as close an imitation of the glitter of Paris (the
Paris of Dumas and Balzac, be it remembered) as it could
attain. An imitation: for American social leaders were no longer
men of ideas as they had been in the days of Burr and
Hamilton; and monarchial Europe ignored them.[146] When
Europe had been interested in republican ideas, the Americans
had been solid and real; now that Europe had in the main
turned from republican ideas, at least among the upper classes,
the American, striving to enter the exclusive circle, searched

---

[144] Jay Cooke to Pitt Cooke, in Oberholtzer, *op. cit.*, I, 34-35.

[145] However, the influence is not to be ignored. Frederika Bremer, for
example, who visited St. Louis in 1850, writes that "all the hotels" are
run "in French style, with French names for dishes and wines." In St.
Louis she met a remarkable bridal party; the bride's mother was "a
young-elderly beauty, polite but artificial; somewhat above fifty, with
bare neck, bare arms, rouged cheeks, perfumed, and with a fan in her
hand; a lady of fashion and French politeness." *Homes in the New World*,
II, 91, 81.

[146] "An American leaves his country with a heart swollen with pride; on
arriving in Europe he at once finds that we are not so engrossed by the
United States and the great people which inhabits them as he had supposed and this begins to annoy him." De Tocqueville, *Democracy in
America*, II, 660.

with pathetic eagerness for aristocratic connections, denied his very inheritance. Franklin had been accepted for what he was; but not very many years are to go by before the expatriated Americans are to form so distinct a class as to invite the pens of Howells and Henry James.[146a] The bourgeoisie aping the aristocracy are not a pleasing spectacle at any time, and they did not impress Murat who describes them with a trenchant pen (1830):

> . . . the first society of New York . . . is composed of tradesmen. They take advantage of their fleeting days of prosperity to show off as much luxury and folly as their situation will permit them. All who have made a voyage to Europe, try to ape the exclusive manners of which they have been the victims on the other side of the Atlantic; affect to value everything foreign, and consider America as a barbarous country, where nothing elegant has ever been invented—not even the galopade and *gigot* sleeves. The first European swindler[147] who takes the trouble to pass himself off for a duke or a marquis is sure to carry away their suffrages, until it pleases him to join thereto their purses. Men of this stamp will pretend not to trouble themselves about politics, or at least not to talk about them; for it is a subject so vulgar and so unfashionable . . . in London. . . . But apart from this society is that formed by the merchants, shipowners, lawyers, physicians, and magistrates of the city. This is truly American: they do not amuse themselves by apeing European manners; among them, conversation is solid and instructive, and turns upon business and the politics of the day. Society in New York is perhaps more tinged with European manners than in any other of the great towns in the United States.[148]

[146a] The changed character of the few French observers of the United States is interesting. The outstanding figure is, of course, de Tocqueville, who was here ostensibly to study prisons, from May 9, 1831, to February, 1832. He interviewed Albert Gallatin, Governor Throop of New York, John C. Spencer, afterwards Tyler's Secretary of State, Jared Sparks, William E. Channing, John Quincy Adams (then in Congress), Brown and Mazarean, famous Louisiana lawyers, Latrobe and Charles Carroll of Baltimore, Nicholas Biddle in Pennsylvania, Joel R. Poinsett, Justice McLean of the Supreme Court, and the President. These are, however, rather intellectual than social contacts; and the difference results in a profound book. (*Democracy in America,* I, VII.) Travelers like Théodore Pavie (*Souvenirs Atlantiques,* Paris, 1833), who continues the romantico-melancholy tradition of Chateaubriand, and who describes the Quakers (I, chap. ix), the mound-builders (II, chap. vii), and the "wilderness" of Texas and Louisiana (II) seem oddly postdated. Pavie is a thorough romanticist, quoting Hugo and Schlegel, with a melancholy preface to his work, and very little acuity.

[147] Cf. the bogus French count in Mrs. Mowatt's *Fashion.*

[148] Murat, *A Moral and Political Sketch of the United States of America,* pp. 349-350.

Against this spirit of servile imitation there were protests which show how wide-spread was the craze for false cosmopolitanism. Thus in the *Christian Examiner* for September 1831 one reads:

A servile imitation of the faded decorations and unseasonable fabrics of European invention, exhibits a national poverty of design, which is not a credit to our genius. To import from the shops of London and Paris the pictures of a French opera dancer or an English jockey, as models for our own ladies' and gentlemens' personal decorations, to exhibit here in August what was there *en règle* in March; to display cast-off finery as novelty, by which the charms of our beautiful countrywomen can be improved, is a folly so supremely ridiculous, that no quantity of impudence would have the audacity to propose it, if already it had not become familiar to us by inveterate usage.[149]

The change is marked in the character of Americans travelling abroad. There are, it is true, the usual number of official representatives who maintained a kind of intellectual contact between French and American civilization.[150] There is a group of cultured literary men, artists, educators, and cosmopolitan minds in the thirties and forties (and earlier) as always.[151]

[149] *Christian Examiner*, XI (new series VI), September, 1831, p. 78.

[150] Thus, to choose at random, James Fenimore Cooper went abroad in 1826 as Consul at Lyons, staying to 1833, and returning so imbued with French standards that he quarreled with American manners. Lounsbury, *James Fenimore Cooper*, chaps. v, vi, vii. James Buchanan, Minister to Russia in 1832-1833, visited Paris in 1833, staying with the American chargé d'affaires, Harris, saw the sights, called on the Duke of Treviso and General Lafayette, and talked with the Duc de Broglie about the refusal of the Chambers to ratify the American treaty, and with Talleyrand. Ticknor, *Life of James Buchanan*, I, 219-225. Lewis Cass, appointed minister to France, 1836, at the time of the uproar over the spoliations treaty, became "the personal friend of the king," wrote a pamphlet against the British right of search, which was attacked by Brougham and John Adams, and was highly popular both in Paris and at home. Indeed, his reputation as ambassador brought him the presidential nomination. He wrote a very solid book called *France, Its King, Court and Government. By an American* (1840). See McLaughlin, *Life of Lewis Cass*, pp. 165-181, 191 ff. Edward Coles, the second governor of Illinois, was sent on a special mission to Russia in 1816, and toured Europe, being presented by Gallatin to Louis XVIII and to Lafayette. Alvord, *Governor Edward Coles*, p. 38.

[151] Cooper has been noted. Joseph C. Cabell, Jefferson's right hand man in founding the University of Virginia, kept in touch with European educational interests after his trip abroad in 1802. See Patton, *Jefferson, Cabell and the University of Virginia*, pp. 24-25. Washington Irving made his first journey to Europe in 1804, visiting Bordeaux, Paris, Marseilles, Genoa, etc.; went again in 1814 to England; and again in 1826, after a year spent in France, Germany, and Italy, he visited Spain, returning only in 1832. John Sanderson, a teacher in the Clermont Seminary (Philadelphia), visited Paris in 1835, and wrote *Sketches of Paris in Familiar Letters to His Friends by an American Gentleman* (2 vols.), 1838; and *The American in Paris*, 1838. Scharf and Westcott, *History of Philadelphia*, II, 1139-40.

But a new type of American travel book appeared to satisfy the taste of the middle class[152]—books by ministers, school teachers, pillars of society, who write good solid accounts with no nonsense in them, books which, like the *Memoranda of Foreign Travel* of Robert J. Breckenridge, D. D. (he was a Presbyterian clergyman), picture France as a country full of open and general contempt for religion; or like *The Old World and the New* by the Rev. Orville Dewey, like Breckenridge's, in two volumes, which cry aloud the superiority of democracy to the effete aristocracy of Europe. Page through Isaac Appleton Jewett's *Passages in Foreign Travel,* 2 vols, Boston, 1838, and you get the run of these tedious works—"a Parisian Sabbath" (so different from our good American Sunday—"Shakspeare in Paris"— "Taglioni" (he shudders, but he attends)—"Italian Opera"— "Cafés"—"Children's Theaters"—"Markets"—"St. Denis"— "Restaurants, Opera" — "Theater" — "Politics" — "Museums"— how odd and un-American these Frenchmen are![153]

Elliott, in charge of the patent office in Washington in the 1830's, had a nephew, Jonathan Elliott, who travelled in Great Britain and France. Stuart, *Three Years in North America,* II, 90. Emerson visited France in 1832, though he said himself that in Paris he lived alone and seldom spoke; and returned to England in 1847, where he spent three weeks with A. H. Clough; the Revolution Year proved to be the richest social experience he ever had. He returned in July, 1848. Woodberry, *Ralph Waldo Emerson,* pp. 39, 102-4. Longfellow visited Europe in 1826-29; again in 1835-36, and on his first visit "Latin colour and picturesqueness meant more to the young traveller" than German romanticism. France, Spain, where he met Irving, and Italy . . . were in turn visited, their manners noted, their literatures studied, their languages in more than polite measure mastered." *Cambridge History of American Literature,* book II, chap. xii, vol. II, p. 33; and Higginson, *Henry Wadsworth Longfellow,* chaps. v and vii, Bryant went abroad in 1834, and was in Paris in July, returning in March, 1836; and went again to Europe in 1845. Godwin, *Biography of William Cullen Bryant,* I, chap. xvi; II, chap. xxiii. John Watts de Peyster went abroad at thirteen in 1834, and again in 1838. Allaben, *John Watts de Peyster,* I, 144-152, 184-201. I have purposely picked these instances at random; a hundred more could be gathered together with some research.

[152] On love of middle-class for travel books see Nichols, *Forty Years of American Life,* I, 343.

[153] Zachariah Allen, *The Practical Tourist, or Sketches of the State of the Useful Arts . . . in Great Britain, France and Holland,* Providence, 1832. Breckenridge, Robert J., D.D., *Memoranda of Foreign Travel,* 2 vols. (1845) (he was in Europe in 1834-35); Rev. Orville Dewey, *The Old World and the New,* 2 vols. (1836); Isaac Appleton Jewett, *Passages in Foreign Travel,* 2 vols. (1838) (parts of this appeared serially), etc. Medical gentlemen reported heavily on their travels: for instance, John Griscom, who was professor of chemistry and natural philosophy in the New York Institution (*sic*), and a member of the Literary and Philosophical Society of New York, wrote *A Year in Europe . . . in 1818 and 1819,* also 2 volumes, but not published until 1823; William Gibson, M.D., is responsible for *Rambles in Europe in 1839* (1841)—he was professor of surgery

Clearly this is a different world from that of Lady Kitty Duer. "Fifty, or even forty years ago, the conceit of this people was a byword," wrote James Bryce in the eighties, adding shrewdly that the Americans "are too proud for a province, too large for a colony."[154] One begins to understand why this is so when one finds Mrs. Fenimore Cooper writing home such patronage of the French ladies as this, in describing a soiré at the Princess Galitzin's in Paris:

> . . . the manners of the French women in high life are highly polished —they are perfectly lady like and well bred—but you would be surprised to hear how trifling is their conversation; their dress, their Mantuamaker, their Marchande de Mode, form the great subject with them.

She speaks of their jewelry and the oddest mixture of colors in their clothes, and concludes:

> I must say that so far as I have been, and all, and whatever I have seen would only serve to endear the manners, and customs, and above all the simplicity of our Country.[155]

in the University of Pennsylvania, and his book is heavily surgical; L. J. Frazee reported on *The Medical Student in Europe* in 1849; he was in Europe in 1844, and the book is published at Maysville, Kentucky. The most characteristic travel-books are perhaps those by "females"; for example, Emma Willard, *Journal and Letters from France and Great Britain,* Troy, 1833; Mrs. Kirkland's *Holidays Abroad* (she was the author of "A New Home," "Forest Life," etc.), published in the inevitable two volumes in 1849; *Over the Ocean; or, Glimpses of Travel,* by a "Lady of New York," 1846; and Miss C. M. Sedgwick, not unknown to fame as "Hope Leslie," whose *Letters from Abroad to Kindred at Home,* likewise in 2 volumes, appeared in 1841. N. H. Carter's *Letters from Europe,* 2 vols., which reached a second edition in 1825, represents an interest in Napoleon. Henry Colman's *European Life and Manners,* 2 vols., 1849, is the work of an agricultural enthusiast. Ik Marvel's *Fresh Gleanings; or, A New Sheaf from Old Fields of Continental Europe* (1847) is full of pleasant chit-chat about cooking and restaurants and French society. Cooper's travel books (*Sketches from Switzerland,* 1836, 4 volumes; *Gleanings in Europe,* 6 vols., 1837-1838) are curiosities, as is *Homeward Bound,* 1837, and *Home as Found,* 1837, with the amazing Effingham family. *Sketches of Paris; in Familiar Letters to His Friends* were prepared by "an American gentleman" and published by Carey and Hart at Philadelphia in 1838. Herman Humphrey, D.D., President of Amherst College, wrote *Great Britain, France, and Belgium,* "a short tour in 1835," which Harpers brought out; and Wilbur Fiske described his *Travels in Europe: viz., in England, Ireland, Scotland, France, Italy, &c.,* which, with the two preceding books, were reviewed in the *North American* in July, 1838 (XLVII, 272). The *North American,* by the by, did not believe that Cooper displayed enough tolerance in dealing with French customs (XLVI, 1-20, review of *Gleanings in Europe,* January, 1838). But the mind staggers at the amount of this dull stuff.

[154] *American Commonwealth,* II, 650, 653.

[155] *Correspondence of James Fenimore-Cooper,* I, 111, Mrs. Cooper to her sister, from Paris, November 28, 1826. "What did I ever get from

Compare with this a passage from *The Daguerreotype* in 1847:

A Frenchman, more than other men, is dependent upon things without himself. . . . For his best enjoyment he must have a succession of factitious excitements. Out of this want Paris has grown to be the capital of the world for superficial amusements. Here are the appliances—multiplied and diversified with the keenest refinement of sensual ingenuity—for keeping the mind busy without labor, and fascinated without sensibility. The senses are beset with piquant baits. . . . Here the sensual can pass years without society and the slothful without ennui. Paris is the Elysium of the idler, and for barren minds a Paradise."[155a]

Americanismus triumphans!

But of course there was more genuine cosmopolitanism than this. Wharton selects as typical of the thirties Mrs. James Rush of Philadelphia, the rival of Mrs. Bingham. Born Phoebe Ann Ridgway in London, in 1799, Mrs. Rush received a continental education, married the son of Dr. Benjamin Rush, and continued her European experiences among art, music, and books. In the opinion of Judge Carleton she was the most intellectual woman he had met in America. When she returned to Philadelphia she established the custom of an "at home"— a European innovation which was at first decried—but being a vigorous individual—she could be seen wrapped in a green velvet mantilla eating raw oysters at an outdoor booth of a fine day—she won out. All her visitors' cards are preserved. Some are in French, some in Italian, some in Spanish. To her house came Joseph Bonaparte, Murat, Louis Maillard, the Generals Henry and Charles Lallemand, Dr. Monges, and Charlotte Bonaparte, who sketched, painted, and drew, whose lithographs were published in a volume[156] and exhibited at the Philadelphia Academy of Fine Arts. Thither flocked opera singers like Madame Caradoni, conversationalists like Moncure Robinson, William D. Lewis, who translated Russian poems,

France or Continental Europe? neither personal favors or money. But this they cannot understand, for so conceited is a Frenchman that many of them think I came to Paris to be paid." Cooper to S. F. B. Morse, August 19, 1832, *ibid.,* I, 283. It is only fair to add that in Lounsbury's judgment, "the polish, the grace, the elegance, and the wit of French social life made upon him an impression which he not only never forgot, but which he was afterwards in the habit of contrasting with the social life of England and America, to the manifest disadvantage of both, and with the certain result of provoking the hostility of each." *James Fenimore Cooper,* p. 69.

[155a] "Scenes and Thoughts in Europe. By an American." *The Daguerreotype,* I:7:319 (October 30, 1847).

[156] *Vues Pittoresques de l'Amérique,* 1834.

Peter du Ponceau, a variously gifted man,[157] Mr. and Mrs. William Jackson, Mr. and Mrs. James Dunas, and other social lights, no less than literary men and foreigners of distinction—Bancroft, Channing, Van Buren, Cooper, Dickens, Harriet Martineau, Longfellow. By and by she established her "Saturday mornings" at eleven, when her house was crowded with men and women of distinction like Clay, Thomas Wharton, and others.[158] The "Wistar parties" of an earlier epoch were, meanwhile, degenerating into "fashionable and sumptuous eating and drinking parties,"[159] according to one not very trustworthy observer. At any rate social life is becoming more mixed: there is the genuine salon spirit, there is the sham cosmopolitanism of the bourgeoisie, there are the solid circles which Murat describes.[160] Meanwhile, the old centers of cosmopolitan culture—New York,[161] Charleston,[162] and New Orleans con-

---

[157] For brief accounts of du Ponceau, cf. Scharf and Westcott, *History of Philadelphia*, II, 1122-23; and *Cambridge History of American Literature*, IV, 448.

[158] Wharton, *op. cit.*, pp. 235-271.

[159] *Autobiography of Charles Caldwell, M.D.*, p. 135.

[160] No account of "cosmopolitanism" in these years would be complete without some account of Anna Cora Mowatt. She was brought up as a child in "a beautiful old country seat, called La Castagne, and situated two miles from Bourdeaux, in France" (p. 14). Her memoirs give an account of life there; among other things the children used to act plays in French (pp. 14-23). Soon after her arrival in New York, "we were placed at Mrs. Okill's boarding school—and there I appeared for the second time on a mimic stage" in a little French play for the amusement of the parents and guardians. She was later placed with two sisters "at boarding school in New Rochelle" where, at the mature age of 14, she acted Voltaire's *Alzire* in English (pp. 30-37). After an amazing courtship, she was married at 15 to "Mr. Mowatt", who continued to instruct her in French (p. 61), She devotes chap. vi to describing a trip to Paris. Mr. Mowatt's bankruptcy threw her genteelly on the stage. She wrote *Fashion* in 1845. See Anna Cora Mowatt, *Autobiography of an Actress; or, Eight Years on the Stage*.

[161] Pavie speaks of the society " moitié européenes, moitié yankees" of New York in 1832. "Les habitans de même que ceux des (*sic*) Charlestown, se distinguent de ceux des autres villes des États-unis, par leur politesse, leur gaieté et leur hospitalité." He left New York with reluctance. "Les réunions, ornées de tout ce qui peut embellir nos salons d'Europe, transplantés sur le sol de l'Amérique, sont de précieux trésors pour un Français." *Souvenirs Atlantiques*, I, 260, 358, 235.

[162] "The society of Charleston is the best I have met with in my travels, whether on this or on your side of the Atlantic. In respect to finish, and elegance of manners, it leaves nothing to be desired, and what is of more value with people who, like you and me, attach little importance to mere politeness, it swarms with real talent, and that without the alloy of pedantry." (This in 1833 or earlier.) Murat, *A Moral and Political Sketch of the United States of America*, p. 14.

tinued to flourish, and Mrs. Trollope reported an "abundance of French dancing masters" in the land.[163]

"The customs and fashions which we imitate as *Parisian*," wrote Mrs. Mowatt, "are not unfrequently mere caricatures of those that exist in Paris. . . . We only *follow* the fashions; we do not conceive the spirit which dictated them. So in our modes of dressing. Expensive materials, worn here (Paris) only at balls, are imported by American merchants and pronounced to be 'very fashionable in Paris.' They are universally bought by our belles, who, instead of wearing them at proper seasons, parade the streets in what is meant exclusively for evening costume."[164] But though the fashions may be awkwardly copied in this, the flourishing period of the bourgeoisie, they are nevertheless copied. "If it were not for the peculiar manner of walking, which distinguishes all American women, Broadway might be taken for a French street," observes the acid Mrs. Trollope in 1832, "where it was the fashion for very smart ladies to promenade. The dress is entirely French (except perhaps the cotton stockings must be English) on pain of being stigmatized as out of fashion. Everything English is decidedly *manvais ton.*"[165] Of conservative Boston in 1832 Wied-Neu-wied writes: "La plupart (des femmes) étaient coiffées de chapeaux de paille avec des rubans verts ou noirs. On portait beaucoup de drap, et les modes étaient absolument semblables à celles d'Angleterre et de France."[166] The historian Schouler rightly observes that when women were copying the latest fashion of London or Paris in the thirties, the cobbler's wife was copying the copiers[167]—it is thus that Paris came to dominate American fashions. Let us glance more closely at this domination.

It struck Pavie with astonishment to find in Baltimore in

---

[163] *Domestic Manners of the Americans,* p. 27.
[164] *Autobiography of an Actress,* p. 125.
[165] *Domestic Manners of the Americans,* p. 317.
[166] *Voyage,* I, 8.
[167] *History,* IV, 21. Schouler finds little "culture" in the West. "The Philadelphia 'Wistar parties' brought local celebrities together; New York literati met at 'the lunch'; Boston had good repute in the art of high converse and hot suppers; there were choice libraries here and there, mostly of the subscription sort, besides those attached to the chief seminaries of advanced learning. We had some general societies for music, art, and sciences; but of club-life on the whole one found very little in the larger centres. Society had a prejudice against clubs of the English pattern. Americans lived at home for the most part, and the source of their sterling qualities was the domestic virtues." *Ibid.,* IV, 12.

1832 "un goût parfait" presiding over the "plus petits détails" among men whom he had imagined to be "presques barbares." Boardman, viewing New York "females" in 1833 (how the word expresses the epoch!) found them "ultra Parisian in their dress. The attire of the gentleman, also, savoured rather more of Paris than London; but no male of any class had whiskers," which peculiarity was striking,[169] especially, one imagines, to a Briton. Hamilton confirms his opinion about New York fashions.[170] Indeed, more than fashions are diffused: Boardman was struck by the presence of French time-pieces in the hotel drawing-rooms,[171] and Abdy, in the same year, found a "French clock in a glass case with several neat ornaments" in the home of a Boston negro.[172]

Somehow the reputability of Louis Philippe lent solid respectability to French fashionableness. Hamilton describes a "splendid ball" given by the newly arrived French minister in 1833, which all Washington attended;[173] Abdy assures us of New York in 1833-34 that "in many respects the manners and customs of New York are rather French than English; and one is reminded by the dress and furniture more of Paris than of London."[174] Of the trans-Mississippi country in the same epoch Chevalier tells us that in a Missouri village you might see "Yankee" girls "dressed in almost the last Paris fashion."[175] Does the recital grow tedious? I trust not. There is something very curious about this conquest of a blatantly self-conscious nation by imported fashions. For instance, in Mobile in 1835 Power saw a merchant's lady, whose French ball-

---

[168] *Souvenirs Atlantiques*, I, 313.
[169] *America and the Americans*; pp. 13-14, 62.
[170] "The fashions of Paris reach even to New York (in 1833), and the fame of Madame Maradan Carson has already transcended the limits of the Old World, and is diffused over the New." Hamilton, *Men and Manners in America*, I, 33.
[171] *Op. cit.*, p. 62.
[172] Abdy, *Journal*, I, 180.
[173] Hamilton, *Men and Manners in America*, II, 37-38.
[174] Abdy, *Journal*, I, 69.
[175] Chevalier's *United States*, p 119. Perhaps Chevalier should have been noted in the discussion of cosmopolitanism in the thirties and forties. Ramon de la Sagra found him useful in securing introductions to good society. "Michel Chevalier, que viaja para cuenta del gobierno frances, y cuyo conocimiento deseaba yo hacer, ha publicado algunas cartes sobre este pais en el Diario de los Debates de Paris, y parece dedicarse mucho á la politica." He gave the Spaniard letters to many scientists and politicians after their meeting in Washington. Ramon de la Sagra, *Cinco meses en los Estados-unidos*, p. 136 (1835).

dress cost one hundred and fifty dollars, dancing in the same set with the modiste who made it up.[176] In the same year Lieber visited Philadelphia. "Go out on a fine afternoon," he writes, "and you will be astonished at the numbers of women neatly and tastefully dressed, even in streets which the fashionable world never enters. American women have, I think, generally, considerable tact in dressing. There are few even third or fourth rate mantua-makers, in any of the larger places, who have not their Petit Courier des Dames of Paris, in order to let their customers choose the newest fashions. This little code of fashions is also found in most millinery shops in Cincinnati as well as in New York. I saw it in the window of two shops in Buffalo."[177] Or if we visit Saratoga with Caroline Gilman, in 1836, where the life of the party at the United States Hotel was "a lovely demi-French family of celebrity, with five attendants and their foreign friends," we shall find that at "the hop" the demi-French and the foreigners enjoy themselves, and are envied because they can dance a cotillion or waltz on occasion, and because they produce Italian or French music—all very fashionable, indeed.[178] Perhaps the feminine eye is better at this sort thing, anyway: "almost the first small sleeves that have been seen in America for seven years" appeared at Carusi's in Washington in 1836 "on the person of a Virginia lady, who had been to France. What a sensation! There was half a shudder among the company as they felt the immense sacks on their arms, contrasted with those new sleeves without one relieving plait, tight—tight as a suit of armor, from the shoulder to the elbow. A pair of black mits were on the arm, which rendered the novelty more striking."[179] This is refreshingly concrete.

The clerk or shopman in Philadelphia wore "as fine English or French broadcloth as his employer" in 1838.[180] The younger men among the fashionables at Saratoga in 1838 and 1839 were almost all copyists of the dress, style, and manners of European young men about town; chiefly, to the unsympathetic eye, they were remarkable for foppery of dress, for the assumption of beards, mustachios, and other exotic fashions, as if they were

[176] Power, *Impressions of America*, II, 225.
[177] Lieber, *The Stranger in America*, pp. 102-3.
[178] *The Poetry of Travelling in the United States*, pp. 84-85.
[179] *Ibid.*, p. 13.
[180] Buckingham, *America: Eastern and Western States*, II, 5.

either foreigners themselves, or had travelled so long on the continent of Europe as to bear about them the marks of their sojourn at Rome, Naples, and Paris.[181] Male fashionables were encouraged by the visit of the Prince de Joinville to Boston in 1841; of course there was a ball, and all the young ladies went, looking their best.[182] Meanwhile increasing ease of communication brought New Orleans into more intimate contact with the union—New Orleans, where the shops were full of French goods, where there were restaurants, cafés, cigar shops, billiard rooms, where, along the narrow streets, the houses were "built chiefly in the French fashion (which is questionable), and the whole appearance was quite French, or, as the people thought, Parisian"[183]—a most satisfactory place for planter and traveller to revel in. "I do not think I ever saw so large a proportion of highly dressed men and women" as in America, said Godley of the forties. "The Parisian fashions of the day are carried out to their extreme, detestably ugly as they are"; the women, he complains, look like "something between a trussed fowl and an hour-glass."[184] Are not the plates from *Godey's Lady's Book* treasured among the knowing? Plates which prove that "Paris is the school of manners as well as of dress for the travelling Americans of both sexes; its sentiments . . . imported with its fashions by the young *elegans* of New York and New Orleans?"[185] In little New Lebanon (New York), there is a most brilliant gathering of Americans which Ramon de la Sagra attends, all very fashionable;[186] in Macon, Georgia, at the end of the forties, Lyell's attention is called to "two of our fashionists"—two gaily dressed ladies wearing the latest Parisian costume.[187] By the end of the epoch the *Journal des Modes*

[181] Buckingham, *op. cit.*, II, 439.
[182] "During our stay at Boston, the citizens gave a splendid ball to the Prince de Joinville, and the Mayor politely sent us tickets of invitation." Lyell, *Travels in North America*, I, 122. He went, and admired "the beauty of the young American ladies."
[183] Cf. McMaster, VII, 229-231.
[184] Godley, *Letters from America*, p. 44.
[185] *Ibid.*, p. 65.
[186] "Hallamos en esta posada (Columbia-House) un concurso brillantisimo de mas de quinientas personas distinguidas de las principales ciudades de los Estados-Unidos. Hallabanse tambien varios españoles, familias de la Habana, y mis amigos los hermanos Santos-Suarez, el consul español Staughton u muchos conocidos." It is needless to remark that Havana followed Paris styles. Ramon de la Sagra, *Cinco meses*, p. 306.
[187] Lyell, *Travels in the United States, Second Visit,* II, 23. An Alabama girl, the daughter of a candidate for the legislature, visited Mobile, and returned home with a dress made with flounces in the latest Parisian mode, wherefore her father lost the election. The dress cost $20, four times its cost in London or Paris, II, 62.

reached New York every fortnight, so that the ladies might conform strictly to Parisian costume; except at balls and large
parties, they wear high dresses; and they spare no expense.
They prefer embroidered muslin of the finest and costliest
kind, they sometimes spend sixteen guineas on a pocket handkerchief; they buy extravagantly expensive fans, and ruby
and emerald pins. Lyell learned when he was in France that
no orders sent to Lyons for furnishing private mansions were
on so grand a scale as some received from New York where
houses are fitted with satin and velvet draperies, rich Axminster
carpets, marble and inlaid tables, and large Parisian looking
glasses.[188]

And in 1843 "C. A." in *The Ladies' Repository* was complaining that "the young female"

left to her own devices (in fashion) and her own imprudence [neglects
her health]; and amidst the frosts of winter, and the damps of spring,
the devotee of fashion may be seen walking the streets with no more
substantial covering for her feet than the silken hose and the Parisian
sole—affording scarce greater protection than the stocking itself; and
this notwithstanding the many instances in which such exposure annually results in early death, or what is more lamentable, in a broken
constitution. [For the fashionable opinion is that it is] "a mark of the
greatest vulgarity for a *lady* to wear anything but a Parisian slipper.[188a]

And so our period ends in that blaze of glory, the record of
which is so amusing to read in Minnegerode's *The Fabulous
Forties*. It is the period of "elegance," that fashionable and
melancholy elegance which one associates with the portraits of
Lamartine and young Hugo (which the pictures of N. P.
Willis so startlingly resemble), that sickly elegance which resented the brutalities of Balzac and preferred the dying fall
of Willis's fashionable cadences—*Hurry-graphs,* for instance,
and *The Rag-bag,* which are to be written within the next decade. But let the fashionable Willis speak for himself: he is on
a Hudson river boat (no longer, alas! fashionable), he has
just described Chabert the fire-king, and he continues:

[188] *Ibid.,* II, 248. When Cooper returned to America, his home in Bleecker
Street, New York, was filled with French furniture and administered by
French servants. Phillips, *James Fenimore Cooper,* p. 260. Cf. with this
catalogue the description of the hotel St. Louis, New Orleans, given by
Lyell in his *Second Visit,* II, 90-91, the rooms being fitted in French style
with muslin curtains and scarlet draperies, a drawing-room being à la Louis
Quatorze, etc.
[188a] The writer concludes with a moving tale of a society belle who died
of French fashions. *The Ladies' Repository and Gatherings of the West,*
III, (August, 1843), 225-7.

For the mass of women, as far as satin slippers, hats, dresses, and gloves could go, a Frenchman might have fancied himself in the midst of a transplantation from the Boulevards. In London, French fashions are in a manner Anglified; but an American woman looks on the productions of Herbault, Boivin, and Maneuri, as a translator of the Talmud on the inspired text. The slight figure and small feet of the race rather favor the resemblance; and a French milliner, who would probably come to America expecting to see bears and buffaloes prowling about the landing-place, would rub her eyes in New York, and imagine she was still in France, and had crossed, perhaps, only the broad part of the Seine.[189]

The fabulous forties! Ladies (should one rather say females?) employed nothing but French toilette articles—Guerlain's lustral water, esprit de cedrat, eau de Botot, sirop de Boubie, blanc de neige, citromane, Micheaux's freckle wash; Pelletier's odontine cleaned the teeth; and French perfumes spilled their fragance over the elegant toilets—caprice de la mode, bouquet de Victoria, and what not.[190] Forgotten epoch! When there was a beau monde and Paris was its capital; when all Frenchmen were wicked, frivolous, and delightful; when good Americans died and went to Paris. It was then, as perhaps never before or since, that these serious republicans imported from France that most important counter-charm to their own seriousness—frivolity. Perhaps it is not the least important of the contributions of French culture to the United States!

6. SUMMARY AND SIGNIFICANCE OF THE LAST TWO CHAPTERS.

A code of manners reaching back to the court of Louis XIV and its imitation, the court of the Stuarts, involving gallantry, duelling, gambling, perhaps even a little wit—these were the first contributions of French culture to the manners of the colonial aristocracy. Dress and deportment are stressed in the colonial capitals for the sufficient reason that they are stressed in Paris, and occasional great ladies play their part in the intellectual life of early America because great ladies were playing a similar role in France. At the end of the eighteenth century, at the beginning of the nineteenth, the salon spirit is abroad in the United States; and we can scarcely question the indebtedness of the American salon to that of France. Dancing

---

[189] Willis, *Here and There*, p. 120. See his article on "French Society, Apropos of the Society of New York," in *The Rag-bag*, pp. 178-183.
[190] See the amazing descriptions which Minnegerode has put together from the magazines, in *The Fabulous Forties*, pp. 92-99.

and dances are French, and all the little accompaniments of frivolity like fans and mirrors and laces are most esteemed when they come from the capital of all the pleasures. Follows then, from about 1810 through the 1820's a confused epoch of social change; the empire of French ways continues but it changes its dominion as in the 1830's the bourgeoisie solidify their positions, and if the salon spirit wanes, the empire of fashion increases. Dresses, hats, bonnets, vests, perfumes, soaps—these articles are in or out of fashion as Paris dictates. The imitation of manners has changed to the imitation of fashions in the main, though on the dance floor and at the formal dinner society is following, often at second and third hand, the modes of a Gallic aristocracy. Is it not remarkable that the greatest political experiment of the nineteenth century should have yielded so abjectly to the universal dominion of the French milliner and the French dress-maker? At any rate, one thing is certain: all this frivolity, these laces and mantuas, these light pleasures and social forms have helped to fix in the American consciousness the conception that a Frenchman is a frivolous creature, vain, fickle, changeable, full of politeness and empty of meaning, of exquisite courtesy and irritating insincerity—a conception as potent in the 1820's as it is in the 1890's, and one that has played its share in shaping the American conception of Paris and its inhabitants.

IX

The Influence of French Art in America

ARTISTIC DÉPENDENCY OF THE UNITED STATES

THE ARTS in the United States are necessarily importations. If in the art history of the republic we note here and there an interest in such indigenous cultures as that of the Amerindian, the Pueblo, the Aztec or the Toltec, we must yet observe that this interest represents a sophisticated return upon primitivism in the hope of recapturing a lost innocence of the eye.[1] It is probable that in any event no satisfactory basis for American art could have been found in Indian culture; however, the historical fact is that, barring the negro, primitive arts in America have on the whole been ruthlessly crushed by the invading settlers; and that the negro has been tolerated rather than developed. In turn the culture of the white invaders, largely because of the vast extent of free land, failed to develop a peasant class which might nourish or develop an indigenous culture like that of European peasants.

As the feeling of nationalities grew and there came a desire to produce artistic work which would be "American," one means of approach which had proved possible in similar movements elsewhere was therefore closed, or rather, had never existed. When, for example, in nineteenth century Russia it was felt that the artist and the literary man should concern themselves with a culture essentially Slavic which would replace the artificial cosmopolitan court culture of the eighteenth century, it was possible to "go among the people," it was possible in Turgeniev's phrase to "become simplified," that is to say, to return to the peasant as the custodian of the essential Russian spirit. So, too, in Norway, it was possible on the one hand to return to a long forgotten tradition, that of the sagas, and on the other, to evolve from peasant dialects a new language

[1] An interest of this kind in the Amerindians is of course no late development. Indeed, a curiosity fed by religious, anthropological, and social inquiry was manifested in the culture of indigenous Americans by white settlers from early times. Not to speak of partisan works like that of Las Casas or romantic evocations like those of Chateaubriand or Longfellow, our earlier national history has to present the solid achievements of Schoolcraft and Catlin. But this interest differs *toto caelo* from an esthetic interest in the primitive or from an interest in a cultural movement like that represented by the contemporary Mexican renaissance.

felt to be characteristically national. In some sense European art, Antaeus-like, is thus perpetually renewing itself from the soil. But no such possibility presents itself in the United States. Here, on the contrary, the whole movement has been towards "Americanization"—i.e, toward the destruction of those values which in his native land the peasant, now an emigrant, had preserved. To return to the people in America is impossible—there is no people.[2]

The present study has of necessity been a two-fold one. Lacking any very clear statement of the cultural forces in American life, we had to discover them; and at the same time we have had to study the impact upon varying levels of American life of French culture. In the present chapter this necessary dichotomy is peculiarly embarrassing: one is tempted to write *in extenso* of the whole problem of American art. But for such a discussion there is not space. We may simply note one or two general considerations regarding the arts in America, and then proceed to a more detailed study of certain aspects of French art with respect to American life. And first, the general considerations.

1. THE COSMOPOLITAN SPIRIT, THE MIDDLE CLASS SPIRIT, AND THE FRONTIER SPIRIT IN RELATION TO AMERICAN ART.

Since the arts were importations, and since the United States began as a British colonial possession, it is a commonplace that we were for a long period an artistic dependency of England. Our literature, it is said, is a branch of British literature; our painters for a long time received their training from English painters; our early music was British; our architecture is—or was—overwhelmingly British; our attitude toward the theater and the opera, the dance and the concert, has its parallel in England. But the implications of this fact are not always well understood. Roughly speaking, it is the eighteenth century which saw the transplantation of the arts to America, and therefore the transplantation of the British attitude toward art existent at that time. Now in eighteenth century England artistic culture was still dominated by the aristocratic ideal; that is to say, the support of the arts was the business of the great man, the patron, the dilettante; and only gradually was

---

[2] One is cognizant of Uncle Remus and Paul Bunyan and Jesse James, and of sporadic interest in folk-lore and ballad, but the most partial advocate cannot hold that these movements bulk large in American cultural history.

there developed that secondary attitude which by and by was to dominate Victorian England; namely, the notion that art is a means of instruction. The first of these attitudes is clearly the cosmopolitan attitude; the second grows with the development of the middle class.[3] The American colonial leisure class accordingly took over the attitude of the British upper classes; the development of the second notion of the function of art grows in the United States *pari passu* with its development in England. In either case there was no possibility for the development of an indigenous art life in America, since the aristocratic attitude looks abroad, and the bourgeois attitude looks away from art to the practice of ethical virtue.

This is not to deny the feeling which is manifest from the earliest times that there should be an American art life. Symbolical, however, is the title of Anne Bradstreet's book, *The Tenth Muse Lately Sprung Up in America,* for the phrase exactly sets forth the attitude: Europe, under the leadership of the nine muses, was to be joined without sense of difference by a tenth. The American scene was accordingly beheld through European eyes; the subject is new, the form, the manner, the accent, are old. The *Sketch Book* takes its place with Addison, the Hudson River school range themselves alongside of Poussin and Claude Lorraine, Benjamin West shakes hands with Sir Joshua Reynolds, colonial "Georgian" architecture proves upon examination to be modified Palladian, and "American" music as written by Foster and others is blood brother to Michael Balfe and Mendelssohn. It is useless to complain that such products are not American; on the one hand the measure in which the *Legend of Sleepy Hollow,* the landscapes of Cole and Doughty, colonial houses, and *Way Down upon the Swanee River* differ, however slightly, from their European prototypes, is the measure of their "Americanism"; on the other hand, this traditionalism is what the dominant intellectual class in the New World wanted, and unless we are prepared to read all American history in terms of modern industrialism and the jazz age, we must agree that the American arts reflect pretty faithfully the art consciousness of the American people as far as they had any. Beginning under the patronage of the eighteenth century colonial leisure class and as long as that class controlled expression (even longer), the arts necessarily retained the spirit of the European tradition, a spirit which, working

[3] Contrast Congreve and Richardson!

upon new raw material, would engender, it was hoped, an "American" genius.[4]

That the dominance of the cosmopolitan attitude in America lasted longer than the social dominance of the class which produced the formula, is due to the peculiar nature of the next classes to rise into social control, namely, the middle class and the frontier. Of course, for the purposes of this chapter, the middle class is more important, although the frontier can not be ignored. The middle class, which stood next to the cosmopolitan group in line of succession was not, as a class, art-minded; bourgeois art, it is notorious, runs to the didactic, the sentimental, the merely pretty, the otiose, and all these qualities have their expression at that lower level of artistic history which seldom or never gets its place in the cultural chronicles of a nation. The Sunday School story, the gift book, the middle-class magazine, the moral novel, the mezzotints and the engravings which "embellished" these publications, the Scriptural oil painting, the false Gothic style, the false Italian style—these are elements in the vast morass of bourgeois culture which was to drive true artists like Poe and Hawthorne underground. Mr. Mumford puts the case in a striking sentence or two: "Two generations before, Thomas Jefferson could lay out and develop the estate of Monticello; now with many of Jefferson's capacities, Poe could only dream about the fantastic domain of Arnheim. The society around Poe had no more use for an architectural imagination than the Puritans had for decorative images; the smoke of the factory chimney was incense, the scars on the landscape were as the lacerations of a saint, and the mere multiplication of gaunt sheds and barracks was a sign of progress, and therefore an earnest of perfection."[4a] And yet the middle class, too, wrought its image of America: Benjamin Franklin and the solid qualities of the New England school are the reflection of its better parts in literature—in literature because here alone could moral idealism reach articulate expression at white heat, and so be satisfactory, not alone to the artist, but also to the audience which supported him.

---

[4] See Eberlein, *The Architecture of Colonial America;* Kimball, *Domestic Architecture of the American Colonies and of the Early Republic;* Mumford, *Sticks and Stones;* Myers, *The History of American Idealism;* Elson, *The History of American Music;* Lahee, *Annals of Music in America;* Caffin, *The Story of American Painting;* and the histories of literature cited in chap. i.

[4a] *Sticks and Stones,* pp. 82-3.

It is essential to note that in literature only does the middle class spirit come to anything like expression. In painting, in music, in dancing, in architecture, in sculpture, they merely imitate at third and fourth hand, or fail altogether. Indeed, they scarcely even produce. And the middle class attitude toward these arts is important. They either fought shy of them or grovelled before them. They fought shy[5] for obvious reasons: that clarity of ethical import which they could find in literature, they could not find in landscape, in portrait painting, in symphony, in opera, in ballet. On the contrary these arts were involved to their thinking in a whole complex of immorality; and all that could be said of the best of them was that it was not ethically bad. But again (and this fact is of supreme importance for the history of American art in the nineteenth century), the instinctive desire of the middle class to get on in the world, led them to adopt as many of the attributes of the cosmopolitan spirit as possible; and since the leisure class traditionally patronized art, the middle class as it became prosperous (the *nouveau riche*) adopted the same attitude.[6] Thus the opera, originally imported as the amusement of the leisure class, became an object of attention from the middle class as they acquired money and leisure. The movement toward art museums, a marked feature of nineteenth century cultural life, is due in part to the theory that museums are improving; it is also an obvious European importation; it, too, represents the colonization of European works of art in the United States. For these reasons it had the support of the middle class. Other instances will readily occur, but the imitative spirit of the middle class is best seen in literature.

As late as the eighties James Bryce wrote that "so far . . . as regards American literature generally, I do not believe that there is in it anything specifically democratic."[7] This is an amazing statement but it is true.[8] Why should American literature be "democratic"? The cosmopolitan class in the first instance, and the middle class in the second instance, looked to the

---

[5] But see below, pp. 317-18.

[6] See chapters xi and xii of Myers, *History of American Idealism*. Mr. Myers does not take into account the different social levels of American life, and he is misled by phrases like "the arts must be freed from the shame of patronage," which is good propaganda but bad social history; nevertheless a careful reading will show the essential rightness of my contention with reference to the art academies of the United States.

[7] *American Commonwealth*, II, 635.

[8] Some will wish to except Whitman.

European tradition for its literary norm. Writing of Philadelphia in 1797 McMaster assures that "with a couple of exceptions the whole trade in books was in the hands of foreigners,"[9] and there is food for reflection in the fact. In 1820 only 30 per cent of American publications were by native authors; in 1840, 50 per cent, though school books, extensively produced in the thirties, account in part for the increase.[10] A noted bookseller in Philadelphia told Mrs. Anne Royall in 1824 that "American works do not pay the expense of publishing, owing to the rage of the American people for foreign productions."[11] Defining the literary interests of the lower South, Professor Dodd says shrewdly of their reading: "The planters were consciously returning to a former allegiance. It was the English, not the budding New England literature, which won them, though Dickens is not to be included in the one group, and Longfellow must be mentioned in the other"[12]—Longfellow, the most cosmopolitan of the poets. English works, wrote Godley in 1844, are read largely, American authorship is not encouraged by the publishers—why should it be in the lack of an international copyright law?[13] When Lyell was here on his second visit, he asked why there were so few theaters in America; he was answered that if he "went into the houses of persons of the middle and even humblest classes," he would "find the father of a family, instead of seeking excitement in a shilling gallery, reading to his wife and four or five children one of the best modern novels, purchased for 25 cents," and that one could often buy in two or three successive numbers of a penny newspaper entire reprints of Dickens, Bulwer, or other popular writers.[14] The same writer informs us that the Harpers in 1845 sold two million volumes of uncopyright English fiction, that 40,000 copies of ordinary English novels were printed that same year, and that 60,000 copies of Macaulay's *History* were sold in the United States in 1849.[15] The fall in the purchase price to 25 cents for "one of the best modern novels" represents the triumph of the middle class: in 1800, for example, when the

---

[9] *History*, II, 333.

[10] *Cambridge History of American Literature*, IV, 542.

[11] *Sketches*, p. 200. Mrs. Royall is not always trustworthy, but there seems no reason to doubt the statement.

[12] *The Cotton Kingdom*, p. 81.

[13] *Letters from America*, II, 66.

[14] *Travels in the United States, Second Visit*, I, 152-3.

[15] II, 252.

cosmopolitan spirit is still regnant, standard works that cost more than five dollars, works in two, three, or four volumes, or works likely to have a large sale, were printed at only a slightly lower cost than the English price; books of this sort went to press only when 300 or 400 subscribers had been secured.[16] But it is useless to multiply proof, for the facts are open and notorious; the triumph of democracy strengthened, rather than diminished, the American taste for European books, and the reason is to be sought, I think, in the desire of the middle class to be as cosmopolitan as they could, and in the fact that British literature in these years was on the whole solid, moral, and respectable. Desirous of manifesting an imitative interest, the middle class found a European literature in their own language which presented exactly the qualities they admired.

The effect of this situation upon the native American writer was impressive. It made him less "American" in theme and treatment, but essentially more American in attitude—if we assume, as we must, that a literature which faithfully meets the need of national life is by so much nationalistic. Pattee puts the situation from 1820 to 1860 in a paragraph:

But even as it (the age) sighed over its *Charlotte Temple* and its *Rosebud* and its *Lamplighter,* it longed for better things. It had caught a glimpse, through Irving and Willis and Longfellow and others, of the culture of older lands. America had entered its first reading age. In 1844 Emerson spoke of "our immense reading and that reading chiefly confined to the productions of the English press." In its eagerness for culture it enlarged its area of books and absorbed edition after edition of translations from the German and Spanish and French. It established everywhere the lyceum, and for a generation America sat like an eager school-girl at the feet of masters—Emerson and Beecher and Taylor and Curtis and Phillips and Gough.[17]

Writing of Bryant, William Ellery Leonard says significantly:

All his translations, many of them made before Longfellow's now widely recognized activities as spokesman in America for European letters, are a witness to Bryant's knowledge of foreign tongues and

---

[16] McMaster, V, 280-1.

[17] Pattee, *American Literature Since 1870,* p. 8. It is not without meaning that there were few lyceums in the south. "Europe colors the whole epoch. Following Irving's *Sketch Book,* a small library was written by eager souls to whom Europe was a wonderland and a dream." P. 12. Pattee lists eighteen leading travel books by leading American authors, and says quite truly that there were scores of others. Pp. 12-13.

literatures, to his part in the culturization of America, to the breadth of his taste and a certain dramatic adaptability . . . and to his all but impeccable artistry.[18]

And by reference to the work of such persons as Percival one can see the minor poets following in the footsteps of their betters. Perhaps, however, no figure is more significant of the peculiar predicament of the American literary man, desirous of being "American" and compelled to be European, than Cooper. He began by writing an imitation of an English society novel. This he followed with a novel on an American theme in the traditional British form, and the influence of British technique upon his fiction is easy to see. In 1826 he went to France where he finished *The Prairie;* a residence of seven years there had a large effect upon his life and works—in Paris he was something of a lion, in Paris he was "charmed with a gayer and more brilliant society than he could have known before." And so Cooper was caught between two forces; the only difference between him and the middle class generally being that in his case the predicament is painfully clear. Unabashedly American, he felt called upon to resent foreign ignorance of the United States; in 1828 he wrote *Notions of the Americans,* a book full of information about American opinion, but too partisan to convince a European reader. In three novels (*The Bravo,* 1831; *The Heidenmauer,* 1832; *The Headsman,* 1833) he showed the superiority of democracy to aristocracy. But alas! when he returned to the United States in November, 1833, he had become "fatally cosmopolitan." Accordingly he lectured and wrote and scolded and sued his countrymen, not that they should become less American, but that their Americanism should conform to the European tradition.[19] No writer more clearly exemplifies the effect upon American culture of the I-would-and-I-would-not cosmopolitanism of the middle class.[20]

[18] *Cambridge History of American Literature,* book II, p. 273.
[19] *Letter to His Countrymen,* 1834; *The Monikins,* 1835; *Homeward Bound,* 1838; *Home as Found,* 1838; *The American Democrat,* 1838, are characteristic documents. Lounsbury, *James Fenimore Cooper; Cambridge History of American Literature,* I, book II, chap. vi.
[20] De Tocqueville, observing that "America has hitherto produced very few writers of distinction; it possesses no great historians, and not a single eminent poet," finds the cause in the fact that "the inhabitants of that country look upon what are properly styled literary pursuits with a kind of disapprobation," but for once the astute Frenchman failed to look beneath the surface. He was keen enough to see the roots of the situation in other fields. "The Americans have lawyers and commentators, but no jurists; and they furnish examples rather than lessons to the world. The

Mingling with the bourgeois spirit is the spirit of the frontier. "Equality," wrote de Tocqueville, "begets in man the desire of judging of everything for himself: it gives him, in all things, a taste for the tangible and the real, a contempt for tradition and for forms,"[21] and nowhere is equality more powerful than on the frontier, which, hostile to all forms of life but its own, peculiarly despises the useless arts and graces of sophisticated society.[22] The one book which illumines as with a lightning flash the attitude of the frontier toward cosmopolitan culture is *Innocents Abroad* (1869). The naive honesty, the contempt for the traditional because it is traditional, the suspicion of anything that looks like cant, especially in relation to art, the sterling good sense and the wild humor of Twain on his pilgrimage show why it is that, impatient of all traditions, the frontier spirit came to expression only late in American history—only, indeed, as the frontier was passing away.[23] Eventually the frontier spirit was to produce an authentic literature; but in the period of our study the frontier, naively ignorant, is on the whole of negative importance. And yet the frontier is not so much distrustful of art as distrustful of what is foreign to its spirit. The untutored poet, the crude painter, the humble musician receive on the frontier the awed tribute due to overwhelming genius. Consider *Roughing It* or Hamlin Garland's *A Son of the Middle Border,* and learn from these books how thoroughly appreciative is the frontier of native talent. Or consider the innumerable literary histories of particu-

same observation applies to the mechanical arts. In America, the inventions of Europe are adopted with sagacity; they are perfected, and adapted with admirable skill to the wants of the country. Manufacturers exist, but the science of manufacture is not cultivated; and they have good workmen, but very few inventors." *Democracy in America,* I, 339. (De Tocqueville is using "inventors" rather in the sense of researchers than in the usual sense of the term.)

[21] II, 523. "In aristocratic society," on the other hand, "the class which gives the tone to opinion, and has the supreme guidance of affairs, being permanently and hereditarily placed above the multitude, naturally conceives a lofty idea of itself and of man." *Ibid.,* p. 527.

[22] In 1835 Power ran into an exhibition of pictures in Natchez, very bad, purporting to be from England. One, "Bacchus and Ariadne," was finely painted. "The proprietor informed me that they were to be brought to the hammer and sold without reserve in a few days, when he anticipated a lively sale for the large pictures, the quantity of raw material used up in the work being a great consideration with the lovers of art here." *Impressions of America,* II, 204.

[23] See the illuminating chapter on "The Laughter of the West" in Pattee.

lar regions;[24] genius struggles everywhere, and the frontier, quietly proud of Milton's more or less ingloriously mute, cherishes the records of their pathetic failures. And finally, as *Innocents Abroad* and *Roughing It* also show, the frontier kindles to the genuine in the cosmopolitan tradition; it is only the sham, or that which, not being understood (alas! this is a great deal), seems to conceal sham, that the frontier spirit receives with Homeric scorn.[25]

Such, over the period of our study, is the composite picture of the artistic life of America. Let us briefly resume what is said. In the eighteenth century the artistic life of the colonies is almost wholly dominated by the cosmopolitan class who take over the artistic traditions of the British leisure class. At the turn of the century, and until 1848, with the triumph of the middle class the situation becomes more complex: the cosmopolitan tradition lingers because the cosmopolitan spirit does not disappear, and because the bourgeoisie, avid of social advancement, acquire by imitation the attitude of the leisure class. But the middle class also moves away from the cosmopolitan tradition because of its instinctive fear of what is not didactic; and the frontier spirit will, on the whole, have nothing to do with the arts until a date beyond the period of our survey. Let us now turn from these general considerations to a particular study of the French elements in the various arts as they are absorbed by America.

2. AMERICANS AND THE FRENCH ARTS OF THE TABLE

It will not do to neglect the minor arts in the composite picture. We have seen in previous chapters how American manners and fashions began by imitating British manners at a period when British manners themselves were influenced by the French; and how, for a variety of reasons, American manners, particularly among the upper classes, came to have a close and intimate relation with Parisian modes. We may note in passing that this general type of situation is true for most of the arts, but let us stress here the fact that the hold of French

---

[24] Venable's *Literary Culture of the Ohio Valley* is a good example of the type. And on the whole subject see Rusk, *Literature of the Middle Western Frontier*.

[25] It is useful in this connection to remember the social history of the California nabobs as recorded by Mark Twain and Bret Harte. The Indian millionaire who, in the recent Oklahoma oil boom, ordered seven expensive automobiles, one for each day of the week, was paying genuine, if mistaken tribute, to the arts and graces of the cosmopolitan tradition.

manners upon the American imagination was strengthened by the presence in this country of numbers of French *petits maîtres*. They represent the most immediate impact upon America of French arts. For manners are a kind of art, and in that art the French were particularly skilled. The American attitude varied. John Adams in Paris in 1778 was delighted with French conduct:

The delights of France are innumerable. The politeness, the elegance, the softness, the delicacy, are extreme. In short, stern and haughty republican as I am, I cannot help loving these people for their earnest desire and assiduity to please.

The cookery and manners of living here, which you know Americans were taught by their former absurd masters to dislike, is (*sic*) more agreeable to me than you can imagine. The manners of the people have an affection in them that is very amiable.[26]

Watson in 1780 was of much the same opinion.

I trust that our alliance and intercourse with France may enable us, as a nation, to shake off the leading-strings of Britain—the English sternness and formality of manner; retaining, however, sufficient of their gravity, to produce, with French ease and elegance, a happy compound of national character and manners, yet to be modelled. The influence of this alliance will tend to remove the deep prejudice against France.

In 1781 he prepared and sent to America an article suggesting that his countrymen adopt certain French customs. Taught by the British that the French eat frogs, that they make soup from old bones, that they are half-starved, let them learn from him and France that in no other country is there such genuine politeness. And, returning to America in 1784, he "was gratified to observe an infusion of French manners and habits, in the social amusements of the people, and in the aspect of their refined circles."[27] In so far as American manners differ from the manners of Great Britain, it is evident that the French have had an important part in the change.[28]

Let us not even despise cooking—did not Brillat-Savarin, a visitor to America, write of American dishes in his *Physiologie du Goût?*[29] There is an art of the table, and French cooking

[26] *Letters*, II, 20-21, 51. See also 24, 43, 45, 66-70.
[27] *Men and Times of the Revolution*, pp. 104, 159-60, 276.
[28] See chaps. vii and viii for a discussion of this topic in greater detail.
[29] See pp. 71-79 especially, "des dindonphiles." The café Savarin, 120 Broadway, New York, is named for him. There is an excellent special article on him in *The New York Times*, February 14, 1926.

has its place among the French arts. Indeed, the assimilation of a French cuisine began early. Thus at New Rochelle, that most influential of Huguenot settlements in the North, though the inhabitants failed to surpass the English in roasts and pastries, or the Dutch in rich dishes, sweet cakes, and preserves, the Huguenot cooks were particularly noted for the economical preparation of wholesome dishes for daily consumption, preparing even the coarsest food with a skill which puzzled others. Particularly in bread-making they were unsurpassed; they were the first to introduce yeast instead of the leaven universally employed by their neighbors. Eventually the delicately flavored French soups, the light omelettes, the delicious entrées, were adopted by non-French colonists, though the change came slowly; some special forms of buns and rolls were first adopted. However, the praise of French cooking began early and stands at the head of a tradition which has colored our whole picture of French ways.[30] Nor did the French bring only yeast to the national cuisine. The seed of the tomato was brought over by emigrants from France, and it is to French immigrants that we owe the artichoke and the okra plant.[31] Despite British prejudices against French wine,[32] it was early introduced into America.[33] French settlements again and again attempted to cultivate the vine.[34] Imlay, describing the flora of the Ohio coun-

[30] Smith, *Colonial Days and Ways*, pp. 149-50; Fosdick, *French Blood in America*, pp. 411-412.

[31] McMaster, I, 97, note. The tomato was long used for ornamental purposes only; the fruit, called the love-apple, was thought to be poisonous. Mitchell argues that Crèvecoeur introduced "the sainfoin, the luzerne, the vêches, the vignon, and the racine de disette" into this country. *St. Jean de Crèvecoeur*, p. 162.

[32] "Our native gentry, when they took wine, preferred Madeira, Oporto or Malaga, to French wines, true to English prejudices." Schouler, *Americans of 1776*, p. 99.

[33] On wine in New England see Weeden, *Economic and Social History*, I, 144, 148; Stauffer, *New England and the Bavarian Illuminati*, p. 20. John Boydell advertises in *The Boston News-Letter* for November 6-13, 1721: "These are to Notify all Persons Interested or Concerned in Ten Hogsheads of Claret, 1 Cask of White Wine, 2 Butts and 3 Anchors of Brandy supposed to be the growth of France (seized in the Town of Lynn on the 7th and 9th Instant) to Appear at a Court of Admiralty, to be Holden at Boston," etc. Similar advertisements point to a considerable smuggling trade. The Virginians in 1720 drank Madeira or Fayal and "besides this, are plentifully drunk with the better sort, of late years, all kinds of French and other European wine, especially claret and port." Hugh Jones, *The Present State of Virginia*, 1724, in Stedman and Hutchinson, II, 285.

[34] See chaps. iv and v. M. Chaptal's *A Treatise Upon Wines* was translated by John H. Sargent and published in Charleston in 1811. But even earlier there was published a treatise *On the Art of Planting and Culti-*

try, speaks of the melons of France, Spain and England, and indicates that these were importations.[35] And as late as 1832 Pavie remarks with interest that he ate French melons in Philadelphia.[36]

Particularly in the epoch of the French Revolution was the effect of French food upon the American appetite an important one—for as one ate, so were his politics. Thus when Jefferson brought back from Paris a fastidious taste for French wines and cookery, Patrick Henry denounced him on the stump as a recreant to roast beef—one who "abjured his native victuals."[37] One frequented pro-French or pro-British taverns according to his politics; and in the pro-French inns, at any rate (such, for instance, as the "Sign of the Alliance" in Boston, kept by Tahon), the cuisine was of a conscientiously French order[38]—one proved his republicanism by eating omelettes. But before the French Revolution aroused gustatory acrimonies, there were eating-places kept by Frenchmen—such, for example, as that described by Schouler: "In the suburbs of Philadelphia, a Frenchman opened a place called 'Lebanon,' and offered to his patrons of both sexes choice tea, coffee, bottled mead, cakes, fruits, and comfits. He praised his place as well adapted to those who came to visit the bettering-place or hos-

---

vating the Vine; also, of Making, Fining, and Preserving Wines &c. according to the most approved methods in the most celebrated wine counties in France, etc., for the benefit of the French colony at New Bordeaux. The book is by "Louis de St. Pierre, Esqu., one of His Majesty's Justices of the Peace for Granville County and Captain of the Company of Militia, consisting of the French Vine-Dressers Established at New Bordeaux in South Carolina. London, J. Wilkie: 1772." My attention was called to this book through the kindness of Professor Yates Snowden of the University of South Carolina. I find in the *State Gazette of North Carolina* for 15 January, 1789, a "description of the Illinois Country" which offers as an inducement to emigrate that in the year 1769 110 hogsheads of strong wine were made by the French settlers from wild grapes. The colonial newspapers often carry advertisements of imported French wines. See, for an instance, the *North-Carolina Gazette* for December 19, 1787. James Carney, at Newbern, is selling the best Bordeaux claret in bottles and by the hogshead. *Blowe's Emigrants' Directory* says in 1820 (p. 576) that in Illinois "the French have made excellent wine from a wild grape, which grows here luxuriantly."

[35] *Topographical Description*, p. 241.
[36] *Souvenirs Atlantiques*, I, 291. Kalm in 1748 had "spoken with both *Englishmen* and *Frenchmen*, who assured me that they had eaten of (the skunk), and found it very good meat, and not much unlike the flesh of the pig." Perhaps this is a further mark of French influence! *Travels Into North America*, I, 217-8.
[37] Schouler, *Americans of 1776*, p. 100; *History*, II, 83.
[38] Stevens, *Albert Gallatin*, p. 12.

pital near by; and none, he assured his patrons, would be admitted on his premises but orderly, genteel, and reputable people."[39] The American palate, educated to French food and drink, came to demand more of both.[40]

The influx of émigrés at the close of the eighteenth century seems to have fixed the notion of a relation between fashion and food when both were French. The most important phenomenon of the epoch in gastronomical history is the residence of Brillat-Savarin in the United States from 1794 to 1797. The *Physiologie du goût* contains many references to this sojourn—to chocolate, turkey, hunting adventures in Connecticut[41] and gustatory adventures in New York. Brillat-Savarin and his Swiss friend, J.-A. de Rostaing kept themselves alive in New York as best they could—the gourmet by tutoring; and they frequented Little's Tavern, until the yellow fever drove them to Hartford and Boston in 1795 and 1796. In Boston Brillat-Savarin proudly boasts that he taught Julien, the French restauranteur, to make "des oeufs brouillés au fromage," a dish which "fit fereur." This prince of gourmets visited Providence, New London, Philadelphia, and other places, leaving, as we may guess, a gustatory trail behind him; he was well received and taught Americans much.[42] In 1794 and 1795 Captain Collet made money in New York by preparing ices and sorbets. "The women especially never tired of so novel a delight—nothing could be more amusing than their little grimaces while partaking thereof."[43] In fact, fashionable society went in for French food: Jefferson, for instance, who brought a French cook to the White House, and John Jay, of whom Mrs. William S. Smith wrote to her mother on May 20, 1788, that Mrs. Jay entertained the *corps diplomatique* and "the dinner was *à la*

[39] *Americans of 1776*, p. 119, note.
[40] Schoepf notes the increasing importation of French wines in 1783-4. *Travels in the Confederation*, II, 184. Crèvecoeur gave special attention to the wine trade, and urged Rochefoucauld to establish a national wine cellar in New York. Mitchell, *St. Jean de Crèvecoeur*, pp. 211, 234-5.
[41] Abbé Robin, writing of Connecticut, says that the inhabitants have fine wheat but that they do not know how to use it—they only half-cook it on an iron plate. The French army could not become accustomed to it, and taught the inhabitants to improve their manner of cooking. Cf. Sherrill, *French Memories*, p. 101.
[42] Baldensperger, "Le séjour de Brillat-Savarin aux États-unis," *Revue de la littérature comparée*, 1922, pp. 94-5.
[43] Sherrill, *French Memories*, pp. 101-2. They could not understand how it could be kept so cold when the Réamur thermometer registered 26.

mode Française."   On February 6, 1789, the French chargé
entertained the Vice President, the heads of departments, and
various distinguished guests at dinner on the anniversary of
the French Alliance.[45] In Philadelphia Breck reports that dinners were got up in elegance and good taste. "Besides Bingham
and Morris and the President who had French cooks, as well
as most of the foreign ministers, there was a most admirable
artist by the name of Marinot, who supplied the tables of
private gentlemen, when they entertained, with all that the most
refined gourmands could desire."[46] In 1802 Brillat-Savarin, returned to New York, was having turtle soup in the morning at
Little's Tavern with the Vicomte de la Massue and Jean
Rodolphe Fehr of Marseilles, and treating them to Welch
rarebit in return.[47] In the same city de Singeron opened a pastry
shop. "The gilt gingerbread he sold was made in the figures of
the king and queen, and the marchpane he made was fashioned
to represent the façade of the Tuileries. Wonderful blanc-
mange he made, too, in the form of bewigged gentlemen and
ladies in court costume." "He was the first to decorate New
Year's cakes with Cupids wreathed in rose-garlands,"[48]—a
doubtful boon, perhaps, but one which goes to show the spread
of French pastries![49]

French wines became increasingly popular. The indefatigable
Brissot produced "Thoughts on the cultivation of vines—and on
the wine trade between France and America," printed, among
other places, in the *American Museum* for December, 1788:
French wines, he argued, "must obtain the preference in the
United States."[50] He was encouraged to find them cheaper;[51]
and cheap they remained. In 1808-9 Jefferson was paying less
than a dollar a bottle for the best champagne; for the best

[44] Griswold, *Republican Court,* pp. 91-92.
[45] *Ibid.,* p. 217.
[46] *Recollections of Samuel Breck,* p. 188. In this year the *Columbian
Magazine* (III, 724-5, December), was printing a "method to make pota-
to-bread without the admixture of flour, by M. Parmentier, Member of
the College of Pharmacy," etc.
[47] *Magazine of American History,* III, 262; VI, 61.
[48] Lamprey, "French Exiles in New York," *Americana,* V, 702-3.
[49] This influence takes curious turns. La Rochefoucauld-Liancourt reports
that in Charleston, after the arrival of a great number of families from
the West Indies who took up gardening, vegetables became better and
more common in Charleston menus. *Voyages,* IV, 65.
[50] IV, 568-571.
[51] Cf. *Travels,* I, 206, 212.

Bordeaux he paid a dollar. Incidentally we may note that his French cook and cook's assistant were paid about $400 a year.[52] And in 1818 Cobbett reported that French wine cost a sixth of the English price.[53] Wine, in truth, figured in the tariff—at least in 1826 and 1832.[54] The vogue was such that by 1833 Hamilton was writing, "The gentlemen in America pique themselves on their discrimination in wine, in a degree which is not common in England."[55] And Louis Philippe in 1834 wrote a personal letter to Andrew Jackson representing to him "that a war between the United States and France would be especially disastrous to the wine-growing districts, and that the interests of those provinces could be relied upon to oppose it."[56] But let us return to eating.

The acquisition of Louisiana opened new and delightful pastures to the gourmands. Apparently a good many Louisiana negroes were employed on ships. Montulé found one on his way to the West Indies in 1817,[57] and on the Mississippi River boats their art was famous:

The fare served on these steamboats at a time when so large a part of America was still in the trencher-pawing, hands-were-made-before-forks stage of ref(l)ectorial procedure, was exquisite in its conception and concoction, and elegant in its serving. Old gourmets recall with many sighs the gustatory pleasures of a trip on the Mississippi when river navigation was at its prime. Cookery in some parts of the world is an acquired art; in other parts, a developed science; but the negro and mulatto *chefs* on the floating palaces that plied the western

[52] Madeira was drunk in pipes at the White House at a cost of between 50c and 60c a bottle. Adams, *History,* IV, 370.

[53] *Year's Residence,* part II, 337.

[54] When James Gordon Bennett was correspondent for the *Washington Enquirer,* he wrote: ". . . we that are liberal, and catholic, and tolerant in our potations, and hold all good wines to be good, have the pleasant prospect opened to us of being enabled, as Mr. Rush promises us, to drink 'the superior wines of France, those of the Rhine, Spain, Portugal, and the Italian States, and perhaps of some other countries,' at a reasonable rate. The imagination warms, and the brain absolutely turns round and grows giddy at the thought of it." It certainly does. Pray, *Memoirs of James Gordon Bennett and His Times,* p. 86. By act of July 13, 1832, duties on French wines were reduced according to terms of the treaty with France; so, too, were silks. Curtis, *Life of James Buchanan,* I, 246-7.

[55] *Men and Manners in America,* I, 121. Writing of Charleston in June, 1819, Faux complains "I am here paying 33s. 6d. a bottle for boxed London porter, just 700 l. percent (*sic*) above cost, and 18s. 8d. a gallon; three times dearer than real French brandy, or any other spirits, the best of which is sold at a dollar and a half a gallon." *Memorable Days in America,* p. 88. *Sic transit gloria vini.*

[56] Curtis, *Life of James Buchanan,* I, 235, note.

[57] *A Voyage to North America,* p. 11.

rivers from New Orleans at one end, to Natchez, Vicksburg, Memphis, St. Louis, Louisville, or Cincinnati at the other, had it born in them and exercised their gift as it inspired.[58]

It is a pity to touch this poetic paragraph; but the fact seems to be that the creoles taught the negroes how to cook.[59]

The French cookbook and the French restaurant or tavern were principal sources of diffusion for a liking of French foods. There may have been in 1831, as Schouler reports, "a prejudice against dishes with French names";[60] possibly the proximity of this year to the embroglio over the French claims explains the sentence, but there was no lack of interest in French cooking. Under Monroe "Mons. de Neuville, at his dinners, used to puzzle and astound the plain-living Yankees by serving dishes of 'turkeys without bones, and puddings in the form of fowls, fresh cod disguised like a salad, and celery like oysters,"[61] but though they were puzzled, they continued to attend. In 1817 the *Analectic Review* thought it worth while to reprint from the *London Monthly Magazine* a "letter from Meaux" dilating on the economy of French cookery.[62] The same magazine in the same year carries an article on wine, largely based on Beauvilliers' *Art du cuisinier;* the article is by "A Constant Reader," who notes that "Beauvilliers' eating house at Paris has been considered as the best in Europe."[63] *The American Register or Summary Review* for the same year notices *The Royal Parisian Pastry Cook . . . by* A. Careme (sic), with 70 engravings (Paris, 1815), in two volumes: "the work is proclaimed to be without a rival in the gastronomic department of literature," says the reviewer.[64] Bernhard, while in New York, stayed at a French boarding house at 72 Broad street in 1825,[65] and many other travellers

---

[58] Chambers, "Early Commercial Prestige of New Orleans," *Louisiana Historical Quarterly,* no. 4, p. 459.

[59] Something of the gourmand possibilities in New Orleans can be gleaned from reading the advertisements in *L'Ami des Lois & Journal du Soir* and *L'Abeille.* I refrain, however, from making the imaginative either hungrier or thirstier than they are.

[60] *History,* IV, 11.

[61] Morse, *John Quincy Adams,* pp. 103-4. He also had dancing on Saturday evenings which the New England ladies had been "educated to consider as holy time."

[62] October, X, 348-9.

[63] December, X, 470-483.

[64] I, 358.

[65] *Travels,* I, 119.

comment on the French boarding house as an institution in eastern cities. In the thirties, Lieber, a good cosmopolitan, reports that "in general, it may be said that American cookery has somewhat engrafted the French upon the English."[66] In 1830 Hamilton found "an excellent French café in New York, which afforded all manner of refreshment to an overheated pedestrian."[67] Power in 1833 says that in Boston at the Tremont Hotel the French cooking was the best in the country.[68] Ramon de la Sagra reports on Delmonico's in New York, which he visited in May, 1835, as follows: "fuimos al restaurador Delmonico, único que ecsiste aquí de semejante especie para comer ó almorzar a cualquiera hora, y los platos que se piden por una lista impresa, como es costumbre general en Francia."[69] Grund, surveying the general situation at the close of the thirties, speaks thus of the menus of the hotels: "the table d'hôte contains all the luxuries of the season, in the shape of viands, condiments, and pastries which are to be found in the market, dressed partly in the French, and partly in the English fashion," and complains of the wine list: "the high price of wines in the American hotels is the more surprising as claret and hock pay but a small duty, and may be procured at a wine-merchant's at about one half or one fourth the prices I have named."[70] Every great American hotel had its chief cook, usually a Frenchman, says Nichols. He used to meet Fitz-Greene Halleck "almost every day at a quiet little French café, in Warren-street, opposite the City Hall. He came there to take his demi-tasse and petit verre, and read the evening papers. On the walls hung pictures of the barricades of Paris, surmounted by the tricolour. . . . Frenchmen, Germans, and a few English and Americans who had got into continental habits, played chess and dominoes, and sipped absinthe, or, in the warmer weather, iced claret punch or orgeat. It was the stillest public house, I believe, in New York."[71] In the forties the interest in French cooking increased, as the magazines evi-

---

[66] *The Stranger in America,* I, 226.
[67] *Men and Manners in America,* II, 382-3.
[68] *Impressions of America,* I, 119.
[69] *Cinco Meses en los Estados-Unidos,* pp. 41-42.
[70] *The Americans,* II, 234, 235 (two volume edition). Madeira was 3 to 10 dollars; hock, 2 to 3 dollars; claret, the same; sherry, 1 to 2 1/2 dollars; champagne, 2 or 3 dollars. Port was little drunk. P. 235.
[71] Nichols, *Forty Years of American Life,* II, 12; I, 351.

denced,[72] so that, at the close of our epoch Schouler can observe that Americans "travelled much and came in contact with the Europeans of many countries"; that the American "did not blindly imitate, but adopted the ideas of all lands to suit his liberal taste. No insular prejudices confined him to particular dishes; but whatever was found relishing in English, French, or German cookery he applied to his own palate."[73] In the degree that American cookery differs from the heavy foods of England, the change may be credited in large measure to the assimilation of a French cuisine. This is in itself important. but when one considers how prevalent is the American misconception that France is largely inhabited by *chefs* and that the cook's uniform is a kind of national costume, the details of the table are seen to have their place in fixing the American attitude toward the Gallic world.

3. THE AMERICANS AND FRENCH ENTERTAINERS

The notion that the French are skillful contrivers of little amusements is also part of the picture, and if our illustrations under this head are fragmentary, it is because much was not recorded and because lack of space crowds out many items that could be cited. In some sense the dancing-master and the music teacher belong under this division. What we have in mind more particularly is that kind of entertainment represented by the museum, the worker in wax-works, the rope-dancer, the singer,

[72] Thus *Campbell's Foreign Semi-Monthly Magazine* for June, 1844 (VI, 241-252), reprints an article from *Frazer's Magazine* for May, on Gastronomy, reviewing the *Classiques de la Table*, tome i, which contained works by Brillat-Savarin, Berchoux, Grimod de la Reynière, Colnet, le Marquis Louis de Cussy, M. F. Roques, Dr. Bourdon, Fayot, Antonin Carême and Mazors. It is an amusing and sympathetic account; this work, we read, assures us of the continuance of the French dynasty! In 1846 the *American Whig Review*, noticing *French Domestic Cookery, combining elegance with economy*, remarks that there "are many things in the French cuisine which it is desirable to have better known in this country" and says the book will be useful to those who know no French (IV, 214). A review of the same publication in the *Democratic Review* (XIX, 236-7) remarks that the heavy foods of England have yielded of late to the light, wholesome, and more varied *repas à la Française*. The French nation "has long regarded cookery as an art worthy of the exercise of 'genius.' " *The Daguerreotype* for January 8, 1848 (I :2 :518-24) reprints an amusing story of how an abstemious young Frenchman ate his way into the affection of a gourmand in order to win his daughter; and the story is prefixed with the remark that in Paris "alone eating can be said to have reached the dignity of an art."

[73] *History*, V, 429. Incidentally, Newark became the great champagne factory of America, where much "imported" champagne was made. Mackay, *Western World*, I, 127.

the dancer (up to the level of aesthetic dancing) ; and, roughly speaking, this sort of thing was on the increase in the United States from the coming of the émigrés. The "museum" in the eighteenth century and later was often the creation of a Frenchman.[74] These "museums" were curious affairs. Baron Wied-Neuwied devotes a paragraph to them in 1832 :

Tous les prétendus musées des grandes villes des États-Unis, à l'exception peut-être de celui de Peale à Philadelphie, ne sont que des ramassis de toutes sorts de curiosités hetérogènes, dont le choix est souvent fort étrange. Dans celui-ci, on trouve à la fois des productions naturelles, des figures en cire, horriblement faites, des instruments de mathématiques et autres, de mauvais tableaux et estampes, des caricatures, et jusqu'aux planches colorées des journaux de mode de l'Europe, le tout exposé ou suspendu pêle-mêle. Parmi les animaux, il y en a quelques-uns de fort intéressants, mais sans aucune étiquette ou explication quelconque. Cette collection occupe plusiers étages d'une maison très-élevée, et remplit une foule de petits chambres, de cabinets, de corridors et de recoins auxquels on arrive par plusiers escaliers, tandis que pour amuser le public, un homme joue du clavecin pendant toute la durée de l'exposition. Ce concert . . . no nous parut pas fort attroyant.[75]

Peale's museum had its replicas over the country. As indicated, French wax-works and subjects from French history in wax-work were objects of popular support, especially during the period of the French Revolution and after. In New York M. Maison in 1797 was exhibiting Le Citoyen Démocrate, Monsieur l'Aristocrate and Madamoiselle Modérée "dans leurs étonnants exercices,"[76] There was one in Philadelphia in 1784 depicting Citizen Sans Culotte and M. Aristocrat, the royal family, and the execution of Louis XVI.[77] There was another

[74] Thus Chastellux found that the cabinet of natural history at the University of Pennsylvania had been "formée par un Peintre Genevois, appelé M. Cimitière." *Voyages,* I, 192. Schoepf visited the collection. "Mr. du Simitière (*sic*), of Geneva, a painter, is almost the only man at Philadelphia who manifests a taste for natural history. Also he possesses the only collection, a small one, of natural curiosities—and a not inconsiderable number of well-executed drawings of American birds, plants, and insects . . . the Americans take most pleasure in a pair of French courier-boots and a Hessian fuseleer's cap." *Travels in the Confederation,* I, 85-86. The interest of persons like Franklin, Dr. Benjamin Rush, and Jefferson in the collection of curiosities, sometimes of scientific worth but oftener merely trivial objects, worthy of a dime museum, was fed by an interchange of notes and objects with French "philosophers" and travellers, as the early magazines and their correspondence testify. See, for an example of this sort of thing, the records of the "Early Proceedings of the American Philosophical Society (1744-1838)," *Proceedings,* XXII, part II.

[75] Wied-Neuwied, *Voyages,* I, 15.
[76] *Gazette Française de New York,* February 8, 1797, quoted in Faÿ, p. 276.
[77] McMaster, II, 550, note ; 551, note.

in Albany of "Louis, all pale and emaciated," "seated with a guard standing round him and others on horseback. A hideous blood-thirsty figure is setting (*sic*) with his eye on a watch, which lies before him; he is watching the minute-hand to ascertain the fatal moment. Robespierre is also present, out-looking vengeance itself. The scaffold upon which Louis is to suffer, stands near; both that, and the steps leading to it, are covered with black."[78] In Charleston in 1794 an Italian named Colomba was showing the execution of Louis XVI, of Marie Antoinette, and the rest. One saw the guillotine fall, and the head roll into the basket; "the whole is done by an invisible machine without any visible aid," says the *South Carolina State Gazette*.[79] In 1810 Dr. Scudder opened the American Museum in New York. "There were on exhibition glass cases of stuffed animals, a live anaconda, a tame alligator, and a gallery of paintings, said to be national portraits. There was also a small room where lectures on various subjects were given. John Scudder devoted his life to the museum, and acquired a competency from it."[80] It was in such curious collections that French objects were frequently found. Thus Bernhard describes the New England Museum at Boston as a private establishment with wax figures, stuffed animals, portraits, French caricatures, and a good working model of the Bastille.[81] Thus in 1820 Audubon was hired to stuff fishes by the Western Museum Society in Cincinnati at $125 a month.[82] "Every town, great or small, has a museum of plaster casts and daubs, dignified with names of the first painters," wrote Murat in 1830; the frontier spirit, the middle class spirit combined to nourish the monstrosity; by and by its great master, Barnum, was to arise; by and by the "dime museum" and the art gallery were to bifurcate, but in the meantime the French were vaguely associated with the "museum" of the forties.

The stage entertainer was somehow vaguely French also. We may begin with the Placides who came to Charleston, and whose appearances are written at length in Miss Willis's

---

[78] Mrs. Anne Royall, *Sketches*, p. 278. This was in 1824 or 1825, and is apparently the same group seen by Francis Hall in 1816. *Travels in Canada and the United States*, p. 26.
[79] October 17, 1794; quoted in Faÿ, p. 308.
[80] Allston, *History of the New York Stage*, I, 71. Barnum bought the contents in 1841.
[81] *Travels*, I, 38.
[82] Herrick, *Audubon the Naturalist*, I, 304-5.

invaluable *History of the Charleston Stage*.[83] Hallam, finding
his season unsuccessful, later "engaged Monsieur Placide, first
rope dancer to the King of France, and his troop" in January,
1792; the engagement continuing for over a year.[84] Placide was
a great celebrity, as he well deserved to be since he "danced
with two boys tied to his feet, and after that with two men in
the same manner."[85] The French juggler, the French sword-
swallower, the French fire-king,[86] the French trick dancer came
apace. Indeed, stage dancing in this country has always been
associated with Paris until the advent of the Russians. To
confine ourselves to New York for purposes of illustration, we
note a succession of French dancers, particularly in the first half
of the nineteenth century. Henry Placide, at the mature age of
fourteen made his debut at the Anthony Street theater in 1813
where he remained for one year; shortly afterwards Jane
Placide made her bow on the same stage. The next year (1814)
Mlle. Adolphe, who was afterwards Mme. Blanchard, appeared
there as a tight-rope dancer, the first woman to give such performances in America, it is said.[87] In January, 1828, the Lafayette Theatre was rented to M. Villalave, a rope dancer; on July
7 the ballet, "The Marriage," was first seen at the Lafayette;
the roll of the company contained such French names as "Mlle.
Estelle, Adrie, Ravenot, Clara, Louise, Esther, and Hyacinth,
and MM. Feltman, Duruissell, and Benoit." The theater burned
on July 11[88]—perhaps it was a judgment. At any rate, when,
two years earlier, Mme. Francisquy Hutin had made her first
American appearance at the Bowery Theatre on February 7,
she introduced the "modern French school of dancing" with

[83] See the index. There were other French dancers in Charleston: Mr.
Francisquy who performed a "Pastoral Dance" and sang the Marseillaise,
in February, 1794 (p. 200); Mons. Carré and an anonymous "foreign
gentleman" who "will perform a few choice pieces with a Pantomimical
Dance called 'L'Amour du Vin'" July 11, 1786 (p. 108); M. Plasidora
who had "performed before the Kings of France, Spain and Portugal and
the Emperor of Germany, and all the Nobles of the different courts with
universal applause" and who danced a Hornpipe on twelve eggs "to admiration" in 1785. P. 94.

[84] Brown, *History of the New York Stage*, III, Index, under Placide.

[85] Sonneck, *Early Opera in America*, p. 81.

[86] Chabert made frequent visits. In the autumn of 1831 he was in New
York, entering red-hot ovens, swallowing boiling oil, putting his hands in
melting lead, and doing other marvels of a similar character, to the admiration of James Gordon Bennett. Pray, *Memoirs of James Gordon Bennett
and His Times*, p. 133.

[87] Brown, pp. 82, 83.

[88] Brown, I, 100.

disastrous results. "During her first dance every lady in the lower tier of boxes left the house; and when she sprang upon the stage in her abbreviated skirts, a storm of hisses greeted her, and the curtain was rung down on the trembling, affrighted Frenchwoman, and she was never allowed to appear again."[89] The audience did not have the stomach of Abigail Adams.[90] Stage dancing was long in recovering from the reproach of moral shame; indeed it may be said that Fanny Elssler was the first to lift it into a higher plane of art in the minds of the great middle class. At any rate, in 1829 the famous Vestris made their debut at the Bowery.[91] They had been preceded by Mlle. Constance at the Park Theatre June 10, 1828, who danced in the opera *John Rock,* as well as by Mlle. Rosalie, a French danseuse, who appeared June 14.[92] In the fall of the year a French ballet opened at the Park Theatre,[93] whither in 1832 came the Ravel family—ten in all, who made their first American appearance at the Park Theatre July 16, 1832, and who had a long and interesting career at the Park, Niblo's Gardens, and other New York houses. "Their performance consisted of rope dancing, herculean feats, and pantomimic ballets in four parts, in which young Gabriel Ravel sustained the principal characters."[94] Mme. Celeste, a great figure of the thirties, was very popular; she played at the National Theatre in 1836, for instance, producing the ballet of *The Maid of Cashmere, or Le Dieu et la Bayadère* October 3, which took the town by storm, and *La Tentation* October 26.[95] In 1837 Mme. Leconte first appeared in America (November 23) as Helen in *Robert le Diable* at the Park Theatre;[96] the next year

---

[89] Brown, p. 102. The Bowery saw the debuts of a number of French dancers in 1827. M. et Mme. Achille made their bow on March 1; Mme. Heloise on July 7; Mme. Celeste on June 7; M. Barbierre on September 18. Pp. 102-103.

[90] Who went to theater and wrote to her friend, Mrs. Cranch, in 1785, that stage dancing first shocked her, but that now she was reconciled. At her first dance, "I felt my delicacy wounded. Girls, clothed in the thinnest silk and gauze, with their petticoats short, springing two feet from the floor, poising themselves in the air, with their feet flying, and as perfectly showing their garters and drawers as though no petticoat had been worn, was a sight altogether new to me." *Letters of Mrs. Adams,* II, 72.

[91] Brown, I, 104-5, August 30.

[92] *Ibid.,* p. 35.

[93] *Ibid.,* p. 36.

[94] Brown, I, 41; and see index, vol. III, under Ravel.

[95] *Ibid.,* I, 242-3.

[96] *Ibid.,* pp. 49-50.

Augusta Maywood Williams, known as La Petite Augusta, the first American to be admitted to the Academy of Dancing at Paris, appeared in a speaking character in Philadelphia (January 15); in September she appeared at the Park Theatre as a dancer in *La Bayadère*.[97] Celeste, who had filled repeated engagements in New York, reappeared September 27, 1838, at the National Theatre in *St. Mary's Eve,* given then for the first time in America, doing Madeline's speaking character in French and English; after the drama she danced *La Cachuca,* and later that same evening, *La Chatte.* October 1, 1831, she danced *La Cracovienne;* October 10, she appeared in *St. Mary's Eve, The French Spy,* a wild Arab dance, and "the last Parisian Quadrille."[98] October 29 at the same theatre a troupe of dancers consisting of Josephine Stephan, Mme. Hazard, M. P. H. Hazard, Rosalie and Sophia Mallet, with a corps de ballet from Europe, made their American debut.[99] Then on May 14, 1840, at the Park Theatre the "divine Fanny" Elssler made her debut; she was fresh from Paris, or so the booklets said; almost she succeeding in banishing the curse from aesthetic dancing; at any rate her tour of two years was a triumphal conquest of moral America.[100] Let us go no further; the divine Fanny closes an epoch; we have seen how definitely French ways were associated with these varying entertainments.[101]

[97] *Ibid.,* p. 50.
[98] *Ibid.,* p. 247. Brown credits her with having first introduced on the British stage an American drama by an American.
[99] *Ibid.,* pp. 237-8.
[100] See the amusing and graphic chapter devoted to her in Minnigerode, *The Fabulous Forties.* I have read somewhere that, after much searching of the conscience, Emerson and Margaret Fuller decided to attend a performance by her in Boston. They sat in silence for some time; then Emerson, turning to Margaret, said, "Margaret, this is poetry." "No, Waldo," she answered, "this is religion."
[101] Some injustice is done artists like Fanny Elssler by associating them with fire-eaters, balloonists, and sword swallowers. It is to be feared, however, that in the American consciousness there was little difference between the two before Fanny's coming; and perhaps not much afterwards. Much has been omitted, of course; French balloonists appeared in Philadelphia, Charleston, Boston, etc.; animal magnetisers like Charles Poyen thrilled the country in the thirties; there was a French "circus" by M. Perez in New Orleans in 1815; French dancers in Philadelphia in 1795-6 (Mons. Lege, who danced an "Egyptian Festival"); occasional discussions of the morality of French ballets (cf. *American Monthly Magazine,* new series, IV, 17-24 on Taglioni), etc., etc. When Power was on a steamboat in the Alabama River in 1834, a huge branch burst open the dining-room door, and "nearly impaled a French conjuror of celebrity on his way to New Orleans." *Impressions of America,* II, 157.

4. THE AMERICAN INTEREST IN FRENCH PAINTING
AND SCULPTURE

If we pass from these dubious arts to those of more conventional standing, we confront a history of intense interest from the social point of view, however much it may lack in genuine artistic worth. In painting and such poor sculpture as there was, the colonial tradition was derived from England and reflects the poor condition of British painting, particularly in portraits, before Reynolds and Gainsborough. The American painter was as likely as not one who had graduated from carriage painting.[102] Despite the stately grandeur of the South, American painting mainly began in Philadelphia[103] and Boston —cities in direct communication with Great Britain; and the biographies of the early American painters are those in truth of British artists temporarily living in America—frequently, indeed, moving from the colonies to Great Britain.[104] The concentration of the art interests in America in cities overwhelmingly dominated in cultural activities by the cosmopolitan merchant princes is of the highest significance: it is the

---

[102] Like John Smibert (died Boston, 1751). Caffin, *Story of American Painting*, p. 2. See also Dunlap, *History of the Rise and Progress of the Arts of Design in the United States*, I, on our early art history. As evidence for the importation of European objects of art the following advertisement from *The Boston Weekly News-Letter*, October 10-17, 1734, is typical:
"John Smibert, *Painter*,"
"SELLS *all Sorts of Colours, dry or ground, with Oils and Brushes, Fanns of Several Sorts, the best Metzotinto, Italian, French, Dutch and English Prints in Frames and Glasses or without, by Wholesale or Retail; at his House in Queen Street, between the Town-House and the Orange-Tree,* Boston."

[103] Colonial Philadelphia boasted this imposing array of artists: Gustavus and John Hesselius, John Woolaston, Robert Feke, John Watson, Henry Bembridge, Matthew Pratt, West, Charles Willson Peale. Later on came James Peale, Sully, W. R. Birch, Pierre Henri, Edward Miles, J. Henry Brown, John Sartain, Stuart, Inman, Trott, Harvis, Malbone, and Freeman. "The concentration of art interest in Philadelphia for some years was doubtless due to the great patronage given to artists, especially to portrait painters during the early sessions of Congress and later, when Philadelphia was the seat of government." Wharton, *Salons Colonial and Republican*, p. 212.

[104] Thus West, Peale Copley, Gilbert Stuart, Robert Pine, Pratt, Trumbull, and Washington Allston were either British by birth or training; and many of them spent most of their lives in London. Caffin, pp. 10-55. Many of course studied in Rome. Engravers like Nathaniel Hurd and Revere were either self-taught or came from London. Cf. Dunlap, I, especially chap. xii. John Ramage of Boston was Irish; James Peale was taught by his brother; Mather Brown studied in London; Thomas Spence (d. 1831) and Duché (d. 1790) studied under West. Thomas Coram (d. 1811) was self-taught.

American parallel to the patronage of the artist by the British leisure class. Consider the portraits of Copley, for example, the Van Dyck of New England; these citizens of Boston in their rich costumes look at you out of their massive settings in self-conscious dignity, a dignity born of gentle blood, class consciousness, position in the community. However inferior the execution may be, the intention of artist and sitter is to rival the stately portraits of Reynolds, to show that even in the colonies the merchant class can hold its own. And as the colonial had his portrait painted by a London artist, so he was likely to order costly paintings direct from England.[105] If he desired, not an oil painting but a miniature, he employed a "limner," a miniature painter from Europe temporarily residing in the colonies. He decorated his walls from the stock of dealers in mezzotints and engravings who sold and advertised them for household adornment in company with maps, looking-glasses, and picture frames.[106] There were no American sculptors until after the Republic, and these were instructed in Europe.[107] Indeed, until after the War of 1812, wherever one turns, art in America is literally European. Thus William Russel Birch, employed by Sir Joshua Reynolds to copy his portraits (he also did portraits in enamel), a great figure at the close of the eighteenth century, a man patronized by the Binghams, is thoroughly British. Again, when Gilbert Stuart came to America to paint Washington's portrait, he came from England, introduced by a letter from John Jay; fashionable society, recognizing him as one of their own, made his Philadelphia studio a salon.[108] This was in 1794. Robert Field, a British

[105] Thus Washington ordered works of sculpture to adorn Mount Vernon from London. Schouler, *Americans of 1776*, p. 18.
[106] Schouler gives lists of fashionable importers in Philadelphia in 1772. The allegorical largely figured. There were, for instance, The Seasons after Soalba; Peace and Plenty; Flora; Joseph and Potiphar's Wife; Venus attired by the Graces; the blinding of Cupid; the letter woman; the oyster woman; the bathing beauty; views of old-world cities; scriptural pieces; sea pieces; sporting pieces; whale fisheries; floral sets of twelve monthly flowers in beautiful frames; a series designed to exhibit the various passions of the human soul in the countenance, and so on. French influence is occasionally to be seen in this department of art. Schouler, *Americans of 1776, passim*. For the influence on household decoration of the French arts nothing is more illuminating than to study chronologically the rooms in the American wing of the Metropolitan Museum. See in this connection, *A Handbook of the American Wing*, 3d. ed.
[107] Like Greenough and Crawford.
[108] Wharton, *Salons Colonial and Republican*, pp. 216-7, 231, 219, 221, 224.

miniaturist famous in America, came in 1795.[109] The school was English, or Italian as interpreted by English artists; "the fascination of grandiloquence is over all," but it has its seamy side: Peale, the founder of the Pennsylvania Academy of Fine Arts, stuffed birds, practiced dentistry, ran a museum, and mended clocks to keep himself alive.[110]

Nor did independence and the interest in the French Revolution do much to change the style.[111] The classical movement which is part and parcel of the romantic revolt in Europe, had its effect upon American life: the epoch which saw the founding of villages strangely named Athens, Rome, Utica, Corinth, and Sparta, and gave to children such cognomens as Eleutheros,[112] sought to express the national genius by the application of the classical formulae of David and Hubert Robert to American history. Trumbull, who learned from West, expresses the ideals of 1815 in the grandiose historical canvasses in the National Capitol which show how heavily the weight of European tradition rested upon artistic work. And as in France classicism softens from David to Proud'hon, as English painting weakens from the solemnity of Gainsborough to the prettinesses of Reynolds, so in American art the grand classical school gave way to the false classic of Washington Allston, the product of Rome and London, him who painted Spanish girls without ever having been to Spain. Even the Hudson River school, the first to go to American "nature," saw its landscape through European spectacles; the landscapes of Cole are in color the equivalent of Volney's *Ruins,* of Bryant's *Thanatopsis*—classic grandeur degraded and sentimentalized. Such men "looked on nature with an eye at once too niggling and too comprehensive."[113] When London and Rome ceased to attract the American student, Düsseldorf took their place; by the middle of the century everybody went there, ceaselessly hunting some formula to express America in paint, unconscious that it is not the subject alone but the form of the work

[109] *Ibid.,* p. 231.
[110] Caffin, pp. 21, 25.
[111] But see Réau, *L'art français aux états-unis,* the section "Première Période."
[112] The father of Jay Cooke was so named. He was cheated out of an election to the Ohio legislature because the voters could not spell his name, and in consequence he named his boys Pitt and Jay. Oberholtzer, *Jay Cooke, Financier of the Civil War,* I, 2, 9.
[113] Caffin, p. 75.

as well, that expresses national genius. From the Düsseldorf tradition of genre painting, from Hogarth prettified, came those canvasses beloved of the middle class, "conversation pictures," dramatic scenes of contemporary life, seen at remote distance, prettified romanticism—chubby bootblacks that swore not, crossing-sweepers incredibly clean, children that never whined, puppies that did not bark. Whereas the merchant prince had imported his pictures from London, the bourgeoisie now took their art from Germany or got it at second hand— they too were "European."[114] Nor did the British tradition die out: Sully, influenced by Lawrence and Stuart, Inman, sent to England by James Lenox, Harding, who had a great vogue in the British Isles, continue the English school.[115]

What place had France in all this history? So far as any influence upon "American" painting is concerned, very little; the time when Paris was to supplant Düsseldorf had not come by 1848. What one has to report is rather the presence of French artists and of French *objets d'art* in America. It is to this record that we must now briefly turn.

Before 1763 there were very few French painters in the colonies; perhaps none; thereafter, however, they begin to appear.[116] Michelson Godhart de Brules, the New York engraver (he was there from 1759 to 1763), was a Frenchman. "Mr. Demilliere," a painter of miniatures in the same city in 1796, was obviously French. Henry Elouis, born at Caen in 1755, who studied under Restout, worked in Baltimore in 1789 and in Philadelphia during the nineties, returning to France in 1807; he was a miniaturist. Du Simitière or Cimitière, a

---

[114] The middle class brought into painting their strong moral prejudices. "Any artist would lose his reputation if he disclosed, in a picture, higher than the ankle or the elbow. Even the ancient statues, deposited in the museums, are carefully veiled; and as to having a living model, that would excite such an indignation that the painter would be obliged to quit the country. The artists and actors are married people, perfectly respectable. . . ." Murat, *A Moral and Political Sketch of the United States of America,* p. 368. The ordering of "art" at high prices is part of this subservience to Europe. Thus the statue of Washington on the Baltimore monument, on which the sculptor was engaged for two years, was ordered by Causici, an Italian, at a cost of $10,000; and the statue of Washington in Raleigh, N. C., by Canova, cost $20,000. Stuart, *Three Years in America,* II, 39, 115.

[115] Caffin, *passim.* Genre painting had as its chief exemplar in the United States John G. Brown. It is to be noted that the frontier has its expression among the Hudson River school, in the mountain landscapes of Moran.

[116] See for Philadelphia the appropriate chapters of Scharf and Westcott, *History of Philadelphia;* and on the whole subject, Réau, *op. cit.* He points out (p. 5) that Henri Couturier painted a portrait of Governer Stuyvesant of New Amsterdam.

Genevan, came to Philadelphia in 1760 where he lived for
thirty years, occupying himself with painting and natural history; his likenesses were engraved "in Paris, for sale,"[117] and
upon his death there was a movement to purchase his collection
in natural history for the state, which failed.[118] Austin Flori-
mont, a "limner" of Philadelphia is mentioned in the *Pennsylvania Packet* in January, 1781. In 1783 or 1784 Schoepf says
that Mr. West and Mr. Duchesne were "particularly mentioned
to me, and a young man of promise, Mr. Copley," the Frenchman being in reality Thomas Spence Duché,[119] a miniature
painter. Madame de Brehon, sister of the French minister
under Washington, made two small portraits of the president,
one of which was engraved in Paris.[120] A more important
figure was "Mr. P. Henri, Miniature Painter from Paris," who
in the *Pennsylvania Packet,* "respectfully informs the Public
that he is living in Front Street, opposite the City Vendue (the
Door facing the Tree) and that he will do himself the honor
to wait on Ladies, at their request,"[121] and who had an honorable career in the city. The great Houdon (1741-1828) seems
to have been sole and singular as a French sculptor in
America.[122] Joseph Wright was placed under Franklin's protection in Paris in 1782, but left before he had learned much.
John James Barrolet (1747-1815) of Philadelphia should,
perhaps, be mentioned here since he was of French-Irish descent; and M. Pigalle designed and etched plates in New York
at the turn of the century.[123] Perhaps we should also note that

---

[117] Griswold, *Republican Court,* p. 352. John Adams wrote his wife from
Philadelphia, August 14, 1776, describing a medal commemorating the surrender of Boston, ordered of du Simitière by Congress. *Letters,* I, 151.
Elouis painted a portrait of Anthony Wayne in the possession of the Historical Society of Pennsylvania.

[118] "He has since died, and his collections are broken up. The Assembly
of Pennsylvania threw out the bill for purchasing them for the University,
although the sum necessary would have been very moderate." Schoepf,
Travels in the Confederation, I, 85, note.

[119] Schoepf, I, 89.

[120] Griswold, *Republican Court,* p. 353.

[121] Quoted in Wharton, pp. 232-3.

[122] See Dunlap, I, 328-7; and see the long and interesting discussion in
Réau, pp. 23-49. Besides his famous Washingtons Houdon executed portrait
busts of Franklin (replicas in the Boston Athenaeum, the Jeanes collection
in Philadelphia, and the Metropolitan Museum; John Paul Jones (Pennsylvania Academy); La Fayette (Richmond); Jefferson (replicas in the New
York Historical Society and the American Philosophical Society collections); Joel Barlow (replicas in Philadelphia and New York); Robert
Fulton; and Gouverneur Morris.

[123] Details not otherwise assigned are from Dunlap, I and II.

in August 1783 Schoepf writes of a "porcelain fabrick . . .
about to be established at Philadelphia by a French regimental
surgeon," the clays to be brought from Maryland; he had seen
"some small specimens of porcelain" that "had been fused out
very successfully," but he does not report on the eventual success of the enterprise.[124] Cyrus Durand, a silversmith, and
Asher Brown Durand, the engraver of Trumbull's "Declaration of Independence" and one of the fathers of American
landscape, were so far French that they were of Huguenot
blood.[125]

The number of notices of French artists in this country
tends to increase in the opening years of the nineteenth century.
Augustin Chevalier executed the basso relievos of the Union
Bank in Baltimore and designed the façade of the Maryland
Insurance Office. In New York in 1814 Chiquet was a well
known engraver. Anthony Imbert, the first lithographer in New
York, was originally a French naval officer; he came to the
United States in 1825. In Boston in 1814 Lavigne was an
engraver, as was Lepelletier. In 1815 Alexander Charles Lesueur (borne at Havre de Grace in 1778) taught painting and
drawing; he returned to France in 1837, but died in America.[126] M. Maras painted miniatures in New York in 1801-2.
D. A. Volozon taught drawing in Philadelphia about 1820.
H. Magenis painted portraits in the same city in 1818; James
Paupiard of Martinique, who came to Philadelphia in 1772,
remained there until 1807 when he went to New York as an
engraver. Charles B. J. F. St. Memin, born in Dijon, France
in 1770, very famous in his day, visited all the principal cities
from 1793 to 1815.[127] Madame Planteau was a painter in

---

[124] Schoepf, I, 119.
[125] Fosdick, *French Blood in America*, p. 429. I have tried to select representative instances, which could of course be indefinitely increased. Thus
the *North-Carolina Gazette* for March 11, 1797, carries an advertisement
of F. Rabineau, "limner from Philadelphia and Washington," who "paints
in miniature, crayon and hair-work" and constructs "Bracelets, Brest-pins,
or Rings, figurative to the wish and desire of the ladies and gentlemen.'
Thomas Sully in his youth was apprenticed to his brother-in-law, Mr. Bel-
zone, a French miniaturist in Charleston. Willis, *The Charleston Stage*, p.
190. Janvier of Princeton (d. 1824) began as a coach painter; he was also
a poet, musician and translator. Hageman, *Princeton and Its Institutions*,
I, 244-5.
[126] Dunlap, III, 289, 290, 310, 314.
[127] See Baldwin, *Life and Letters of Simeon Baldwin*, p. 351 and Réau,
pp. 49-51. There is a collection of over 700 of his miniatures in the Corcoran
Gallery in Washington. His disciple L. Le Met was established in Philadelphia in 1804.

Washington in 1820, and A. Vignier painted landscapes in Philadelphia in 1811.[128] Charles Le Boulanger de Boisfremont painted portraits of some 24 Revolutionary heroes at the turn of the century; Thomas Gimbrède, later professor of design at West Point, was a designer of note, who came here from France in 1802; and in the South, the itinerant miniaturist Belzons, brother-in-law of Thomas Sully, should not be forgotten.[128a]

There was also a growing interest in Paris as an art center, following, one supposes, the artistic buccaneering of Napoleon. Washington Allston went to Paris in 1804 and again in 1817,[129] without, it must be confessed, deriving much benefit therefrom.[130] Rembrandt Peale journeyed to Paris a number of times between 1807 and 1812, visiting the Napoleonic art treasures and painting in the French manner; his "Roman Daughter" is the result of this false classical influence; his equestrian Napoleon (1810) was popular, as was his "Court of Death."[131] Robert Fulton, who was notable as an artist, spent some time in Paris at various intervals from 1797 to 1804; there he secured permission to exhibit his panorama, and painted—in 1800!—a Burning of Moscow.[131a] John Vanderlyn, the first American to matriculate in the Academy of Painting at Paris, went to France in 1796 and stayed until 1801, returning with Allston and not coming back to America until 1815. He was sufficiently in touch with French schools to receive the Napoleonic gold medal for his "Marius Among the Ruins of Carthage," and his pictures helped to encourage

---

[128] Dunlap, II, 283; III, 315, 328, 332, 340. The above list does not exhaust Dunlap, but is representative.

[128a] Réau, pp. 52-53.

[129] Dunlap, II, 324. Trumbull had visited France in 1780 before working with West in London. Réau, p. 83. Joseph Wright was in Paris in 1782. *Do.*, p. 84.

[130] "I never met with a French artist who had a sense of the sublime. One of them defined the sublime to me as the *Très bien.* I never saw a French painting that reached my higher nature. I have seen many such from the Italian, German, Dutch, Spanish, and English, but never from the French." (From an undated letter in Flagg, *Life and Letters of Washington Allston,* p. 366.) Allston belonged to the seraphic school. Born on a plantation owned by a Charleston (S. C.) family, he painted in oils while in school at Charleston. When his first effort was shown "his family were so surprised by its excellence that they feared lest he might disgrace them by becoming a painter" and sent him to Newport to prepare for college. *Ibid.*, p. 8. See also Réau, pp. 89-96 on this period. Charles R. Leslie accompanied Allston on his second visit. p. 110.

[131] Dunlap, II, 184.

[131a] Réau, pp. 85-89.

"classical" taste in this country.[132] Cole, French by birth, had no interest in modern French painting, though he visited Paris.[133] Samuel Morse, who, besides inventing the telegraph, enjoyed some fame as a portrait-painter, came to Paris in 1824, where he painted a picture of Lafayette that hung in the old City Hall in New York; and George Healy, a better artist, came to Paris in 1834 with the intention of staying a year or two, and remained sixteen. Healy is remembered for his "Franklin pleading the cause of the American colonies" and "Webster replying to Hayne," the last gaining him the gold medal of the Salon of 1855. George Catlin, the Indian painter, exhibited two portraits of Indian chiefs in the Salon of 1846, but he seems to have been little influenced by contemporary French art.[133a] Seth Cheney, however, studied under Isabey and Delaroche in the thirties, returning to Boston in the forties.[134] Southern planters went to sit to De Veaux and Fraser in Charleston where the tradition of French miniaturists and portrait-work was a long one.[135] Meanwhile New Orleans was developing a group of French artists.[136]

It is evident from these random notes that the place of French artists in America was rather one of social prestige than of positive influence upon American production.[137] As the biographer of Allston observes, "the prestige of foreign

---

[132] Dunlap, II, chap. xi. John R. Smith had his pictures turned out of the American Academy of Fine Arts; apparently because of jealousy. Vanderlyn helped to encourage the craze for panoramas. See also Réau, pp. 89-92. It is through Vanderlyn that the style of David came to be known in this country.

[133] III, 153.

[133a] Réau, pp. 110-113.

[134] III, 289. Perhaps one should note in this connection the extraordinary career of Francis Martin Drexel, the son of an Austrian officer, who had studied in Rome and who brought letters of introduction to Joseph Bonaparte. He painted portraits for a while, but, tiring of it, went to Bolivia in 1825, and on his return to the United States became a banker. Wharton, *op. cit.*, pp. 232-3.

[135] Dodd, *The Cotton Kingdom*, p. 82.

[136] There is a long list of artists resident in New Orleans in the first half of the nineteenth century in Cline, *Art and Artists in New Orleans.* See also Kendall, *History of New Orleans*, II, chap. ii.

[137] Réau, whose careful study deserves esteem, points out that French artists were most numerous in America in the 30 or 40 years after our independence; and that in the period 1815-1865, relatively destitute of French artists resident in America, an increasing number of American artists visited Paris, pp. 11, 113. The observation is significant in view of the middle-class domination of the second period. J. J. Audubon wrote Miss Maria Martin in April, 1834, that New York, with its 250,000 souls, possessed but two drawing masters. Herrick, *Audubon the Naturalist*, I, 65.

travel, in those days [was] an important factor in the reputation of an artist." If we turn from the artist to his product it is to be observed that while from the years 1776 to 1825 the presence of French painters is not uncommon, the presence of French objects of art is more common from 1800 on, as the museum movement commenced to grow.[138]

After the French Alliance the American government was presented with the portraits of the King and Queen of France, portraits which have a curious history. At one time they were hung in Federal Hall in New York; they were there in 1788 before Congress moved in.[139] When they were moved to Philadelphia with the government, they were hung in the Senate Chamber; when Washington took his second inaugural oath, however, they were covered with a curtain. Previously they had been for a time in the care of Robert Morris, and there is a story to the effect that the French Ambassador was wroth to find the gifts of his sovereign to the American nation, hanging in a private house. Eventually they were moved to Washington, and they disappeared when the British captured the capital in the War of 1812.[140] Louis also gave the patent office the arms of France and Navarre, which have disappeared;[141] in Newport he put up a monument in honor of M. de Ternay, who died there in 1780;[142] he gave the Catholic Cathedral in Baltimore a "Descent from the Cross," described by Mrs. Anne Royall;[143] he presented his picture and the arms of France to Washington;[144] and doubtless proffered other gifts. Jefferson brought back various works of art from France, for when Lafayette visited him in 1824, there was an "Ascension" by Poussin in the "saloon" at Monticello.[145] Dating from the same period are the statues of Washington in the national capitol and of Lafayette in Richmond, where likewise is a replica of the Washington statue.[146]

---

[138] On the museum movement consult Myers, *History of American Idealism*, chaps. xii-xiv.
[139] Griswold, *Republican Court.*
[140] Wharton, pp. 74-75; Bernhard, *Travels,* I, 175.
[141] Bernhard, I, 175.
[142] La Rochefoucauld-Liancourt, *Voyages,* III, 175; Levasseur, *Lafayette in America,* I, 183.
[143] *Sketches,* p. 190 and see below.
[144] Described by Bernhard, *Travels,* I, 179.
[145] Levasseur, I, 214.
[146] For the Capitol Washington see the description by Frederika Bremer, *Homes in the New World,* II, 513. For the Richmond statues see Francis

The émigrés occasionally saved a precious painting or so,[147] but the next influx seems to proceed from Napoleon. Levasseur inspected at the Academy of Arts in New York City a collection of engravings sent that institution by the Emperor.[148] Bernhard in the Philadelphia Academy of Fine Arts discovered that the best collection was owned by the Count Survilliers (Joseph Bonaparte); it included a portrait of the count, of his lady, and his two daughters, all painted by Gérard of Paris; and four busts, one of Madame Mère, one of Madame Murat, one of the Princess Borghese, and one of the Empress Marie Louise, all by Canova.[149] Dining with President Adams in 1825 the same traveller saw several handsome Sèvres pieces and a great chandelier, originally made for Napoleon, and bought by the American minister in Paris in 1815.[150] Emerson saw "a marble copy of Canova's bust of Queen Carolina of Naples" when he visited Murat in Tallahassee in Florida in 1827.[151] When Napoleon's followers came to New Orleans after his downfall, they brought their art treasures with them and attempted to recoup their losses by the sale of them to Northerners.[152]

After Napoleon, the Restoration. Coke admired in the Baltimore cathedral "the altar, a present from France," and some paintings, one by Paulin Guérin, presented by Louis XVIII, the subject the "Descent from the Cross" (it may be identical with Mrs. Royall's picture—that inaccurate lady), as well as a

Hall, *Travels in Canada and the United States,* p. 233, who remarks with surprise that the "sculptures are not mutilated" perhaps because "of the veneration in which the originals are held." His testimony is contradicted by Birkbeck, who, writing from Richmond in May, 1817, says that "it would be well, however, for the patriots of Richmond to repair the mutilated bust of La Fayette in their Capitol, which now stands an object of horror and derision:—La Fayette, the friend of their hero, and his faithful, disinterested, and zealous associate." *Notes on a Journey in America,* p. 28. See also Réau, under "Houdin."

[147] "Many of the residents of French and Spanish ancestry brought fine paintings and family heirlooms with them to this country." Cline, *Art and Artists in New Orleans,* p. 3.

[148] *Op. cit.,* I, 91.

[149] *Travels,* 141. On the art treasures at Bordentown see Lee, "Residence of Joseph Bonaparte in New Jersey," *American Historical Magazine,* I, 178-80; Darusmont, *Views of the Society and Manners in America,* letter VIII; Stuart, *Three Years in North America,* I, 386. The grounds were full of "pagan statues and animals"; and David's "Napoleon Crossing the Alps," busts of Napoleon, and statues by Canova were in the collection.

[150] Bernhard, *Travels,* I, 182.

[151] *Journals, 1824-32,* p. 161.

[152] Cline, *Art and Artists in New Orleans,* p. 3.

crusading subject by an unknown artist, given by Charles X.[153] David sent a bust of Cooper to Charles Wilkes in America, as well as a statue of Jefferson set up in New York.[154] And while these casual instances represent what may be called an official or political intercourse, a constant and increasing stream of private importations was going on.[155] A sense of splendor, of social prestige was cast over French pictures by this association with royal and imperial personages; by the forties the glamor of the French art galleries is reflected in the travel books of the time.

We must note finally some magazine comment on French art. *The American Review of History and Politics* for June, 1811, has "an essay on the history of painting," translated from the French, among its contents.[156] In the *Analectic* for June, 1815, there is a brief discussion entitled *The Raphael of Cats,* translated from a French journal.[157] The same periodical in September, 1816, notices the publication of M. Quatremere de Quincy's *The Olympian Jupiter, or the Art of Antique Sculpture,* a book which combines the "solidity of science" and the "charms of ingenious hypothesis."[158] The report of Joachim le Breton to the Institute of October 28, 1815, is translated in September 1818 as *On the Progress of the Fine Arts in France.*[159] *The Portico* (published in Baltimore by "two gentlemen of Padua") carried a treatise "On Painting upon Glass, and of Mosaick Work in France" translated from the *Musée Impérial des Monumens Français* of Alexandre Lenoir, in 1816.[159a] *The Analectic* in January, 1817, says that

---

[153] Coke, *A Subaltern's Furlough,* I, 73. Hamilton pronounced the pictures inferior. *Men and Manners in America,* II, 11.

[154] He also made a bronze relief of Cooper in 1833. *Correspondence of James-Fenimore Cooper,* I, 313, 147, 351.

[155] See Myers, *The History of American Idealism,* the chapters on art. Hunter, for instance, a real estate magnate of the Catskills, had a collection of pictures made for him abroad which Stuart saw: they included Poussin and Watteau, but seem to have been copies. *Three Years in North America,* II, 20. Stuart adds on the next page the cryptic comment: "Chaste works of art are much wanting in the United States." He saw in Vincennes some French engravings that struck him as good. II, 465. In 1847 in the St. Louis Ball Room 280 pictures were offered for sale, chosen from the collections of 39 Italian noblemen, which included David, Vernet, Poussin, Claude, and many Italians. Kendall, *History of New Orleans,* II, 651; Cline, *Art and Artists in New Orleans.*

[156] I, 367-77.

[157] V, 510-11.

[158] VIII, 272.

[159] *Analectic Magazine,* XII, 222-227, September, 1818.

[159a] I, 288-96, April, 1816.

M. Hacquart is to publish *Les Fastes de Bourbons,* engravings of "acts of beneficence, virtue, and heroism," of that house; and a year later it carries a condensation of two articles in British magazines on French lithography.[160] *The American Monthly Magazine* notes with surprise in 1836 that there are 1,385 artists in France, innumerable art schools and museums. In the thirties one finds an occasional article on French museums. It seemed to J. A. Jewett, writing in the *American Monthly Magazine* for March, 1838, an excellent thing that the Louvre was free; but with toplofty arrogance, he dismissed a thousand paintings as contemptible, and 800 others as less so; only fifty were worth notice, of which canvases by De la Roche and Delacroix are praised—it is the full tide of romanticism. France, it seems "has a very few good painters and sculptors." However, let us be grateful: "the prospects for Art in France are not discouraging."[161] Paris, it appears, was "coming in." However, Mr. Allston who holds "first place among American painters" did not think so. The paintings in Europe which "absolutely enchanted him," which took "away all sense of the subject," were the paintings, not of the Roman nor Lombard masters, but of the Venetian.[162] It is a far cry to Monet and Manet.

5. FRENCH ARCHITECTURE IN AMERICA

The history of American colonial architecture falls into certain well-defined periods overwhelmingly British in tone. The earliest structures in the English colonies, after the colonial huts of branches, rushes and turf with which the settlers began,[163] continued the mediaeval tradition.[164] Roughly speaking, the mediaeval tradition, Dutch, English, Welch, or what not, persisted, with various local modifications to the end of the seventeenth century.[165] The Georgian mode begins to make

---

[160] IX, 86; XI, 163-4. The articles (from the *Edinburgh Magazine* and from the *Monthly Magazine*) describe the work of Count Lasteyrie and M. Engelmann, and Quatremere de Quincy's work on lithography.

[161] V, 217-227, March (new series). For characteristic notices of French books on the history of art see the *North American Review*, XLVI, 83-106; *Campbell's Foreign Monthly Magazine*, I, 424; *North American Review*, LVII, 373-399; *New York Review*, X, 448-74; *The Daguerreotype*, II:6, 287, etc. The last (1848) indicates a waning interest in David.

[162] *North American Review*, L, 358-381 (April, 1840).

[163] See "The Seventeenth Century: Primitive Shelters," Kimball, *Domestic Architecture*, pp. 3-9.

[164] Kimball, *op. cit.*

[165] Mumford, *Sticks and Stones,* chap. I.

itself manifest about 1720 or 1725,[166] its popularity arising
from the desire of the great cosmopolitan classes to found
estates and mansions which would solidify their social standing. The period of Georgian architecture falls into three
epochs: the first phase from 1720 to 1740 or 1745; the second
from 1745 to 1775 or 1780; the third, from 1775 to the end
of the century when the "rejuvenated and direct importation of
classicism" came to dominate public taste for a quarter of a
century.[167] The impetus toward Georgian is English; what is
of more consequence is that in architecture the peculiar love of
the eighteenth century cosmopolitan class for the great cultural
tradition of Europe is even more notable than in other arts.
Mumford speaks of the Georgian period, quite truly, as part of
the heritage of the Renaissance. It is not merely that the origin
of the style was Palladian and therefore Italian, but that in the
eighteenth century every gentleman was his own architect. He
learned what he needed from the various textbooks imported
into the colonies,[168] and with the aid of skillful workmen and
builders he constructed his own house. This is not the spirit
of the frontier; it is the tradition of the Renaissance, of the
gentleman, the amateur of all the arts: the same individual was
skilled in verse-making, dancing, statecraft, making love and
building houses, the art of war, and husbandry; nothing more
clearly indicates how thoroughly the colonial leisure class was
a Europeanized class than their activities in architecture. And
since architecture is a conservative art, the British gentry
simply continued the British tradition, Italian as it was. There

---

[166] "By the end of the first quarter of the eighteenth century there had
been a marked increase in the wealth of the country . . . the general
growth of material prosperity provided the means to indulge the taste for
larger, better, and, in a word, more pretentious domestic environment that
accorded with the affluence and important social position of the prominent
citizens . . . they looked to the current architectural fashions in England
for inspiration to guide them in so momentous a matter as the establishment of a dwelling suited to their estate and fit to be the domicile of
succeeding generations of their name." Eberlein, *The Architecture of
Colonial America*, pp. 101-02.

[167] Eberlein, chap. vi; Mumford, chap. ii; Kimball, pp. 53-142.

[168] See the bibliography and comment in Kimball, pp. 56-60. "In reality,
the adoption of the new style came about in America in the same way in
which it did, as any general or wide-spread matter in England: through
the making of its forms universally accessible to intelligent workmen, or
even laymen, by means of books. . . . Copies of all these works found their
way to America, often within a very few years of their issue," and of these
copies there were "surprising numbers, both of monumental folios and of
pocket handbooks." Pp. 55-56, 60. See also Kimball, *Thomas Jefferson:
Architect.*

is not the shadow of French influence until well toward the close of the century.[169]

It is in the post-colonial period and the period of the classic revival that French influence begins to be felt. The classic enthusiasms of the American Revolution, the French Revolution, and the Empire periods, that same classic revival which goes with romanticism, felt in poetry, in politics, in painting, in fashions, has as its most enduring memorials in the United States, architecture. The situation is well set forth by Mumford:

These educated eighteenth century gentlemen, these contemporaries of 'Junius' and Gibbon, who had read Horace and Livy and Plutarch, had one foot in their own age, and the other in the grave of Rome. In America, Thomas Jefferson exemplified this whole culture at its best and gave it a definite stamp: he combined in almost equal degrees the statesman, the student, and the artist. Not merely did Jefferson design his own Monticello; he executed a number of other houses for the surrounding gentry—Shadwell, Edgehill, Farrington—to say nothing of the Virginia State Capitol and the church and university at Charlottesville.[170] It was Jefferson who in America first gave a strict interpretation to classicism; for he had nothing but contempt for the free, Georgian vernacular which was making its way among those who regarded the classical past as little more than a useful embellishment.[171]
The contrast between the classical and the vernacular, between the architecture of the plantation and the architecture of the village, between the work of the craftsman and the work of the gentlemen, became even more marked after the Revolutionary War. As a result of that re-crystallization of American society, the conditions of classical culture and classical civilization were for a short time fused in the activities of the community, even in the town. One may express the transformation in a crude way by saying that the carpenter-architects of the early republic worked upon a classical foundation. It was the Revolution itself, I believe, that turned the classical taste into a myth which had the power to move men and hold their actions.[172]

The two revolutions combined to bring in the classical taste of contemporary French art.[173] The chief formulae were the

[169] Except as the peculiar architecture of the French settlements on the Wabash, in Illinois, and on the Mississippi may have influenced occasional settlers. The question of New Orleans and Charleston is discussed below.
[170] Jefferson's activities are studied at length in Kimball, *Thomas Jefferson: Architect*, and reproductions of his designs are given there.
[171] See his criticism of Virginia public buildings in the *Notes on Virginia, Works*, VIII, 394. "The genius of architecture seems to have shed its maledictions over this land . . . the first principles of the art are unknown, and there exists scarcely a model among us sufficiently chaste to give an idea of them." It is needless to remark that he is thinking of purely classic buildings.
[172] Mumford, pp. 56-57.
[173] Eberlein, pp. 166-67; Réau, pp. 12-22; Kimball, *Thomas Jefferson: Architect*, pp. 37-46. "Almost within his life-time Washington became Divus

Greek or Roman temple, the formal city plan, and the use of the Greek and Roman orders.[174] In interior ornamentation, particularly, French influence can be specifically traced; Mr. Kimball has done it in his thorough treatise on our early domestic architecture. Even before the classic revival, something of the rococo spirit of Louis XV may be found in American houses; rocaille motifs in ceiling and stair-case for example.[175] In the union of classic form for the exterior and modern conveniences for the interior; the substitution of marble or pseudo-marble for brick; the practice of having a dressing-room and an alcove, rather than a mere bed-room; the notion of a projecting saloon, sometimes elliptical, sometimes circular, sometimes octagonal; an aversion to the visible roof; the use of classical motifs for interior decoration (such as Wedgwood panels, "classic" mantel-pieces and cornices and doorways)— these were the various specific fashions in which French influence was exerted on domestic architecture during the "classic" revival.[176] In public architecture the dominant influence was Jefferson.[177] An ardent student of architecture, his residence in France was devoted among other things to that pursuit; and his contacts with French architects, his detailed analysis of Roman buildings and French adaptations of them, are fundamental in our national architecture, especially in the two forms for capitols and churches—the temple style, and the dome-and-wing style. For good or ill, Jefferson, and through Jefferson, France, is the true parent of our national architecture.[178]

Caesar, and if a monument was not built to him immediately, a city was named after him, as Alexandria had been named after Alexander. Did not the very war-veterans become the Society of the Cincinnati; did not the first pioneers on the westward march sprinkle names like Utica and Ithaca and Syracuse over the Mohawk trail; and did not a few ex-soldiers go back to their Tory neighbor's plow?" Mumford, pp. 59-60.

[174] Particular buildings are the Old Maritime Exchange, Philadelphia; Andalusia on the Delaware, Pennsylvania; Girard College, Philadelphia; the Capitol at Washington; the Bulfinch State House, Boston; the New York City Hall; Monticello; the buildings of the University of Virginia; "Arlington" and the Virginia State Capitol. See the illustrations in Eberlein and the two volumes by Kimball.

[175] Kimball, *Domestic Architecture*, p. 112.

[176] *Op. cit.*, see Index under French Influence.

[177] Who planned the arrangement of public buildings in Richmond in 1776; who designed the Virginia State Capitol, the first use of the Greek temple for public building in America and perhaps in the world; who assisted L'Enfant in planning Washington; who counselled with Thornton, Latrobe, and Hallett in the construction of the National Capitol. For Jefferson's enthusiasm for the Golden House at Nismes, see his letter to the Comtesse de Tesse, *Works*, II, 131-134.

[178] Kimball, *Thomas Jefferson: Architect*, p. 89. This exhaustive volume is sufficient to correct the erroneous view of Flagg ("Influence of the

And in city planning Jefferson and France were pioneers, as L'Enfant and Petitral lived to prove.[179] L'Enfant's famous plan for Washington, a model for city development, was later imitated at Buffalo; and L'Enfant also drew up a plan for "la ville industrielle de Paterson." Nor should one forget that old New Orleans, or at least the "Vieux Carré," was laid out in 1720 by Adrien de Pauger as a kind of fortified camp; or that Chouteau in 1780 drew up a very simple plan for St. Louis—three streets parallel to the Mississippi.[179a] City planning leads to formal gardening and to cemeteries. There were undoubtedly other gardens in early republican days like that which Lieber describes,[180] and as for cemeteries, the melancholy moralists of the thirties and forties occasionally hint at French influence.[181]

French School on Architecture in the United States.") *Architectural Record*, IV, 211-228, that the "classical revival" did not begin until the thirties—*i.e.*, after Napoleon. On the contrary, there is every reason to think that the true father of the so-called Empire classic is Jefferson. Cf. Kimball: "Jefferson's provincial insistence on the support of classic authority thus anticipated by twenty years the attempt of Napoleon to gain the same sanction for his own empire." P. 42. It is not pretended that Jefferson's enthusiasm for classic architecture was begun in France, but that contact with French antiquarians and artists matured and directed his enthusiasm. Kimball's view is confirmed by Réau: "le Capitole de la Virginie . . . est en effet le premier monument de la renaissance classique aux États-unis et même, peut-on ajouter, dans le monde entier." Pp. 79-80.

[179] L'Enfant was also an architect, building a house for Robert Morris in Philadelphia, modelled after the Hôtel Biron of Jacques Gabriel. Réau, p. 17 note. He remodeled the City Hall in New York for the use of Congress. The plan for Washington was submitted and adopted in 1791. According to the *Journal of Latrobe* (who was a Briton and a classical enthusiast), L'Enfant made a mess of the city assembly rooms in Philadelphia. When Latrobe designed the Bank of Philadelphia, he was praised; when he was at work on the famous Schuylkill water-works, people referred to him as another L'Enfant, that "damned Frenchman." Pp. xix-xx. Bernhard saw in Charleston in the twenties "an elegant new plan of the city designed by an emigrant French engineer, M. Petitral." *Travels*, II, 8.

[179a] Réau, pp. 14; 17; 6-7.

[180] "Two large yew trees, cut in the stiff and cramped style of the period of Louis XIV, and brought from Europe at the beginning of the last century, are fondly and justly nursed in the garden of a friend of mine. . . ." *The Stranger in America*, II, 103.

[181] "The cemeteries are laid out in fine taste. Père-la-Chaise at Paris has formed the pattern, and tastefully is it imitated, and even surpassed." Duncan, *America As I Found It*, p. 246. Frederika Bremer says that Greenwood, "the large and new cemetery of New York" is "a young Père la Chaise, but on a more gigantic scale." *Homes in the New World*, I, 15. Buckingham describes the cemeteries of Mount Auburn in Boston and of Laurel Hill in Philadelphia as being "after the earlier example of Père la Chaise in Paris," and says that an association was being formed (1838) in Baltimore to copy the model. *America: Eastern and Western States*, II, 124.

In the lower South there were two possible foci for French architectural influence—Charleston and New Orleans. The buildings which are characteristic of Old Charleston are clearly not British, but alas! neither are they French; they rather represent that mingled Spanish and French style which the creole émigrés brought with them from Santo Domingo and which the need for shade (the typical house has a double gallery along its long side) made popular in a semi-tropical climate.[182] Public buildings like colleges were usually built in the "classical" order popularized by Jefferson and Latrobe.[183] In New Orleans[184] the so-called French quarter, architecturally speaking, is not really French, for the fire of 1788 devastated the city and destroyed the original French buildings, which were replaced by the Franco-Spanish architecture that dominates the quarter today.[185] Nevertheless, some examples of French architecture, public and domestic, remain. The Convent of the Ursulines, now the Archbishop's Palace, built in 1730, is mainly French, (barring the portico), with its plain façade, the stucco finish, the walls pierced with windows, and the three small French dormer windows which relieve the high-pitched roof on either side, and the tall and slender chimneys. In the Spanish buildings erected under Don Andres Almonester y Roxas and his successors, French delicacy tempered the bare effect of the Spanish; and notable in the quarter are the wrought iron railings, often Spanish in motive, but made by French "forgerons," skilled slaves brought from St. Domingo; sometimes the railings were imported from Paris.[186] Thus the

[182] The church at Goose Creek is Spanish, as is the so-called "old Revolutionary Powder Magazine." Cf. Whitehead, "The Old and the New South," *The Architectural Record*, XXX, 1-56.
[183] See "Architecture of American Colleges" by Montgomery Schuyler in *Architectural Record*, XXX, 57-84.
[184] See Embury, "Old New Orleans," *Architectural Record*, XXX, 85-98; Goldstein, "The Architecture of Old New Orleans," *Architecture and Allied Arts*, I: no. 9; Mrs. Philip Werlein, *The Wrought Iron Railing of Le Vieux Carré* (in the Howard Memorial Library); Marguerite Samuels, "Art in the Iron Verandas of New Orleans," *Times-Picayune*, June 6, 1920; Flo Field, "Ironwork of Old New Orleans Balconies," in *Ibid.*, for March 12, 1916; and the collection of pictures and articles on old New Orleans houses by John P. Coleman, originally published in the *New Orleans States* in 1922, and preserved at the Howard Memorial Library.
[185] On the fire see Fortier, *History of Louisiana*, II, 116; O'Connor, *The Fire Department of New Orleans*, pp. 33-36, in the Howard Memorial Library. Property loss in buildings amounted to almost $2,000,000.
[186] Tradition assigns many of the balconies to Lafitte. M. Mangin, whose grandfather came from France in 1832, stopped his work as a maker of artistic railings in iron about 1920—the last of his kind. Cf. Samuels, *op. cit.*

wrought iron balconies on the Cabildo are French; and so, too, are the Tuscan Romanesque mansard roof and the tower, which were added to the original Spanish structure. In the plantation dwellings, not touched by the fire (as here and there in the French quarter) one finds still occasional traces of the original French architecture: brick laid in between heavy joists (the brick often imported from France), the high-pitched roofs, and the chimney midway of the ridge.[187] The Pontalba buildings on Jackson Square are French. The pride of tradition has led to the construction of public buildings in the city after the French manner, such as Sophie Newcomb College (Louis XVI) and an attempt in the domestic architecture of the city to retain many French features. Incident to the architectural history of the city is the work of Gallier, whose classical taste is exemplified in the City Hall and the United States mint, and who spent some years in Paris.[188]

Comment by travellers of what may be called a miscellaneous order is not helpful or rich in the field of architecture for obvious reasons. Here and there one finds some traces of French architecture, but they are not many. For instance, when Samuel Fullerton took his bride in 1815 to Pottsgrove, now Pottstown, in Pennsylvania, and his estate called Stowe, he took her to a mansion originally erected by a Frenchman; there were marble floors and so many rooms and passages that Mrs. Fullerton was afraid she might get lost.[189] Again, Dunlap notes that "Mr. Godefroi," driven here by the French Revolution, married and lived in Baltimore, where he built the "Gothic Chapel," St. Mary's College, and the Unitarian Church; he designed and erected the Battle Monument; and with Latrobe, he built the Exchange.[190] Power describes (December, 1833) the New York Opera House; it was arranged after the French fashion, having stalls, a parterre, and a "balcon" below; and above, two circles of private boxes fitted up in a style of extravagance he never saw elsewhere.[191] In Abdy's

---

[187] The illustrations to Embury, op. cit., show both the Hispano-Moresque and French type of private house.

[188] Autobiography of James Gallier.

[189] Dall, Spencer Fullerton Baird, pp. 6-7. Later the Reading railroad trains used to stop to allow the passengers a glimpse of it and its garden.

[190] Dunlap, History of the Arts of Design, III, 173-4; Réau, p. 20.

[191] Impressions of America, I, 164. The Park Theater in New York, built in 1798, was planned by Mark Isambord Brunel, who had been connected with the London Thames tunnel project. Brown, History of the New York Stage, I, 12.

opinion Sing Sing prison was modelled after the Maison de Force at Ghent.[192] French buildings in the West occasionally drew the comments of travellers.[193] In the South travellers note that the great houses are occasionally French in style. Latrobe, ascending the James River, found "fine, old, aristocratical-looking mansions built in the French or English styles," the French ones being "like French chateaux, with terraces in front, backed by stiff clumps of trees."[194] Power comments on the European quality of the domestic architecture of Savannah;[195] and in Mississippi Lyell found that many of the elegant country places were English, some were French, and the gardens in each case partook of the quality of the houses.[196] Stuart's single comment on the fine houses of Charleston is that "many of them are inclosed like the great hotels in Paris, and all of them covered with verandas." Travellers visiting New Orleans naturally commented on its architecture. And just beyond the borders of our period were Richardson and the influence of the Romanesque, which, building upon the work already sketched, made a profound impression upon America. All in all, the influence of French architecture upon the United States has been great and important.

6. FRENCH MUSIC IN AMERICA

If the history of French architectural influence can be determined with fair exactness, that of French music is more vague and diffuse. In both music and drama the initial impulse was in the main British. American music, in the sense of music written by Americans, begins with psalms sung by the Puritans. By the end of the eighteenth century a straggling group of native composers had appeared, William Billings and Francis Hopkinson being among the earliest native com-

---

[192] *Journal*, I, 17.
[193] For example, Buckingham, writing of Detroit in 1842, says that "among the prettiest houses of this description, are those of the old French and English merchants and traders, built before the Revolution and spared by destructive fires. These are situated in the suburbs of the town, running along the bank of the Strait, to the south of the present city, with much larger gardens, orchards, and even fields adjoining them . . . they are chiefly occupied by the very few Anti-(ante)Revolutionary families, or their descendants, that remain here." *America: Eastern and Western States*, III, 387.
[194] *Rambler in North America*, II, 5.
[195] *Impressions of America*, II, 117-8.
[196] Lyell, *Travels in the United States, Second Visit*, II, 153.

posers.[197] But, at least so far as the eighteenth century is concerned, we must not conceive the musical life of the country as being merely primitive; rather, it was provincial. The first song recital on record in America was given in Charleston in 1733; Boston had a concert in 1731 and Charleston in 1732.[198] The ballad opera of *Flora, or Hob in the Well* was given in Charleston as early as 1735;[199] and as early as 1767, the *Pennsylvania Chronicle* announces the forthcoming performance of *The Disappointment,* "a new American Comic Opera in two Acts" by Andrew Barton. The opera was not performed; and the next "American" opera seems to be Francis Hopkinson's *The Temple of Minerva,* 1781, an allegorical piece in which the Genius of France and the Genius of America sing pleasant things of the alliance.[200] In the meantime something of a concert life had developed.[201] "We had more or less regular operatic seasons in New York, Philadelphia, Baltimore, Annapolis, Charleston, the répertoire consisting, of course, mostly of English ballad-operas, and later a few French and Italian operas. . . . We had regular orchestral subscription or amateur concerts; we had musical societies; we did not neglect chamber music, and music played a prominent part at all College Commencements. The German flute, the

[197] Others were Oliver Holden, Andrew Law, Jacob Kimball. Elson, *History of American Music,* pp. 1-23; Lahee, *Annals of Music in America,* chap. i.
[198] Lahee, p. 2.
[199] *Ibid.,* p. 4.
[200] Sonneck, *Miscellaneous Studies,* pp. 23 ff. *The Temple of Minerva* was made part of a concert given 11 December, 1781, by the minister of France in honor of Washington, Mrs. Washington, General and Mrs. Greene, and "a very polite circle."
[201] Here is a typical musical program in Charleston in 1765:

Act I
French Horn Concerto
2d Concerto of Stanley
Solo on the Violincello
5th Concerto of Stanley
Bassoon Concerto
Song
Overture in Scipio
Act II
French Horn Overture
Concerto on the Harpsichord
Trio
Bassoon Concerto
Song
French Horn Concerto of Hasse

Willis, *The Charleston Stage,* p. 48.

guitar, the harpsichord—the fashionable instruments of the time—the pianoforte, the violin, the bass-viol, were not missing in well-to-do families of Colonial times. Not even the strolling Italian and French virtuosos were wanting, nor the blessed 'Wunderkinder.' "[202] A concert series, vocal or instrumental, in one of the larger colonial cities was usually announced for six or eight weeks, one concert each week drawing "a very polite company." The fashionable hour was half-past six in the evening; the price of admission, half a dollar or its equivalent; the program might include airs and duets, a solo on the violin, French horn, hautboy, or harpsichord, or sometimes numbers by a regimental band. Handel was a favorite, but, since most of the performers were amateurs, few published programs exist, and we know little about the musicians themselves.[203] The general practice in concerts was modelled upon London, just as British taste was followed in the "spinet music" thought to be essential to fashionable education—formal music, indeed, being almost the monopoly of the upper classes.[204] The French dancing master occasionally gave music lessons; and after the French Alliance the number of Gallic musicians considerably increased; indeed, there was a traditional association of Frenchmen with the lighter music.[205] The war itself seems to have increased the taste for music: Schoepf, a conscientious observer, writes that "during the war and after it straggling musicians from the various armies spread abroad a taste for music, and now in the largest towns concerts are given, and conventional balls. In the item of dancing-masters France has supplied the necessary."[206] The asso-

---

[202] Sonneck, *op. cit.,* p. 74. See his essay, *The Musical Side of Our First Presidents* in *Suum Cuique;* and his discussion of Benjamin Franklin and the musical glasses in the same volume.

[203] Schouler, *Americans of 1776,* pp. 107-8. Even New England succumbed. Thus Bayard reports that in Boston at the end of the century, "music, which their Presbyterian ministers formerly described as a diabolical art, is beginning to form a part of their education. The piano is heard in some wealthy homes." He hopes that American women will not acquire the rage for music which distinguishes his own countryman. Sherrill, *French Memories,* p. 42. And see Brissot de Warville, *New Travels in the United States,* p. 72. However, pianos were a rarity in New Hampshire at the opening of the nineteenth century; see the account of Jonas Chickering and the London piano in *The Commemoration of the Founding of the House of Chickering,* pp. 33-34.

[204] Elson, pp. 25-41.

[205] Thus Watson, after travelling in France, remarked that "almost every Frenchman is an adept in playing on some musical instrument." *Men and Times of the Revolution,* p. 120.

[206] Schoepf, *Travels in the Confederation,* I, 90. This was in 1783-4.

ciation of music with foreigners is important to note; here, too, an exotic and fashionable flavor clung to the formal mastery of music.

Miss Willis's exhaustive study of *The Charleston Stage* enables us to study a typical group of French musicians in an American city at the close of the eighteenth century. For instance, the *South Carolina Gazette* in February, 1774, advertises "Mr. Valton's Concert of Vocal and Instrumental Musick" performed at "Mr. Pike's New Assembly Room," at which one Abercrombie, a Frenchman just arrived, played the first violin incomparably well. In April, 1774, there was a "Grand Concert of Vocal and Instrumental Music" at the Theater by Mr. Franceschini under the patronage of the St. Cecilia Society. If we omit other references, and turn to the eighties, we find in the *Columbian Herald* for May, 1786, an advertisement that Mrs. Stras from London purposes to give tuition in the Art of Music—an accomplishment which she has attained by long practice in Paris—particularly the lyre or harp. She will also give instructions for the Violin and "Guittar." In the same year "Mr. Lafar's Music Shop" was located at No. 119 Tradd Street. In the nineties, after the arrival of the émigrés, musical notices increase. On the sixth of March, 1794, the St. Cecilia Society gave a Grand Concert for their benefit: Grand Overture, Haydn; Overture, Gretris; Overture, La Chasse, Goffet; Concerto violin by Mr. Petit. M. Francisque and M. Dainville, and M. and Mme. Val gave a grand Ballet. In February of that year Mr. Gornet was offering to give lessons on violin, tenor, violincello, German flute, clarionet and bassoon; and to tune harpsichords and pianofortes; he was a member of the theatre orchestra besides. So were Lécat, Brunet and Daguetty. In the same year "Mr. De Colland hath the honor to present his respects to the ladies and gentlemen of this city, and acquaints them that he sells music-paper of all sizes. He likewise copies music in the neatest manner."[207] The year 1794-5 was noted for the unusual excellence of its musical entertainments; there were two fine theater orchestras, the St. Cecilia Society, a number of paid singers, and "an equaled chorus for the operas." That year or later Mrs. Pownall and Mr. Leroy gave a concert in Williams' Coffee House, singing French and English songs. M. Poiteaux's Grand Concert with

[207] And "hath to dispose of Airs, selected from the most celebrated French operas, and adapted for any instrument." Willis, p. 249.

orchestra of thirty pieces should be noted; French music and Chinese fireworks were given by Citizen Bulit weekly; and Citizen Cornet had an "excellent French orchestra" in his Vauxhall Gardens. When General Pinckney visited Charleston in 1799, the City Theater had a special program in his honor, which included "General Pinckney's March" composed by M. Foucard.[208] All in all, the French contributed much to the musical life of Charleston, and to the country. The weak spot in operatic performance in America had been the orchestra, but after the Revolution, the historian of American music notes a remarkable change. The troubles in France and the West Indies "added to the English and German a distinctly French element, represented by such artists as Gehot and Victor Pelissier."[209]

In New Orleans we have little information regarding French music teachers in the eighteenth century, but for the nineteenth century a good many details are known.[210] E. John, maître de piano, was established at 184 Bienville Street in 1824; by 1837 he had become the head of a firm of booksellers, printers and publishers. He is said to have been the first citizen to compose and publish original verse; at any rate, jointly with the house of F. Pleyel & Company, he published the *Album Louisianais, Hommage aux Dames de la Nouvelle-Orléans.* He also composed six romances, a waltz, and a polonaise. When he returned from Paris in 1838, he published *Les Magnolias, ou Valses Louisianaises,* by G. P. Monouvre, a work dedicated to Madame Johns, of which a copy is to be found in the Howard Library; and a barcarolle, *Haste, Boatman, Haste,* by another local composer. W. V. Wallace of that city published his *Grand Fantasia* in 1847, having previously composed other works. One Curte, whose name appears in a city directory of 1820, was a famous music teacher who trained a generation of singers, and who also composed various forgotten compositions. Nor should we forget the association of the Patti family with New Orleans; a brass tablet marks the house where the famous Adelina lived. And at St. Peter near Dauphine street the famous Gottschalk was born on June 23, 1837. Most of these musicians belonged to the romantic school in taste.

[208] Willis, pp. 65, 67, 104, 118, 202-3, 197, 210-2, 249, 277, 421-2, 289-90.
[209] Sonneck, *Miscellaneous Studies,* pp. 54-55.
[210] See Beard, "Composers of Music and Music Publishers in New Orleans," *The Daily Picayune,* February 18, 1912.

Early opera in America was of course British; and the ballad opera (like *The Beggars' Opera* given in New York December 3, 1750)[211] predominated. But the association of opera with British performers necessarily died away during the Revolution, and in place of the British, the French and the Italians appeared. *La Servante Maîtresse,* adapted from Pergolisi's *La Serva Padrona,* was given in Baltimore, June 14, 1790; in the fall of 1790 (October 7) the City Tavern in New York was honored by the première of *Le Tonnellier* of Audinot Gossec;[212] and in 1791 a company of French comedians and singers gave vaudeville and operas in New York—works by Grétry and Rousseau being among the number; it would appear that the early establishment of opera in New Orleans had some part in this movement.[213] Native American "operas," such as they were, got themselves written at the end of the eighteenth century by expatriated Frenchmen; besides these, occasional French operas may be noted. From the authoritative list of musical productions at the Park Theater in New York, 1793-1800, compiled by Sonneck, I extract the following names of French works, or of works by Frenchmen resident in America:

Ariadne Abandoned by Theseus in the Isle of Naxos, melodrama by Pelissier, April 26, 1797
Bourville Castle, by Carr and Pelissier, January 16, 20, 25, 1797
Demolition of the Bastille, pantomime, June 25, 1795
Don Juan, pantomime-ballet (apparently based on Mozart and Molière), given each year except 1798
Edwin and Angelina by Pelissier, December 19, 1796
Fontainebleau, May 12, 1797
Forêt Noire, pantomime, given 1795, 1796, 1798
The Fourth of July (probably a "spectacle") by Pelissier, July 4, 1789
Gil Blas, pantomime, December 28, 1798
Jeanne d'Arc, May 4, 1794
Pygmalion by Rousseau (in English), March 13, 1796
Richard Coeur de Lion by Grétry (in English), March 13, 1796
Sophia of Brabant, pantomime by Pelissier, 1794, 1795
Sterne's Maria by Pelissier, 1799[214]

Sonneck's invaluable study gives other lists for later decades, but the above is representative, both of fashionable taste and of the extent and variety of French influence at the end of the

[211] See Elson, early chapters.
[212] Willis, pp. 236-7; Lahee, p. 11.
[213] Elson, pp. 94-95; Sonneck, *Early Opera in America;* Lahee, p. 11.
[214] Sonneck, *Early Opera in America,* Table B, pp. 89-90.

century. The "operas" were of course of the simplest variety. French refugees gave occasional operatic performances in New York, or else helped to augment the meagre orchestras of the day, and this Pelissier, whose name figures prominently in the above list, was, for instance, a horn-player.[215] In addition to New York, Charleston and Baltimore, cities where French cultural influence was strong, were two important opera centers at the opening of the nineteenth century,[216] and there was always New Orleans.

New Orleans has a long and honorable history in opera,[217] and indeed, may be said to have been the most important operatic center in the United States until after the Civil War. Louis Tabary with a troupe of comédiens gave performances in one place or another, sometimes in a tent, sometimes in the open air, until in 1791 the company fixed its abode in the Spectacle de la Rue St. Pierre. This company seems to have been recruited from Paris, and offered drama, operas, ballets and pantomimes winter and summer except for a few months respite.[217a] The building itself degenerated, and was at one time closed by the police. The director announced the events of the day before the rise of the curtain on the evening's performance, and as the artists were French, and the audience mostly so, and "ferocious demagogues" besides, the result of the director's speech was frequently a disturbance, punctuated with *La Carmagnole* and *Ça Ira,* and, later, the *Marseillaise.*

[215] *The Vintage,* libretto by Dunlap and score by Pelissier, seems to be the earliest opera with a book based on American themes. Elton, p. 98.

[216] Elton, pp. 98-9.

[217] Now being written by Professor J. S. Kendall of Tulane University. Until Professor Kendall's book appears, the most available sources are J. M. Augustin, "Fifty Years of French Opera," the *Daily Picayune* for October 24, 1909; J. G. de Baroncelli, *Le Théâtre Français à la Nouvelle Orleans;* Fischer, "The Story of New Orlean's Rise as a Musical Center," *Musical America,* March 14, 1914, pp. 3-5; Loeb, *The Opera in New Orleans;* Straus, "Interesting History of New Orleans Theaters," *Times-Picayune,* May 9, 1920; the *Historical Sketch Book and Guide to New Orleans* of 1885; Mrs. Bishop, "The Musical History of Louisiana," *Times-Democrat* of October 31, 1909; Loeb, "Opera in New Orleans," *Publications of the Louisiana Historical Society,* IX, 29-41; Higgins, "New Orleans Has Romantic Opera History," *The Item-Tribune* for December 20, 1925; Straus, "The Old New Orleans and Its Opera, The Repertory, Theaters, Audiences," *The New York Times* for December 6, 1925; Price, "Le Spectacle de la Rue St. Pierre," *Louisiana Historical Quarterly,* I, 215-223; and the files of programs and libretti in the library of the Louisiana Historical Society and the Howard Memorial Library.

[217a] Price, *op. cit.,* says there is no proof that opera was given before 1806, but that it is extremely likely.

In 1799 a half dozen actors and actresses from Santo Domingo were added to the theatrical life of the city and gave "acceptable performances" of comedy, drama, and vaudeville. In 1807 the Spectacle de la Rue St. Pierre, then a "long, low wooden structure, built of cypress and alarmingly exposed to the dangers of fire"[218] was closed; the Théâtre de St. Pierre, erected on the same site, was opened September 14, 1808, with *Le Prince Tékéli, ou Le Siège de Montgatz,* a three-act melodrama, and *Le Secret,* a one-act opera. Here performances of a varied nature were given until the building was sold at auction, December 28, 1810. In that year there were three theaters in the city: the St. Philippe, erected in 1808, and rather pretentious; the Théâtre d'Orleans, and the St. Pierre.[219] In the Théâtre de St. Pierre certain operas were regularly given, where Tabary was manager and de Rigny, son of an admiral in the French navy, was a star.[220] Thus from 1803-1808 one finds *Richard Coeur de Lion, Pizarre ou le conquérant de Pérou, Eugénie,* drame en cinq actes (Beaumarchais), *Deux Chasseurs et la Laitière, Le Distrait* (comédie en cinq actes), *Une Heure de Ménage, Crispin Médecin, Le Petit Page,* etc., etc., among the offerings; and the artists included Drigny, St. Martin, Fontaine, Champigny, and Mlles. Alice, Joséphine and Remusat.[221] The St. Philippe, built at a cost of $100,000, opened its doors January 30, 1808; it held 700 people and its auditorium consisted of a parquet and two tiers of boxes. The initial performance was a double bill under the direction of Tabary: *Les Fausses Consultations,* a one-act comedy in prose, and *Une Folie,* an opéra comique in two acts, the words by Bouilly, the music by Méhul. The course of its career was stormy, and the management frequently changed; nonetheless operas of the rank of *Mon Tante Aurore* by Boieldieu, *Romeo*

---

[218] See Price, *op. cit.* The City Council voted to allow M. Fournier to manage the theater, if it was repaired. On November 16, 1804, he advertised that the repairs were completed.

[219] According to one account the St. Philippe was built in 1810, but this seems to be an error. Douvallier was manager of the St. Peter in 1808, and was followed by Daudet.

[220] From *Le Moniteur de la Louisiane,* December 30, 1809: "Dimanche prochain, Le Collatéral, ou la Diligence de Joigny, comédie en cinq actes de Picard, suivie de L'Amour Filial, ou La Jambe de Bois, opéra en un acte de Gaveaux." Loeb, *op. cit.* This is a typical program, in which the short one-act opera follows the play.

[221] Baroncelli, p. 8. This was in the St. Pierre, it must be remembered. Seventy different operas were given at the St. Pierre, 1806-1811. Price, *op. cit.*

et Juliette, Le Jugement de Midas, and *Le Billet de Loterie* were given; and a corps de ballet was organized at vast expense. The year 1816 was said to have been a specially brilliant one at the St. Philippe, but by 1817 all the performances at the St. Pierre and the St. Philippe alike were given, under the direction of Ludlow, in English.[222] But the St. Philippe went the way of the St. Pierre in 1819.[223]

In the meantime the redoubtable John Davis, gambler, adventurer, and manager of genius, had come to New Orleans in 1811, and after running a gambling hall for a year or two, had decided to enter the theatrical business. The famous Théâtre d'Orleans, begun in 1809 under the direction of Lacarière Latour, had housed a commercial company after November, 1809, which produced plays and operas; but the building was destroyed by fire in 1813. It was rebuilt by the architect Thibaut at a cost of $180,000; it was managed by John Davis, the head of a corporation; and a feature of the house was the grilled loges for those in mourning. Here, from 1813 till 1859,[224] when the famous French Opera House was erected, opera was given season after season with a completeness and splendor not equalled anywhere in the country. Each year the manager went to Paris to recruit the best Parisian artists for his company; each year saw some notable addition to the repertoire of the company; each year the ballet, the scenery, the orchestra, the lovely creole ladies in the audience, drew the delighted attention of residents and visitors. A list of the performances is a list of the notable operas of the epoch: the following, compiled from *L'Ami des Lois et Journal du Soir,* Loeb, and other sources indicates something of the resources

---

[222] So says Baroncelli in his pamphlet, which is not wholly reliable. According to the *Historical Sketch Book* English plays alternated with French opera in 1819 (p. 138).

[223] It probably became the place where the famous quadroon balls were held. However, performances were given after that date. In 1821 the building was altered to permit an equestrian troupe to perform; in 1832 it was occupied by a company of acrobats, and became the Washington Ball room.

[224] In November, 1836, the Council of Municipality No. 1 voted, over the Mayor's veto, to subscribe $200,000 to the New Orleans Theatre Company, in shares of $100; the investment taking the form of municipal bonds payable thirty years after date. The legislature incorporated the company in March, 1836; and an act of March, 1837, recognized the municipality as a stockholder in the enterprise. The first dividend (1858) brought $6,000 into the treasury. See Edgar Grima, "Municipal Support of Theatres and Operas in New Orleans," *Publications of the Louisiana Historical Society,* IX, 43-45.

of the theater. Important productions for 1815 include *L'Amant Jaloux,* opera in three acts by Grétry, followed by *Gulnare,* opera in one act; *L'Oncle-Valet,* a new opera by Della Maria, preceded by *L'Epreuve Villageoise,* opera in two acts by Grétry; *La Rosière de Salency,* opera in three acts; *D'Azemia ou les Sauvages,* opera in three acts; *Le Calife de Bagdad,* opera in one act by Boieldieu; *Zemire et Azor,* fairy opera in four acts; *Felix, ou l'Enfant trouvé,* opera in three acts by Monsigny; *Ariadne abondonnée dans l'Isle de Naxos* of Edelmane (grand opéra musique); *Bion,* opera in one act by Méhul; *Paul et Virginie,* opera in three acts, etc. Such was a representative offering for three months—and the list omits all comedies, *drames,* and the like. Or, to take the matter another way, consider this list of important operas compiled by Fischer, and augmented from the libretti available in the library at the Cabildo:

1828, March 9, *Le Barbier de Seville*
1836, December 6, *La Muette de Portici*
         December 15, *Fra Diavolo*
         December 24, *Robert le Diable*
1837, February 16, *L'Éclair* (Halévy)
         May 1, *Semiramide*
1839, April 29, *Les Huguenots*
1840, January 14, *La Sonnambula*
1841, March 16, *Zanetta* (Auber)
         December 28, *Lucia di Lammermoor*
1842, March 2, *La Esmeralda* (Prevost)
         March 21, *Beatrice di Tenda* (Bellini)
         March 28, *Il Furioso* (Verdi)
         December 13, *William Tell*
         December 31, *Norma*
         January 24, *Lucia di Lammermoor*
1843, February 9, *La Favorita*
         March 7, *La Fille du Regiment*
1844, February 13, *La Juive*
         April 25, *La Favorita*
         April 27, *Lucrezia Borgia*
         La Reine de Chypre [Halévy]
1845, March 3, *I Puritani* (in Italian)
         March 10, *Belisario* (in Italian once)
1846, February 5, *Der Freischütz*
         March 24, *Les Martyrs*
         Les Mousquetaires de la Reine (Halévy)
1847, *Charles VI* (Halévy)
1848, January, *Ne Touches pas à la Reine* [Baissleot][225]

[225] Fischer, *op. cit.* In 1846-7 opera was regularly reviewed in the *Revue Louisianaise,* the advertisements of which also give considerable information.

Opera began at six-thirty and lasted until eleven or twelve. The crowded condition of the streets led to duels among the patrons and the accessibility of gambling dens sometimes caused the disappearance of escorts, nor was the scenery all that our modern taste might desire. Yet French opera in New Orleans was then, as it was after the building of the French Opera House in 1859, a brilliant affair which drew the attention of the country.

The rise of "grand" opera in the United States, aside from New Orleans, is definitely associated with the French and Italian schools. Thus in New York in 1810 one finds that Paisiello's *Barbiere di Seviglia* was given, and that opera seasons more or less regularly followed. The first great opera company was the troupe of Manuel Garcia, which began a New York engagement November 29, 1825, with the *Barber of Seville*. They remained in the city until September 30, 1826, offering 79 performances, a truly remarkable record.[226] The orchestra of twenty-five was under the direction of a Frenchman, de Luce.[227]

The artists of the New Orleans opera often paused on their way to or from the Crescent City to give operatic performances in New York or Philadelphia, as various records exist to show. Thus they opened a summer season July 13, 1827, at the Park Theatre in New York with Nicolo's *Cendrillon*, the repertory including *Les Deux Journées* of Cherubini, *Joconde* by Nicolo, *Ma Tante Aurore* by Boieldieu, *La Dame Blanche* by Boieldieu, *Le Calife de Bagdad* (one act) by Boieldieu, *Le Maçon* by Auber, *Le Petit Chaperon Rouge* by Boieldieu, *Aline, Reine de Golconde* by Berton(?), etc.[227a] The same company played in the Chestnut Street Theatre in Philadelphia in 1827, 1828, 1831, 1833, and other years, nor did they fail to return to New York. Thus in 1833 they gave in the Park Theater Auber's *Le Philtre* and his *La Fiancée*, Hérold's *Zampa*, Rossini's *Le Comte Ory*, Castil-Blaze's *Les Folies Amoureuses* and so on.[227b] In 1843 the New Orleans company with Mlle. Calvé as

[226] Elton, p. 101. See Russo, *Lorenzo da Ponte,* chap. vii, on the absence of critical standards in the audience. On the first production see also Pray, *Memoirs of James Gordon Bennett and His Times,* p. 63. On the whole subject see Mattfeld, *A Hundred Years of Grand Opera in New York, 1825-1925.*

[227] Brown, *History of the New York,* I, 30.

[227a] Mattfeld, pp. 24-25.

[227b] Mattfeld, p. 30; Scharf and Westcott, *History of Philadelphia,* II, 1080.

their bright particular star (an earlier Calvé than the famous Carmen) played from May to October in Niblo's Gardens, offering *Lucia di Lammermoor, Gemma di Vergy, Anna Boleyn, La Fille du Régiment,* all by Donizetti, Auber's *Le Domino Noir,* Halévy's *L'Éclair,* Hérold's *Le Pré aux Clercs,* Adam's *Le Châlet,* Auber's *Les Diamants de la Couronne,* and his *L'Ambassadrice* among others.[228] Libretti indicate that *La Reine de Chypre* by Halévy was produced at Niblo's Garden in New York in 1845; and that *Esmeralda, ou Notre Dame de Paris,* a dramatic ballet pantomime was first performed in New York at the Park Theater September 1, 1848. But from 1825 to 1832 New York had mainly to depend upon amateur performances of opera in which French residents took an important share, singing operas like *Jean de Paris* and *Le Calife de Bagdad,* often in mutilated versions. The French and Italian schools were both popular; the question from 1832 to 1848 was mainly whether a company should call itself one or the other. Through the efforts of Lorenzo da Ponte, librettist to Mozart, who died in New York in 1838, the city boasted an opera house in 1833, but it proved to be a financial white elephant, and when it burned in 1839 a long warfare between opera in a foreign language and opera in English was temporarily suspended. In 1829 a wandering French opera company visited Boston.[229] Whether in opera troupes or alone, the tradition of the French professional musician is an important one for the period.[230] The magazines printed articles on the Parisian opera[231] and on French methods for cultivating the voice.[232] American musical critics sometimes took occasion to

[228] Mattfeld, p. 35.

[229] Elson, p. 107.

[230] Thus in Baltimore in 1824 Lafayette heard a "music mass . . . delightfully sung by Baltimore ladies, under the direction of Mr. Gilles, an accomplished professor, who has diffused a taste for music in the city for several years, and has instructed numerous distinguished pupils." Levasseur, *Lafayette in America,* I, 161-2. American bands welcomed him with *La Marseillaise* and *Où peut-être mieux qu'au sein de sa famille.* In 1833, Hamilton, coming to America, found on board the boat Master Burke, "the Irish Roscius" and his French music master. *Men and Manners in America,* I, 5. M. Maillard was pianist for the Vauxhall Gardens in New York (July, 1845). Brown, *History of the New York Stage,* I, 174.

[231] *American Monthly Magazine,* n.s., IV, 443-450 on the Théâtre aux Italiens; *American Quarterly Review,* XI, 30-66 on opera in France. (The French are "destitute of a sensibility to tune and time"!); *Democratic Review,* IX, 417-22, on French opera: *Boston Quarterly Review,* III, 332-7 on Otis's *Biographie Universelle des Musiciens,* etc.

[232] *Christian Examiner,* September, 1841, pp. 83-90, review of *Methode de Vocalisation* by Auguste Panseron of the Conservatory, is an example.

defend French orchestral music against the claims of other nationalities.[233] Certain moral qualms were felt against French theatricalism, to be sure,[234] yet by the end of our period there was a long list of foreign musicians resident in America, among whom the French were prominent, and French and Italian operas were being patronized by the chief metropolises.[235] Then as now opera carried with it a sense of the exotic and of social distinction,[236] and in this attitude French artists and French works of art necessarily shared.

7. THE FRENCH THEATER IN AMERICA

Some glimpse of the French drama in the United States has been given in the foregoing section. American introduction to French drama was either in the printed book, French or English, or in such occasional British versions of Molière and the tragic writers as may have been produced in America.[237] We find *The Orphan of China* being produced in Charleston in 1765, and *The Oracle,* translated from the French by Mrs. Cibber, in 1766.[238] Aside from New Orleans the great focus of French theatrical influence in the eighteenth century was Charleston.[239]

In Charleston the "American" theater had occasionally produced French pieces in translation before 1794,[240] and there

---

[233] *American Quarterly Review,* March 1830, reviews a work entitled *Music in Germany,* in which the writer defends French instrumental music from censure as being superior to the English and to "almost all the European nations." P. 222.

[234] "There are two theatres at Boston, not differing much in the interior from the smaller British theatres, very well filled while we were there owing to some British and French performers of eminence, especially as *dancers,* who were loudly applauded by the puritans of New England, although the French *danseuses* se(e)med to me *saltare elegantius quam necesse est probae.* The more *outré* the dancing, the more applause." Stuart, *Three Years in North America,* I, 304.

[235] Schouler, *History* V, 430-1.

[236] "Me han dicho, que el gusto de los Américanos no está decidido en favor de la ópera," wrote Ramon de la Sagra in 1835. *Cinco Meses en los Estados-Unidos.* Opera was almost wholly the plaything of the leisure class. "They do not dislike the ballet (in Philadelphia), but they have no enthusiasm for its extravagances." Mackay, *Western World,* I, 144.

[237] To be treated in a subsequent study.

[238] Willis, *The Charleston Stage,* pp. 44, 52.

[239] The Charleston stage of the period is exhaustively studied in Willis.

[240] The Charleston Theater was erected by Bignall and West in 1792; the Church Street Theater in 1786; in the nineties the latter was managed by Mr. Solee, a Frenchman. Hornblow, *A History of the American Theatre,* I, 236. Party feeling ran high by 1793. At the Charleston Theater, after the

Frenchmen had been influential in the theater.[241] After the influx of the émigrés the French Theatre was opened in Solee's Hall with an excellent company of comedians, pantomimists, and rope-dancers. Rivalry between the French house and the established American company continued until the end of the season when the French forces, including the Placide family (who later went to New York), went over to the American forces under Bignall and West.[242] Performances of course were in French, and the *Mahomet* of Voltaire (staged, however, at the Charleston Theatre, December 20, 1794) is said to be the first French tragedy performed in America.[243] French themes,[244] adaptations of French plays,[245] and French actors and performers, as well as scene painters and designers, continued to color theatrical life in Charleston throughout the nineties. Thence the French actors dispersed over the country. Thus, by 1796 Miss Sully and Mrs. Val had gone to the American Company in New York; Mrs. Villiers, to Boston; and the old American Company had engaged Francisquy and others to give ballets and pantomines in New York and Philadelphia.[246] The Placides of course became famous.

production of "the celebrated comic opera," *The Surrender of Calais, or Gallic Heroism,* written by George Colman, jun., Esqu., and the Music by Dr. Arnold, Mr. Bignall was compelled to insert an advertisement in the local paper to the effect that as some had thought the opera reflected on Englishmen or Frenchmen, he believed that "it breathes only sentiments of pure heroism, genuine patriotism, and refined humanity equally on the part of the British as on that of the French nation." Willis, p. 174.

[241] In 1793 the name of Mons Odin (Audin) commences to appear in the playbills cited in Willis. He and his son were scene painters. He apparently trained a corps of assistants; at any rate the Audins were succeeded by Mr. Schultz, who had been his subordinate.

[242] Willis, chap. x.

[243] *Ibid.,* p. 281.

[244] *The 14th. of July, 1789, or the Destruction of the Bastille,* produced about November, 1794, with remarkable scenic effects; *America Preserved, or the Americans and French at the Siege of Yorktown,* written by the Rev. Mr. Coste, produced in May, 1795; *Louis XVI, or the Dawn of Freedom,* produced in February, 1795; *First Love; or, the French Emigrant,* produced in March, 1798, are typical instances. Willis, pp. 263, 277-8, 395, 397. *Louis XVI* was taken on tour, as appears from an advertisement in the *Wilmington Gazette* of March 2, 1797. When *The Old Soldier* was played in the French Theater May 8, 1795, the management requested all the citizens to join in singing the Marseillaise, which they did with tremendous enthusiasm, the small boys beating tattoos in time to the music, says a contemporary. P. 243.

[245] Mrs. Inchbald's "celebrated comedy" of the *Child of Nature,* from the *Zébé* of the late Countess of Genlis, was produced January 27, 1794; Aaron Hill's (?) *Zara,* an adaptation of *Zaïre* by Voltaire, January 10, 1795; the *Barbier de Seville,* translated by Mr. Williamson as *The Spanish Barber,* February 1, 1798. *Ibid.,* pp. 194, 272, 380, 397.

[246] Willis, p. 320.

In New York, meanwhile, American interest in the French Revolution commenced to take form on the stage: when, for example, Hodgkinson appeared on the scene as Captain Flash, wearing a British uniform, the play was interrupted by the tumult of the anti-British audience, until he explained that he was impersonating a coward and a bully.[247] As a consequence of this enthusiasm William Dunlap commenced to turn his attention to the translation and adaptation of plays from the French which would supplant the previous interest in German melodrama. He adapted eight French plays from 1797 to 1828, two melodramas, one *The Voice of Nature,* and the other *The Wife of Two Husbands,* being most successful. However, *The Widow of Malabar, or The Tyranny of Custom* as adapted by David Humphreys and played at the Southwark Theater in Philadelphia, May 7, 1790, seems to have the distinction of being the first adaptation from the French.[247a] Following Dunlap, John Howard Payne made over some twelve French plays. He was followed by Richard Penn Smith, of whose twenty plays, ten, it is said, are from the French, many of them being melodramas.[248] By the end of our period the adaptation of French plays had become a regular industry in America as well as in Great Britain.[249] The French Revolution, moreover, offered occasion for American playwrights to write original themes on French subjects or related ones.[250] Cosmopolitan New York attracted various French actors and theatrical people: Mrs. Val and the Placides, as we have seen; and on July 19, 1800, Joseph Corré (Corrie), formerly chef to a British army officer, opened the first summer theater in New York, called Mt. Vernon Garden, where entertainments were given Mondays, Wed-

---

[247] Schoenberger, *American Adaptations of French Plays,* pp. 8-9.
[247a] The "Prologue to the widow of Malabar, or, The Tyranny of custom: A Tragedy. Imitated from the French of M. le Mierre. Spoken by Mr. Hallam," appears in the *American Museum,* VIII, Appendix, 38-39 (1790); and the Epilogue in Vol. IX, Appendix, 37-38.
[248] See Schoenberger's monograph for the details.
[249] See Quinn in the *Cambridge History of American Literature,* I, book II, chap. ii; Hornblow, I, 181; Dunlap, *History of the American Theatre,* pp. 65, 105 ff., 163.
[250] For instance John D. Burke published *Female Patriotism, or the Death of Joan of Arc* in 1798. Faÿ, pp. 308-9; Kellogg, *Life and Works of John Davis,* pp. 101-2. Saint-Méry describes a play in 1795 in New York on the taking of the Bastille, supposed by the ignorant to be the work of Madame de Staël. *Voyages,* pp. 267-269. This may be the same play as that produced in Charleston in 1794.

nesdays, and Fridays.[251] A French company in Philadelphia played varieties and vaudevilles in the South Street Theater in 1807, afterwards removing to Sicard's ball-room.[252] In 1833 the New Orleans company was giving French plays in New York in the summer;[253] they also appeared in Philadelphia.[254] At Harvard they even gave selections from Molière at commencement.[255] French influence even penetrated to the frontier.[256]

New Orleans was of course a great center for French play-giving.[257] In that city both American and French theaters existed side by side. Of the French playhouses we have already heard. N. M. Ludlow brought a company to New Orleans to present English drama in the St. Phillippe in 1817; half the audience did not understand English, but the season is said to have been a success. Then came John Davis at the Orleans; and in 1820 James H. Caldwell opened at the St. Philip with an English-speaking company. The Camp Street theater, the first American playhouse in the city, was opened January 1, 1824; it is said to have been the first building to be illuminated by gas. In 1835 Caldwell built the St. Charles, a house famous for its luxurious furnishings. Playbills in the Schwartz library indicate that performances at the Camp Street Theater were not, however, exclusively "American": for example, on May 2, 1829, a play in French was given for the benefit of Celeste, in which Booth played the part of a mute; the previous April Celeste, Constance, and Mlle. Placide had benefits; and there are occasional French plays in English versions. Playbills for the

---

[251] Hornblow, I, 258-9; Brown, *History of the New York Stage*, I, 70; Dunlap thought that Corré was a better business man than he (Dunlap) was.
[252] Scharf and Westcott, *History of Philadelphia*, II, 969. Some of the pieces were *Le Directeur dans l'Embarras, L'Avocat Pathelin* (by Palaprat), *On fait ce qu'on peut et non pas ce qu'on veut, Heureusement,* and *Le Sourd, ou l'auberge pleine.*
[253] Boardman saw them in that year. *America and the Americans,* p. 81.
[254] Power (*Impressions of America*, I, 87) saw them at the Chestnut Theater. He saw at the Park Theater in New York an "American actor called Placide, descended of a long line of excellent players," who was admirable in old men's parts (1833), I, 65.
[255] Mrs. Anne Royall, *Sketches,* p. 353. This was in 1824 or 1825. *The Imaginary Invalid* was performed in Philadelphia in 1813. Scharf and Westcott, *op. cit.,* II, 957-8.
[256] The *Jodolet* of Corneille was translated by René Paul, a St. Louis merchant. Fielding's translation of Molière's *The Mock Doctor* was performed, as was *La Tour de Nesle,* in various frontier towns. See Rusk, I, 418-425.
[257] See the references on New Orleans opera given above; and Hornblow, *History of the Theatre in America,* I, 399, 340-342.

St. Charles indicate much the same sort of thing: *The Marriage of Figaro* was given December 3, 1835; *John of Paris* on December 5; *The French Spy* (with Mlle. Celeste) on December 14 and December 18, the same lady being featured in programs during the latter part of December. It is interesting to note that a performance of *Hamlet* on December 21, 1835, included, besides the inevitable farce, selections from a French overture. The author of *The Americans as They Are* (to return to the Camp for a minute) reports that a rough audience frequented the American theater; at the French theater he saw Corneille, Racine, and the French classics, but unfortunately the playbills for the French theater are not preserved in anything like the quantities of American playbills.[258] But the influence of French drama upon the American theater still awaits its historian; these scattering references indicate, however, that this influence must have been varied and extensive.[259]

[258] The French company sometimes produced French plays in New York. A playbill in the Schwartz collection announces a performance of *Andromaque* at the Park Theatre, September 18, 1827, accompanied by Méhul's opera, *Une Folie*. Pray tells us that "the French ballet was illustrated by Hutin, Achille, and Celeste" in New York at that time. *Memoirs of James Gordon Bennett and His Times,* p. 88.

[259] For instance, *Napoleon Bonaparte* was played at the Park Theater in New York December 15, 1831 (Dumas's spectacle drama?); *The French Spy* was a vehicle for Mrs. Carrie Lewis in 1835; *Don Caesar de Bazan* by Dumanoir and Dennery was first seen in America December 16, 1844, at the Park Theater and simultaneously at the Bowery; *The Battle of Waterloo,* introducing fifty horses, two hundred supers clothed in new and handsome uniforms, cannons, artillery, baggage-wagons, and moving magazines, a spectacle which had had a great run in London, was staged at the Bowery in 1840 with Charles Mason as Napoleon; *The Exile and Death of Napoleon the Great* was produced for Mason's benefit December 21, 1841; *The Mysteries of Paris,* October 27, 1843; *The Bohemians of Paris* was produced September 4, 1848, and *The Destruction of the Bastille* September 11, 1848; *Robert Macaire* was produced at the National May, 1839, and at Mitchell's Olympic December 30, 1839, etc. Brown, *History of the New York Stage,* I. 41, 63, 119, 120, 121, 248, etc. These are entries in an old history of the New York stage chosen almost at random. The subject of the character and amount of French adaptation on the American stage should furnish material for two or three monographs.

X

The Influence of French Religion

Upon my arrival in the United States," wrote de Tocqueville, "the religious aspect of the country was the first thing that struck my attention; and the longer I stayed there the more did I perceive the great political consequences resulting from this state of things, to which I was unaccustomed."[1] In this passage is the epitome of two civilizations: the Latin, accustomed to keep his religion in one department, his practical endeavors in another; the American, in theory at least desirous of mixing the two; and here also is the astonishment of the Latin at the result of the mixture. Clearly, in any study of American culture, the place which religion occupies is an important one. It colors our social life, our education, our philosophy, our politics, our diplomacy. And yet it is surprising how little attention the absorbing subject of American religion has received. It has been left almost wholly to professional sectarian historians. In such a work as Tyler's *History of American Literature, 1607-1765,* religious literature, it is true, necessarily occupies most of the space; and yet, in general treatises on our national culture, in histories of American thought, of American literature, even of American social movements, it can not be said that the religious element has been properly studied or properly appreciated. Latterly, of course, cultural pronouncements have been hostile to the assumed qualities of Puritanism, but perhaps Puritanism is not so characteristic of our religious life as the great evangelical denominations such as the Baptists, the Methodists, the Presbyterians, with their peculiar history and their peculiar social effectiveness. We can not hope in this brief essay to do more than indicate the situation; and yet, in dealing with a culture overwhelmingly Protestant as it draws from a culture overwhelmingly Catholic, the religious issue can not be ignored. Indeed, religious prejudice colors a large part of the picture of Frenchmen and their ways of thought in the period under survey.

[1] *Democracy in America* I, 331.

1. THE COSMOPOLITAN SPIRIT OF THE AMERICAN RELIGIOUS
   COLONIES LEADS TO AN INTEREST IN FRENCH
   THEOLOGICAL LITERATURE

The popular conception of the early colonists in North America—Puritan, Pilgrim, Huguenot, Quaker, Moravian, Roman Catholic—is that of peoples fleeing from a hostile Europe in order to set up in the new world religious customs satisfactory to themselves. The error in the popular view is not that the facts are wrong but that the interpretation is one-sided. I have already hinted that the seventeenth century colonies partake, by the very fact that they were fleeing from persecution, and afterwards themselves persecuting others, of the cosmopolitan spirit of their times. They came, most of them, not with enthusiasm but with reluctance; the new world was less a refuge than a last resource. The Huguenot preferred the Low Countries or England so long as he could stay there;[2] the Puritan fled to Holland first and to America afterwards. And having fled, it was their business in many instances to keep up their European connexions, to pretend that they were still in Europe, and to participate in the stream of European controversy as far as might be. Read in the textbooks the system of New England Calvinism: it is a complete body of thought, it has its ontology, its cosmology, its epistemology, its psychology.[3] It is not, like Mormonism, the eccentric product of isolation. It belongs in short to the same trend, the same century, which gave birth to the systems of Spinoza and Descartes, of Leibnitz and Gassendi; and the debate on free will and determinism, on revelation and reason, on the substance of God and the nature of man, is but extended to America. Look at the vast bibliographies of controversial works compiled by the New England ministers—they are not intended for home consumption alone, they are directed at an international audience, and in such writers as Jonathan Edwards[4] and Sam-

---

[2] With respect to the Huguenots it must not be forgotten that despite occasional outbursts of generosity, under the Stuarts London was full of French police spies seeking to hound them out; nor that the pro-Catholic James II was not the monarch to attract French Protestants, in view of the close relations between the Bourbons and the Stuart kings.

[3] See Riley, *American Philosophy: the Early Schools*, pp. 38 ff. "Especially in Massachusetts Bay they established an ecclesiastico-political regime, recalling in many of its features the Genevan system of John Calvin." Merriam, *History of American Political Theories*, p. 5.

[4] Who "seems to have anticipated Berkeley, rather than have been influenced by him." Tyler, *op. cit.*, II, 183, note.

uel Johnson, the friend of Berkeley, America does not so much repay its debt to Europe as take its place in the cosmopolitan movement. Or look at the libraries of these divines; they are an epitome of European knowledge; the same ill-digested quartos, the same dusty and unreadable controversialists furnish the spiritual food of thinkers on both sides of the Atlantic. Are they mainly polemic theologians? The seventeenth century is the great century of theological polemics.

Necessarily the theocratic colonies were the heirs of the intellectual tradition of Great Britain. In that tradition in theology there was a marked anti-papal strain. Since our interest is in things French, we note therefore that the Americans were the heirs of that fierce detestation of all things papistical which, in this country, led to their fear of the pope, their dark suspicion of the Jesuit, and their distrust of the Huguenot in time of war as a possible spy of that wily tool of the church; and this is a dominant note in their attitude toward things French until the American Revolution. Indeed, there is no more remarkable intellectual revolution in American history than the *volte-face* not merely toward the French but towards the Catholics wrought in that struggle. But of this more in a moment.

If the theocratic colonies were the heirs of an anti-French tradition of one type, they were also heirs of a pro-French interest of another order. We must remember that in France and Switzerland in the seventeenth century, and earlier, there is a rich body of French Protestant literature extremely interesting to Englishmen, and often available to them. As a careful student has remarked:

The greatest documents of the Protestant faith—sermons, commentaries, and argumentative treatises—were in great demand in English versions, and the most familiar piece of literature in England for a time was Joshua Sylvester's translation of the French epic of Protestantism, the *Semaines* of Du Bartas.[5] In the first three decades of Elizabeth's reign more than twenty separate translations from John Calvin were offered to the English public. During the years that followed, an almost equal popularity was extended to the writings of Pierre Viret, Théodore de Bèze, John de l'Espine, Odet de la Noue, Duplessis-Mornay, and Pierre du Moulin.[6]

[5] English version in 1598.
[6] Upham, *French Influence in English Literature*, pp. 11-12; see his chap. iv on Du Bartas in English.

It is often works by these authors and by others like them that are found in seventeenth century American libraries.[7]

In fact, Puritanism, wrongly regarded as a unique American institution, is rather a part of the Renaissance. What are the grand debates of the Renaissance—what is its intellectual life? Is it not the question whether human nature can be trusted, whether it is so weak that man must seek out Divine Grace, or whether it is competent by the exercise of reason, divinely implanted in the human frame, to achieve perfection by free will?

François Rabelais and Jean Calvin are respectively the positive and negative poles of the Renaissance. Drawing alike their inspiration from the newly discovered classics, with an equal opposition to mediaeval pedantry, they yet represent the parting of the ways in their conflicting ideals: Rabelais the exuberant apostle of freedom, and Calvin, the rigid disciplinarian. To the one, human nature appeared essentially healthy and hence trustworthy; to the other it appeared totally depraved and therefore in pressing need of renewed contact with the Deity.[8]

Well, this debate is but transferred to New England, and the same books are read on this side of the Atlantic as are read in Europe,—including Rabelais and Calvin. The famous controversy over the Half-Way Covenant in the New England Synod of 1662,[9] is a debate over the same question: shall a man be a church member without any verifiable religious experience—i.e., a man in some sense self-sufficient, one who does not flee from the corruption of this world to Divine Grace, alone sufficient to save sinners? Man's free mind is as much an

[7] Rather than spot the page with footnote references, let me say that for books and their owners mentioned in the following discussion I have consulted the lists of books in Wright, *Literary Culture in Early New England;* Weeden, *Economic and Social History of New England, 1620-1789;* Weeden, "Ideal Newport in the Eighteenth Century," *Proceedings of the American Antiquarian Society,* XVIII, pp. 112 ff; Marsden, R. G., "A Virginian Minister's Library, 1635," *The American Historical Review,* XI, 328-332; Dexter, "Early Private Libraries in New England," *Proceedings of the American Antiquarian Society,* XVIII (n.s.), 135-147; the list of books belonging to William Brewster in *Proceedings of the Massachusetts Historical Society,* second series, V, 37-85; Ford, *The Boston Book Market, 1679-1700;* Tuttle, "Libraries of the Mathers," *Proceedings of the American Antiquarian Society,* XX, 279-290; the list of Harvard College Library duplicates in *Publications of the Colonial Society of Massachusetts,* XVIII, 407-417; the list of books belonging to John Harvard in *Proceedings of the American Antiquarian Society,* II, 296-356; the list of books belonging to William Byrd in his *Writings* edited by Bassett; Winsor, *The Prince Library;* Herrick, "The Early New-Englanders: What Did They Read?" *The Library,* IX, 1-17; Farnham, *A Glance at Private Libraries.*

[8] Nitze and Dargan, *A History of French Literature,* p. 145.

[9] See Murdock, *Increase Mather,* pp. 80 ff.

issue at Harvard College as it is at Port-Royal or the Sorbonne; and the triangular quarrel among Jansenist, Jesuit, and Calvinist on the Continent, is, if one may trust the library lists, eagerly followed in America. In fact, the Reformation is the basis of New England life, and the Reformation continued in the seventeenth century its activities against Louis XIV and the Catholics as in earlier ages it had fought the Medici and the League.

There is, for instance, the question of theology, dry and dusty to us now, debating the eternal question of free will and determinism, pessimism and optimism, man's inherent powers, and life's inherent depravity. And in this discussion New England thought was profoundly indebted to French and Genevan writers. To begin with, we must see that even Calvinism was a liberating influence. Henry Osborne Taylor speaks, I think rightly, of

this new religious scholarship [which] would pierce the once living spells of mediaeval symbolism, custom, and tradition, to the sure records of the pristine Faith, read them with fresh eyes, and re-interpret them according to their evident meaning, rather than follow traditional acceptances. The final systematized and ordered culmination of the Reform, [he continues] which came through Calvin, represents still further intellectual or logical advance.[10]

The essence of Calvin's teaching is individual judgment, exercised under wise supervision, and directed toward a knowledge of God and of ourselves; and as such, Calvin's true doctrine must in time disintegrate Calvinism, must in time liberate the individual judgment and lead on to democracy. Calvin's constitution for Geneva[11] is a model of the theocratic state, a model admired in New England, and the charter of Calvinism, the great *Institution de la religion chrétienne,* published in Latin in 1536, in French in 1541, is found in Latin, in French, in English—in Dutch even—in every colonial library of any importance in the seventeenth century. John Cotton esteemed Calvin "to be greater than all the fathers and all the schoolmen" and "was accustomed to read in him last of all every evening,"[12] and his opinion is the opinion of New England. In fact, Calvinism is so profoundly stamped upon the New World that the most powerful philosopher of the early

[10] Taylor, *Thought and Expression in the Sixteenth Century,* I, 388.
[11] There is a brief summary in Taylor, I, 398-400.
[12] Tyler, *History of American Literature, 1607-1616,* I, 214.

period can do little more than re-write Calvin on the freedom of the will.[13]

But even the *Institut* is not enough. There is beside Calvin a host of warriors in New England libraries ready to spring to the defence of the new religion. For example, there is the great Théodore de Bèze (1519-1605), who taught Greek at Lausanne, who attacked Servetus and Castallion in a tract justifying the civil magistrates in punishing heretics, whose textual discussion of the Old and New Testaments was part of the equipment of every protestant minister, whose *L'Histoire ecclésiastique des églises réformées au royaume de France*. published in 1580, is a great apology for the Huguenots—his works are spread from New England to Virginia, from the library of William Brewster who owned Beza's *Discourse of the true visible marks of the Catholique Church,* translated by T. Wilcox, London, 1622, to the library of the great Colonel Byrd who owned Beza's Greek and Latin testaments. There is Jean Claude (1619-1687), the most celebrated protestant pastor of his time, who fought with the great Arnaud and with Nicole and who, according to Bayle, carried off the honors in the eucharistic controversy: Cotton Mather knows him and quotes him. There is the great jurisconsult and protestant theologian Lambert Daneau (1530-1595), author of sixty works, including one on witchcraft and one against dice-playing and card-playing and another against dancing: John Harvard had four of his works in Latin. There is the famous Pierre Dumoulin, 1568-1658, the terror of the Jesuits who called him "erit mundo lupus" in an anagram: both the Prince and the Harvard libraries possessed some of his great controversial writings. There is Philip du Plessis-Mornay (d. 1549), that famous scholar and polemical writer who escaped from the Massacre of Saint-Bartholomew by a miracle, a man whom Sir Philip Sidney admired: William Brewster read his *Of the trewnesse of Christian religion* as translated by Sidney—the fourth edition, if you please, published in London in 1617, not to speak of *A Notable Treatise of the Church,* published in London in 1606. Alas, time has forgotten the mighty Pierre Jurieu, (1637-1713), who held his own against Bossuet, an ardent defender of political liberty who, under Louis XIV, dared to advocate the sovereignty of the people; but his con-

[13] Becelaere remarks in *La Philosophie en Amérique*, p. 43, that Jonathan Edwards' *Essay on the Freedom of the Will* is only "a re-edition of the doctrines of Calvin."

temporaries did not forget him, even in New England: Cotton Mather quotes his *Traité de l'unité de l'église,* and his books were found in the Prince Library. Indeed, there are how many more!—Pierre Viret, the Vaudois reformer and the friend of Calvin who converted 8,000 to protestantism at Nismes—William Brewster read him; Daniel Chamier, whose articles of the reformed churches of France were in the Prince Library; L. Dupont; R. Estienne, whose *Latin Thesaurus* still is famous, but whose *Exposition sur S. Matthieu* attracted the Puritans; Antoine de la Fay, whom John Harvard bought; Isaac d'Huisseau; N. Jannot; François (Franz) Lambert; Bénédict Pictet; Josué La Placette; Pierre Poiret; André Rivet; Bénédict Turretin—or was it his son, François Turretin, who died in 1687 that the Mather family admired? Alas, they are names now to be looked up in histories of theology and encyclopaedias, but in seventeenth century New England these French theologians were exciting to read. Clearly here is the first great intellectual impact of French thinking upon the New World—this great system of protestant thought as framed by French thinkers into the doctrine of Geneva.

We must not think that the New England divines confined their reading to but one side of the great controversies of the age. On the contrary they often had in their libraries the books of their ablest Catholic opponents, the books of Jesuit and Jansenist no less than of Huguenot and of mystic. That great Catholic controversialist, Cardinal Bellarmine, whose blows, dealt from the chair of controversies in the Roman College, seriously injured protestantism, against whom special chairs had to be founded in protestant colleges that proper reply might be made—he who revised the Vulgate and tactfully corrected the errors of Sextus V, he who upheld papal authority as no other Jesuit quite did, he, too, was known in New England: John Harvard had his *de faelicitate* (sic) *sanctoru,* and several other works; Samuel Sewall bought two volumes of his polemical works; Cotton Mather quoted him; and in 1682 Harvard College listed him among its duplicates. François Bourgoing, (1585-1662), one of the founders of the congregation of the oratory, who joined in the quarrel over the sacraments, has a work in the Prince library. Cornelius à Lapide (Corneille de la Pierre, or von der Stein), (1568-1637), a Catholic exegete of great importance, was widely known in New England: Harvard, for example, possessed his *Opera* in eight volumes.

Fénelon was widely distributed throughout the seventeenth and eighteenth centuries—indeed, he was regularly reprinted in French or in translation throughout our whole period; and even such minor figures as that unscrupulous pamphleteer François Feuardent (1539-1610) and Henri-Louis Chasteignier de La Rocheposay, an able anti-Calvinist, were read, besides what others not now to be identified we know not.

If such were the Catholic authors, so, too, the Jansenists were not forgotten. The great Antoine Arnauld or Arnaud, (1612-1694), the apostle, the theologian, the polemicist of Jansenism, was studied in the New World. When in 1662 the quarrel over the Half-Way Covenant occurred in New England, did no one consult *La fréquent communion,* designed to explode the Jesuit doctrine that the more one feels he is denuded of grace, the more frequently he should take communion? It does not seem quite credible, since in 1670 interest was still keen enough for Henry Oldenburg to send John Winthrop "a small discourse . . . against yt great Sorbonist, Monsr Arnaud, touching ye Perpetuity of ye Romish Faith about the Eucharist." He it was who, with Nicole, wrote the *Port-Royal Logic* in 1662, a book sufficiently widespread in America to fall into the hands of Franklin in 1722, with whom it served, together with Locke, to convince him of the futility of philosophy.[14] As for Pascal, John Winthrop Junior had *Les Provinciales* in 12mo. in his library, and there are other traces in New England, even in Virginia, that the greatest of the Jansenists was read in America. Pierre Nicole, the friend and supporter of Arnaud, the "true heir of Pascal,"—he, too, was not unknown; and as for Jean Bodin, 1530-1596, he who approved religious toleration, thought the state should be operated as a family is run, who believed that the supremacy of the state is based on divine will, but who was sufficiently ahead of his time to see the effect of climate and environment on society, whatever he might believe about witches, him the Mathers quoted, and William Brewster had his *The six Bookes of a Commonweale* in R. Knolles' London translation of 1606.

It is true that we do not know always what book was in any given library;[15] and even when we do know, we can not, with-

---

[14] Jones, *Early American Philosophers,* p. 12.
[15] Sometimes it is impossible without more research than our study warrants to identify an author. For instance, I have not been able to locate G. Barjac, *Introductio in artem jesuiticam.* Geneva, MDXCIX, in the Prince Library. Often there is only a name to go on, as Bovet, Carion, A. Chau-

out more research than is appropriate to our present study, estimate precisely what effect the author's thought may have had upon the mind of his reader. Nevertheless, we must remember that in the sixteenth and seventeenth centuries, France was the great center of protestant theology outside of England; that Germany had, for one reason or another, declined in importance; and that in the sixteenth century, French protestant thinking was probably much more important than English. Accordingly it is fundamental to our study to realize that the theology of France, as it presented itself to New England readers in the seventeenth century, painted a picture of a France wherein Protestantism was not safe; on the one hand, Saint Bartholomew, and on the other the Revocation of the Edict of Nantes; and everywhere the Jesuit and the Jansenist. What wonder therefore that Huguenots were welcomed as refugees from an iniquitous situation; or what further wonder, when war broke out, that even Huguenots fell under suspicion, and that Acadians, simple and harmless as they seemed, were viewed with dark disfavor in an America overwhelmingly protestant, and overwhelmingly convinced by New England divine, Episcopalian controversialist, and military propaganda, that France was the home of Romanism and Satan? We shall not understand the American picture of France until we have looked into the libraries of the New England divines in these early years.

Even the remarkable richness of French theological works in seventeenth century American libraries in Massachusetts does not represent the whole of the story. Not merely theology, but philosophy is represented. Ramus (1515-1572), beginning with his master's thesis in 1536, *Quaecumque ob Aristotele dicta essent, commentitia esse,* led the attack upon the scholastic Aristotelianism which the Renaissance was to overthrow; and his *Aristotelicae animadversiones* of 1543, banned by the Sorbonne, accuses Aristotle of sophistry in reasoning. To Ramus

mette, Cluin, F. Gorgres (somehow this last fascinates me). Sometimes there are two or more writers by one name. Is J. de Laet Jean or Jacques de Laet? Usually in the lists at my disposal only some such entry as "Lavater de spectris" is given. Even when one is able to identify the author, one does not always know what book is meant, although, considering the expense of importation and the cost and scarcity of books, it would seem that only important controversial works would tend to get transported to New England. Nevertheless, even when one allows for all this multiple possibility of error, one is astonished at the amount of reading which must have been done in French theology and philosophy in seventeenth century New England.

man was equipped with the faculty of reason; logic was but the precepts for the right employment of reason, and in his elementary logic of 1543, the *Dialecticae partiones,* he tried to substitute for traditional scholastic rules, a deductive system of reasoning, based upon the practice of the classic philosophers. Ramus is like Calvin essentially of the Renaissance; essentially one who believed in the inherent worth of the individual; and Ramus was part of the intellectual food of the Puritans.[16] Most of the great Puritan thinkers owned one or another of his works. When Increase Mather presented a thesis for the B.A. degree at Harvard, August 12, 1656, Cotton Mather tells us that the president (Charles Chauncy) "upon a Dislike of the *Ramaean* Strains in which our Young Disputant was carrying on his Thesis, would have cut him Short, but Mr. *Mitchel* Publickly Interposed, *Pergat Quaeso, Nam doctissime disputat.*"[17] Richard Mather had been early impressed by Ramus as one who freed men's minds from the yoke of authority; Michael Wigglesworth studied him and fell "under the spell of the 'Ramoean' confidence in the power of reason and in the observation of human nature as the basis of philosophy";[18] copies of his works were in the Prince library and were owned by John Harvard and bought by booksellers.

After Ramus, Descartes; after the anti-Aristotelian, the disciple of Euclid. Both, whatever their differences, believe in reason; Descartes so profoundly that he sought to make philosophy as simple and rational as mathematics. Descartes likewise is known to these omnivorous readers. There are two editions of the *Meditationes* (first published in 1641) in the Prince library, as well as Legrand's *Institutio philosophiae secundum principia R. Descartes,* and an anonymous book on the same subject. The Harvard Library had the *Meditationes;* so did the Redwood Library; so did the Mathers; so did many more. The *Philosophical Principles* (an English translation) appears in the library at Westover, and so does "Des Cartes's Musick," which I take to be the *Compendium musicae* in Eng-

---

[16] "La logique qu'on suivait était celle de *Ramus,* écrivain français de l'époque de la Renaissance et victime de la Saint Barthélemy, dont l'opposition à Aristotle et la condemnation par le concile de Trente constitutaient évidemment un grand mérite aux yeux des puritains." Becelaere, *La Philosophie en Amérique,* p. 30.

[17] Quoted from the *Parentator* in Murdock, *Increase Mather,* p. 54.

[18] *Ibid.*

lish dress. Samuel Lee owns Descartes; and when William Brattle published his logic in 1734, a book written, in all probability before 1696, the title was *Compendium Logicae secundum principia D. Renati Cartesii plurumque efformatum,* and the book was used at Harvard up to 1765. It is, according to one writer, "all Des Cartes" and there are "no marks of Locke's influence" in the text—only in the notes, which were added later.[19] By and by the influence of Descartes was to be re-enforced by the influence of Malebranche, whose *Traité de la nature et de la grâce,* 1680, condemned by the Congregation of the Index, was naturally attractive to Puritans, not to speak of his various *Méditations* and the *Recherche de la vérité* of 1674-5.

But Descartes did not hold the field alone. The anti-Aristotelian philosophy of Ramus was continued by Gassendi, whose epicureanism does not seem to have frightened certain seventeenth century Americans from his writings. Gassendi, who preaches sensationalism, for whom there are no immortal atoms but immortal souls, who opposed Descartes on one hand, and mysticism on the other—this same Gassendi prepares the way for the doctrines of Locke and Berkeley and by and by Condillac. To recite the titles of his works in American libraries in the seventeenth century would be but to recapitulate the lists we have already made; sufficient is it to say that he was attractive, as much by his philosophical daring as by his scientific interests, and that much of the astronomy of seventeenth century America seems, if one can trust the evidence, to be based upon Gassendi's exposition of Copernicus and Galileo. In fact, rationalism is very much the fashion; even so unexpected a person as Jean Buridan, nominalist of the fourteenth century, has his *Quaestiones in X Libros Ethicorum Aristotelis* in the Harvard library. Increase Mather cites Cardan's *de Rerum varietate* and *de subtilitate;* and "Mountignes Assayes" are not uncommon. But we are passing beyond the realm of theology and metaphysics. Still, even Montaigne is a kind of philosopher. One thing is certain: despite the number of book lists that have perished, despite our inability to identify books and authors, the great intellectual currents of sixteenth and seventeenth century France fertilize men's minds in that strange new world which seemed like the dream of a lost Atlantis. Nathaniel Mather of Dublin, writing in 1686 of

[19] Jones, *Early American Philosophers,* p. 10. It was possible for Brattle to have seen the Port Royal Logic. P. 2. See also Becelaere, pp. 33-34.

Harvard College says, "But I perceive the Cartesian philosophy begins to obteyn in New England, & if I conjecture aright the Copernican System too."[20] "It is not to be doubted," says Becelaere, "that Edwards owed much to Malebranche, translated into English in 1694 and 1704."[21] Before his graduation from Yale in 1714 the American Samuel Johnson had been exposed to "some of the speculations and discoveries of Descartes, Boyle, Locke and Newton."[22] Clearly a certain kind of French thought was making its impression.

2. THE RISE OF DEISM, THE GROWTH OF THE SPIRIT OF TOLERANCE, AND THE INTEREST IN FRENCH CATHOLICISM IN THE EIGHTEENTH CENTURY

Protestantism, according to the argument of Bossuet, is essentially negative and therefore carries the seeds of its own destruction in its bosom. Certain it is that the dream of a pure theocratic state in the New World presently disappeared in a cloud of schism and controversy. Congregationalism began to decline as soon as the Half Way Covenant of 1662 had been reached;[23] the seeds of Unitarianism were already being sown. When Governor Bellomont at the end of the seventeenth century required Harvard College to draw up an address for a new charter for that institution, they asked for the introduction of a clause restricting the right to hold office in the college to Presbyterians and Congregationalists, so necessary was it that orthodoxy be preserved among the shifting currents of New England thought, but the Governor refused to permit the restriction to stand.[24] We can not pause to trace all these obscure quarrels, but it is interesting to note that religious people were sometimes encouraged by the translation and publication of devotional treatises from the French. For instance, they might read Guy de Bretz's *Rise, Spring, and Foundation of the Anabaptists or Rebaptized of Our Times,* 1565, translated from the French by "J.S." and published at Cambridge by M.

[20] Wright, *Literary Culture in Early New England,* p. 103.
[21] Becelaere, *La philosophie en Amérique,* p. 38, note. And see Allen, *Jonathan Edwards,* p. 348.
[22] *Cambridge History of American Literature,* I, 81. Johnson went to England about 1731, visiting Pope, Dr. Johnson, and the universities, and it is highly probable he came into contact with French thought there also.
[23] Such, at least, is the conclusion of so careful and painstaking a scholar as Murdock. *Increase Mather,* p. 83.
[24] Murdock, pp. 353-5.

Johnson in 1668.[25] Or they might read *A Letter from Father La Chaise, Confessor to the French King, to Father Peters, Confessor to the King of England; in which is contained the Project and Design of that Faction to introduce the Prince of Wales. Also a Letter from William Penn to Father La Chaise,* all "printed in the City of Philadelphia, in the Land of Promise, by order of Father Penn. 1688," in which they would be comforted to learn the unhistorical truth that Penn was a Roman Catholic, and that he was in league with the French Jesuits.[26] Then next year they could read Ezechiel Carré's *The Charitable Samaritan. A sermon on the Tenth Chapter of Luke, ver. 30-35, pronounced in the French church at Boston* and translated into English by N. Walter (Boston, 1689), from which they would be reassured that the Huguenots were not in league with the Jesuits, even though they were Frenchmen; and in 1690 they could learn to know what Jesuitism really is in Echantillon's *De la Doctrine que les Jesuites enseignent aux Sauvages du Nouveau Monde, pour les convertir, tirée de leurs propres manuscrites,* etc., with a preface by the Rev. Dr. Cotton Mather (Boston, 1690).[27] Or in New York in 1696 they could buy *Le Trésor des consolations divines et humaines* from the press of William Bradford. After the turn of the century one might be edified with Isaac Jacquelot's *An Abstract of the History of the Cruel Sufferings of the Blessed French Martyr Louis de Marolles. Translated from the French. To which is Added, a Relation of the Barbarities lately exercised toward several eminent persons at Montaubon, in a letter dated January 29, 1713.* (Boston, 1713); and four years later *The Triumphs of Grace, or, The Last Words and Edifying Death of the Lady Margaret de la Musse, a Noble French Lady, who Dyed when but Sixteen Years of Age. Englished by P.L.* and reprinted in Boston in 1717 from the London edition.[28] In fact this sub-literary religious literature runs through the rest of the eighteenth century,[29] and its popu-

---

[25] Thomas, *History of Printing,* II, 309.
[26] Evans, item 438.
[27] Evans, items 464, 504.
[28] Evans, items, 775, 1611, 1933.
[29] Some other instances will show its variety. *A Dialogue betwixt a Burgomaster of Rotterdam and Monsieur Jurieu, a French Calvinist preacher, concerning a question of great importance; viz., whether the civil magistrates ought in conscience to take cognizance of ecclesiastical disputes so as to prevent them, or any ways punish the authors of them.* Philadelphia, 1724; *The French Convert: Being a true relation of the happy conversion*

lar effect is to strengthen the belief that the French papists are a wicked lot, that France is to be distrusted.

But the world does not stand still, even in Atlantis. However buttressed by edifying works, French and otherwise, orthodoxy eventually gives way. In England by 1689 religious toleration has become a fact, if not altogether a matter of law, to be described for the applause of Europe by Voltaire in 1734. In America they cease to hang witches; the persecuted may fly to Rhode Island; in cosmopolitan New York there is a great variety of churches; in Pennsylvania every one may worship God as he pleases; in Maryland the Catholics are undisturbed. In fact Peter Kalm, travelling in the colonies in 1748 reports with honest amazement on American toleration. November 2, 1748, he writes in his diary that "there are many Jews settled in *New York,* who possess great privileges. They have a synagogue and houses, and great country seats of their own, property, and are allowed to keep shops in town. They have likewise several ships, which they freight, and send out with their own goods. In fine, they enjoy all the privileges common to the other inhabitants of the town and providence."[30] He has

of a noble French lady from the errors of popery to the Reformed Religion by means of a Protestant Gardener, her servant. New York, 1724, and regularly reprinted throughout the century; Charles Chauncy, *The Wonderful Narrative; or a Faithful Account of the French Prophets, their Agitations, extasies, and inspirations,* etc. Boston, 1742 (may be by Benjamin Coleman) ; Drelincourt, *The Christian's Defence against the Fears of Death.* Boston, 1744, and often reprinted; Fénelon, *Dissertation on Pure Love* (plus an account of Madame Guyon). Philadelphia, 1738, and often reprinted; Jeanne de la Nativité, *Daily Conversation with God, exemplified in the holy life of Armelle Nicholas, a poor ignorant country maid in France,* etc. Philadelphia: Benjamin Franklin (!), 1741; André Lemercier, *The Christian Rapture: A Poem.* Boston, 1747; *ibid., The Church History of Geneva.* Boston, 1732; and *ibid., A treatise against detraction.* Boston, 1733; the Prince de Conti on stage plays, Philadelphia, 1754, etc. Evans, items 2523, 2532, 2637, 4915, 5381, 4246, 6498, 5399, 6143, 6322, 4732, 5983, 3557, 3673, 7175. For items not found in Evans consult Thomas, *History of Printing* II, 309-666.

In connection with the next to the last of the above books, the following advertisement from *The Boston Weekly News-Letter* of April 6-13, 1732, is of interest: "Some Persons having desired the Author of the Church History of GENEVA, to write also an Account of the Political State of that Place ; He hath composed a Small Treatise, containing a Description of the City and it's (*sic*) Territories, of the Lake and River *Rhone,* an Account of it's Trade, Riches, Academy, Civil Government, Laws, Customs, Interest, &c. In all which things he hath rectifyed a great many English and French Authors, related things never published before and set almost every thing in a New Light." Subscriptions were to be received at M. Gerrish's bookshop. On July 20 the book was ready for delivery.

[30] Kalm, *Travels Into North America,* I, 191. He attended a service in the synagogue.

come to New York from Philadelphia where he observes that
"the *Roman Catholicks* have in the south-west part of the town
a great house, which is well adorned within, and has an
organ."[31] In February, 1718 *The Boston News-Letter* prints
"A Letter from the Clergy of the Diocese of Montpellier to
their Bishop" (of March 13, 1717), and adds: "N.B. There's
a much greater Number of Bishops, and other Church Dignitaries and Clergymen who now do actually dispute the Pope's
infallibility and his Superiourity over the Church of France,
than there were Bishops and Clergymen in England, who con-
curr'd in K. Hen. VIII.h's Time to throw off the Pope's
Supremacy in England." Interest in the quarrel (over the Bull
Unigenitus) was such that the paper printed various documents in the debate during the rest of the year.[31a] In 1721
the same paper prints from Salem, Dec. 13, 1717, the following doggerel:

"A Specimen of *New-English Celibacy.*
"THO *Rome* blaspheme the Marriage-Bed,
And Vows of Single-life has bred:
Chast PARKER, STOUGHTON, BRINSMEAD, NOYES,
Shew us the Odds 'twixt *Force,* and *Choice.*
These Undefil'd, Contracted here,
Are gone to Heav'n, and Marri'd there,"

with more like it.[31b] At Yale in 1743 a number of the senior
class reprinted Locke's *A Letter concerning Toleration* as a
protest against the intolerance of the president and board of
governors. The president reprimanded them, and ordered them
to confess, which they all did but one, who said he would appeal
to the king in council; thereupon "they treated him with much
complaisance" and gave him his degree.[31c] Orthodoxy, somewhat confused by all this novelty, is compelled to suffer a peculiar phenomenon, shortly to become common in America, a
great revival—for we must not forget the Great Awakening
of 1740. Whitefield is welcomed to New England by the clergy,
who, however, are shocked by his methods. Harvard in
1744 protested; so did Yale in 1745. When old ministers
were possessed of authority as scholars, they did not look
with approval upon the antics of the inspired potboy, whose
meetings can be best imagined by "supposing that half the

[31] *Ibid.,* I, 33, September 16, 1748.
[31a] *The Boston News-Letter,* nos. 710, 722, 729, etc.
[31b] *Ibid.,* no. 883.
[31c] Evans, *Bibliography,* II, 242.

respectable classes of New England should fervently abandon their earthly affairs, and, enrolling themselves under the
banners of the Salvation Army, should proceed to camp-
meetings of the most enthusiastic disorder."[32] It is to such
straits that orthodoxy is reduced. And there is no help from
across the water; deism is rampant, and English religious life
is never at a lower ebb than in the first forty or fifty years
of the eighteenth century.

In fact, orthodoxy in western Europe, Catholic or Protestant, is not comfortable. As a great protest against religiosity,
deism, rational or sentimental, is a dominant note in that interesting epoch; and with the deists march the various dissenting
battalions of atheists and materialists, sensualists and sceptics,
who assault in their respective fashions, the citadel, as they believe, of obscurantism. It is idle to think that America, because
she is distant, stands aloof; on the contrary, as fast as the
means of communication will allow, the warfare is extended
across the ocean; in the future republic the story of religious
and philosophic thought in the eighteenth century is the story
of the rising tide of deism, of the receding waves of orthodoxy.
Toleration and rationalism go hand in hand. We must look
into this movement if we are to understand the amazing
welcome given the French in 1778.

Of the forces which might oppose deism in America, the
Anglicans suffered from the sloth prevailing in the church
everywhere, and from the suspicion of the colonists,[33] the
Catholics were too few and too generally uncertain of their
standing to be effective;[34] and a liberal movement in New Eng-

[32] Wendell, *A Literary History of America*, p. 75. See his admirable discussion of the Great Awakening, pp. 74-76; and see Allen, *Jonathan Edwards*, pp. 181-2.
[33] "Controversies of a religious character kept the colonists suspicious of
encroachment by the Anglican Church." C. H. Van Tyne, "The Clergy and
the American Revolution," *The American Historical Review*, XIX, 45. On
Anglican control see A. L. Cross, "Schemes for Episcopal Control in the
Colonies," *Annual Report of the American Historical Association for 1896*,
pp. 233-41; and *The Anglican Episcopate and the American Colonies*.
[34] As late as 1784 there were hardly 30,000 Catholics in the United States,
two-thirds of them begin in Maryland and Pennsylvania. Carroll, *Religious
Forces of the United States*, p. 53. They were free of political disabilities
only in these states. In 1756 it is the estimate of a Catholic historian that
there were twelve missionaries and 16,000 Catholics in Maryland; and five
missionaries and 600 or 700 Catholics in Pennsylvania. Other estimates
are 3,000 communicants in Pennsylvania and 10,000 in Maryland for the
same year. Shea, *History of the Catholic Church in the United States*, II,
68-69. After 1705 Catholics were disqualified for holding office in Pennsylvania. Merriam, *History of American Political Theories*, p. 29, note. It is

land, concomitant with the growth of a worldly mercantile class, divided the one church which might have presented a united front to the enemy.[35] Based upon the rationalism of protestant theology, Cartesian philosophy, and the sensationalism of Gassendi and others, there was a movement toward Locke. Indeed, Locke may be said to be the great contributory cause to the spread of American deism.[36] At fourteen Jonathan Edwards had read Locke's *Essay on the Human Understanding,* a book "which made an era in the history of his mind."[37] At Harvard Cotton Mather early wrote his book on "Reasonable Religion," published in London in 1713.[38] At Yale, Samuel Johnson, warned against the reading of Descartes, Locke, and Newton as a student, waited until he was a tutor and introduced all three authors into the college library, to which Berkeley, the heir of Locke, left 880 volumes,

interesting to note, as a mark of growing toleration, that upon the conclusion of the Seven Years War General Gage in New York, December 30, 1764, announced to the inhabitants of the Illinois country, now a British territory, the liberty of the Catholic religion. Fortier, *History of Louisiana,* II, 306. Louisiana was Catholic, but did not affect the history of the colonies until later. Contrast this liberalism with an item in the *Boston News-Letter* for December 17-24, 1705, in which the writer, learning that the seminary at Quebec had burned, that shingles flew to a chapel, set it on fire, and that a neighboring crucifix and cross "was consumed," wrote "this short Elegy:"

> "Gallica crux aquam flammam sentire coacta est:
> Ista salus fallax, igne probata perit.
> Idolum nihil est; restat de stipite longo
> Nescio quid cineris, quem capit urna brevis."

[35] Of later New England thought a writer in the *Cambridge History of American Literature,* II, 196-7, observes quite truly that there were two schools, one hardheaded, deriving from Aristotle, Calvin, and the later commonsense philosophy; and the other, tender-minded, deriving from Shaftesbury, the deists, Rousseau, Coleridge, etc. The split may be traced to the seventeenth century, as I have hinted in section I of the present chapter. For the controversy over deism in New England from 1720 to 1789 see *ibid.,* I, chap. v. See in this connection the account of Edwards's dismissal at Northampton in Allen, *Jonathan Edwards,* pp. 263-272; and in *Jonathan Edwards, a Retrospect,* the discussion by Henry T. Rose, pp. 104 ff.

[36] On the enormous vogue of Locke in eighteenth century America see F. Emory Aldrich, *Proceedings of the American Antiquarian Society,* April, 1879, pp. 23-39, "John Locke and the Influence of His Works in America"; Riley, *American Philosophy: The Early Schools,* pp. 10 ff.; Becker, *The Declaration of Independence: A Study in the History of Political Ideas;* and Merriam, *A History of American Political Theory.* And see the discussion of John Wise in Tyler, *op. cit.,* II, 115-6, author of *The Churches' Quarrel Espoused* (1705) and *A Vindication of the Government of New England Churches* (1717).

[37] Tyler, *op. cit.,* II, 178.

[38] Riley, *op. cit.,* p. 207.

some thirty of them being deistical.[39] When Whitefield (it is true, he is a prejudiced witness) visited Harvard in 1740 he found that "bad books are become fashionable among them (the students). Tillotson and Clarke are read instead of Shephard and Stoddard, and such like evangelical writers," though he also adds that after his preaching the students "in general" were "wonderfully wrought upon."[40] In 1758 the Rev. Dr. Hales and the Rev. Dr. Thomas Wilson presented the Harvard Library with 100 sets of Leland's *View of the Principal Deistical Writers*.[41] In 1756 William Smith, Provost of the College of Pennsylvania, recommended that candidates for the B.A. degree read the *Spectacle de la Nature, or a Course of Natural and experimental Philosophy calculated for the instructions of youth*.[42] Franklin, it is notorious, was "converted" to deism by reading arguments against it;[43] his Library Company was founded in 1731, and the catalogue of 1764 shows that it had "the largest collection of rationalistic literature in the country."[44] Charles Chauncey wrote a work on the benevolence of deity; Edward Holyoke, lecturer on the Dudleien foundation "for proving and explaining . . . the proper use and improvement of the principles of natural religion" in 1775, was necessarily a deist.[45] John Randolph of Roanoke read Voltaire, Rousseau, Hume, Gibbon, and the like and was as deistical as any of them. The Christian religion was hateful to him, as it was to Tom Paine; he loved everything hostile to it.[46] On July 1, 1772, Francis Asbury enters in his journal that "I set off for Philadelphia with unprofitable company; among whom I sat still as a man dumb; and as one in whose mouth

---

[39] Riley, *op. cit.*, pp. 210, 211-212. Ezra Stiles read the thirty deists.
[40] Quincy, *History of Harvard University*, II, 41. Harvard was not too far gone, however; Langloissorie had been dismissed for his religious opinions in 1735. *Ibid.*, I, 574-6.
[41] *Ibid.*, II, 528.
[42] Riley, *op. cit.*, p. 232.
[43] When Franklin was in London in 1724 he was "in the proselyting stage of infidelity" and published *A Dissertation on Liberty and Necessity, Pleasure and Pain*, which made him known to London free-thinkers. As early as 16, however, "Shaftesbury and Collins, efficiently aided by the pious writers who had endeavored to refute them, had made him 'a real doubter' in religion." However, he had no desire to combat infidelity or fidelity either. Morse, *Benjamin Franklin*, pp. 9, 24, 26. See the letters quoted on pp. 27-28.
[44] Riley, p. 243.
[45] Riley, p. 59.
[46] Henry Adams, *John Randolph*, pp. 13-14. He was at Princeton in 1787; at Columbia in 1788.

there was no reproof. They appeared so stupidly ignorant, sceptical, deistical, and atheistical, that I thought if there were *no other* hell, I should strive with all my might to shun that."[47] On March 2, 1777, he preached "to a deistical audience" in the playhouse in Annapolis, where "many people openly deny the holy Scriptures, as well as the power of inward religion"; on March 29 he records having gone one afternoon to a schoolhouse near Annapolis where "there was very little appearance of spiritual feeling," and declares that his "brethren are inclined to leave the continent." In June, when he "intended to preach in Annapolis," there was no house open for him.[48] In fine, looking back over such evidence as this, we must agree with Faÿ that in the years 1760-1770 a profound change was being wrought in American religious and intellectual life; that "dans toutes les colonies du Sud, en principe anglicanes, la pratique religieuse disparaissait, dans les colonies du centre où la tolérance régnait entre Protestants les sectes se multipliaient et devenaient de plus en plus populaires, optimistes et anti-dogmatiques, enfin en Nouvelle Angleterre, rempart du puritanisme, un schisme se préparait. La confiance de l'homme en soi-même pour aller à Dieu, sinon pour le créer, était marquée et croissante."[49] Little wonder that the fathers of the republic were often deists, like Franklin and Jefferson. As late as 1800 Locke was a college textbook, and few clergymen had learned to deride the idealism of Berkeley.[50]

The consequences of this deistical movement are of great

---

[47] *Journal*, I, 20.

[48] *Journal*, I, 179, 181, 182, 188. He did preach in June in a church.

[49] Faÿ, p. 22. He attributes the change to the isolation of the Americans, who in their simple life, could not long retain their sense of the values of severe and subtle dogmas. I am sceptical of this mystic cause, but I am sure of the facts. Certain it is that this attitude "correspondait à leur effort pour se libérer en religion comme en politique de toute tutelle étrangère, et pour se trouver des cadres spécialement adaptés à leurs qualités." Is it not true, however, that America is until the Napoleonic period, so far as its intellectual life is concerned, mainly an extension of Europe; and that we must wait until the great evangelical movement had reached the frontiers for a peculiarly American religious movement? The situation in 1760-1800 in America does not on the whole seem to me to be essentially different from the religious situation in Great Britain; and as Professor Faÿ himself points out (p. 7), the general French movement after 1770 was away from atheism and materialism and toward religiosity. France was tired of negation and discussion. "Un appel au sentiment et une protestation contre la stérilité et le négation" was heard; "on affecte la spontanéité." The European movement was away from theology toward a sentimental deism, and in America we had our share of the movement.

[50] Adams, *History*, I, 124.

importance. On the one hand Locke the political philosopher went hand in hand with Locke the sensationalist; the politics and the theology of the eighteenth century mutually re-enforced each other. The adoption of the contract theory of government set forth in Locke's *Two Treatises of Government,* 1689, as it was combined with Montesquieu, led the way to the Revolution.[51] The Presbyterian and Congregational ministers taught their flocks the political doctrines of Locke and Milton, especially the right of the people to choose their own rulers; and Professor Van Tyne instances a long line of revolutionary sermons based upon the contract theory; the pulpit was, as he says, in that day the most direct and effectual way of reaching the masses.[52] On the other hand the spread of deism capped this teaching by breaking down respect for authority, and did not negate the contract theory.

In the next place, deism combined with other intellectual movements to make for indifference or toleration—the term depends upon the point of view; certainly for godlessness, viewed with the eyes of the subsequent religious reaction. There was, for instance, an increasingly tolerant attitude toward Catholics. The Puritan expedition against Louisbourg had been a Protestant crusade; the flag bore the motto, *Nil desperandum, Christo duce;* they spoke of the "rascally Roman Catholics," and the colonial bitterness against the Quebec Act shows the state of popular feeling.[53] The newspapers before 1763 "teemed with articles and passages full of hostility to the

---

[51] Merriam, *History of American Political Theories,* p. 90. Merriam points out that colonial political theory was mainly derived from Milton (*Areopagitica, The Tenure of Kings and Magistrates,* and the *First and Second Defence of the English People*), Sydney (*Discourse Concerning Government*), Montesquieu, and Locke (pp. 89-92). I should be inclined to add to these as an important influence the Genevan theologians. The influence of Rousseau was negligible. See Becelaere, section II of *La Philosophie en Amérique.* "The French radical influence upon the Revolution was comparatively small. . . . The greatest of the revolutionary philosophers of France, Rousseau, did not write his classic work, *The Social Contract,* until 1762, whereas the revolutionary doctrines of Otis were uttered in 1761. The general philosophy of the colonists shows little likeness to that of Rousseau, and but infrequent reference to his theory is made. Indeed, the fundamental ideas of the French writer were very similar to those of Locke." Hence, why drag in Velasquez? Merriam, pp. 91-92. However, when the declaration of independence was being debated and signed, an edition of extracts from Rousseau had just appeared in Philadelphia. Faÿ, p. 55.
[52] Van Tyne, "The Clergy and the American Revolution," *The American Historical Review,* XIX, 48-54.
[53] Van Tyne, *op. cit.,* p. 61.

Church,"[54] and the colonial presses turned out a vast deal of bitter anti-Catholic propaganda,[55] which was to affect the standing of Huguenots and the reception of the Acadians. But the newspapers "assumed a different tone after the conquest of Canada, and anti-Catholic items become rare."[56] Shea prints a list of nineteen titles of Catholic books printed in America before 1783; of these only five antedate 1763; fourteen are after the peace; most of them are in the Revolutionary epoch.[57] How far this tolerance is due to French philosophy is debatable,[58] but certain it is that the French alliance strengthened the movement for tolerance. Perhaps, as Professor Faÿ remarks,

[54] Shea, *History of the Catholic Church in the United States*, II, 83.

[55] See pages 362-63 of this chapter for some titles. Here are more: *Some Considerations on the Consequences of the French Settling Colonies on the Mississippi*. Boston, 1720; Seguenot, *A Letter from a Romish Priest in Canada to One* (Mrs. Christina Baker) *who was Taken Captive in her Infancy and Instructed in the Romish Faith, But Some Time Ago returned to her Native Country, with an Answer thereto, by a Person to Whom it Was Communicated* (Governor William Burnett of Massachusetts). Boston, 1729; *An Ode, for the Thanksgiving Day. By Titus Antigallicus, Esq.*, Boston, 1749; Doolittle, Benjamin, *A Short Narrative of Mischief done by the French and Indian Enemy, on the Western Frontiers*, etc. Boston, 1750; and a whole literature on the Louisbourg expedition for which consult Evans, *passim*, under Canada and Cape Breton. Evans, items 2176, 3216, 6277, 6488.

[56] Shea, *op. cit.*, II, 84.

[57] Shea, pp. 236-7, for the list.

[58] Faÿ naturally capitalizes the French philosophical influence. "Un adoucissement de la morale, un assouplissement du lien sociale et politique, une sentimentalité douce et dans l'ensemble une tendance à faire plutôt crédit aux hommes et aux instincts qu'aux gouvernements, tels sont les traits que l'on retrouve chez les Américains soumis à l'influence philosophique française vers 1780 et ce sont les meilleurs esprits du pays." P. 86. Faÿ is a careful student, and his opinion must have great weight; nevertheless his opinion is not the general one, and he is likely to over-estimate rather than under-estimate the effect of the *philosophes* on American religious thought. Thus an examination of the writings of S. Sewall, Jeremiah Dummer, James Otis, Jefferson in his younger days, Tom Paine in *his* younger days, Franklin, John Adams, Dickinson, Lee, Jay, and others by Rosenthal, shows citations of Montesquieu, and a few from Rousseau, but an overwhelming confidence in Locke and British precedent. Rosenthal, "Rousseau in Philadelphia," *Magazine of American History*, XII, 46-55. The mass of the people were ignorant of French theories. "The Americans of education read the Bible, Milton, Sidney, the Treatises of Locke, the Tracts of Somers for their political guidance." P. 47. "College bred Americans almost invariably alluded to French scientists, not to French politicians, when mentioning the French at all in their letters." Pp. 53-4. Nor is Faÿ able to cite many magazine and newspaper references to publication of extracts from French writers; when one considers the size of the country and the small circulation of these periodicals, one must minimize, I think, the influence of French thought in this direction (toleration) during the period 1770-1793.

the American clergy, preaching the destruction of the papacy and of Catholicism, did not realize that their blows were really being dealt against themselves.[59] Certainly there is a remarkable change in public sentiment after the alliance. When Samuel Adams held forth to the inhabitants of Philadelphia on the steps of Independence Hall, just after the adoption of the declaration, he denounced popery and monarchy as twin evils;[60] yet as early as November 5, 1775, Washington had issued a general order to the army forbidding the celebration of "Pope Day" (Guy Fawkes Day); Rhode Island, with a French fleet in her waters, blotted from her statute books a law against Catholics,[61] and Roosevelt is undoubtedly right in saying that "the wonderful increase in the spirit of tolerance shown after the Revolution was due in part to the change of the Catholic French into our allies, and of the Protestant English into our most active foes."[62] Perhaps some, like the Adams's, were not shaken greatly in their anti-Catholic attitude;[63] certain it is that Tory papers, seeking a handle against the Revolution, ridiculed popery, but the Americans refused to take alarm.[64]

[59] Faÿ, p. 228.
[60] Cf. Schouler, *Americans of 1776*, pp. 242-3.
[61] Shea, *op. cit.*, II, 166.
[62] Roosevelt, *Gouverneur Morris*, p. 39.
[63] John Adams writes his wife on October 9, 1774, describing a visit to a Roman Catholic church. "Led by curiosity and good company, I strolled away to mother church, or rather, grandmother church. I mean the Romish Chapel. I heard a good, short, moral essay upon the duty of parents to their children founded in justice and charity, to take care of their interests, temporal and spiritual. This afternoon's entertainment was to me most awful and affecting." He describes the "poor wretches" fingering beads and chanting Latin, the service, the dress of the priests, the altar, the music; "the assembly chanted most sweetly and exquisitely." "Here," he concludes, "is everything which can lay hold of the eye, ear, and imagination. Everything which can charm, and bewitch the simple and ignorant. I wonder how Luther ever broke the spell." *Letters*, I, 35.
Some ten years later Mrs. Adams was in France. On January 18, 1785, she wrote the Rev. John Shaw from Auteil on the subject of Catholic churches, which, it seems, are damp. The people use them without ceremony. She describes auricular confession, and repeats the familiar calumny: the confessor will "absolve the transgressor, and very often makes an assignation for a repetition of the same crime, or perhaps a new one. I do not think this a breach of charity (O Mrs. Adams!); for can we suppose, that, of the many thousands whom the religion of the country obliges to celibacy, one quarter part of the number can . . . conquer those passions which nature had implanted in man, when the gratification of them will cost only a few livres in confession." *Letters of Mrs. Adams*, II, 72.
It is fair to state that, however, John Adams as President assisted in the erection of a Roman Catholic chapel in Boston. See below, p. 373.
[64] On this propaganda consult Faÿ, *passim*, but especially chap. ii.

Luzerne brought Congress to hear a sermon preached by a Catholic in a Roman Catholic chapel—the Abbé Bandole, chaplain of the French embassy, was the officiating clergyman[65]—and we may take the fact as symbolical.[66] The Revolution, indeed, represents a period of Catholic growth.

"Our French alliance," says Scharf in his history of Baltimore, "aided Romanism in Baltimore. French troops from victorious Yorktown, one of his legions anyway, remained in Baltimore until the end of the war. An unfinished Catholic chapel was here opened for their benefit, and mass celebrated, a French military band accompanying the service."[67] The first Catholic priest came to Charleston in 1786—an Italian; he was followed by the Rev. Mr. Ryan in 1788.[68] By 1785 there were according to Carroll 15,800 Catholics in Maryland, 7,000 in Philadelphia, 200 in Virginia, 1500 in New York. In the same year the King of France offered eight free places in the seminary at Bordeaux for the education of American priests; St. John de Crèvecoeur organized a Catholic church in New York city, and sought financial aid from the French king, and the growth of Catholicism under this favoring sky may be traced in many ways.[69] Thus in Boston young Breck, who thought he had been converted to Catholicism in France, but who turned protestant again in Massachusetts, seems to have had no difficulty in helping his friend, the Catholic abbé Thayer, to establish a Catholic chapel in 1789; it is perhaps symbolic that "a dilapidated and deserted meeting-house in School Street, built in 1716 by French Huguenots, was turned into a chapel for the French Romanists." Breck was present

[65] Faÿ, pp. 86, 120; *Diary of Ezra Stiles*, II, 517-9; *The American Museum*, IV, 28-30 (July, 1788).
[66] The religious spirit in the Congress may be discovered in a letter of John Adams to his wife, September 16, 1774: "When the Congress met, Mr. Cushing made a motion that it should be opened with prayer. It was opposed by Mr. Jay of New York and Mr. Rutledge of South Carolina, because we were so divided in religious sentiments; some Episcopalians, some Quakers, some Anabaptists, some Presbyterians, and some Congregationalists, that we could not join in the same act of worship. Mr. Samuel Adams arose and said, 'he was no bigot, and could hear a prayer from a gentleman of piety and virtue, who was at the same time a friend to his country.'" The Rev. Mr. Duché was secured, who read the Thirty-fifth Psalm and made an extempory prayer "which filled the bosom of every man present," and "had an excellent effect upon every body there." *Letters*, I, 23-24. Note the positive quality of this tolerant spirit.
[67] Quoted in Schouler, *Americans of 1776*, pp. 243-4.
[68] *Year Book (1897) of the City of Charleston*, p. 433.
[69] Shea, II, 147, 257, 264, 266.

at the first mass; and the presence of Catholic émigrés from France and the West Indies helped to give social tone to the enterprise. Thayer was succeeded by M. Martignon, and he by Cheverus, afterwards archbishop of Bordeaux, who stayed for twenty-seven years and almost refused to return to France.[70] Indeed, as marking the increased social esteem in which Catholics were held, one notes that when Cheverus, who "gained the respect and admiration of all classes and sects," opened subscriptions for a church, President John Adams was the first to subscribe. Cheverus was a prominent promoter of art, science, and literature in Boston, and one of the founders of the Boston Athenaeum.[71] In Baltimore there was established in this epoch a tradition of enlightened princes of the church. Bishop Carroll, one of the great Carroll family, lent prestige to a once despised religion; in 1795 he headed the movement to establish a public library there, and the Rev. Mr. Périgny, a French priest, a doctor of the Sorbonne, became the first librarian.[72]

The one jarring note in the situation had been the attempt of the French government to control the Catholic Church in the United States, but it is doubtful whether this piece of political trickery was generally known.[73] American vanity was gratified in the appointment of John Carroll by the Holy See as head of the missions of the new republic, with the title of prefect apostolic, and later of archbishop,[74] when, in 1808, the diocese of Baltimore was created.[75] Meanwhile (for we are

---

[70] *Recollections of Samuel Breck,* pp. 116-8. The "liberal part of the inhabitants" were highly pleased, according to the *State Gazette of North-Carolina* for February 5, 1789.

[71] Breck, p. 118. The best seat in this church was (1791) reserved for the French consul. Shea, II, 391.

[72] Shea, II, 413.

[73] After the French alliance, when the British Roman Catholic clergy had abandoned control of the American Catholics, a scheme was broached at Paris, with Franklin's cognizance and that of the French ministry, to appoint a French apostolic nuncio, residing in Paris, as the head of the American church. The scheme was fully matured by September, 1783. But the Roman Catholic church in America had already begun to develop its own organization, and protested; Franklin retreated; the French government changed, and Carroll was appointed. See Guilday, *The Life and Times of John Carroll, Archbishop of Baltimore,* pp. 178-201, 212-214; Shea, II, 204-248; Humphrey, *Nationalism and Religion,* pp. 403 ff.

[74] Guilday, p. 201. The appointment was made June 9, 1784. The whole transaction gave color to S. B. Morse's later pamphlet, *Foreign Conspiracy Against the Liberty of the United States.* See Guilday, p. 193, note 23.

[75] It became a metropolitan see with four suffragan bishops, New York, Philadelphia, Boston, Beardstown. In 1803 the diocese of New Orleans was created. Carroll, *Religious Forces of the United States,* p. 69.

getting ahead of our story) Philadelphia had witnessed a Catholic burial of some ceremony, that of Don Juan de Mirallès, when the piety and edifying air of the papists surprised the onlookers; the edict of Louis XVI for toleration of protestants, and various liberal decisions by the French government made a great noise; and the preachers themselves admired the French, whom once they had hated.[76] "The greater part of these happy results," said the *Massachusetts Centinel* on June 21, 1788, "must be attributed to our independence and our alliance with our great and good ally, Louis of France, the protector of the rights of man against tyranny."[77]

Thus it was that toleration went hand in hand with the contract theory of government and with deism. Nor was this all. It affected the schools. Whereas Harvard in the seventeenth century had sought to confine its government to Presbyterians and Congregationalists, the charters of various colleges granted in the eighteenth century make express provisions for one or another variety of toleration. A manuscript bill providing for the establishment of a South Carolina college sometime after 1723 (possibly the work of John Rutledge) seems to waive the question of denominational difference.[78] The original charter of the College of New Jersey (Princeton) guaranteed freedom to all denominations in 1746,[79] although the design of the college was to raise up a pious and learned ministry.[80] There was at first considerable opposition to the founding of King's College (Columbia) for fear it would be a church establishment; and under the charter granted October 31, 1754, the college was forbidden to exclude anybody "on account of his particular Tenets in matters of Religion," and King's was perhaps the only college in the country without a theological faculty. In 1784 the act creating Columbia University provided that "no Professor shall in any way whatsoever be accounted ineligible for or by reason of any religious tenet or tenets that he may or shall profess, or be compelled by any bye law or otherwise to take any religious test-oath whatsoever."[81] Its

---

[76] Faÿ, pp. 146-7, and references to sermons there given.
[77] Quoted in Faÿ, as above.
[78] Laborde, *History of the South Carolina College,* pp. 15-16. The college was not incorporated until 1801. P. 27.
[79] Maclean, *History of the College of New Jersey,* I, 51, 61.
[80] It is curious to note in this connection that there was felt the need of a religious revival in 1757; and again in 1770 and 1772. *Ibid.,* I, 388-9. Princeton operated under the revised charter of 1748.
[81] Mathews (ed.), *A History of Columbia University,* pp. 5-6, 7, 16, 17, 60.

president from 1754 to 1763 was, by the way, that Samuel Johnson who had been exposed to Descartes, Boyle, Locke, and Newton. In 1785 the charter of the University of Georgia provided, it is true, that "all officers" of instruction and government "shall be of the Christian religion" (section IX), which seems sufficiently broad; but section XI explicitly provides that nobody shall be excluded from studying because of "speculative sentiments in religion."[82] Clearly, here is a different temper from that which saw in the university at Geneva or the university at Cambridge the defender of orthodoxy. This, too, is owing to the spread of deism and tolerance. Let us examine the movement a little more closely.

With increasing tolerance, what may be called religiosity declined.[83] On the one hand philosophy, which had hitherto been ancillary to theology, was pursued more and more as an independent branch of knowledge, becoming increasingly non-religious and even anti-religious. On the other hand there was a positive lowering of the religious life. Let us briefly trace these two movements in the eighteenth century.

Professor Riley distinguishes three streams of foreign influence upon American philosophy: the British, the French, and the German. The British begins with the sensationalism of Locke and the idealism of Berkeley and follows with the Scotch realism of Reid and his school. The French influence includes the naturalism of Montesquieu, French deism, and the ma-

---

[82] Hull, *A Historical Sketch of the University of Georgia*, p. 7.

[83] For purposes of reference it may be well to give Humphrey's census (estimated) of the churches in the United States at the outbreak of the revolution:

	Clergy	Churches
Episcopal	250	300
Presbyterian	77	417
Congregational	575	700
Baptist	424	471
Methodists (not a separate body)		
Lutheran	25	60
German Reformed (no figures)		
Dutch Reformed	30	82
Associate	13	6 or 8
Roman Catholic	26	52

Nationalism and Religion, p. 13, note.

It will be seen that the Congregational clergy offered the most numerous fighting force against irreligion; but even this regiment of shock troops was quarreling among itself over the unitarian movement, then in its beginning. The German and Dutch Reformed churches may be disregarded; and the Roman Catholic clergy seem to have had little effect upon American life at this time. As for the Episcopalian clergy see the discussion in the text.

terialism of La Mettrie (and in the nineteenth century, the influence of Cousin and Comte). The Germans are not effective until the nineteenth century. The analysis is not very satisfactory: it ignores the seventeenth century French influence altogether, but it will serve for our present purpose. The important thing now is to note with Riley that deism, scepticism, sensationalism, atheism, materialism—all these are found in varying degrees among American thinkers in the eighteenth century,[84] many of whom are in the colleges and therefore influencing the rising generation. To him there is a correspondence between philosophical and political movements: Puritanism, which is passivity, determinism, pessimism (?), corresponds to the monarchical politics of the seventeenth century; the dualistic naturalism of the eighteenth century reflects, and is reflected by the dualistic political philosophy of the time, whether that philosophy takes the form of the theory of a limited monarchy (monarch and people), or of the contract theory (sovereignty and subjects); and the pantheistic philosophy of the nineteenth century has its analogue in the liberal democracy of the epoch. The progress is from theology to natural rights; and from natural rights to democracy.[85] The theory is more symmetrical than sound; but notably with reference to the eighteenth century it gets at the main point, which is that theology and philosophy are part of the cosmopolitan movement, that the cosmopolitan movement was making for tolerance and the international mind.

The breakdown of the theocratic state—to continue with Professor Riley—was achieved in three ways. One was political: it is a movement from a state church to a liberty of philosophizing. One was naturalistic: it is a movement from supernaturalism to science. The best example of the first is Jefferson; the best representative of the second is Franklin. And the third is rationalistic: it moves from the authority of revelation to the authority of reason, and Professor Riley chooses as its best examplar, Ethan Allen's *Oracles of Reason,* (1784), written with the aid of a Bible and a dictionary;[86] its logical goal is materialism. "In the place of Paley and Watts and Butler and the Bridgewater treatises are to be found books dealing with the mental processes of the individual.

[84] Riley, *American Philosophy: The Early Schools,* pp. 10-11.
[85] *Ibid.,* pp. 1-4.
[86] *Ibid.,* pp. 11-12.

From England come Locke's Inquiry on Human Understanding and Hartley's Observations on Man; from France Condorcet's Progress of the Human Spirit and La Mettrie's Man a Machine;[87] from Scotland come the similar humanistic treatises of Hume, Reid and Stewart." And Professor Riley tells us that "materialism in America . . . was an orderly reproduction of the European movement—deriving its mechanical notions from Newton, its psychological from Hobbes, its physical from Hartley and Darwin, and, as the last step in this historic succession, approaching the sensualistic philosophy of the French schools." It is in marked contrast with the austere idealism of Puritan theology; its center is Philadelphia and the South is its sphere; and as a scientific movement among the doctors it has considerable importance.[88] Against this heavy attack the dominant theological note of American life was compelled for a time to give way; and one of the striking results of the movement was the inculcation of the frontier with deism—a point we shall presently discuss.

The best testimony to the spread of irreligious sentiment in the late eighteenth century is the alarm—perhaps exaggerated —of the churches. A historian informs us that:

The two decades from the close of the War of Independence include the period of the lowest ebb-tide of vitality in the history of American Christianity. The spirit of half-belief or unbelief that prevailed on the other side of the sea, both in the church and out of it, was manifest also here. Happily the tide of foreign immigration at this time was stayed and the church had opportunity to gather strength for the immense task that was presently to be devolved upon it. . . . The demoralization of army life, the fury of political factions, the catchpenny materialist morality of Franklin, the philosophic deism of men like Jefferson, and the popular ribaldry of Tom Paine had wrought . . . to bring about a condition of things which to the eye of little faith seemed almost desperate.[89]

A second writer tells us that the war-peril of the revolution was

much increased by the alliance, which brought groups of French officers into contact with the people in every important seaport, and with the army at large. The frivolous and scoffing deism of the school of Voltaire was thus naturalized, and an irreligious tone began to per-

---

[87] On this topic consult Chinard, *Jefferson et les philosophes; Volney et l'Amérique; La Correspondance de Madame de Staël avec Jefferson* in *Revue de la littérature comparée,* II, 621-640; and *Les amitiés américaines de Madame d'Houdetot,* as well as Faÿ, *passim.*

[88] Riley, *op. cit.,* pp. 17, 20, 47. See in this connection the *Autobiography of Charles Caldwell, M.D.*

[89] Bacon, *A History of American Christianity,* pp. 219-230.

vade society, especially its public life. Religion was valued, if at all, as a supplement to the jail and the police; belief in a disclosure of God to His creatures was thought a jestworthy superstition.[90]

One may trace this irreligious spirit in various places. Thus it is significant that of ten colleges founded by 1776 only one was non-sectarian, whereas of fourteen colleges founded in the next twenty years, only four are denominational schools, and, outside of New England, there are only two—Dickinson College in Pennsylvania (Methodist Episcopal) and Georgetown in the District of Columbia (Roman Catholic).[91] In Cambridge in the church where Dr. Thomas Coke was to preach December 5, 1784, there had been no service for several years, and prior to his arrival, it had been used for cattle and hogs.[92] At Yale, before the coming of President Dwight in 1795, the college was, according to Lyman Beecher's *Autobiography*, "in a most ungodly state. The college church was almost extinct. Most of the students were skeptical, and rowdies were plenty. . . . Most of the class before me," he says, "were infidels, and called each other Voltaire, Rousseau, D'Alembert, etc.," and the cause seemed to be that they had read Tom Paine.[93] When the authorities tried to stop the flood, a policy of suppression "led to an explosion of free thinking upon the advent of the Franco-American deism of Citizen Paine and Thomas Jefferson."[94] When Bishop Asbury visited New Haven he remarked, "New Haven! thou seat of science and of sin! Can thy dry

[90] Thompson, *A History of the Presbyterian Churches in the United States*, p. 58.
[91] See the table in Boone, *Education in the United States*, p. 77. There should be added to the denominational colleges, however, Cokesbury College, near Baltimore, founded by the Methodists and shortly destroyed. Dr. Thomas Coke and Bishop Asbury drew up a pronunciamento on Cokesbury College in 1789, declaring that Locke and Rousseau were the greatest writers on education any age has produced, although the latter's religious system is mistaken. As recreation for the students agriculture and architecture were recommended, since Peter the Great, the early Romans, and the Georgics especially recommend agriculture. The reasons for including architecture do not appear. Manual training and gardening were part of the curriculum; and the simple life was led by all. See Drew, *The Life of the Rev. Thos. Coke*, pp. 122-5, where the rules governing student life are included.
[92] Drew, *Life of the Rev. Thos. Coke*, p. 94. Anti-Methodist feeling was strong and Asbury was compelled to preach in the open air.
[93] Bacon, *op. cit.*, p. 231. "That was the day of the infidelity of the Tom Paine school. Boys that dressed flax in the barn, as I used to, read Tom Paine and believed him." Dwight preached six months on the subject, "Is the Bible the Word of God." P. 243.
[94] Riley, *American Thought from Puritanism to Pragmatism*, p. 66.

bones live? 'O Lord, thou knowest.' " "At Middlebury we find college-craft and priest-craft," wrote the good bishop.[95] At Princeton, which had been closed for three years of the Revolution, there were in 1782 only two professed Christians in the whole student body.[96] At Columbia Samuel Johnson and William Livingston had combined to make deism popular.[97] And the infection had spread to southern schools.

Deism, in fact, was not in bad odor. Allowing for the ambiguous meaning of the word "atheists," Griswold is probably right in saying that "in the days of Washington," atheists were "comparatively much more numerous and more dignified in talents and positions" than at any time since.[98] In Philadelphia in 1790 they formed a society under the leadership of John Fitch, the inventor of steamboats; the membership ran to forty, the meetings were held in Church Alley, and were usually occupied with essays and debates, in which the God of Nature was the central theme and a rigid code of morals was urged.[99] In 1794 Boston papers were publishing letters commenting on and praising Robespierre's Discourse on Science and Religion of April 21, 1794;[100] Tom Paine was being read by the young in New England and "the impression that Paine had aided and abetted the cause of impiety and irreligion was general."[101] Meanwhile deism was spreading to the frontier.[102]

In the churches themselves there was a general disaffection. An Episcopal church could not be organized in the South;[103] Bishop Provost of New York laid down his episcopal functions, not expecting his church to survive; Bishop Madison of Virginia and Chief-Justice Marshall despaired of reviving the Episcopal faith.[104] In New England Puritanism was breaking

[95] He was of the opinion that Boston was "famous for poor religion and bad water." Strickland, The Pioneer Bishop, p. 472.
[96] Bacon, op. cit., p. 230.
[97] Riley, op. cit., p. 66.
[98] Republican Court, p. 290.
[99] Scharf and Westcott, History of Philadelphia, II, 1404-5, note. The society tried to get the Rev. Elihu Palmer, a Dartmouth graduate who had been expelled from the "Universal Baptists" for denying the deity of Christ, as their minister, but Bishop White prevented their procuring a suitable hall, and by and by the society "became invisible."
[100] Faÿ, p. 228 and references.
[101] Stauffer, New England and the Bavarian Illuminati, p. 76. See his chapter i on the New England situation.
[102] See below, pp. 381 ff.
[103] Faÿ, p. 146 and references.
[104] Bacon, pp. 230-1.

down until "to a very considerable number of earnest lovers of religion in New England and elsewhere throughout the nation, the century's sun seemed to be setting amid black and sullen clouds of the most ominous character;"[105] the logic of Edwards had proved too unbearable, and people refused to tolerate it longer,[106] particularly the Baptists. In 1798 the Congregational clergy of Massachusetts in their annual convention unanimously expressed their sorrow and concern on account of "those atheistical, licentious and disorganizing principles which have been avowed and zealously propagated by the philosophers and politicians of France; which have produced the greatest crimes and miseries in that unhappy country, and like a mortal pestilence are diffusing their baneful influence even to distant nations."[107] The same year the Presbyterian General Assembly resolved that there is "a general dereliction of religious principles and practice, "a visible and prevailing infidelity, which in many instances tends to atheism."[108] "Unbelief became the fashion of the day. There was a decay of zeal in the churches, and in the eastern part of Massachusetts a rapid spread of Socinianism. . . ."[109] As marking the un-religious tendency of the epoch we may note the increasing vagueness of creeds, the decline of tithing, and the character of the religious sections of the national constitution and of many state constitutions adopted at this time. So strong was the tide that Schouler

[105] Stauffer, p. 102. See his various quotations from contemporary sermons. Thus the Rev. Joseph Lathrop, preaching on May 4, 1796, at West Springfield, Massachusetts, under the title, "God's Challenge to Infidels to Defend their Cause," remarks that "this is a day when infidelity appears with unusual boldness, and advances with threatening progress, to the hazard of our national freedom and happiness as' well as to the danger of our future salvation." On April 6, 1798, the Rev. Nathan Strong at Hartford, preaching a fast-day sermon, oratorically thundered that "there are dark and ominous appearances. I do not mean the wrath and threatening of any foreign nations whatever, for if we please God and procure him on our side, we may bless his providence, and hear human threatenings without emotion. But the dark omens are to be found at home. In our hearts, in our homes, in our practice, and in a licentious spirit disposed to break down civil and religious order. In affecting to depend on reason in the things of religion, more than the word of God; so as to reject all evangelical holiness, faith in Jesus Christ, the Son of God, and the ministrations of the spirit in the heart. In substituting anarchy and licentiousness, in the room of rational and just liberty," etc., etc. (pp. 97-98). Of course a large part of this is due to the anti-revolutionary movement of the day. But see Stauffer's bibliography of anti-Paine literature.
[106] See Brissot de Warville, *Travels,* pp. 70-82.
[107] Quoted in Stauffer, p. 101.
[108] Bacon, pp. 230-3; Stauffer, pp. 99-100.
[109] Thompson, *op. cit.,* p. 73.

believes it had an important influence in shaping the future destinies of the church in American life.[110] Imlay, writing at the close of the century, advised preachers not to emigrate to America.[111] Let us conclude our paragraph with a quotation from the reminiscences of Joshua Bates who ascribes this decline in faith to

the infidel philosophy which led to the French revolution of 1790, and which found its way across the Atlantic in the writings of Voltaire for the learned, and Paine for the illiterate; and, through the medium of political sympathy, obtained a lodgment in the American mind. Some of them might be discovered in the perverting and degrading influence diffused through the writings of Dr. Priestley, and other speculative writers of that period, who claimed the Christian name, and yet denied the plenary inspiration and infallible authority of the Christian Scriptures. And some of them might, unquestionably, be traced back to the influence of the war of the American revolution on the principles and habits of American society.[112]

But it was in the South and on the frontier that irreligion and deism became especially characteristic marks of culture. Thus, writing of Pennsylvania and western New York in 1795, La Rochefoucauld-Liancourt assures his reader that:

Quant à la religion, elle occupe peu les esprits en Pennsilvanie, et moins encore au milieu des déserts du Genessée. Il y a dans les villes des lieux destinés au culte, ainsi que dans les campagnes habitées d'une population un peu considérable; mais la religion est plus généralement regardée comme un ressort politique que une voie de salut.[113]

"They have no preaching in some parts of the back settlements," wrote Mr. Richard Boardman, a Methodist preacher

[110] "American thought, with its English tincture of sobriety, had never descended in sacred things to the depths of French scepticism; yet the influence of Jefferson and his party must have tended steadily to unseat the illiberal priesthood of whatever denomination, and by making its members wholly dependent upon private maintenance, subject them and their polity to the influence, if not the direction, of their supporters." His reference is 1821, but the influence begins earlier. *History of the United States*, III, 221.

[111] "With respect to divinity, I doubt whether individuals of any class of that profession, orthodox or heterodox, would be much in request. If any, those of the arian or socinian persuasion would be so in New York and Philadelphia: there are many unitarians in the two last-mentioned towns, and in Boston; where I believe there is one congregation, which is the only one of that description I know of in America. Were divines to emigrate, they would probably succeed best as schoolmasters, who are much in request everywhere on the American continent." In Imlay, *Topographical Description*, pp. 190-1. His discussion of the geology of the western country is eminently non-Biblical, not to say Cuvieresque. See pp. 94-97.

[112] "Them" is causes. In Allen, *Memoir of John Codman, D.D.*, pp. 177-8.

[113] *Voyages*, I, 280.

in 1770.[114] For one thing a formal church is almost impossible on the frontier;[115] for another, the frontier was indifferent: where each man's safety depends upon himself, the aid of the minister is not so likely to be sought. Again, the frontier wanted emotion and not philosophical argument in religion.[116] Finally, the frontier was settled by the dissatisfied, and the dissatisfied, especially at this period, made Paine their Bible and spread deism into the wilderness.

> A fig for those by law protected,
> Liberty's a glorious feast;
> Courts for cowards were erected,
> Churches built to please the priest,

was their motto. The first edition of *The Age of Reason* was spread broadcast through the free-thinking societies, the Illuminati and the Jacobin clubs, and appealed everywhere to the same class as that which Ingersoll was later to sway. "Within two decades the pamphlet was found on the banks of the Genessee and the Ohio; within two more it circulated among the readers of Volney and Voltaire in those places in Tennessee and Kentucky whose names still attest the French sympathies of their first settlers." The president of Transylvania University was suspected of teaching naturalism; in Indiana at a later date a friend of Lincoln said it (Paine) passed from hand to hand and was discussed at the village store. And the influence of Paine was strengthened by the vogue of Volney's *Ruins,* translated by Barlow and printed in New York and Philadelphia. "Associated with his popular book of travels, the Ruins helped the Age of Reason and the twin volumes, hand in hand, went wandering through the woods."[117] And a historian informs us of the lower frontier that "for the moment a good deal of the religious inheritance from Jonathan Edwards, Whitefield, and Wesley, which the 'new light' preachers had delivered to the poorer white people of the South, was lost in the migration to the cotton country. The frontier

---

[114] Drew, *Life of the Rev. Thomas Coke,* p. 51.
[115] On frontier religion see Roosevelt, *Winning of the West, passim,* but especially volume I; Rusk, *Literature of the Middle Western Frontier,* I, 38-51; Francis Asbury's *Journal,* especially the last part of volume I, and volume II, *passim;* and Humphreys, *Nationalism and Religion.*
[116] "In general it may be said that, with the exception of extremists such as the Mormons and Shakers, Protestant sects succeeded in the pioneer West in inverse ratio to their intellectual attainments, and in direct ratio to their emotional appeal." Rusk, I, 46.
[117] Riley, *American Philosophy: the Early Schools,* p. 306.

has always been indifferent to formal religion."[118] "Immorality and scepticism abounded in Kentucky and Tennessee"; in 1793 the Kentucky legislature voted to dispense with prayers at its sessions,[119] and as late as 1827 it seemed to one traveler that Kentucky "rails . . . at every form of worship." He notes that the Kentucky constitution excluded all ministers from public office.[120]

If such was the condition of the frontier, the end of the century found the South equally indifferent to faith. Neither the Catholic[121] nor the Anglican clergy were able or desirous to save men's souls. Here where, as we have seen, the cosmopolitan spirit held, and was to hold, long sway, the cosmopolitan indifference to formal faith held sway also. Infidelity spread from Philadelphia downward as well as from England and France. Preaching at Cape May, New Jersey, in 1786, Asbury enters in his journal that "there is a great dearth of religion in these parts. . . ."[122] "I think, for ignorance of God and religion, the wilds and swamps of Delaware exceed most parts of America with which I have had any acquaintance," he wrote in January 15, 1781; indeed, of a Presbyterian meeting at, or near, Dover in 1779, he had written that "the unfeeling people" "are so full of politics they seem to have turned all religion out of doors."[123] In Virginia the propagandist of Methodism, preaching to the inhabitants of Winchester, observes generally that "religion is greatly wanting in these parts. The inhabitants are much divided, made up, as they are, of different nations, and speaking different languages, they agree in scarcely anything, except it be to sin against God;" and at Yorktown he reports that "the inhabitants are dissolute and

[118] Dodd, *The Cotton Kingdom,* pp. 20-21.
[119] Thompson, *op. cit.,* p. 73.
[120] *The Americans as They Are,* pp. 50-52.
[121] "The lower South had been and still was an outwardly irreligious dram-drinking, and dueling section. The French priests had built a compact religious community in and about New Orleans, but they had not pushed this work up the rivers and out into the great stretches of country where plantation life was dominant." (Cf., however, Rusk, I, 38-40.) "The faith of the Roman Catholic Church was, therefore, comparatively stagnant in the lower South. Aside from a few churches in Louisiana and Charleston, firmly established parishes in Mobile, and a diocese in Florida, this branch of the Christian Church had not become a force in the planter civilization." This of course refers to the opening decades of the nineteenth century. Dodd, *The Cotton Kingdom,* pp. 13, 14.
[122] *Journal,* II, 4.
[123] *Ibid.,* I, 324, 248.

careless."[124] If this seem the jaundiced view of a revivalist, let us remember Jefferson's wish to keep religion as such out of the University of Virginia—in which connection it is surprising to learn that in 1819 John Adams "opposed the selection of foreign professors because they would teach Christianity."[125] Jefferson tried to force the election of Dr. Thomas Cooper;[126] religion and politics combined, it is true, to thwart him, but Cooper merely transferred his activities to South Carolina where he became president of the college at Columbia, and where he wielded a remarkable influence. Teachers and models of propriety were trained under him and became deists; "young men from all the cotton region flocked to his institution," says Dodd, who adds that "he was perhaps the first teacher in this country to break down the faith of men in the literal inspiration of the Bible. South Carolinians liked the scientific spirit which took nothing for granted—at least that was their attitude in 1819."[127] Despite his defeat over the election of Cooper, Jefferson managed to give the University of Virginia a strongly agnostic bias which continued long after Jefferson's death.[128] In this connection it is interesting to note that the Rev. Mr. Garrettson, a Methodist, met a man in the region of the Cypress Swamps about 1800 in Virginia, and asked if he was acquainted with Jesus Christ. "Sir," said he, "I know not where the gentleman lives."[129] In North Carolina Asbury found "a hardness over the people here; they have had the Gospel preached by Presbyterians, Baptists, and Methodists, the two former appear to be too much in the spirit of the world," but he reports that "there is life amongst some of the Methodists." Four days later he writes that "the Baptists appear

[124] *Ibid.,* I, 357-385.
[125] Trent, *English Culture in Virginia,* p. 22, note 2, for the Adams reference; see the whole book for an account of the founding of the university, particularly with reference to the religious question.
[126] Dr. Thomas Cooper of Pennsylvania was born in London in 1759 and was then in Pennsylvania. He was offered the professorship of chemistry and law; had practiced law in England; and was one of the representatives sent by the English democratic clubs to France. He accepted the chair, but when a clamor arose respecting his religious opinions, he resigned. Trent, pp. 18-19. See Riley on his philosophic importance.
[127] Dodd, p. 97.
[128] Trent, p. 98.
[129] *Reminiscences of the Rev. Henry Boehm,* p. 68. Garrettson, supposing the man misunderstood him, repeated his question, and to the astonishment of the preacher, he replied, "I don't know the man."

to be very dead."[130] In the same state "at the widow Kembrough's" he was "Wonderfully entertained with a late publication by Silas Mercer, a Baptist preacher, in which he has anathematized the whole race of kings from Saul to George III, his is republicanism run mad." He asks sadly, "Why afraid of religious establishments in these days of enlightened liberty?"—that is, in 1784.[131] In Charleston he notes in 1785 that "the Calvinists, who are the only people who appear to have any sense of religion, seem to be alarmed" at his preaching, and adds that "there is a great dearth of religion here; some say, never more so than at this time." And when he left the city, he left, he says, "the seat of Satan, dissipation and folly," though he had been hospitably entertained.[132] The influences of deism were meantime being re-enforced from Kentucky where, at Transylvania University, "true republicanism" was taught by Horace Holley to some four or five hundred students, many of them preparing to be lawyers, physicians, and teachers.[133] Twenty or thirty thousand Roman Catholics and twenty thousand Episcopalians could not, or would not, stem the tide.

3. SUMMARY AND SIGNIFICANCE OF THE CHAPTER

So it is that the cosmopolitan spirit dominates the religious history of America in the first two centuries; in the seventeenth by developing the spirit of religious zeal and religious bigotry; in the eighteenth, by developing the spirit of toleration and later of indifference and even of hostility to religion. The movement, it is obvious, develops *pari passu* with similar movements in England, Germany, and France; there, too, the persecuting spirit dominates for a while, then yields to the spirit of toleration and finally of indifference; there as here (what we have not had time to develop) the scientific spirit increases toleration and replaces an interest in the invisible world with an interest in the visible one. By 1789 it was the hope of liberal European minds, whether they were domiciled in the New World or the

[130] *Journal*, I, 292 ff., for complaints of the lack of religion in this state.
[131] *Journal*, I, 365. Asbury was not narrowly denominational. He read, or had read to him, the sermons of "Mr. James Saurin, a French Protestant minister at the Hague" and found them "long, elaborate, learned, doctrinal, practical, historical and explanatory." *Journal*, II, 366-7 (January 19, 1800).
[132] *Journal*, I, 382; II, 108, 185. Of all the Southern states Asbury reports favorably of Georgia alone where "many that had no religion in Virginia have found it after their removal into Georgia and (western) South Carolina." II, 30.
[133] Dodd, p. 99. See Rusk, index under Transylvania University.

Old, that the brotherhood of man might obliterate national and sectarian divisions. What is the significance of this situation for the American reception of French culture?

Partly indebted to Huguenot and Calvinist theology the religious spirit of seventeenth century New England (and to a less degree, of the other colonies in the same epoch) implanted in men's minds that there was an alliance between papacy, France, and the devil. Had this spirit continued, there might have been a French alliance in the Revolution, but the cordial relations between the two peoples traced in Professor Faÿ's study, would have been impossible; there would have been no Jacobin party and no enthusiasm for Genêt and no feasts of liberty. In 1682 France was being preached against by Increase Mather as the great persecutor of orthodox Christianity; in 1795-6 the victories of France were being celebrated in many churches as the victories of liberty.[134] The causes of this change of front are many; but one of the most important is the breakdown of religious prejudice against the French.

Protestantism, especially Calvinism, (to recapitulate) by its very nature could not endure unchanged. Under the impact of theological and philosophical rationalism in the seventeenth century; under the impact of a varied and cosmopolitan immigration; under the impact of the increasing commercial spirit which is impatient of religious warfare, the narrower zeal of the first century slowly gave way. Rhode Island and Pennsylvania set examples of religious toleration; and across the water in England the sectarian differences of the time of Cromwell die away under the House of Orange and the House of Hanover. Open-mindedness was in a sense forced upon America. But warfare with France continued, with brief interruptions until 1763, and as a result of Indian massacre and Jesuit propaganda, the prejudice against the French continued also. Beginning, however, in the sixties of the eighteenth century, the rising tide of tolerance commences to make itself felt until by the time that Protestant Great Britain was the enemy and Catholic France was the ally, many Americans were prepared to receive the French sympathetically and even admiringly. Liberal religious minds were ready at least not to decry the papists; and under the impact of rational philosophy and sentimental deism, British and French, whole groups of leaders were prepared to take a more positive stand, to decry all sec-

[134] Faÿ, p. 255.

tarian difference and even religion itself. The decline of religion in eighteenth century America represents a kind of letting down the bars of French influence. But not all of America, even in the eighteenth century, was liberal, deistic or agnostic; there were, it is true, many who were uneasy; and as the excesses of the French Revolution commenced to be made known, there began in the United States a religious reaction as remarkable as the religious decline. Let us turn to this in our next chapter.

XI

The Reaction to French Religious Influence
(continued)

1. THE RELIGIOUS REVIVAL AFTER THE REVOLUTION AND THE ATTACK ON FRENCH AND AMERICAN DEISM

WHILE bishops were resigning in despair, while the godly believed that the infidels were triumphant, while there was a vague fear of the Illuminati and a marked fear of the religious scepticism and political radicalism of Jefferson, there were yet forces at work to overturn the triumph of infidelity. Just at the turn of the nineteenth century there began one of the most remarkable epochs in the religious history of the United States; and America, which had slid smoothly into the cosmopolitan stream, now swung sharply away from that current and chose another. An American religion commenced to emerge; the spirit of nationalism came to overcome the cosmopolitan spirit; a great religious reaction began, which took on the character of a revival. Nor is revival quite the right word. It is rather a renaissance; the protestant church in the United States after 1800 bears little relation to the protestant church in the eighteenth century, nor does it have much resemblance to the protestant church anywhere else in the world. Let us trace the currents and counter-currents of this religious renaissance.

The roots of this remarkable phenomenon are obscure, nor can we hope to find them all. There was, of course, that natural reaction which follows any period of marked infidelity and agnosticism. There was, after the Revolution and the setting up of the new government, a conservative movement in politics which tended to strengthen the church, for we have seen already that many who were not themselves notably religious, yet felt that the church was useful as a police force, however dubious as a means to salvation. But perhaps the most important forces at work were the importation from England of a new conception of religious proselyting, the American reaction to the French Revolution, the influence of the frontier, and the rise of the middle classes. The general result was to seal the religious mind against the influence of all but one particular brand of European thought for some decades, and to create a unique, novel, and not uninteresting American church, or rather system of churches.

Even in the last quarter of the eighteenth century the religious interests of American life had been obscured rather than fatally injured. Whatever the deficiencies of the American Constitution in this regard, the Continental Congress was, *pro forma* at least, a body with a profound sense of religious responsibility.[1] Humphrey collects from their papers a great concatenation of phrases which give their legislation ecclesiastical coloring;[2] "we find them," he writes, "legislating upon such subjects as morality, sins, repentance, humiliation, divine service, fasting prayers, reformation, mourning, public worship, funerals, chaplains, true religion, and Thanksgiving. The Sabbath is recognized to a degree rarely exhibited in other countries; Congress adjourns and all official business is suspended." Moreover, whatever the rationalist tendencies of the leaders might be in 1776, religious qualifications held a conspicuous place in the state constitutions formed during the epoch. Toleration was recognized, but religious tests were not unfrequently set up as qualifications for office. In New Hampshire, New Jersey, North Carolina, and South Carolina, the governor must be a protestant; in Maryland and Massachusetts he must be a Christian. In Georgia, New Hampshire, North Carolina, South Carolina, and New Jersey, the legislator must be a protestant; in Massachusetts and Maryland he must be a Christian; in Delaware and Pennsylvania he must believe in God, a future life, and the inspiration of the Scriptures. In New York and Rhode Island only there were no religious qualifications for office.[3] Indeed, the very fact of the existence of an anti-religious tendency strengthened the American church and helped to give it individuality.

The general character of American ecclesiastical institutions was determined by the development of the period under discussion. All of the churches worked out their national institutions under the stress of mutual jealousies. No one or two sects were strong enough to maintain exceptional pretensions over the others when in combination, and

---

[1] "Seul le Congrès comme corps réagit dans une certain mesure contre le flot général (en faveur de France). C'est qu'il n'acceptait pas l'idéal moral et philosophique dont Vergennes était imbu, et que les Français croyaient légitime d'attributer aux États-Unis comme nation. Le Congrès sentait que cette terre était appelée à un grand destin, mais il ne percevait pas l'influence décisive qu'aurait la révolution d'Amérique sur Europe. Il rêvait bien plus de grandeur terrestre et de puissance matérielle." Faÿ, p. 89. Note the bourgeois attitude and the providential mysticism.

[2] Humphrey, *Nationalism and Religion*, p. 407.

[3] Merriam, *History of American Political Theory*, pp. 86-87. On the other hand almost every state constitution forbade the clergy to hold office.

French philosophic thought as interpreted by the searching deistic criticism of such men as Benjamin Franklin and Thomas Jefferson, kept them on their mettle and made them justify every act. All of the churches seem to have felt the effects of the prevalent doctrinaire political theories of Rousseau, Montesquieu, and their contemporaries. So we find American ecclesiasticism, like the American political state, stamped with the contract theory of government, with the doctrine of the separation of powers, and with the ideal of the consent of the governed. These theories we find combined with the more distinctive American principles, which had grown from the early independent movement—equality of all religious communions before the law and non-interference on the part of the state with religion. Above all the Revolution compelled distinctively American churches to a complete independence from foreign ecclesiastical control.[4]

Thus it was that the general movement toward tolerance, by freeing the church of all entanglements with politics, cleared the way for denominational growth.

Meanwhile deism was riding rough-shod over powerful enemies. A new attitude toward religious life had been introduced into America by the preaching of Whitefield and the emissaries of Wesley.[5] Wesley's first visit to Georgia had been a failure; but in 1769 he sent Joseph Pilmoor and Boardman as missionaries to America; in 1771 came Richard Wright and Francis Asbury, later first bishop of the church in America. It was Asbury who first initiated regular circuit work in America;[6] and his work was so successful that on July 14, 1773, the first conference of the Methodist Church was held in Philadelphia, and the denomination had grown to ten preachers and 1116 members. In the summer of that year in Virginia, home of Jefferson, five or six new circuits were formed, and 500 or 600 souls were converted. By the next conference (May, 1775), there were 3000 members and nineteen preachers on "stations"; 1800 were converted in Virginia that same year. The conference of 1776 found that there were 104 preachers and 15,000 members. Then in 1777 there were but 27 preachers.

For the Methodist revival had met certain difficulties. It is true that, as in England, the early preachers had not been

<hr>

[4] Humphrey, p. 14.
[5] See Buckley, *A History of the Methodists in the United States;* Strickland, *The Pioneer Bishop.*
[6] See his *Journal* for his account of his experiences. For the work in Virginia see volume I, 157-175.

cordially received.[7] But the special difficulty was the attitude of Wesley toward the colonists. His *Calm Address to the Colonies,* advising them to return to their allegiance, had been echoed by itinerant preachers; wherefore the patriots naturally looked upon the Methodists as enemies to the cause of liberty, secret instruments of despotic power, and men unworthy to be cherished in the midst of the republic. The storm was so great that the preachers were compelled to withdraw, and even Asbury went into hiding in Delaware. In the words of the Rev. Thomas Coke: "the clergy abandoned their flocks; and in many instances the British missionaries, following their example, forsook their spheres of action." In addition, the anti-slavery views of Wesley were viewed with prophetic suspicion, and the odium directed against the British was soon shared by native preachers, who were compelled to take an oath of allegiance to the new nation and who often suffered fine and imprisonment.[8] It was resolved to formulate an address to President Washington after his inauguration, professing loyalty to the new government. Washington replied in general terms, but even then suspicion had not died down: Dr. Coke, preaching in Baltimore after Asbury's ordination in 1784, was compelled to explain and defend Wesley's episcopation of Asbury and himself, failed to be tactful, and left the impression that the Methodists contemplated some kind of American episcopalian establishment.[9] However, in spite of difficulties, in 1784 there were 18,000 members and 104 traveling preachers.[10] The other evangelical denominations, studying these methods and not entangled with Wesley, were able to develop similar methods of conversion and revival, and became the most formidable foes of the spread of deism.

But it was in the reaction away from the French Revolution that the return to religion found its great impetus. This reaction is of such political consequence that we have discussed it elsewhere.[11] Here let us note that American criticism of the French constitution; American horror at the death of Louis XVI and at the Reign of Terror; the French hostility to relig-

---

[7] A single instance will serve for many. When Asbury visited Newcastle, Pennsylvania, in 1772, he found that the courthouse could not be used for his preaching, although it was open for dances and balls. *Journal*, I, 14.
[8] Drew, *Life of the Rev. Thomas Coke,* pp. 53-5, 56, 102-3.
[9] Drew, pp. 96-98, 98-102.
[10] Strickland, *The Pioneer Bishop,* p. 159.
[11] See chapter xv.

ion as indicated by the sequestration of church lands and the separation of church and state as noted by such men as John Adams, Patrick Henry, Alexander Hamilton, and Noah Webster; the conservative fear of the doctrine of equality, and a strong distrust in formal minds of the French rebellion against conventions, however puerile[12]—these caused the Americans to inquire whether there was any relation between anarchy and the goddess of reason. The conservative reaction was undoubtedly helped by the views of Burke and the British generally, as also by certain scandals in the conduct of émigré Frenchmen in this country.[13] It was "ces incidentes choquants et quelques autres, colportés adroitement, comparés avec les romans libertins de France et les déclarations irréligieuses de Volney" which "suffisaient à développer la légende d'une France athée et coupable."[14] The New England minister was not yet ousted from social control. "Did an individual defy their authority," writes Henry Adams, describing the situation in 1800, "the minister put his three-cornered hat on his head, took his silver-topped cane in his hand, and walked down the village street, knocking at one door and another of his best parishioners, to warn them that a spirit of license and of French infidelity was abroad, which could be repressed only by a strenuous and combined effort."[15] At Yale Timothy Dwight, president in 1795, thundered against atheism, deism, and materialism, ironically dedicated his *The Triumph of Infidelity* to Voltaire:

> There stood the infidel of modern breed,
> Blest vegetation of infernal seed,
> Alike no Deist, and no Christian, he;
> But from all principle, all virtue, free.
> To him all things the same, as good or evil;
> Jehovah, Jove, the Lama, or the Devil,
> Mohammed's braying, or Isaiah's lays;
> The Indian's powaws or the Christian's praise.

[12] Hazen's summary; see "The French Revolution as seen by the Americans of the Eighteenth Century," *Annual Report of the American Historical Society, 1896*, pp. 462-6. See in this connection Faÿ, chapter v.

[13] Talleyrand went about the streets of Philadelphia escorting a colored woman; Jean de Marsillac, received here as a persecuted French Quaker, changed to a worldling in France; M. Tilly ran off with Miss Bingham; and above all, the publication of the X. Y. Z. correspondence proved the French to be dishonorable. See Bowers, *Jefferson and Hamilton*, pp. 135, 364-367; and Faÿ, pp. 304-6.

[14] Faÿ, p. 306. See his references.

[15] Adams, *History*, I, 79.

With him all *natural* desires are good;
His thirst, for stews; the Mohawk's thirst for blood:
Made, not to know, or love, the all beauteous mind;
Or wing thro' heaven his path to bliss refin'd;

and in his *Century Discourses* arraigned the deist, as in his five volumes of *Theology Explained and Defended* he defended Christian theology against unitarian and sceptic and pilloried France for its want of religious faith.

Infidelity [said he] was first theism, or natural religion; then mere unbelief, then animalism, then scepticism, then partial, and finally, total atheism. The infidel writers have used terms so abstract, and a phraseology so mysterious as to attract readers fond of novelty, but the common people, never honored by Voltaire with any higher title than rabble or mob, have been caught by these writers, who volunteered to vindicate their wrongs and assert their rights. Happily it was soon discovered that the liberty of infidels was not the liberty of New England; that France, instead of being free, merely changed through a series of tyrannies; and that man, unrestrained by law and religion, is a mere beast of prey.[16]

In place thereof let us, he argues, return to the faith of our fathers. He set the senior class to debating the question, "Are the Scriptures of the Old and New Testament the Word of God?" and after the students, who had overwhelmingly chosen the negative, had delivered their arguments, he refuted their speeches and delivered a powerful argument for Christianity.[17] Nor was this all. Year after year he delivered his series of 173 sermons designed to prove a complete system of theology, so overwhelming that he boasts that the infidels have carried on warfare "in every manner which has promised them the least success," and failing argument, have been reduced to ridicule.[18] Does one require more positive proof? Let him read

[16] Cf. Riley, *American Thought from Puritanism to Pragmatism*, pp. 90-91.
[17] Dwight, *Theology Explained and Defended*, I, pp. xli-xlii.
[18] *Ibid.*, V, 544. See especially sermon xxiii, designed to prove the soul is not material, directed against Priestley (I, 361-376); sermon xxiv, designed to prove that the soul is not a chain of ideas and exercises (I, 377-392), since this notion contradicts intuitive certainty; sermon xxxi (I, 498-518) on the depravity of man, with its statistics of Parisian murders, suicides, divorces, and bastards and prostitutes ("this tremendous recital admits no comment," he says, p. 515); sermon xxxiv, proving that apostate man can not be justified by works of law (II, 38-54), directed against unitarian thinking; sermon xl (II, 150-169) on the divinity of Christ, which gives his objections to unitarian systems; sermon lx on the miracles (II, 151-464), directed against Hume; and the two concluding discourses, showing the superiority of divine truth to all moral schemes whatsoever, V, 529 ff. The series was first reduced to writing in 1809, but had been worked over for years.

Dwight's *Travels;*[19] with a wealth of detail Dwight proves the superiority of Christian and democratic New England to all infidel countries whatsoever.

Meanwhile Samuel Hopkins was addressing a letter to Aaron Burr, Vice-President of the United States, saying that "it is reported and believed by a number, that you do not believe in divine revelation, and discard Christianity as not worthy of credit;" this Hopkins can not believe, although the age is infidel, but nevertheless he straightway sets to expounding the superior virtues of Christianity.[20] There are many articles like that in the *American Museum* for November, 1788, entitled "Thoughts on deism. Ascribed to his excellency William Livingstone, esq., governor of New Jersey," in which a series of rhetorical questions were intended to reduce the deistic position to absurdity.[21] Straws show the direction of the wind. This in the *North-Carolina Journal,* February 18, 1799, one finds that "the Bishop of Landaff's answer to Paine's The Age of Reason" is for sale at the newspaper office in Halifax, and the advertisement is kept standing through a number of issues.[22] In 1794 there is published from the press "at Franklin's Head, no. 41, Chestnut Street" in Philadelphia, *A Gospel Alarm to Christendom: which Exhibits Vital Truth and Reprobates all her most lauded Notions of Religion, both Natural and Revealed. By Henry Casson, Dec. late of Maryland;* the book, which was printed by William Woodward, is frantically anti-deistic, anti-Quaker, and anti-Anglican: the Christian religion must, and shall, be preserved. Davis, prefacing his *Travels in America, 1798-1802,* expressly repudiates the "frantic crew of Deists," in dedicating his book to Jefferson,[23] and describes the "Infidel *Palmer,* who delivers lectures on Deism at New York," as one who "is securing for himself and followers considerable grants of land in hell."[24] By 1807 *The Balance* was summarizing a whole change in thought when it printed *The Dying Atheist,* the last stanza of which reads:

[19] *Travels in New-England and New-York,* 4 volumes, New Haven, 1822.
[20] See Stedman and Hutchinson, *Library of American Literature,* III, 89-91.
[21] *American Museum,* IV, November, 1788, pp. 440-442.
[22] P. 314.
[23] P. 3.
[24] P. 23.

"Ye erring mortals see the promis'd bliss—
By which a brother's exit is seren'd,
Hell opes its jaws, its fiery tenants hiss,
To hail the advent of another fiend."[25]

Deism was going down in a storm of popular disapproval. "It is a singular fact, that a person of the same name, Thomas Paine," wrote Stuart, "to whom a prize had been adjudged, about the beginning of this century, for writing a prologue at the opening of the Boston Theatre, afterwards obtained an act of the legislature of Massachusetts, authorizing him to change his name to Robert Treat Paine, 'because he was unwilling any longer to bear that of a certain noted infidel, and reviler of religion.' "[26] Thus the drama received its own.

Now that Franklin was dead, denunciation centered upon Jefferson.[27] Part of this denunciation, it is true, was purely political, but a large part of it was sincere, if ignorant. The opinion that he was a lost soul was founded partly on books and partly on stories spread by his foes. His opponents declared that he had denied that shells found on the mountain-tops are proofs of the great flood; that he had said, if the contents of the whole atmosphere were water, the land would only be overflowed to the depth of fifty-two and one half feet. He did not believe the Indians emigrated from Asia after the settlement of that continent by the descendants of Adam and Eve. He insisted that the negroes were a specially created and inferior race. He insisted that children should study Greek and Roman history instead of the Bible. His daily speech was that of an infidel.[28] In Massachusetts "pulpits had been set like so many Plymouth rocks, against Jeffersonism, the democracy, and the lax tendencies of French philosophy. It was," says a historian, "a sad, a painful sight from 1809 to 1814 to see these New England illiberals in their utter distrust of those in national power, whom they sincerely believed to be in secret league with Tophet, Napoleon, and the Jacobin clubs, riding the lean shank of Federalism straight towards the abyss of

[25] *The Balance,* VI, no. 27, July 7, 1807, p. 216.
[26] Stuart, *Three Years in North America,* II, 18.
[27] See the excerpts from contemporary newspapers in Bowers, *Hamilton and Jefferson,* index under Jefferson.
[28] McMaster, *History,* III, 501-2. In September, 1800, a pamphlet was published in New York City by an intimate friend of General Hamilton, entitled "The Voice of Warning to Christians on the Ensuing Election," devoted to showing that the *Notes on Virginia* attacked the Scriptures. Forman, *Life and Writings of Thomas Jefferson,* p. 80.

disunion."[29] Men of letters and politicians joined in the cry. Fessenden distinguished himself by his abuse,[30] and Joseph Dennie in the *Portfolio* was equally vehement.[31] So great was the outcry that it has remained almost for the present generation to clear Jefferson from some of the imputations repeated against him by Mrs. Trollope and others, gathering up the libels of this earlier period; as late as 1830 the life and correspondence of the great democrat was refused a place in the Public Library of Philadelphia.[32] Jefferson's language shows how deeply he resented the charges.[33] In effect, "the outcome of formal deism in America was to have the clergy reject it and the colleges thrust it out . . . the public first accepted, then grew tired of it."[34]

In January, 1804, *The Balance* carried a mock "oration on the progress of the Human Mind towards perfectibility, Delivered on a Quarter Day, by a Student in one of the Academies in this State," which sounds the praise of Mary Wollstone-

[29] Schouler, *History*, III, 222. See Stauffer, *New England and the Bavarian Illuminati*, particularly chapter III; and the introduction to Parrington, *The Connecticut Wits*.

[30] I have not been able to see the *Terrible Tractoration*. The most characteristic satire is *Democracy Unveiled, or Tyranny stripped of the Garb of Patriotism. By Christopher Caustic*, the third edition of which (New York, Printed for I. Riley, & Co. 1806) is under my hand. This lively Hudibrastic satire attacks illuminism and mobocracy (cantos II and III), as well as Jeffersonianism (canto IV: The Jeffersoniad). The work is in two volumes, and there is an index of proper names! *The Modern Philosopher* is directed against electrical magnetism and has incidental hits against French pseudo-science and Jefferson. (Philadelphia, 1806). *The Original Poems by Thomas Green Fessenden* (Philadelphia, 1806) appeared under his own name; there are a good many incidental hits at Jefferson. By 1809, the year of *Pills, Poetical, Political, and Philosophical, Prescribed for the Purging the Publick of Piddling Philosophers, of Puny Poetasters, of Paltry Politicians, and Petty Partisans. By Peter Pepper-Box, Poet and Physician* (Philadelphia), the satirist was growing tired. The *Democracy Unveiled* in particular rakes the vilest pits of gossip for mud to throw at Jefferson. Milder, but equally determined, was Alsop's attack in *The Echo*, No. XX, March 4, 1805. (In Parrington, *op. cit.*, pp. 497-514.)

[31] On Dennie see Ellis, *Joseph Dennie and His Circle*.

[32] Boardman, *America and the Americans*, p. 198.

[33] "Systematical in grasping at an ascendancy over all other sects, Presbyterians aim, like the Jesuits, at engrossing the education of the country, are hostile to every institution which they do not direct, and jealous at seeing others begin to attend at all to that object." (Jefferson to Cooper, 1822) Forman, *Life and Writings of Thomas Jefferson*, p. 344. This refers to the state of things in Virginia; Jefferson's denunciation of the New England clergy is well known.

[34] Riley, *American Philosophy: the Early Schools*, p. 317. Cf. the correspondence over questions of deism carried on by John Adams and Jefferson after the reconciliation, particularly in volume X of Adams' *Works*.

craft and the "immortal Godwin," discusses animal magnetism and ridicules galvanism. For the spread of these doctrines Voltaire, Diderot, d'Alembert, Adam Weishaupt, and Frederick the Great are chiefly responsible. "Thomas Paine, Volney, &c, are only under strappers," we learn, and the speaker is made to conclude that "my soul is filled with ecstasy at the sight of a Guillotine."[35] These names, with one exception, are familiarly known to the general reader. But the name of Adam Weishaupt introduces us to one of the most curious aspects of the anti-deistic movement, namely, the excitement over the *Illuminati.*[36]

On May 1, 1776, in Bavaria, Adam Weishaupt, a sincere, if somewhat crackbrained Bavarian liberal, had organized the Order of the Illuminati with a membership of five, the purpose of this secret order being the development of the human race. For a time the society languished; then in 1780 the organizing genius of Baron Adolf Franz Friederich Knigge applied itself to the task of extending the fraternity, and by 1784 there were 2000 or 3000 members, including various German princes of a liberal persuasion, Herder, Goethe, and Pestalozzi. On June 22, 1784, Karl Theodor of Bavaria, who since 1779 had been anti-liberal and ultramontane, launched the first of a succession of edicts against the order which by 1787 had disappeared in Bavaria, and which failed to flourish outside of that state. In the meantime, however, revelations real and imaginary of the purpose of the Illuminati, coinciding with the desire of conservative people everywhere to explain the sudden upheaval of the French Revolution, led to the foundation of the great legend in which Democratic Clubs, Freemasons, the Jesuits, and the Illuminati were equally implicated; namely, that the leaders of the French Revolution and the *philosophes* were secret members of a vast world-embracing society aiming to destroy Christianity and government.[37] This theory was set

[35] *The Balance,* III, no. 2, January 10, 1805, pp. 9-10.

[36] On the relation between the émigrés and the Illuminati see the first two chapters of the second volume of Baldensperger, *Le Mouvement des Idées dans l'émigration française.* For the American excitement the exhaustive study is Stauffer, *New England and the Bavarian Illuminati.*

[37] This theory seems first to have been seriously advanced with reference to Bode and Mirabeau. According to the theory, Mirabeau, during his residence in Berlin in 1786-7, had been inducted into the order by Johann Joachim Christoph Bode (1730-1793), the successor of Weishaupt, and upon his return to Paris he indoctrined that branch of French Freemasonry known as the Philalèthes or Amis Réunis with Illuminism, Bode and Busche coming to Paris in 1787 to assist in founding French Illuminism. French

forth in a once famous book by Professor John Robinson of the University of Edinburgh, the *Proofs of a Conspiracy against All Religions and Governments of Europe carried on in the Secret Meetings of the Free Masons, Illuminati, and Reading Societies,* first published in Edinburgh in 1797.[38] Robinson's theory was supposed to receive support from "revelations" in the *Mémoires pour servir à l'histoire du Jacobinisme* of the Abbé Barruel (1741-1820), a Jesuit priest who had been driven out of France, published in London in 1797-8.[39] The grand point with either book was that there existed a secret world-society devoted to rooting out all the religious establishments and overturning all the existing governments of Europe.[40] Meanwhile, in the United States the Democratic Societies had given trouble until they were suppressed because of Washington's disbelief in them; and Masonry had received a considerable increase by reason of the importation into the United States of various French lodges, not to speak of the enrollment of many of the revolutionary leaders, especially Federalists, and including Washington, among the ranks of Masonry. There was also the Order of the Cincinnati. One or another of these various organizations was distasteful to many. When on March 23, 1798, President John Adams proclaimed a fast day to be observed May 9, he offered opportunity for the Reverend Jedidiah Morse to deliver in Boston and Charlestown a sermon against infidelity which first made prominent the work of Robinson and charged that the Order had its branches established in America, that Paine's *Age of Reason* was one of their damnable products, and that the Democratical Societies were establishing the principles of Illu-

Freemasonry thus became the foundation of a secret revolutionary movement which on July 14, 1789, sprang its mine in the destruction of the Bastille. All subsequent events in the Revolution were traced to the order.
[38] Robinson's book went through a number of editions. There was a second London edition in 1797; a third (*ibid.*) in 1798; a fourth (*ibid.*) the same year. The fourth London edition was reprinted in New York in 1798. A French translation was published in two volumes in London in 1798-9; a German translation in 1800; and a Dutch (n.d.), Dordrecht. The connection between these translations and the émigré interest in Robinson is obvious. Cf. Baldensperger and Stauffer, pp. 199-200.
[39] Reprinted in Hamburg, Augsburg, Braunschweig that same year. A new edition revised and corrected by the author, appeared in Lyons in 1818; an English translation of the first edition was published by Barruel in London 1798, and this was reprinted at Hartford and at Elizabethtown, New Jersey, in 1799. There were also various abridgments and books of excerpts. Cf. Stauffer, p. 215.
[40] For a summary of both books see Stauffer, pp. 199-228.

minism in America.[41] In printing his sermon Morse further charged that the Illuminati were endeavoring to control Freemasonry and hinted that in this design in America, they had partially succeeded. There was shortly precipitated a controversy which continued to rage until 1800. Morse, under attack, returned to the charge in sermon and newspaper article; President Dwight was convinced of the truth of the allegations and thundered against infidelity and illuminism; so did the Reverend David Tappan, professor of divinity at Harvard; so did Dwight's brother, Theodore, domiciled in Hartford; so did various preachers, orators, publicists, and politicians. In vain did the Republicans in New England call for proofs; the Federalist clergymen were determined to believe in the great conspiracy; Jacobins, Freemasons, deists, Quakers, and republicans were at one time or another drawn into the charges; William Cobbett in *Porcupine's Gazette* in 1798 printed Morse's sermons with violent comments of his own; and Morse finally charged that the Grand Orient Lodge of Virginia, the members of which were chiefly emigrants from France and Santo Domingo, represented the Illuminati in the New World.[42] There followed a heated newspaper discussion.[43] When finally it was proved that the Wisdom lodge of Portsmouth, Virginia, was the lodge in question, and that this was a perfectly reputable Masonic organization, the discussion died down; the Masons, who had been continually protesting meanwhile, took the occasion of Washington's Masonic funeral, to ask how so good and great a man could belong to an organization held to be subversive of all he stood for. The agitation quieted, leaving behind it certain characteristic legacies. One was, curiously enough, a spirit of sympathy for the Roman Catholic church which Illuminism, it was charged, had been

[41] Summarized with much detail in Stauffer, pp. 229-235. The eagerness with which Robinson was received in America is indicated by Morse: "The first copies which were sent to America, arrived at Philadelphia and New York, at both which places the re-printing of it was immediately undertaken, and the Philadelphia edition was completely ready for sale in the short space of 3 *weeks*. This was about the middle of April. Happening at this time to be in Philadelphia, and hearing the work spoken of in terms of the highest respect by men of judgment, one of them went so far as to pronounce it the most interesting work that the present century had produced; I was induced to procure a copy which I brought home with me . . ." Stauffer, p. 233, note.
[42] Sermon delivered at Charlestown, April 25, 1799, on the occasion of a national fast. Stauffer, pp. 288-301.
[43] Stauffer, pp. 304-321.

organized to overthrow; one was a suspicion of Masonry
which flared up in the Antimasonic Party of 1826-1832 and
is not yet dead; and one was the conviction that moral and
republican America was well out of the intrigues of the Old
World.[44] While the excitement lasted, men of good sound sense
were prepared to agree with Fessenden that

> democrats, Illuminees,
> Are birds obscene, and of a feather,
> Should therefore all be class'd together.
> They all object to the propriety
> Of law and order in society,
> Think *reason* will supply restraints,
> And make mankind a set of saints.
>
> Such principles, alas, will flood
> Columbia's "happy land" with blood,
> Unless kind Providence restrain
> These demons of the hurricane.[45]

2. THE TRIUMPH OF THE MORAL REACTION OVER DEISM

Meanwhile deism and its associated creeds were fighting a
losing battle. It is too much to say with Professor Faÿ that up
to 1794 no one in general showed any fear of French deism,[46]
but certainly by that date deism had not been overwhelmed.
The influence of Franklin upon the intellectual life of Philadelphia had been profound,[47] and was not lightly to be shaken
off.[48] In New England the reading public knew Herbert,
Chubb, Shaftesbury, Tindal, Wollaston, Toland, and Hume;[49]
and there had appeared, as we have seen, Ethan Allen's *Reason
the Only Oracle of Man* in 1784.[50] Men had been too profoundly shocked by the rigid logic of Edward's theology not

[44] Attempts by the Republicans to fix the charge of Illuminism upon the
Federalists proved on the whole futile. Stauffer, pp. 345-60.
[45] Fessenden, *Democracy Unveiled*, I, 84-5.
[46] Pp. 228-9.
[47] For some notion of the variety and extent of Franklin's correspondence
with, and intimacy with, French philiosophers, scientists, deists, materialists,
and speculators generally, the student should turn over the pages of the
Calendar of Franklin Papers.
[48] Franklin had made Philadelphia "the van of intellectual progress." Riley,
American Thought from Puritanism to Pragmatism, p. 76.
[49] Cf. Stauffer, p. 70.
[50] The entire edition except thirty copies had been destroyed by fire,
thought to have been caused by lightning. The righteous pointed to the
judgment of God on the wicked. Evans, *American Bibliography*, VI, 266.
On the other hand Franklin's lightning rod had removed the early terror of
lightning.

to react in favor of "man's confidence in himself, in the midst of an age characterized by prodigious political initiative and love of liberty, and by conceptions of the Deity which stressed the very vastness of those reaches of space stretching between God and the World." Emphasis upon the divine sovereignty of God seemed quaintly out of date in a world given over to democratic enthusiasm.[51] As a result unitarianism was making progress.[52] The first Unitarian congregation had been one in Gloucester, formed in 1779; but the dramatic moment was to come later when King's Chapel, Boston, swung out of the Trinitarian fold in 1785-7. Even in Connecticut religious liberalism was making some headway.[53] Dr. Charles Chauncy's book, *Salvation for All Men,* was reprinted in America in 1784;[54] in Massachusetts Isaac Backus was obstinately arguing for liberty of conscience,[55] and all in all, even in rock-ribbed New England there was enough liberal thinking to alarm the conservative.[56] Staunch John Adams, though by no means an out-and-out deist, was greatly disturbed in his Christianity, as his Diary shows,[57] and if he repudiated the Encyclopaedists because of their "atheism," Rousseau and Helvétius, for their

---

[51] Stauffer, p. 69.

[52] See Cooke, *Unitarianism in America.*

[53] Consult Brissot de Warville, *Travels,* pp. 70-82. In 1784 liberty of conscience was secured to all Christians in Connecticut, the most hidebound New England state, by act of the General Court. Stauffer, pp. 59-60. "The fact is, new ideals and new forces were working upward in the common life of the age. The new sense of freedom which the War of Independence had ushered in, the steadily growing prosperity of the people, the development of social intimacies as the population of the country increased, the intrusion and growing influence of foreign ideas and customs, the steadily diminishing domination of the clergy—all these tended to inaugurate a new order which clashed more or less violently with the old." Stauffer, p. 26.

[54] Stauffer, p. 69 note.

[55] Author of *Government and Liberty Described and Ecclesiastical Tyranny Exposed,* 1778; *Appeal to the Public for Religious Liberty,* 1773; *Policy as Well as Honesty Forbids the Use of Secular Force in Religious Affairs,* 1779; *Truth is Great and Will Prevail,* 1781; *A Door Opened for Equal Christian Liberty,* 1783, all published in Boston.

[56] Thus Franklin sent to Harvard such "profane and deistic works" as the *Monde Primitif* of Count de Gébelin, who was a regular correspondent of Professor Sewall; and the college gave honorary degrees to Luzerne, Marbois, and Valnais, French consul at Boston, in 1782. Faÿ, p. 84, testimony of a freedom of attitude not found in Yale, when Dwight, issuing *The Triumph of Infidelity* in 1788, was attacking the unitarian Freeman of King's Chapel. The Hartford Wits, by the way, who were so strongly Federal in sympathies, were mostly Yale men. Wendell, *Literary History of America,* pp. 122-23.

[57] *Works,* II.

absurdity, and Diderot and Condorcet, for their materialism, if to him the *Age of Reason* was mainly stolen from Blount's *Oracles of Reason,* Bolingbroke, Voltaire and Bérenger,[58] he had yet read them and was prepared to fence with Jefferson over their merits;[59] his mind was not closed against free thought, and his correspondence shows that many of his neighbors had taken it over root and branch.

Jefferson meanwhile was actively mediating between French philosophy and American thought. "It was his five years' residence in France, before the outbreak of the Revolution, that gave the free-thinking Southerner," writes a historian of American philosophy, "an insight into the possibilities of materialism when carried to its logical outcome," but his "fundamental deism held him back from the atheism of Diderot, D'Alembert, and Holbach."[60] However this may be, the researches of Professor Chinard have put us into possession of precise information regarding Jefferson's acceptance of French thought. In 1793, for instance, Volney was writing to Jefferson; he had some notion of removing to the United States, where Franklin was his friend, and where he hoped to become intimate with Jefferson and Madison.[61] This same Volney wrote *Les ruines ou méditations sur les révolutions des empires* in 1791, sending 1200 copies of the Paris (English) edition to Philadelphia.[62] The book so impressed Jefferson that he translated the first twenty chapters; but the fact that he was president made it impolitic for him to acknowledge the work, which he turned over to Joel Barlow who finished and fathered it.[63] Jefferson translated the invocation with special fervor;[64] he was attracted to the book as much by its Ossianic style as by its anti-clerical tone, and this translation it was which appeared in

---

[58] *Works,* see index.

[59] See especially volume X of his *Works* for this correspondence.

[60] Riley, *American Thought from Puritanism to Pragmatism,* p. 80.

[61] Chinard, *Volney et l'Amérique,* pp. 26-27. The *Ruins* (eighteen editions appeared in England from 1792 to 1878) represents a reaction "contre les théories de Rousseau," and is "au fond la doctrine de l'intérêt, le doctrine de d'Helvétius, et de d'Holbach et celle de Bentham," which "offrait à la fois un traité sur l'origine des sociétés, une histoire des religions qui flattait les passions anti-cléricales de l'époque, une base solide et positive, au moins en apparence, sur laquelle on pouvait construire un nouvel ordre de choses." Chinard, p. 15.

[62] *Ibid.,* p. 133.

[63] The basis of Jefferson's translation was one published by James Lyon in Philadelphia in 1799.

[64] See *ibid.,* pp. 114-5.

Paris in 1802, was reprinted in 1818, and has since been reprinted in America.[65] Through the American Philosophical Society at Philadelphia, as well as by private correspondence, Jefferson kept in touch with movement and thought in France; presently we find him translating Destutt de Tracy's *Commentaries on Montesquieu,* published by Duane in 1811, very useful as anti-Federalist theory;[66] and next he has his hand in an American edition of that part of the French thinker's system which pertained to economics, the *Treatise on Political Economy,* published at Georgetown, D. C., in 1817.[67] Meantime the sage of Monticello has exchanged ideas with groups of French thinkers from the *philosophe* to the *idéologue* movements; from answering the Abbé de Pauw and Buffon in the *Notes on Virginia,* to absorbing the ideas of Condorcet and Cabanis on the progress of the human race and the secretion of thought by the human brain. The works and ideas of such French philosophers as appealed to him he frequently passed on to his lieutenants, such as Madison.[68] Perhaps the Presbyterians and Congregationalists were not entirely wrong in their denunciations.

Certain it is that up to the death of Louis XVI French thought was interesting a good many of the leaders of the United States, as for instance, the American Philosophical Society group in Philadelphia.[69] To that organization were sent

[65] Chinard, op. cit., pp. 112-8, 116-7. Chinard suggests some influence on Jefferson's famous estimate of the doctrines of Jesus. Volney's whole spirit was scientific, despite his fervid style. In 1830 the Religious Tract Society devoted a special tract to him. Eight editions of the *Ruins* appeared in America, the last in New York, 1890. The *Tableau des États-unis* appeared in Philadelphia in 1804 only, translated by Charles Brockden Brown. Chinard finds it the only book of travel in the United States by a Frenchman built on a scientific system; viz., the influence of climate and soil on race and temperament. In view of the various reprints of the *Ruins* in the United States from 1822 to 1835 it would appear that Volney was as useful as Paine against revealed religion. As late as 1857 an author in the *Southern Literary Messenger* couples Paine, Volney, and Voltaire.

[66] Chinard, *Jefferson et les Idéologues,* pp. 31-96.

[67] *Ibid.,* pp. 97-188.

[68] Thus one finds Madison writing Jefferson in 1788, "Mr. St. John has given me a very interesting description of a 'System of Nature' lately published in Paris. Will you add it for me?" Shortly he acknowledges the pamphlets of Marquis Condorcet and Mr. Dupont which Jefferson has sent him. In 1789 he writes Jefferson to thank him for his "attention to the works of the Abbé Barthelemy and the Marquis Condorcet." *Letters,* I, 379, 422, 465.

[69] Consult "Early Proceedings of the American Philosophical Society . . . 1744-1831," *Proceedings of the American Philosophical Society,* XXII, part II.

copies of the principal scientific and philosophical books appearing in France,[70] and to it were elected all the leading Frenchmen who attracted the attention of American thinkers.[71] In Philadelphia it was that Priestley had his discussion with Volney,[72] and there it was that the materialistic theories of Buffon, Cabanis, Chastellux, Condorcet, Lavoisier, whose pneumatic

[70] For instance, on December 17, 1774, Franklin sent them Buffon's *Natural History* and Lavoisier; September 15, 1775, Franklin delivered the Abbé Decquemare's *Essay on Sea Anemones* and Rozier's *Physic;* September 26, 1783, the Count de Gébelin announced he was sending the first four volumes of his *Primitive World;* July 15, 1785, they received three volumes of the Royal French Academy; December 7, 1787, Belin de Villenouve, Moreau de St. Méry, and M. Grevel all presented books; August 15, 1788, Franklin sent Pallanzani's *Opuscules* and Carminati's *Recherches;* September 19, 1788, Mandrillon's *Fragmens de Politique et de Littérature;* November 21, 1788, Brissot de Warville sent a book on the relative situations of France and the United States; March 6, 1789, 22 volumes of Velly, Villaret and Garnier's *History of France,* a *Histoire du Commerce* in 2 vols., the *Œuvres* of Thomas, and various other volumes were received; and the list can be extended indefinitely over the period covered. *Op. cit.*

[71] January 28, 1775, Condorcet, Daubenton, Dubourg, Le Roux, Macquair, Raynal, Lavoisier and Rosier were elected members; January 16, 1784, Count Campomanes, Marquis d'Angeville, and the Comte de Vergennes were elected; July 21, 1786, the Duc de Rochefoucauld, the Marquis de Condorcet (elected twice?), Charles the aeronaut, Cabanis, and L. Crell; January 16, 1789, Crèvecoeur, Captain François, Arthaud, Moreau de St. Méry, Brissot de Warville; January 20, 1792, Anthony R. C. M. de la Forest, consul general of France, Palisot de Beauvois; January 15, 1796, Dr. Grassi, late of Bordeaux and now of Philadelphia, La Rochefoucauld-Liancourt, Fessier de Grandpré, Citizen Adet; April 15, 1796, Alex Leribours, A. J. Larocque, Talleyrand; January 20, 1797, Mozard, French consul at Boston, Volney; April 18, 1800, Dupont de Nemours, etc.
As marking the closeness of relation between scientist and philosopher in France and the United States, the communications to the society are not without interest. Thus on December 30, 1774, Franklin wrote from Paris forwarding certain queries which Raynal wanted answered. (On December 17, 1774, the society "agreed that they were not proper objects of the Society's enquiries" as lying outside their province). December 17, 1774, Franklin forwarded certain queries from Condorcet, and a committee was appointed to answer them. December 10, 1779, the society wrote a letter to Buffon expressing their appreciation of his great work and offering aid. May 3, 1782, they received a letter from Mr. D'Abeville, a colonel of artillery in the French army, describing a partridge with two hearts. September 26, 1783, a letter from the French Minister was received saying the King would receive the orrery presented by the society. October 17, 1783, the society received letters from John Hyacinthe de Magellan, accompanying a gift and asking certain questions, and next month a second letter was received. September 19, 1788, M. le Roy of Paris sent "an elegant copperplate engraving of a Nouvel Hôtel Dieu" and October 17, 1788, M. de Marbois sent from Port au Prince a copy of his treatise on finances in Santo Domingo. This list could be indefinitely increased; the point is that French scientific materialism was known to the members of the American Philosophical Society. *Proceedings, op. cit.*

[72] For bibliography of pamphlets caused by the Priestley-Volney controversy, see Chinard, *Volney et l'Amérique,* p. 73 note.

theory was used to explode Priestley's phlogistic theory, and Volney, were debated and discussed, to be carried southward in the correspondence of Jefferson.[73] In Philadelphia the redoubtable Dr. Benjamin Rush wrote his *Influence of Physical Causes upon the Moral Faculty,* a treatise on the physical basis of mind and the relation of mental suggestion to therapeuty— had not the lightning-rod and Mesmer made anything probable?[74] Such advanced doctrines Dr. Thomas Cooper, son-in-law of Priestley, was to carry southward, re-enforcing the influence of Jefferson and Madison. What wonder that one finds an *Abridgement of the Laws of Nature,* "A Rhapsody by Mons. . . .," the French and English in parallel columns, in the *American Magazine* for February, 1788?[75] Or that the account of Voltaire's death in the *Columbian Magazine* in that same year (attributed to the bustle of Paris, the attempt to do the letter "A" in the French Dictionary, and too much coffee), should conclude that he "died with the resignation of a philosopher"; even though, when the Curate of St. Sulpice asked him, "Do you acknowledge the divinity of Jesus Christ?" Voltaire answered, "In the name of God, Sir, don't mention that man's name to me!" (these were, says the writer, Voltaire's last words). The editor is not shocked.[76] Even as late as 1793 Voltaire was "the judicious Voltaire" to the editor of the *North-Carolina Journal;*[77] six months earlier he is quoted in praise of Madame du Chatelet in the *Columbian Magazine,* a lady "who had too much judgment and was too ardent in the pursuit of truth, to dwell long on the chimaeras of metaphysics; she readily quitted, therefore, the imaginations of Leibnitz in order to give herself up to the clear and perspicuous doctrine of Newton." She was a mother, too,—admirable philosopher!—and her "manners and talents" are both praised.[78] Even as late as 1801 and in rock-ribbed New England, Abraham Bishop could roundly declare that the religion of the country was made a stalking horse for political jockies.[79] And

[73] Riley, *American Thought from Puritanism to Pragmatism,* pp. 98-9.
[74] Riley, *op. cit.,* pp. 102 ff.
[75] Pp. 131-3.
[76] August, 1788, pp. 445-447.
[77] July 10, 1793, no. 52.
[78] November, 1792, II (3d. series), pp. 300-2.
[79] In an oration at Wallingford, published at New Haven, 1801. Cf. Stauffer, p. 65 note.

is not *Thanatopsis,* written in 1810-11, thoroughly non-Christian in its attitude toward death?[80] On June 11, 1800, *The Temple of Reason,* published in New York, remarked that Christ was the greatest deist who ever lived.[81] Naturally this sort of thing could not long endure.

Deism came to its first great stumbling block in the work of Tom Paine. Part one of *The Age of Reason* had its first American edition in 1794, and there was some grumbling. When, however, Paine sent 15,000 copies of the second part to Franklin Bache of Philadelphia in 1796, the storm burst. Atheism, having dethroned Christianity in France, was now, it appeared, making propaganda in America, and we would not be safe in our beds. Behold the Reverend Daniel Dana of Newburyport, Massachusetts, in his pulpit one April Sunday in 1799. "Let me," he tells his congregation, "let me mention a fact which ought to excite universal alarm and horror." And the fact?

The well-known and detestable pamphlet of Tom Paine, written with a professed design to revile the Christian religion, and to diffuse the poison of infidelity, was composed in France, was there printed in English, and an edition containing many thousands of copies, conveyed at a single time into our country, in order to be sold at a cheap rate, or given away, as might best ensure its circulation. What baneful success has attended this vile and insidious effort, you need not be told. That infidelity has had, for several years past, a rapid increase among us, seems a truth generally acknowledged.[82]

When Jefferson was elected president, the turmoil over deism increased. Consider, for example, Joseph Dennie as "the

[80] Aaron Burr, brought up in this atmosphere, carried his tastes abroad with him in his "exile," 1808-12. June 10, 1809, he "read two or three hours this morning in a French work printed in 1804, entitled 'De la Philosophie de la Nature ou Traité de Morale pour le Génie Humain tiré de la Philosophie et fondé sur la Nature.' " He found the author a great advocate for *natural law* as the foundation of all law and morals, but objected to the sentimentalism of the book. In Stockholm, July 21, 1809, he read the 'Histoire de l'Église du japon,' Paris, 1715, and notes with irony that "the *miracles,* as the compiler, a learned priest (R. P. Crassett, a Jesuit), says, are as well attested as any of those in the New Testament!" He also read an 'Essai sur la Mégalanthropogénesie, par Robert le jeune" (1801), an early work on eugenics. He bought Bayle for four louis in Paris April 23, 1810, for the benefit of Theodosia; October 10, 1810, he says that of all the books he bought for Theodosia, Cabanis will afford her most satisfaction: "it is exactly in your line, being at once medical and philosophical." Davis, *The Private Journal of Aaron Burr,* I, 231, 248, 447; II, 55.

[81] Faÿ, p. 313.

[82] Quoted in Stauffer, pp. 75-6. See the bibliography of anti-Paine literature there given. "The impression that Paine had aided and abetted the cause of impiety and irreligion was general."

lay preacher" in his *The Portfolio* as he impartially condemns French philosophy and Virginia deism in 1801:

Those who have been professors of the new philosophy of France, and their servile devotees in America, taint everything they touch. Like the dead insect in the ointment, they cause the whole to send forth an odious and putrid savor. Instead of viewing man as he is, they are continually forming plans for man as he should be. Nothing established, nothing common, is admitted into their systems. They invert all the rules of adaptation. They wish to fashion nature and society in their whimsical mould, instead of regulating that mould according to the proportions of society and nature. They glow with intense love for the whole species, but are cold and chill as death towards every individual. . . .

To men of the complexion of Condorcet and his associates, most of the miseries of France may be ascribed. Full of paradox, recent from wire-drawing in the schools, and with mind all begrimed from the Cyclops cave of metaphysics, behold a Sieyes *(sic)*, in the form of a politician, draughting, *currente calamo,* three hundred constitutions in a day, and not one of them fit for use, but delusive as a mountebank's bill and bloody as the habilliments *(sic)* of a Banquo.

Of this dangerous, deistical, and Utopian school, a great personage from Virginia is a favored pupil. His Gallic Masters stroke his head, and pronounce him forward and promising. Those who sit in the same form cheerfully and reverently allow him to be the head of his class. In allusion to the well marshalled words of a great orator, him they worship; him they emulate; his "notes" they con over all the time they can spare from the "Aurora" of the morning, or French politics at night. The man has talents, but they are of a dangerous and delusive kind. He has read much, and can write plausibly. He is a man of letters, and should be a retired one. His closet, and not the cabinet, is his place. In the first, he might harmlessly examine the teeth of a nondescript monster, the secretions of an African, or the Almanac of Banneker. At home he might catch a standard of weight from the droppings of his eaves, and seated in his epicurean chair, laugh at Moses and the prophets, and wink against the beams of the Sun of Righteousness. At the seat of government his abstract, inapplicable metaphysico-politics are either nugatory or noxious. Besides, his principles relish so strongly of Paris, and are seasoned with such a profusion of French garlic, that he offends the whole nation. Better for Americans, that on their extended plains, "thistles should grow, instead of wheat, and cockle instead of barley," than that a "philosopher" should influence the councils of the country, and that his admiration of the works of Voltaire and Helvetius *(sic)* should induce him to wish a closer connection with Frenchmen. When a metaphysical and Gallic government obtains in America, may the pen drop from the hand, and "the arm fall from the shoulder-blade" of

THE LAY PREACHER.[83]

Paine and Jefferson were the most heartily abused men of their time.

[83] Quoted in Stedman and Hutchison, IV, 249-251.

After 1801 favorable references to French deism become fewer and fewer, and evidences of hostility increase.[84] *The Monthly Anthology and Boston Review* in August 1806, can not decide whether Voltaire died a Christian or no.[85] *The Portfolio* by July, 1810, is firm in its denunciation—not unnaturally. Of *La Pucelle,* the *Dictionary,* and *Candide,* the editor remarks that

Every page is defiled with vulgar pleasantry, gross indecencies, and disgusting ribaldry. No respect is paid to the Deity, none to religion, to virtue, or to morals, and we may add, none to taste; for what can be more opposed to taste, to the perception of what is true, refined and beautiful, than a low and grovelling style delineating manners still more loose and contemptible; than a crude collection of puerile incidents, improbable adventure and forced witticisms, which would disgrace the character of a footman?[86]

The Analectic observes in 1813 that

the whole tribe of French writers who have any pretensions to philosophy in the last several years, are injected with a spirit of indelicacy which is peculiar, we think, to their nation; and strikes us as more shameful and offensive than any other. We do not know how very well to describe it, otherwise than by saying, that it consists in a strange combination of physical science with obscenity, and an attempt to unite the pedantic and disgusting details of anatomy and physiology, with images of voluptuousness and sensuality. . . .[87]

In 1817 the *American Monthly Magazine and Critical Review* "is informed that religion is reviving in France," that "daily pilgrimages . . . of repentant and converted atheists" are to be seen, although things are not going too well: "it has been stated that there are no less than four thousand parishes in France destitute of ministers. The consequences of such a want of religious instruction may be easily conceived."[88] That

[84] They do occur. *The Monthly Anthology and Boston Review* in November, 1803, reviewing the Life of Voltaire by Condorcet, takes a civil and impartial attitude. Voltaire is credited with intelligence of an astonishing degree and the review takes a favorable view of his religion. I, 44. Again, *The Balance* ran through January and part of February, 1803, the "Profession of Philosophical Faith, translated for the Balance, from the French of a Pupil of Rousseau." II, nos. 1-5. An edition of Massillon's sermons (in English), published by Carey in 1818, was introduced curiously enough by D'Alembert's *Discourse on Massillon.*
[85] III, 413.
[86] Article on the "Life, Character, and Works of Voltaire." IV, 11.
[87] This is à propos of Diderot. The article is reprinted from the *Edinburgh Review,* but expresses the American attitude. II, 353.
[88] November, 1817, p. 66; May, 1817, p. 49. See in this connection the "Admonition to the Clergy of France" in the *Christian Disciple,* III (n.s.), 332-338, (Sept.-Oct.), 1821.

year James Madison was writing to John Adams that Condor-cet's idea of government "seems now to be everywhere ex-ploded."[89] Fearon, inspecting the book-stores in New York in 1817, found old books scarce, few standard books, plenty of theological works, English novels and poetry, but "Hartley, Priestley, and the religious writings of Locke are scarce; I may say unknown."[90] Yet James Monroe is president! Such are the whirligigs of time.

It is 1820, and Monroe is still president: the era of good feeling, men say, has come. Perhaps that is why the *Philadelphian Register and National Recorder* is printing the "prayer of Voltaire for toleration" in its issue for January 30.[91] At any rate, deism is not wholly dead: *Blowe's Emigrants' Directory*, mainly devoted to the frontier, declares that there are "a great number who reject religion altogether as unnecessary, inconvenient, and fabulous, and plead the sufficiency of natural religion. Of this description are many of the principal inhabitants throughout the Union, and particularly to the southward," but, it adds, they do not dare to declare themselves openly. "To read the petty and malicious gossip concerning the last days of Hobbes and Hume, Voltaire and Paine, one would be led to think that the compilers had gone mad to meet their private ends," writes Professor Riley of this epoch; and he points out that Hinton's *Lectures to Despisers of Religion* advises that deists be socially ostracized.[92] In fiction, at least, it is done. *Precaution* was published in 1820; and Cooper insists that a mother shall require piety in her son-in-law. "Would our daughters admire a handsome deist, if properly impressed with the horror of his doctrines, sooner than they would now admire a handsome Mohammedan?" Mrs. Wilson asks. When one of the characters asks his wife to go riding on Sunday, the same lady observes that "had he been an open deist, she would have shrunk from the act in his company on suspicion of its sinfulness."[93]

---

[89] Madison *Letters*, III, 41, May 22, 1817.
[90] Fearon, *Sketches of America*, p. 35.
[91] I, 91.
[92] Riley, *American Philosophy: the Early Schools*, pp. 313, 318.
[93] See Lounsbury, *James Fenimore Cooper*, pp. 25-26. The same religious preoccupation runs through Cooper. In *Wing-and-Wing*, the heroine, a French Roman Catholic, will not marry the hero, an infidel; the refusal causes his death. The book was published in 1842. Lounsbury, pp. 243-4. I have not been able to see a copy of *Precaution*.

In 1822 and 1823 Candler declared that "instances of openly avowed deism are rare. Persons who hold deistical opinions generally either keep them to themselves, or veil them under the garb of flimsy hypocrisy. I recollect only two persons of all with whom I conversed on religion, who unhesitatingly proclaimed their disbelief in Christianity. In many parts a man's reputation would be seriously injured if he were to avow himself one." He found that Universalists, Unitarians, and Jews, were "branded as Deists," and of certain English deists who had emigrated to Illinois, he says that they have had to establish weekly worship under the Christian name.[94] In 1824 the *Christian Spectator* was making extracts from one of Dwight's sermons which attributed the French Revolution to Voltairean infidelity.[95] There was in Cambridge at this epoch "an awful whisper" that Mrs. Craigie read Voltaire in the original—at any rate her copy of his works remained in the library at Craigie House.[96] "When I was in America," wrote de Tocqueville of the thirties, "a witness, who happened to be called at the assizes of the county of Westchester . . . declared that he did not believe in the existence of God, or in the immortality of the soul. The judge refused to admit his evidence on the ground that the witness had destroyed beforehand all the confidence of the court in what he was about to say. The newspapers related the fact without any further comment."[97] Bernhard, visiting the library of Bishop Dubourg in New Orleans in 1826 and finding there a complete set of the French Encyclopaedia, observed that the books were difficult or impossible to get in the United States.[98] If on the one hand Murat attributed

[94] Candler, *Summary View of America,* pp. 163, 172, 174. He adds, however, that "a strong deistical feeling is apparent in the opposition made to missionary societies." Pp. 163-4.
[95] VI, 75-79, February, 1824. From the Public Fast sermon of July 23, 1812.
[96] Samuel Longfellow, *Life of Longfellow,* I, 263. On the other hand Emerson recorded in his journal September 21, 1836, that "the French period brought Rousseau and Voltaire into the field and their army of Encyclopaedists, to speak for the people and protest against the corruptions and tyrannies of monarchy. Pascal uttered amidst his polemics a few thrilling words. Paine and the infidels began with good intentions, and the Cobbetts and Malthuses and Benthams have aimed at the same; foolish men, but dominated by a wisdom of humanity." *Journal, 1836-1838,* p. 86.
[97] *Democracy in America,* I, 329. "The revolutionists of America are obliged to profess an ostensible respect for Christian morality and equity. which does not easily permit them to violate the laws that oppose their designs; nor would they find it easy to surmount the scruples of their partisans, even if they were able to get over their own." P. 328.
[98] Bernhard, *Travels,* II, 83.

a considerable anti-religious effect to Owen,[99] if Combe alleges the existence of a society of Scotch deists meeting in Tammany Hall,[100] we must remember that by the 1830's the Unitarian movement in New England was well under way;[101] that the labor movement was beginning, and that labor tends to deism; that in short, by the end of the thirties, the narrow conservatism of the previous years was beginning to crumble— a point to which we shall presently recur.

3. THE RELIGIOUS REVIVAL SPREADS OVER THE COUNTRY

So it is that deism and French philosophy disappear in a mist of objurgation and discussion. So remarkable a transformation, wrought in less than fifty years, could not have occurred purely because of the defects in deism or in the Revolutionary philosophy. This is but the negative side; the positive side of this remarkable movement is to be found in the extraordinary religious revival among the evangelical denominations, the effects of which still color American life. For a brief period the romantic philanthropy of the rights of man philosophy satisfied the ardent, but as a national pabulum it was not sufficient. At any rate, the "revival" movement, already a distinctive characteristic of American religion, took on at the turn of the century a new and fascinating lease of life. The "Great Revival" seems to have begun in a number of places; we may instance New England and Kentucky, for the one was to influence the other. The New England movement proceeded in a series of waves: the historian of Congregationalism tells us that after 1740, the years 1799-1805, 1820-1823, 1826-27, 1830-31, and 1841-42, were remarkable for revivals of that faith in New England and, later, in the West; and that (what

---

[99] "His frank and polished, but irrevocable manner of attacking revelation, produced a very great effect." Murat, *A Moral and Political Sketch of the United States,* p. 140.

[100] Combe, *Notes on America,* II, 170. He does not know "to what extent infidelity prevails." The Rev. Isaac Fidler describes Tammany Hall in 1832 as "a place where the lower and more restless orders meet to discuss political and religious questions, and not a few of whose frequenters, as I was informed, are professed Atheists." Fidler, *Observations in the United States and Canada.*

[101] "Deism took the mild form of Unitarian Christianity," writes Nichols, "merging gradually into the Rationalism of Theodore Parker. . . . This form of theology, Deism—under the name and with the forms of Christianity—has not had much success out of New England." In New England "infidels or Deists called themselves Unitarians and kept up the forms of religious worship." *Forty Years of America Life,* I, 72, 73. See also Cooke, *Unitarianism in America.*

is equally important), the effect of the movement was to send
out home missionaries to Vermont, western New York, Ohio,
Indiana, Illinois, and Michigan, there to convert the frontier.[102]
Simultaneously with the first of these periods the Kentucky
Revival occurred:[103] the first regular general camp-meeting
was held at Gasper River Church, July, 1800.[104] The movement especially involved the Presbyterians, Methodists and
Baptists.[105] The Baptists, whose congregation in Philadelphia
had been scattered in the Revolution, had now recovered and
had grown by 1812 to 2,164 churches with 1,605 ministers
and 172,972 members.[106] The Methodists[107] and the Presbyterians grew in proportion, the latter sect in particular becoming large enough to split in two when the frontier set up its
own brand of Presbyterianism, namely, the Cumberland, a
direct product of the Gasper River revival.[108] In 1810 the
General Assembly resolved on establishing a theological semi-

[102] Walker, *A History of the Congregational Churches in the United
States*, p. 320.

[103] There were 30,000 souls in Kentucky in 1784; by 1787 20,000 more had
migrated thither. Some schools had been established, and there was a college
to which the Rev. John Todd of Virginia had given a library. The Anabaptists were the first to promote public worship in Kentucky; though three
congregations of Presbyterians were soon established near Harrod's station,
the Rev. David Rice of Virginia being the pastor (?). At Lexington there
was another congregation under the leadership of the Rev. Mr. Rankin, also
of Virginia. Imlay could find no other formal religious societies, though
various types of believers were to be found. Imlay, *Topographical Description*, pp. 321-322. Rice and Rankin immediately got into a theological quarrel,
for the details of which see Rusk, I, 219 ff.

[104] McMaster, II, 578-82. This was the revival to which Jefferson's opponents pointed significantly.

[105] See Buckley, *A History of the Methodists in the United States;* Newman, *A History of the Baptist Churches in the United States;* Thompson,
A History of the Presbyterian Churches in the United States.

[106] The distribution of the Baptists is significant of the geography of the
revival. The figures are given as follows:

Virginia	35,665	North Carolina	12,567
Kentucky	22,694	South Carolina	11,821
New York	18,499	Tennessee	11,325
Georgia	14,761	New England	32,373
	Middle States	26,155	

Considering the relative density of population, it is clear that the strength of
the Baptists was in the South and along the frontier. Newman, *op. cit.*, p.
379. Cf. chap. X above, p. 375, note 83.

[107] On the whole character of the religious conquest of the frontier in connection with Methodist growth, cf. Strickland, *The Pioneer Bishop,* especially
chaps. v-xxii.

[108] The Cumberland Presbytery was formed in 1810. There were three
ministers in 1813, 46 in 1822, 114 in 1827. Carroll, *Religious Forces in the
United States,* pp. 289-290.

nary at Princeton, a move that was to have an important influence upon the religious life of the South in particular.[109] The War of 1812 for a time troubled the onward flow of the revival, but the increasing capture of the movement by the middle classes in the North led to a second and even more vigorous moral movement, a reform which, not content with re-invigorating the church, took shape in Temperance Societies, movements for prison reform, for Sunday Schools, and an interest in juvenile delinquents.[110] But postponing for the moment our consideration of moral reform in the North, let us note that the revival movement was aimed especially at the South and at the frontier; and that it is characterized by sending out missionaries to convert the godless. Calvinism in these regions was re-enforced by the character of the emigration. "Between the New Englanders with their modified Calvinism, and the Southerns with their diluted Arminianism, there came a wave of new settlers . . . the Scotch-Irish entering chiefly by way of the ports of the Middle States," who brought with them their religious fervor, their moral zeal, and the philosophy of Stewart and Reid. "They carried along with their Presbyterian connections their philosophy of common sense. To trace this movement into the Alleghany Mountains and down the valleys of Virginia and of the Cumberland, is to trace a kind of intellectual glacier, an overwhelming mass of cold facts which moved slowly southwards and ground out all opposition. . . . Because of it deism disappeared, save in the tide-water counties where planters of English blood still remained, and materialism was wiped out, save in the Gallicised portions of the country, such as the Carolinas, and the Bourbon sections of Kentucky."[111] President Dwight, as we have seen, was the champion of the orthodox hosts, and neither the University of Pennsylvania, nor the University of Virginia, nor Transyl-

---

[109] Hageman, *Princeton and Its Institutions,* II, 267.

[110] At the close of the war "the pauper, dependent, ond petty criminal classes had multiplied with what seemed alarming rapidity" along the seaboard because of the war and the resulting idleness. "All admitted that crime, profaneness, desecration of the Sabbath, intemperance and pauperism, prevailed everywhere to an extent which called loudly for public interference." McMaster, IV, 524-5. In 1815 there was a great revival at Princeton in which the students especially were touched. Hageman, *op. cit.,* II, 110-111. In these years, by the way, Dr. Francis Brown, third president of Dartmouth, was ardently defending Calvinism in pamphlets and sermons. Smith, *The History of Dartmouth College,* p. 120, gives the list.

[111] Riley, *American Philosophy: The Early Schools,* p. 478. On the movement of the Scotch-Irish toward the frontier see Roosevelt, *The Winning of the West,* I, 125-128, 193-201, 219-220; II, 275-278, etc.

vania University could stem the tide.[112] The preachers served as schoolmasters to the frontier,[113] and having conquered the frontier, they found that the frontier in turn could overwhelm the seaboard. "Once they had won over the small farmers of the hills in the two Carolinas and Georgia, these teachers of a stern faith were in a strategic position when small farmers became big cotton-planters."[114] Institutions of liberal thought in that region were compelled to surrender. When Jefferson founded the University of Virginia, he excluded from it, as we have hinted, any ecclesiastical establishment or clergy. But when the news of Cooper's appointment came out (29 March, 1819), "a terrific outcry arose that Atheism was to be publicly taught, that the state would become bankrupt, that the good old times were gone forever, and that war was being waged against the manhood and virtue of Virginia by the arch-scoffer of Monticello, seconded by his deistical follower of Montpellier."[115] With the rise of the Cotton Kingdom the teachings of Jefferson were discredited under the ridicule of John Randolph and Chief Justice Marshall, so that "four years after Jefferson's death the Virginia constitutional convention openly disavowed the equalitarian teachings which had underlain the politics of the South since 1800."[116] Two years later Thomas R. Dew, trained in German universities, began the formulation of a new economics, a new social theory which was to supplant the equalitarianism of the older school: economics and religion combined to strangle deism in Virginia and the lower South; by 1850 Jeffersonian ideals were dead.[117]

[112] Riley, op. cit., p. 479. On Transylvania University see Rusk, I, 28, 58-9. Harry Toulmin, a Unitarian minister and a disciple of Priestley, had been president of Transylvania Seminary, which became a university in 1798-99 (in name). In 1818, Horace Holley, a Boston Unitarian clergyman, resolved to make Transylvania the center of higher education in the West. By 1824 he had a faculty of fifteen eminent men: Charles Caldwell and Daniel Drake, leading physicians; James Blythe, later president of Hanover College; Robert Hamilton Bishop, first president of Miami; Mann Butler, the Kentucky historian; Constantine Rafinesque, the picturesque scientist and cosmopolite, and others.

[113] ". . . preachers of early Prebysterianism, missionaries trained in the methods and the theology of Princeton, carried Latin and Greek wherever they went." Dodd, The Cotton Kingdom, p. 83. There are a good many details in Roosevelt.

[114] Ibid., pp. 100-101.

[115] Trent, English Culture in Virginia, p. 22. On the whole subject see Patton, Jefferson, Cabell, and the University of Virginia, chapters v-vi.

[116] Dodd, op. cit., pp. 48-49.

[117] See Dodd's account of the establishment of the new theory. William and Mary College made Dew its head and "students from the lower South

The symbolical change at the University of Virginia was noted by Frederika Bremer in 1851:

But so clear among this people is the conviction that social life requires religious life, and that the religious teacher must have his place in the community, that, soon after Jefferson's death, a room in one of the buildings of the University was fitted up for a place of worship, and the heads of the University agreed in summoning thither ministers of various religious persuasions, who should alternately perform divine service and give religious instruction.[118]

Cotton and Calvin had triumphed.

When Cooper resigned at Virginia he went, as we have seen, to South Carolina. But the Presbyterian glacier required only time to overcome the Carolinas as well. Let Professor Dodd tell the story:

They (i.e., the Presbyterians) took command in these three states before 1840. Presbyterians became governors and members of Congress without waiting for the consent of their religious seniors. The president of the University of North Carolina was a Presbyterian divine, for all the world like the good Dr. Witherspoon of Princeton. In South Carolina, President Cooper was brought to trial for his "shameful atheism" in 1834[119] . . . John H. Thornwell, a student of Cooper's, was one of the powers behind the movement and not many years passed before he was himself president of the University. Not to be outdone in the matter, Thornwell founded in the very shadow of the University, the Southern Presbyterian Theological Seminary. . . . Even the great Calhoun became interested in Calvinism and manifested a genuine concern in the growing religiosity of the planters.[120]

In the meantime, it is true, the Presbyterians lost the hillfolk, but these the Baptists and the Methodists saved. By 1860 there were a million church members in the South, the majority of them belonging to these two faiths.[121] The Southern Presbyterians, however, became powerful enough to take control of the national organization, with Thornwell as their chief, and had they not split on the subject of slavery, these three organizations would have proved even more powerful factors in the national life than they were. As it was,

hastened to the old institution to sit at the feet of the new Gamaliel." See also *Cambridge History of American Literature,* III, book III, chap. xxi, especially pp. 338-40.

[118] *Homes in the New World,* II, 515.

[119] Cf. Laborde, *History of the South Carolina College,* chapter viii. Laborde reports that Cooper had been in addition, dogmatic and officious. The college was almost deserted in 1834, there being but 20 students. In 1835 a professorship of Christian evidences was established. P. 191.

[120] Dodd, *op. cit.,* pp. 101, 102.

[121] Dodd, pp. 102-3.

the movement of intellectual liberalism was almostly completely annihilated in the greater portion of the country by the evangelical or revivalist movement. The triumph of revivalism was rendered easier by the weakly organized intellectual life and the economic bankruptcy of the older Southern aristocracy as reflected in the financial difficulties which embarrassed Jefferson, Madison, and Monroe in their old age.[122]

Let us look in the next chapter at certain consequences of this movement.

[122] *Cambridge History of American Literature,* III, 227.

XII

The Effects of French Religion

1. THE CHARACTERISTICS OF FRONTIER RELIGION

We HAVE attempted to trace in the last chapter the confusing currents and counter-currents which eddied around deism in the concluding years of the eighteenth century, as well as the remarkable religious revival in the opening decades of the nineteenth century which dealt deism so formidable a blow. Certain other factors originate in this period which we must consider before we go on to discuss the remaining elements in these aspects of the intellectual and emotional life of America which are yet to cover.

We have seen how, particularly in the South, the frontier spirit (which had at first shared with the planters and the tidewater aristocracy the easy indifference of the eighteenth century) caught fire from the northern missionaries, "got religion," and, so converted, rolled back and obliterated the cosmopolitan liberalism of the coast.[1] The transformation need not astonish us. I have already noted that there is not one, but several, frontiers. The outermost frontier remained to the end consistently deistic and even irreligious;[2] it is the second and third frontiers which were thus converted. Nor can we pass to other matters until we have noted that the frontier did more— it contributed so largely to the shaping of the evangelical denominations in this country, that they may almost be called frontier products.[3] In the first place, the frontier enlarged the

---

[1] Bryce noted in the eighties that "six Southern states exclude from office any one who denies the existence of a Supreme Being. Besides these six, Pennsylvania and Tennessee pronounce a man ineligible for office who does not believe in God and in a future state of rewards and punishments. Maryland and Arkansas even make such a person incompetent as a juror or witness." *The American Commonwealth,* II, 571.

[2] Note the unorthodox religious views of the cowboys, the trappers, the California gold-diggers, and the Alaskan fortune-hunters. The church is ever the product of an established social group. It is not, of course, denied, that Christians exist on the frontier, and perhaps the word "consistently" is too strong; the point is that indifference and tolerance characterize the shifting society of the frontier where a belief in God is normally the only great point of agreement.

[3] On this whole topic see the significant and illuminating study of Mode, *The Frontier Spirit in American Christianity,* on which the discussion in the text is based.

missionary horizon to include the Indian and the "home mission" and so strengthened the missionary note long typical of American Protestant Christianity.[4] The revival meeting, the camp meeting, the stress upon "personal conversion" highly characteristic of the Baptist, Methodist, and Presbyterian denominations, took, if not their origin, their American qualities from the history we have just outlined. Then, since the minister was not merely missionary but school teacher as well, the small "freshwater" college, overwhelmingly denominational in its origins, owes its rise and spread to the exigencies of sending Christianity to the frontier. These schools extend through Iowa, Missouri, and Kansas, where, during the process of settlement, small colleges multiply. If, for fifty years, they have ceased to dot the West, it is because methods have changed. Founded originally to "solve the problem of ministerial leadership," they could in the nature of the case offer no highly specialized theological course: Paley's *Natural Theology,* Butler's *Analogy of Revealed Religion,* Wayland's *Moral Science* and *The Evidences of Christianity* were studied, so that, while liberal movements like Unitarianism and Transcendentalism might sweep the East, the West on the whole tended, as it still tends so far as these beliefs are concerned, to stand firm.[5] If the East, with its greater cosmopolitanism, became highly critical of these educational endeavors, they yet multiplied—to keep pace with "Romanism," their proponents argued, and Hamlin Garland in his *A Son of the Middle Border,* has showed their importance in the cultural life of his youth. Nor is this all. The frontier with its particularistic spirit tends to break up into small sects; with its uncritical spirit it tends to accept eccentric religious doctrine, and Mode devotes a whole chapter to the discussion of some characteristic evidences of this tendency.[6] The multiplication of small sects has long been noted as characteristic of American religious life.[7] Mode shows, too, how the opposite tendencies of church coöperation and church

[4] "It thus appears that from its earliest stages the settlement of the frontier served as a training school in which East and West alike had brought home to them the world-horizon of missionary responsibility, *and the constructive value of Christianity in the upbuilding of society.*" Mode, p. 30. (My italics.) Note the meaning of this statement for the Eastern attempt to keep a cultural control of the West.
[5] Western radicalism is mainly political, not philosophical.
[6] Mode, chap. v. The multiplication of religious sects should not be confused with a "non-religious" movement like deism.
[7] See the list of sects in Carroll, *Religious Forces in the United States;* and for a discussion, de Tocqueville, chap. xxiii.

rivalry[8] are again a part of the frontier spirit. He has also something to say about the tendency towards centralized control in church government, not found among the colonists,[9] but required by the necessities of missionary work on so large a scale; and, what is perhaps more significant still, he notes that the frontier tends towards irreverence, to the secularizing of the religious mind—the counterpart to what Professor Pattee has justly called the laughter of the West. Finally, it would be unfair to pass over the challenge to the heroic in mankind which the frontier has flung to the religious, and which found expression in the circuit-rider who, with the pony express, has now melted into epic legend. So thoroughly has the frontier stamped American Protestant Christianity that it has been the problem of an industrial age to re-shape the church to its needs. The significance of all this for our study is that the frontier in religion has tended to increase the differentiation between American protestantism and European religious life, whether protestant or Catholic.

2. THE CHARACTERISTICS OF BOURGEOIS RELIGION

While religion was capturing the South and the frontier, in the North the bourgeois spirit was capturing religion. The characteristic note of the Southern movement with its missionary zeal, its camp-meetings, its exhorters, is emotional; the characteristic note of the northern movement is moral. There, in a growing industrial society which was gradually taking control of state governments, the middle classes with their serious ethical interests, deepening into prudery, shaped the religious movement to their own ends and shaped their beliefs to the religious movement: the phenomenon is paralleled in Great Britain. In fact the American religious revival is but part of a world movement, that movement which brought about the Catholic Revival on the Continent, and the Oxford movement and muscular Christianity in England.

Our understanding of the capture of the religious revival by the middle class will be helped less by a quantitative than by a qualitative study.[10] If the increase in membership of the evangelical churches is written in their histories for all to read,

---

[8] Compare the tendency of the frontier in social life to be pulled two ways between individualism and equalitarianism.
[9] Cf. the quotation from Humphrey, chap. xi, pp. 389-90, above.
[10] See, for a summary of views and interpretations conveniently collected, Mesick, *The English Traveller in America,* chap. viii.

it yet tells us nothing; it is the peculiar quality of the ethico-religious movement which we must grasp; and here we are helped by a reference to eighteenth century sentimentalism and to the literature of the Victorian period in Great Britain. Serious, moral, godly, the attitude yet saw no inconsistency in a society which created temperance organizations and manufactured New England rum; which preached the need of Christian brotherhood to all the world and followed the doctrines of laissez-faire economics at home; which combined thriftiness with a painless altruism, condemned the Catholic without taking the trouble to understand him, and felt for the negro without ever having known him. Built upon the ethical code of Benjamin Franklin—is there a more typical example in all the world of the strength and weakness of middle-class standards than the *Autobiography* and the *Almanac?*—and upon the economics of Adam Smith[11] and Bentham, and the common-sense philosophy of the Scottish blood,[12] it reared that extraordinary structure of religion and morality which it is the despair of the historian to describe, the irritation of the artist to combat. One traces it everywhere: in the Sunday School movement,[13] in the attitude toward vice and crime, in the solemn figures of the pillars of local churches who were also pillars of business; in the defeated lives of its good wives and excellent daughters; in the runaway escapades of people like Dana and Melville, and in the cheap and tinsel romanticism with which, in its magazines, it strove to make compensation for the color

[11] There is a close connection between Smith and Franklin. See Eliot, "The Relations between Adam Smith and Benjamin Franklin Before 1776," *The Political Science Quarterly*, XXXIX, March, 1924, pp. 67-96. "Franklin's economics represent the common-sense reactions of a powerful mind to the problems of the day, reinforced later on by the general reflections suggested by the Physiocrats and Adam Smith." (*Cambridge History of American Literature*, IV, 428.) Of the *Wealth of Nations* McMaster writes that "it may well be questioned whether in 1784, there could be found from Boston to Savannah one hundred copies of the book" (*History*, I, 25). On the other hand, a hundred copies, properly placed in the hands of influential leaders, is a good many; and by 1793 the book was well enough known for Hamilton's reports to be compared to Smith, derogatorily, in the Second Congress (II, 115). On the Lancasterian system which went hand in hand with laissez-faire theory, see Fitzpatrick, *The Educational Views and Influence of DeWitt Clinton.*

[12] Brought in as "an aid to faith, a safeguard to morality as against the scepticism of Hume and the atheism of Voltaireans," and advocated by the denominational colleges and churches as "an eminently safe philosophy which kept undergraduates locked in so many intellectual dormitories." Riley, *American Philosophy: The Early Schools*, pp. 476-477.

[13] See for an interesting account by a Latin, Ramon de la Sagra, *Cinco meses en los Estados-Unidos*, pp. 92-95.

it had washed out of real existence. Perhaps its symbol is the rocking chair—"the New England 'rocking-chair,' the *ne plus ultra* of all comforts in the shape of furniture," which had "acquired an European reputation."[14] It developed in time its own peculiar literature—the goody-goody books, the solemn magazines, the periodicals calculated to do good, the volumes of sermons, the ethical poetry, the gift-book of the era. One notes how, hand in hand with the revival of religion at Princeton, for example, there comes a company of periodicals calculated to spread good lessons and inculcate morality.[15] *The Christian Disciple,* the *Christian Examiner,* the *Christian Union & Religious Memorial,* the *Evangelical and Literary Magazine,* the *Home Missionary,* the *Literary and Theological Review,* the *Massachusetts Missionary Magazine,* the *Monthly Religious Magazine,* the *Mother's Magazine,* the *New York Ecclesiologist,* the *Religious Intelligencer,* the *Religious Magazine,* the *Sailors' Magazine and Seamen's Friend, The Christian Citizen*—how much more redolent of the epoch are these actual titles of magazines than any picture one can give! Nor is this moral urge confined to the theological magazine alone. Of the 41 magazines established between the administrations of Washington and Adams, McMaster observes that their editors "were moralists, philanthropists, censors, whose duty it was to lead, not to follow,"[16] and this instinct to urge, to reform, to see life only in terms of moral categories, the editors of general magazines followed thereafter: such magazines,

[14] Grund, *The Americans,* II, 158.
[15] *The Princeton Religious and Literary Gazette* begins the stream in 1824, edited by the Rev. Robert Gibson; after a few issues it expired. *The New Jersey Patriot,* 1825, a newspaper, was distinguished by a crusade against dancing. A *Series of Monthly Tracts* in 1824 told the story of good Christian men. The next year the Rev. Robert Gibson edited the *American Journal of Letters, Christianity and Civil Affairs*—a weekly— how the title sums up the attitude! *The American Magazine of Letters and Christianity,* 1826, had in its opening number a lecture by Samuel Miller of the Theological Seminary. *The Princeton Courier and Literary Register* ran from 1831 to 1835. *The American System and Farmers' and Mechanics' Advocate,* founded in 1832, became eventually the *Princeton Press.* And under the editorship of the Rev. Charles Hodge, the *Biblical Repertory and Princeton Review,* 1825, achieved a national reputation. Hageman, *Princeton and Its Institutions,* chap. xvii. In the meantime, in 1823, of 126 students at Amherst, 98 were "hopefully pious." Tyler, *A History of Amherst College,* p. 43. Because of its reputation as the stronghold of orthodoxy (as contrasted to Harvard) Amherst grew to 259 by 1836-7; then it fell to 118 in 1845-46 when the zeal for orthodox piety was no longer at white heat and the passion for ministers and missionaries had cooled, and the revivals became fewer. *Ibid.,* pp. 86-7.
[16] McMaster, V, 269.

writes the historian, "rarely contained what could be called light literature," and no one who has examined them can deny the characterization. And as in their magazines, so in their books they seek only the practical, the useful, the didactic, and they compel others to follow them. "The people when they read anything read newspapers, political pamphlets, novels of English origin, poetry sometimes the product of native authors, fast-day sermons, fourth-of-July orations, treatises on manners and morals, and such literature was especially prepared for them. . . . For young women there was a class of books designed to inculcate morality of the most unhealthy sort."[17] Light reading they will not have.[18] Thus in 1790 we find that novels "hold up *life,* it is true, but it is not as yet *life* in America. . . . As yet the intrigues of a British novel are foreign to our manners, as the refinements of Asiatic vice. Let it not be said, that the tales of distress, which fill modern novels, have a tendency to soften the female heart into arts of humanity. The fact is the reverse of this."[19] And in 1880 we read of Zola's *Nana* that it is not even a useful warning: "we unconsciously take on the character of our social surroundings, and in the reading of fiction we subject our minds to the influences which its scenes are calculated to produce. . . ." The book "is no preacher of virtue, but a guide to debauchery."[20] Between these two utterances, almost a hundred years apart, lies a terrain colored by the desire of the middle class to turn art and speculation to moral ends.

In a house in Louisville in 1829, said Caleb Atwater, "on entering the drawing room, the mother and daughters, I found employed in sewing or some other labor, all except one, who was reading aloud to the others; or they were discussing some topic growing out of the remarks of the author. I scarcely saw one novel, among the books thus read—but History often, Scientific works frequently, and Mr. Walsh's Review, or the National Gazette, almost always."[21] Read Henry Beecher's *Norwood;* or read again the opening chapters of *Tom Sawyer* or *Huckleberry Finn*—they are complete pictures of a moral

[17] *Ibid.,* p. 277.
[18] For a discussion of the middle-class attitude toward fiction, see above, chap. iii, 58 ff.
[19] *Columbian Magazine,* IV, 212, April, 1790.
[20] A. R. Fiske, "Profligacy in Fiction," *North American Review,* CXXXI, 82, July, 1880.
[21] Atwater, *Remarks Made on a Tour to Prairie du Chien in 1829,* p. 23.

civilization, its strength, its domestic virtue, its necessary and inevitable compensations in the way of coarse pleasures and crude vices.[22] These people invented Sunday in America.

Let a foreigner sharpen the sense of difference between America in the twenties and thirties of the nineteenth century, and Europe. It is Achille Murat; he is Latin; he can not understand this sobriety, this gloom:

. . . religion is the only feature which disgusts a foreigner. A Sunday, particularly in the north and east, is a day of gloom, and well calculated to make one regret other countries, even Austria, to an exile *(sic)*. . . . On that day there is no theatre, no visitings; the shops are shut, the streets deserted, the communications interrupted. The post-office of the United States is barely permitted to send despatches, and this thanks to the southern representatives. People go out only to go to church. Every body wears a sullen and taciturn air. Families have no cooking on that day; they live on the leavings of the day before. The women assemble in a circle, each with a Bible in hand, which she makes believe to read while yawning. The men do the like, or under that pretext shut themselves up in their closet and look into their private business, sure of not being interrupted on the sabbath, as it is called. But, who do they mean to deceive? . . . The fact is that nobody is deceived, although there is a desire to deceive everybody.[23]

When these people go to New Orleans or to Paris, they are shocked by the Continental Sunday. For instance, here is the report of a godly traveller in New Orleans in 1817: it could be duplicated in ten other books:

The little respect paid to the Sabbath is a relic of the French revolution and of Buonaparte, for whom the French and the creoles of Louisiana have an unlimited respect, imitating him as poor minds generally do, as far as they are able, in his bad qualities, his contempt of venerable customs, and his egotism, and leaving his great deeds and the noble traits in his character to the imitation of others.[24]

"An American Author," writing in a periodical in 1848, reports on "A Parisian Sabbath":

[22] Commenting upon travellers' observations on the coarseness of American manners in 1800, Henry Adams adds that "public and private records might be searched long, before they revealed evidence of misconduct such as filled the press and formed one of the commonest topics of conversation in the society of England and France." *History,* I, 48-9. See also Nevins and Mesick for impressions of middle-class America.
[23] Murat, *A Moral and Political Sketch of the United States of America,* pp. 142-3. See also the description of a middle-class Sunday in 1835 in Ramon de la Sagra, *Cinco Meses en los Estados-Unidos,* pp. 45-46.
[24] *The Americans as They Are,* p. 148. However, there was hope in sight for godless New Orleans: swarms of needy Yankees and Kentuckians were purchasing land. P. 170.

. . . a Sabbath in this metropolis, so far from being set apart as a day of seriousness for its religion, is only set apart as a larger receptacle for its amusements. . . . Paris wants a Luther in 1837.[25]

It is the attitude of all the travel books about France: the American travellers take their prejudices with them. This is the attitude which explains why a mild scandal about a married woman that in Europe would have been a subject for the comic papers, wrecks Jackson's cabinet and becomes a national issue;[26] why it is that the fireside, home, and heaven occupy so large a place in our literature; it is the national strength and the national weakness.

Let us take this matter of the mails which Murat comments upon.[27] So long as it was merely a matter of moving the mails, there was little complaint—such is not the middle-class habit; such matters, in Franklin's famous phrase, were "seldom, snug, and gave no scandal." But in 1810 the postmaster-general, one Granger, directed the postmasters to keep their offices open on Sunday if the mails arrived on Sunday; and how is it done? The postmaster-general is not in sympathy with the plan, "feeling it tended to bring into disrepute the institution of that Holy Day," but he does not act upon his feeling; he directs the office to be open one hour after the arrival of a mail, or one hour after the usual time for church services. Thus God and Mercury are served to the benefit of each. And though protests come to Congress in 1815 to stop the Sunday mails, and again under McLean (1823-29) protest is made, nothing is done; it is too convenient for business to have the mail moving on the Sabbath Day—it is a "necessary work."[28] This morality can not stand slavery—it is by and by to put it down, after business has begun to feel the need of its abolishment; but the inevitable by-product of a moral urge like this is hypocrisy and prudery.

Thus about 1784 Pine came to America, bringing with him the first plaster cast of the Venus de Medici ever seen in the United States. But the Philadelphia women are prudes; the statue is nude. The "cry of shame that went up was so strong

---

[25] *Holden's Dollar Magazine*, I, 100-105, February, 1848.
[26] Contrast the comparatively slight political result flowing from Hamilton's adulterous intrigue some forty years earlier.
[27] Discussed at length, with reports and petitions, in Stuart, *Three Years in North America*, II, 49-78.
[28] Rich, *History of the United States Post Office*, pp. 105-6.

that Pine was forced to show it to his friends in private."
Twenty-one years later, when a new generation had grown
up, the exhibition of the Philadelphia Academy of Fine Arts
was held in the Rotunda. Among the pictures thus shown were
fifty casts of famous statues in the Louvre; but many of them
were naked, were pronounced indecent; and the managers were
compelled to set apart one day in each week for women, and
on such days to keep the naked figures covered up.[29] When
Story's Greek Slave is exhibited, there is a tremendous moral
upheaval; when in 1831 two paintings representing Adam and
Eve before and after the fall, are shown over the country, they
have to be called a scriptural show in order to justify the scant
attire.[30] In 1846 Mackay visits Newport; to his horror, there
is mixed bathing in the surf. "I confess I thought this," he
says, "more in accordance with the social habits of Paris and
Vienna than those of the United States"—he, too, is of the
middle class.[31] Or let the inquirer turn to Minnegerode's *The
Fabulous Forties;* he will find there instance after instance of
the same attitude—it is the result of this moral urge, this
religious obsession.[32]

And the effect of all this is to deepen the gulf, not merely
between the United States and Europe, but between the Protestant United States and Latin Europe—that is to say, Catholic Europe. The abhorrence of the Revolution ideas which we
have remarked, was increased by an abhorrence of another
ethical system, another religion; France, as it was pictured by
the travelling ministers, the school-teachers, the professors—
France, as they read about it surreptitiously in translated novels
or directly in the denunciations of French life and literature
which continually appeared in their magazines—France became
for them not merely the home of tyranny, but more: Paris was
the capital of immorality, the modern Sodom, and all that
threatened to disintegrate a civilization founded upon middle-
class premises was attributed to Catholicism and to France.
Let us look a little at this hatred of Catholicism, at this tendency to attribute immorality to all Frenchmen, and to attribute
immorality to the lack of the blessings of a Protestant church.

[29] McMaster, I, 82.
[30] Schouler, *History,* IV, 19.
[31] *The Western World,* I, 220.
[32] For further instances of prudery see chap. iii above, pp. 58-61.

3. THE ANTI-CATHOLIC MOVEMENT, 1815-1848, AND ITS
EFFECT UPON THE INTERPRETATION OF FRENCH RELIGION

Two opposite and contradictory tendencies characterize the
attitude of these religious and moral people toward France.
On the one hand, we must note that the fear of French infidelity is not dead. The Americans can not forget the horrors
of the Reign of Terror which they attribute to French atheism,
not does any fairer picture of the Revolution appear, for the
most part, even as late as 1848. For instance, Stephen Girard,[33]
of French descent, founds Girard College in Philadelphia, where
300 boys are to be instructed in every kind of handicraft trade,
leaving his large property for the endowment of the school.
This school will surely please the middle class. But no. Girard,
in his will, "expressly ordered that no religious instruction
should be given in his institution to the young, and that no
teacher of religion should have a place, either among the
teachers or the directors of his establishment." This is French
infidelity, and it will never, never do. "So decided is the view
which these people take of the necessary relationship of religious instruction both with the men and the school, and so
strong is their attachment to it, that they always find some expedient for evading such prohibitions"; they adhere to the letter
of the will because the college is useful, but "every morning at
Girard college, as in all other American schools, a chapter of
the New Testament is read aloud to the assembled youths."[34]
It is a rebuke to the dead Frenchman.

Or again, Calvin Colton who wants an established church in
America, lest civilization perish, admits in 1839 that the French
are "a very gallant and rather ambitious race," but they are not
"addicted to be religious." In Paris, it seems, they have got up
La Société de la Civilisation, which alas! lacks the soul of
Christianity. "It is enough to point the finger to those scenes
which were enacted around the falling, and upon the fallen
throne of Louis XVI, to determine the claims of the French
nation, while living without God, to the highest degree of
human civilization; or what civilization is, without Christianity."[35] That the French are part of a great Christian church
does not matter; it is not a middle-class, protestant Christian
church.

[33] For interesting discussions of Girard in the period see Coke, *A Subaltern's Furlough,* I, 60-63; and Buckingham, *America,* II, 39-41.
[34] Bremer, *Homes of the New World,* I, 404.
[35] Colton, *A Voice from America to England,* pp. 176-7.

Are the newspapers growing too bold? Is yellow journalism creeping in? That, too, is the working of French infidelity. "A licentious and disorganizing press," says the New York *Journal of Commerce* in 1842, "was among the fore-runners of the French revolution; if it did not assist in causing that terrible convulsion, it showed the moral feeling of the people to be depraved and full of mischief, and in fit condition for the horrors that ensued; and we sometimes fear that the downward progress of our American press . . . portends evils near at hand."[36] If the middle-class had its way, it would seal the American mind against popery, Gallicism, and the claims of French culture.[37]

But just now it is not infidelity, but popery that we must consider. As late as the middle of the eighteenth century, as we have seen,[38] popery and France were the great enemies to be combatted. Then as the war ended, as fear died away, as England became the enemy, as the cosmopolitan spirit increased and tolerance throve, as the nation drew closer and closer to Catholic France, men commenced to ask themselves whether papists were so bad, after all. The death of Louis XV and the accession of Louis XVI removed a reproach against the most Catholic throne.[39] In vain the British propagandists and the Tory agitators raised the cry of popery and Jesuitism; Catholicism seemed less and less dreadful; and when it finally presented itself in the shape of the well disciplined French army, it did not seem dreadful at all: Congress heard a sermon in a Catholic church by the abbé Bandole, chaplain of the French ambassador, and seemed none the worse for it; Philadelphia witnessed a Catholic funeral, and the foundations of the earth were not rocked; in Massachusetts John Thayer became a Catholic,[40] and presently (1788) there was, as we

---

[36] Quoted in Buckingham, *Eastern and Western States*, I, 459.

[37] "Rousseau, Voltaire, Diderot, &c., were read by the old federalists, but now they seem known more as naughty words than as great names. I am much mistaken if a hundred untravelled Americans could be found, who have read Boileau or La Fontaine. Still fewer are acquainted with that delightful host of French female writers, whose memoirs and letters sparkle in every page with unequalled felicity of style." Mrs. Trollope, *Domestic Manners of the Americans*, pp. 281-2. (This of the period, 1827-1831.)

[38] Cf. chap. x above.

[39] Cf. Faÿ, pp. 29-31.

[40] And became an abbé and called on Abigail Adams in Auteuil in January, 1785. "We had a visit the other day from no less a personage than Abbé Thayer, in his habit, who has become a convert. . . . He told us that he

have seen, a Catholic church in Boston![41] Came then the émigrés—from 10,000 to 25,000 of them, no one knows just how many: there were among them many who were anti-clerical, but most were not—indeed, that was why they were émigrés; and by and by they turned everywhere to the consolation of religion, especially in England and the New World. By 1790 there were 25 Catholic priests in the first states of the union, and a flock of 20,000; and the Sulpitians, disembarking in Baltimore, had made the place the center of Catholic action on the coast.[42] Meanwhile, it is Christianity which is being persecuted in France; and Christians forgot their sectarian differences to sympathize with religion.[43] Louisiana is annexed, and a large Catholic population added to the country. In the Northwest Territory, it is true, Catholicism has done little;[44]

had spent a year at Rome, that he belonged to a seminary of St. Sulpice in Paris, that he never knew what religion was, until his conversion, and that he designed to return to America in a year or two, to see if he could not convert his friends and acquaintance." "Mr. Adams took him up pretty short," and he "took his leave after some time, without any invitation to repeat his visit." Mrs. Adams to the Reverend John Shaw, *Letters of Mrs. Adams*, II, 73-74.

[41] See chap. X, 372-3.

[42] Baldensperger, *Le mouvement des idées dans l'émigration française*, II, chap. iii (Expérience religieuse et christianisme de sentiment), traces the pro-Catholic movement among the émigrés. The figures in the text are his, pp. 199-200. Carroll (*Religious Forces of the United States*, p. 53) estimates, however, that there were nearer 30,000 Roman Catholics in the country by 1784. Rosengarten collects some interesting facts on the distribution of French Catholics at the close of the eighteenth century. In Philadelphia a French Benevolent Society was organized in 1793, and schools were kept by the Picot, Guillou, Segoigne, Bolmar and Grellot families. In Wilmington, Delaware, on the authority of Montgomery's memoirs, representative Catholics included M. Martel, tutor to Theodosia Burr; Dr. Bayard and Dr. Capelle, who had served under Lafayette in the Revolution; I. Isambrie, a soldier who had served under Napoleon in Egypt; the Marquise de Sourci; Dr. Didie; the Garesché family; Peter Provenchere, the tutor of the Duc de Berri, one of whose relatives became Mrs. John Keating of Philadelphia; Mrs. Capron, a school teacher; M. Bergerac, later professor in St. Mary's College, Baltimore. John Bouvier came to Philadelphia in 1803 with his family. In the same year a colony of French Trappists settled in Baltimore, but later removed to Louisville. Rosengarten, pp. 87-89. In 1792 French bishops in the United States included Cheverus of Paris in Boston; M. Flaget of Auvergne in Kentucky; M. David of Nantes, his coadjutor; M. Dubourg of St. Louis. Faÿ points out that before 1800 only one American student had entered the Sulpitian seminary in Baltimore, but that from 1800 to 1810 more than twenty entered the order, which evangelized the West. Pp. 312-13.

[43] Cf. Stauffner, *New England and the Bavarian Illuminati, passim.*

[44] The Church of St. Anne in Detroit, founded about 1700, had only two priests as late as 1832. St. Louis at the beginning of American occupation had one church but no priest. The French settlements on the Wabash and associated territories seem to have been wretchedly served. Rusk, I, 39.

but following the French Revolution there is a movement westward.[45] The Catholics slowly increase. In 1803 the Diocese of New Orleans was created; in 1808, the Diocese of Baltimore. By 1807 there were 80 churches and 150,000 of the faithful. By 1820 the latter number had doubled; by 1830, there were 500,000 or 600,000; by 1840, a million and a half; by the end of our period something over three million.[46] The cause? Mainly immigration. Of the 5,055,938 aliens admitted into the United States from 1820 to 1860 the Irish led with 1,880,943; the immigration from France from 1820 to 1848 varies from 2696 in 1835 to 20,040 in 1847.[47] Indeed, the Catholic Irish, it seemed, would ruin Protestant democracy, and in 1837, in the midst of rioting, destruction, and religious bitterness, the Native American party was formed to keep them down.[48] But we are running ahead of our story.[49]

During the Directory, the Consulate, and the Empire the principal energies of American religious controversialists were directed, as we have seen, to the battle against infidelity. Moreover, during a great part of this period we were cut off from Continental Europe, and in the years 1812-1814 we were actively at war. When the veil lifted and we looked again at Europe, we found that the Restoration had gone hand in hand with a Catholic Revival; we did not like the one, and although we rather approved of the restoration of religion in France, we tended to attribute the unlucky performances of the Bourbons to their Catholic policies. That is to say, the Protestant Revival, the nationalistic movement, and perhaps a sympathy with

---

[45] A group went out from Bardstown, Kentucky, in 1785, followed two years later by a priest. In 1793 the whole Catholic population of Kentucky was estimated at 300 families. A group of Trappist monks removed from Kentucky to the French towns on the Mississippi and later returned to Europe. *Ibid.*

[46] Carroll, *op. cit.*, p. 53, 69. By 1832 the Diocese of Detroit was established; by 1847 the Diocese of St. Louis; by 1850, the Dioceses of Cincinnati, and Vincennes.

[47] *Emigration Conditions in Europe*, pp. 7-8.

[48] Lasting throughout our period, and passing into the Knownothing movement of the fifties, ancestor of the Ku Klux Klan.

[49] As illustrating the spread of the Catholic Irish and the attitude toward Catholicism in 1829, the following anecdote from Pavie, *Souvenirs Atlantiques,* is not without interest (I, 50-51). Pavie was in Albany when the news of Catholic emancipation reached the place. An Irish woman in the same hotel woke him early that morning with loud expressions of joy, thinking that a French traveller would be happy over the event and would want to attend mass and the Te Deum. He went; the church was too small for the crowd, and many stood outside. Protestant neighbors were scandalized by the vehemence of the demonstration.

émigrés (now Bonapartist rather than Bourbon) and with emigrants in the twenties, led all good Americans to see a connection between European tyranny and European Catholicism; with respect to France, we returned to the attitude of the seventeenth century with our prejudices strengthened; our belief in democracy and our hatred of monarchy intertwined with our suspicion of the Pope and the Jesuit.

The attack began early. Timothy Dwight referred in these pleasant terms to the pope in *The Triumph of Infidelity* (printed in 1797):

> Full in his church I (Satan) fix'd my glorious throne;
> Thrice crown'd, I sate a God, and more than God;
> Bade all earth's nations shiver at my nod;
> Dispens'd to men the code of Satan's laws,
> And made my priests the columns of my cause.
> In their bless'd hands the gospel I conceal'd,
> And new-found doctrines, in its stead, reveal'd;
> Of gloomy visions drew a fearful round,
> Names of dire look, and words of killing sound.
> *   *   *   *   *   *   *   *
> To this bless'd scheme I forc'd the struggling mind;
> Faith sunk beneath me; sense her light resign'd;
> Before rebellious conscience clank'd the chain;
> The rack, the wheel, unbosomed all their pain;
> The dungeon yawn'd; uprose the faggot pyre,
> And, fierce with vengeance, twin'd the livid fire.
> These woes I form'd on earth; beyond the tomb,
> Of dreams, I built the purgatorial doom;
> Hurl'd round all realms the interdictive peal;
> Shut kings from heaven, and nations scourg'd to hell;
> All crimes forgave; those crimes indulg'd again;
> Disclos'd the right divine to every sin;
> To certain ecstasies the faithful led;
> Damn'd Doubt, when living; double damn'd, when dead;
> O'er bold Inquiry bade all horrors roll,
> And to its native nothing shrunk the soul.

Thus spoke the true-blue Protestants of Connecticut.

The magazines took up the theme. For instance, in 1815 the *North American Review* has an account of the death of Madamoiselle Raucour, an actress refused burial by the priests of St. Rocque who followed the ancient rule of the church regarding members of her profession. The king would not interfere until all the actors in Paris threatened to turn Lutheran (or so the story runs), when he ordered the services performed, services so imperfect that the editor refers to them as "one of the most barbarous and absurd pieces of ancient superstition."[50] In

---

[50] I, 143, May, 1815.

1816 the *Analectic* reprints an article from the *Eclectic Review* discussing Helen Maria Williams' *On the Late Persecution of the Protestants in the South of France*: the interest of the article is clearly that the writer protests against the theory that persecution of Protestants by Catholics ceased with the Revolution and Napoleon; on the contrary, it is continuing under the Catholic Bourbon regime.[51] In the same year the *North American Review* prints an excerpt from the "Literary Panorama" on the *Excommunication of Mice!!!*, which relates how a priest went into the Catholic districts of Basle and exorcised all the worms, caterpillars, mice, etc., using the same terms as are used in the excommunication of human beings. The writer asks if this is "not using the Lord's name in vain," and if not, "what is? . . . If these and similar customs be revived, the time is not far off that may teach Popery more effectual lessons."[52] An Orangeman could hardly be less tolerant. Of the Jesuits *The Portico* observed in 1816 that although "much of the civilization of the world, of the excellence of science and literature; and numerous discoveries in unknown parts, are exclusively owing to this inquisitive society," nevertheless they "poisoned the source of human virtue, and the fountain of happiness; and became a pest, instead of a blessing." The magazine, it is curious to note, was published in Baltimore.[52a]

The battle in France between orthodoxy and Christian socialism was watched with profound interest. A translation of Massillon's sermons, which reached a second edition in 1818, was published in Philadelphia, since being "unconnected with local or temporary events in France," they would be "an acceptable present to Christians of every denomination." In 1821 the *North American Review* in an article of fourteen pages notices the *Essai sur l'Indifférence en Matière de Religion* of "F. de la Mennaise." "Nothing," says the writer, "has been published in France upon the subject of religion, since it was decreed, that God might exist, and the soul be immortal, which has attracted so much attention as this essay of the Abbé de la Mennais," the fourth edition of which is before him. The learned abbé is "without a rival since the time of Bossuet."[53] Two years later the *Christian Disciple* notes the *Journal de la Société de la Morale Chrétienne,* of which the first and second

[51] *Analectic Magazine*, VIII, 145-150, August, 1816.
[52] III, 58-61, May, 1816.
[52a] *The Portico*, I, 146-154, February, 1816.
[53] XII, 371-385, April, 1821.

volumes have been published in Paris; La Rochefoucauld-Liancourt, it seems, is president, and a Christian social economy is being taught.[54] To the *Christian Examiner* of July, 1831, it appears there has been a rebirth of religion in France; the writer quotes Constant on *Religion* to prove that "a scoffing derision of Christianity is not esteemed a necessary passport to good society" now. But, *mirabile dictu*, it is the Protestants who are bringing about the change:

This increased interest in religion, after the universal prevalence of infidelity, appears to have been felt, in some degree, by all classes of the French community, but especially among the intelligent and literal members of the Protestant church.

The domination of France by the Catholic clergy in the eighteenth century, it appears, resulted in the death of the spirit and life of Christianity; and though the reformation then brought about, which ran to deism and atheism, exceeded all bounds, the need of religion in nineteenth century France, can not, it appears from Vincent's *Vues sur le Protestantisme en France* (1829), be brought about by the "priesthood," whose authority is inadequate, since their historical succession has been broken. Men wish free inquiry, not authoritarianism; they wish in France to fill the imagination, to listen to the inward voice, to live under moral government: therefore let them discard Catholicism, Calvinism, and Arminianism, and take up a kind of Rationalism, which seems to be universalism.[55] Returning to Lamennais' *Words of a Believer,* the *North American Review* in 1835 found it a "work of great power and interest," filled with "sentiments of deep religious faith," the doctrine, however, being open to two corrections: the author excites the animosities of the people instead of cultivating in them a love for constitutional rights, and he misapplies "his admirable religious principles" in sanctioning popular violence. In 1838 *The New York Review* summarized Lamennais' career, à propos of his *Affaires de Rome,* in an article sympathetic with Lamennais but sharing the same fear that he had not sufficiently impressed upon the people "the salutary lesson of the dangers and duties of freemen." The Pope's absolutism must, however, disappear.[55a]

[54] *Christian Disciple,* new series, V, 469-77, November-December, 1823.

[55] *Christian Examiner,* X (n. s., V), 273-296, July, 1831. Review of *Vues sur le Protestantisme en France.* Par J. L. S. Vincent, l'un des Pasteurs de l'Église Réformée de Nisme. 2 vols., Paris, 1829.

[55a] *North American Review,* XL, 269-298, April, 1835; *New York Review,* II, 146-174, January, 1838.

But perhaps the good Vincent was over-enthusiastic. In 1834 the *Quarterly Christian Spectator* is alarmed over the growth of the Romish Church, but it takes comfort in reviewing Villers' *Spirit and influence of the Reformation,* a prize essay of the French Institute, which has just been translated by Samuel Miller, D.D., and published in Philadelphia in 1833. This work, it appears, is effectually combatting Romanism in France, since it proves, first, that the unchanging principles of popery are destructive of civil and religious liberty; second, that "truth" is a power sufficient to overthrow this despotism; and third, that a single mind may work astonishing changes.[56] Perhaps the proofs of this latter statement are to be found in the *New York Mirror,* for November 14, 1835, wherein it appears that certain reforms are being worked in infidel French literature, such as the prohibition of philosophical works and of Diderot's novels![57] Or perhaps the growth of French Methodism is responsible, which *The Ladies' Repository* found encouraging in 1842; the French, it seems, are reading the *Life of Wesley,* the *Life of Nelson,* Wesley's *Sermons,* Pipe on Sanctification, and other improving works.[57a]

In the meantime, as we have indicated, the Catholic Irish had been pouring into the country,[58] settling particularly in the New England states and in the central states. Native Americans became alarmed. Hostility to the Catholics, it developed, had been smouldering rather than extinguished. As late as 1821 every foreign-born Catholic in New York was compelled to abjure allegiance to the Pope before he could become a citizen; as late as 1833 Catholics in Massachusetts were still compelled to pay taxes for the support of the Protestant church; New Jersey retained an anti-Catholic constitution until 1844; and so did New Hampshire until 1877. The Protestant Americans who retained provisions such as these in their fun-

---

[56] *Quarterly Christian Spectator,* VI, 169-187, June, 1834.
[57] XIII, 159.
[57a] *The Ladies' Repository,* II, 128, April, 1842.
[58] From 1820 to 1845 they constituted the largest single group of emigrants; in 1846 they were temporarily ousted from first place by the Germans (often Catholic), but resumed their primacy from 1847 to 1850. The figures for the Irish are 1820, 3,614; 1821, 1,518; 1822, 2,267; 1823, 1,908; 1824, 2,345; 1825, 4,888; 1826, 5,408; 1827, 9,766; 1828, 12,488; 1829, 7,415; 1830, 2,721; 1831, 5,772; 1832, 12,436; 1833, 8,648; 1834, 24,474; 1835, 20,927; 1836, 30,578; 1837, 28,508; 1838, 12,645; 1839, 23,963; 1840, 39,430; 1841, 37,772; 1842, 51,342; 1843 (nine months only), 19,670; 1844, 33,490; 1845, 44,821; 1846 (Germans predominate); 1847, 105,536; 1848, 112,934. *Emigration Conditions in Europe,* pp. 7-8.

damental laws naturally looked with uneasiness upon the flood of Catholicism.[59] Plain democracy went to work in vigorous fashion. For instance, on the night of the eleventh of August, 1834, they attacked the Ursuline Convent in Charlestown and set it on fire while the nuns and the pupils hurried out of the building. On the 29th of May, 1833, Bishop Dubois laid the cornerstone of a Catholic college at Nyack on the North River, an act which aroused such opposition that the Rev. Dr. Brownlee came to preach against the Pope and Catholic colleges; whereupon the college was burned—accidentally, said the Protestants, deliberately, said the Catholics. Down in New Orleans there were riots in the autumn of 1835; up in New York there were disorders, and in the latter city there was formed the Native American Democratic Association which, in the fall of 1835, nominated James Monroe for Congress, on the platform, "Elevate no person of foreign birth to any office of honor, trust, or profit in the United States," which honor the said Monroe prudently declined.[60]

Such events have their originators. In the thirties and forties, Lyman Beecher "toured the cities of the Atlantic seaboard exhorting his countrymen to be alive to the dark designs of the potentates of Europe on the civil and ecclesiastical liberties of the western pioneers," which, it seemed, were being threatened by Romanism.[61] Various papers arose like *The Protestant, The Protestant Vindicator,* and *The Downfall of Babylon* to inform New England and New York Protestants regarding the machinations of the wily Catholics. "One hundred and thirty Protestant clergymen," according to Catholic historians, "many of them from Princeton, New Brunswick, and Yale," wrote an introductory address to a reprint, issued

[59] See McMaster, VI, 84-85. "Great alarm seems to prevail among the Protestant sects in general," wrote Buckingham in 1838, "as to the progress making by the Catholics in the west, and it is undoubted that large and costly churches are springing up in every city, the funds of which are believed to be transmitted from Europe, as there are no visible sources of income for such undertakings here." *America,* III, 38-39. He notes that the increase goes hand in hand with the increased immigration of German, Swiss, and Irish.

[60] McMaster, VI, 85-86, 367-368; de Courcy and Shea, *History of the Catholic Church in the United States, passim; Catholic Encyclopaedia* under *Knownothingism.* There is greatly needed an impartial study of the Native American movement. For that matter, the Knownothing party is only imperfectly known.

[61] Stephenson, "Nativism in the Forties and Fifties, with Special Reference to the Mississippi Valley," *The Mississippi Valley Historical Review,* IX, 191. December, 1922.

in 1834, of the New Testament as translated by the English College of Rheims in 1582, together with the original notes, "replete with impiety, irreligion, and the most fiery persecution." There appeared in 1835 *Six Months in a Convent* by Rebecca Theresa Reed, printed in Boston, of which, it is said, 35,000 copies were sold in a few days; the burning of the Ursuline Convent was one of the fruits of the book. Lyman Beecher, in his *Plea for the West,* amid his difficulties with the presbytery and synod of Cincinnati in June, 1835,[62] takes time to point out that the millenium will probably begin in America, and more probably still, in the West, but not, one gathers, while "three-fourths of the foreign emigrants whose accumulating tide is rolling in upon us, are, through the medium of their religion and priesthood, as entirely accessible to the control of the potentates of Europe as if they were an army of soldiers." It is true that an anti-Catholic mob burned down the Ursuline Convent, but then, these curious Catholics insist on preaching their religion and on building schools, as various sermons, and citations from the *Quarterly Register* for 1830, are garnered in to prove. Alas,

it is notorious that the Catholic immigrants to this country are generally of the class least enlightened, and most implicit in their religious subjection to the priesthood, who are able, by their spiritual ascendency, to direct easily and infallibly the exercise of their civil rights and political action.

If they dared to think for themselves, the contrast of Protestant independence with their thraldom, would awaken the desire of equal privileges, and put an end to an arbitrary clerical dominion over trembling superstitious minds. If the pope and potentates of Europe held no dominion over ecclesiastics here, we might trust to time and circumstances to mitigate their ascendency and produce assimilation. But for conscience sake and patronage, they are dependent on the power that be across the deep, by whom they are sustained and nurtured; and receive and organize all who come, and retain all who are born; while by argument, and a Catholic education, they beguile the children of credulous unsuspecting Protestants into their own communion.[64]

"No design?" exclaims the pious Beecher. "They do design the subversion of our institutions," as Russia, Austria, St. Domingo and signs "of the coming on of the next European conflict, . . . a war of liberty against despotism" exist to prove.[64] Mr. Beecher's rhetoric was buttressed by S. F. B. Morse's *Brutus, or a Foreign Conspiracy Against the United States*

[62] See Beecher's *Works,* III, for the documents in this caes.
[63] Beecher, *A Plea for the West,* pp. 10, 56, 138, 129.
[64] *Ibid.,* pp. 129, 152-159.

(New York, 1835) and *The Confession of a French Catholic Priest,* edited by the same gentleman, books which, according to the *Quarterly Christian Spectator,* indicate that "much is to be done."[65] *The New York Review* in 1838 (II, 225-6) hoped that the *Outlines of a History of the Court of Rome* (Philadelphia, 1837), supposed to be from the French of Daunou, would have a wide circulation, especially among American Romanists, since the book proves that the "temporal power originated in fraud and superstition" and has been injurious to religion, civilization, and knowledge. Meanwhile the less intelligent were being pleasantly thrilled by the "Awful Disclosures of Maria Monk," written, it would seem, by one Timothy Dwight, which purported to be the disclosures of revolting crimes committed in the Hôtel Dieu in Montreal.[66] Two editions of this thrilling narrative sold to the number of 40,000 copies, and presently a sequel appeared.[67] It was in vain that moderate Protestants and Catholics protested. Various pretended confessions by renegade priests and others fed the flames.[68]

By the forties masses of people were ready to believe anything about the Catholics. Dowling's *The History of Romanism* passed into twelve editions by 1846; it was published in 1845, and is a diligent compilation of all the gossip and error about that body which its compiler could put together, running to 671 pages, and copiously illustrated with "numerous accurate and highly finished engravings of (Catholic) ceremonies, superstitions, persecutions, and historical incidents."[69] In May,

[65] IX, 670-1, November, 1837, for review of the last.
[66] *Awful Exposure of the atrocious plot formed by certain individuals against the Clergy and Nuns of Lower Canada, through the intervention of Maria Monk.* New York. Printed for Jones & Co., of Montreal, 1836.
[67] *Farther Disclosures by Maria Monk, concerning the Hotel Dieu Nunnery. Also her visits to the Nun's Island, and disclosures concerning the Secret Retreat.* New York, 1837.
[68] Stephenson observes that "the anti-catholic literature of the forties and fifties is . . . voluminous." For representative titles see him, p. 194, note; and de Courcy and Shea, *History of the Catholic Church in America,* chap. xvi.
[69] The "description" of the emblematical title page" is worth recording as a curiosity. "The central portion of the engraving is an emblematical representation or picture of Popery as it is, and has been. On the right and left, standing upon two pedestals, are two Reformers in monkish dress, implying that like many eminent reformers, they have been converted from the errors of Popery. These two reformers are lifting up the curtain to exhibit to the world a genuine picture of the Romanish Anti-Christ. In the background is seen the Church of St. Peter's, against which the lightnings are flashing, implying that Popery is destined to fall before the light of Heaven. Near by are seen two martyrdoms, implying that Popery has ever been drunk with the blood of the saints and martyrs of Jesus. In

1844, an anti-Catholic riot began in Philadelphia over the use of the Bible in the public schools. There was intense disorder; placards were posted to the effect that "the bloody hand of the Pope is upon us; the modern St. Bartholomew has begun; the Irish papists have arisen to massacre us"; on the eighth of May St. Michael's Church, the house of the Sisters of Charity, and St. Augustine's Church were fired; on the ninth martial law was proclaimed; on the fifth of July the church of St. Philip Neri was invaded by a mob; and throughout the whole summer feeling was at a tension,[70] lives were lost, and property destroyed. As a result of such feeling Whigs and Democrats found themselves seriously embarrassed by the Native American party movement; it became necessary to prove that Polk was not a Catholic in order to get him elected; and the feeling simmered, even after 1845, to flare up again in the Knownothing movement of the fifties.[71]

Acts of violence were, it is true, confined to the mob, but among the intellectual leaders there was a great deal of disturbance. Beecher's alarm we have noted. Leaders of Protestantism beheld with grief the dissensions and schisms which rent the Church of Christ.[72] Presbyterianism was split into

front is seen a Pope, dressed in his tiara and pontifical robes, trampling under foot the Bible, and pronouncing an absolution upon a couple of devotees who are kneeling before him. These have both their rosaries in their hands, and the man has a dagger in one hand, implying that Popery does not hesitate to authorize its use to remove a troublesome opponent, and that more than one assassin has been commended with priestly benedictions, to the *holy* work of assassinating heretical monarchs and nobles. In the hand of the Pope is a purse of money, which he has received as the price of his pontifical indulgence or absolution. While the Pope is trampling under foot the Bible, one of his soldiers is seen behind him, pointing with his sword to the Decrees of Lateran, Lyons, Constance and Trent, the most celebrated and bloody of all the Romish Councils—as much as to say 'you must obey these decrees or suffer the consequences.' . . . On the left are seen the representatives of the four divisions of the globe, Europe, Asia, Africa and America, with a queen, who may represent Victoria of England, looking on, as interested spectators of the picture thus exhibited. In the centre, is a Protestant minister with the Bible before him, pointing to and describing the scene; and on the right, the living Pope, a cardinal and other dignitaries, horrified that this curtain should be removed, and this faithful picture of Popery exhibited to the world."

This preposterous stuff is printed on page 2. The other pictures are of the same general merit, but the book is carefully compiled to give chapter and verse for its paragraphs.

[70] de Courcy and Shea, pp. 240-248; McMaster, VII, 375-385.

[71] There was something to be said on the other side, for the foreign language groups had undoubtedly been something of a nuisance, and even of a menace. Consult Stephenson, pp. 199-202.

[72] Consult Bacon, *A History of American Christianity*, chap. xvii, on the period from 1835 to 1845.

Old Calvinism, modified Calvinism, and Hopkinsianism, taught by Taylor at Yale; the faithful were edified by trials of Lyman Beecher, Edward Beecher, J. M. Sturtevant, William Kirby, and George Duffield, for heresy; presently 533 churches and 100,000 communicants (in 1837) found themselves "excommunicated by a majority vote." Congregationalism had already given birth to Unitarianism; now Unitarianism itself divided over Emerson's Harvard *Divinity School Address* (1838) and Theodore Parker's *The Transient and the Permanent in Christianity* (1841), which boldly discarded the supernatural. In 1844-45 the Methodists were split wide open over the problem of slavery. The Episcopalians were struggling with the High-Church principles of Bishop Hobart, endeavoring to digest the Oxford Tracts, while "every mail brought to America the names of new converts (to Catholicism) among the clergy, and lists of eminent laymen who followed their teachers," as a Catholic historian jubilantly remarks.[73] At an ordination in 1843 two of the leading presbyters in the diocese of New York rose and read solemn protests against the ordaining of one of the candidates on the ground of his Romanizing opinion;[74] and various important clergymen, like Dr. Ives, Bishop of North Carolina, went over to Rome.[75] And protestant orthodoxy was ever struggling with the problem of the Unitarian.

Not unnaturally French theological thought and French religious history was seen through this cloud of controversy. It was known that the French religious situation was not satisfactory; the restoration of Catholicism in its old form by the Bourbons had been followed by a recrudescence of Protestant theology, and the battle in France was remarked with anxious eyes by American ministers. In the whole interpretation put on French religious expression, French philosophy, and French politics affecting the church, one finds mainly confusion, hesitation, and fear. If the French religious situation was confused (and between de Maistre and Lamennais, Cousin and Chateaubriand, the coronation of Charles X and the "discovery" of the holy oil, and the "religion of humanity" of Comte, it may be called so), the American interpretation of it was likewise confused. On one point and one point only, the American inter-

---

[73] de Courcy and Shea, p. 421.
[74] Bacon, pp. 307-8.
[75] For a representative list, see de Courcy and Shea, p. 423.

preters were agreed; namely, to hail all evidences of French protestantism as marking a return to liberty and morality, and to accept all evidences of French catholic "modernity" with joy. Let us turn to some evidences of the American attitude.

Fénelon had ever been a favorite Catholic author in America.[76] There was a recrudescence of interest in him in the thirties and forties—indeed, before. As early as 1822 the *Christian Disciple* was printing "Sketches of the Life and Character of Fénelon," translated from the French.[77] In 1829 the *Christian Examiner,* reviewing a book of selections from Fénelon published in English at Boston that year, after remarking on the dullness of most religious literature, declares that Fénelon, "if not a profound," was "an original thinker, and . . . though a Catholic, he was essentially free." His works come fresh from the soul; he saw far into the human heart, and especially into the workings of self-love. Nevertheless, his view of human nature is too dark, and his priestly profession narrows him; he applied too rigorous a standard to the multitude. What were Fénelon's characteristic views? God is the Universal Father; he yearns for human perfection: which means self-crucifixion and the love of God. But, objects the reviewer, crucifixion of the self leads to self-contempt and to the misuse of body and mind; self-love can not be renounced, and thus the Protestant banner is raised.[78]

The American Monthly Review observes in 1832 that there is little in *A Treatise on the Education of Daughters, Translated from the French* of Fénelon, Archbishop of Cambray "to which a Protestant can object, and little that is inapplicable to our republican institutions and manners"; the book "imparts highly valuable lessons."[79] Of Madame Guyon (whom he calls Lady Guion), the *Christian Review* remarks in 1838 that she fell into "Catholic errors," but the chivalric writer "would not speak lightly of that broken-hearted, holy woman." Chivalry

[76] Two editions of the *Télémaque* were published in America in the eighteenth century, both in Philadelphia, one in 1784 (Evans, item 18466) and one in 1791 (Evans, item 23366). The *Télémaque* was a favorite school text.
[77] IV (n. s.), 421-33, November-December, 1822.
[78] *Christian Examiner,* VI (n. s., I), 1-35, March, 1829. The article contains a passage on the virtues of the Catholic church, which has produced Charlemagne, Alfred, Dante, Raphael, Michael Angelo, Tasso, Bossuet, Pascal, Descartes—and Fénelon. But the writer hastens to add that he is not a Catholic. P. 9.
[79] *American Monthly Review,* 1832, p. 257.

or not, it appears that her "unreasonable mysticism" is the result of the fact that "her mind was impaired," as appears in her *Short and Easy Method of Prayer*.[80] In 1843 the *Christian Examiner* believes that "everything of Fénelon is welcome"; his *Thoughts on Spiritual Subjects,* as translated at Boston, "breathes of heaven and devotion."[81] This book was a kind of supplement to Mrs. Follen's *Selections from the Writings of Fénelon: with a Memoir of His Life,* by Mrs. Follen which reached five editions by 1844; "L" considers the demand for "so pure and elevated a writer as Fénelon" "an indication of sound public taste."[82] In 1847 Upham's *Life and Religious Opinions and Experience of Madame de la Mothe Guyon with an Account of Fénelon* is full of instruction and interest, an example of purified mind and exalted faith;[83] Fénelon is "the most tolerant and humble-minded of Roman Catholics," Madame Guyon "a pious transcendentalist"(!)[84] To another reviewer the Doctrine of Pure Love set forth in this volume is most misapprehended; to call Madame Guyon a fanatic, as many do, is to misjudge her diary, since she is as powerful in intellect as Bossuet. "Love constitutes my crime," she wrote, and Bossuet and the church are vigorously scourged for condemning her—albeit the Church of Rome is no more inconsistent than other churches.[85]

The same gentleness is extended to the anti-Jesuitism of Pascal. As early as 1828 "V," writing in the *Christian Spectator,* calls attention to the desirability of an American edition of the *Provincial Letters,* "an admirable antidote for Popery," "the finest production of one of the first geniuses that ever wrote."[86] The same periodical contains an article, "Pascal's Thoughts on Religion," together with a brief life, which stresses the occasion of the letters, and gives a series of excerpts from the *Pensées*.[87] Cousin's *Rapport à L'Académie Française* on the necessity of a new edition of the *Pensées*

---

[80] III, 449-467, September, 1838. Article: "Lady Guion and some of her Religious Views."
[81] *Christian Examiner,* XXXIV (3 s., XVI), 262, May, 1843.
[82] *Christian Examiner,* XXXVII (4 s., II), 418, November, 1844.
[83] *Democratic Review,* XXI, 187, August, 1847.
[84] *Columbian Magazine,* VIII, 96, August, 1847.
[85] *Christian Examiner,* XLIII (4 s., VIII), 317-24, November, 1847. Upham was professor of mental and moral philosophy in Bowdoin College. The book, published in New York in 1847, was in two volumes.
[86] *Christian Spectator,* n. s., II, 23, January, 1828.
[87] *Ibid.,* pp. 28-31.

(Paris, 1843), is discussed at length in the *Democratic Review* for February, 1845.[88] In 1846, reviewing a translation of the *Thoughts* published at Andover in 1846, the *Christian Examiner* remarks that the book "can never lose its value," since "there is something sublime in the plan which he seems to have formed"; yet the book must be received with caution— "thoughts . . . suggested by (men's) emotions" are "untrustworthy as guides."[89] However, so genteel a periodical as the *Evergreen* has room for "Human Weakness," translated from the French of Pascal by "P. L.,"[90] and to the *Democratic Review* it seemed that "Pascal himself is known to every man who pretends to any education. He is the pride, not only of France, and of Catholicism, but of the whole Christian and civilized world."[91] *The Dial* had already announced that "Mr. Alcott and Mr. Lane have recently brought from England a small but valuable library, amounting to about one thousand volumes, containing undoubtedly a richer collection of mystical writers than any other library in this country," which included seven books by Madame Guyon, six by Fénelon, two by Malebranche, Pascal's *Thoughts,* Du Bartas and Bellarmine.[92]

Comment on what may be called undiluted Catholic literature was, however, more variable. *The American Monthly Magazine and Critical Review* notices Massillon's *Sermons,* selected and translated and published in a second American edition in 1818, without much comment.[93] The *Christian Spectator* in 1827 remarks on the modesty and humility of Massillon's life, says that the letters on charity are "said to be masterpieces of eloquence and pathos," and Massillon's reputation for unrivalled fervor is due to his uncompromising spirit and to his knowledge of the human heart.[94] And the *Evergreen* carries a moral tidbit from Massillon entitled "Our Conversation too often but a Concealment of the Truth."[95] But seventeenth century writers were not, so to speak, so dangerous.

[88] XVI, 137-144.
[89] XLI (4 s., VI), 141-2, July, 1846.
[90] IV, 47-48, February, 1847.
[91] XXI, 15-22, July, 1847. Account of Pascal's sister, based on *Jacqueline Pascal* by Victor Cousin. Paris, 1845. *The Eclectic Magazine* the same year reprints an article from the *Edinburgh Review* on the genius and writings of Pascal. X, 433-56, April, 1847.
[92] III, 545-48, April, 1843.
[93] December, 1818, p. 138. The translation was by William Dickson.
[94] I (n. s.), 131-4, March, 1827. D'Alembert's account of the first discourse at Versailles is quoted, and there is a eulogy of D'Alembert.
[95] III, 284, September, 1846.

Confronted by Joseph de Maistre's *Les Soirées de St. Peters-bourg,* the *American Monthly Magazine* for 1838 finds it a "strange book." De Maistre "is said to be one of the greatest geniuses of the age, and this book is the proof of it," it is "an encyclopaedic book," "not in the least *frenchified,*" whatever that may be. The work is summarized; the author is comforted that de Maistre "laughs at the natural philosopher," Rousseau, but alas!

The Count is a Jesuit, and believes in the infallibility of the Church in authority therefore, and indulgences; he thinks war divine as well as monarchy, and private judgment upon religious matters ridiculous; that priests, nobles, and statesmen alone have a right to revolve and present truths, *as the people have the natural sciences to amuse themselves with!*[96]

The *American Eclectic* in 1841, reprints a British article reviewing Bouvet's *Du Catholicisme, du Protestantisme et de la Philosophie en France* to show that the battle of the world is between the Catholics and the Protestants.[97] A French life of Cardinal Cheverus (formerly Bishop of Boston) is condemned, together with a life by an American Catholic, as a specimen "of Popish credulity and French exaggeration" in the *Christian Examiner* for 1839; the reviewer thereupon proceeds to give an "American" estimate of Cheverus.[98] The same magazine, viewing the situation of French Catholicism in 1844, declares that Protestants must rally.[99] *The American Whig Review* for July, 1847, seems surprised that Salverte's *Philosophy of Magic, Prodigies, and Apparent Miracles,* which had just been translated by A. T. Thompson, should omit all reference to Scripture miracles; apparently any Frenchman was expected to be wrong on that subject. The book is praised.[100] The *Christian Examiner* in January, 1848, regrets the general belief that the French are irreligious; there are those who renounce Catholicism, and for such Coquerel has written his *Le Christianisme*

[96] VI (n. s.), 291-3, September, 1838.
[97] *American Eclectic,* November, 1841, pp. 440-454. The author ignores the book he is supposed to review.
[98] XVI (3 s., VIII), 88-100, March, 1839. Article by "J. H. M." reviewing lives of J. Huen-Dubourgh, American translation, 1839, and by Robert M. Walsh, Philadelphia, 1839. See also *North American Review,* XLVIII, 565; *Boston Quarterly Review,* II, 357-9 (July, 1839), the last a plea for tolerance. *The New York Review* (IV, 500-501, April 1839) found the book "an animated sketch of a good man," "revered and loved alike by all of every class and profession."
[99] XXXVII (4 s., II), 289-308. Article by "C. B." reviewing two works on French theology, one by Vincent and one by Athanase Coquerel.
[100] VI, 109-110. Arago is quoted in praise of it.

Expérimentale (Paris, 1847), which, far from being rationalistic, contains good sound Unitarian doctrine.[101] And the struggle of France with the Jesuits was followed sympathetically by Protestants in the forties,[102] as well as the struggle in Switzerland. The *History of the Jesuits* by MM. Michelet and Quinet, designed to show the pernicious influence of the order, was especially debated by American magazines.[103] "They have suspended their ordinary labors," said the *Eclectic,* quoting the *Foreign Quarterly Review,* "to ring an alarm upon the revival of the Jesuits in France."[104] In the opinion of the *Democratic Review* the two historians "are contending in the sacred cause of liberty."[105] The *North American* went even farther. Briefly dismissing this famous volume with the statement that Michelet says that "jesuit" is to the French "a word of terror," the reviewer is alarmed to find that "Jesuitism is spreading, and silently acquiring strength in the United States; for good or for evil, it is gaining ground among us; and many, whose eyes are open to the fact, see in our future history auto-da-fés and inquisitions, and Protestantism destroyed by

[101] XLIV (4 s., IX), 1-21 January, 1848. The Daguerreotype (II:12, 512-8, October 21, 1848) found Pius IX a courageous reformer.

[102] Almost immediately upon the coronation of Charles X at Rheims (May 29, 1825) the Jesuits were secretly re-admitted to France. The government of Villèle (June, 1828) introduced two ordinances into the chamber restricting their operations, which were carried; but almost immediately (April, 1829) the Villèle ministry was ended and the Polignac cabinet called in (August 9, 1829). By 1845-46 the Guizot ministry under Louis Philippe found itself engaged in a struggle to allow free teaching at the University of Paris as well as the free development of religious bodies. Twice before (1841 and 1844) Villemain had attempted to secure liberty of education, but the Jesuits did not obey the legislation intended to restrict their activities, the number of their schools increased, and their influence became greater. The government then sent Rossi to Pope Gregory XVI, asking him to dissolve the order. On July 6, 1845, the official *Moniteur* announced that the Pope had agreed to dissolve the Jesuits. In the meantime a similar struggle had occurred in Switzerland; the Catholic cantons were allied against the Protestant cantons, and a state resembling civil war had been created. The Helvetic Diet ordered the expulsion of the Jesuits, who had been invited by the canton of Lucerne to superintend the schools of that district. The intervention of France in behalf of the Catholic cantons was asked and was refused. Moreton-MacDonald, *A History of France,* III, 271-2; Guizot, *History of France,* VIII, 362-368.

[103] See *The American Protestant,* I, September, 1845, for example, for representative articles on the Jesuits, French Protestantism, and the like.

[104] I, 144, January, 1844. A sketch of the controversy is given.

[105] December, 1845, XVII, 477-8. Review of an American translation of Quinet's *The Roman Church and Modern Society* and of *The Jesuits.* The same periodical, reviewing Michelet's *Du prêtre, de la femme, de la famille* (XVII, 127-137, August, 1845), had denounced the Catholic clergy.

a new St. Bartholomew." A life of Loyola would, he thinks, be revealing; and as for remedying the situation, "let Protestantism quit scolding, and live out a better Christianity than Romanism, and Jesuitism, and these latter cannot succeed." For alas, if they form the church militant, while Protestantism continues to be only the church termagant, the power and the growth will be theirs."[106] Michelet's book on auricular confession illustrated "the baneful influence of the established system of confession and spiritual direction" on family life in France and America, although the book mainly applies to France and is unfair to Fénelon and to quietism.[107] Even Brownson was compelled to admit that the anti-Jesuit history of Michelet and Quinet had a wide vogue in America.[108] If the government of the bourgeois Guizot was engaged in a death grapple with Jesuitism, what might not happen in America? The struggle of French Protestant theology was watched with anxious eyes.

From the midst of all this confusion the extraordinary figure of Orestes A. Brownson commenced to emerge as the champion of Catholicism in general, and of French Catholicism in particular. The career of this singular mind illustrates better than anything else the curious intellectual confusion of the time. Born in Stockbridge, Vermont, the 16th of September, 1803, he was brought up a Congregationalist; then, in October, 1822, he joined the Presbyterian church. But he was repelled by their harsh doctrine; at the age of twenty—that is to say, in 1824—he avowed himself a Universalist, of which faith he was ordained a pastor in June, 1826, and for which he preached and wrote up to 1829. But he was growing uneasy; and at length, denying the possibility of any divine revelation, he associated his views with those of Robert Dale Owen and Fanny Wright, carrying on his campaign in the *Free Enquirer* and later founding a paper in the interest of the Workingmen's Party. He had embraced the religion of humanity. In 1831 he began preaching as an independent minister; at which time he

[106] *North American Review*, LIX, 412-434, October, 1844. The *North American*, reviewing a French translation of Voigt's history of Gregory VII, was glad that Protestant historians dared to present the truth about mediaeval Catholicism. (LXI, 20-54, July, 1845).
[107] *Christian Examiner*, XLI (4 s.), 1-18, July, 1846. The reviewer (A. P. P.) observes of Quinet's book that "the substratum of facts is slender and indefinite; the steps of ratiocination faintly marked; the inferences vague and illogical." P. 3.
[108] *Brownson's Quarterly Review*, III, 135, January, 1846.

published *The Philanthropist.* Then Channing converted him to Unitarianism; in 1832 he became pastor of the Unitarian church in Canton, Massachusetts; in 1836 he organized the Society for Christian Union and Progress, to whom he preached in Tremont Street in Boston. During this period he was a regular contributor to the *Christian Examiner,* the Unitarian organ which we have frequently cited. In January, 1838, he founded the *Boston Quarterly Review,* writing most of the articles, especially those on religion and philosophy, himself, though others were contributed by A. H. Everett, George Bancroft, George Ripley, A. Bronson Alcott, and Margaret Fuller. By 1840 he had become a Saint-Simonian, and in the *Review* for July, 1840, he advocated the abolishing of formal Christianity. The Democrats were horrified; Van Buren said the article helped to defeat him. In 1842 this magazine was merged with the *United States Democratic Review* of New York, for which Brownson soon ceased to write; and seeking an organ, he founded *Brownson's Quarterly Review,* which ran from January, 1844, to October 1875, although it was suspended from 1865 to 1872. In the meantime his views had swung around to Catholicism; and he was received into the bosom of the church in Boston in October, 1844. He then became the most active advocate of Catholicism outside the clergy in the United States; not unnaturally, his writings were praised by the Church Council held in Baltimore in 1849. The student may trace these changes in the edition of his works in twenty volumes.[109]

Brownson struggled to prove that Catholicism was a liberal doctrine, and that the Americans should not take *au pied de lettre* the detractions which came from across the water. There is no middle ground, he wrote in the *Boston Quarterly Review* in 1838, between the Catholicism of de Maistre (Absolutism) and the democratic Christianity of Lamennais. "Christianity must enlist on one side or the other," unless religion be "a mere police force." And by long quotations from the *Paroles d'un Croyant* the article seeks to prove that Christianity must choose Catholic democracy.[110] In 1840 he sought to draw pub-

[109] Brownson, Henry F., *The Works of Orestes A. Brownson, Collected and Arranged.* Twenty volumes. Detroit, 1898-1908. My sketch of Brownson's singular career is based on this, and on the article in the *Catholic Encyclopedia.* See his own account of his conversion in *Brownson's Quarterly Review,* I, 1-28 (January, 1844).
[110] I, 444-473, April, 1838, article on *The Democracy of Christianity,* reviewing a group of books, mainly by Lamennais.

lic attention once more to Lamennais. The author of *The People's Own Book* (a translation by Nathaniel Greene, Boston, 1839) is, in Brownson's opinion, "one of the most remarkable men of the day, and one of the ablest and most vigorous writers of the French language." *The Essai sur l'Indifférence* "arrested the attention of the best thinkers and most distinguished literary men in France." Prior to the Revolution of July, Lamennais had been, it is true, anti-liberal, but since, he has "exerted himself nobly in the cause of freedom both religious and political for which he has had the high honor of being deposed by the Pope." (Brownson had not yet joined the church.) The remarkable doctrine of Lamennais is that religion and liberty are compatible, "a new doctrine for France." *The Words of a Believer* has had no parallel since Jeremiah; it is at once a prophesy, a curse, and a hymn, fraught with deep, terrible, and joyful meaning. Lamennais discusses both rights and duties; he is a social reformer, advocating justice and love, and the book "should be the pocket companion of every citizen of the Republic. It should lie on the table with the Bible, Pilgrim's Progress, and the Psalm Book; and if the Board of Education wish to escape utter damnation, they will obtain leave to make it a volume in their common school library."[111]

Then in 1844 Brownson was received into the church, and his attitude toward Lamennais necessarily changed. Now it is that "all Protestants" should read de Maistre's *Letters on the Spanish Inquisition* in an American translation—de Maistre, the great enemy of Lamennais![112] By 1847 Lamennais is a heretic,[113] and de Maistre, although as a theologian he stresses too much the analogies between the Catholic religion and heathen faiths, has written "works admirably" fitted to the times and temper of the age. The *Essay on the Generative Principles of Political Constitutions* exists, it seems, to show that the human race has always assented to the general principles underlying Catholicism; and the profound change in France has been due to de Maistre and to Lamennais before his "fall." Hobbes, Locke, Rousseau, and Paine are now overthrown in their falsity; Providence, it appears, shapes human constitutions; and the truth of de Maistre is amply illustrated by the Revolution of July and the troubles of Ireland.[114]

[111] *Boston Quarterly Review*, III, 117-127, January, 1840.
[112] *Brownson's Quarterly Review*, I, 415, July, 1844. T. J. O'Flaherty had published a translation in Boston in 1844.
[113] *Ibid.*, IV, 460, October, 1847.
[114] *Brownson's Quarterly Review*, IV, 458-85, October, 1847.

Naturally Brownson took up the cudgels in favor of the Jesuits. The famous history of Michelet and Quinet is merely anti-Catholic propaganda suited to the times; and Brownson proceeds to defend the Jesuits and attack the historians.[115] In 1846 he is attacking Quinet for having described Voltaire, Rousseau, and Montesquieu as the triple crown of the new Papacy with which France shook the earth; he alleges that the "new Christianity" of Quinet is the deism of the eighteenth century come to life again; he rushes to the defence of the church and of liberty and winds up with a grand attack on materialism.[116] By April Brownson, under fire from his late allies of the *Christian Examiner,* is talking about the "infamous work" of Michelet and Quinet, and writing scorchingly of Eugène Sue,[117] trying to free Saint Dominic from blame in the matter of the Albigensian crusade,[118] trying in short to get Catholicism understood. "The Roman Catholics," wrote Colton in 1839, "are generally found on one side, viz., the most thoroughly democratic and radical. And as that is at present the dominant party. it may be said that the Roman Catholics govern the country."[119] It did not happen either that Brownson was democratic and radical or that the Catholics were governing the country. In the fifties the Knownothings were to appear.

4. SUMMARY

So it is that the Protestant reaction captured the country and kept down the Catholic vote. France, instead of being a country to admire and pattern after, was now a nation to pity and

---

[115] *Ibid.,* III, 135, January, 1846; IV, 305-334, July, 1847.

[116] *Ibid.,* III, 107-127, January, 1846. Brownson was also calling attention to various pro-Catholic writings, such as the *Life of St. Vincent de Paul,* by M. Collot (translated, Baltimore, 1845), *Review,* III, 407-8, July, 1846; books of Catholic ethics, III, 137-153 (April, 1846); *La Reforme contre la Reforme, ou Retour à l'Unité Catholique* from the German of Hoeninghaus (French translation), III, 127-132 (January, 1846); *History of the Variations of the Protestant Church* of Bossuet (N. Y., 1845), "welcome to all good Catholics," III, 134 (January, 1846); *Lorenzo, or the Empire of Religion. By a Scotch Non-conformist, a Convert to the Catholic Faith.* From the French; by a Lady of Philadelphia• (Baltimore, 1844), IV, 216-49 (April, 1847); Thomas à Kempis, etc., IV, 411-412 (July, 1847).

[117] *Ibid.,* III, 173-202, April, 1846, in an article defending the Jesuits and based on Crétineau-Joly's *Histoire de la Compagnie de Jésus.* Paris, 1844, 5 volumes.

[118] *Ibid.,* V, 539-562, October, 1848. Review of Lacordaire's *Vie de Saint-Dominique,* 2d. edition, Paris, 1841.

[119] *A Voice from America to England,* p. 161. De Tocqueville was of the opinion that America must, as a democracy. become Catholic.

despise. The French, it is true, had struggled out of the horrors of infidelity, but only to fall into the arms of the Pope; de Maistre and the Jesuits had replaced Robespierre and the Goddess of Reason; and it was hard to say whether the last state of France (especially under Charles X, but not excepting Louis Philippe) was, or was not, worse than the first. And again, France was once more the insidious foe, the seat of subtle propaganda and of a mysterious secret force; the Catholic Church supplanted the Illuminati in popular imagination, and the French bishops and priests became as dreadful in the popular mind as ever were French deist or scoffing émigré. And this profound protestant upheaval is more than another instance of human folly; it affects the politics of the two countries, it affects the interpretation of literature, of art, of drama, it affects the whole problem of intellectual exchange between France and the United States in the nineteenth century. If France had been atheistic, it was now both atheistic and Catholic; and the dreadful immorality of French fiction was laid to one or another or both of these causes, just as Lamartine and Chateaubriand were received, not on their own merits, but as they upheld a Catholicism held to be in league with monarchy, tyranny, and darkness. But we have yet to deal with two or three matters of moment in the religious and philosophical life of America as it touched things French before we go on to other matters.

XIII

French Philosophical and Educational Influences

1. AMERICAN INTEREST IN FRENCH AND SWISS THEOLOGY, 1815-1848

WHILE the anti-Catholic movement was sweeping over America, certain more thoughtful men did not lose interest in contemporary movements in French theology. As early as 1819 one finds French religious news appearing in American theological journals.[1] French authorities on the influence of Christianity are quoted by "F. H. W." in his article, *The Influence of Christianity on the Political and Social Interests of Man* in the *Christian Spectator* in 1823, including Vattel, Neckar's work on the influence of religion, Villers on the Reformation, and Chateaubriand's *Genius of Christianity*.[2] The *Christian Review* in 1840 cites M. Dupin's refutation of Salvador's *The Trial and Condemnation of Jesus* in 1840 to show that Christ was not tried but persecuted.[3] The *American Eclectic* clips reviews of French religious works from French religious publications in 1842.[4] In 1843 a long article by "A. L." is devoted to theological education in Paris. It appears from the pastoral letter of the Archbishop of Paris that the French Catholics are seeking "to combat the errors and counteract the sinister influence of the times, and to reëstablish the reign of piety and virtue." The document in question "is quite a manly production, and is no less creditable to the talents and discernment of the archbishop, than to his piety," largely, it appears, because the archbishop is against romanticism. A discussion of French theological schools closes the account.[5] Two years later the

---

[1] In the *Christian Disciple*, I (new series), 159-162, March-April, 1819, for example (and again in the May-June number, pp. 237-239), one finds religious news gleaned from the *Archives du Christianisme* and the *Chronique Religieuse*. Both were taken at the "Reading Room" at Harvard.

[2] V, 409-421, August, 1823. He regrets that he has not seen Loget's sermons. Chateaubriand and Lamartine will be discussed in the second part of this study.

[3] *Christian Review,* V, 33-46, March, 1840. Article, "The Trial of Jesus," reviewing Dupin's work, translated and published in Boston, 1839.

[4] September, 1842, reviews of three French religious books appear, two from *Le Semeur,* and one from the *Revue Théologique.*

[5] *Christian Examiner,* XXXIII (third series, XV), 265-79, January, 1843.

same magazine has a long article on Alexander Vinet's *Vital Christianity*, which has just been translated and published by Robert Turnbull in Boston in 1845. The reviewer is "at a loss to explain the very high praise bestowed on this volume," which is not stirring, which has little depth, which is not an original exposition of Christian doctrine. Vinet, it seems, can not overcome the scepticism of the age, but insofar as he is anti-Trinitarian and anti-Calvinistic, he is "good."[6] The *Christian Review* is gentler; the market for sermons is nil, but Vinet is a great man, as Turnbull and D'Aubigné agree, and a great—Protestant—preacher, one "rich in Christianity": the sermon on the mysteries of Christianity, and one on grace and law, are quoted at length.[7] In the meantime de Gérando's *Visitor of the Poor* had been translated[8] and had attracted some attention: in the *Christian Examiner* for 1832[9] the book is made the text for a sermon on Christian benevolence; and in the *North American Review* for 1833,[10] the work receives a good deal of attention. De Gérando, we learn, "writes, too, with an amiable enthusiasm which does his heart the highest credit. Whether he can inspire equal enthusiasm in his readers, may be questioned; but one cannot read his book without feeling respect for him, nor without wishing to be as good and charitable as he seems to be." He is known also "to have written the best work which the French possess on the History of Philosophy." His latest work is on the very American theme of Self-Education; and (returning to the *Visitor of the Poor*) the review closes with a good many edifying excerpts and cases of the poor-widow-ill-and-many-children-plus-drunken-husband variety. Brownson, now converted to Catholicism, fires away at Protestantism behind a list of titles of theological works, some of them French, in 1845,[11] and even such works as the *Iconographie Chrétienne: Histoire de Dieu* of Didron (Paris, 1843) are pressed into service by the Unitarians as sticks to beat the

[6] *Ibid.*, XXXIX (fourth series, IV), 130-1, July, 1845.
[7] *Christian Review*, X, 295-309, June, 1845. *The American Quarterly Observer*, I, 341-45, October, 1833, denotes considerable space to the *Life of Julius Charles Rieu*, pastor of the Reformed French Church of Paris (American translation by the Rev. A. Alexander, D.D., Philadelphia, 1833).
[8] By "A Lady of Boston. With an Introduction by Joseph Tuckerman." Boston, 1832.
[9] XIII (new series, VIII), 137-163, November, 1832.
[10] XXXVI, 99-112, January, 1833.
[11] *Brownson's Quarterly Review*, II, 194-222.

Trinitarians with.[12] The same magazine attacked John Daille's *Treatise on the Right Use of the Fathers* as being too high· church.[12a] Poujalat's *Saint Augustin* (Paris, 1845) is noticed in 1846[13] and two French works on Saint Francis of Assisi in 1847.[14] *Brownson's Quarterly Review* necessarily carries a good deal of theological artillery, some of it from the French,[15] but the *Christian Examiner* and other papers were not far behind.[16]

But in theology the great interest of the thirties was in French protestant theology no less than in the state of French Catholicism or in such miscellaneous books as we have already noticed. With the growth of the Unitarian and Transcendental movements in America, there was a renewed interest in the foundations of Protestant theology; and as a result Americans either returned to the foundational works of Calvin or took a remarkable interest in the anti-Calvinistic movement which took place in Geneva and occupied some attention in France during the last two decades of our period. Calvin, indeed, becomes in the thirties and forties the same dominant figure that he was in the seventeenth century.[17] Judging from the magazines, it can not be said that an interest in Calvin ever died out. For instance, in 1814 we find the *Analectic* devoting seven

[12] *Christian Examiner*, XLI (fourth series, VI), 365-80, November, 1846.
[12a] XXXVII (4s. II), 270-2, September, 1844. Daille was a minister in the reformed church in Paris.
[13] *Christian Examiner*, XL (fourth series, V), 1-24, January, 1846.
[14] *Eclectic*, XII, September, 1847, 83-105. By Delecluse and de Malon.
[15] IV, 555, October, 1847, a notice of a translation by M. E. K. (Baltimore, 1847) of the *Catechism of an Interior Life*. By J. J. Olier, Founder . . . of the Seminary of St. Sulpitius, V, 255-265, April, 1848, Ventura's *Oraison Funèbre d'O'Connell*, criticized for political views; V, 233-55, April, 1848, an article on the social effects of protestantism, reviewing *Le Protestantisme comparé au Catholicisme dans ses Rapports avec la Civilization Européenne* by the Abbé Jacques Balmes, Paris, 1842.
[16] I see I have omitted *The Basket of Flowers; or Piety and Truth Triumphant. A Tale for the young, translated from the French, and altered and arranged.* By G. Y. Bedell, D. D., Rector of St. Andrew's Church, Philadelphia. Philadelphia, 1833. 144 pp. Reviewed at length in the *American Quarterly Observer*, I, 341-5, October, 1833. About the same time *The Art of Being Happy: from the French of Droz,* translated by Timothy Flint (Boston, 1832), attracted some attention among reviewers. The *American Monthly Review* for August, 1832, doubts whether Flint "will escape the censure of just criticism for such unmerciful cutting and mangling as he has deemed necessary in order to transplant this exotic from a Parisian hot-bed of sentimentality to the virgin soil of New England." Moreover, Mr. Flint is too "inclined to the philosophy of feeling." The reviewer exhibits no knowledge of the original (*Sur l'art d'être heureux*).
[17] See chap. x, 353 ff.

pages to a review of the *Memoirs of the Life and Writings of
John Calvin* compiled by the Rev. Elijah Waterman, and published at Hartford in 1813. "The life of Calvin," says the
reviewer, "is one of the noblest subjects which can be selected
by the philosophical historian." He agrees that Calvin is the
magister sententiae of the Reformation; and for biographer,
he deserves a Gibbon or a Horsley. The Rev. Elijah Waterman
is not a Gibbon, alas! but a simple follower of Beza's *Life;* he
has, however, vindicated Calvin from the aspersions of Roscoe
in his *Life of Leo X*.[18] In 1819 the proposal to publish a new
translation of the *Institutes* drew from *The American Monthly
Magazine and Critical Review* the remark that "the Christian
world never has been blessed with an uninspired man of greater
and more vigorous intellect, more fervent piety, and eminent
holiness."[18a] In 1821 the *Christian Spectator* is engaged in
exculpating Calvin from the charge of bad faith in the matter
of Servetus;[19] and in the same year a major interest in this
Calvinistic revival appears in the *Christian Disciple* with a
history of the rebellion against Calvinism in Geneva.[20] The
debate was to wax warmer in America. A history of the quarrel
appears in the *Christian Spectator* for August, 1822.[21] Geneva
is a home for Christians; but it possesses also "the fascination
of the sophistical sentiment in Rousseau" and "the brilliancy"
and "atheistical principles" of Voltaire among its associations.
In the eighteenth century it was the most religious and the best
informed community in Europe, but now—how changed, how
fallen—Voltaire's depraved sentiments are still popular there;
and its present irreligious state is probably due to "the incon-
clusive reasonings and brilliant theories" of Rousseau. Arian-
ism and Socinianism walk abroad; the work of reform is opposed by the pastors, including Vernet, and the story of the
suppression of Malan (a neo-Calvinist) is told at length. What
else can one expect? Society there is easy and sociable, and the
French officers of Napoleon spread atheism around them! The
controversy was continued in a debate between the *Christian
Spectator*[22] and the *Christian Disciple* (in which Professor

[18] *Analectic Review,* July, 1814, pp. 42-49.
[18a] February, 1819, p. 292.
[19] III, 408-410, August, 1821.
[20] III (new series), 214-30, May-June, 1821. "The Genevan Church," a
review of six French works on Geneva, all by ministers.
[21] IV, 412-9, August, 1822. Article, "Geneva," by "M. B."
[22] V, 196-224, April, 1823; VI, 310-37, June, 1824; VI, 360-374, July, 1824.

Norton had attacked Calvin), with the effect of "gentling" Calvin's views. By 1828 the speaker at the Andover Anniversary Celebration was admitting that Calvin "possessed . . . a harsh and impetuous temperament—a reckless energy of soul," that "he convulsed, agitated, roused, the sleeping elements of society—stirred the public mind to active and independent investigation." However, he is the master who regulated the storm; he himself was "calm, intellectual, collected"; his *Institutes* won him eminence; he was skilled in law, wise in counsel, prudent in zeal, decided in character. Slandered by all society, Calvin yet "deserves the thanks and not the curses of posterity."[23] The Unitarian movement was beginning to tell.[24] The speaker at Andover seems uneasily conscious of the blows dealt Calvinism by Channing in his *The Moral Argument Against Calvinism*.[25]

The situation at Geneva continued to engage the attention of American theologians. "That ridicule, persecution, and banishment should be resorted to, in this nineteenth century, by the Unitarians of Switzerland, against their orthodox fellow citizens, is an act of defiance to the spirit of the age not less surprising than its contradictions to their own published system," says *The Christian Spectator* spiritedly in 1828.[26] In the United States—*felix Arcadia!*—discussion is confined to pen and pulpit; in Geneva, brute force is employed, and men are ejected from college and academy. Once again, the writer mounts upward to Voltaire, Rousseau and D'Alembert, who announced to the world the triumph of Socinianism. A spirited history of the controversy follows, including the obligation imposed on young pastors by the Venerable Company, and the protests of Malan, Chenevière, Cellérier and Gaussen are outlined. The *Quarterly Christian Spectator* carried a similar article in 1830,[27] based upon French publications; and so does the *Chris-*

[23] *Christian Spectator*, new series, II, 239-241, May, 1828.
[24] On the origins of Unitarianism see volume X of the *American Church History* series; and Channing's *Works*, I, 530 ff, *Discourse at the Ordination of the Rev. Jared Sparks*. Baltimore, 1819. On the association of Unitarianism with the *Anthology and Boston Review* (predecessor of the *North American Review*), see Adams, *History*, IX, 201-205.
[25] Reprinted in *Works*, I, 160-172: "It is plain that a doctrine which contradicts our best ideas of goodness and justice, cannot come from the just and good God, or be a true representation of his character." The attack is made on the doctrine of inherited sin and that of predestination.
[26] New series, II, 86-98, February, 1828.
[27] II, 366-79, June, 1830, article, "Review of Religious Liberty in Switzerland based on Observations sur l'article sur les sectaires, inséré dans la Gazette de Lausanne du 13 Mars, 1829"; and *Essai sur la Conscience et sur la liberté Religieuse*, etc., by Venet. Paris and Geneva, 1829.

tian Examiner in 1831, the latter article being mainly devoted to Gaussen.[28]

The *Christian Examiner,* indeed, devoted itself to discussing the chief figures in the Geneva controversy. In 1827 it reviewed three books, two by Chenevière and one by Curtat,[29] rehearsed the history of the controversy, described the government of Geneva, a city exhibiting "a remarkable purity of manners" even when "occupied by the French, at the maddest period of their vices," and closed with a general burst of admiration for Switzerland.[30] M. Cellèrier the elder and M. Chenevière are the most celebrated preachers in the city. In 1832[31] the same periodical carries a brief and sympathetic summary of Chenevière's attack on Calvinistic Trinitarianism, which is unknown to the primitive church, incapable of direct proof, lacks any direct proof of its reasonableness, and is not essential to salvation. The same general line of argument is continued in a second article that same year.[32] In 1833 Chenevière's *Essais Théologiques* (Geneva and Paris, 1832) are "a lucid and satisfactory exposition of the great fundamental principles of Protestantism, defending them not only against the adherents of the Pope, but against the inconsistencies of Protestants." Faith requires evidence to be believed: it must be reasonable. The opposite view, it appears, is that held by "de la Mennais" who praises authority—that "precious process of ratiocination" of the "plausible Abbé" which Chenevière so courteously refutes. The writer quotes with approval Montaigne's dictum that "Christians have only to meet a thing incredible to find an occasion for believing" and praises the Swiss for taking a middle path between Faith and Reason, which are mutually supplementary. The argument against a

[28] XI (new series, VI), 225-240, "Recent Events in Geneva." Gaussen refused to teach Calvin's Catechism. This article is a continuation of a previous one. See *ibid.,* IV, 37 ff. In July, 1842, the same magazine "repudiates" Gaussen's *Theopneusty* (XXXII, 3 S, XIV, 319-37), whereas the *Christian Review* (June, 1842) finds his theory very sound (VII, 311), a view confirmed by Leonard Woods in March, 1844 (IX, 1-20).

[29] *A Summary of the Theological Controversies which of Late Years have Agitated the City of Geneva* by M. J. J. Chenevière, translated, London, 1824; *Causes qui retardent, chez les Réformés, le Progrès de la Théologie.* Ibid., Geneva, 1819; *De l'Etablissement des Conventicles dans le Canton de Vaud,* 2d. ed. L. A. Curtat, Lausanne, 1821.

[30] IV, 37-61, January-February, 1827.

[31] XII (new series, VII), 39-47, March, 1832.

[32] XII (new series, VII), 380-85, July, 1832. The writer is unable to agree with Chenevière's attempt to allegorize Genesis.

formal creed is then discussed at length: the apostles did not require one, there was none in the primitive church, the reformers were opposed to one, it is not Christian in spirit, the origins of creeds are in the doubtful fields of controversy, and the consequences of them are bad.[33] In 1834 the same periodical calls attention to the "truly admirable Discourses" of Cellèrier le jeune who will become as favorably known as Chenevière.[34] Cellèrier's *The Authenticity of the New Testament* as translated by "a Sunday School Teacher" (Boston, 1838) is better adapted for Sunday Schools than is Paley or Norton.[35] Unitarian scholars, it appears, know the elder Cellèrier as the eloquent pastor and devoted scholar; but the younger is equally eminent; and these two, with Chenevière are "prominent amongst that noble band of Genevan Reformers, who have risen up in the nineteenth century to complete the Reformation begun in the sixteenth." The two principles of the Reformation are the sufficiency of the Scriptures as a guide of life and the unlimited right of private judgment in religion, and both are being defended in the Swiss cantons where "Unitarianism is now making an advance."[36] Alas, Brownson thought Cellèriere's book "a poor concern."[37]

However, Calvin had his defenders. Reviewing a German edition of *Joannis Calvini in Librum Geneseos Commentarius,* the *Christian Review* thought it remarkable that Hengstenberg, "one of the strongest opponents of Calvinism should be an admirer of his genius." Why are the Germans doing work in Calvinism? They now believe that the scriptures teach the doctrines of the Reformers; that a mere philologian can not interpret them and that Calvin has "a rare union of the higher qualifications of an interpreter"—sympathy, linguistic skill, critical feeling and "sound morals." He excels as a commentator on Paul's epistles, on Genesis and the Psalms. "Ardent piety, great knowledge of the human heart, strong feelings, and a susceptibility to poetical impressions give (Luther and Calvin) a deep insight into that ancient treasury of spiritual

[33] *Christian Examiner,* XV (new series, X), 137-153, November, 1833.
[34] XV (new series, X), 344-350, January, 1834.
[35] XXV (third series, VII), 399-400, January, 1839. *The New York Review* also liked the book (IV, 245-6, January, 1839).
[36] *Ibid.,* XXVI (third series, VIII), 319-343, July, 1839. Review of *Esprit de la Legislation Mosaïque* by the younger Cellèrier, Geneva and Paris, 1837, a book of "lucid and beautiful order."
[37] *Boston Quarterly Review,* II, 261-2, April, 1839.

experience."[38] And on the subject of Calvin, the *Democratic Review* burst into verse:

> While angry zealots boast of CALVIN'S fame,
> Or load his memory with reproaches dire;
> Let truth and justice speak, and they conspire
> To praise, to bless, to canonize his name.
> Say that he clothes in too austere a guise
> The sacred doctrines of the Christian page;
> Say that he shares the spirit of his age,
> And stands unmoved while poor Servetus dies—
> Shall specks like these forbid us to revere
> The brightest day-star of the blessed hour
> When Europe, waking from her night of fear,
> Shook off the incubus of papal power?
> Helvetia, Holland, Britain, answer No!
> And from our own broad land, the like response doth go.[39]

Brownson had his doubts. Indeed, he was impolite enough to speak of the great man as a "fiend in human shape" in reviewing a French life of Calvin, translated and published in 1845.[40] However, the *Christian Examiner*,[41] reviewing the same volume, helped to hold the balance even; the book is by a Catholic, it is true, but it does Calvin justice as a thinker and writer, it is a fair specimen of the Catholic temper of the age in dealing with a disputed subject, although the style is bad. Calvin remains great, if not lovable; subtle and strong in mind, if narrow, definitive and hard; genuine and sincere, if intolerant in opinion; and void of idealism, sympathy, beauty, and social intercourse—lacking, in short, the humanity of Luther. With which verdict we shall leave him.

One general effect of all this discussion was, it is clear, to accentuate the difference between Catholic and Protestant. This same difference was deepened by the remarkable vogue of D'Aubigné's *History of the Reformation* in the United States. Before the book appeared there had been, it is true, an interest in the religious history of the French Protestants, and in various historical works by Frenchmen dealing with the Protestant past. Thus, among the new publications listed in the *North American Review* for 1826 (October), one finds Holmes' *Memoir of the French Protestants Who Settled at Oxford, in*

[38] IV, 620-2, December, 1839.
[39] IX, 382, October, 1841.
[40] *Brownson's Quarterly Review*, II, 540-4, October, 1845. *History of the Life, Works, and Doctrines of John Calvin*, from the French of J. M. V. Audin. Baltimore and Louisville, 1845.
[41] XLIII (fourth series, VIII), 161-86, September, 1847.

Massachusetts, A.D. 1686; with a Sketch of the Entire History of the Protestants of France.[42] Villers' *An Essay on the Spirit and Influence of the Reformation* was translated by Samuel Miller and published at Philadelphia in 1833.[43] Michelet's *Life of Martin Luther,*[44] Bonnechose's *The Reformers Before the Reformation* and *Letters of John Huss,*[45] and Coquerel's *Histoire des Églises du Désert chez les Protestans de France* (Paris, 1841)[46] are typical of the volumes reviewed in American magazines. But the great figure was D'Aubigné, a Genevan Calvinist, contemporary of Chenevière and the Cellèriers, father and son. *The History of the Great Reformation in the Sixteenth Century,* usually known in the three-volume London translation, marched over the land. One can trace its vogue in the magazines. Thus in the *Christian Examiner* for 1840 and again for 1842[47] "G. E. E." reviews the successive volumes, which he finds admirable for "candour, discrimination, and a generous feeling and a reverence for faith"; the work has the fascination of fiction and a graphic style, the sole fault being that it takes too narrow a view of the causes and issues of the Reformation. The *Christian Review*[48] found "unusual pleasure" in the mastery of the subject, the dramatic interest, and the deep religious sentiment of the volumes, which combine German diligence with French vivacity and have the manner of Ranke, save that D'Aubigné is more of a general writer than the Germans. The work gives a comprehensive view of the moral and social influence of modern Christianity and leaves no room for new research; it is not so much scientific as apologetic and—this is significant—it too painfully parallels the present world. The *Democratic Review* observes that the book is to be had in a cheap reprint, 15c per monthly

[42] XXIII, 495.
[43] Cf. *American Quarterly Observer,* II, 363-4, April, 1834.
[44] Translated by G. H. Smith. New York re-publication. *Democratic Review,* XIX, 80, July 1846. Also noticed in *North American Review,* LXIII, 433-466, October, 1846; and *The Christian Examiner,* XLIII (4 s. VIII), 98-118, July, 1847.
[45] British translations. *North American Review,* LXV, 265-304, October, 1847.
[46] *North American Review,* LXVII, 445-464, October, 1848. Coquerel was a reformed preacher in Paris, whose works were sometimes made known in America. Cf. *Christian Examiner,* XL (fourth series V), 331-2, May, 1846; and *ibid.,* XLV (fourth series, X), 363-389, November, 1848.
[47] XXVIII (third series, X), 20-44, March, 1840; XXXII (third series, XIV), 19-37.
[48] VI, 621-5, December, 1841.

number[49] in 1843; and declares that the same author's *Puseyism Examined* (which of course is strongly Protestant) has
"an immense circulation in England and the United States."[50]
Brownson admitted that the book "has been circulated very
extensively and very generally read," when he reviewed an
American edition (Baltimore, 1844) by Spaulding, though
of course he attacked it.[51] When the *Discourses and Essays of
D'Aubigné* were translated by Charles W. Baird, reviewers
spoke of "his high popularity."[52] In 1846 there were editions of
the *History,* one for thirty-eight cents a volume, one for fifty,
and one for seventy-five.[53] D'Aubigné, said the *Christian Review,* holds a large place in the public eye, and if the editor does
not altogether agree with the *History,* which displays "too much
imagination," the minor works show the author in a "new and
pleasing attitude."[54] This enthusiasm carried over into other
fields; for one thing, it floated other Huguenot histories;[55]
and for another, it called attention to D'Aubigné's other
works.[56] Published in these various forms, the *History* was
widely distributed[57] and helped to increase the feeling that the
Protestants were right and the French Catholics wrong.

[49] XII, 331, March, 1843; *The Ladies Repository* (III, 62, February, 1843)
was delighted with the dollar edition; and in April (III, 127) notes with
equal pleasure the monthly arrangement.
[50] *Ibid.,* XII, 442-3, April, 1843.
[51] *Brownson's Quarterly Review,* I, 410-11, July, 1844.
[52] *American Whig Review,* III, 674, June, 1846; *Democratic Review,*
XVIII, 478, June, 1846.
[53] *Columbian Magazine,* V, 192, April, 1846.
[54] XI, 556-83, December, 1846. The reference is to *Puseyism Examined*
and the *Discourses.*
[55] One by Browning, *A History of the Huguenots,* Philadelphia, 1845,
"succinct but not philosophical." Cf. *Democratic Review,* XVII, 475, December, 1845; and an anonymous one published at Cambridge in 1843 in
two volumes. Cf. *Christian Examiner,* XXXVI (fourth series, I), 74-82,
January, 1844.
[56] For instance, *Germany, England and Scotland,* reviewed in the *Christian Review,* XIII, 455, September, 1848 ("will richly repay perusal");
and his vindication of Cromwell for which see *Christian Examiner,*
XLIV (fourth series, IX), 205-222, March, 1848; and *The Church Review,*
I, 413-33, October, 1848. The latter, being Episcopalian, is violently anti-
d'Aubigné. *The Daguerreotype* (I:3, 122-32 September 4, 1847) declared
the *Life of Cromwell* was intended "to arouse anti-Catholic feelings,"
and finds D'Aubigné inconsistent.
[57] Professor Vernon Howell of the University of North Carolina informs
me that in the eighties, for instance, D'Aubigné and the Bible were the
total library in many homes in his state.

2. THE LIBERAL MOVEMENT IN AMERICAN THOUGHT, AND
FRENCH PHILOSOPHY IN THE SAME PERIOD

The moral reaction of the opening decades of the nineteenth century could not last. The regime was too rigorous. Even in the citadel of Calvinism, in the one-time theocratic state, there is a movement toward liberals. In the Era of Good Feeling the Anglicans of Connecticut, the Unitarians in Boston, the Universalists and Baptists, all worked for the overthrow of the established New England church.[58] The rigid Calvinism of an older generation had somehow to give way; human nature is not depraved, and a group of young Boston clergymen, drawing its inspiration from Harvard College in the very epoch when Jefferson was still holding sway, began to preach a more human Christ. At Harvard in 1805 Henry Ware was made Hollis Professor of Theology, with the result that, as Harvard became more and more liberal,[59] the Calvinists were compelled to create Andover Seminary. The Reverend J. S. Buckminster preached from 1805 to 1812; the Rev. S. C. Thacher from 1811 on, but the head and forefront of the movement was Channing.[60] In 1803 the Anthology Club became the rallying-ground for Boston liberals. Simultaneously the Universalist movement gathered force; Hosea Ballou in Portsmouth, following the doctrines of Dr. Benjamin Rush, Priestley and others, preached a liberal doctrine, embodied in the Winchester Profession of Belief of 1803[61] and warred against by Yale College and the Congregationalists. *The Panoplist* called upon the church to refuse communion to the heretics. But Channing, in his *Letter to Samuel C. Thacher* and his *Sermon on the Ordination of Jared Sparks, 1819,*[62] stoutly defended his creed,[63] and by and by victory was with the liberals. Of the old school Adams writes: "Obliged to insist on the infinite justice rather than on the infinite mercy

---

[58] Adams, *History*, IX, 133.
[59] Allen and Eddy, *A History of the Unitarians and Universalists in the United States*, pp. 187-8; Quincy, *History of Harvard University*, II, 284-291; Adams, *History*, IX, 176-8. The first Episcopal Church in New England (King's Chapel, Boston) became the first Unitarian Church in America in 1785. Predecessors of the movement were Jonathan Mayhew and William Bentley.
[60] Adams, IX, 176-8; Allen and Eddy, pp. 186-198.
[61] Allen and Eddy, p. 431.
[62] *Works*, I, 530-551.
[63] He was, however, opposed to French "atheism." Cf. *Works*, II, 521-528.

of God, they shocked the instinct of the new generation which wanted to enjoy worldly blessings without fear of future reckoning. Driven to bay by the deistic and utilitarian principles of Jefferson's democracy, they fell into the worldly error of defying the national instinct, pressing their resistance to war until it amounted to treasonable conspiracy."[64] "You will ask me, probably," wrote Murat in 1838,

after reading this, if religion, supported by such means, and disposing of such capitals, does not make great progress, and if it does not bid fair soon to penetrate everything? On the contrary; with difficulty does it keep its footing: it is like a ship sailing against the tide, which seems to make much way if we look at the water, and remains stationary in respect to the shore; in the same way is the church carried away by the great current of opinions, literature, and modern philosophy, which nothing can resist. This, above all, is the great opposing power, and which *(sic)* will certainly end by overthrowing the Christian religion; perhaps even this overthrow, considered as that of a complete system, is more advanced in the United States than is generally believed. But, besides that, other causes conspire to the same effect; the rising influence of the Unitarian sect is, perhaps, one of the most powerful. Pure theists, enlightened and virtuous philosophers, they do not, it is true, openly attack superstition, but they take away the support of their names, which is much. Boston, for instance, was the centre of bigotry; it is become that of this philosophic sect, and the chief seat of letters. Every distinguished man in that city, whether in politics or literature, is an Unitarian. The University of Cambridge, which is near by, is the head quarters of the sect, and it spreads from one end of the Union to the other. But, in addition to this, there are other philosophic sects which make a direct war on religion.[65]

So it is that the cosmopolitan spirit begins to exhibit new signs of activity. Writer after writer comments on the high social and intellectual attainments of the New England Unitarians. Beginning in the heart of Boston, Unitarianism went abroad;[66] we have already seen its interest in Swiss theological controversy, and presently the influences of German and

---

[64] *History*, IX, 87. The reaction against dogma was so pronounced that for thirty years society seemed less likely to resume the ancient faith in the Christianity Trinity, thinks Adams, than to establish a new Trinity in which a deified humanity should have place. IX, 182-3.

[65] I.e., Moravians, Shakers, "armonists," etc. Murat, *A Moral and Political Sketch of the United States of America*, pp. 135-6.

[66] "It cannot be denied that pantheism has made a great progress in our age. The writings of a part of Europe bear visible marks of it: the Germans introduce it into philosophy, and the French into literature. Most of the works of imagination published in France contain some opinions or tinge caught from pantheistical doctrines, or they disclose some tendency to such doctrines in their authors." De Tocqueville, II, 513.

French philosophy were to be brought to bear upon it.[67] So the gates to Europe that threatened to close are once more forced open; Boston becomes the Athens of America, a port to which European ideas may flow and, there transformed by a group of thinkers and writers, spread abroad over the republic to counter-act the narrowing tendency of too much morality. Transcendentalism becomes "the renaissance of New England culturally and spiritually"; here again the cosmopolitan spirit is strong. Channing, after spending some time at Harvard, went for two years as a tutor to Virginia where he "became acquainted with the works of Rousseau, Godwin and Mary Wollstonecraft, and from that time the kinship of many of his ideas with those of French Revolutionary origin can be clearly traced, though in passing through his serene and profoundly Christian mind," they become almost unrecognizable.[68] At the same epoch, that is to say with the return from Göttingen in 1819 of Ticknor, Bancroft, Everett, and others, a new force entered the history of our ideas,[69] that of Germany. But our present concern is with the interests of the transcendentalists in French thought, for French thinkers played an honorable, if not a leading part, in this renaissance of the human spirit in New England.[70]

To estimate the exact quality of the influence exerted upon the transcendentalists by French thought is a task beyond the scope of our present discussion. Much depends upon the interpretation given the word. Girard would like to depreciate the whole German influence and substitute in first place that of

[67] Frothingham, *Transcendentalism in New England;* Goddard, *Studies in New England Transcendentalism.*

[68] *Cambridge History of American Literature,* I, 331. "When, speaking to his classmates on their graduation from college, William Ellery Channing made the address entitled "The Present Age" (1798), (*Works,* I, 488 ff), the note that he uttered was one that henceforth reverberated throughout our national life and literature. It showed affiliation with the French Revolution, and with the England of Burns, Shelley and Wordsworth; and notable is the emphasis on the possibility of all human progress, not alone American progress, and on the importance of that culture which shall be shared by all classes of mankind." *Ibid.,* III, 109.

[69] Cf. the Appendix to Goddard, pp. 202-206.

[70] The exact amount of French influence is under strenuous debate. See Frothingham and Goddard; Riley, *American Thought from Puritanism to Pragmatism,* pp. 397-408; Leighton, *French Philosophers and New-England Transcendentalism;* Girard, *Du transcendantalisme considéré essentiellement dans sa définition et ses origines Françaises,* and the review of this by Sherburn in *Modern Philology,* XV, 125-128; Michaud, "Le Transcendentalisme d'après l'Histoire," *Modern Philology,* XVI, 113-412. War psychosis seems to underlie at least two of these anti-German articles.

Cousin, Jouffroy, Maine de Biran and Madame de Staël, but as Sherburn points out in his review of Girard, this is possible only by ignoring the facts and shifting the method of investigation.[71] Michaud, who likewise fails to agree with the conclusions of Girard, believing that the transcendental movement is not a religious movement, but an attempt to reconcile philosophy and religion, argues "à Cousin principalement, et par son intermédiare aux métaphysiciens allemands à qui Cousin l'emprunte, ils doivent la théorie de la Raison conçue comme un moyen direct et infaillible de connaissance transcendante."[72] Leighton, whose excellent earlier study both parties to the quarrel have overlooked, points out more sanely that the influence of French philosophy was not particularly predominant, mixing as it did with Oriental, Greek, German, and British thought;[73] that "the greater surge, boldness, originality of the German idealists apparently appealed more strongly to the young idealistic philosophers of New England than did the more rational, urbane, compromise philosophy of the French Eclectics."[74] Yet Cousin, Jouffroy, and Fourier exerted their influence, which Leighton, more particular than others in the discussion, traces in detail. He notes that the wide learning of Cousin and Jouffroy (and I should add, de Gérando) helped "to extend the intellectual horizon" of the transcendentalists; that the rationality and urbanity of the French tended to check stylistic and intellectual excess; that the French shared with the Americans an appreciation of the value of common-sense;[75] that the idealism of the French appealed to the Americans, as did their union of literature with philosophy.[76] On the whole Leighton makes out a better case than does anybody else, and

[71] Sherburn believes that even when the evidence is collected that shows a considerable knowledge of French thought on the part of the transcendentalists, it means rather that they turned to French simplification of German thought than to original French thought. *Op. cit.*, pp. 126-7.

[72] *Op. cit.*, p. 75.

[73] Leighton finds that in the sixteen volumes of *The Dial*, for instance, Cousin, Jouffroy, and Fourier are referred to only about fifteen times, whereas there are over thirty references to Plato alone, and twenty to Fichte; he also indicates that in Ripley's *Specimens of Foreign Standard Literature*, it was proposed to translate only four French writers, as opposed to 21 in German. *Op. cit.*, p. 93.

[74] Leighton, p. 94. This statement should be balanced against Sherburn's sound observation that most clergymen felt a peculiar horror for German theology (pp. 126-7) and Michaud's point that Kant was unintelligible to many. *Op. cit.*, p. 400.

[75] However, see Girard, *op. cit.*, pp. 444-7.

[76] Leighton, pp. 92-99.

it is surprising that his study is not better known. In what particular ways was this influence exerted?

We must note first of all a considerable amount of translation of French philosophy done by members of the transcendentalist-unitarian group. Leighton summarizes this as follows:

George Ripley, in his "Specimens of Foreign Standard Literature," had published his translations of Cousin's "Mélanges philosophiques" and Jouffroy's "Mélanges philosophiques." W. H. Channing had published in two different editions (1840;1848) his translation of Jouffroy's "Introduction to Ethics." C. S. Henry had published in New York (1838) his translation of Cousin's "Elements of Psychology." H. G. Linberg published in Boston in 1832 his version of Cousin's "Introduction to the History of Philosophy." J. C. Daniel translated in 1849 Cousin's "The Philosophy of the Beautiful." The translation by O. W. Wight of Cousin's "History of Modern Philosophy" was published in New York, 1852. R. N. Tappan, in 1862, published a version of Jouffroy's "Moral Philosophy."[77]

Some nine of Cousin's works were translated during the flood tide of transcendentalism, five of them before 1842 being especially influential in New England;[78] and seven translations from Jouffroy.[79] This seems to indicate a marked interest in French thinking.

In the second place, we must note a lively magazine discussion of French philosophy—an even livelier one than that of French theology we have just outlined. It is to this magazine discussion that we must turn to catch the intellectual manners of the time.

Aside from Madame de Staël,[80] whose work was influential in bringing light to bear upon German literature, and aside, too, from some feeble discussion of Constant,[81] the first French philosopher of the contemporary movement to draw attention to himself, seems to have been de Gérando. As early as 1824, the *North American Review* (not a transcendentalist organ by any means) was calling attention to the *Histoire Comparée des Systèmes de Philosophie* which was later to delight Emerson;

[77] P. 21. There were certain minor translations.
[78] Three by Ripley: *Preface to Tenneman's Manual; Preface to Philosophical Fragments; Preface to New Philosophical Fragments;* C. S. Henry, *History of Moral Philosophy of the Eighteenth Century;* and Linberg, *Introduction to the History of Philosophy,* Leighton, p. 30.
[79] *Ibid.,* p. 41.
[80] The entire discussion of Madame de Staël is postponed to the second part of this work. See, however, Girard, pp. 413-419. The *De l'Allemagne* was not known in the United States until the twenties, when it was rather widely discussed.
[81] Likewise postponed, but see Girard, pp. 420-427.

the book has already been translated into the German, M. Gérando is recognized as the first metaphysician of France, and he outlines the history of philosophy from the beginning to the present in an "elegant and perspicuous" manner.[82] This was the work which Emerson read in the fall of 1830, and from which he transcribed into his notebooks whole paragraphs relative to Greek philosophers, and sections which tend to build up his thought of circles, harmony, and law.[83] And reviewing the same writer's *Du Perfectionnement Moral, ou de l'Éducation de Soi-même* (translated, Boston, 1830), the *Christian Examiner* in 1830 is "glad, moreover, as Christians, to welcome among us a work like this, from the new school of French philosophy. We are weary of the thread-bare sophism, sanctioned by the former philosophers[84] of that country, and repeated by superficial declaimers since, which tends at once to cast contempt on the nature of man and the truths of the gospel. It is well to have their fallacy exposed by a writer, like de Gérando, who, singularly free from prejudice himself, is well qualified to soften the prejudices of others."[85] The style is "clear as the sun." Joseph Droz's *Essai sur l'Art d'Etre Heureux* in 1828 does not seem to be representative of this "new school"; whereas Franklin wishes us to frequent

> The marble porch where wisdom wont to talk
> With Socrates and Tully,

Droz "would conduct us, in preference, to certain pleasure gardens of somewhat doubtful fame, which were laid out in olden times in the neighborhood of the said porch, but were never much patronized by the good society of Athens."[86] However, the new school was presently to be on us in force.

And mainly in the shape of Cousin's eclecticism. In 1829 the *North American Review* was discussing his *Œuvres de Platon,*

[82] XVIII, 234-266, April, 1824.
[83] *Journals, 1824-32,* pp. 283, 332-345. Thus Emerson is interested in finding from de Gérando that there are certain universal philosophical principles which would be "a simple and sure means of marking in a general manner the primary conditions, the essential characteristics of each doctrine, and from these determining "the terms which compose one of the most important laws of the intellectual world." P. 333.
[84] Cf. James Buchanan, writing to Mrs. Slaymaker from St. Petersburg: "I fear I cannot with truth defend the chastity of the Empress Catharine. She was a disciple of the school of the French philosophers, and was therefore wholly destitute of religion—the surest safeguard of female virtue." October 31, 1832. Curtis, *Life of James Buchanan,* I, 154.
[85] IX (new series, IV), 70-107, September, 1830.
[86] *North American Review,* XXVII, 115-138, July, 1828.

Fragmens Philosophiques, Cours de Philosophie, and *Nouveaux Fragmens* in an article of almost sixty pages,[87] which is grateful for the Plato and highly critical of the philosophy. The *American Quarterly Review* tried to clarify the matter in a similar article published in December, 1831.[88] Cousin's eclecticism is hard to present, but in Europe "he is at the moment conspicuous for the novelty and comprehensiveness of his views, and for the energy and eloquence with which he urges them upon his hearers." Traces of Platonism, of idealism, of mysticism, of the free-thinker, and of the Catholic are in him. The eclectic philosophy assumes that all error contains some truth, and believes that it should analyze the beginnings of systems and extract truth therefrom. Cousin, however, omits the necessary postulate that new truth shall direct this operation, especially in the realms of sensualism and idealism, for the reviewer is wary of a trap. Cousin is "an eclectic in the most lofty sense of the world," but alas, the light of his principles "grows dim much too soon," as a general account of his work is apparently intended to show. The *History of Philosophy* is now examined; the "leading ideas of this volume" have been long known but "have never been so distinctly put forth, never so logically arranged, and never made to throw so bright and beautiful a light over the vicissitudes of humanity." Is this excessive? Is there anything "more bold, clear and philosophical" than Cousin's "establishment of (the) principle" of an idea of Providence? Thence flows, it appears, the idea of order, therefore of purpose, therefore of progress, which works alike in world history and in the individual mind. However, the victor is not always right, and the principal of progress will "need some, not to say, very great qualification"—especially in the eighteenth century. If the lectures do not "contain new truths" or "combine the fragments of old hypotheses into new unities," yet idealism is right and sensationalism is wrong as the Coleridges and the Cousins exist to show, even though the latter end in "indeterminate and barren generalities." The writer should have been comforted by the assurance of the Rev. Edmund D. Griffin: "I never shall forget the animated dignity with which (Cousin) made profession of his own belief in Christianity."[89] The *North American Review* charitably held that even those

[87] XXIX, 67-123, July, 1829.
[88] X, 291-311, December, 1831.
[89] *American Monthly Review,* January, 1832, pp. 22-23.

who could not adopt Cousin's system, "cannot fail to admire the profoundness of his views, and extent of his learning, his fearless but catholic spirit, his reverence for religion, and his just respect for humanity," for "his soaring genius, rising above all the particulars of periods and sects, comprehends in its splendid generalizations, not the actual merely, but the possible, and embraces in one vast idea, God, man and the universe."[90] Admirable man! He strongly reprobated "the practice of excluding clergymen and religious books, from schools."[91] Is it any wonder that "the sceptre of philosophy, though it seems to have passed from Germany to France, where it is now wielded by the distinguished Cousin, still lingers on the continent of Europe?"[92] What if he misapprehends Locke? He is a "perspicuous" psychologist, this Cousin;[93] even Brownson, not yet a Catholic, is gratified at the "considerable attention" given Cousin, whose works "are beginning to exert no little influence on our philosophical speculations," works which will aid "in rescuing the church, and religious matters in general, from their present lamentable condition." "Everybody," he says, "knows that our religion and our philosophy are at war," but M. Cousin is the truce-maker; his works indicate a revolution in French philosophy to which "as Americans, we cannot be indifferent." Gone is French sensualism; gone are Cabanis, Destutt de Tracy, Volney, de Gérando, Condillac; and now Providence and eclecticism, "the only true method," will rule the world.[94]

But the *Christian Review* is far from satisfied.[95] The eloquent Cousin—yes, but many of his doctrines are founded in error and their tendency is injurious to philosophy and religion. Shall we have to throw away Paley because absolute infinity is not possible except with particular finites to define it, as this deplorable Cousin argues? No, such relations are not *necessary,* though they may exist. Alas, when Cousin says that men are responsible only for their volition, not for their thoughts, he destroys the moral character. The same necessity does not attach to all our judgments as necessarily attaches to our perception of first and necessary truths; and though "great pains have

[90] XXV, 19-36, July, 1832.
[91] *American Quarterly Observer,* I, 177, July, 1833. See also III, 354-6.
[92] *North American Review,* XLI, 372 (article on Channing).
[93] Cf. *Quarterly Christian Spectator,* VII, 89-127, review of *Cousin's Psychology,* translated by C. S. Henry. Hartford, 1834.
[94] *Christian Examiner,* XXI (third series, III), 33-64, September, 1836.
[95] III, 590-613, December, 1838; IV, 21-36, March, 1839.

been taken to recommend this system to the young men of our country," it will "expire in France," though not before it has helped "to expel the poison of German transcendentalism." For —whisper it not in Gath—Cousin's system is not "Christian." This terrible Cousin has argued that war is necessary, but he is clearly wrong as J. Q. Adams and Brownson are prepared to show.[96] And this eclecticism that was to save us all, "I would say," said Emerson in his *Journal,* "that there is an optical illusion in it."[97] However, Brownson comes to the rescue of eclecticism in the *Boston Quarterly* with whole armies of metaphysical artillery.[98] And he has something to say of the spread of eclecticism:

The friends of the modern school of Eclecticism in France have abundant reason to be gratified with the reception which its principal doctrines have found in this country. . . . The youthful student has welcomed them as leading to a higher eminence, commanding a more elastic and refreshing atmosphere, than the popular theories of English sensationalism; while the politician and the theologian have begun to look into their influence and either to claim their support or to attempt their refutation. . . . Such an impulse has been communicated, in no small degree, to a numerous circle of minds, by the eloquent writings of M. Cousin; they have spread fear in many high places; the usual portion of reproach and misrepresentation has been administered to them; but still they are studied with more interest than any philosophical system we are acquainted with; they are scattered far and wide over the land, in some of the various forms, in which they have been represented or reproduced.[99]

For in the meantime the doctrines *are* popular; as early as 1829 President Marsh remarked that Paris is the place where doctrines of rational and spiritual form are taught by Jouffroy and Cousin, and eclecticism was spreading by the end of the thirties to Ohio and Wisconsin and the old frontier, where Calvin Stowe and the Beechers argued with Ephraim Peabody, James Freeman Clarke, James H. Perkins, and Channing.[100] By 1848 De Bow was running *The Science of History* (Linberg's translation) in installments in his *Commercial Review.*[101]

[96] *Boston Quarterly Review,* I, 152-161, April, 1838.
[97] *Journal, 1836-38,* pp. 404-5; see also p. 400.
[98] II, 27-53, January, 1839; 169-187, April, 1839; October, 1839.
[99] *Ibid.,* pp. 435-6. He attributes their spread in New York and Boston to the moral and religious character and the psychological method of the system.
[100] Cf. Riley, *op. cit.,* pp. 397-408; Rusk, *Literature of the Middle Western Frontier,* I, 51.
[101] V, 58-65, 127-134, 211-220, 346-357, 445-454.

Under the shadow of Cousin the minor people tend to shrink. Nevertheless the indefatigable Brownson calls attention to Matter's *De l'influence des moeurs sur les lois* (Paris, 1832) in the *Christian Examiner* in 1836, whence he draws the lesson that the Christian clergy should educate the people.[102] And Jouffroy begins to attract attention, "one of the most distinguished of the French Eclectics," according to Brownson, one who tries to find a basis for the sense of obligation, seeking the end of man's existence in the primitive and instinctive tendencies of human nature and in the concept of another life. He is, one reads, "less peculiarly French than most French writers," which seems to be intended as a compliment.[103] And George Ripley's *Philosophical Miscellanies* of 1838 called attention to Cousin, Jouffroy, and Constant.[104] The project of the *Specimens of Foreign Standard Literature* "meets with encouragement to a degree beyond the expectations of its proprietors"; Jouffroy promises "to do more for the advancement of mental science than any other living author."[105] So month by month the discussion went on. Morality, religion, democracy, and philosophy were to be somehow welded into a living unity by eclecticism, and the transcendentalists rejoiced.

By 1840 they were rejoicing in *The Dial*. "Few if any living writers upon Ethical Philosophy," one reads in July, 1840, "stand so high in the estimation of those who have made this science a study" as Jouffroy, the translation of whose *Ethics* by Channing (Boston, 1840) is under discussion; and Paley, it seems, is "psychologically wrong."[106] In Boston bookstores "Jouffroy is admirable for his genuine liberality, as well as his lucid order. He knows where to stop; and if he does not satisfy you, never makes you dissatisfied."[107] The *Boston Quarterly*

---

[102] XX, 153-169, May, 1836. Cf. *Boston Quarterly Review*, I, 126-7, January, 1838; *Christian Examiner*, XXIV (third series, VI), 112-129, March, 1838.

[103] *Christian Examiner*, XXII (third series, IV), 181-217, May, 1837.

[104] Cf. *Boston Quarterly Review*, I, 433-444, October, 1838; *New York Review*, III, 487-8, October, 1838. See also *Christian Examiner*, XXV (third series, VII), 137-157, November, 1838, on the scepticism of the present age as discussed by Jouffroy.

[105] *Christian Examiner*, XXIV (third series, VI), 270-4, May, 1838.

[106] I, 99-117. Cf. Michaud, *op. cit.*, pp. 58-59. Cf. the review of Brownson's novel, *Charles Elwood* in *ibid.*, I, 22-46. "The philosophical basis of religion, which, in the main, coincides with the theory of M. Cousin, is exhibited in several conversations between Elwood and the ancient minister." P. 41.

[107] *Boston Quarterly Review*, III, 330, July, 1840. A Chat in Boston Bookstores.

gallantly defends the transcendentalists from the attacks of Andrews Norton and the *Princeton Review,* for, though the transcendentalists—some of them, at any rate,—have read Cousin, "the movement is really of an American origin, and the prominent actors in it were carried away by it before ever they formed any acquaintance with French or German metaphysics; and their attachment to the literatures of France and Germany is the effect of their connexion with the movement, not the cause." However, Cousin is cleared from charges of atheism, pantheism, egotism, and fatalism.[108] The embattled *Christian Examiner,* after examining all possible moral systems, agrees that "no French writer has appeared, whose labors can be so agreeable to the English mind . . . as Jouffroy, who combines [one must get over this as best he can!] enthusiasm and Scotch caution." We need a system of Christian ethics; perhaps we can found one on Jouffroy's "noble charity, as well as singular lucidity."[109] The *North American,* which is relatively neutral in the contest, bears witness to the vogue of Cousin by 1841:

The writings of Cousin form the popular philosophy of the day. Their success in this country by the appearance of the three translations, of which the titles are given above,[110] one of which has already passed to a second edition, and has been introduced as a textbook in some of our principal colleges. . . . His manner, after all, is one much to the taste of sober and accurate thinkers; but it has qualities which are sure to please the majority of readers. Evidently formed in the lecture room, it is sometimes eloquent, but more frequently declamatory. Profound subjects are treated without any affectation of profundity of manner,—the capital vice of the German metaphysicians; and the general lucidness of the views set forth is due partly to the clearness of the writer's mind, and partially to the superficial character of the inquiries. . . . His conclusions lie but a step from the premises, when they have any premises at all, and they are repeated with frequency.[111]

So the *North American* gives with one hand and takes away with the other. Meanwhile Brownson was building up a whole system of philosophy on Cousin,[112] who was becoming the

---

[108] III, 265-323, July, 1840. In reply to two articles in the *Princeton Review.*

[109] XXVIII (third series, X), 137-147, May, 1840.

[110] Linberg's *Introduction,* Boston, 1832; the *Specimens* of Ripley, Boston, 1838, and Henry's *Elements of Psychology,* New York, 1838.

[111] *North American Review,* LIII, 1-40, July, 1841. *The Ladies Repository* this same year thought that Cousin had "wrought wonders" toward the reformation of philosophy from materialism and infidelity. I, 118, April, 1841. Jouffroy's *Prolégomènes au Droit Naturel* in Channing's translation was a text-book at Harvard by 1843. *Democratic Review,* XII, 464.

[112] *Democratic Review,* XI, XII, a series of articles in 1841-2-3.

interpreter of Kant to America—Cousin, "the best equipped living writer to interpret the 'critical philosophy.' "[113] When Leroux arises to refute Cousin, the *Boston Quarterly* gives him short shrift: "we do not like the spirit manifested towards Cousin, nor the virulent personal attacks on him," though Leroux "has the merit of great ability and uncommon philo-sophic powers."[114] However, a writer in the *North American Review* in April, 1842, is not so certain: even if the popularity of Cousin's philosophy in France has driven out that of Con-dillac, "there would be good reason to suspect the reality, and the pure character, of a religious movement produced by such a cause and conducted by such a guide."[115] And Brownson, the ever-versatile, is beginning to doubt Michelet, Cousin, and Jouffroy in the *Democratic Review;* one is a Manichaean and introduces fatalism; one has a false idea of human develop-ment, and Cousin's "impersonal reason," borrowed from Hegel, "leads to pessimism."[116] Brownson, become Catholic, burned what he had adored.[117] Barring one or two minor articles,[118] the great discussion died away.

Regarding the vogue of French eclecticism, Professor Riley has some interesting things to say. Cousin, as we have seen, was exactly fitted to the temper of an age and a movement revolting alike from sensationalism and religious formalism, not to speak of utilitarian economics. But the word "eclectic" itself was in ill-repute; it had covered polite forms of literary piracy, had denoted a form of medicine between allopathy and homeopathy, and had been used to characterize political mug-wumps. Nevertheless these negative factors were offset by the

[113] A translation of Cousin's *Kant and His Philosophy* in the *American Eclectic,* I, 276-87, March, 1841.
[114] *Boston Quarterly Review,* V, 126-7, January, 1842.
[115] LIV, 356-97.
[116] XII, 457-74, May, 1843. A subsequent article (pp. 569-86, June, 1843) vigorously defends the providential theory of history.
[117] The first of his anti-transcendental articles in *Brownson's Quarterly* (I, 137-174, April, 1844) attacks Cousin's classification of knowledge and defends scholastic philosophy against the Frenchman. In January, 1845 (II, 53-76) he falls afoul of Jouffroy; hints that man must follow, not Nature, but God, and declares that Cousin perverted Jouffroy's original Catholic faith.
[118] Such as a notice of Cousin's *Early Greek Philosophers* in *Campbell's Foreign Monthly Magazine,* II, 20-37, January-April, 1843; one in the *Democratic Review,* XV, 17-32, July, 1844, justifying transcendentalism as both democratic and Christian, which adds nothing to the argument; a notice in the *Eclectic Magazine,* VI, 217-225, October, 1845, of a post-humous work of Jouffroy, etc.

close personal connection between Cousin and Americans; his correspondence with his translators and friends was heavy, and he worked for cordial Franco-American relations. Moreover, his philosophy, besides being debated in New England, was taught in the West by people like William E. Channing; it had its curious combinations of common-sense qualities and soaring cloudinesses, and all in all, was well calculated for the American latitude.[119] If Cousin was not the European foster-father of transcendentalism—and he was not—no single French thinker in the nineteenth century was more vigorously debated and discussed in the United States in our epoch.

One scarcely knows whether to include the ambiguous figure of Fourier in this group or not. Certain it is that no such discussion of his theory exists as in the case of Cousin, and McMaster may be right in saying that it is extremely doubtful whether the mass of our countrymen ever heard of his schemes of social reform before 1840, when Albert Brisbane published his *The Social Destiny of Man,* compounded of Fourierism.[120] In that year there is a good deal of writing about associationism in the various numbers of *The Diamond.* In the *Boston Quarterly Review* in 1841 Brownson has a long article discussing Fourierism, and is sceptical about it; Brisbane replied in a subsequent issue.[121] The *Dial* article of July, 1842, is largely compounded out of Brisbane.[122] As late as 1844 "E.P.P." is writing in the *Dial* that "the works of Fourier do not seem to have reached us, and this want of text has been ill supplied by various conjectures respecting them." The convention in Boston of December 1843, January 1844, is "the first publication of Fourierism in this region," but the vague horror in which Fourierism had been held was supplanted by respect after Channing's exposition. Stress is laid on the fact that the Associationist, to succeed, must be a Christian.[123] *The Democratic Review* devoted a good deal of space to Associationism in 1844, the *Christian Examiner* was sceptical,[124] and Brownson was dead against it.[125] The *American Whig*

---

[119] *American Thought from Puritanism to Pragmatism,* pp. 389-97.
[120] VII, 142.
[121] IV, 265-91, July, 1841; 494-512, October, 1841.
[122] III, 86-96, July, 1842.
[123] IV, 478-83, April, 1844.
[124] Cf. XXXVII (fourth series, II), July, 1844, 57-78.
[125] *Brownson's Quarterly Review,* I, 175-194, April, 1844; I, 450-87, October, 1844.

Review in 1848 referred pleasantly to the "pollutions of Fourierism" in an article on Societary Theories and argued that the socialist was anti-Christian,[126] and by the same year the *Democratic Review* was definitely hostile.[127] Whatever importance the associationist theory had for the Brook Farm colony, it would seem as though the country at large, already accustomed to various communistic experiments, was prepared to look upon it as an oddity which might have dangerous possibilities. Meantime, Comte was just around the corner.[128] As yet he was little known.

The reader must have observed that these various French philosophers are at one time or another brought to the test of Christianity. If no country was less philosophical, it was because the overwhelming preoccupation of men in things metaphysical was religious. The question was simply how far the moral reaction of the first decades could be stretched out of its narrowness. "Christianity," wrote de Tocqueville, "itself is a fact so irresistibly established no one undertakes either to attack or to defend it." The Americans tacitly accept its theology and its morals. "Hence the activity of individual analysis is restrained within narrow limits, and many of the most important human opinions are removed from the range of its influence. . . . Everybody there adopts numbers of theories, on philosophy, morals, and politics, without inquiry, upon public trust."[129] On this discouraging note, let us leave the philosophical problem.[130] It can not be said that Kantian or Eclectic, Transcendentalist or Unitarian greatly affected the intellectual condition of the great mass of the people.

3. FRENCH INFLUENCE UPON AMERICAN EDUCATIONAL SYSTEMS

We ought in any thorough study of American culture to devote a larger space to education than is possible in this survey, for here, too, the conflict of forces exhibits certain char-

[126] VII, 632-646, June, 1848.
[127] XXIII, 375, November, 1848.
[128] The *Democratic Review* carried a discussion of the Positive Philosophy through February, March, April, and May of 1847, vol. XX. On the general vogue of Comte see Riley, *op. cit.*, pp. 397-408. Interest waxed in the fifties
[129] *Democracy in America*, II, 488, 493.
[130] It must not be forgotten that the thirties were the decades of Millerism and Mormonism, and of various other religious sects which flourished only to disappear. The official historian of American religion refers to the ten years from 1835 to 1845 as "the dreary decade." Bacon, *History of American Christianity*, p. 312.

acteristics; here too, the French touch us. In the present chapter we can but hint at the situation.

In the popular mind the United States is the parent of the great public school system, unique in the world's history, devoted to the intelligent upbringing of a democracy; and this school system develops (so runs the legend) from the beginning; from 1619 when the "records of the Virginia Company show that . . . a proposition . . . came up to build a college in Virginia 'for the training and bringing up of infidels' children to the true knowledge of God and understanding of righteousness' ";[131] and from the statutes of the Massachusetts colonies establishing schools; and in such development the Ordinance of 1787 and the state university system are document and evidence. But this popular view is open to considerable correction; the Ordinance of 1787 is a product of the time when the back country was temporarily in the saddle, and the evidence goes to show that the American public school system is relatively a late development, and that there was a class grip upon education, a monopoly on learning in America, until well towards the end of the period we are traversing.

Thus "until 1805, in fact, there were hardly any but Church of England parochial and private schools in New York City";[132] and New York, as a matter of fact, created a university long before it established public schools, although state lands had been set aside for both in 1789. Indiana founded Vincennes University in 1807, but it did not enact a general school law until 1824. In New York City in 1828 there were twenty-four thousand two hundred children between five and fifteen years of age who did not attend any school whatever. In his message of January 1, 1822, Governor John Collins complained that not even primary schools existed in Delaware at that date. Rhode Island in 1800 passed an act for free schools "to contribute to the greater equality of the people," but at the instance of the rich the act was repealed in 1803; not until 1828 was an act got through the legislature establishing common schools. And in the South the public school system came only slowly; in the Louisiana legislature, for instance, Mr. Eustis complained in 1846 that the children of the state took away $200,000 annually by getting an education elsewhere.[133]

---

[131] Myers, *History of American Idealism,* p. 85.
[132] Myers, p. 88.
[133] The facts are from Myers, chap. vii. Cf. Cubberley, *Public Education in the United States,* chaps. v-vi.

And indeed, generally speaking, the American public school system dates from Horace Mann's endeavors; in 1837, the first Massachusetts state board of education was created, and coincident with that year a popular wave of public school enthusiasm struck Ohio and the West.[134] It is not without meaning that the first labor movement runs from 1824 to 1836;[135] that the "struggle between labor and capital begins under Jackson in 1835";[136] labor—the democracy—shut out from education, was demanding the education it had not opportunity to enjoy.[137]

What type of education was prevalent in America before Horace Mann? It was almost wholly class education, and indeed it was because of this insistence on class differences that the labor party complained. The characteristic institution of the seventeenth and eighteenth centuries was the college, and the college in an eminently aristocratic form, whether its origin be in Massachusetts or in the South—a quality so marked that today, even, a suspicion of the collegiate aristocracy lingers in many minds with respect to the educational institutions of the East. We need not rehearse the familiar story of the founding of Harvard, Yale, Princeton, King's College, and William and Mary; a glance at their curricula, a glance at the student body is sufficient: these institutions are for the aristocracy of intellect, the aristocracy of breeding; their courses are the courses of European universities as far as may be, and the institutions belong to the cosmopolitan spirit. Nor, later, when the republic was created, had the attitude greatly changed; if colleges increased, if universities were founding, it is a striking and significant fact that "universities were actually established before a general public school system; in many instances they long preceded it." Why should this surprise us? It was but the carrying out of the dominance of the interests of the cosmo-

---

[134] Dexter, *History of Education in the United States,* pp. 101-105. See in this connection the maps in Cubberley showing the "expansion" of New England.

[135] Simons, *Social Forces in American History,* chap. xvii.

[136] Schouler, *History,* IV, 201.

[137] Thus the Workingmen's Party in New York was bitter in its denunciation of the then existing system in New York City. "According to the *Workingmen's Advocate* of May 1, 1830, nearly half the children in New York City did not go to school because their parents could not pay tuition fees or would not take the bounty of the Free School Society. The *Mechanics' Magazine,* in August, 1833, stated that 80,000 children remained unschooled in New York State." Myers, pp. 101-2. See in Cubberley, p. 120, the list of interests for and against the public schools; and see him, pp. 125-127 on the labor interest.

politan classes. "According to their view the future adminis-
trators of the American Republic would be members of legislatures and of the courts and of the learned professions in
general."[138] Not to educate the democracy—except by way of
charity[139]—but to educate the leaders of a democracy—this is
the note of education in colonial times and in the early republic.

In such a situation European ideas, especially during the first
century of the colonies, and later on during the post-Revolutionary epoch, might easily penetrate, and particularly those of
France. One notes, to begin with, that the Huguenots in New
Rochelle and elsewhere helped to mould the children of the
gentry to the pattern of an elegant and useless curriculum:

The French boarding and day schools for young ladies which were
established in New Rochelle were eagerly patronized by the English
and Dutch, whose daughters hitherto had possessed few educational
advantages. These schools were the originals of the young ladies'
seminaries and fitting schools, or finishing schools, which held the field
until the day of women's colleges, which were ushered in by a Huge-
not descendant—Matthew Vassar. . . . From the first the French
language was taught, and all the "ladylike accomplishments" of the
time were imparted. English teachers were employed to teach the
grammatical use of their own tongue, written and spoken . . . accomplishments included enough of music to enable a young woman to play
a little for dancing, or to warble a few songs in her fresh, sweet tones
to the accompaniment of the spinet; enough of French to read it easily,
write it fairly well, and hold a not too monosyllabic conversation.
Then much was made of instruction in the arts of painting and embroidery, and more of that truly high art, gentle manners. . . . The
pupils were taught how to avoid all awkwardness of movement or
carriage; how to bear themselves gracefully erect; how to enter and
leave a room, to greet properly all ages and conditions, to arrange and
preside at a dinner table with elegance, to dress with taste and effect,
and to dance gracefully.[140]

So it is that the French establish in the United States the superficial but cosmopolitan tradition of the boarding school.

Nor is this the sole way in which the French were to influence American education. Education for women, generally

---

[138] Myers, pp. 94-5.
[139] "Both in the Middle and Southern colonies, however, down to the era
of final separation from England, and so long as the influence of the
Crown lasted, schemes of education for the people partook to a considerable degree of the nature of almsgiving and patronage, so far as the poor
man and his children were concerned." Schouler, *Americans of 1776*, p. 199.
As to the situation in New England, however, see Cubberley, pp. 37-46.
Unfortunately the development in New England of something like a modern common school system was checked by the Revolution.
[140] Fosdick, *French Blood in America*, pp. 413-4. See the description of the
jeu de courtoisie for children in Smith, *Colonial Days & Ways*, pp. 164-6.

speaking, came in at the end of the eighteenth century,[141] and barring such exceptions as the Penn Charter School at Philadelphia which admitted both sexes, and the Moravian school for girls in Bethlehem, founded in 1745, academies for young ladies begin to multiply only with the powerful impetus given to "female education" by Rousseau and the English radical feminists.[141a] One notes, for example, that the Philadelphia Female Academy dates from the Revolution. Dr. Dwight's Young Ladies' Academy at Greenfield, Connecticut, was founded in 1785. The Medford School near Boston, founded in 1789, was long the resort of young ladies from the Eastern states. In Boston in 1787 Caleb Bingham proposed to open a school for girls, and instances could be multiplied.[142]

With the French Alliance and the French Revolution, Gallic influence upon American education increased. "Frenchmen saw in the United States a wide field for planting French science, art, and culture. It is scarcely an exaggeration to say that a propaganda was organized, or at least was on the point of organization in France, looking to that end."[143] One point of influence was the learned society in America, of which two types existed. One, represented by the American Philosophical Society, founded in 1769, represented the English idea, modelling its organization on the Royal Society of Great Britain. The other, like The American Academy of Arts and Sciences of Boston, incorporated in 1780, was French in conception, and modelled itself upon the Royal Academy of Paris. Whereas the Academy published its *Memoirs,* the Philadelphia organization issued its *Philosophical Transactions.* Franklin was the progenitor of the one, and John Adams, returned from Paris, was the originator of the other. However, by an ironic reversal of fortune, the Boston group came in time to be thoroughly British, whereas the Philadelphia organization, as we have seen, admitted a number of French to membership, and was thoroughly in touch with French science.[144]

[141] Dexter, *op. cit.,* pp. 426-8.
[141a] Andrew Eliot presented "Rousseau on Education" to Harvard in 1774. Quincy, *History of Harvard University,* p. 529.
[142] Boone, *Education in the United States,* p. 69. A writing school for girls was established in Boston in 1700. The Penn Charter School was founded in 1698.
[143] Hinsdale, *Foreign Influence upon Education in the United States,* I, 597.
[144] See the *Early Proceedings of the American Philosophical Society;* Hinsdale, I, 596; Faÿ, *passim,* but specially chaps. ii and iii.

Certain French writers are of interest in this connection. The wide vogue of Fénelon would be of more interest, were it not for the not uncommon fear of an aristocratic education expressed by many, who did not practice what they preached.[145] The exact vogue of Rousseau awaits investigation.[146] Montesquieu was occasionally cited in educational discussion.[147] Certainly the wide diffusion of French instructors is a marked feature of the epoch.[148] Perhaps more interesting was the dream of Quesnay de Beaurepaire, who travelled in the United States, and conceived the idea of establishing at Richmond an Academy of Sciences and Fine Arts to have branches in all the principal cities and to be affiliated with European cities. In Richmond there were to be French professors, masters, and artists. Twenty-five resident, and one hundred seventy-five non-resident associates were to be chosen from both hemispheres. John Page, the lieutenant-governor of Virginia, encouraged him in 1778; by 1786 he had obtained from prominent Baltimoreans and Virginians a subscription of sixty thousand francs, and in Paris he got a favorable report on the idea from the Academy of Sciences, signed by Lalande, Thouin, Lavoisier and Condorcet, as well as one from the Academy of Painting, signed by Vernet and others. The French court patronized the enterprise; Lafayette, Beaumarchais, Houdon, Malesherbes, Luzerne, Montalembert, and La Rochefoucauld were all benevolently disposed. Jefferson stood behind it, and by 1788 Quesnay was publishing a program in Paris, for in 1786 the foundations of the building were laid in Richmond in the presence of local authorities and various French supporters like Raguet, Audrin, La Case, Noel, Dossière, and others. One professor, John Rouel, was appointed—mineralogist and professor of natural history and chemistry—but it is doubtful whether he ever came to America, for the French Revolution resulted in the withdrawal of support from France, and the building, when completed, served only to house the state convention that ratified the Federal constitution. "Had it succeeded there would,

---

[145] Cf. Faÿ, pp. 139-40.
[146] Bayard observed that "Dr. Benjamin Rush has in vain recommended the humane methods of J. J. Rousseau to schoolmasters." Quoted in Sherrill, *French Memories,* p. 234.
[147] As in *The American Magazine* for April, 1788, p. 3. There was an attempt to introduce Montesquieu into the study of law at Harvard. Cf. Faÿ, p. 142. Faÿ also points to the authority of Montesquieu, Burlamaqui, Grotius, and Vattel in legal education. P. 304.
[148] See chap. vi; Faÿ, p. 142.

478 PHILOSOPHY AND EDUCATION

perhaps, have been no University of Virginia."[149] But if the scheme failed, it was not without results. For the Academy was really a sketch for a graduate school, and when in 1779 Jefferson was developing his own ideas regarding the future of William and Mary College, he had Quesnay's ideas in mind, and he carried over the same notion in shaping the University of Virginia.

In Louisiana the work done by the Huguenots in the North was accomplished by the Catholic nuns. The Ursuline convent at New Orleans, founded in 1727, educated generation upon generation of the ladies of New Orleans and Louisiana,[150] and (to anticipate) the tradition thus founded was continued for many years. The convent of the Sacred Heart, just above New Orleans, educated the "daughters of the rich in the most elegant and fashionable manner." In the suburbs of Mobile Nichols found that the Convent of Visitation was training the belles of Alabama; and he finds French convents doing similar work for Protestant and Catholic alike in Galveston, Memphis, St. Louis and other cities in this vast region. For instance, in one of the "wildest regions" of Ohio he reports discovering an Ursuline convent, the Mother Superior of which had been educated in France; the second in authority was of noble French blood; the third, a Belgian, and two French priests had charge of the spiritual welfare of the place.[151]

French ideas also helped to shape, not merely the social education, but the intellectual education of the upper classes in Louisiana. The College of New Orleans, a non-sectarian school created by the legislature in 1805 in New Orleans, was created on the plan of the University of France.[152] Jules D'Avezac, a native of Santo Domingo, was put in charge of it; he was succeeded by Rochefort, another Santo-Domingan. The professor of mathematics was Teinturie, whose accomplishments included gardening and piano-tuning; and the curriculum included Latin, French, Spanish, English, mathematics,

[149] Hinsdale, pp. 597-8; *Cambridge History of American Literature,* IV, iv, 447; Rosengarten, *French Colonists and Exiles,* pp. 75-76; Gaines, "Richmond's First Academy," *Proceedings of the Virginia Historical Society (Collections),* VI (new series), 167-175; Quesnay de Beaurepaire, *Memoirs Concerning the Academy of the Arts and Sciences of the U. S. A.,* translated by Rosewell Page; Réau, *L'art français aux états-unis,* 54-55.
[150] Ficklen, "Education," in Rightor, *Standard History of New Orleans,* chap. ix. Bienville asked for a college in 1742, and was refused.
[151] *Forty Years of American Life,* II, 96-106.
[152] Dexter, p. 132.

and fencing. Actual work was not begun until 1811. The college had a stormy career until 1826. In its latter days it was under the charge of Lakanal, who had been chairman of the committee on education of the revolutionary convention, and who had voted for the death of Louis XVI, an act that did not make him popular in New Orleans. After his appointment, the college closed.[153] To the College of New Orleans succeeded the College of Louisiana at Jackson, which was later sold to the Methodists, when it became Centenary College. The College of Jefferson, incorporated in 1831, was supposed to represent French influence, as the College of Louisiana represented English influence, for the state was bitterly divided in feeling. Neither was highly successful.[154] The interesting point is to see that the whole endeavor of the state is given to establishing higher education; common schools were not created until the constitution of 1845.[155]

While these developments were going on in the far South, Jefferson, the most powerful single force in higher education in the upper South, was meditating his university ideas. When he was in Paris, in addition to his other studies, he carried on investigations in education, and was wholly devoted to French ways.[156] He found that Geneva and Rome were the best schools upon the continent; and the "idea of distinct schools of art and science in the University of Virginia is the enduring product of Jefferson's observation in the schools of Paris."[157] Nor was the influence of his Parisian observations the sole force at work in shaping Jefferson's ideas: he encouraged Dupont de Nemours to write for him on the problem of education.[158] The result was one of the most interesting of the early theoretical works on education. After congratulating the country on its educational advance, Dupont de Nemours urged upon congress the desirability of offering prizes for educational books, and

---

[153] Fortier, *History of Louisiana,* III, 192-4; Ficklen, *op. cit.;* Breaux, "Early Colleges and Schools of Louisiana," *Publications of the Louisiana Historical Society,* VII, 136-142.

[154] Breaux, *op. cit.*

[155] Fortier, III, 194.

[156] The name, Germany, does not occur in the indexes to the nine-volume edition of his works. Hinsdale, I, 598.

[157] Hinsdale, *op. cit.;* Patton, *Jefferson, Cabell and the University of Virginia.*

[158] *Sur l'éducation nationale dans les états-unis d'Amérique.* The second (Paris) edition was published in 1812. The American edition has been reprinted by the University of Delaware, but I have not been able to see a copy.

480   *PHILOSOPHY AND EDUCATION*

advises that there be established a college in every county.
Indeed, he draws up a scheme of organization for these, as
well as a financial budget—six professors, seven classes, ten
courses, twenty sciences, forty "methods" to a college; each
class is to vote a prize to its most deserving members; and at
the end of every seven years the winners are to receive university fellowships. The cost will be small: one president, $500;
six professors, at $300; two supervisors, at $200; a cook at the
same salary; three servants, at $150; prizes and repairs, $150;
total cost, $3,500. For $35,000 the country may have ten colleges. If each has fourteen free scholarships, the cost will be
$56,000. Special schools will cost $10,500; and provision for
fifty free students will eat up $10,000—result, an educational
system at $76,500, at an annual fee per student of $150. The
author provided likewise for special schools in theology, law,
medicine, and arts, and the whole was to be known as the University of North America. Such was the Napoleonic dream of
Dupont de Nemours in 1800.

If French ideas were helping to create the leading university
of the South, they were also to shape a future leading university
of the North. In the whole history of American higher education, there is nothing quite so amazing as the scheme for the
Catholepistemiad, or University of Michigania, adopted by the
first territorial legislature on the plan of the University of
France. The plan was forwarded by Judge Woodward, adopted
in 1817, and, though never put in force, furnished the ground
work for the subsequent act of 1837, especially in the provision for religious freedom, which established the University
of Michigan.[159] Meantime, we are ignoring the project of the
college of Geneva to remove bodily to the United States.[160]

The upper class cosmopolitan spirit shaped American education until about 1820,[161] and in higher institutions of learning
it controlled them much beyond this date. The characteristic
expression of the period dominated by the middle class is the

[159] The complete text is in Hinsdale, I, 601 ff. The president was to draw
$25 annual salary; the vice-president, $18.75; each professor, $12.50; each
instructor or instructrice, $25.00 (!) German influence in 1837 modified
the scheme.
[160] Cf. Hinsdale, I, 599.
[161] Cf. Cubberley, pp. 76-77. It is significant that the Constitution does
not mention education, and that only once was anything relating to education brought before that body, that instance, being an inquiry to the chairman whether the new government might establish a national university!
P. 52.

academy, and we have noted in another connection,[162] how thoroughly this respectable institution satisfied the need of the bourgeoisie for education; how religion and morality combined to nourish it and spread it over the eastern half of America. But the middle class found itself theoretically committed to a democratic idea; the problem in education was one of educating their own children, and at the same time of educating, or seeming to educate, the children of the increasing "lower classes." The solution was characteristically bourgeois. Inheriting from the colonial past the idea of public schools as charity schools,[163] the middle class, with their belief in benevolence, simply continued the system and strove to educate the poorer classes according to the Lancasterian formula.[164] Governor Lewis of New York declared in 1803 that "common schools, under the guidance of respectable teachers, should be established in every village, and the indigent should be educated at the public expense"—a complete formulation of the attitude; note the "respectable teachers," the charity tang. Governor de Witt Clinton, committed to a democratic program, enthusiastically advocated the Lancasterian system. The upper classes and the middle classes necessarily drew away from public schools of this order; the poorer classes refused to accept this interested benevolence.[165] In 1819 the Massachusetts Senate voted that "it is a source of satisfaction to learn that successful efforts are making to diminish the mass of pauperism and vice. Charity schools, founded on new and enlarged modes of instruction, have brought down the elements of education within the reach of multitudes of mendicants; and their operation has been so efficacious as to reclaim a neglected populace from the waste of

---

[162] See chap. iii, pp. 63-65.

[163] In the colonial period "public schools were looked upon by poor parents or guardians as a species of public charity, the acceptance of which implied the open humiliation of acknowledging poverty." Laws were passed in Connecticut (1700) for establishing such "free schools"; in South Carolina in 1710, etc. But the South Carolina school was "boycotted by both poor and dissenters"; and "such laws . . . only accentuated the visible difference between children attending schools where tuition fees were paid, and those going to the free school, often termed pauper schools." Myers, pp. 88-89.

[164] Cubberley, chap. iv; Fitzpatrick, *Educational Views and Influence of de Witt Clinton.*

[165] *Cambridge History of American Literature,* III, chap. xxiii; Dexter; Boone; Myers; Cubberley. "In Massachusetts where officials showed the greatest anxiety if a single child escaped schooling, there were hundreds of children, many of whose parents would not send them to the charity schools." Myers, p. 96. Attendance was under the supervision of the Overseers of the Poor.

ignorance and crime to lead. to the manufactory and the field who would otherwise become tenants of the prison."[166] But alas! the mendicants so approached often refused to accept as philanthropy what they claimed as a right; and with the breakdown of middle-class domination, with the extension of manhood suffrage, the growth of cities, the rise of manufactures, and the increasing class consciousness of the workers, something had to be done.

In such a situation (prior to the thirties) the influence of France was nil.[167] The Americans were suspicious of the success of French educational theories. Said *The Daguerreotype* in 1847:

It has been observed, that if the French had been an educated people, many of the atrocities of their revolution would never have happened, and I believe it. Furious mobs composed, not of enlightened but unenlightened men—of men in whom the passions are dominant over the judgment, because the judgment has not been exercised, and informed, and habituated to direct the conduct. A factious declaimer can much less easily influence a number of men who acquired at school the rudiments of knowledge, and who have subsequently devoted their leisure to a Mechanics' Institute, than a multitude who cannot read or write, and who have never practised reasoning and considerate thought. And as the education of a people prevents political evil, it effects political good. Despotic rulers well know that knowledge is inimical to their power. (I : 4, 173, September 18, 1847).

Why should American democracy look abroad? Complacent and self-satisfied, the United States viewed Europe with distrust. Jefferson, as we have seen, advised young men to stay

[166] Quoted in Myers, p. 96. On middle-class schools see Ramon de la Sagra, *Cinco Meses en los Estados-Unidos, passim.*
[167] Except in the useful work of training the unfortunate. Thomas H. Gallaudet returned to Hartford in 1816 after learning in Paris the methods of the Abbé Sicard of the Royal Institute, and began his pioneer work in training the deaf-and-dumb with seven pupils in 1817. By 1842 he had 150, and the system had been extended over the country. See *North American Review,* VII, 127-136 (May, 1818; also V, 435, September, 1817; XXXVIII, 307-358, April, 1834) ; Ramon de la Sagra, *Cinco Meses en los Estados-Unidos,* pp. 25-26; Buckingham, *America: Eastern and Western States,* I, 345, Abdy's *Journal,* I, 226-233, 241-243. French works on the training of deaf-mutes received some attention in American magazines. See, for instances, the *North American Review,* XXXVIII, 307-358 (April, 1834), and the *Quarterly Christian Spectator,* IX, 521-53. Gallaudet brought Laurent Clerc, himself deaf-and-dumb, to assist him. Mrs. Anne Royall, *Sketches,* pp. 296-7; Levasseur, *Lafayette in America,* 1, 80.
In 1833 the *North American* called attention to the improved methods of teaching the blind to read in Paris through the invention of raised type (XXXVII, 20-58, July, 1833) ; and in August, 1831, Dr. Howe of Boston, commissioned to study European methods abroad, had returned to establish his school. Ramon de la Sagra, *op. cit.,* p. 364.

at home; in Georgia there was a popular distrust of foreign travel; and the attitude of Jefferson Brick in *Martin Chuzzlewit* was only too characteristic. Even as late as 1843 and in so liberal a publication as *The Dial,* one finds that "Europe has lost weight lately. Our young men go thither in every ship, but not as in the golden days, when the same tour" showed a good many celebrities to look at.[168] Perhaps Emerson's *The American Scholar* was not an unmitigated boon. In this epoch the textbooks are "flamboyant and rhetorical,"[169] the ideal is "Americanism," the demand is for a cheap, moral, and utilitarian education for the masses. When the change for the better came, it came largely because America was compelled to turn to that Europe which it had so gratuitously despised.

A group of American travellers brought news of new possibilities in a democratic education. We have to note the return of Ticknor and others from Göttingen in 1819; and the publication in that year of *A Year in Europe* by Professor John Griscom of New York, who had been visiting educational institutions abroad. In addition to Griscom, Woodbridge of New England discovered Pestalozzi to American readers in his *Letters* appearing in the *American Journal* in the twenties.[170] Doubtless there were those who, like Mrs. Emma Hart Willard, visited Europe to inspect school systems.[171] The Rev. Charles Brooks, visiting Europe in 1834, became enthusiastic for Prussian ideas and lectured in the eastern states. In 1836 President A. D. Bache of Girard College went abroad to visit European teacher-training schools; his book helped to spread the idea in America. At about the same time Calvin E. Stowe reported to the Ohio legislature on the elementary schools of Europe.[172] But in this renewed interest in European methodology, no single document is more conspicuous than Cousin's *Report on the State of Public Instruction in Prussia,* published in 1831, but not translated until 1834.[173] It was this report

[168] III, 512-3.
[169] *Cambridge History of American Literature,* III, 401.
[170] Cubberley, pp. 27-271.
[171] She opened a school for young women in Middlebury, Vermont, in 1808; and later founded the celebrated Troy Female Seminary, Boone, p. 364.
[172] Boone, pp. 129-30; Cubberley, chap. ix.
[173] Discussed, among other places, in the *American Quarterly Observer,* III, 354-6, October, 1834; *North American Review,* XL, 511-536 (April, 1835).

which laid the foundation for the modern school system of France (Law of 1833),[174] and which became known in the United States at the critical period of the development of the new public school system.

> It gave support to the demands of the few leaders of the time who were struggling to reduce the rampant district system to some semblance of order, and who were trying to organize the thousands of little community school systems in each State into one state school system, under some form of centralized control . . . the two main ideas gained from it were the importance of some form of centralized state control, and the training of teachers in state normal schools.[175]

Particularly was Cousin's report influential in shaping the public school systems of Massachusetts and Michigan; and one notes that the first normal school was established in Massachusetts in 1839.[176]

Throughout the period one finds a minor French influence on American education through the translation and adaptation of French textbooks, particularly in the sciences. No complete lists of these are obtainable, but random instances, cited in the lists of new publications in various magazines of the epoch, indicate the character of these schoolbooks. An early nineteenth century instance is the *Narrationes excerptae ex Latinis scriptoribus servato temporum ordine dispositae,* or extracts from standard Latin authors, by Dumanchel and Goffaux, of which the first American edition was published in Philadelphia in 1810. Willis B. Fowle published *An Introduction to Linear Drawing,* adapted from the French of Francoeur, in Boston in 1826; and in the same year Noble Heath published in Baltimore *A Theoretical and Practical Arithmetic,* also adapted from the French. Among mathematical textbooks John Farrar's version of Legendre's *Elements of Geometry,* intended for the use of Harvard University, of which a new edition is listed in 1832; and Bowden's *Elements of Algebra* (Boston, 1832), are typical. Chemical and medical textbooks are legion; indeed, it is not too much to say that in the first half of the nineteenth century, most of the scientific textbooks in use among American schools and colleges derived, directly or indirectly, from the French. Language textbooks have already been noticed. These clear and perspicuous manuals did much to clarify methods of teaching in the United States.

[174] Reisner, *op. cit.,* 130 ff, 47-62.
[175] Cubberley, p. 273.
[176] Cubberley, p. 291. There had been previous private schools.

Another interesting and important influence on American educational policy is found in the department of military instruction. Throughout the eighteenth century the discipline of the colonial troops was of course modelled on that of the British army, but with the French Alliance the Continental Congress availed itself of the opportunity to re-organize its system of military instruction on French (and Prussian) models. As early as February 23, 1776, the Congress paid Francis Daymon to translate the rules of war from the French for the benefit of the army; and shortly a group of textbooks appeared, such as *L'ingénieur de campagne,* "written in French by the Chevalier de Clairac, and translated by Major Lewis Nicola" (Philadelphia, 1776); and *The Art of War* from the French of M. de Lamont (Philadelphia, 1778).[177] French muskets served as models for American artificers as early as 1777;[178] and certain Frenchmen lingered in America to teach American manufacturers of cannon and musketry.[179] After the Napoleonic wars General Bernard, recommended to the United States by Lafayette, had an active part in designing our coastal fortifications, and in teaching artillery officers;[180] and the total French influence was such that Lafayette, visiting a camp at Savin Hall, near Boston, (or rather his secretary), was "not a little surprised to recognize our French models perfectly imitated" in the park of artillery belonging to the militia.[181] Coke, a British officer, observes of the fieldpieces turned out at the Georgetown arsenal in 1832 that "the French system had been

[177] Faÿ, p. 109.
[178] Bernhard, *Travels,* I, 56.
[179] La Rochefoucauld-Liancourt reports in 1796 that 7000 "fusils" in the Springfield arsenal were modelled after a 1763 pattern, but he adds that M. Pourcheresse Bourguignon, formerly an officer in the Royal-Suédois regiment, was assistant director of the arsenal, a man much esteemed by the inhabitants. The cannon and fortifications of Castle Island, Boston, were imperfectly imitated from those of M. de Gribeauval, according to the same authority; and the fortifications of Governor's Island, New York, begun in 1794, were planned by M. Vincent, a French engineer.' *Voyages,* V, 243; 244-5; 210; VII, 133. On the distribution of French cannon over the country, see Schoepf, *Travels in the Confederation,* especially volume II. The Americans came in time to equal, and even to surpass, their models in small arms. "On a very critical survey and examination (Jefferson) did not hesitate to say, that he had in no instance seen any work or specimens equal to Mr. Whitneys, excepting in one factory in France in which the owner had desined the various parts of his Muskets on the principles of Mr. Whitney that Mr. Whitney equalled his specimens." (Elizur Goodrich to Simeon Baldwin, January 8, 1801). Baldwin, *Life and Letters of Simeon Baldwin,* p. 429.
[180] Bernhard, *Travels,* I, 128; Schouler, *History,* III, 8.
[181] Levasseur, *Lafayette in America,* I, 58.

approved of, and will be adopted in the American service, on account of the uniform size of the ammunition-wagons, and a trifling difference in some other respect."[182] In fact, West Point, the heart of the system, was "a school upon the system of the polytechnic school of Paris," and it is not surprising to learn that "the organization of the regiments, the manoeuvres, and exercises" of the regular army in the thirties "are entirely in the French manner, although the word of command is given in English."[183] Bernhard made an exhaustive examination of the curriculum in 1825, when Colonel Thayer was commandant. Thayer had just remodelled the school after visiting French military schools; and the list of textbooks given by Bernhard shows how profound was the French influence, including, as it did:

Programme d'un course de construction, par Sganzin
Traité des Machines, par Hachette
Traité du Calcul Différentiel et Integral, par Lacroix
Essai de Géometrie Analytique aux Courbes et aux Surfaces du second
    order, par Biot
Complément des Élémens d'Algèbre, par Lacroix
Bérard's Lecteur Français
Bérard's Grammaire Française
Histoire de Gil Blas
Histoire de Charles XII, par Voltaire

The model of topographical drawing was the Carnmontaigne system, as improved by French engineers.[184] By 1840 Captain Robert Anderson had translated and adapted from the French his *Instructions for Field Artillery, Horse, and Foot* (Philadelphia)[185] and about the same time Scott's *Infantry Tactics, or Rules for the Exercises of the United States Infantry,* appeared in three volumes (New York, 1840), a work frankly based on the tactics and organization of the Napoleonic armies.[186] Scott thought for a while of keeping the words of command in French. But if the formal instruction in military affairs was thus influenced by France, the Americans failed to take over the democratic spirit of the French army, preferring the caste system of their British originals.

[182] Coke, *A Subaltern's Furlough,* I, 104.
[183] Murat, *A Moral and Political Sketch,* pp. 259; 255.
[184] Bernhard, *Travels,* I, 110-117. See also Grund, *The Americans,* II, 332.
[185] *North American Review,* L, April, 1840, "New Publications."
[186] See *The New York Review,* VIII, 358 ff, April, 1841.

4. SIGNIFICANCE OF THE FINDINGS OF THE LAST
FOUR CHAPTERS

What have we learned from our long survey? In the fields of religion, philosophy, and education, French influence is at work. In philosophy European systems struggle for a hearing against the moral and religious convictions of the New World, and only rarely do they secure a hearing—only, in case they have, like Cousin and Jouffroy, a marked ethical interest. In religion the field is dominated now by the cosmopolitan spirit, now by the bourgeois spirit, now by the spirit of the frontier, but only the first of these is not hostile to the French and to Catholicism. In education the story is the story of a gradual drift downward of education until the frontier, too, makes its contribution—the state university. We have seen in each department of interests how the American spirit at one or more of our three levels, was now drawn to, and now driven from, the culture of the French. Hostile at first, the eighteenth century developed an American mind more and more open to French ideas; the reaction from the French Revolution and from Napoleon sharply swung-to the door on Europe. But the situation is never simple; there are curves and recurrences at all periods, and the problem of cultural relationships is complex and contradictory. If the body of French culture were a static thing, it would be easier to estimate the relations between a constant and a variable factor, but both elements in the equation vary; precisely at the period when the Americans were most open to French influence—that is to say in the last quarter of the eighteenth century—the state of literature, the state of the arts, the state of philosophy in France was confused and contradictory. Then, curiously enough, just as the American mind turns away from things French—that is to say from 1815 to 1848 (with obvious exceptions), French culture took on a sudden cohesion—there is that efflorescence of new ideas which we call French romanticism, which, however, failed to command the interest of Americans. Suppose the romantic movement in France had come from 1776 to 1800! How different the cultural history of the United States might have been!

XIV

Conflicting Forces in Politics

SOCIAL analysis is deceptive. At the beginning of this study we sought to find the essential characteristics of our literature, whence we were led to an analysis of American life; and the necessity for clearness compelled us to reduce to three shaping elements the forces at work in the making of American culture. We should not, however, be deceived: the rich, complex, and highly energized life of the republic wherein, in Henry Adams' thesis, the virgin has been dispossessed by the dynamo, can not be reduced to such simplicity without loss. Aside from the fact that our analysis carried us only through the first half of the nineteenth century, we have had to omit much, even there; nevertheless we are not writing history in the conventional sense, we are determining the character of immaterial forces, of ideas, ideals, projects, desires, necessities, out of which the national expression comes. We may in the main rest satisfied with our analysis as we embark upon the most discussed phase of our relations with France (namely, the political one), provided always that we realize our three forces only as a working hypothesis. If they are not the truth, they are something sufficiently near the truth for the pragmatic purposes of this study.

We have traced these forces at work, sometimes clearly, sometimes obscurely, in the realm of manners, of arts, of religion and philosophy; let us now turn to politics and observe the action and interaction of these forces as they work upon French culture. In the field of politics we shall have to note both the internal and the external, or international, expression of our political mind; we shall note the periods of attraction and repulsion between the United States and Europe. But first, we must briefly describe the fundamental American attitude.

1. THE CONFLICT IN POLITICS AND THE WESTWARD-FRONTING ATTITUDE

The conflict between the cosmopolitan seaboard and the interests of the frontier began almost immediately; as soon, in other words, as the straggling little plantations on the edge of the oceans commenced to throw out settlements into the primeval wilderness behind them.[1] The history of this conflict has been

[1] Mumford points out an interesting parallel between the multiplication of colonies in Massachusetts and in ancient Greece. "The early provincial vil-

written at length.[2] It is not now our business to rewrite it, but to summarize it and to draw from it that which may illumine the attitude of the American toward foreign culture. But in so doing we can not ignore even such apparently unrelated matters as canal-building and Indian wars, for they tend to promote American isolation, and American isolation has much to do with problems of international cultures.

The conflict in politics between the frontier and the cosmopolitan seaboard begins, then, with the earliest periods of American history; we have indeed, traced some of its earlier manifestations. Rather than repeat ourselves, let us simply note how typically in colonial Virginia the conflict arose. There where the county was the political unit, the assembly jealously retained the power of creating new counties, and there, "as the colony grew in wealth the oldest counties were more conservative than the newer ones, and were unwilling to create the latter as rapidly as the growth of population seemed to demand, lest the control of the assembly pass into the hands of 'back counties.' "[3] So bitter grew the battle in North Carolina that for eight years the colony may be said to have had no government.[4] So from the beginning the seacoast sought to dominate the West; by gerrymandering in established colonies; by obtaining titles to unoccupied land,[5] titles which the squatter cheer-

lage bears another resemblance to the early Greek city; it does not continue to grow at such a pace that it either becomes overcrowded within or spills beyond its limits into dejected suburbs; still less does it seek what we ironically call greatness by increasing the number of its inhabitants. When the corporation has a sufficient number of members, that is to say, when the land is fairly occupied, and when the addition of more land would unduly increase the hardship of working it from the town, or would spread out the farmers, and make it difficult for them to attend to their religious and civil duties, the original settlement throws out a new shoot. So Charlestown threw off Woburn; so Dedham colonized Medfield; so Lynn founded Nahant." *Sticks and Stones,* p. 16.

[2] See the references to chaps. ii and iii.

[3] Bassett, *Short History of the United States,* p. 135. See Wertenbaker's illuminating Study, *Virginia under the Stuarts.*

[4] See Bassett p. 135. "By 1760 the opposition between new and old settlements had taken on a territorial character."

[5] Land speculation was the foundation of any number of colonial fortunes. Cf. Bassett, *The Writings of Colonel Byrd,* Introduction, on the growth of the Byrd estate. "The surveyor, who from his travels into all parts of the forest had opportunity to find the best tracts of ungranted land, was much concerned in the operation, either buying outright and selling later when the advance of population had raised the price, or becoming the agent of some rich man who could make the investment." Bassett, *Short History,* p. 136. See also Simons, *Social Forces in American History,* pp. 58, 66. There is a considerable literature on the subject: these summarize the findings. Oklahoma simply repeats the story of western Virginia.

fully disregarded, the result being rich provender for the rapidly
increasing lawyer class; by attempting to draw the line of
terminus beyond which the frontier might not go[6]—in sum, the
conflict is at bottom a conflict over land.[7] So, too, the East,
by sending out home missionaries and by multiplying rural
churches and small colleges, has, at least, tried to force the
West to its chariot wheels in culture; it is the Eastern teacher
who has "school-marmed" the American language, established
the list of high school classics as norms in literature, and retained Latin and Greek in the public school systems of Colorado
and Idaho, states which would have never dreamed of the
necessity of such subjects except for her and her male compeer.

If until 1760 the seacoast was on the whole successful, it
was not always so to be. War is a great upsetter of what is
customary, as it is also an intensifier of social differences, making the rich richer and the poor poorer; and the French and
Indian Wars, by freeing the back country for development,
by establishing an uncertain paper currency,[8] and consequently
a dissatisfied debtor class, and (in the capture of Louisbourg
and the defeat of Braddock) by encouraging colonial self-confidence, brought to a head the unrest of the back country, which
the mercantile interests, pinched by British regulations, and
almost to their undoing, capitalized, with the aid of the rising
legal classes, until it grew to revolution. In the period from
1776 to 1789 the seacoast almost lost control of the situation.
The period of hostilities had seen great political concessions to
the "lower classes." To enlist their support, to finance the war,
it had been necessary to issue still greater quantities of paper

---

[6] The Webster-Hayne debate arose over a resolution offered by Foote of
Connecticut to restrict the sale of western lands. Benton of Missouri and
the Western senators charged that this was an attempt to build up the East
at the expense of the West; and the South saw an opportunity to enlist the
injured Western members under the banner of state rights. The splendor of
the oratory has obscured the occasion of the speeches.

[7] The Northwest Territory represents the practical solution of a squabble
in land ownership among the states.

[8] The first paper money in America was issued by Massachusetts in 1690
to pay for an unsuccessful expedition against Quebec. Other colonies followed her example. By 1745 a silver dollar was worth eleven dollars in
currency. The expedition against Louisbourg in that year was paid for in
pounds sterling, and the currency became specie. Virginia yielded to the
movement in 1755, and in Rhode Island, New Jersey, Pennsylvania, and the
Carolinas, there was a paper money craze, against which the merchants and
the governors struggled in vain. The French and Indian War (1754-1763)
brought another flood; and the attempt of the British government to check
the movement for cheap money, increased colonial irritation. See Bassett,
History, pp. 157-8, for brief account.

money, later repudiated when the struggle had been won. When, in the midst of the terrible poverty of the post-Revolution era, Shay's rebellion occurred (1786-7), when paper-money mobs arose in New Hampshire and Rhode Island, it became necessary to stage a counter-revolution, the document of which is the American Constitution. In fine, it was necessary to originate a strong central government of gentlemen by gentlemen around which the Boston merchants, the Pennsylvania manufacturers, and the commercial magnates of South Carolina might rally.[9] It was an act of the highest wisdom, and very necessary, but no student of the constitution has failed to see in its elaborate system of checks and balances (which later amendments have attempted here and there to break down) a severe check upon the ebullient democracy of the West. The government went into operation. So did the financial system of Hamilton. But the frontier, which wanted new issues of paper money, a moratorium, restrictions on the power of the courts, economy, and low taxes, was not pleased. It flared up in the Whiskey Rebellion of 1791[10] which Washington put down with a firm hand. Then the Jay treaty, necessary but unpopular, was forced on the country in the mercantile interests. The crushing of the Whiskey Rebellion meant that "social control had been invested in the class whose lineal descendants have held it until the present time,"[11] a statement not quite accurate but sufficiently illuminating.

If the administrations of Washington and Adams represent the dominance of the seacoast interests, those of Jefferson mark the first break in the system of political control by the cosmopolitan interests; and Jefferson's purchase of Louisiana Territory, his attempt to purchase Florida, his desire to confine

[9] For a brief, brilliant, and biased account of Hamiltonianism, see Bowers, *Jefferson and Hamilton,* chaps. I-IV, VI, VIII. On the restricted property qualifications of the Revolutionary constitutions see Merriam, *History of American Political Theory,* chapter ii; and see him, chapter iii, on the post-Revolutionary conservative reaction. Parrington, *The Connecticut Wits* is a convenient collection of some of the conservative propaganda.

[10] One reason why the insurrection was so easily controlled, aside from the personal prestige of Washington and the desperate demand for some kind of stability, was that it was supposed to be a product of Revolutionary theory. When in 1794 a convention was called to settle the excise issue, Brackenridge wrote: "Our hall was a grove and we might well be called 'the mountain,' "—an allusion to the radical left in the French convention. Bradford was accused by contemporary authorities of imitating the methods of the French Jacobins. Stevens, *Albert Gallatin,* pp. 75, 78. Cf. Bowers, *op. cit.,* 250-256 for an account from the Jeffersonian point of view.

[11] Simons, *Social Forces,* p. 119.

the judiciary within limits,[12] (in which he was checked by Marshall) are all concessions to the frontier spirit. But there is something doctrinaire in Jefferson's democracy; when he walked to the Capitol for his oath of inauguration he walked from the sincerest motives, no doubt, but it did not occur to a genuine frontiersman like Jackson that it was necessary to walk to prove that he was a democrat. Despite the pronounced democratic theorizing of Jefferson, he is a democrat in the sense that liberal French noblemen of the eighteenth century were democratic.[13]

Meantime, however, the frontier was capturing more and more political power; *western* New York and *western* Virginia were to force liberal suffrage upon those states;[14] the constitutions of the West are in successive periods more and more liberal[15] than those of the East—with exceptions, like Maryland.[16] It was the West which hopefully fought the War of

[12] The impeachment proceedings in the case of Judge Chase have an importance beyond the merits of the case. In the first place, the impeachment of Warren Hastings had taken deep hold on the imagination of the United States. Then, "whether Judge Chase should be removed from the bench was a trifling matter; whether Chief-Justice Marshall and the Supreme Court should hold their power against this combination of States-rights conservatives and Pennsylvania democrats was a subject for grave reflection. Men who did not see that the tide of political innovation had long since turned, and that the French Revolution was no longer (1805) raging, were consumed with anxiety for the fate of Chase. . . ." Adams, *History*, II, 226-7. Cf. the account of Aaron Burr's trial in Wandell and Minnigerode, *Aaron Burr*, II, part VIII.

[13] "The government (under Jefferson) was still in the hands of the freeholders and the gentry. The theory of the Jeffersonians was in many respects an advance upon that of the government party, but its practice was still in many ways aristocratic." Merriam, *History of American Political Theories*, p. 175.

[14] See Fox, *The Decline of Aristocracy in the Politics of New York*.

[15] During the ten years from Washington's administration on, eight state constitutions were made and amended and "by almost every one the rights of man were extended." McMaster, III, 149. "In general it may be said that church and state were parted; that religion ceased to be a qualification for civil office; that the property qualification was greatly reduced; and that the democratic principle of universal suffrage was spreading fast." The first Ohio constitution (1800) was the "full expression of the most advanced ideas of free government." The tendency was toward a unicameral legislature, a weak executive, and an elected judiciary—ideas that John Adams combatted in his *Defence of the Constitutions of Government of the United States of America, against the Attack of M. Turgot in his Letters to Dr. Price.* (*Works*, IV.) As state after state changed from Federalist to Republican, the popular control of judges became a great question. See McMaster, III, 151-153. Note also that Judge Alexander Addison who issued a pamphlet against the French Revolution was impeached. *Ibid.*, III, 156-7.

[16] "The State of Maryland, which had been founded by men of rank, was the first to proclaim universal suffrage, and to introduce the most democratic forms into the conduct of its government." De Tocqueville, I, 45.

1812 after the mercantile East had gone sulking to its tent. If in the succeeding administrations the Virginia and New England lines were restored in the persons of Monroe, Madison, and John Quincy Adams, partly because of the inevitable conservative reactions of a post-war period, and partly because the nascent manufacturing interest had come to reënforce the mercantile interest, yet the war marks a distinct change in the American political scene. "The wars of the French Revolution and of 1812," wrote that shrewd observer, de Tocqueville, "had created manufacturing establishments in the North of the Union by cutting off all free communication between America and Europe."[17] The result was a new feeling of nationalism which tended to isolation. "With the repeal of the embargo ended the early period of United States history, when diplomatists played a part at Washington equal in importance to that of the Legislature or the Executive. . . . Thenceforward the government ceased to balance between great foreign powers, and depended on its own resources."[18] And Adams, perhaps the greatest historian who has dealt with the period, adds at the conclusion of his remarkable survey:

The Rights of Man occupied public thoughts less, and the price of cotton more. . . . Although in 1815 Europe was suffering under a violent reaction against free government, Americans showed little interest and no alarm, compared with their emotions of twenty years before. Napoleon resumed his empire, and was overthrown at Waterloo, without causing the people of the United States to express a sign of concern in his fate; and France was occupied by foreign armies without rousing among Americans a fear of England.[19]

The unity of the nation was established and "its probable divergence from older societies was also well defined."[20] Thereafter the Americans looked within: as the mercantile dynasty ebbed; as the manufacturers, the cotton planters, and the frontier came to grips, treaties, commercial bounties, and

[17] *Democracy in America*, II, 450. And see Bogart, *Economic History of the United States*, chapter xi.
[18] Adams, *History*, VII, 395.
[19] Adams, *History*, IX, 104. "The war gave a severe shock to the Anglican sympathies of society, and peace seemed to widen the breach between European and American tastes. Interest in Europe languished after Napoleon's overthrow. France ceased to affect American opinion." *Ibid.*, p. 221.
[20] Adams, *ibid.*, p. 220. Paxson draws the line earlier. For him the year 1800, when Jefferson, with the western democracy behind him, came into power "becomes the dividing point between two chapters of history." *The History of the American Frontier*, p. 111. I can but feel that this is at least fifteen years too early.

international politics failed to occupy the public mind so much as internal improvements, tariffs, public lands, the currency, banks, state sovereignty, and the slavery problem.[21]

We can not do more than indicate how our method of disposing of the public lands, our Indian wars, and our Indian problems,[22] the public policy with respect to grazing, timberlands, and mineral claims, and, by and by, such matters as woman suffrage, the initiative, the referendum, and the recall, bear stamped upon them the mark of the frontier with its strong individualism, its strong equalitarianism. It is sufficient to point out how, before industrial imperialism set in, during the very perod we are traversing, the first phase of American imperialism is thoroughly of the frontier. Westward the star of empire led the way to the Pacific—northward and southward as well; and the belief in manifest destiny is bone and sinew of the frontier. So it is that Clark conquers the Illinois country; so it is that Burr and Blennerhassett seek to detach New Orleans from Spain; so it is that Louisiana is bought, Florida conceded; so in the War of 1812 the first aim of the campaign is to conquer Canada and the last battle is fought by Jackson and his frontier militia at the mouth of the Mississippi; so it is (but there the Southern interest in the extension of the cotton area commences to play a part) that there are projects to annex Cuba, Mexico, and Central America; that Texas is added to the Union, the Mexican War fought, the Spanish-American republic torn in two by a war which "nobody in society defended,"[23] the Gadsden purchase made; and so it is that after another flare-up of nationalism—"fifty-four forty or fight"—Oregon is added to the Union. Whatever the subsequent vagaries of the imperial spirit, the foundations lie in the frontier.

But if there is not time to retrace American history, one can, by sitting at the White House and watching the presidents come and go, observe the rise and fall of the cosmopolitan spirit and the spirit of the frontier. There is first of all the great succession of Virginian and New England presidents: Washington, inaugurated with the stately ceremony of the day, wearing

[21] Simons, pp. 151-2.

[22] At Washington the Indians are treated with the dignity of separate nations, and the public faith is pledged to treaties with them. The West, strongly feeling that the Indian is one of the wild beasts, either disregards the treaty or forces its abrogation.

[23] Lyell, *Travels in the United States, Second Visit,* II, 256.

on his second inaugural a suit of black velvet, ornate with an abundance of silver lace and diamond-studded buckles—a truly republican king; John Adams of the mercantile aristocracy (in fact, a lawyer), obscured by the glory of his departing predecessor, scornful of Jacobin democracy; Jefferson handing on the powers of the dynasty to Madison; Madison and Dolly Madison, with whom the White House becomes an informal salon; Monroe, and Mrs. Monroe, who strove to restore formality, who laid down rules for the costumes of her guests as though she were a queen, who required the men to wear small clothes and silk stockings, even excluding her relatives if they were not properly dressed; John Quincy Adams, last of the cosmopolitan line. For ten administrations the president comes from the East; out of six presidents four are from Virginia, two from New England; for forty years the cosmopolitan spirit resides in the Capitol. And then, like a cataclysm, the West comes down. In 1829 Andrew Jackson became the eleventh president of the United States.

The inauguration has been often described. A wild mob stormed the White House wearing muddy boots and spitting on the carpets; they broke the furniture, smashed the glass, crowded the president against the wall until his comrades had to form a barricade around him with their bodies. There were refreshments for twenty thousand; punch and lemonade were carried about in tubs and buckets, and in the fight to get at these the crowd became a struggling, cursing mob. It was a fit beginning for an administration that was less a government than a campaign, a campaign against all that the West resented —the bank, disunion, the finesse of diplomacy; an administration which, in the Berserker fashion of the frontier, sought revenge on its enemies and rewards for its friends. Then, barring the Van Buren episode, the West demanded another president, and William Henry Harrison rode into office. The theory was that he had lived in a log cabin and had fought a great battle against an overwhelming Indian force, whereas the truth is, he was born on a tide-water plantation on the lower James in Virginia, and possessed means and a comfortable home. It was not the fault of the West that he died in office, and that Tyler succeeded him. Texas was annexed and Polk fought the Mexican War. In short, from 1815 to 1848, "Americanism," the obverse of the cosmopolitan spirit, had its way. Let us briefly look at its workings, and then take up the international story.[24]

We might, indeed, trace this nascent separatism back to colonial times, but to save space, we shall deal with the relations of America and France in this period when we come to the problem of international diplomacy. Equally, in the conflicts of the American and French Revolutions, we can find this chauvinistic nationalism at work. But we are now defining attitudes; let us begin later. Let us begin when the "Americanism" we are describing is in full bloom. It is in the administrations of Monroe that the political terminology of the early republic had lost its meaning: "Federalist" as a name disappeared and "Democrat" was for a time dropped; it was the era of good feeling, of America for the Americans, and the political expression of it is the Monroe Doctrine.[25] This is the gentle prelude to the arrogant nationalism of Jacksonian democracy.[26] The hostility of England, the treachery of France, had disgusted Americans with foreign embroglio, and they returned to Washington's inaugural address. They evolved the "American system" of Clay. "Americanism" is both positive and negative; its negative aspect is a distrust of the non-American. One finds "Americanism" expressed in various ways. Thus Governor Robertson delivered a curious message on international affairs to the Louisiana legislature in January, 1824:

Fortunately for mankind, the principles on which liberty and happiness depend, are, of all others, the most simple and easiest understood. Strip them of the tinsel, clear them of the rubbish with which they have been artfully surrounded by tyranny and superstition, they exhibit themselves with a native grace, an attractive charm, that none but the inveterately perverse have either the inclination or the power to withstand.

Wherefore he abhors Europe. Americans are "citizens of the only free, peaceful, and enlightened government on earth." In Spain an atrocious war is waging and France, "once the friend of freedom and of man" is helping that despot, Ferdinand VII. All Europe is hostile to free government; and only Greece

---

[24] See the amusing survey of American presidents by Don Seitz, "Our Presidents," *The Forum*, LXXIII, February, 1925, pp. 239-248; and Minnigerode, *Some American Ladies.*

[25] Schouler, *History*, III, 12.

[26] ". . . the word 'Democratic,' once affixed for reproach and deprecated, this section of the old Jefferson Republican fold, into which Monroe had absorbed all parties, fearlessly accepted in 1832." Schouler, IV, 73.

commands "the warmest sympathy" of republicans.[27] Thank God, in other words, we are not as other men are. Or again, when Simon Bernard, one of the most useful of American benefactors, was in charge of the engineer corps in 1825, he found himself treated very coolly, and he was not given any real rank in the army—in contradistinction to Steuben, Kosciusko, LaFayette, and others in the Revolution—and, says a German observer, one finds "the cause of this coolness undoubtedly . . . in a silly misconception of patriotism, for the general is a foreigner, and frequent experience has shown that a foreigner in military service seldom enjoys satisfaction."[28] Indeed, foreigners were not made to feel at home. "In every part of the United States," wrote Bristed in 1818, "individual Englishmen feel themselves to be Americans; and individual Frenchmen find themselves to be as completely strangers, as if they were animals of different species at least."[29] This is a partisan observation, to be sure, but it has its truth. Indeed, as Europe flowed in on America, the native spirit protested, sometimes with words, sometimes with violence, as the anti-Catholic riots existed to prove.[30] Memorials poured into Congress in 1838 to complain of the morals of foreigners and of their hostile political principles, and especial complaint was lodged against the Leopold Foundation, resulting from the Schlegel lectures of 1828, which proved that Catholicism favored monarchy—Protestantism, revolution.[31] "The Italian and French never give up the hope of regaining their native land," wrote Lieber in the 1830's, who says also that the Germans, English, Scotch, and Irish assimilate much easier with the natives of this country than do the Latins.[32] Why don't they assimilate? The acrid Godley tells us very clearly:

[27] Fortier, *History of Louisiana*, III, 199-200.
[28] Bernhard, *Travels*, I, 128.
[29] Bristed, *Resources of the United States*, p. 379.
[30] See chap. xii, pp. 427-38. It was urged that the Roman Catholic clergy were spreading; that protestants should arise to prevent nunneries, the Jesuit order, the inquisition; that there were already twenty colleges for Catholic males, sixty for females; that seventeen convents had already been established; that six hundred missionaries of the Catholic faith had arrived in six months. Hence the rise of the "Native American" party to "protest, as it were, against foreign influence in our national affairs and religion, under the secret propagation of the Vatican and the Jesuits." Schouler, IV, 177-179. The results were, first the Native American movement; next the Locofoco party and lastly the Knownothing movement, all seeking restrictions on immigration.
[31] McMaster, VII, 371-5.
[32] Lieber, *The Stranger in America*, II, 39.

I had a good deal of conversation the other day upon the subject of Texas, and the progress generally of the Anglo-American race over the western continent. I find the doctrine of what may be called polit- ical fatalism very generally held, though not perhaps openly avowed or defended—the doctrine that Providence has so obviously destined America for the Anglo-Saxons, and the Anglo-Saxons for America, that the means by which its designs are promoted should not be too roughly scrutinized.[33]

Or behold Cooper fresh from his quarrels with critics of the United States abroad, returning to New York in 1833, greeted with an American salvo:

Sir
    A number of young former friends, pleased with your return among them, are desirous of testifying to you the continuance of their friend- ship, of the respect in which they hold your talents, and of their appro- bation of your manly defence, while abroad, of the Institutions of our Country.
    They therefore beg your acceptance of a Dinner at such time as shall be agreeable to you.[34]

It takes the said Cooper but very little while to diagnose the ills of the country:

The foreigners have got to be so strong among us that they no longer creep but walk erect. They throng the prisons, control one or two of the larger cities, and materially influence public opinion over the Union. By foreigners, I do not mean the lower class of Irish voters, who do so much at the polls, but the merchants and others a degree below them, who are almost to a man hostile in feeling to the country, and to all her interests, except as they may happen to be their interests.[35]

    Foreign criticism, in all periods of our history, but particu- larly after 1815, helped to fix and embitter the attitude. It was perhaps expected that the subjects of continental despots should not understand us, but when the British turned on us, espe- cially after we had, by beating them, shown we were better men

---

[33] *Letters from America,* p. 19.
[34] There are 29 signatures, including P. A. Jay, Thomas Morris, M. M. Noah, George P. Morris, W. C. Bryant, and F. G. Halleck. *Correspondence of James Fenimore-Cooper,* I, 327.
[35] Cooper to Horatio Greenough, June 14, 1836. *Ibid.,* I, 358-9. It is true there was a good deal of excuse for the attitude in question. For example, Lieber writes: "The French form, in the larger cities, where there is a sufficient number of them, a circle much for themselves; and I have known a lady, who came to this country when fifteen years old, from St. Domingo, at the time of the insurrection of the negroes in that island, and whose hus- band was a zealous admirer of American institutions; who nevertheless, had not learned to speak, still less to read English, when I became acquainted with her, but a year ago." Lieber, *The Stranger in America,* II, 40.

than they were, the thrust hurt. "As the commercial quarrel between America and Great Britain grew fiercer and fiercer, and the second war approached, the belief gained ground that behind these attacks of (British) travellers lay a deeply premeditated policy of the British ministry; that it was their deliberate purpose to belittle and abuse the United States; and that the men who seemed to be travellers were hired lampooners in disguise."[36] After the war, came the period of Tory criticism.[37] "Critics of reputation, men of influence, periodicals of standing began to join in the hue and cry, till readers on this side of the water were convinced that a deliberate and well-laid scheme to decry the United States was on foot in Great Britain." When about 1823 the dispute ended, "there had been engendered in this country a hearty detestation of Great Britain which strongly affected international relations for many years to come."[38] It was not unnatural; it flowed from the premise which had been established by Continental Europe two centuries before; namely, that something new and good was being shaped in America, that a radical political and social experiment was being tried out. Hence the contempt of Americans for Europe and its fear of democracy, which took awkward and uncouth shape. "An American," said de Tocqueville, "should never be allowed to speak of Europe; for he will then probably display a vast deal of presumption and very foolish pride. He will take up with those crude and vague notions which are so useful to the ignorant all over the world."[39] By 1845 the anti-British sentiment of the Americans was as great as the anti-American sentiment of the British Tories. The burning of the *Caroline,* the trial of McLeod, the Webster-Ashburton Treaty, the redline map, the dispute over Oregon, the charge of British meddling in Texas, the default of the states in payment of interest, had made the abuse of this country popular in Great Britain, and the abuse was naturally returned.[40] Read in Lyell's *Travels*

[36] McMaster, V, 307-8.
[37] See Nevins, *American Social History as Recorded by British Travellers,* especially the introductions; and Mesick, *The English Traveller in America, 1785-1835,* especially chapter X; McMaster (as above); Schouler, IV, opening pages.
[38] McMaster, V, 309. The year 1819 was especially prolific in attacks from the *Edinburgh Review,* the *British Review,* and the *Quarterly Review.* One matter which irritated Americans was the reproach of irreligion. An interesting result was the grateful reception of de Tocqueville's work.
[39] I, 342.
[40] McMaster, VII, 92-3.

the anecdotes he collects about the Oregon affair—it is a study in one-hundred-percent Americanism before the invention of the term.[41] "If we must have a war about Oregon," said a friend to him, "it will at least be attended with one blessing— stopping of the incessant influx of hordes of ignorant adventurers who pour in and bear down upon our native population. Whether they call themselves 'the true sons of Erin' or the 'noble sons of Germany,' they are the dupes and tools of our demagogues."[42] The failure of Kossuth's visit to secure aid in 1851-2 shows how well settled was the American policy of isolation; the congressional debate soon evaporated, our interest being in the West, and it is just at the close of our period that Marcy tried to get our diplomats abroad to abandon court dress.[43] For the American of Thoreau's generation, history began with the musketry of the embattled farmers at Concord bridge,[44] says a historian, and if we exclude the saving remnant, the statement is true enough.

2. EARLY COLONIAL HOSTILITY TO THE FRENCH

I have been thus specific and even tedious about the definition of the American attitude, with reference to a phase of our period which chronologically comes last, because it is fundamental to an understanding of the whole drift of our political relations with foreign countries during the epoch under survey. One must realize that from the earliest times a westward-fronting spirit gives to political discussion the importance which, said de Tocqueville, is with us a substitute for culture.[45]

[41] *Second Visit,* I, 193, 194, 225-6, 241, 243; II, 32-3, 211 for representative instances. See also Stevens' *Gallatin,* pp. 332, 363, 357.

[42] Lyell, *op. cit.,* I, 90. In this connection it is interesting to have the observations of Grund, a careful and thoughtful observer: "Not only is emigration from France exceedingly limited, but those who emigrate are so seldom inclined to interfere with the policy of the country that *as a political party* (with the exception of the French Creoles in Louisiana) they are hardly forcing themselves on the notice of Americans. The French do not take an active part in politics, at least nothing to compare with the English or the Germans, and, where they cannot conform to the custom of the country, follow their own with so much modesty and so little intrusion on the established rules of society, that their conduct is approved and commended in every part of the country." *The Americans* (American edition), pp. 65-66, (1837).

[43] Schouler, V, 226-9.

[44] *Cambridge History of American Literature,* II, 11.

[45] "The cares of political life take a most prominent place in the occupation of a citizen of the United States, and almost the only pleasure of which an American has any idea is to take part in the Government, and to discuss the part he has taken. This feeling pervades the most trifling habits of life;

But though the frontier element is basic in all discussions of American politics, the cosmopolitan spirit, which may at times be conquered, is never absent. If we turn to our foreign relations, to wars and the rumors of wars, to treaty-making and boundary disputes, we may see that there the cosmopolitan spirit struggles with this feeling of isolation which is characteristic of the frontier. It is convenient for our study that the story of the foreign relations of the United States to 1848 is mainly the story of our relations to England and France; Germany does not count; Spain is a minor problem.[46]

The seventeenth century in America, as we have seen, shares in the cosmopolitan spirit of the time by participating in religious controversy and religious persecution.[47] Necessarily the English colonies partake of the policy of the mother country which was, with intervals of calm, anti-French. Naturally therefore, out of this war of Protestant and Catholic, of Briton and Gaul, there springs a remarkable detestation of the French, which prevailed in America until about 1770. To the Americans the warfare against Louis XIV and his successors was in some sense a Protestant crusade; to them the French kings were the focus of Catholic Europe. The French therefore connoted the Scarlet Woman, the profligacy of priests, the deceits of the Jesuits, and the horrors of the Inquisition. When, in addition, there was the added horror of Indian warfare, supposed to be instigated by the French, the name of Frenchman became an object of peculiar detestation—save when the Frenchman was Huguenot, and sometimes even then.[48] For the Huguenot

even the women frequently attend public meetings and listen to political harangues as a recreation after their household labors. Debating clubs are to a certain extent a substitute for theatrical entertainments: an American can not converse, but he can discuss; and when he attempts to talk he falls into a dissertation." *Democracy in America*, I, 266.

[46] On this whole subject see the clear and able survey of R. G. Adams, *A History of the Foreign Policy of the United States.*

[47] One curious feature of colonial life is that the colonies are, with reference to each other, independent nations. Read the accounts of the embassies they send back and forth among themselves, Massachusetts Bay and Hartford, Rhode Island and New Amsterdam, Pennsylvania and the New England states; treaties are drawn up, negotiations entered into by solemn companies of ministers and ambassadors, a gravely ludicrous parody of the statesmanship of Europe, which yet helped to prepare diplomats for the struggles of the eighteenth century. As in Europe, a grand alliance is forced by the threat of an alien foe—France (Albany Congress of 1754).

[48] See chap. iv. The eagerness of the colonials for European news is indicated in William Parks' address to subscribers of *The Maryland Gazette* (June 9, 1730) "I made it my particular concern, whilst I was in England, to settle such correspondence there; by which, upon all occasions, I shall be furnished with the freshest intelligence, both from thence and other Parts of Europe. . . ." Quoted in Evans, I, 373.

contributed his share of anti-French bitterness. Solomon Legaré was accustomed to tell his children:

Ah, my children! the blood-soaked soil of France cries to heaven for vengeance, and vengeance it will have, just as surely as righteous Abel's blood, crying from the earth to God for vengeance upon his murderer, brought down the curse upon Cain, so will a blasting curse rest upon France. Mark well what I say to you! France, guilty France, will never be blest with peace, prosperity and quiet; but, on the contrary, trouble, violence, and revolution after revolution will vex and rend those who have thus troubled and murdered the people of God. Therefore, my dear children, never do you return to France—keep yourselves clear of it, if you would keep clear of the fearful curse which hangs over it.[49]

We may put together some typical instances of this feeling.

For instance, Increase Mather preached in 1682 a sermon "Wherein is Shewed that the Church of God is sometimes a Subject of Great Persecution," the sermon being occasioned by news from France of the sufferings of the Protestants under Louis XIV; and a little later the fact that Sir Edmund Andros was of French extraction and sympathies was used by Mather against him in pamphlets published during Mather's mission in Great Britain in 1688-89.[50] In 1698 Governor Bellomont wrote to the Board of Trade from New York that "I must acquaint your lordships that the French here are very factious and their numbers considerable. At the last election they ran in with the Jacobite party, and have been since so insolent as to boast they had turned the scale and could balance the interests as they pleased"[51]—a state of affairs that did not make for good feeling. When in 1689 the French through treachery captured

---

[49] Fludd, *Biographical Sketches of the Huguenot Solomon Legaré*, p. 39. He died in 1760 at the age of 98. "The Huguenot refugee ceased to speak his own language as speedily as possible. My grandmother and her many brothers and sisters were only the fourth generation in this country. As their own grandfather had been left behind in France and educated there, they might well be accounted as the third generation here. Yet, with the exception of some of Marot's psalms, two or three childish rhymes, a proverb or two, and a few chance expressions, their speech betrayed no traces of their national origin. Though their great-grandfather, the refugee, taught his own language for several years, the household use of his beautiful mother-tongue was distinctly discouraged by him." This, because the Huguenot was not a colonist, but a refugee. Smith, *Colonial Days and Ways*, p. 151.

[50] Murdock, *Increase Mather*, pp. 136, 225. The first book printed in New York was anti-French: *A Narrative of an Attempt Made by the French of Canada Upon the Mohaques Country*, by Nicholas Bayard and Charles A. Lodowick, including a collection of official papers on French and Indian affairs, printed by William Bradford in 1693. Evans, Item No. 632.

[51] Quoted in Fosdick, p. 224.

Block Island, the fact was remembered; and in Samuel Niles'
Summary Historical Narrative of the Wars in New-England,
not completed until 1760, one finds that the narrative of the
capture lays emphasis upon the cunning of the French.[52] When
in 1690 Cuthbert Potter travelled from Virginia to New England to ascertain the truth about the Andros uprising—and was,
like some other seventeenth century ambassadors, jailed—he
arrived in New York in July, where he found the citizens in
consternation: "the alarm of the French Pyrates being then upon the Coast, caused them to prepare a force for their defence.
. . ." This was July 23. A week later he went "from Sebrook
to New London," where he "was told that the French Pyrates
had come to anchor before the town, but finding too great an
appearance to oppose them, they departed without doing any
dammage (*sic*). . . ."[53] John Williams, carried off to Canada,
returns to write *The Reedemed Captive Returning to Zion* in
1707; he has escaped the Deerfield massacre and the captivity;
he tells how the Governor of Canada lied to him about the number of French dead; how he disliked being carried "to a Popish
country"; and how he refused to go to mass in spite of the wiles
of the Jesuits.[54] Almost simultaneously a combined French and
Spanish force besieged Charleston, S. C., to the consternation
of the inhabitants who, however, beat them off.[55] Narratives
like John Gyles' *Memoirs of Odd Adventures, Strange Deliv-
erances, etc.* (1736), telling of captivity among the French and
Indians, helped to inflame public feeling.[56] Consider the state
of mind engendered among pious Quakers by the state of
things described by Peter Kalm in 1748:

At the close of the last war, a *redoubt* was erected here, on the south
side of the town, near the river, to prevent the *French* and *Spanish*
privateers from landing. But this was done after a very strong debate.
For the quakers opposed all fortifications, as contrary to the tenets of
their religion. . . . Several papers were then handed about for and
against the opinion. But the enemy's privateers having taken several
vessels belonging to the town in the river, many of the quakers, if not
all of them, found it reasonable to forward the building of the fortification as much as possible, at least by a supply of money.

And there was a similar scurry in Wilmington.[57]

[52] See Stedman and Hutchinson, II, 464 ff.
[53] "Cuthbert Potter's Journal" in *Mereness, Travels in the American
Colonies,* pp. 6, 7.
[54] Stedman and Hutchinson, II, 241 ff.
[55] See the narrative in Ramsay, *History of South Carolina,* I, 130-5.
[56] See Stedman and Hutchinson, II, 314 ff.
[57] Kalm, *Travels into North America,* I, 36, 123-4.

The early files of the *Boston News-Letter* are full of anti-French propaganda, which it is curious and interesting to examine. The first issue (April 17-24, 1704) includes a dispatch from the *London Flying-Post* expressing apprehension that the French king might send troops to' Scotland, and similar apprehensions are expressed in subsequent numbers. The eighteenth number (August 14-21, 1704) prints with pride the Governor's address to the Massachusetts General court, August 16, 1704, to the effect that:

The Forces Eastward under Col. *Church,* with the Assistance of Her Majesties Ships, have past thro' all the Eastern parts of *L'accadie* and *Nova-Scotia,* and have burnt and destroyed all the French Settlements except the town of *Port-Royal*: And kill'd their Cattel, & broken their Dams; and have brought home about 100 Prisoners, and a good Plunder: so that I am not sensible there are five Houses left in any part of the French Settlement out of sight of the Fort, or any manner of support for the Inhabitants; which was what we projected in the Spring. And the Forces are returned and disbanded without the loss of any more than Six men, for which we have all reason to render thanks to Almighty GOD.

In the issue of June 3-10, 1706, one reads Lord Cornbury's address to the New York General Assembly, which voted £3000 for the fortification of the Narrows against the French; in Boston the inhabitants have voted £1000 for repairing the fortifications. Maps "curiously engraven and painted" of "the Glory of the Confederate Arms" at Blenheim are advertised by Benjamin Eliot in January, 1707 (No. 195); and the particulars of the treaty of peace fill up a great deal of the space in the issues of 1713. But the treaty did little to allay suspicion. June 16-23, 1712, one reads that

They write from Albany that the French of Canada have debauched our five nations of Indians and insinuated to them, that the English design to Murder all the Indians on the Main, &c—And 'tis reported our Indians design to surprise Albany, and Murder all the English;

and some years later (June 6-13, 1723), we learn that the Governor of Canada has been inciting the Indians against New England, and has been rebuked by the Regent of France. Three years later (April 7-14, 1726), Lieutenant-Governor Dummer's speech to the General Assembly is quoted:

I have lately received Letters from the *Indians,* which I think proper to be communicated to you, by them you will perceive that the *French* (as they used to do) have been early at work by false Suggestions & perverse Interpretations of the Treaty to disaffect and perplex them.

And the same year (July 28-August 4) the paper printed the alarming news that "Four Mississippi Savages" visiting France had uttered speeches showing the closeness of the Franco-Indian alliance. "It is apprehended that if these encroachments of the French (the building of a fort at Crown Point) are not prevented, they may prove of the last Consequence to this and the rest of His Majesty's adjacent Colonies here in America," says the paper October 21-29, 1731. French gambling, French murderers, French trade rivalry, French piracy, and French boastfulness, French espionage, and French barbarity all have their place in the tale.[57a]

The natural result of such affairs was suspicion and distrust of the French. The French, wrote William Douglass about 1748, "are the common nuisance and disturbers of Europe, and will in a short time become the same in America, if not mutilated at home, and in America fenced off from us by ditches and walls, that is, by great rivers and impracticable mountains."[58] And this attitude was wide-spread. Colonel Johnson, answering a series of inquiries from the Lords of Trade in January 1719-20, which includes the question how the French settlements on the Mississippi may affect the Carolinas, replies that the French are very strong, that they number five thousand or six thousand fighting men, and that more are coming daily to Pensacola, and that they already have a fort and forty men among the Halbamas (Alabamas):

These great preparacons of setling the Mississippi cannot but very much alarm all ye continent of America, and especially Carolina, that lies soe near them, for even in time of Peace they underhand incence ye Indians against us and incourage them to make inroads upon us to the great damage and hasard of our utmost Settlements.[59]

And he prophecies that in case of war the province will fall an easy prey. Or again, when the helpless Acadians to the number of four hundred fifty-five were dumped upon Philadelphia, the city of brotherly love, by the British fleet, one finds a contemporary account which includes the passage: "May God be pleased to give us success against all our copper-coloured can-

---

[57a] *Boston News-Letter,* issues of January 23-30, October 22-29, 1724; February 18-25, April 22-29, 1725; September 29-October 6, 1726; *Boston Weekly News-Letter,* January 17-24, 1734; February 7-14, 1734, and generally for the year. "There is hardly any reading of the Stories of the Barbarous Manner of Making War of the French and Muscovites, without shedding Tears." (August 15-22, 1734).

[58] Quoted in Tyler, *History of American Literature,* II, 156-7.

[59] See Rivers, *A Chapter in the Early History of South Carolina,* p. 97.

nibals and French savages, equally cruel and perfidious in their natures"; while the Acadians are "no better than so many scorpions in the bowels of the country."[60] Perhaps it is not surprising: the Acadians came in November, and in the previous September three Frenchmen had been arrested for poisoning wells.[61] Similar reception awaited the Acadians in almost every province.[62] Nor were the Huguenots, despite their professed Protestantism, able to escape suspicion and sometimes persecution. One finds in 1708 that there appeared from the press of William Bradford in New York a *Full & Just Discovery of the weak & slender foundation of a most pernicious slander raised against the French Protestant refugees inhabiting the Province of New York generally, but more particularly affecting Capt. Benj. Faniel* (sic), *a person of considerable note amongst them*. The title is self-explanatory; the work was "printed and published by License of his excellency Edward, Viscount Cornbury, Captain General and Governour in Chief of the said Providence, in favour of Justice."[63] In April, 1707, the Huguenots of Manakin-town in Virginia were sending a petition to the President and Council of that province, complaining of the treatment that had been accorded them; and after a good deal of debate, they withdrew to North Carolina whence they were driven by a war between the Corees and Tuscaroras.[64] And in South Carolina, despite explicit directions from the Royal government, naturalization had been accorded the Huguenots only grudgingly about twelve years before.[65] These are but isolated instances, it is true, but they could be multiplied; the colonial press teemed with pamphlet and document designed to expose the subtle schemes of that arch-enemy, the Frenchman,[66] and Huguenot and Acadian naturally suffered.

[60] Quoted from the Shippen papers in Scharf and Westcott, *History of Philadelphia*, I, 248; II, 1369.

[61] *Ibid.*, I, 248. The unfortunate Acadians were supported by the private benevolence of their Huguenot compatriots—Benezet, Le Fevre, de Normandie—by public subscription and by state bounty. I, 249-250.

[62] See chap. iv, pp. 107-111.

[63] Evans, item, 1352.

[64] See the Gaillard MSS. printed in the *Transactions of the Huguenot Society of South Carolina*, no. 14 (1907), particularly pp. 18-19.

[65] For details see chap. iv, pp. 00-00; and also *Transactions*, no. 5 (1897), pp. 19-26.

[66] See the earlier volumes of Evans for titles. Here are some representative ones: *Some Considerations on the Consequnces of the French Settling Colonies on the Mississippi*. Boston, 1720; *An Account of the French Settlements in North America, showing from the latest authors, the towns, forts,*

The patriotic spirit cared as little in 1759 for fine distinctions as it did in 1917. The *Pennsylvania Gazette,* November 8, 1759, hearing of the death of Wolfe on the Plains of Abraham, bursts out into rhymed chauvinism:

> Like Britain's genius shouldst thou then appear,
> Hurling destruction on the Gallic rear—
> While France, astonished, trembled at thy sight,
> And placed her safety in ignoble flight.
> The last great scene should melt each Briton's heart,
> And rage and grief alternately impart.

The dying general learns that his

> bold troops o'er slaughter heaps advance,
> And deal due vengeance on the sons of France,

before he cries out, "I'm satisfied," and dies.[67] And the result was that Americans thoroughly misunderstood the French. "Before the Revolution," wrote Samuel Breck in his *Recollections,* "the colonists had little or no communication with France, so that Frenchmen were known to them only through the prejudiced medium of England. Every vulgar story told by John Bull about Frenchmen living on salads and frogs was implicitly believed." Indeed, when Mr. Nathaniel Tracy entertained the officers of the French fleet at dinner in Boston after the Alliance, he served a whole green frog in each plate of soup, and seemed astonished at the resulting laughter.[68] It is all natural and human enough, but whatever the sources, the attitude is the frontier attitude, it is the attitude of suspicion and alienation, even of chauvinism—that same expression which we have defined in the first section of this chapter. We may say that up

---

islands, lakes, rivers, &c. of Canada, claimed and improved by the French king. . . . By P. Charlevoix. Boston, 1746; *An Ode, for the Thanksgiving Day.* By Titus Antigallicus, Esq. Boston, 1749; *A Short Narrative of Mischief done by the French and Indian Enemy,* etc. (Dr. Doolittle). Boston, 1750; *A Plan of the City & Fortress of Louisbourg, with a small plan of the Harbor,* etc. Boston, 1746; *A Letter from William Shirley, Esq., Governor of the Massachusetts Bay to . . . the Duke of Newcastle: with a journal of the siege of Louisbourg,* etc. London, 1746; Boston, 1746; *A Scheme to drive the French out of all the continent of America.* Boston, 1755, by C. T.; William Clarke, *Observations upon the late and present conduct of the French with regard to the encroachments upon the British colonies in North America,* etc. Boston, 1775. *Etc., etc.* (Evans, items 2176, 5725, 6277, 6488, 5783, 5863, 7377, 7389. There is really an enormous literature of anti-French propaganda, as anyone who will take the trouble to turn over the pages of Evans will see.

[67] Stedman and Hutchinson, II, 477-8.

[68] *Recollections of Samuel Breck,* pp. 24-26. The Bostonese were astonished at the strong, vigorous aspect of the French sailors.

to the conclusion of the Seven Years War, the general political situation in America reflected this opinion of hostility toward the French.

3. THE REVOLUTIONARY PERIOD

But wars have an end and opinions change. As we have indicated elsewhere, the cosmopolitan classes did not believe that Frenchman was synonymous with devil. To the world convulsion of the Seven Years War, there succeeded, in the words of Professor Faÿ, a sort of universal calm,[69] and in this universal calm the voice of cosmopolitan intelligence could now and again be heard. Considering religion, government, liberty, shipping, arts, sciences, population, and virtue, it did not seem to John Adams in 1761 that England was superior to France; on the contrary he was inclined to believe that France was superior to England.[70] French was, as we have seen, getting itself taught in American colleges; the French tutor, dancing-master, or fencer was instructing the polite youth of the land; and the newspapers were beginning to cite French authors, especially Montesquieu and Voltaire and Raynal.[71] As we have indicated elsewhere, there was a constant importation of French literature, and necessarily of French ideas.[72] It was flattering to read in the Abbé Raynal's *Histoire des Indes*[73] that Europe was decadent, that America was the hope of the world, even though his book was full of recognizable errors and he refused to agree that the colonists had the right of rebellion.[74] Frank-

[69] "L'image, que les livres et les journaux publiés de 1770 à 1775 donne du monde politique et intellectuel à cette date, est caractérisée par un contraste : une sort d'accalmie universelle s'est produite, les grandes puissances occidentales s'observent, cherchent à éviter des conflits violents, les gouvernements s'efforcent de se renforcer et de durer, et les grands écrivains eux-mêmes semblent prolonger une époque dont la période la plus brillante serait écoulée. Toutefois une fièvre de nouveauté commence à se répandre, une impatience aiguë et indistincte règne partout." *L'Ésprit Révolutionnaire*, p. 5.
[70] *Works*, II, 110.
[71] See previous chapters of this study; and for the citation of French writers in colonial newspapers, Faÿ, p. 27, and references.
[72] Faÿ (p. 26) estimates that about a quarter of the books imported at New York in 1770-1774 were in French, and a less proportion in other seaport towns. His estimates are based on careful search among the contemporary newspapers.
[73] Vol. IX of the edition of 1820. See especially section xv of vol. X, "Réflections sur le bien et le mal que la découverte du nouveau-monde a faits à l'Europe."
[74] See the excellent discussion of Raynal in Faÿ, pp. 8-11; and see *Writings of Franklin*, II, 463-467; I, 205-6 for an account of some of Raynal's errors.

lin, being in Paris in 1767, received "the strongest Impressions of the French Politeness,"[75] though, to be sure, "that intriguing nation would like very well to meddle on occasion, and blow up coals between Britain and her colonies; but I hope we shall give them no opportunity."[76] However, as the quarrel between Parliament and the colonies increased, so did Franklin's correspondence with Frenchmen increase, his friends including Père Berthier (1702-1783), the scientist; M. Thomas-François Dalibard, the physicist; M. Barbeu Dubourg, the translator of Bolingbroke and of Franklin;[77] Dupont de Nemours; Jean Baptiste LeRoy (1724-1800), the physicist, and his three brothers, Pierre, Charles, and David; Condorcet; Cabanis; and others.[78] Montesquieu became popular in the papers;[79] articles appeal to the French king;[80] and the ideas of the French philosophers were "in the air."[81] From 1763 to

[75] Franklin to Mary Stevenson, September 14, 1767, *Writings*, V, 53.

[76] Franklin to William Franklin, August 28, 1767, V, 47.

[77] *Œuvres de M. Franklin, Docteur ès Loix, Traduites de l'Anglois sur la quatrième édition.* Paris, 1773.

[78] See the list of correspondents in *Writings*, X, 511-535.

[79] See Faÿ, p. 27. For instance, May 3, 1770, the *New York Journal* is cited by Faÿ as saying that the moment prophesied by Montesquieu has come when the British constitution shall be ruined since the legislative is now worse than the executive; in 1772 the *Gazette* of New London quotes Montesquieu's definition of servitude and indulges in a tirade against oppression, etc. Merriam (*History of American Political Theories*, p. 79) notes that the theory and the facts of Montesquieu were well known among the Americans and that "consequently they readily accepted and acted upon Montesquieu's theory."

[80] For instance, Faÿ cites the *Boston Gazette* of September 20, 1768, as printing such an article.

[81] Unfortunately I must trust to the authority of others for much that I should like to say from first-hand information. The following paragraph from the *Cambridge History of American Literature* (I, 119) seems to me to state fairly the case: "The ideas of the French philosophers were in the air, and there is plenty of evidence in the colonial newspapers for fifteen or twenty years before the Revolution, that the French influence was increasing. Even during the French and Indian war, booksellers advertised French texts, grammars, and dictionaries in the papers, while courses in French were often announced. Before the close of the war we find *The Boston Gazette* printing extracts from Montesquieu's *The Spirit of Laws*, with an apology and the expressed hope that it may not be 'political Heresey' to suppose that 'a Frenchman may have juster Notions of Civil Liberty than some among ourselves.' After 1760 all the important works of Rousseau, Montesquieu and the Encyclopaedists as well as many other French books were advertised for sale in the colonial press. Such advertisements indicate the taste of the reading public more accurately than do catalogues of private libraries, which represent individual preferences. Voltaire had long been known in the colonies. Rousseau's *Social Contract* was advertised as a *Treatise on the Social Compact, or The Principles of Political Law*. He himself is referred to again and again as 'the ingenious Rousseau' or 'the celebrated Rousseau.'

1773, remarks Faÿ, American public opinion took on a remark-able coherence as journalism developed. Papers printed Whig news from England and all the European intelligence they could secure.[82] It is by such steps that public opinion was influenced and the French alliance gradually prepared for.

It is true, however, that there is manifest no overwhelming love for France anywhere between 1763 and 1776. Listen to Professor Faÿ on the subject:

On a beaucoup dit qu'elle (France) jouissait d'une haine bien établie. Et cela est plausible, après les années de guerre qui ont séparé les deux peuples. J'ai bien trouvé dans les livres et journaux américains de l'époque les imprécations que l'on m'avait prédites. Stansbury, en 1771, rappelle Crécy, Poitiers et Azincourt et incite à continuer. En 1774 J. Adams lui-même affirme que la France est trop turbulente pour ne pas faire de guerre. Mais ce sont surtout les journaux qui fournissent une riche moisson de déclamations antifrançaises.[83]

And this dislike of France took certain definite forms. The newspapers instanced Louis XIV as the perfect example of tyranny and intolerance.[84] In the sermons the anti-papal note was still being stressed by parsons like Mayhew and Hitch-cock.[85] The newspapers announced that France was buying naval stores for nefarious purposes; that France was a decadent country; that France was on the verge of a revolution; that Madame du Barry was no better than she should be; that France, in acquiring Corsica, had violated the laws of nations.[86] Whoever, wrote a contributor to the *New London Gazette* in 1770, maintains that France is in life and spirit the gayest of the nations, deceives himself; all that gaiety is found only at

And *Emile* and *La Nouvelle Hélöise* were evidently in demand. . . . Reports of French interest in American inclined the colonists still more to the French philosophy of government." Such reading necessarily made France more attractive in proportion as Great Britain seemed more arbitrary. On the other hand Carl Becker denies, and is probably right in so doing, any great French influence on the Declaration of Independence. *The Declaration of Independence,* chapter ii. I think, too, that the influence of Rousseau is greatly exaggerated in the above quotation.

[82] Faÿ, p. 23.

[83] Faÿ, p. 24.

[84] "When he says, that the king's dominions must have an uncontrollable power coextensive with them, I ask whether they have such a power or not? and utterly deny that they have, by any law but that of Louis XIV and the king of Sardinia." "Novanglus" (John Adams) in the *Boston Gazette* of 1774. *Works of John Adams,* IV, 38.

[85] Faÿ cites J. Mayhew, *Papist Idolatry,* Boston, 1765, for example. See Evans, *passim,* for many other examples.

[86] See the references cited by Faÿ, pp. 24-25.

Paris, the peasants being miserably poor; and a kingdom of eighteen million is held in subjugation by a standing army.[87] Naturally the Tories painted France as black as possible[88] in order to whiten England, and pointed with alarm to the "foreigners" in the colonies, who, in the opinion of Peter Kalm, had "no particular attachment to Old England."[89] But the attack, as its historian comments, was really a boomerang; every attack on the standing army of France led men to think of the danger of a standing army in the colonies; every description of arbitrary monarchy in France compelled them to remember the arbitrary acts of monarchy in Great Britain.[90] By the winter of 1775-6 colonial newspapers were printing articles on the good disposition of France,[91] for Louis XV had yielded to Louis XVI, regarded as a model young man and a "good" king, who was willing to listen to the philosophers.[92] By 1776 John Adams and Samuel Chase (of Maryland) were proposing a mission for the negotiating of a commercial treaty with France, to the Continental Congress.[93] So it is that, while among the lower classes, Frenchmen are perhaps still detestable, among the cosmopolitan groups, their status changes: to the Loyalists the Frenchman is a menace, to the Whigs, rebels, or insurgents,[94] he is a promise of aid. As trade grows, as commerce increases, as parliament and the British merchant combine in the true spirit of mercantile economics to exploit the colonies rather than to develop them, the inevitable consequence follows: colonial prejudice against Great Britain increases and the sense of hostility toward France inevitably wanes.

In France America had passed into a legend, and the coming of Franklin justified the legend.[95] In France, after 1770, people

[87] Faÿ says this letter was reproduced in more than twenty colonial newspapers, p. 25.
[88] See Faÿ's references, p. 46.
[89] *Travels into North America*, I, 206-7.
[90] Faÿ, p. 25.
[91] Faÿ, p. 53.
[92] See Faÿ, pp. 29-31.
[93] *Works of John Adams*, I, 199-201; II, 454-9.
[94] "You are too early, *Hussy*, (as well as too saucy,) in calling me Rebel. . . . Here (in France) the Ladies are more civil; they call us *les Insurgens*, a Character that usually pleases them: And methinks all other Women who smart, or have smarted, under the Tyranny of a bad Husband, ought to be fixed in *Revolution* principles, and act accordingly." Franklin to Mrs. Thompson, Feb. 8, 1777. *Writings*, VII, 23.
[95] Faÿ, pp. 16-17, 15-16, 65 ff., 95 ff. He was regarded as the typical American, possessed of all the primitive republican virtues, sage, serious,

began to affect spontaneity,[96] and naturally they saw a spontaneous civilization in the new and primitive world, a belief that was shared by the Americans.[97] France had, moreover, certain legitimate grounds of complaint against England. The humiliations of the Treaty of 1763 were not forgotten; nor was the presence at Dunkirk after 1713 of a British commissioner, kept at the expense of France, to prevent the re-building of the fortifications of the town. The ministry, which seemed to be doing nothing to avenge the national honor, was unpopular among a growing number of partisans—an unpopularity that engendered in turn a sense of grievance. Moreover, from 1773 and 1774 down to the Treaty of Alliance, the continual trading between the French West Indies and France, on the one hand, and the insurgents on the other, led to irritation: the English vessels not merely cruised the open sea, but sailed under the very cannon of the French forts to stop suspected vessels.[98]

and simple; and he was himself conscious of the value of the role, and sought to dramatize it. See *Writings,* VII, *passim* for instances. Here is a typical one: "Figure to yourself an old Man, with grey Hair Appearing under a Martin Fur Cap, among the Powder'd Heads of Paris." Franklin to Mrs. Mary Hewson, VII, 10. Franklin "became, in fact, the one conspicuous interpreter to Europe of the grievances and the purposes of America, and the one conspicuous interpreter to America of the attitude of Europe." Tyler, *Literary History of the American Revolution,* II, 372.

[96] Cf. Faÿ, p. 7. Free-masonry was growing; Perkins, *France in the American Revolution,* chapter XI.

[97] For instance, Timothy Dwight wrote in *The Conquest of Canaan* in 1785, such lines as these:

"Then o'er wide lands, as blissful Eden bright,
Type of the skies, and seats of pure delight,
Our sons with prosperous course shall stretch their sway,
And claim an empire spread from sea to sea;
In one great whole th' harmonious tribes combine,
Trace Justice' path, and choose their chiefs divine;
Teach laws to reign, and save the Rights of Man.
Then smiling Art shall wrap the fields in bloom,
Fine the rich ore, and guide the useful loom;
Then lofty towers in golden pomp arise,
Then spiry cities meet auspicious skies;
The soul on Wisdom's wing sublimely soar,
New virtues cherish and new truths explore;
Through Time's long track our name celestial run,
Climb in the east and circle with the sun;
And smiling glory stretch triumphant wings
O'er hosts of heroes and o'er tribes of kings."

Quoted in Adams, *History,* I, 96. Dwight recanted this doctrine in *The Triumph of Infidelity,* 1797.

[98] See for an admirable summary of the situation, chapter I of Merlant, *Soldiers and Sailors of France in the American War for Independence.* For example, the Governor of Martinique (Comte d'Argoult) complains on March 26, 1776, that the English frigate, *The Lynx,* has captured a brigan-

Naturally, the Americans grew in popularity:

> Bravo, Messieurs les Insurgents!
> Vainquers dans une juste guerre,
> Vous donnez par vos sentiments
> Un peuple de plus à la terre.
> Fermes, courageux, patients
> Doués d'une franchise altière,
> Libres surtout! voilà mes gens.[99]

Vergennes, the ablest minister that Louis XVI ever had, waited and calculated his chances, for an alliance between France and America meant a complete change in the habits of the two peoples, a boldness in diplomacy so strange that no one could divine where it led.[100]

Insofar as the Alliance of 1778 was the work of particular persons, it was the work of Vergennes and of Franklin. The friends of Franklin in France were men like Vergennes, Lafayette, Mirabeau, Quesnay, La Rochefoucauld-Liancourt, Condorcet, Lavoisier, Buffon, d'Alembert, and Voltaire—physiocrats and philosophers, and it was among these that he spread his propaganda. He was interested, for example, in the secret lodge of the Nine Sisters, a branch of the Illuminati, among whom he spread propaganda for constitutionalism,[101] and if, as colonial agent in England in 1757-62, he had played up the policy of crushing the commercial rivalry of France, this was now forgotten.[102] He moved among influential circles, and was everywhere received.[103] When Deane had come to Paris in June, 1776, he had not been received by Vergennes; with the arrival of Franklin and Arthur Lee in the fall, it became increasingly evident that the colonists meant business; the commissioners on February 2, 1777, unanimously resolved that "if France or Spain should conclude a Treaty of Amity and Commerce with our States, and enter into a war with Great

tine coming from the Carolinas just as she was about to cast anchor. The crew of *La Rosière d'Artois,* a French ship retained at St. Augustine, were told that they could go where they pleased, but that the English had promised the Indians 120 pounds for each Frenchman's scalp. pp. 8-9.

[99] By du Couëdic, quoted in Merlant, p. 8.

[100] Faÿ, p. 46.

[101] The other members were Bailly, Bonneville, Brissot de Warville, Condorcet, Danton, Desmoulins, Hilliard d'Auberteuil, Pétion, Rabaut Saint-Étienne, Sieyès. Cf. D. J. Hill, "A Missing Chapter of Franco-American History," *American Historical Review,* XXI, 709-719.

[102] Cf. Sherman in *Cambridge History of American Literature,* I, 106.

[103] Cf. Hale, *Franklin in France;* and see *Writings,* especially VII and VIII; and Perkins, *op. cit.,* chap. vii.

Britain," it would be right and proper to agree not to conclude a separate peace, and that "if it should be necessary," they would "pledge our persons or hazard the censure of the Congress by exceeding our Instructions."[104] And to secure this end Franklin made propaganda orally and by printed pamphlets and letters.[105]

As for Vergennes, the story of his manouevres towards the American alliance is a lesson in adroit diplomacy.[106] The aims of France interested him more than fine words about the rights of man, nor should we be deceived by the talk of the idéologues or the generous enthusiasm of Lafayette and others into thinking that Vergennes was not a master of *Realpolitik*. Professor Corwin, after examining the French archives, concludes that:

The line of reasoning by which France was brought into the American Revolution comprised for the most part the following ideas: that France was entitled by her wealth, power, and history to the preponderating influence in Continental affairs; that she had lost this position of interference largely on account of Great Britain's intermeddling; that Great Britain had been able to mingle in Continental concerns by virtue of her great naval strength, her commercial prosperity, and her preparedness to maintain Continental subsidiaries; that these in turn were due in great part to her American colonial empire, and especially to the policies controlling her trade therewith; that America, become independent, would be an almost total loss from the point of view of British interests; that this loss would mean a corresponding diminution of British power; that, since the two were rivals, whatever abased the power of Great Britain would elevate the power of France.[107]

The rights of man are not invading diplomacy, although Vergennes was not unwilling to employ the idealistic enthusiasm of the intelligentsia to gain his end. But Europe, we must always remember, was yet under the dynastic system: the balance of power, the balance of trade—these are the cruxes of diplomacy, and in this diplomacy the future United States is an integral part—in this diplomacy American representatives at various European courts participate. We are far from the shirt-sleeve

---

[104] *Writings of Franklin*, VII, 20.
[105] See, for example, *The Sale of the Hessians, A Dialogue between Britain, France, Spain, Holland, Saxony and America, A Catechism relating to the English National Debt.*, etc., in *Writings*, VII, all written and printed for European circulation.
[106] Told with great skill in Faÿ, chap. ii; and Perkins, chaps. iii-xiii.
[107] Corwin, "The French Objective in the American Revolution," *American Historical Review*, XXI, pp. 59-60. The whole article (pp. 33-61) should be read in correction of Faÿ's somewhat idealized picture.

diplomacy of later days. Moreover, it would appear from the findings of Professor Van Tyne that the American representatives impressed Europe with the fact that the New World was still a part of Europe—we have not yet come to the era of Washington's Farewell Address or of the Monroe doctrine. The cosmopolitan spirit is temporarily in the saddle.

France entered into alliance with the United States in the spring of 1778, because the king and his ministry were convinced that France was doomed to a war with Great Britain . . . and . . . it was the better policy to join with America and thus win her support rather than wait for England to make peace with America and then make war in company with her upon the House of Bourbon whose insular possessions would lie so completely at her mercy.[108]

Here is no "American" policy as yet; all this is in the eighteenth century manner, the period of the reversal of alliances, of secret treaties,[109] and a cheerful disregard of obligations.[110] The United States was still a part of Europe.[111] But let us return to our story.

Long before there was an open break between the colonies and Great Britain, France had her secret agents in the New World. Under the reign of Louis XV Choiseul dispatched M. de Pontleroy to America in 1764 on a tour of observation; Pontleroy continued to send reports to Choiseul for two years, reports which gave a glowing account of the strength and resources of America.[112] In 1765 we know from an anonymous

---

[108] C. H. Van Tyne, "Influences which Determined the French Government to Make the Treaty with America, 1778," *American Historical Review*, XXI, 541. See the whole article, pp. 528-541.

[109] In negotiating the Treaty of Paris after the Continental Congress had placed the negotiations under French control—a policy brought about by Luzerne—the envoys (Franklin, Jay and Laurens) concluded a treaty with England without informing Vergennes of the fact until after the treaty was signed. However justified by the results, the performance was far from being an example of covenants openly arrived at. Cf. Faÿ, pp. 113-118.

[110] By the treaty of alliance the United States was bound to protect French possessions in the West Indies. After the French Revolution, when the British threatened these possessions, the United States refused to keep its obligations.

[111] ". . . in every case from 1689 to 1815 there was not a single great European War (and there were seven of them) in which American lives were not lost, American property destroyed, and in which American soldiers and sailors were not involved." During the colonial period English "victories in America were traded off for land in India, or balanced against defeats elsewhere. That Americans might have something to say in the matter was not frequently considered." Adams, *A History of the Foreign Policy of the United States*, pp. 21, 22.

[112] He described the land as rich and prosperous, the people as being hardy seamen and skillful shipbuilders along the coast; and said that the colonists were beginning to feel their strength. Perkins, pp. 25-26.

diary published in the *American Historical Review*[113] that a secret French agent reviewed Patrick Henry, Charles Carroll, and other prominent American leaders. Sometime before that a French agent reported from London to Choiseul that "only arms, a leader, and a feeling of self-reliance were required to secure the independence of the American colonies."[114] In 1768 Choiseul sent Kalb to America; Kalb was not so encouraging, and Choiseul told him on his return in June, 1768, that he need not send in any more reports.[115] But now Choiseul had departed and Vergennes was in power: he, too, sent his agent to America —Achard de Bonvouloir (perhaps the name was prophetic) who interviewed John Adams, Samuel Chase, and Franklin; and one d'Annemours, later French consul at Baltimore, who came, it is said, as early as 1773.[116] Bonvouloir was instructed to say that as long as the colonists remained subject to the King of Great Britain, France could do nothing: the mission was very secret, Bonvouloir was allowed only two hundred louis a month, and his chief activity was to send back glowing reports of American military discipline, which misled Vergennes.[117] Came then to France the unfortunate Silas Deane, to be succeeded by the American mission (Franklin and Lee were associated with Deane), and Vergennes was getting ready to act. Action took the curious form of the mythical house of Roderigue Hortalez and Company, "merchants"; really Beaumarchais, who had undertaken to act between Vergennes and a secret committee of the Continental Congress in surreptitiously forwarding supplies and money to the insurgents,[118] and who

[113] XXVI, no. 4, pp. 726-47; and XXVII, no. 1, pp. 70-89.
[114] Perkins, p. 26.
[115] Perkins, pp. 26-30.
[116] Faÿ, p. 34; and notes on p. 44. Unfortunately I have not been able to see the authoritative work of Doniol, *Participation de la France à l'Établissement des États-unis*, on which Perkins and Faÿ both draw.
[117] Perkins, pp. 45-59.
[118] "Hortalez and Company" sold "general merchandise" to one "Timothy Jones" of Bermuda (Silas Deane); the King of Spain and the King of France each advanced a million livres; and the "house" forwarded something like 30,000 stands of arms, 250 cannon, and supplies of clothing to the insurgents. See Kite, *Beaumarchais and the War of American Independence,* especially vol. II; Rivers, *Figaro: the Life of Beaumarchais;* Perkins, chap. v; Faÿ, pp. 36-39; Loménie, *Beaumarchais et son temps.* The "house" was under way before the arrival of Franklin and Lee. I am unable to identify the two Frenchmen who have gone to English America as agents to the Congress, concerning whom Vergennes inquires 22 April 1776, and of whose existence Beaumarchais denies any knowledge on the 27 April. Stevens, *Facsimiles,* No. 1327; No. 1331.

went bankrupt out of sheer zeal for humanity. But there were others bitten by the same madness; Franklin found that "a sort of crusading ardor" had seized on the French, that Deane had been sending them over in swarms, and that Congress was put to heavy expense in sending most of them back. He tried to check the flow, and permit only picked men to go over.[119]

News of the Declaration of Independence "excited a degree of enthusiasm among the French people which had been aroused by no other public document." The news came in August, 1776, and Vergennes was ready to declare war openly if only Spain would act, which she would not.[120] Moreover, there were certain difficulties in the way. For one thing, the American commission at Paris had taken to quarreling among themselves, until Franklin only was left to act, for Lee withdrew and Deane was something of a subordinate. The British Ambassador, Lord Stormont, refused to believe Vergennes' assurances that Franklin was only a private gentleman; and there arose certain difficulties about American privateers in French ports.[121] Unfortunately, also, the news of the Declaration was followed by news of the Battle of Long Island, and American stock sank.[122] And in the New World, French adventurers had not showed themselves to advantage.[123] France had sent a number of scapegrace sons to the Antilles, and these, seeing the opportunity for plunder, embarrassed Congress with their importunities until, when an attempt was made to raise a French legion in the West Indies to serve under Washington, the offer was refused.[124]

However, Franklin was a host in himself; in March, 1777, ten vessels of the "firm" sailed for America;[125] engineers commenced to arrive;[126] and, to the wonder of Europe and the

[119] Morse, *Benjamin Franklin,* pp. 239-243.
[120] Perkins, pp. 119-125.
[121] See Perkins, chap. viii.
[122] Perkins, pp. 125-8.
[123] Deane had been "hourly fatigued with . . . applications and offers, which we are obliged to refuse, and with hundreds of letters which we can not possibly answer to their satisfaction." Perkins, p. 166. In consequence, when Congress asked for four engineers, it received a host of volunteers like du Coudray who demanded a major-generalship, and whose death by drowning in the Schuylkill seemed to Lafayette a happy accident. American officers did not relish the superiority of these French gentlemen. Perkins, pp. 166-9. On these early volunteers see Balch, *The French in America during the War of Independence,* pp. 79-82.
[124] Faÿ, pp. 46-7, and references, 58-59; Perkins, pp. 164-7.
[125] Merlant, *op. cit.,* p. 21.
[126] For instance, Potter de Baldivia and Gille Lomont; de Gouvion, La Radière, and Launoy, the first arriving in 1776, the last on July 29, 1777. De Kernovan came and was commissioned as engineer July 4, 1776. Balch, *op. cit.,* pp. 79-81.

admiration of America, Lafayette left home, wife, and children, disobeyed his king, and sailed to America,[127] arriving in Philadelphia with Kalb and twelve French officers just in time to participate in the battle of Brandywine.[128] The reception of Lafayette throws a flood of light on American opinion of the French. They landed near Georgetown, South Carolina; these idealists, at night, proceeded to a house nearby, and had it not been for Kalb, who knew some English, might have been shot for marauders. Once known for what they were, Charleston proved hospitable; and writing his wife (19 June, 1777), Lafayette says he has been overwhelmed with politeness and attention, and can only praise his reception. So, too, on his journey to Philadelphia, he experienced nothing but courtesy,[129] although the journey was a difficult one, lasting thirty-two days. Their reception by Congress was chilly, the committee at first treating them as additional troublesome adventurers, but when it appeared that Lafayette asked only two things, viz., that he should serve as a volunteer in any capacity, and that he should pay his own expenses, it was soon discovered that a new order of Frenchman had arrived, and by resolution of July 31, 1777, Lafayette was given the rank of major-general.[130] He and his comrades were charmed by General Washington and much loved by the auxiliary troops. If Franklin became the ideal type of American for France, Lafayette, known as "the Marquis," became the ideal type of Frenchman for Americans; and it is safe to say that this tact and charm resulted in a popularity which, as much as anything else, prepared American public opinion for the French alliance. Finally, Lafayette returned to France in February, 1777, a visit which resulted (after the alliance) in the sending of seven ships-of-the-line, ten or twelve

[127] For a brief and accurate account of Lafayette see Perkins, chap. ix; also Merlant, pp. 21-37; Faÿ, pp. 59 ff.

[128] The officers were de Mauroy, de Gimat, Pontgibaud, Armand de la Rouërie, (known as Colonel Armand), Mauduit du Plessis, de Fleury, de Buysson, the Sennevilles, du Bois-Martin, Amaryton. See *Mémoires de Lafayette*, I., especially pp. 9-16, for the romantic story of his departure from France.

[129] Lafayette to his wife, 19 June, 1777; 17 July, 1777. *Mémoires*, I, 121, 126.

[130] Perkins, p. 188. Lafayette was wise enough to see that there was reason for American distrust of foreigners. "Ils (les étrangers) ont essayé par toutes sortes de piége de me dégouter et de cette révolution et de celui qui en est le chef." (To his wife, from Valley Forge, 6 January, 1778) *Mémoires*, I, 178. He found himself "overwhelmed" by the goodness of the Americans, and their confidence in him. II, 182.

thousand men, and six million livres to America.[131] But this
is to anticipate.

The turning point in the negotiations came with the arrival
of the *Perch* at Nantes, November 30, 1777, carrying J. L.
Austin of Boston with messages from the Massachusetts Council of the surrender of Burgoyne—news so joyful that Beaumarchais, in his eagerness to carry the tidings to Paris tipped
over his carriage and nearly broke his neck.[132] On February 6,
1778, treaties of alliance were signed between the French ministers on behalf of Louis XVI and the three American commissioners. Really two treaties were signed, one providing for
the alliance, and one being a treaty of commerce. The only condition imposed by France on her new allies was that the Americans should make no peace until their independence was recognized, and that the allies should unite in making a peace. News
of the treaty was received in the United States in April with
unfeigned enthusiasm.[133] A French representative, Gérard de
Rayneval, was dispatched to the Congress, who was officially
received on August 6, 1778,[134] and who was succeeded in September, 1779, by the Count de la Luzerne. Gérard watched
assiduously over the interests of France,[135] and among other
matters, subsidized a writer named Leonidas to advocate independence, liberty, and the French alliance. Luzerne continued
the policy of subsidizing authors; he paid Tom Paine to continue his writings and to refrain from attacking France; and
he hired Samuel Cooper at $1,000 a year to preach in the

[131] Balch, *The French in America during the War of Independence*, pp.
97-98. On the difficulties in the arrival of French troops consult Perkins,
chaps. xiv-xvii.
[132] Perkins, pp. 230-31.
[133] On the details of the enthusiasm see Faÿ, pp. 70-71; Perkins, pp. 244-6.
See also Chotteau, *Les Français en Amérique*.
[134] The details of Gérard's reception throw a good deal of light on the
attitude of the day towards the importance of diplomatic etiquette. Congress, not knowing how to receive a foreign ambassador, appointed a committee to investigate the matter; the finding of the committee was that if
he were an ambassador, three members of Congress should wait upon him
in a coach belonging to the nation, and that the chairman of the committee
should return with the ambassador and his secretary in the coach. The ambassador, on reaching the hall of Congress, should be seated in a chair raised
eighteen inches from the floor. But, alas! Gérard was only a minister, so
that he was waited on by only two members, and his chair was not raised
from the floor. However, he and the president of Congress had the largest
chairs. Perkins, pp. 251-2.
[135] Cf. Perkins, pp. 253-4.

interests of the alliance, which he did for three years[136]—by which time Puritan clergymen, who had formerly prayed for the fall of the Pope, were praying for the health of the Catholic King of France.

The immediate results of the alliance were war between France and England and the dispatch of d'Estaing, who proved to be a better maker of apothegms than he was a naval strategist, to the New World with a fleet. On the part of the Americans there followed a deepening dislike of England and an increasing enthusiasm for France. D'Estaing, however, sailed too slowly; he failed to catch Howe either at Philadelphia or at New York; and he failed to take Newport, though in the last of these events the fault was not all his, and he withdrew to the West Indies. At first, criticism of these failures was swallowed up in general enthusiasm for the allies. John Adams, who had sailed on February 13, 1778, to France as American commissioner, receiving from his wife an account of the reception of d'Estaing and his officers, replied in a letter which faithfully reflects the enthusiasm of the moment:

I am extremely obliged to the Comte d'Estaing and his officers for their politeness to you, and am very glad you have had an opportunity of seeing so much of the French nation. The accounts from all hands agree, that there was an agreeable intercourse and happy harmony, upon the whole, between the inhabitants and the fleets. The more this nation is known, and the more their language is understood, the more will narrow prejudices wear away. British fleets and armies are very different from their's *(sic)*. In point of temperance and politeness, there is no comparison.[137]

Hatred of England became, as Lodge remarks, "well-nigh universal in the United States."[138] But agreeable intercourse and happy harmony did not remain the rule. After the failure to take Newport, while the French fleet was in Boston and despite good will shown by the mercantile classes to the officers, there was a riot, in which two officers of the fleet were dangerously

[136] Faÿ, pp. 87-8, from the Archives of the French Office for Foreign Affairs. Of Luzerne Faÿ writes that he was "gros, rouge, myope, et d'assez belles manières. On le trouvait correct et un peu routinier." Luzerne was especially useful in calming quarrels in Congress. Pp. 77-9. The Rev. Dr. Cooper was noted for his bold expressions; "although," wrote de Broglie, "he expresses himself with difficulty in French, he understands it perfectly well, knows all our best authors, and has sometimes cited, even in the pulpit, passages from Voltaire and Jean Jacques Rousseau." "Narrative of the Prince de Broglie," *Magazine of American History*, I, 378.

[137] John Adams to Abigail Adams, Passy, 18 December, 1778. *Letters*, II, 38.

[138] *Life of Washington*, II, 168.

wounded, one dying from his injuries.[139] In Congress there was continual quarreling about the personnel of commissions sent abroad, so that two parties developed: those who believed with Arthur Lee in the policy of playing France against England, and those who believed, like Franklin, in the equal union of two great nations; and the inevitable result of this unhappy squabbling was to throw suspicion on the good intentions of France.[140] Adams, back from France in 1779, reported that the American delegation was rent with jealousy,[141] and when he returned that same year, his blunders secured the ill-will of Vergennes and Franklin, the Frenchman coming to distrust and hate him.[142] D'Estaing, back from the Indies, failed to take Savannah in 1779, whereas the English over-ran Georgia and South Carolina, and the question asked by Americans more zealous than sensible, was why the French failed to do more.[143] Something of the sentiment of many may be gained from a speech by Simeon Baldwin, then an undergraduate at Yale, on the question, whether the alliance had been beneficial to America. What, asked the young debater, were France's motives? "A Nation so Subtel, So skilled in political affairs" hopes advantage from American products which she will exchange for "her Vices & Religion." America was now compelled to go to war with any enemy of France. "Though the Inhabitants of America will never introduce the Popish Religion of ourselves," yet climate, free land, glory, and "free toleration we allow, are sufficient invitation for those Popish Idolaters to spring to her extended Arms" and Catholicism "will soon spread with universal acceptance among the lo(o)ser & more vitious part of the People, & from them to others of more note till great part of the Inhabitants are tainted with it. There are not many Arts but what we understand as well as they, except those of Luxury & debauchery," and the French will soon "make us their military vassals."[144] There were many who thought so, including

[139] Perkins, p. 270; Stevens, *Albert Gallatin,* p. 13. The City Council voted a public funeral, which was declined.
[140] Faÿ, pp. 76-7. One of the unfortunate results of these quarrels was that Beaumarchais was not repaid for his losses.
[141] Morse, *Life of John Adams,* p. 154.
[142] *Ibid.,* pp. 180-2. This was June-July, 1780. Adams was then transferred to the United Provinces. Morse charges that Vergennes worked to prevent the recognition of the independence of the United States by Holland, and that Adams outwitted him. Pp. 193-4.
[143] See Faÿ, p. 90.
[144] Baldwin, *Life and Letters of Simeon Baldwin,* pp. 60-62.

English Whigs,[145] Boston merchants, Philadelphia Quakers,[146] and the Tories, who carried on a continual pamphlet warfare against the French, saying that they had not sent sufficient aid, that monarchical and Catholic France intended to gobble up the United States, that the king was stupid and the queen no better than she should be.[147]

The situation called for action. Lafayette pleaded and argued for a French army, and in February, 1780, it was decided to send one under Rochambeau.[148] John Paul Jones added to the prestige of America in French eyes by his enterprise under the fostering care of Franklin;[149] and in America Washington, who was looming larger and larger as the real executive, writing Reed, President of the Assembly of Pennsylvania, demanded responsible heads of affairs.[150] And if the Tory papers could spread propaganda, so too could the patriot press, supplied by the French ambassador with articles and discussions.[151] Freneau, released from his prison ship, published in 1781 his *Cantos from a Prison Ship,* sang Arnold out of New York in a Horation ode, and celebrated the patriots and anathematized the British and Tories from 1780 to 1783.[152] On May 12, 1780, Rochambeau sailed from Brest with 5,500 men.[153] Greatly to the disgust of Lauzun, de Ternay, in command of the squadron, unlike d'Estaing, conceived it his business to get to America as quickly as possible, and refused to engage an inferior English squadron.[154] French stock in America went up again: the army from Europe was extraordinarily well behaved;[155] Rochambeau and Washington got along fa-

[145] See Faÿ, p. 75. They regarded France as "la plus implacable ennemie des idées philosophiques et de la liberté."
[146] *Ibid.,* p. 74 ff.
[147] The principal Tory organ was Rivington's *Royal Gazette,* analyzed by Faÿ, p. 74.
[148] On Lafayette's negotiations, see Perkins, pp. 284-297.
[149] Consult *Writings of Franklin,* VIII, for Franklin's share in equipping Jones, almost in spite of the court.
[150] Cf. Merlant, pp. 106-110.
[151] Faÿ, pp. 88-89, cites a number of instances. He notes that in comedies of the day one finds that the Tories curse the French Alliance as the principal cause of American independence (*The Motley Assembly,* a farce, Boston, 1779); that Pelatiah Webster was insisting that the Americans should revise their tax-systems to avoid imposing on French generosity; and that the papers, to avoid the Tory charge that the French were governed by an absolute monarch, insisted on the alliance between the two peoples.
[152] Austin, *Philip Freneau,* pp. 121-138.
[153] So says Lauzun in his *Mémoires,* p. 141. Perkins says May 3.
[154] *Ibid.*
[155] Robin, *Nouveau Voyage,* pp. 35 ff.; Lauzun, *Mémoires,* pp. 142-3

mously, and the young French officers agreed that if Franklin was the Nestor of America, Washington was its Agamemnon.[156] Straws show the direction of the wind. When the coach containing Rochambeau broke down on its way to the American camp, a wheelwright, stricken with malaria, worked most of the night without pay that the French general might keep his engagement.[157]

But Howe had thirteen thousand men in New York, Rodney arrived from the West Indies with thirty-one ships, and an attack on New York did not seem feasible.[158] Washington, feeling the need for more men, dispatched young Colonel Laurens to Paris to ask for more men and money. Laurens was dashing, if nothing else; he delivered a spirited rebuke to Vergennes and insisted on presenting his memorial to the King in person; but, backed by the genius of Franklin, Laurens was assured of a further loan of 1,500,000 livres, and told that de Grasse would be directed to sail to America with twenty-five ships-of-the-line.[159] It was the beginning of the end. On the news of the arrival of de Grasse the Philadelphians crowded in front of the house of the French minister, shouting "Vive le Roi!"[160] There followed the famous march of the French and American armies to Yorktown,[161] and the surrender of Cornwallis. Despite some naval encounters, the war, in Merlant's phrase, ceased of itself,[162] and there followed a remarkable period of fraternization between the French, quartered in Newport, and the Americans.[163] The French squadron under

---

[156] See for a characteristic view of Washington the selections from de Broglie in Balch, pp. 60 ff.

[157] Balch, pp. 120-21.

[158] Stevens, *Facsimiles*, No. 730.

[159] Garden, *Anecdotes of the American Revolution*, pp. 12-19. For a less enthusiastic view of Laurens see Perkins, pp. 333 ff. There is a certain irony in Franklin's letter to Laurens of May 17, 1781: "I would not attempt persuading you to quit the military Line, because I think you have the Qualities of Mind and Body that promise your doing great service & acquiring Honour in that Line. Otherwise I should be happy to see you again here as my Successor; having sometime since written to Congress requesting to be reliev'd, and believing as I firmly do, that they could not put their Affairs in better Hands." *Writings*, VIII, 259-260.

[160] Robin, *op. cit.*, p. 91.

[161] Robin, pp. 87-96; Lauzun, pp. 148-50; Perkins, chap. xviii; Merlant, chap. ix.

[162] P. 187.

[163] Perkins, chap. xxii; Lauzun, *Mémoires*, pp. 150-156.

Vaudreuil left Boston December 24, 1782.[164] There remained only the question of the peace.

If the years 1781-1783 were marked by fraternization between the French officers—by travels over the country, by hospitality received from Americans, by the gathering of materials for travel-book and diary by such officers and observers as Chastellux. and others—in the diplomatic sphere things were not so satisfactory. In Congress the division over France had never been wholly healed, and the future Federalists succeeded in placing John Adams on the commission to negotiate the peace.[165] Adams, despite his enthusiasm for French culture in 1778, had perceptibly cooled.[166] Jay, who was a member of the commission, believed that France had already secured sufficient benefits from the alliance.[167] Franklin, with whom Vergennes was on good terms, was not well most of the time, being confined to his bed. Vergennes, on his side, had many complicated interests to watch over, and his conduct in the negotiations aroused, perhaps unfairly, the suspicions of the American commissioners.[168] At length, after various complications had arisen, at the instance of Jay and with the approval of Adams, the American commissioners opened separate negotiations with England, and on November 30, 1782, signed a preliminary treaty of peace, despite the express conditions of the original treaty of alliance. Vergennes put a good face on this, but when immediately after Franklin asked him for a loan of twenty million francs, and when Vergennes had learned that the English would not surrender Gibraltar, he wrote Franklin that he was "at a loss to explain your (Franklin's) conduct, and that of your colleagues on this occasion. You have concluded your preliminary articles without any communication between us, although the instructions from Congress prescribe, that nothing

---

[164] The French during the war had 63 ships of the line, 3,668 cannon, 32,609 officers and sailors; 697 army officers and 11,983 soldiers engaged in the American cause; the total expense amounting to about $50,000,000. Keim, quoted in Merlant, p. 204.

[165] Morse, *Life of John Adams,* pp. 204-226. For Adams' early enthusiasm for French culture see his *Letters,* II, 20-23, 43, 51, 66-70, 35-36. For his opinion of Franklin in 1783, see *Works,* III, 300.

[166] His reaction against French ideas is shown in his *Defence of the Constitutions of Government of the United States . . . against the Attack of M. Turgot,* not published until 1787, but in answer to Turgot's *Letter to Price* of 1778.

[167] Faÿ, p. 116.

[168] Perkins, pp. 474-484; Faÿ, p. 114; Bassett, *Short History,* pp. 214-5.

shall be done without the participation of the King."[169] Franklin apologized,[170] and Vergennes lent the money— an unheard of piece of generosity.[171] Yet perhaps Faÿ is right in regarding the treaty as rather a hint of Anglo-American reconciliation than the crown of the Franco-American alliance.[172]

If there was hostility in diplomatic affairs, it was not perceptible to the great mass of the people in either country.[173] Perhaps, as Schoepf remarked in 1783-4, when he was travelling south from Philadelphia, the tavern signs bore the heads of Frederick II and some of the Georges, rather than that of Louis XVI,[174] but the fact was not significant. The people kept their sympathy for France in 1783 and subsequent years. Even after Vergennes ceased to pay members of Congress to vote for France,[175] newspapers in Baltimore, Philadelphia, New York, and Boston took pride in understanding France and doing her justice: the French press, they said, was not servile nor were the Catholics bigotted; Louis XVI was, despite British opinion, the benefactor of the United States; and on the death of Vergennes, they were loud in his praise.[176] French officers became members of the Order of the Cincinnati.[177] The ideas of the French philosophers were discussed in American newspapers, side by side with news of the French officers who had battled for America,[178] and in the great debate in the critical period, over American government, the theories of Turgot, Target, Montesquieu, and Rousseau were discussed by Jefferson, Madison, Monroe, and other leaders.[179] Marbois,

[169] *Writings of Franklin,* VIII, 641.
[170] *Ibid.,* p. 642.
[171] Franklin had asked for twenty millions; Vergennes could lend only six.
[172] Faÿ, p. 113.
[173] *Ibid.,* p. 119.
[174] Schoepf, *Travels in the Confederation,* I, 125.
[175] Faÿ, pp. 118-9, from the French Archives.
[176] See the instances collected by Faÿ, p. 139 and notes. Chastellux (*Voyages,* I, 32) says that Governor Trumbull was working on a history of the American Revolution when he visited him in Hartford in 1780; the introduction was addressed to Luzerne. Chastellux later bought a copy and found the work superficial.
[177] Fosdick, *French Blood in America,* p. 399. The Order was denounced by many including Ædanus Burke of South Carolina. On the whole debate see Faÿ, p. 131.
[178] Faÿ, pp. 138-9.
[179] Target in 1784 sent a long letter to the New York journals, whence it passed into all the American papers. He told the Americans that Europe had its eyes fixed on them, that they were bound to make their constitutions succeed; and that they must follow virtuous manners if they would be happy. He advised them to develop national education, avoid riches and conquests, have fraternal feasts, and cultivate virtuous passions, Faÿ, p. 131.

who succeeded Luzerne, and Otto, who succeeded Marbois, continued to keep up relations with the intellectual life of the country.[180] Crèvecoeur suggested to Ethan Allen in 1785 that new towns in Vermont be given names that would commemorate the alliance, and tried to get the royal engravers to make a seal for the state and one for the college of Vermont.[181] Countless engravings, decorating the walls of so many old-fashioned American 'sitting-rooms' and 'best parlors' showed Franklin and Voltaire embracing at the memorable sitting of the Academy of Sciences, April 29, 1778.[182] The word "dauphin" apparently became common.[183] French manners came in,[184] and in Pennsylvania a constitution was adopted according to the ideas of Turgot.[185] Despite British propaganda,[186] despite the fact that after the peace, commerce between England and the United States had been resumed to the detriment of French commerce,[187] Franco-American friendship, it seemed, was on a firm foundation. The cosmopolitan spirit ruled in international affairs, and who could foresee the events of 1789?

[180] Faÿ, p. 119, and see chaps. x and vi above.
[181] Mitchell, *St. Jean de Crèvecoeur,* pp. 145-6. Luzerne county, Pennsylvania, is named for the ambassador.
[182] Morse, *Benjamin Franklin,* p. 286.
[183] "Mrs. Meigs is safely put to bed with a young *Dauphin* (in her esteem)." Baldwin, *Life and Letters of Simeon Baldwin,* p. 245, Nov. 3, 1782.
[184] *I.e.,* uni-cameral. Faÿ, p. 86. Cf. Adams' *Works,* IV, on democratic republics.
[185] Consult Faÿ, pp. 117, 138.
[187] Consult Mitchell, *St. Jean de Crèvecoeur,* chapter on trade relations, for the history of attempts to divert trade to French ports. Vergennes had hoped to please the Americans by giving them a free port in the West Indies. Faÿ, p. 118. Crèvecoeur circulated commercial propaganda among the American newspapers. See, for example, the *State Gazette of North Carolina,* IV, 158, January 15, 1789.

XV

Conflicting Forces in Politics
(continued)

1. ANTI-BRITISH FEELING AFTER THE REVOLUTION

DURING the troubled time of the critical period of France
behaved with an exemplary patience which contrasted strongly
with the dilatory tactics of England. On the part of Great
Britain there was no haste to compensate for the slaves she had
carried off, or to surrender the frontier posts in the North and
West, from which, it was alleged, she was still inciting Indians
to massacre American pioneers. It is true that the United
States, on the other hand, had been unable or unwilling to pay
British debts as guaranteed by the treaty, or to change the
American regulations against royalists.[1] No ambassador to the
infant republic from the Court of St. James arrived until the
autumn of 1791, and when he came he was without power to
negotiate a treaty of commerce.[2] France, on the contrary, had
been most amiable. France had negotiated a treaty of commerce
along with the treaty of alliance, from which great results
were expected to flow; it is true that American commerce had
not gone to France, despite the efforts of Crèvecoeur and
others to direct it thither, and American trade with England
and the British West Indies, it was amazingly discovered, had
now to pay tariff duties;[3] but still the French had made a generous gesture, they did not press too heavily for the repayment
of their loans, and American universities had got into the habit
of asking Louis XVI for books and professors, American
learned societies carried on correspondence with French savants,
the while that French savants wrote books to prove how good
and wise and virtuous the Americans were.[4] And although a
case could be made out to prove that the French government

---

[1] Schouler, *History,* I, 91.
[2] Bassett, *Short History,* p. 262.
[3] Schouler, *op. cit.* On French commerce see Madison's letter to Moustier in 1788, *Letters,* I, 430-3.
[4] Consult Faÿ, *Bibliographie Critique des ouvrages français relatifs aux
États-unis (1770-1800).* By 1781 "the Continental currency had ceased to
circulate and the springs of Continental credit were fast drying up. But
for the French alliance and timely loans procured by agents in Europe,
the American cause would have grown desperate." Schouler, I, 20.

preferred the Articles of Confederation, which left the country weak, to the adoption of a new constitution which would strengthen the government, it does not appear that any active interference occurred.[5] On the other hand, the views of French theorists in regard to the new instruments were studied and debated.[6] Almost all of the delegates were familiar with the theory of the separation of powers taught by Montesquieu, and written into the constitution.[7] Madison and Jefferson had for some years been collecting treatises on republican government, some of which were in French.[8] Franklin, observing the success of the Pennsylvania constitution, advocated the idea of his friend Turgot, that the legislature should consist of a single chamber,[9] an idea denounced by such Federalists as John Adams.[10] The American constitution, however, though it embodies the theories of Montesquieu, can not be said to have been greatly influenced by French theory, for Montesquieu admittedly codified English practice, and the constitution is a conservative document. France, however, looked benevolently on a government headed by the admirable Washington, in which Jefferson was secretary of state.

It is, however, to be noted that feeling in regard to Great Britain was beginning to divide. There were those, particularly among the New England Federals and the commercial princes, who found the need of closer commercial relations with their former sovereign, among whom, indeed, an Anglophile atti-

[5] Cf. Duniway, "French Influence on the Adoption of the Federal Constitution," *American Historical Review*, IX, 304-309.
[6] Cf. Faÿ, pp. 147-151; Duniway, *op. cit.*; Bourne, "The Use of History Made by the Framers of the Constitution," in *Annual Report of the American Historical Association for the Year 1896*, pp. 223-228; Haines, "Ministerial Responsibility versus the Separation of Powers," in the *American Political Science Review*, XVI, no. 2, May, 1922; McLaughlin, "Social Compact and Constitutional Construction," in *American Historical Review*, V, 470-490.
[7] Montesquieu had influenced the voting in the Continental Congress. Cf. *Works of John Adams*, II, 490-500.
[8] Cf. Bourne, *op. cit.*, 225-227. Besides Montesquieu, these included the *Mémoires* of Sully, Comte d'Albon, Gillies, Félice's *Le Code de l'Humanité* (13 vols.), and Stanyan's *Dictionnaire de Suisse*.
[9] Cf. Faÿ, pp. 149-50 and references.
[10] Livingston found fault with the two-chamber system in his *Examination of the Government of England* which praises Turgot; whereas Adams in his *Defence* (*Works*, IV, 271-588) attacked Turgot and upheld Montesquieu. The *Discourses of Davila* (*Works*, VI) were even more violently anti-French. The two works "were the cause of that immense unpopularity which fell like the tower of Siloam upon me." (Adams to Jefferson, 13 July, 1813.) *Works*, X, 54.

tude had been rather obscured than eradicated.[11] There were those who favored a monarchical government, including, it must be admitted, some who were friendly to France.[12] On the other hand, friction between the two countries was almost constant from 1775 to 1814. Adams, appointed minister to Great Britain in 1785, found his stay in London "far from comfortable," and reported that England had embarked on a policy of crushing the colonies commercially.[13] When, over the remonstrances of Ames, Lawrence, Smith, and the mercantile interests, a policy was initiated of setting up a tariff wall against Great Britain, the measure was only thwarted in the Senate by the powerful British lobby in New York.[14] The president sent Gouverneur Morris to London in 1789 to negotiate a treaty of commerce but in vain; the total result of Morris's mission was that "he never found the English congenial as friends or companions; he could not sympathize or indeed get along well, with them."[15] The British minister, when one arrived, was, as we have seen, without full powers, and the total result was that by 1794 the Republicans were clamoring for war; in 1797 "McClanachan told the President that, by God, he would rather see the world annihilated than this country united with Great Britain; that there would not remain a single king in Europe within six months."[16] Clearly something had to be done. In May, 1794, Jay was sent to negotiate some

---

[11] For example: "Congress received yesterday from Mr. Adams several letters dated September, not remarkable for anything unless it be a fresh display of his vanity, and prejudice vs. the French course and his venom vs. Doct. Franklin." Madison to Jefferson, February, 1783. Madison, *Letters,* I, 33.

[12] For the various projects looking toward the establishment of an American monarchy, consult Dunbar, *A Study of "Monarchical" Tendencies in the United States, from 1776 to 1801. University of Illinois Studies in the Social Sciences,* X, 1-164. The Comte de Broglie had some notion of founding an American monarchy, 1776-7. That the fear of monarchy was genuine and deep-seated we are prone to forget. As late as 1789 the *State Gazette of North Carolina* (January 29) reprints from a "London rank ministerial print" a paragraph applauding Rhode Island for rejecting the Federal constitution and the "French faction" in their "insidious attempt to raise up an Emperor and a Roman Senate upon the ruins of those divided commonwealths." (IV, 160).

[13] Morse, *Life of John Adams,* pp. 234, 238-9.

[14] Schouler, I, 92.

[15] Roosevelt, *Gouverneur Morris,* p. 229. The truth is that "he was at this time much more friendly to France, and was even helping the French ministers concoct a scheme of warfare against their neighbor." P. 230.

[16] Stevens, *Albert Gallatin,* p. 143. See in this connection chap. xi in Bowers, *Jefferson and Hamilton.*

530 CONFLICTING FORCES IN POLITICS

kind of treaty in the mercantile interests, and he sent back in 1795 the most unpopular treaty ever entered into between the United States and a foreign nation.[17] A storm of protest broke; the Republicans were furious, charging the Federalists with taking British gold; it was reported that the British had seized vessels carrying provisions (largely grain) for France,[18] and the Federalists were, despite the "Camillus" essays of Hamilton in defence of the administration, lukewarm in their support. If, the treaty once ratified, the indignation subsided,[19] we chafed under the imputation of inferiority. War and diplomacy combined to alienate us from Britain and to send us farther in the direction of France. With France we had a treaty of alliance; to France, as it seemed, British stupidity was driving us; and then, as if to cement the bond between the two nations, France, too, had her revolution, an event so important in the history of our relations with French culture that we must study it in some detail.

2. THE FRENCH REVOLUTION AND THE AMERICANS

The first news of the Revolution was hailed by Americans with universal delight.[20] France, which had hitherto mainly interested the cosmopolitan class because of its culture, was discovered by the country as a whole: "on cessa de parler des lumières des philosophes français pour louer la nation dans son ensemble."[21] The news was hailed with expressions of ardent

[17] No settlement was made for ships seized by Great Britain. Americans might trade with the British East Indies, but no ship of more than 70 tons burden might trade with the West Indian ports, and no American vessel might carry West Indian products to Europe. Privateers should not be fitted out in American ports against England's enemies; Americans serving against England were to be treated as pirates; and British trade with the United States was to be on the footing of the most favored nation. The senate rejected the articles relating to the West Indian trade. Bassett, pp. 272-3.

[18] Stevens, *Albert Gallatin*, p. 106. The "real and proper ground" of Republican antipathy "lay in its concession of rights of capture of French property in American vessels, while the treaty with France forbade her to seize British property in American vessels." P. 120. On American opinion of the treaty see Faÿ, pp. 243-9.

[19] Cf. Lodge, *Life of Washington*, p. 207.

[20] Lodge, *Alexander Hamilton*, p. 158. See on this whole subject, Bowers, *Jefferson and Hamilton;* Faÿ, chaps. iv-v; Hazen, "The French Revolution as Seen by the Americans of the Eighteenth Century," *Annual Report of the American Historical Society for 1895*, pp. 455-66. For accounts of the celebrations in various cities see McMaster, II, 90-93; Griswold, *Republican Court*, pp. 292 ff; Mrs. Lamb, *History of the City of New York*, II, 390-395; Scharf and Westcott, *History of Philadelphia, passim.*

[21] Faÿ, p. 184. "Le mélange de ces deux races (in the American Revolution) a permis au sentiment de l'égalité de se développer extraordinaire-

enthusiasm and lively sympathy, broken only here and there, in widely isolated cases, by some subdued utterance of distrust or doubt.[22] Americans had indeed scented the coming event from afar.[23] Freneau, attached to the Department of State in 1790, had served in his poems to keep Revolutionary spirit alive;[24] Joel Barlow in 1787 had written his *Vision of Columbus,* in which, as Voltaire had done in the *Henriade,* he had pictured the future greatness of his country, and had praised Louis XVI as the pride of the Bourbons.[25] Even Fenno, April

ment, car elle a rapproché des hommes placés aux extrêmes de la société." Faÿ, p. 90. In Picardy, said the *Columbian Magazine* in March, 1789 (pp. 173-5), the most virtuous girl has been for many years crowned with roses. What could one not expect of this admirable race? In the preceding year (II, 160-161, March, 1788), the magazine had praised the just and noble manner of Louis XIV!

[22] Hazen, *op. cit.,* p. 456. Madison to Pendleton (October 20, 1788): "France is certainly enough occupied with her internal fermentation. At present the struggle is merely between the Aristocracy and the Monarchy. The only chance in favor of the people lies in the mutual attempts of the competitors to make their side of the question the popular one. The late measures of the Court have that tendency. The nobility and Clergy, who wish to accelerate the States-General, wish at the same time to have it formed on the ancient model, established on the feudal idea, which excluded the people almost altogether. The Court has at length agreed to convene this Assembly in May, but is endeavoring to counteract the aristocratic policy, by admitting the people to a greater share of representation. In both the parties there are some real friends to liberty, who will probably take advantage of the circumstances to promote their object. Of this description on the anti-court side is our friend the Marquis. It is not true, I believe, that he is in the Bastile, but true that he is in disgrace, as the phrase there is." The next day Madison sent the identical information to Washington. *Letters,* I, 429.

[23] An important event was Lafayette's visit to this country in 1784. Madison to Jefferson: Lafayette has received in New York "a continuation of those marks of cordial esteem and affection which were hinted in my last. The Gazettes herewith enclosed will give you samples of them. Besides the personal homage he receives, his presence has furnished occasion for fresh manifestations of those sentiments toward France which have been so well merited by her, but which her Enemies pretended would soon give way to returning affection for Great Britain. In this view, a republication of those passages in the Gazettes of France may be of advantage to us. They will at least give pleasure to the Friends of the Marquis." *Letters,* I, 101. As evidencing the good relations between the two countries, one notes that when Washington visited Portsmouth in 1788, he received a royal salute from the French ship Teneriffe. Griswold, *Republican Court,* p. 195.

[24] Faÿ, p. 144; Forman, *The Political Activities of Philip Freneau,* p. 26-7; Austin, *Philip Freneau,* chap. viii.

[25] On the other hand the Hartford wits published in 1786-87 *The Anarchiad,* a satire directed against the French philosophers like de Pauw, Target, Raynal, Mably, Mirabeau, and Hilliard d'Auberteuil, who insisted on giving advice to the Americans when they had themselves not thrown off despotism. Faÿ, pp. 145-6. See Parrington, *The Connecticut Wits.*

18, 1789, said that although the American Revolution was to have a great influence on Europe, no one could foresee the astonishing events which have occurred since "our generous and magnanimous ally, the French nation, by its published expressions of the laws, its government, and its liberty, gives proof of a noble ardor in the best of causes."[26] Long extracts began to appear in American papers from speeches and discourses by Moreau de Saint-Méry, Rabaut Saint-Étienne, Voltaire, Necker, and Mirabeau; memoirs of the Bastille, real or feigned, and poems in praise of its capture. Nobody is blamed except the privileged classes, and the king; Lafayette, the patriots, and the army are praised.[27] In 1788, "a French gentleman of distinction at New York" had written that "the flame of revolt, which she fostered in America, recoils on the vitals of France; and, tho' smothered for a time, by the habits of popular subjects, it will yet break forth with irresistible rage, and, in the end, extinguish her monarch,"[28] but for the moment Louis XVI was more popular than ever. It was known that American constitutions, state and national, had been translated into French and circulated for the benefit of the "patriots"; Franklin himself had helped to disseminate them, and Vergennes had had a copy; and American constitutional precedent played its part in the earliest deliberations of the assembly.[29] In Congress, the party of Jay diminished; and even John Adams, disgusted with England, praised the policy of Wash-

---

[26] Quoted in Faÿ, pp. 184-5, who notes that in the smallest towns and villages newspapers that had hitherto given no news from France, carried information on the French Revolution.

[27] Faÿ, p. 185 and references. "Thank God, the Bastile is no more, "exclaimed the *State Gazette of North Carolina* (November 19, 1789), express-the common American attitde.

> The scene is chang'd—the infernal walls are raz'd,
> And let the people—and high Heaven be praised.

Ibid., October 5, 1789.

[28] *American Museum*, IV, August, 1788, p. 74.

[29] It was responsible for the declaration of rights; and as the framing of a constitution went on, discussion was illuminated by an ardent debate among Turgot, Price, John Adams, Mably, William Livingston, Condorcet, Dupont de Nemours, and Brissot de Warville. Among the later revolutionary groups Mounier was in constant consultation with Lafayette; Jefferson continually gave advice, and is to some degree responsible for the absence of any system of checks and balances in the French constitution. Bourne, "American Constitutional Precedents in the French Assembly," *American Historical Review*, VIII, 466-86. *The Discourses on Davila* of Adams was a reply to Condorcet. Merriam, *History of American Political Theories*, p. 124. The Declaration of the Rights of Man was often reprinted in American newspapers.

ington, as did the clergy and the conservative classes.[30] Jefferson, writing from France, supplied his friends with accounts of the struggle,[31] and served as an intellectual liaison officer between groups in the two countries.[32] Jefferson, it is true, knew only the upper class, and neither the French bourgeoisie nor the peasants came within his ken,[33] but on his return he profoundly impressed American opinion by his serenity.[34] The Americans rejoiced.

Why not? The particulars of the French Revolution from day to day filled the journals and flooded the drawing-rooms.[35] Not only the drawing-rooms rejoiced—there the idéologues held sway—but in the streets the people of no importance, in Hamilton's unfortunate phrase, accepted the news of the French Revolution as evidence of the progress of democracy. Let us borrow from Mr. Bowers' excellent study for the moment:

As the real significance of the struggle began to take form, with the crowned heads of the Old World marching in serried ranks under the leadership of Brunswick on the French frontier, the excitement was electric; and when they were turned back by the gallant resistance of the Revolutionists, the floodgates of enthusiasm broke. One prolonged, triumphant shout went up from the masses. The "people of no particular importance" somehow felt that the victory was theirs. They had been a little indifferent, these men of the shops, taverns, wharves, and the frontier, over the disputed financial and economic policies of their country, but they could understand the meaning of "liberty, equality, fraternity." It meant democracy. Thus the news of the French victories shook the bells in the New York steeples, Tammany celebrated with song, shout, and speech in her wigwam, and the bung was knocked out of the barrel of illiterate oratory in the beer saloons. . . . The enthusiasm swept over the country, and the scenes of riotous joy at Mr.

[30] Faÿ, p. 187. Morse visited Moustier, the French ambassador, the latter consenting to insert in Morse's *Geography* passages on France, and the only American geography was pro-French in tone. Moustier was popular. "I have informed you already that Madam Brehan is every day recovering from the disesteem and neglect into which reports had thrown her, and that Moustier is also become more and more acceptable, at least less and less otherwise. His commercial ideas are probably neither illiberal nor unfriendly to this country. The contrary has been supposed." Madison to Jefferson (1789), *Letters,* I, 472-3.
[31] He was the American minister in Paris from 1784-1789.
[32] See his correspondence with James Madison, Jay, John Adams, Shippen, and others, *Works* (Washington edition), II, 553-591; III, 3-123. Madison in turn often passed on this information to others. Cf. Madison *Letters,* I, 429, 493-4 (to Pendleton) for this relaying of information.
[33] Cf. Faÿ, pp. 162-4, 173-8.
[34] Faÿ, p. 186; Stevens, *Albert Gallatin,* p. 105.
[35] Griswold, *Republican Court,* p. 296; Bowers. *Jefferson and Hamilton,* chap. x; Willis, *The Charleston Stage,* p. 236

Grant's fountain tavern in Baltimore, were imitated at Plymouth, Princetown, Fredericksburg, Norfolk, Savannah, Charleston, Boston, Philadelphia.

In Boston there was a salute of cannon at the castle, and a picturesque procession moved, fluttering French and American flags, bearing a roasted ox of a thousand weight for the barbecue and a hogshead of punch to wash it down, while girls and women waved from the windows, boys shouted from the roofs, and the frenzied throng roared approval to the eloquence of Charles Jarvis, the Jeffersonian leader, and to the Revolutionary poem by "Citizen" Joseph Croswell. The cheers of Boston were echoed back from Charleston, where the artillery boomed in the day, mingling its thunder with the bells of Saint Michael's.[36] Only "the pen of a Burke could describe the scene on State Street" packed with exultant humanity, with men looking down from the chimney tops, while "bevies of amiable and beautiful women" blessed the marchers with their smiles from the balconies of the houses. On to Saint Philip's tramped the crowd for religious exercises, for these men were . . . decent citizens, moved to the depths by the defeat of the persecutors of France.[37]

The newspapers and magazines were filled with news from France, either directly or by way of Great Britain.[38] Jefferson,

[36] See note 81 below.

[37] Bowers, *op. cit.*, pp. 207-8. The phrases in quotations are from the contemporary accounts in the *Centinel*.

[38] Perhaps a good notion of the extent and character of these items can be gained by following through the files of the *State Gazette of North Carolina* (Edenton) for 1789, a paper neither violently pro-Gallic nor pro-British. On January 26, 1789, there is a London despatch of December 10, giving news of the Assembly of Notables on the question of equality of representation. April 16, reprinted from a London letter, there is "intelligence from Paris" which gives news of the debate over the status of the Tiers État and the question of representation; as also a paragraph abusing the *lettre de cachet*. June 18 a "gentleman from Paris" writes to his friend in Boston under date of February 20, saying that "France has a most fortunate time to establish her constitution. Light and knowledge are springing up, and the gospel of civil liberty is spreading like the rays of the morning. Pamphlets and hand-bills without number circulate as they did in America, and have the same spirit. A great degree of order is preserved. The assembling of the States-General, will be the epoch of the glory of this country; by uniting the Majesty of the King with the greater majority of the people, that union will be produced which will render this the most powerful nation in Europe." (New York heading.) On June 25, a letter from Paris dated March 16 announces that 'all . . . bears a very unfavorable appearance for the general tranquility of the kingdom," but another letter from Kingston of April 22 announces that the French now make themselves happy in the idea of a free press. July 16, there is a fragment of a letter from Paris (reprinted from a London paper) describing an uprising at Thoulouse and the burning of nineteen "puppets" of the royal tribunal. On July 30 a letter (Berlin to London, March 7-April 23) gives a laudatory account of the possibilities of liberty and progress. On July 23 a London letter describes corn riots in the French provinces (April 10). August 20 the King's Speech to the States-General of April 27, 1789, is given in summary, together with the royal instructions to that body; and a Boston

before he returned, was telling his friends that "there is not a crowned head in Europe whose talents or merits would entitle him to be elected a vestryman by the people of any parish in America."[39] He also had something to say, as his enemies were not to forget, about "once in twenty years watering the tree of liberty with the blood of tyrants."[40] As early as 1788 (July 22) paper is quoted as saying that the eyes of the French are on the States-General. September 3, "by express from Paris" to London of May 27, one learns that the clergy are sagacious and moderate, that the Commons are startled at the view of their own importance, and that all agree "THAT THE PEOPLE SHOULD BE FREE." Extracts from Necker's speech of May 9 and the instructions (cahiers) to put down the slave trade are given. September 17, a London despatch (June 18) announces the determination of the Third Estate to constitute itself the States-General. September 24 there is a despatch from Paris of June 21 containing an account of the Oath of the Tennis Court: "All Paris is in the greatest consternation"; and a long and favorable history of the Revolution to date, comes from London (June 29). October 1, the storming of the Bastille occupies over a third of the paper, together with a description of uprisings at Rennes, Rouen, etc. October 8 one finds a Paris despatch of July 18, telling of the King's going to Paris where "two hundred thousand citizens, orderly, and all in arms," await him; Bailly's speech of welcome; the national cockade in the royal hat; and speeches by Moreau de St-Méry and Lally Tolendal. This is "one of the greatest and most glorious revolutions that ever took place in the annals of mankind." A London dispatch of July 15 in the same issue gives ten articles of the new constitution as reported by a committee to the Assembly. October 15 one finds a good deal of French news, including a colorless account of Foulon's death, although the grass-eating speech is known and quoted. The correspondence between Louis and Necker is given in full; as also a good many items in the new constitution. One-half the paper is devoted to French news. October 22, Paris and London dispatches are darker in tone: there is want of supreme power in France; there are mobs in the provinces and banditti in the country; and various tales of atrocities. The Declaration of the night of August 4 is given in full. November 29 the same kind of dispatch is given, and mob violence and politics constitute the French news for the rest of the year. November and December issues contain a good many poems and articles on the Bastille. The issue for December 31 contains this gem, reprinted from the London *Morning Chronicle:*

"What is the King?
A poor thing.
What is the Queen?
In the spleen.
What is the nation?
Kick'd out of its station.
What are the States?
What all the world hates.
What are they doing?
Undoing.
            etc., etc., etc.

By December 1789 and the opening months of January 1790 the tone of the dispatches is distinctly hostile. Edenton, it will be remembered, is a provincial "city" and a fair representative of the average opinion of the country.

[39] Quoted in Schouler, I, 64.
[40] Cf. Lodge, *Life of Washington,* II, 27.

Brissot de Warville found that the wife of the innkeeper in Salem and her daughters were admirers of M. D'Epréminil, "a Brutus, just arrested by the parlement of Paris,"[41] and the same writer describes the toast that was drunk to Lafayette in New York.[42]

Indeed, from 1789 to 1793 our politics became Gallican, and so did the topics of our conversation, the plays in our theaters, the topics of our letters, the articles in our magazines. Thus *The Columbian Magazine* in February, 1790, prints the congratulations of the British Revolutionary Society to the National Assembly of November 4, 1781; and throughout the year minimizes the disturbances in France.[43] When, at Gray's Gardens in Boston a concert was held on July 5, 1790, there was an "ode," which the *Columbian* promptly printed:

> May Gallia's and Columbia's hands
> Be joined by freedom's sacred bands,
> Till time shall be no more,

they sang on that interesting occasion.[44]   Down in Fredericktown, Maryland, they were debating the merits of the two Revolutions, as well as the merits of Brissot, Chastellux and Crèvecoeur.[45] By 1793 the *North-Carolina Journal* was lyrically proclaiming:

> O FRANCE! the world to thee must owe
> A debt they ne'er can pay:
> The rights of man you bid them know,
> And kindle reason's day.
> COLUMBIA, in your friendship blest,
> Your gallant deeds shall hail,
> On the same ground our fortunes rest,
> Must flourish or must fail,

and, in *Stanzas on the Unfortunate Emigrants from Cape-Francais,* poetically hoped that the heart of Charity would expand and that the poor exile might bless the happy land "That chear'd his heart oppress'd with many a woe," all in the

[41] *Travels,* I, 385.
[42] *Ibid.,* p. 137.
[43] Vol. IV.
[44] V, July, 1790, p. 57. In April, 1791, pp. 217-24, the *Columbian* was printing extracts from Mr. Paine's celebrated "Answer to Mr. Burke's Attack on the French Revolution," together with the "Observations on the Revolution in France, and the genius of the French Nation, etc., from a Young American gentleman, residing in London." (Pp. 215-6.)
[45] Bayard, *Voyage dans l'intérieur des états-unis,* pp. 36-38.

stanzas of Gray's *Elegy*.[46] When Franklin died, America was gratified to know that the National Assembly paused in its labors long enough to hear addresses by Mirabeau, Lafayette, Rochefoucauld, Sieyès, Fauchet, and Condorcet; that mourning was worn for three days; and that the "grain market," the place of meeting was draped in black.[47] Morris, who had succeeded Jefferson in Paris, wrote back home of the events. Joel Barlow published in France his *Address to the Privileged Orders* and offered the Americans *The Conspiracy of Kings* to read.[48] In *The American Museum* for July, 1792, Lafayette is poetically exhorted by "An American" to "Cover the despot with disgrace and shame," and "him exalt who now in slavery groans," whatever that may mean.[49] Noah Webster, classmate

[46] January 16, 1793, August 21, 1793. The second poem is by "Orlando."

[47] Griswold, *Republican Court*, pp. 222-223; Morse, *Benjamin Franklin*, p. 413; *Works*, X, 490-3. There were commemorative sessions by the "Society of 1789," the Commune of Paris, and the Academy of Sciences.

[48] Faÿ, p. 202. *The Conspiracy of Kings* paints the league of tyrants; the advice to the privileged orders is to abolish feudalism. There are extracts from both in Parrington, op. cit. Here is a section of *The Conspiracy of Kings*, printed in the *Fayetteville Gazette* September 25, 1792, by "Jowel Barlow, Esquire."

> Say then fraternal family divine,
> Whom mutual wants and mutual aids combine,
> Say from what source the dire delusion rose;
> That souls like ours were ever made for foes;
> Why earth's maternal bosom, where we tread,
> To rear our mansions and receive our bread,
> Should blush so often for the race she bore,
> So long be drenched with floods of filial gore;
> Why to small realms for ever rest confin'd
> Our great affections, ment (*sic*) for all mankind?
> Though climes divide us shall the stream of sea
> That forms a barrier 'twixt my friend and me,
> Inspire the(e) with his peaceful state to war,
> And meet his falchion in the ranks of war?
> Not seas nor climes nor wild ambition's fire
> In nation's minds could e'er the wish inspire;
> Where equal rights each sober voice should guide,
> No blood would stain them, and no war divide.
> 'Tis dark deception, 'tis the glare of state,
> Man sunk in titles lost in small and great;
> 'Tis rank distinction, all the hell that springs
> From those prolifick monsters, Courts and Kings.
> Those are the vampires nurs'd on nature's spoils;
> For these with pangs the starving peasant toils,
> For these the earth's broad surface teams (*sic*) with grain,
> Theirs the dread labours of the devious main.
>   etc., etc., etc.

[49] XII (Appendix), pp. 9-10. In the same magazine for October, 1792, "the illustrious Fayette" is the subject of a brief eulogy by "Americus" "That such a man can be a traitor cannot, and will not be believed" (p.

of Barlow, published in 1794 a critical review of the French Revolution—he was editing a daily paper at the time. In the newspapers French news crowds out foreign news from less interesting places; and among the books advertised are Mirabeau's *Speeches,* the *Memoirs* of *Dumouriez,*[50] Rabaut's *History of the French Revolution,* Robespierre's *Reports,* translations of the different French constitutions, Paine's *The Rights of Man,* Barlow's pamphlets.[51] The stage became political and democratic: *Tammany,* one of the early American operas, was widely popular; it was "seasoned high with spice hot from France." There were other productions: *Helvetic Liberty, or the Lass of the Lakes; The Demolition of the Bastile; Tyranny Suppressed;* and *Louis XVI* by William Preston. The year 1792-3 is without parallel in American history. When the Allies retreated from the soil of France, "Americans gave themselves up to a most extraordinary series of celebrations in honor of the achievements of another country, which in no way directly concerned them."[52] South, west, north went the contagion: February 6 (the date of the French alliance), May first (St. Tammany Day), the anniversary of the battle of Bunker Hill, July 4, July 14, the Tenth of August, Thanksgiving Day, the anniversary of the surrender of Yorktown, were each made the expression of a "real French frenzy."[53] The Jeffersonians were delighted. The people were beginning to think for themselves.

But frenzies do not last, and enthusiasms wane. The democracy might sing *Ça Ira,* but the machinery of government was nonetheless in the hands of the Hamiltonians—that is to say,

196). In November (p. 290), Lafayette "stands completely acquitted from all suspicion" and in December (pp. 348-9) "the citizens of America" send an "Address from Americans to Fayette."

[50] When the news of Dumouriez's victory over the Duke of Brunswick was received in New York, the church bells were rung, the shops were closed, the taverns were filled; "never had there been such excitement since the great day, five years before, when Pennsylvania came under the new Federal roof," and yet New York was the center of the English interest. There, however, the Republicans put up in the Tontine Coffee-House a crimson silk liberty cap, inscribed "Sacred to Liberty," and declared it to be under the protection of the old Whigs, and defied the aristocrats to take it down. McMaster, II, 89, 106.

[51] Hazen, *op. cit.,* pp. 455-66. Cf. Faÿ, chap. iv.

[52] The news reached here in December, 1792; on the twentieth there was a celebration at Baltimore in the Fountain Inn; on the twenty-seventh a Tammany banquet in New York; on January 23, 1793, there was a "Civic Feast" in Boston; and religious services were held in Plymouth, January 24.

[53] Hazen, *op. cit.*

of the upper class, and the upper class did not look with favor on the revolution. Jefferson, writing to Hamilton, analyzed the situation with customary sagacity: "On the one side are, 1. The fashionable circles of Philadelphia, New York, Boston, and Charleston (Natural Aristocrats). 2. Merchants trading on British capital. 3. Paper men (all the old Tories are found in someone of the three descriptions). On the other side, are 1. Merchants trading on their own capital. 2. Irish merchants. 3. Tradesmen, mechanics, farmers, and every other description of our citizens."[54] There were some early doubters, including Franklin.[55] Dr. Thomas Coke, after vainly striving to convert the Parisians to Methodism in 1791, "retired from the country, carrying with him a full persuasion that the French were too much enamoured with their revolution, and too much enlightened by their new philosophy, to regard either the truths of Christianity, or the salvation of their souls,"[56] a view he was to propagate among American Methodists. "We have," wrote Madison to Jefferson late in 1789, "no late information from Europe except through the English papers, which represent the affairs of Paris as in the most ticklish state. . . . It can be little doubted that the patriots have been abandoned, whether from impotency in France, misconduct in them, or from what other cause, is not altogether clear."[57] British propaganda did not fail to dwell upon the rumor of massacre and bloodshed, and to ridicule the events of the Revolution.[58] The French Revolution ceased to be a distant adventure and became for many a menace and a danger. "The bolder half of republican America inveighed against the perfidy of monarchs, the more timid shrank shuddering from the spectacle of a fickle populace,"[59] and two parties were formed, the republicans and the federalists, the jacobins and the monocrats, the Jefferson-

[54] Forman, *Life and Writings of Thomas Jefferson*, p. 51.
[55] Note the dubious tone of his letter to Hartley (pp. 72-3) and to Jean Baptiste Le Roy (pp. 68-69) in the latter part of 1789. *Writings*, X. "Will the struggle in Europe be anything more than a change of imposters and impositions?" John Adams asked a correspondent in 1790. *North American Review*, III, 153-154, July, 1816.
[56] Drew, *Life of the Rev. Thomas Coke*, pp. 244-5.
[57] Madison, *Letters*, I, 380.
[58] Thus the Stockbridge *Star*, as quoted by Faÿ, p. 205, says (December 15, 1789) that France is in a state of complete anarchy; by 1790 many journals were playing up the massacres; and the New York *Weekly Register* by September, 1790, was referring to the foolish and despotic revolutionary régime.
[59] Schouler, I, 169.

ians and the Hamiltonians. Sometimes it was hard to say whether the divisions of American opinion were formed by the French Revolution, or whether the division of opinion toward that event was a result of the previous bias of men's minds. Certain it is that the conservatives in the United States followed the lead of the Tories and the Old Whigs in Great Britain.

For some years there was, it seemed, a pro-Gallican party and a pro-Anglican party; the pro-American party seemed to consist mainly of Washington. The first effect of opposition to belief in the goodness of the Revolution was necessarily to intensify the partisanship of enthusiasts.[60] Thousands of refugees from Santo Domingo and of émigrés from France helped to embitter the feeling—helped, on the other hand, to make everything Gallic *à la mode*. "Dancing schools, fencing schools, language schools, conducted by Frenchmen, French dishes, names, expressions, customs, dress, music, books, were the rage. Inns and taverns became hotels, bakers and pastry cooks became restauranteurs, French advertisements appeared in the newspapers." There was published in New York the *Gazette Française;* at Philadelphia *Le Courier Politique de l'Univers, Le Courier de l'Amérique,* and *La Chronique des Mois ou les Cahiers Patriotiques;* at Charleston, *Le Moniteur Française* and *L'Oracle.*[61] In English Fenno's *Gazette of the United States* derided Jefferson and the Revolution; and Freneau's *National Gazette* (both in Philadelphia) responded in like terms;[62] the one paper ran serially Adams's *Discourses of Davila* (this was the summer of 1790), widely copied by administration papers over the country, while its rival used the opportunity to destroy what popularity Adams had acquired and supported Paine.[63] Presently in the *Columbian Centinel* of Boston there appeared a series of essays signed by Publicola, denouncing Paine and the Jeffersonians; essays really by John Q. Adams, but popularly attributed to the elder John.[64] Jeffer-

---

[60] McMaster speaks of "the wild craze of 1793, with its liberty poles and red caps, civic feasts, Citizen This and Citizen That, the intense outbursts of democracy which made it impossible for a true republican to walk on Prince Street, or Queen Street, or King Street, or worship God in a church on whose wall was a rude imitation of the royal arms." McMaster, V, 279-80.

[61] McMaster, *op. cit.*

[62] See the studies of Freneau already cited.

[63] Cf. Bowers, pp. 82-87.

[64] This was in the summer of 1791. See also Faÿ, p. 209.

son, returned from France, gazed on the turmoil in mild dismay. Full of Paris enthusiasm, he had come to New York expecting to find there the same glow of enthusiasm for liberty, equality, and fraternity, that agitated his friends in France. But he found that the city was a hotbed of British Toryism, where people openly expressed their preference for kingly government. When he went to Philadelphia, he was ignored by cosmopolitan society.[65] So in 1790-91 party strife deepened in bitterness.

In the thirties and forties the ever active Franklin had founded numerous societies over the colonies, societies with an elaborate system of inter-communication. Now, in imitation of Franklin's scheme and in emulation of the Jacobin societies in France,[66] the idea was revived, and the extraordinary spectacle was offered to Washington's eyes of Democratic (Jacobin) societies scattered over fifteen states,[67] all clamorous against the policy of neutrality on which the administration had (1793) embarked. Behind the Jacobin societies there was a seething mass of excitement such as the country had never before witnessed. For instance, when young Stephen Decatur and a friend, J. K. Hamilton, were returning from a fishing expedition, they found an enormous crowd at Buck's Head Tavern, Philadelphia, celebrating the presence of the French minister, wearing the tri-colour and singing Jacobin songs. Decatur, who wore the blue (American) cockade was involved in a general fight, for the mob insisted that he and his friend don the cockade of the French Republic; and only the arrival of his father's apprentices saved him.[68] In the same city an innkeeper whose sign was a portrait of the Queen of France,

[65] Schouler, I, 174; Bowers, pp. 173-4, 354. Even in Virginia the cleavage between town and country over the Revolution added bitterness to the feeling. Madison to Jefferson, 1793: "The great danger of misconstruing the sentiment of Virginia with regard to liberty and France is from the heretical tone of conversation in the Towns on the post roads. The voice of the country is universally and warmly right. If the popular disposition could be collected and carried into effect, a most important use might be made of it in obtaining the contributions of the necessaries called for by the danger of famine in France. Unfortunately, the disaffection of the Towns, which alone could give effect to a plan for the purpose, locks up the public gratitude and beneficience." *Letters,* I, 582.

[66] Morse, *Benjamin Franklin,* p. 34.

[67] David Rittenhouse was president of the Democratic Society of Philadelphia. Peter du Ponceau, an officer of the Continental army and the best known Frenchman in the city, was secretary; and Alexander J. Dallas, secretary of state and once editor of a monthly magazine, was a member. McMaster, II, 109.

[68] Mackenzie, *Life of Stephen Decatur,* pp. 15-16.

was forced to daub a streak of red around the royal neck and stain her clothes with blood.[69] In New York the Indian Queen tavern across the street from Brannon's Tea Gardens was nightly frequented by Frenchmen and their partisans and there, when the moon was up, they sang *Ça Ira* and the *Marseillaise;*[70] and in New York John Butler preached unitarianism in 1794, for "the city was much infected with French infidelity, Mr. Butler was liberal, the people went in crowds to hear him, and the clergy vainly attempted to shut him up."[71] In the spring of 1791 Jefferson had received *The Rights of Man*. He straightway sent the pamphlet to the printer with a note of approbation reflecting on John Adams. The pamphlet had appeared in print with the note prefixed, there was much stir, and the published comment pro and con increased in bitterness until Jefferson's resignation in 1793.[72] At a dinner in Philadelphia which Governor Mifflin of Pennsylvania attended, a decapitated roast pig was passed around to represent Louis XVI; each guest put on the liberty cap, exclaimed, "Tyrant!" and plunged his knife into the pig[73]—so the excitement mounted. When Priestley

[69] McMaster, II, 175; Griswold, p. 295.
[70] McMaster, II, 237.
[71] *Ibid.*, pp. 237-8. The spread of the Revolution philosophy and of deism was undoubtedly helped by the growth of the Masonic order. (Faÿ, p. 228 and references.) The first Boston lodge, founded in 1733, has a large number of Huguenot names; it was followed by the Lodge of St. Andrew, chartered in 1756. Huguenots were favorable to Free Masonry because it was anti-Catholic; moreover, Washington, Paul Revere, and other leaders of the American Revolution, were Masons; and it was easy to receive sympathetically the doctrines of liberty, equality, and fraternity. The Friendship Lodge, established in 1793, had a considerable French element; and the Perfect Union Lodge, of 1781, was distinctively French. In Philadelphia the L'Amenité Lodge, organized by French refugees in 1797, seems to have been active. Fosdick, pp. 387, 392-3, 395, 296. In Charleston and New Orleans especially, whole lodges were transferred from Santo Domingo to the new world. See Rightor, *History of New Orleans,* the chapter on fraternal organizations. As late as 1824, when Levasseur inquired why Freemasonry was so much in favor in the United States, he was given an answer which shows the connection between the West Indies and the American lodges: the Americans "are often exposed to the risk of falling into the hands of the pirates who infest the waters of the West Indies, which we often visit. These pirates who rob and hang all without distinction of religion, have a particular respect for Freemasons, whom they almost always treat like brothers. I could show you, without going out of Richmond (Virginia), a great number of individuals, who owe the safety of their lives and property, to a masonic sign timely made, under the scimeter of the robbers of the sea." His informant was a Frenchman. *Lafayette in America,* I, 210.
[72] Lodge, *Washington,* II, 222. Jefferson was violently abused for offering Paine a passage from France on an American ship. McMaster, II, 594.
[73] Griswold, *Republican Court,* pp. 294-5.

came to New York in 1794 it was sufficient that he had answered Burke's *Reflections* and that he had been maltreated by an English mob for him to be hailed as a martyr.[74] By 1795 Fisher Ames was observing in the house that Britain had no influence. "France, possessed of popular enthusiasm, or party attachments," he said, "has had and still has *too much influence* on our politics."[75] In the West, following the proclamation of neutrality by Washington, writers in *The Kentucke* [*sic*] *Gazette* called loudly for American participation on the side of France—a policy echoed in many another Western paper.[76]

The year 1793 proved to be the turning point. From abroad came the news of the execution of Louis XVI and afterwards, that of Marie Antoinette. New England, which had been tepid in sympathy, was now the stronghold of Federalism, and was shocked by the regicide.

> When *Mobs* triumphant seize the rheisn *(sic)*,
>   And guide the *Car* of *State,*
> Monarchs will feel the galling chains,
>   And meet the worst of fate:
> For instance, view the *Gallic* shore,
>   A nation, *once* polite
> See what confusion hovers o'er,
>   A *Star,* that shone so bright.
> Then from the scene recoil with dread,
>   For LOUIS is no more,
> The barb'rous *Mob* cut off his head,
>   And drank the spouting gore.
> Shall we, the *Sons* of FREEDOM dare
>   Against so *vile* a *Race?*
> Unless we mean ourselves to *bare*
>   The *palm* of their disgrace.
> No! God forbid, the man who feels
>   The force of *pity's* call,
> To join those *Brutes,* whose *sentence* seals,
>   Whose hearts are made of gall.[77]

So ran the broadsides. And among the upper classes men were exchanging letters in which they wrote:

The spirit of ambition and of conquest, which the French republic in its cradle has already discovered, has alarmed England and Holland. France has been execrated in Europe for their ambition for universal monarchy; but the passion was imputed to their kings, Henry 4th. and Louis 14th. But the people are already giving unequivocal proofs of

[74] McMaster, II, 207.
[75] Stevens, *Albert Gallatin,* p. 124.
[76] Rusk, I, 149.
[77] Stauffer, *New England and the Bavarian Illuminati,* p. 80, note.

an equal lust after a universal republic. . . . I can only sigh at the prospect of calamities opening on the human race and pray God to avert them.[78]

In Philadelphia the ladies sang a plaintive air, composed on the execution of Marie Antoinette; sometimes they varied the words to Bradford's impromptu verses on Washington's sorrow for Lafayette's imprisonment[79]—whence presently some enthusiastic South Carolinians were to try to rescue him.[80] The refugees were naturally horrified, and succeeded in imposing their views on many in the cosmopolitan circles of Charleston, Philadelphia, and New York.[81] Conservative schoolmasters and divines joined in denouncing atheism and anarchy.[82] Hamilton was writing Wolcott, as he had written Lafayette, that there was need to fear the Jacobins,[83] and "Peter Porcupine" (William Cobbett), come to this country in 1792, joined with Fenno to denounce the French,[84] centering his attack especially on Priestley. The views of Burke, circulated in the original or in extract, influenced many, as did the anti-French

[78] John Adams to his wife, *Letters,* II, 125 (12 February, 1793), "Danton, Robespierre, Marat, &c., are furies. Dragon's teeth have been sown in France and come up monsters." Ibid., II, 120.
[79] Griswold, p. 337.
[80] Cf. "Olmütz," in bibliography.
[81] Faÿ, p. 211. On the other hand the pro-Revolutionary spirit in Charleston reached perfectly absurd dimensions. A statue of Lord Chatham which stood at Broad and Meeting streets obstructed traffic, and it was resolved to remove it in March, 1794. "By some mismanagement in the tackling for removing the statue it fell, and the head was broken off. The day following, a truculent article noticed this incident in one of our papers, as a happy prognostic of the success of the guillotine—to use their own words, 'as ominous to the aristocrats.' " Fraser, *Reminiscences of Charleston,* pp. 35-36. See his accounts of the civic feasts, pp. 39-47. Nothing is more delightful than the account of the procession of January 11, 1793, in honor of the National Assembly. The evening before, the bells chimed and a salute of thirteen guns was fired, which ceremony was repeated the next morning. The parade was headed by the Governor, the Chief Justice, Consul Mangourit, the orator of the day, Mr. Coste, the pastor of the French church, the judges, the chancellor, and other dignitaries. When he passed by the French Protestant Church, the Consul, as an expiation for the persecutions of Louis XIV, halted the procession, took off his hat, and saluted with the national colours! The day concluded with an evening fête at Williams's Coffee House, with toasts in French and English. Pp. 404-41. See the anecdote of the little French hairdresser who had seen the execution of Marie Antoinette, p. 43.
[82] Cooper attended a school in Albany taught by the Rev. Thomas Ellison, who contrasted Mr. Jefferson's "libertinism" with the approved morals of George III. Phillips, *James Fenimore Cooper,* p. 32. Cf. Adams' *Letters,* II, 172, 130; Dwight's *Travels, passim.*
[83] Lodge, *Alexander Hamilton,* pp. 253-4.
[84] McMaster, II, 208; Bowers, under *Porcupine's Gazette* in index.

publications of Rivington.[85] Even Jefferson had a few early doubts.[86] Morris, the American representative who succeeded Jefferson, had little love for the French nobility, but he despised the theorists who began the Revolution even, and hated their cruelty; he came to distrust French character until at length his original antipathy to England was swallowed up in his hatred of France.[87] Hamilton of course never varied in his detestation, differing from his friends only in believing that the United States could not go to war with this "vicious republic."[88] The age seemed restless. The spirit of inquiry, no longer confined to scholastic questions, was spreading far and wide, the people were uneasy and expectant and felt that the social system was threatened, especially by Rousseau and his king; even Gallatin, a *citoyen du monde,* by temperament, grew cool.[89] With the news of the death of the king and the excesses of the Revolution, a marked conservative and moral reaction set in, aided in upper circles by the utterances of the émigrés.[90]

But even then there would have been no open hostility, had it not been for the untactful diplomacy of the French, who seemed determined to provoke a breach. Moustier, recalled at the opening of the trouble, had not been sent back to the United States, although he was a good minister and a friend of Washington, the cause of the situation being, it is said, the intrigues of the

[85] Faÿ, p. 249 and references.

[86] Thus as early as 1787 he wrote Mrs. John Adams of the Assembly of Notables that "the occasion more than anything I have seen, convinces me that this nation is incapable of any serious effort but under the word of command. The people at large view every object only as it may furnish puns and *bon mots;* and I pronounce that a good punster would disarm the whole nation were they ever so seriously inclined to revolt. Indeed, Madam, they are gone when a measure so capable of doing good as the calling of the Notables is treated with so much ridicule; we may conclude that the nation is desperate and in charity pray that heaven may send them good kings." Forman, *Life and Writings of Thomas Jefferson,* p. 216.

[87] Roosevelt, *Gouverneur Morris,* pp. 170, 173, 175, 187. "Taine, in his great work on the Revolution, ranks (Morris) high among the small number of observers who have recorded clear and sound judgments of those years of confused, formless tumult and horror." P. 183.

[88] Lodge, *Alexander Hamilton,* p. 200. "It is more and more evident that the powerful faction which has for years opposed the government, is determined to go every length with France. I am sincere in declaring my full conviction, as the result of a long course of observation, that they are ready to *new model* our constitution under the *influence* of coercion of France, to form with her a perpetual alliance, *offensive and defensive,* and to give her a monopoly of our trade by *peculiar* and *exclusive* privileges." Hamilton to Washington, 1798. *Ibid.,* p. 258.

[89] Stevens, *Albert Gallatin,* p. 6.

[90] Cf. Faÿ, last chapter.

British faction and of Gouverneur Morris.[91] He was succeeded by Otto, whose conduct was certainly ambiguous.[92] Came next the notorious Genêt, the first minister of the Republic, whose conduct has become a standard instance of diplomatic maladroitness. Landing at Charleston April 8, 1793, he was received with unparalleled enthusiasm; and since under the terms of the treaty of alliance of 1778 he conceived that he was empowered to enlist troops and fit out ships, he proceeded to do so. His progress to Philadelphia was an ovation, and when he was coolly received by the unenthusiastic Washington (whom he described as a weak, foolish old man), he determined to appeal to the people, to the embarrassment of Jefferson, who finally was compelled to disown him. When in July, *The Little Sarah* sailed against the express orders of the government, Washington convened the cabinet, which determined to ask for the recall of Genêt and to exclude French privateers from American ports.[93]

To Genêt succeeded Fauchet, who had been sent to arrest his predecessor—a measure that Washington stopped by refusing him extradition.[94] Fauchet was the head of a commission of

[91] *Ibid.,* pp. 204-5.
[92] *Ibid.*
[93] Lodge, *Washington,* II, *passim;* Stevens, *Albert Gallatin;* Faÿ, pp. 214-224; Bowers, pp. 218-224; McMaster and Schouler, *passim.* Washington had refrained from seeing émigrés like the Vicomte de Noailles and many who had actually given aid to the United States during the American Revolution for fear of alienating French sympathy, so that he can not be accused of unfriendliness to France (Lodge, II, 148-9). Genêt proved impossible. Even Jefferson ended by denouncing the unfortunate fanatic with asperity. (Morse, *Life of Jefferson,* p. 141). Something of the opportunities which Genêt threw away may be glimpsed from certain passages in the Madison-Jefferson correspondence. On March 2, 1794, Madison writes Jefferson, upon hearing that the British fleet was being supplied from New York by American vessels, that "this is really horrible. Whilst we allow the British to stop our supplies to the French Dominions, we allow our citizens to carry supplies to hers, for the known purpose of aiding her in taking from France the Islands we have guaranteed to her, and transferring these valuable markets from friendly to unfriendly hands." What can one expect, however, after "the vast exertions by the British party to mislead the people of the Eastern states. No means have been spared. The most artful and wicked calumnies have been propagated with all the zeal which malice and interest could invent," and the blackest have fallen upon Madison, the mover of the Virginia Resolutions. *Letters,* II, 2-5. Or again, John Adams writes his wife on January 2, 1794: "The news from France, so glorious for the French army, is celebrated in loud peals of festivity, and elevates the spirits of the enemies of government among us more than it ought, for it will not answer their ends." *Letters,* II, 135. Genêt had merely to capitalize this popular spirit, and it is a miracle that the country did not go to war with Great Britain as an ally of France.
[94] Bassett, p. 267. On Fauchet see the excellent article by James, "French Diplomacy and American Politics," *Annual Report of the American His-*

four whom the new Revolutionary government had sent to gain the confidence of Washington and the government; to propose a new treaty of commerce; to allow French privateers to outfit in American ports. When an embargo act was proposed, he endeavored to enlist his "friends" in Congress to prevent its passage or secure its modification; and although he at first profited by Genêt's example, he soon allied himself with the extreme republicans, he was unable to frustrate the sending of Jay to England, and he concluded, as Genêt had done, by making a general appeal to the country. "A foreign minister," Randolph told him, "has a right to remonstrate with the Executive to whom he is accredited . . . but it will ever be denied as a right of a foreign minister that he should endeavor, by an address to the people, oral or written, to forestall a depending measure, or to defeat one which has been decided."[95] He was succeeded by Adet, who was little better,[96] the chief events of whose term of office were an unfortunate presentation of a French flag to Congress and Washington, the publication in Bache's *Aurora* of some pompous letters threatening vengeance if pro-Gallic measures were not carried out, and the discovery that the French had tinkered with Randolph who was compelled to resign as Secretary of State. In the meantime, Monroe, appointed ambassador to France, had got himself entangled in an unfortunate flag-presenting incident of another order, and presently Washington was obliged to recall him in favor of the cool-headed Pinckney.[97] With the coming on of the Adams administration, French affairs approached a crisis.

Party bitterness had never been fiercer.[98] Over the question of international relations and of internal government, the country was split wide open. On the one hand Britain had by 1794 succeeded in alienating the affections of her former subjects by a stubborn and dilatory maritime policy; and on the

---

torical Association for 1911, I, 153-163. Madison to Jefferson, June 1, 1794: "The bill for punishing certain crimes, including that of selling prizes, has been unexpectedly called up at the last moment of the session. It is pretended that our citizens will arm under French colors if not restrained. . . . The bill for complying with Fauchet's application for a million dollars passed the House . . . by a large majority. The Senate will certainly reject it." *Letters*, II, 18.

[95] James, *op. cit.*, p. 162. Cf. Faÿ, pp. 252-4, 224 ff, 229-232. For Adams' opinion of Fauchet, see *Letters*, II, 145; for Madison's, *Letters*, II, 4.

[96] Faÿ, pp. 254-5.

[97] Stevens, *Albert Gallatin*, p. 136; Faÿ, pp. 257-61.

[98] Bowers, chap. xv-xviii.

other hand the adoption of Jay's treaty in 1795[99] and the neutrality policy of Washington had practically, if not formally, destroyed the French alliance. Hammond, the English minister, had a large budget which he used generously where members of congress were concerned, or where writers, like Cobbett, could be subsidized.[100] When Ames denounced a set of resolutions in Congress in 1794 as having French stamped upon their face, "I wish," said Parker of Virginia, "there was a stamp on the forehead of every member to show whether he is for France or England. For my part I will not sit silently to hear that nation abused to whom America is indebted for her rank as a nation." The galleries applauded.[101] But when Adet was suspended in 1795, no successor was appointed, so much was the Directory offended by the Jay treaty; and American shipowners were told to look out for themselves and their goods.[102] Adams dispatched Pinckney, Marshall, and Gerry to Paris in an attempt to smooth out the differences which had arisen over the interpretation of the Treaty of 1778 and the regulation of trade, while at home the Federalists struggled for war with France, and the Jeffersonians fought to maintain peace. Unfortunately the French again blundered, and there followed the famous attempt to bribe the American commissioners on the part of Talleyrand, which, reported at home, first to the Federalists[103] and afterwards to the country at large in the publication of the XYZ correspondence in 1798, "utterly discredited the party . . . friendly to France."[104] A cry arose for war,

[99] Jay's treaty substituted a defensive alliance with England for a defensive alliance with France in effect if not *pro forma.* Faÿ, pp. 245, 246 ff. See Madison, *Letters,* II, 39.

[100] Faÿ, pp. 248 and references.

[101] Schouler, I, 266.

[102] *Ibid.,* p. 325. France in 1796-7 was at war with the two most formidable powers of Europe, Austria and England, one the mistress of Central Europe, the other mistress of the seas. The United States was the only maritime power which could be opposed to Great Britain; consequently the Directory tried to appeal to the American people over the head of Adams. Stevens, *Albert Gallatin,* p. 136.

[103] Bowers, p. 364. On the whole affair see him, chap. xvi; and Magruder, *John Marshall,* chap. vii.

[104] Lodge, *Hamilton,* p. 202. ". . . in the press and at public meetings . . . men rivalled each other in denunciation of France. . . . In the House of Representatives the change of sentiment was especially remarkable. The few Republicans who stood firm could do nothing more than urge that no action should be taken until the truth could be more clearly known. This is the tone, also, of Jefferson's letters during the intensity of the excitement. His disgust was as strong as that which he felt during the Genêt affair. He wrote as a man who felt his cause discredited; nor can we entirely

and Frenchmen became extremely unpopular.[105] By 1798 the over-zealous Federalists had succeeded in passing the infamous Alien and Sedition laws, under cover of which they hunted down the pro-French, Jeffersonian opponents.[106] The country expected war. Adams refused to send another minister to France until he was assured that the ambassador would have proper reception. In February, 1798, he informed Congress of the outrages which French privateers had committed within the limits of American territorial waters, including the burning of English merchantmen at Charleston, and an act was passed authorizing merchant vessels to defend themselves by force of arms, and another, authorizing the purchase and equipment of twelve ships for the navy,—all to the consternation of the Jeffersonians.[107] Out in Kentucky the furious frontiersmen were grimly passing the Kentucky Resolutions of 1798.[108] The Fourth-of-July celebrations saw the wearing of the Federalist black cockades.[109] What had become of the dreams of fraternity and the rights of man? Ten thousand copies of the XYZ dispatches were distributed, Talleyrand was burned in effigy, and the *Aurora* and other Republican papers saw their circulation dwindle.[110] When the Quaker, James Logan, went on his self-appointed mission to France, he returned to find himself hugely

acquit him of a species of intellectual juggling, when he maintained that not the conduct of Talleyrand, but Adams' address of May, 1797, was the chief obstacle to reconciliation and friendship between the two nations." Forman, *Life and Writings of Thomas Jefferson*, p. 71. See also Faÿ, p. 280.

[105] Volney remarks (1795-98) that while Englishmen, Scotsmen, Germans, and Hollanders settle easily in the United States, the contrary is true of Frenchmen. "I have observed with much regret, none of that friendly and brotherly good-will, in this people toward us, with which some writers have flattered us. On the contrary, they appear to me to be strongly tinctured with the old English prejudice and animosity against us. . . . There is nothing in the social forms and habits of the two nations, that can make them coalesce. They tax us with levity, loquacity, and folly; while we reproach them with coldness, reserve, and haughty taciturnity." *View of the Soil and Climate of the United States*, p. 17.

[106] For a clear, if over-colored, account of this man-hunt, see Bowers, chap. xvii, "The Reign of Terror."

[107] Consider, for example, John Dickinson, who by 1797, writing as Fabius, declared that the French Republic was the heir of Louis X who in 1315 had declared all Frenchmen to be equal; and of Louis XVI who had freed the United States. She was the daughter of Rome, and England was "Carthage." Faÿ, p. 256.

[108] On western pro-Gallic and pro-Jeffersonian literature in this period see Rusk, I, 211-2.

[109] Stevens, *Albert Gallatin*, p. 158.

[110] Schouler, I, 391.

unpopular in Philadelphia.[111] Presently American ships were
playing havoc with French commerce in the West Indies, and
fighting occasional glorious battles with French frigates on the
high seas—it was our "naval war" with the ally we had sworn
to cherish.[112] But the war fever died out in both countries.
Adams, courageous and lonely and deserted by his party, performed a great act of statesmanship when, after assurance by
way of Holland that the envoys would be received, he swung
over to the Republican view of things, and on October 16,
1799, dispatched a fresh set of envoys who, by September 30,
1800, had negotiated a new convention with the Directory.
The treaty was not wholly popular,[113] but the war—and taxes
—had been less so, and the Federalists had simply prepared
their own doom. In spite of the violence of the campaign
against Jefferson as an atheist, a libertine, and an idéologue,
in spite of American loss of faith in France, the Republicans
had their majority. Perhaps—who knows?—the election of
Jefferson was, as Faÿ would like to believe, a triumph for
French philosophy.[114]

3. THE REACTION UNDER JEFFERSON

Federalism was defeated, and John Adams stayed not to
welcome Jefferson into office, preferring to leave Washington
at four in the morning, a disappointed and bitter man. But
Federalism, in defeat, or rather in the process of defeat, yet
had a good many guns to fire. Every conceivable term of abuse

[111] *Ibid.,* p. 417.
[112] See Adams, *History of the Foreign Policy of the United States,* pp.
106-111; Faÿ, pp. 270-5; Bowers, pp. 414-428. The immediate cause of the
trouble was a Decree of the Directory of May 9, 1793, authorizing the
French navy to seize foodstuffs and private property of the English even on
neutral ships. For a complete history of the "war" see Allen, *Our Naval
War with France.* The value of condemned prizes was $700,000; the number,
85, not including recaptured vessels and small boats.
[113] Schouler, p. 478.
[114] Faÿ argues that the quasi-religious aspect of the doctrine of the sovereignty of the people is not derived from the Anglo-Saxon tradition as in the
American Revolution, but, as developed and interpreted by Jefferson, takes
on a character of universality, an absolute quality that shows the influence
of French philosophy and discussion. The fact that the interpretation and
application of the American constitution from 1788 to 1799 was a Federalist
interpretation strengthens him, rather than weakens him, in his belief. Faÿ,
pp. 295-6. Curiously enough, he has the support of Chevalier, who believed
(1834) that Jefferson "had imbibed in Paris the doctrines of the philosophy
of the eighteenth century." *United States,* p. 341. Jefferson's biographers
(Morse and Forman, for example) are inclined to flout the claim—perhaps
from patriotic motives.

was heaped upon the head of the sage of Monticello, but chief among these was the charge that he was a French infidel. New England, which, since 1793, had looked on the French Revolution and its consequences with horror led the country in that reaction against France which, beginning in 1797-1798, mounted in vehemence as the Directory pursued its crooked ways. In vain did Volney, Letombe (the French chargé d'affaires), Collot, Moreau de Saint-Méry, and the *Courrier Français* battle against the mounting tide.[115] In Philadelphia people were shocked by the XYZ correspondence, Volney's deism, the elopement of Alexandre de Tilly with Miss Bingham, and the flaunting immorality of Talleyrand.[116] In New England a great moral and religious "revival" which quaintly linked Federalism and Christian theology, under the leadership of men like Dwight, who had repudiated his early enthusiasm, taught the faithful that the Americans were the chosen people and that France was Anti-Christ.[117] In the universities and colleges of the East, students were saying that France had been governed by a succession of tyrants, to whom the Neros and Caligulas of antiquity are not worthy to be compared; and that the French Revolution had its origin in the intrigues and basenesses of certain individuals, while its progress has been marked by violence and horror.[118] Frenchmen themselves were no longer popular. Thus in 1797 Latrobe remarked that "there is in the minds of us Virginians a practical English unsociability to the French, and we are apt to mistake all but English, Irish, and Scotch for Frenchmen, as soon as we hear them open their

---

[115] Faÿ, pp. 275-8.

[116] Faÿ, pp. 305-6. Count de Tilly's "advertisement" seems to have been widely reprinted; I quote from the *North-Carolina Journal* of May, 13, 1799:

"From Philadelphia Paper.
1000 Dollars Reward

"As I have been deprived of my lawful beloved wife, **Maria Matilda Countess de Tilly** (late Maria Matilda Bingham, daughter of William Bingham, esquire) of Philadelphia, ever since the 12th. instant, any person giving information where she is, so that I may be restored to her presence and society, shall receive the above reward.

April 27   Count Alexandre de Tilly."

[117] On the character and amount of anti-Gallic literature from 1798 to 1800 see Faÿ, p. 283.

[118] This was at Princeton in 1798. At Harvard one learned that the French Revolution had annihilated society. In William Bigelow's poem on *Education* (1797), the French eat like swine and drink the ocean; they pillage even France itself. Cf. Faÿ, p. 303; Baldwin, *Life and Letters of Simeon Baldwin*, pp. 418-9.

mouths."[119] Talleyrand felt in 1798 that "in every part of America through which I have travelled, I have not found a single Englishman who did not feel himself to be an American; not a single Frenchman who did not find himself a stranger."[120] Dwight, travelling through New England in 1797, collected evidences of French boastfulness and French perfidy,[121] and published that same year his *Triumph of Infidelity* as a palinode to the *Conquest of Canaan*.[122] In Maryland La Rochefoucauld-Liancourt found that the Revolution was due to the destruction of the Jesuit order; Catholic Maryland was attached to France, but not to the Revolution.[123]

The incoming of Jefferson was fought with bitterness and foreseen with dismay:

New England looked upon the bloody and blasphemous work with such horror as religious citizens could not but feel. Thenceforward the mark of a wise and good man was that he abhorred the French Revolution and believed democracy to be its cause. . . . The answer to every democratic suggestion ran in a set phrase, "Look at France!" The idea became a monomania with the New England leaders, and took exclusive hold of Fisher Ames, their most brilliant writer and talker, until it degenerated into a morbid illusion. During the last few months of his life, even as late as 1808, this dying man could scarce speak of his children without expressing his fears of their future

[119] *The Journal of Latrobe*, p. 46.
[120] Quoted in Adams, *History*, II, 52-53.
[121] See his *Travels*, in which he collected all the hateful memories of the French and Indian Wars. Thus, in discussing King Philip's War, he writes: "To the efficacy of these causes of suffering (Indian cunning, treachery, and cruelty), were superadded, in those originated by the French, the power of all such motives, as the sinuous ingenuity of that singular nation could invent, their wealth furnished, or their bigotry adopt." ". . . the aid of European officers and soldiers was conjoined; the devastation and slaughter were sanctioned by the Ministers of religion; and the blood-hounds, while their fangs were yet dropping blood, were caressed, and cherished, by men, regarded by them, as superiour beings, and professing themselves to be followers of the Saviour." He contrasts with this Pitt's denunciation of the use of Indians in warfare. "At the same time," he writes elsewhere, "it has for ages been a primary characteristic of the French, as a nation, to study all means of rendering themselves agreeable to those, from whom they hope for any advantage," and he contrasts with this pliant spirit the "grave, unbending spirit of a Briton." *Travels*, I, 156, 157, 152. See his description of the attack on Haverhill by M. Perrière, and M. Hertel de Rouville, "the Gallic savage, who a little before had destroyed Deerfield," and who was now planning to "butcher defenseless women and children." I, 414-415. See also II, 260-261, 154-5.
[122] On Dwight see Adams, *History*, I, 96-97.
[123] *Voyages*, VI, 112-120. It is interesting to note that Francis Hall (*Travels in Canada and the United States*, p. 37, note) complains that "it is a curious circumstance that, while we accuse them (the Americans) of favouring the French, French writers invariably attack them for their rooted, and, as they deem it, blind partiality to the English."

servitude to the French. He believed his alarm to be shared by his friends. . . . In theory, the French Revolution was not an argument or a proof, but only illustration, of the workings of divine law; and what had happened in France must sooner or later happen in America if the ignorant and vicious were to govern the wise and good.[124]

When fires broke out in Savannah, Baltimore, Philadelphia, and New York, they were clearly the result of design: "The Jacobins, the shouters of *Ça ira,* the friends of the Sage of Monticello, had applied the torch" and "having commenced to burn the cities, they would soon begin to murder the citizens," and to attribute the fires to their natural causes was to pronounce oneself a Jacobin."[125] New England clergy warned their congregations in 1800 that the election of Jefferson would be the signal for breaking down the pulpits, burning the Bibles, and enthroning the goddess of reason.[126] No calumny was too black to circulate about the terrible atheist. He was a *sans-culotte,* a red-legged Democrat;[127] and Gallatin, his secretary of the treasury, was a Genevan by birth, a Frenchman in accent, a Jesuit in morals—he spoke the speech of the French, that nation that has robbed our ships, rejected our ministers, and, in the name of liberty, perpetrated horrors.[128] When Paine returned to America from France in October, 1802, aboard an American ship, New England was horrified, and the Federalists dubbed him Citizen Egotism.[129] In 1803 Alexander Addison, circuit judge in Allegheny County, Pennsylvania, published *The Rise and Progress of Revolution: A Charge to the Grand Juries of the County Courts of the Fifth Circuit of the States of Pennsylvania at December Session, 1800.* There are, the book declares, three great revolutionary conspiracies: anti-Christian, anti-Monarchical, and anti-social, and the author denounces the books and pamphlets of the democrats, the debating societies, the Jacobin clubs, and the Illu-

[124] Adams, *History,* I, 82-3.
[125] McMaster, II, 538-9.
[126] Schouler, II, 85.
[127] Stevens, *Albert Gallatin,* p. 107.
[128] McMaster, II, 584. Gallatin was Swiss, not French, in temperament wholly different from the crack-brained zealot, whiskey insurrectionist, and frog-eating foreigner depicted by the imagination of those who had never beheld him, and one of the ablest financiers in the country. Schouler, II, 70.
[129] Adams, *History,* I, 315 ff.; Schouler, II, 35-36. Paine's subsequent conduct was not tactful; Congress refused him a pension, and he died obscurely on a New York farm in 1809, the last years of his life having been spent as a hanger-on at Washington.

minati; vengeful democrats got him impeached.[130] Washington
Irving[131] and the Hartford Wits[132] joined in the hue and cry.
And the Republicans, though they could retort bitter phrases
about monocrats and monarchists, had little to say regarding
France, for in the midst of the Revolutionary troubles, there
was rising the ominous figure of Napoleon.[133]

The paradox of the Jefferson regime is that, whereas Jefferson rode into office on the votes of the democratic and frontier
elements, no president played so adroitly the cosmopolitan game
of international diplomacy. Indeed, no administration during
our period had quite so many or so difficult foreign situations
to meet. The United States was caught between the giant forces
of Napoleon and Great Britain. In French affairs Jefferson
had to deal with Talleyrand, the subtlest diplomat, and with
Napoleon, the most powerful ruler, of the age. At home, the
problem set by the Alien Sedition laws and the Naturalization
Act, inheritances from the Adams' regime, was still to solve;
not to speak of popular bitterness or the feeling engendered
by the rumor "that the failure to elect Jefferson president
would be construed as the sufficient inducement for hostilities
against the United States" by France.[134] Once again, whatever
internal interests may be paramount, the cosmopolitan spirit
ruled our diplomacy.

England, Spain, and France appear in bewildering succession as opponents in the chess game which Jefferson played.
In addition he was compelled to wage war (1801-5) against
the Barbary pirates. If, out of this muddle, Jefferson secured
so distinct an advantage as the purchase of Louisiana, if he
laid the foundations for the subsequent purchase of Florida, if
his presidency is starred with the Burr conspiracy with its
haunting shadow of international diplomacy,[135] Fox's blockade,
the Berlin Decree, the First and Second Orders in Council, the
Embargo Act of 1807, the Non-intercourse Law of 1809,
Rose's futile mission of 1808, and the Chesapeake-Leopard
tragedy of 1807, one sees how thoroughly the United States

[130] McMaster, III, 155-7. B. C. Lucas, a French juryman, tried to respond
to the original charge.
[131] Wilhelmus Kieft the Testy in *Knickerbocker's History of New York*
is a satire on Jefferson. Adams, *History*, IX, 210-211.
[132] See the parody on Jefferson's inaugural address in Stedman and
Hutchinson, III, 426-7.
[133] For the Republican "rally" of 1798-1800, see Faÿ, pp. 285-7.
[134] Morse, *Life of Jefferson*, p. 160.
[135] See Wandell and Minnigerode, *Aaron Burr*, II.

played the international game. Read in Henry Adams the story of Jefferson's diplomacy; it is instructive. He seeks in the best manner of the eighteenth century to play off England against Napoleon, Spain against France, Toussaint L'Ouverture[136] and the Louisiana Purchase—it is exhilarating, those crowded years, and on the whole, despite the Crillon fiasco[137] and the unfortunate results of Jefferson's Florida policy,[138] the United States played the game with considerable skill—for the mercantile economics which, despite Adam Smith, still reigned, could not foresee the disastrous results of the non-importation and embargo acts; or else the merchants over-estimated the importance of their carrying trade to France and England.

The United States swung alternately between Great Britain and France, but the swing toward France was not dictated by any great love for France on the part of the president.[139] A paragraph from the biographer of Gallatin whom we have found so valuable, is illuminating:

Freed from the menace of immediate war, the people of plain common sense recognized that the friendship of Great Britain was more dangerous than the enmity of France. They dreaded the fixed power of an organized aristocracy far more than the ephemeral anarchy of an ill-ordered democracy; they were more averse to class distinctions protected by law than even to military despotism, which destroyed all distinctions, and they preferred, as man always has preferred, and always will prefer, personal and political equality.[140]

It was gratifying to see the young Napoleon feed fat the ancient grudge the young republic owed the mother country. The First Consul (despite the intricacy of negotiations behind

---

[136] Adams, I, chap. xvi.

[137] "Count Edward Crillon," really a French secret police agent, made a social sensation in Washington in 1812, and, with one Henry, was instrumental in selling some worthless letters to the government for $50,000. McMaster, III, 444-7; Adams, VI, chap. ix.

[138] "Jefferson, in his pursuit of Florida, lost what was a thousand times more valuable to him than territory—the moral leadership which belonged to the head of democracy." Adams, IV, 339.

[139] In connection with the XYZ negotiations Jefferson wished that there were "an ocean of fire between the new and the old world." Stevens, *Albert Gallatin,* p. 144. "The more he saw of other countries, the more highly he appreciated the superiority of his own. He never ceased to make the abuses of the civilization of Europe, and even of England, a text from which to preach the education of the masses of his own country. This spirit was especially characteristic of his attitude toward France. It must be remembered that he saw that country under conditions never paralleled in the history of the world." Forman, *Life and Writings of Thomas Jefferson,* p. 39. For Jefferson's final view of Napoleon, see *ibid.,* p. 149.

[140] Stevens, *Albert Gallatin,* p. 168.

the scenes)[141] seemed promptly to assent to the convention for the purchase of Louisiana (March 2, 1802), ratifications were exchanged, and the purchase deprived the Federalists of their remaining laurels.[142] American admiration for Napoleon began early, wavered only as he took on despotic character, and, after his death, his faults forgot, wove around him their own version of the Napoleonic legend. Jefferson's first term marked the completion of four years of successful diplomacy directed toward peace.[143]

But worse remained behind. The stormy years of Jefferson's second administration are in marked contrast to the calm triumphs of the first. Grievances against British interference with American policy swung sharply toward France in the winter and kindred wrongs, gathered head and found impressive official statement in the president's message of January 17, 1806. The party of Pitt had been in power; it was the business of that party in England to win the war. As an inevitable result American policy swung sharply toward France in the winter of 1805-6,[144] a policy dictated in part by Jefferson's own distrust of England.[145] But the winter of 1806-07 promised to undo the work and even to bring the country to the verge of war with France. Jefferson urged the suspension of the non-importation act; and there followed the Berlin decree (November 21, 1807), harshly enforced, and the Milan decree of December 17, declaring that any vessel submitting to search by British cruisers would be forfeited. Jefferson was compelled to draw away from France. Opposition increased, especially in New England where British prepossession was strong, and the influence of the Congregational clergy and the ruling families were constantly pro-Federal; it was said in Massachusetts,

---

[141] In which Volney played an important part. See Chinard, *Volney et l'Amérique,* chap. iii.

[142] Schouler, II, 17, 40-45.

[143] Turreau "had resided hardly six months in the United States (this was in 1805) before he announced to Talleyrand the conviction of all American politicians that any war would end in driving from office the party which made it." Adams, III, 83. See him also II, 269.

[144] The winter of 1805-06 had been favorable to Turreau, who saw France control American policy toward Spain and St. Domingo; while a stringent Act of Congress prohibiting the importation of British manufactures brought within his sight the chief object of French diplomacy in America— a war between the United States and England. Adams, III, 423.

[145] "The dislike of England that showed itself so emphatically in Jefferson's subsequent career may be ascribed largely to Cornwallis' general devastation of Virginia, his own experience of wanton outrage lending a personal tinge to his bitterness." Forman, *op. cit.,* p. 31.

which looked on Jefferson "as a man of low cunning and French preferences,"[146] that the president had entered into a secret alliance with France against England,[147] that the Embargo Act was proof positive that England was to be ruined.[148] If, under the stress of circumstances, war was eventually declared against Great Britain rather than France, it was only because France would desist under protest, nominally at least, and because England would not.

Love of France grew fainter and fainter, however. In 1807 Cobbett, who, it is true, saw only what he wanted to see, averred that "more than half the people of America were already disgusted with the French bias of their government."[149] Hamilton's death had been laid to French influence, though minute guns were fired by the English war ship *Boston* and the French frigates *Cybèle* and *Didon* in 1804 when he died.[150] Barent Gardinier, Congressman from New York, wrote, or is said to have written, the letter composed during the secret session of December 19, 1807, and published in the *New York Evening Post,* which began the cry of French influence, charging that American policy was being made subservient to France.[151] But it is when we cross the line into Madison's administration that the hostility to France seems to increase. In 1811 in Massachusetts "the downfall of the Bank, for which those Southern lordlings were responsible, their project of new states to be composed of French Jacobins and monarchists, their war on Spain by invading her territories, but most of all their revival of non-importation against Great Britain at Napoleon's behest" were loudly denounced. Pickering wrote a series of articles in the Boston *Centinel* and the spirit of 1776 was invoked against France.[152] In 1812, after the Republican press had made no concealment of its active sympathy with Napoleon, even in Spain, "what wonder if large numbers of good citizens who believed Napoleon to be anti-Christ should be disposed to resist, even to the verge of treason, the attempt to use their

[146] Schouler, II, 175.
[147] *Ibid.,* p. 163.
[148] *Ibid.,* pp. 176, 180. Giles repudiated the idea in the senate. "He asked what are the means of French influence in this country? None. Of British? Language, jurisprudence, literature, Tories, and their descendants, blood connections, mercantile capital and partnership." *Ibid.,* p. 186.
[149] Adams, IV, 45.
[150] McMaster, III, 53.
[151] Adams, IV, 203.
[152] Schouler II, 323.

lives and fortunes in a service (of war) they regarded with horror."[153] This was the year of the "Baltimore Massacre"— a riot against Wagner, publisher of the *Federal Republican* and opponent of the War of 1812. The riot recalled the excesses of the French Revolution, and the murder of Lingan shook the foundations of society.[154] When Napoleon was finally driven from power, the French reaction to the event served merely to convince Americans of the essential irresponsibility of the Gallic mind.[155] Opponents of the war "rejoiced over Leipsic as if it had been won by American generals on American soil. The downfall of the tyrant of the world," it was said, "must give consolation to every virtuous American." And a public dinner was held at Philadelphia in honor of the Emperor Alexander, the King of Sweden, the German people, and the Spanish and Portuguese patriots, and liberated Holland; similar rejoicings were held in various Eastern cities.[156] On June 29, 1814, Gouverneur Morris addressed a New York audience on the overthrow of Napoleon:

And thou, too, Democracy! savage and wild! thou who wouldst bring down the virtuous and wise to the level of folly and guilt! . . . See the objects of thy deadly hate! See lawful princes surrounded by loyal subjects! . . . Let those who would know the idol of thy devotion seek him in the island of Elba![157]

In the Federal Street Church, Boston, the citizens adopted resolutions of congratulation to the Bourbons and to Christianity, praising Alexander the Deliverer, a document signed by the leading men of Boston, one which expresses the sentiments of New England and New York. In New York, Napoleon was a fiend, the French a nation of atheists, Frenchmen and frogs, Irishmen and bulls were equally the objects of ridicule. On June 5, 1813, at a meeting in Georgetown, Bonaparte is a second Lucifer, Russia has emancipated the world, and Madison concurred in the view, for he attends the meeting.[158] The Napoleonic regime, it is clear, drove us away from France. But not to England: there followed the War of 1812-1814.

[153] Adams, VI, 218-9. As indicating the attitude of the frontier, it is interesting to note that Cairo, Tennessee, was named in commemoration of Napoleon's capture of the Egyptian city. Michaux, *Travels,* p. 256.
[154] *Ibid.,* p. 408.
[155] Cf. McMaster, V, 34.
[156] I have postponed the intricate problem of the American opinion of Napoleon to the second part of this study.
[157] Quoted in Adams, VIII, 19-20.
[158] Fearson, *Sketches in America,* pp. 115-121, 365-7, 326-332.

Three times since its founding the American Republic had, by reason of its commercial interests, been forced into war: once against France; once against the Barbary pirates; and once against Great Britain. It is not without meaning that the Naval War with France resulted in a working agreement with the Directory for the furthering of American trade, or that the War against the Barbary states protected that trade, or that the War of 1812 was fought to further the interests of that trade. Here is expressed the cosmopolitan spirit of the seacoast cities as it dictates the international policy of the United States; throughout these years the republic is forced to consider itself a part of Europe. But the War of 1812 marks the ending of this domination by the cosmopolitan spirit. Begun in the interest of commerce, its results were temporarily to check commerce; begun by the mercantile interests against the hostility of the West, it ended in being fought by the West in spite of the mercantile interests of the East; begun as a war to protect seamen, it ended with a treaty which ignored all the questions at issue; begun because we were entangled with Europe, it ended by completely isolating us from the Old World. Henceforth our interests turned inward and landward; manufacturing increased; and on December 2, 1823, the Monroe Doctrine, that expression of the spirit of isolation, was enunciated. In international diplomacy the interests of the West came in time to triumph over the interests of the East.

3. FRANCO-AMERICAN RELATIONS, 1815-1848

The ending of the War of 1812 left a feeling of soreness towards both France and England. "In the event of a pacification with Great Britain," wrote Madison to Joel Barlow in August 1812, "the full tide of indignation . . . will be directed against France, if not obviated by a due reparation of her wrongs. War will be called for by the nation almost *viva voce*. Even without a peace with England the further refusal or prevarications of France on the subject of redress may be expected to produce measures of hostility against her at the ensuing session of congress."[159] And as late as 1819 Madison was complaining of the commercial policy of France toward the United States.[160] But the fall of Napoleon meant the downfall of the

---

[159] Madison, *Letters,* II, 541. See also his letter to Jefferson of May 25, 1812, II, 535.
[160] See his letter to Richard Rush of May 10, 1819. *Letters,* III, 130. The feeling was returned, if one can consider Beaujour's *Aperçu des Etats-*

Napoleonic system and the removal of grievances. However, American sympathy went out to the proscribed Napoleonic exiles who sought refuge in this country; and the untactful meddling of the French ambassador, Hyde de Neuville, who saw conspiracies where there were none, and threats of un-neutral conduct in paper warfare,[161] mildly perturbed the diplomatic relations between the two countries. The Napoleonic agitations eventuated in nothing more terrible than the Champ d'Asile experiment in Texas, and the attempt of certain devoted Louisianans to rescue the Emperor from St. Helena, an attempt thwarted by the death of the great man. The official Bonapartist paper in America, *L'Abeille Américaine,* advised the exiles to behave with more care.[162] On the other hand, Americans viewed the restoration of kings with abhorrence. "The principles proclaimed by France ought," said Madison, "to excite universal execration, and the alarm of every free people not beyond the

unis (Paris, 1814), typical. After discussing the physical characteristics of the United States, Beaujour goes on to discuss its political make-up; he thinks the balance of powers bad, and the government feeble; the people have no sufficing guarantee against their own indiscretions. (Pp. 70-71.) He traces the rise of the factory system (pp. 97-107), and thinks that the French, especially those from Santo-Domingo, have given industry and especially agriculture "une grande impulsion." But American commerce is growing rich at the expense of French and Spanish losses. (P. 101.) He does not like the army, the militia, nor the police. (Pp. 121-133.) He thinks the democrats love France only because the federalists love England, (p. 135), and though religious tolerance is admirable (152-3), our manners are crude, and the republic must soon split into separate parts. (153-5, 170-1.) He regrets that the balance of Franco-American trade is in favor of the United States to the extent of four millions of dollars (p. 179), and endeavors to teach the French how to meet American demands (179-187), a difficult thing since the Americans are prejudiced against the French by the British (187-8.) And against the maritime tyranny of England and the commercial greed of the Americans he inveighs bitterly in the last chapter of his book.

[161] Studied at length in Philips, *Les Réfugiés Bonapartistes;* and in Reeves, *The Napoleonic Exiles in America.* Hyde de Neuville was, however, helpful in the negotiations with Spain over the boundaries of Louisiana. Morse, *John Quincy Adams,* p. 115.

[162] This was the paper that Hyde de Neuville referred to as a "journal atroce, infâme, et dégoûtant." (Philips, p. 17). In January, 1818, Simon Chaudron addressed the Bonapartists in the United States as follows: "Le Français est trop prompt à s'offenser des ridicules qu'on lui donne avec une plate prodigalité, tant sur la scène dramatique que dans ses rapports particuliers avec des hommes aussi vains et moins bons que lui. Dans cette situation, qui lui rest-il à faire dans les États-Unis pour rentrer en possession de la considération à laquelle tout honnête étranger a le droit de prétendre. Nous osons avancer qu'il ne lui faut pour cela qu'un peu plus de discrétion dans son empressement à juger de tout et d'un peu moins d'affectation dans les démonstrations de sa politesse et de sa gaité, de tout observer sans rien critique, de profiter des avantages qu'offre un pays où les lois politiques sont plus hospitalières que les habitants, sans se plaindre de ces derniers." Philips, p. 18.

reach of her power. . . . She not only revives the obsolete and impious doctrine of the divine right of Kings, but asserts the right in every Govt to overthrow a neighboring one which reproaches its corruption by the precedent of the reformation"[163]—the turgid reference being to the French invasion of Spain. In the same year that this was written, the admirable Gallatin[164] was negotiating with Chateaubriand over the eighth article of the Louisiana treaty: Chateaubriand insisted on connecting a discussion of American claims with the treaty, and Gallatin refused to link the two matters, so that a deadlock ensued. Gallatin felt "that there was at that time no disposition to do us justice."[165] France as it was had lost the sympathy of America; France as it had been still called forth the liveliest expressions of gratitude and interest, as evinced by the triumphant tour of Lafayette in 1824.[166] But the affection evinced for the Marquis did not suffice to change American opinion of his countrymen, and the general detestation of Americans exhibited in the newly acquired state of Louisiana simply confirmed our citizens in their distrust of Frenchmen.[167]

Our relations with Great Britain were scarcely satisfactory. At first it seemed that, under the impulse of rejoicing over the downfall of Napoleon, anti-British prejudice had decreased. In 1820 Blow, speaking of the "supposed partiality of the Ameri-

[163] Madison to Richard Rush, *Letters*, III: 330. July 22, 1823. For an opposite view see *The North American Review* I, 91-110 (May, 1830).

[164] "Mr. Gallatin is highly respected by every one in Europe, and excessively admired for his talents. I fear it would be difficult to represent the country half as well, if he should decline continuing minister." Madame Jerome Bonaparte (Betsy Patterson) to her father, May 6, 1823. Didier, *Life and Letters of Madame Bonaparte,* p. 135.

[165] Stevens, *Albert Gallatin,* p. 353.

[166] See Levasseur, *Lafayette in America.* In Washington there were Lafayette ribbons, Lafayette waistcoats, Lafayette feathers, hats, caps, and so on. "Everything was honored by his image and superscription—even the ginger-cakes were impressed with his name. . . ." Mrs. Anne Royall, *Sketches,* pp. 175-6. Towns and counties were named for him; for instance, La Grange, Mo., was named for Lafayette's country-seat. Buckingham, *America: Eastern and Western States,* III, 163.

[167] See chapter iv, pp. 117-23. Genêt had caused trouble in Louisiana in 1794, when he induced the French Jacobins in Philadelphia to circulate an address in which the colonists were urged to establish an independent government. His principal agent in Kentucky, Auguste de la Chaise, a native Louisianan, endeavored to prepare an expedition against the Spanish possessions, the said la Chaise dying in 1803 as a general in the French army of Santo Domingo. Fortier, *History of Louisiana,* II, 155. On the attitude toward American occupation see the quotations from Laussat's *Memoirs, passim* in the same volume. Louisiana in general had been pro-Revolutionary and was pro-Napoleonic. II, 152. See also Butler, *Judah P. Benjamin,* p. 65.

can government to the French nation," says on the contrary
that "the influence of Britain preponderates in an eminent
degree."[168] In 1824 Francis Gilmer wrote to Jefferson that
"the tone of feeling in England is undoubtedly favorable to us
of the United States."[169] But the entente prophesied in these
passages did not take shape;[170] a series of irritating international problems arose which served to keep the two countries
apart through the period.[171] The very period of Canning's
acceptance of the Monroe Doctrine was a period of uneasiness
in the office of the Secretary of State over England's designs
on Cuba. Irritation over the restrictions on the West Indian
trade lasted from 1815 to 1830; the Maine Boundary and the
"Aroostook War" of 1838 did not make for good feeling, nor
was the Webster-Ashburton Treaty of 1842 received with
entire favor in the United States. There is also to be noted the
flare-up of anti-British feeling in 1844 over the question of the
Oregon boundary.[172] When in addition to these sources of irritation, the South felt that British influence tended to check
American expansion towards Cuba, Nicaragua and Mexico;[173]
and when Tory travellers and Tory magazines sneered at
American manners,[174] it is easy to see that an *entente cordiale*

[168] *Blowe's Emigrants' Directory*, p. 75. Blowe was violently anti-Gallican.
[169] Trent, *English Culture in Virginia*, p. 63.
[170] An amusing instance of anti-British feeling in 1824 is given in Levasseur's account of Lafayette's visit. Just outside of Baltimore Lafayette and
his party passed the Waterloo Inn; his conductor thought it would hurt his
feelings to stop there, and the militia accompanying him were disposed to
make the innkeeper take down his sign. They rode on to a second inn some
two or three miles distant, where Lafayette was informed that a Tory had
let the first house on condition that it should be called Waterloo; "but,"
added his informant, "everybody ridicules it; and nobody will enter his
house; so that the owner is obliged to indemnify the tenant." *Lafayette in
America*, I, 166.
[171] Gallatin was sent to England in 1826 to settle, if he could, the New
England boundary line, the boundary west of the Stony Mountains, the
question of navigation of the St. Lawrence and of American intercourse with
Canada, and the problem of colonial trade. In his negotiations with Canning
he "did not fail to bring to bear the pressure of a possible change in the
relations of the United States and Great Britain which might arise from
the war which seemed imminent between that power and Spain." That is to
say, a threat of British occupation of Cuba and the old question of the
impressment of American sailors (not settled by the Treaty of Ghent)
might bring the United States into collision with England. Stevens, *Albert
Gallatin*, pp. 355-6, 358.
[172] Lyell's *Travels in the United States, Second Visit*, is rich in anecdotes
illustrative of an anti-British sentiment.
[173] Cf. Schouler, V, 221-13, 306, 309-11.
[174] See Mesick and Nevins; and Cairns, *British Criticisms of American
Writings, 1783-1815*; and *ibid.*, for 1815-1833.

could not come. Nevertheless, the identity of interests between British manufacturers and American manufacturers was perhaps as remarkable as their divergence; it was impossible for the Americans to ignore their British origin, even though a large Irish immigration tended to fan the flame of hatred. There is accordingly no such flamboyant animosity in the period from 1815 to 1848 as distinguished certain previous epochs. A thousand ties held the nations together. Moreover, the choice for the United States was no longer, as it had been, England *or* France; the period is the period of splendid isolation.

Keen interest in French affairs abated. The Revolution and Napoleonism continued to be discussed in books and magazines from varying points of view,[175] nor is it to be denied that hostility to England played a great part in the American estimate of the little Corsican. Roughly speaking, the mercantile interests, the moneyed classes, and the middle class continued to hold the conservative views of Burke, which the religious reaction[176] tended to strengthen. Roughly speaking, the masses continued to look upon the French Revolution and Napoleon with favor.[177] But whether the Virginian and New England dynasties held sway, or whether the frontier occupied the White House, the United States with one or two striking exceptions, took no hand in French affairs.

Tidings of the collapse of absolute government in Spain reached the United States in March, 1820, and were welcomed with unconcealed delight. Congress quickly passed a bill to appoint ministers to the South American republics then in revolt (1822).[178] France had intended to propose a Congress of powers to deal with the rebellions in South America;[179] in

[175] To be studied in a subsequent treatise.
[176] See chaps. xi and xii.
[177] "It is not to be denied that the masses in America look with a far more friendly feeling upon France than upon England," a fact to be "accounted for by traditional recollections of the revolutionary war." It is "also in some measure attributed to the more amicable and sympathetic sentiments which distinguish French travellers, as compared with English, when writing on the subject of America. . . . M. de Tocqueville or M. Chevalier . . . appreciate America better than we do. . . . They have neither time nor inclination to laugh at and 'show up' the manner in which the Americans eat their meals or the posture in which they sit at the theatre, or any such minor peculiarities as in their larger view are lost in comparison with more important features." Godley, *Letters from America*, pp. xii-xiii.
[178] McMaster, V, 41-42.
[179] "It was no new rumor in court circles in Great Britain that France had intrigued to set up a Bourbon dynasty in the western Hemisphere." Schouler, III, 284.

April, 1823, a French army, led by the Duc d'Angoulême, crossed the frontier and entered Spain; and it is significant that Monroe's famous message followed in December—a message received with delight by English papers "and denounced by the French administration journal, *L'Étoile.*"[180] When in 1825 a great French fleet appeared on our coasts, it was feared that the French, having stamped out constitutional government at home, were about to invade Cuba and Porto Rico, and Clay instructed our minister at Paris to say that the United States would not consent to the occupation of the islands by a foreign power.[181]

By a peculiar juxtaposition of events the Jackson administration and the Revolution of July came in almost together. News of the latter event was received in America with enthusiasm. There was a public meeting in New York at which Monroe attended.[182] Minor celebrations were held elsewhere. In Louisiana the House of Representatives addressed congratulations to the French people, which the government of Louis Philippe very properly refused to receive.[183] On the Ohio river steamers were named for the French king,[184] the rumor of whose death, in 1837, threw St. Louis into official mourning.[185] Caleb Cushing wrote his *Review, Historical and Political, of the Late Revolution in France* (Boston, 1833) to explain the event, and the magazines, reviewing the book, thought that "in this country . . . Americans rejoiced at the downfall of the selfish, bigoted, impotent tyrant," for they had "trembled for France," which must now "re-invoke her insulted and rejected God and re-hallow the profaned Sabbath, and re-acknowledge the despised Bible."[186] Some years later the *Democratic Review*

[180] McMaster, V, 44, 48; Schouler, III, 284.
[181] McMaster, V, 54.
[182] Described in Boardman, *America and the Americans,* pp. 314-392; Hamilton, *Men and Manners* in America, I, 59-70; Stuart, *Three Years in North America,* II, 567-576.
[183] Gayarré was chairman of the committee. The address said among other things that "the voice of France, whether in glory or in grief, ever finds an echo in Louisiana. . . . Liberty is then about to commence her triumphal march around the globe, and we hope, if it be necessary, a French car will carry the divinity." Fortier, III, 219-20.
[184] Cf. Nichols, *Forty Years of American Life,* I, 165-7.
[185] See the letter from Jay Cooke to Pitt Cooke, January 17, 1837, in Oberholtzer, *Jay Cooke, Financier of the Civil War,* I, 36. All the shops and places of amusement were shut up, mass was said, and processions formed to escort the effigy of the "late" king to its final resting place.
[186] *American Quarterly Observer,* April, 1834, pp. 353-5.

expressed a general sentiment when it said that Louis Philippe was not a great man, that he would not stand a week before the genius of Bonaparte, and that he was but an interlude in the history of France, a phrase sufficiently prophetic.[187] Yet it is to be suspected that the principal impression made on the American consciousness was to deepen our impression that the French were unstable and light-headed.

Despite the national grief for the death of Lafayette in 1832, when Congress decreed funeral honors, and John Quincy Adams was chosen to deliver the oration,[188] the principal event of the thirties in French affairs was the imbroglio over the reparations claims. By a convention signed in Paris, July 4, 1831, the government of Louis Philippe agreed to settle American claims for spoilation under the Napoleonic regime.[189] In 1834, however, the French Chamber refused to pay the claims due under the treaty, and Jackson sent a truculent message to Congress demanding settlement.[190] There was a storm in the French Chamber; in February it looked as though France meant to fight, for the French minister was recalled and Livingston in Paris was offered his passports.[191] Adams' speech in the senate insisted on payment, but the senate hung back and dropped the bills for defence.[192] In March, 1835, a bill was introduced into the French Chamber,[193] largely at the instigation of Louis Philippe, who was personally popular in America

[187] *Democratic Review,* I, 125-9, October, 1837.
[188] Schouler, IV, 168.
[189] Schouler, III, 504; McMaster, VI, 235-241, 299-302. For the early status of these claims see the *North American Review,* XXII, 136-626 January, 1826; XXIII, 385-414 (October, 1826).
[190] The French in Charleston took Jackson's message as a personal affront. See Power, *Impressions of America,* II, 106.
[191] Schouler, IV, 184.
[192] Crittenden in the senate, responding to Benton's allusion to the probability of war, remarked: "The gentlemen think it is indispensable to our dignity to *compel* France to pay the sum of money which, by treaty, she owes. I have not sensibility enough to discover that the *honor and dignity* of the country is concerned. The question affects our *interests* and not our *honor.*" If five millions is owing, "shall we go to war *for that?* A war with *whom*—for what? *With* France, our *first,* our ancient ally! France, whose blood flowed for us, flowed with our own, in that great struggle which gave us freedom. A war for money—a paltry sum of money! . . . Could we *pocket* that blood-stained purse without emotions of pain and remorse?" Coleman, *Life of John J. Crittenden,* I, 91-92.
[193] A minor cause of friction had been an unfortunate quarrel between Lafayette, Cooper, M. Saulnier, and others over the relative cost of government in France and the United States. Cooper rushed into print in both France and Philadelphia. Lounsbury, *James Fenimore Cooper,* 111-116.

and who was friendly to the United States, to pay the claims, and was passed in April.[194] In February, 1837, Calhoun in the senate "proved beyond contradiction that . . . in a war between the United States and France the former would have infinitely more to suffer, while neither could derive any advantage from it," and the "sober second thought of the people entirely agreed with Calhoun."[195] An interesting by-product of the episode, which had no lasting consequences, was the appointment of Lewis Cass as minister to France in June, 1836. Cass became as popular as Morris had been. He was a personal friend of the King, who had toured the backwoods of Pennsylvania and Ohio from which Cass came; and he wrote a pamphlet against the British right of search, printed in Paris in 1842, which had considerable effect upon European diplomacy. "For the first time in our history," wrote Wheaton from Berlin with pardonable exaggeration, "could it be said that the American government had exerted an influence on the policy of Europe."[196]

The remaining diplomatic incidents of the thirties and forties had no serious consequences. At the French attack on Vera Cruz in 1838 Farragut was an interested observer,[197] and for a time the United States had some anticipations of a war between France and Mexico.[198] French conduct in the Argentine in 1837-1840 drew some protests from the magazines.[198a] In 1843 there was some fear that France might establish a colony in Texas; there "England and France, while careful not to come into collision with our government, were trying to circumvent our designs."[199] But Rufus Choate summed up an attitude when he said in the senate in a debate on the Oregon question, that war would be futile, that peace was necessary, and that we ought to "look on England as we look on France."[200] We were not interested in France. Even the proclamation of the Second Republic in 1848, though it

---

[194] Schouler, IV, 22-24. Great Britain served as a mediator. There had been talk of tariff reprisals against the United States which would hurt the South, since cotton was "the principal article of export from the United States to France." Chevalier's *United States,* p. 183.

[195] Von Holst, *John C. Calhoun,* p. 183.

[196] McLaughlin, *Life of Lewis Cass,* pp, 181, 165-180.

[197] Mahan, *Admiral Farragut,* pp. 75-88.

[198] Pray, *Memoirs of James Gordon Bennett and His Times,* p. 254.

[198a] See *The New York Review,* VI, 74-123 January, 1840, for an article denouncing French and British intervention on the Rio de la Plata. See the *Democratic Review,* XVIII, 163-184 (March, 1846).

[199] Schouler, IV, 448-532.

[200] Brown, *Life of Rufus Choate,* p. 118.

operated for the benefit of American industry and commerce, and though Rives, the American minister, caused a small diplomatic stir in his criticism of the method of the election of Louis Napoleon,[201] was received with mild interest and friendly comment, as something that did not much concern Americans.

5. SUMMARY OF THE LAST TWO CHAPTERS

What now have we learned? On the whole that American diplomacy is under the dominance of the spirit of the frontier, which tends to draw the United States away from Europe. On the other hand, the cosmopolitan interest in war and diplomacy, alert to the international movement, desires to take an appropriate part in international affairs. In politics the general tendency of the one is to close the American mind to foreign influence, and to withdraw it from the world of events; whereas the general tendency of the other is to open the American mind and to insist that the United States shall play its part on the international scene. Nor should the fact that the cosmopolitan spirit sometimes leads us into war blind us to its general tendency. War, it is true, cuts off intercourse; but it is also an expression of power, it stimulates curiosity, it leads to an interchange of goods and ideas. Seen from the point of view of politics alone, the American mind seems most open to foreign influence in the last thirty years of the eighteenth century, and least open in the epoch of Jackson and his successors. But there is a difference between influence and knowledge, and it will not appear that our knowledge of French ideas greatly decreased during the years after 1815. We close our sketch, however, as we began it, with the policy of isolation—of suspicion—of withdrawal— once more in the saddle; at the opening of our hundred years the Frenchman is fickle, unstable, the ally of the Indian and the Jesuit; at the close he is still fickle, still the ally of the Jesuit, but he no longer has power to do us positive harm—he is in popular opinion but one of the effete types of Europe.

Implicit in our discussion, particularly in the latter portion of it, has been the political attitude of the middle class. The middle class, with its conservative and compromising spirit, is eager for information where it is closed to culture. United now with the dominant West, and now with the aristocratic South, the weight of middle class influence was thrown first on one side of the scale and now on the other. But although it is possible to

---

[201] Schouler, V, 121. Our government disavowed the "insult." P. 234.

see this spirit at work in our international relationships, it is easier to define these relations in terms of a conflict between the spirit of the frontier and the spirit of the cosmopolitan mind, the latter dominant from 1770 to 1815, the former (despite the wars of the colonial period) dominant in the rest of our epoch.

Conclusion

I⊤ ɪs against the rich and complicated background studied in this work that the problem of the American reception of French letters must be seen. This analysis has been, indeed, defective if it does not appear that we are dealing with two variable quantities. On the one hand the changing panorama of American life in which at one time or another the cosmopolitan spirit, the middle-class spirit, or the frontier spirit dominates, yet never wholly crushing out the interests of the other two groups, is one side of the problem; on the other hand is French culture which, through the hundred years or so which have been our main preoccupation, goes through a series of violent and revolutionary changes. There are varying levels of American life; there are varying aspects of French culture, and in the relation between the two lies the fascination and complexity of the problem. And yet while the situation is thus a dynamic rather than a static one, certain elements remain the same: French culture, whatever the internal upheavals may be, continues to present to American eyes certain permanent traits; and although one or another of the strands of American culture may be most important in any given decade, there are always present the three factors of American culture, even in very early times. It is to a brief consideration of these permanent characteristics that this brief conclusion is directed.

The great obstacle to a sympathetic reception of things French by the Americans has been, it appears, a *sense of religious difference*. This sense of religious difference carries with it a suspicion of French morality, of French infidelity, and of French Catholicism. Weakest in the concluding quarter of the eighteenth century when both countries were dominated by a movement of tolerance and even of scepticism, this sense of difference is yet always present and is basic to an understanding of the American attitude. In the seventeenth century the Americans are suspicious of French Catholicism; in the last decade of the eighteenth century, they are suspicious of French infidelity, and they carry this attitude into the opening decades of the nineteenth century; and in the last twenty-five or thirty years of our study, they are impartially suspicious of both infidelity and Catholicism. Most obvious in the fields of religion and philosophy, this spirit of distrust is yet at work in other

[569]

ways; it colors our whole attitude towards things French. It explains the varying reception of the different groups of French immigrants who have come to America; it underlies the American legend that in the arts of the theater, the table, and music, of painting, sculpture (and we may add, literature), the French are immoral, sensuous, or light-minded. It helps to explain the distrust with which the teaching of French has sometimes been greeted during our period; and in certain sections of our political history, the presence of this sense of religious difference is a conditioning factor, avowed or implicit, of political policies.

But this sense of religious difference is weakest among those who possess the cosmopolitan spirit. Hence, a second important element which has developed in our history is that things French come to *possess social prestige* for the Americans. This opposite and contradictory attitude exhibits itself most clearly in the fields of fashion and manners, as we have seen, but it is not confined to these departments. The glamor of social prestige, by virtue of the dominance of the cosmopolitan class over so important a period of American history as the eighteenth century (and, in lesser degree, the opening years of the nineteenth), has been thrown over the French stage, French opera, French painting, French sculpture, French architecture; it has made the French chef a "smart" possession; in the field of politics, it has its force in giving a glamor to diplomacy, and perhaps it has helped to build up that distrust of European diplomatic methods felt by the plain American. No other foreign influence in the United States has had this peculiar quality of social prestige; and even at moments when American distrust of the French was highest, certain contacts between the two cultures, by virtue of this prestige, have been maintained.

Caught between these two contradictory attitudes, the Americans, and the middle-class Americans in particular, have developed a third belief concerning the French which has been powerful in the relations between the two people. Viewing the political kaleidoscope of France with alarm, touched by British propaganda, distrustful of the animation and gaiety which the French, as he believed, possess, the average bourgeois has developed the idea that the French are predominantly a *fickle and unreliable people*. The very fact that the most unchanging factor in the cultural relation has been the social prestige given French manners and French arts, has likewise helped to build up this notion. To the average American in our period the most obvious facts about the French were, first, that they were politically unstable; and second, that their principal productions were articles of luxury, fashions, millinery, the dancing master, an exaggerated sense of punctilio, and various other things or qualities which seemed to him unworthy of serious consideration by a truly great and important people. What trust can be placed in a people who take so seriously the frills and little accomplishments of life? While the Americans were engaging in the gigantic task of civilizing the continent and conducting a great political experiment, the French were—dancing! The average American did not know, but had he known, he would have quoted with approval, Voltaire's line:

"On s'abîme à Lisbonne, et on danse à Paris."

Yet (and this will appear in a subsequent study and is only implicit in the present one) in contradistinction to this widely prevalent belief, one must also remember that to a certain group of the Americans, the French have also possessed *intellectual prestige*. The great achievements of the German technological methods were of course not known in our period. British thought and British science had its place, although, in the nineteenth century at least, a candid appreciation of the achievements of the British was impossible because of the common American idea that the British were violently hostile to the Americans. But the achievements of French philosophers and scientists have always been seriously considered by intelligent Americans, even when they have not found agreement in this country. With Great Britain France has been over our period the great intellectual center of Europe. Until the rise to prestige of Germany, this attitude has been fairly constant in the New World. Calvin, Montesquieu, Buffon, Cousin, Comte have been seriously regarded and seriously discussed. The connections between American scientific and learned societies and French *savants* have been, on the whole, remarkably intimate, especially when one considers the political situation and the linguistic and geographical obstacles.

That these several attitudes are mutually contradictory need not especially disturb us. The popular mind is not distinguished for logic, and finds little difficulty in believing two opposite things at once. Moreover, the American mind is not a homogenous one. To the frontier type of thinking, the French were simply another effete European nation to which the United States was obviously and providentially superior. To the cosmopolitan classes the regrettable crudities of American life seemed but the more crude beside the polish and superior *savoir faire* of the French. The middle classes vibrated between the two attitudes.

On the whole it is in the departments of manners and fashions that the French have exerted their most notable influence in shaping American culture. In intellectual matters they have had vogue rather than influence. The popular notion that the representative institutions of America owe much to Rousseau does not appear to be historically sound; and if Montesquieu played an important part in shaping the constitution, he yet derives from English thought and was useful largely because he so clearly represented the English idea at a time when hostility to England was great. In the arts it is only at the end of our survey that Paris commences to exert a real influence upon cis-Atlantic painters; and if in architecture the French have contributed through Jefferson to the stylization of American public buildings, they have had little influence upon domestic architecture, which remain in these hundred years mainly British. It does not appear that a knowledge of the French language was widely diffused except in upper social circles; nor has the total French immigration seriously colored the complexion of the American people. And yet, when all this is admitted, it yet remains true that no continental nation until the rise of German influence has possessed the social prestige of France. I believe that in the decades following 1848 we should see the result of much that is begun in the years covered by our study.

Bibliography

BOOKS AND ARTICLES

A Voyage to Mexico and Havanna including some general observations on the United States. By an Italian. New York, 1841.

Abdy, E. S., *Journal of a Residence and Tour in the United States of America, from April, 1833, to October, 1834.* Three volumes. London, 1835.

"Account of the First Boston Public Library, 1656-1747, founded by Captain Robert Keayne," *Publications of the Colonial Society of Massachusetts,* XII, Transactions, 1908-1909, pp. 116-133.

Adams, Charles Francis, *Charles Francis Adams (American Statesmen Series).* Boston and New York, 1900.

Adams, Charles Francis (editor), *Letters of John Adams, Addressed to his Wife.* Two volumes. Boston, 1841.

Adam, Charles Francis (editor), *Letters of Mrs. Adams, the Wife of John Adams, with an introductory memoir.* Two volumes, third edition. Boston, 1841.

Adams, Charles Francis (editor), *The Works of John Adams, Second President of the United States, with a Life of the Author, Notes and Illustrations.* Ten volumes. Boston, 1850-1856.

Adams, Henry, *History of the United States (1801-1817).* Nine volumes. 1891—(variously published).

Adams, Henry, *John Randolph (American Statesmen Series).* Boston, 1882.

Adams, Randolph Greenfield, *A History of the Foreign Policy of the United States.* New York, 1924.

Agassiz, Elizabeth Cary, *Louis Agassiz: His Life and Correspondence.* Two volumes. Boston, 1888.

Aldrich, P. Emory, "John Locke and the influence of his works in America," *Publications of the American Antiquarian Society,* April, 1879, pp. 22-39.

Allaben, Frank, *John Watts de Peyster.* Two volumes. New York, 1908.

Allen, Alexander V. G., D.D., *Jonathan Edwards.* Boston and New York, 1889.

Allen, Gardner W., *Our Naval War with France.* Boston and New York, 1909.

Allen, Joseph Henry, and Eddy, Richard, *A History of the Unitarians and the Universalists in the United States (American Church History Series).* New York, 1894.

Allen, William, *Memoir of John Codman, D.D., with reminiscences by Joshua Bates, D.D.* Boston, 1853.

Allison, Young E., *The Curious Legend of Louis Philippe in Kentucky.* Louisville, Kentucky (privately printed), 1924.

Alvord, Clarence Walworth, *Governor Edward Coles: Collections of the Illinois State Historical Library,* XV, *Biographical Series,* I. Springfield, Illinois, 1920.

Americans as They Are, The. Described in A Tour Through the Valley of the Mississippi. By the Author of *Austria As It Is.* London, 1828.

L'Amérique Septentrionale et Méridionale, ou déscription de cette grande partie du monde, etc. Par une société de géographes et d'hommes de lettres. . . . Paris, 1835.

Anburey, Thomas, *Travels through the Interior Parts of America.* Two volumes. Boston and New York, 1923. (Reprint of edition of 1789).

Angell, James Burrill, *The Reminiscences of James Burrill Angell.* New York and London, 1912.

"Appendix to the Report of the Board of Regents of the Smithsonian Institution, containing a Report on the Public Libraries of the United States of America, January 1, 1850." By Charles C. Jewett. *House Miscellaneous Documents,* Number 50. Thirty-first Congress, First Session. Washington, 1850.

Armstrong, Emma Kate, "Chateaubriand's America. Arrival in America and First Impressions," *Publications of the Modern Language Association of America,* new series, XV, pp. 345-370.

Art and Letters. New Orleans, n.d. (in Howard Memorial Library).

Asbury, Rev. Francis, *The Journal of Rev. Francis Asbury, Bishop of the Methodist Episcopal Church, from August 7, 1771, to December 7, 1815.* Three volumes. New York, 1821.

Ashe, Thomas, *Travels in America, performed in 1806, for the purpose of exploring the Rivers Alleghany, Monongahela, Ohio, and Mississippi, and ascertaining the produce and condition of their banks and vicinity.* Three volumes. London, 1808.

Atwater, Caleb, *Remarks made on a tour to Prairie du Chien; thence to Washington City in 1829.* Columbus, Ohio, 1831.

Autobiography of Charles Caldwell, M.D., with a preface, notes and appendix, by Harriot W. Warner. Philadelphia, 1855.

Augustin, J. M., "Fifty Years of French Opera," *The Daily Picayune,* October 24, 1909.

Austin, Mary S., *Philip Freneau, the poet of the revolution.* Edited by Helen Kearny Vreeland. New York, 1901.

Bacon, Leonard Woolsey, *A History of American Christianity (American Church History Series).* New York, 1897.

Baird, Charles W., *History of the Huguenot Emigration to America.* Two volumes. New York, 1885.

Balch, E. W. (translator), "Narrative of the Prince de Broglie," *The Magazine of American History,* I, pp. 180ff, 231ff, 306ff, 374ff.

Balch, Thomas, *The French in America during the War of Independence of the United States, 1777-1783.* A translation by Thomas Willing Balch, etc. Philadelphia, 1891.

Baldensperger, Fernand, *Le Mouvement des Idées dans l'Émigration française, 1789-1815* .Two volumes Paris, 1924.

Baldensperger, Fernand, "Le séjour de Brillat-Savarin aux états unis," *Revue de la littérature comparée,* II, 1922, pp. 94-95.

Baldensperger, F., and Carré, J. M., "La première histoire indienne de Chateaubriand et sa source américaine," *Modern Language Review,* VIII, 1913, pp. 15-26.

Baldwin, Simeon E., *Life and Letters of Simeon Baldwin.* New Haven, n.d. (Privately printed).

de Baroncelli, J. G., *Le théâtre-français à la Nouvelle Orleans.* New Orleans, 1906.

Bassett, John Spencer, *A Short History of the United States*. New York, 1913.
Bassett, John Spencer (editor), *The Writings of "Colonel William Byrd of Westover in Virginia Esqr."* New York, 1901.
Battle, Kemp Plummer, *History of the University of North Carolina*. Two volumes. Raleigh, North Carolina, 1907-12.
Bayard, Ferdinand-M., *Voyage dans l'intérieur des États-Unis, a Bath, Winchester, dans la vallée de Shenandoah, etc., etc. Pendant l'été de 1791*. Second edition. Paris, An. VI.
Beard, Charles A., *Economic Origins of Jeffersonian Democracy*. New York, 1915.
Beard, James Carter, "Composers of Music and Music Publishers in New Orleans," *The Daily Picayune*, February 18, 1912.
Beaty, John O., *John Esten Cooke, Virginian*. New York, 1922.
Beaujour, Félix (Louis Auguste), Chevalier, *Aperçu des états-unis, au commencement du XIXᵉ. siècle, depuis 1800 jusqu'en 1810, avec des tables statistiques*. Paris, 1814.
van Becelaere, L., *La philosophie en Amérique depuis les origines jusqu'à nos jours (1607-1900)*. New York, 1904.
Becker, Carl, *The Declaration of Independence. A study in the history of political ideas*. New York, 1922.
Beckwith, Paul, *Creoles of St. Louis*. St. Louis, 1893.
Beecher, Lyman, *A Plea for the West*. Second edition. Cincinnati and New York, 1835.
Beecher, Lyman, *Views of Theology; as developed in three sermons, and on his trials before the Presbytery and Synod of Cincinnati, etc.* Boston and Cleveland, 1853.
Beer, William, *Checklist of American Periodicals, 1740-1800*. Reprinted from the *Proceedings of the American Antiquarian Society*. Worcester, Massachusetts, 1923.
Belisle, Alexandre, *Histoire de la presse Franco-Américaine*. Worcester, Massachusetts, 1911.
Belloc, Hilaire, *The Contrast*. New York, 1924.
Belote, Theodore Thomas, "The Scioto Speculation and the French Settlement at Gallipolis. A Study in Ohio Valley History," *University of Cincinnati Studies*, series II, III, number 3, September-October, 1907.
Benwell, J., *An Englishman's Travels in America: his observations of life and manners in the Free and Slave States*. London and Edinburgh. (1853?).
Bernhard, Duke of Saxe-Weimar Eisenach, *Travels through North America, 1825-1826*. Two volumes. Philadelphia, 1828.
Bernheim, Gotthardt Dellman, *History of the German Settlements and of the Lutheran Church in North and South Carolina*. Philadelphia, 1872.
(Beverley, Robert), *The History of Virginia, in four parts. . . . The Second Edition revis'd and enlarg'd by the Author*. London, 1722.
Birkbeck, Morris, *Letters from the Illinois*. Philadelphia; printed for the author. Dublin: 1818.
Birkbeck, Morris, *Notes on a Journey in America, from the coast of Virginia to the Territory of Illinois: with proposals for the establishment of a colony of English, accompanied by a map illustrating the route*. Dublin: (printed from the last Philadelphia edition), 1818.

Birket, James, *Some Cursory Remarks made by James Birket in his Voyage to North America, 1750-1751.* New Haven, 1916.

Bishop, Mrs. J. T., "Musical History of Louisiana," *The Times-Democrat* (New Orleans), October 31, 1909.

Blanchard, Claude, see Duane, William.

(Blowe's) *Emigrants' Directory. Geographical, historical, commercial, and agricultural view of the United States of America; forming a complete emigrant's directory through every part of the republic.* London, 1820.

(Boardman, James), *America, and the Americans.* By a citizen of the world. London, 1833.

Bogart, Ernest Ludlow, *An Economic History of the United States.* Fourth edition. New York and London, 1924.

Boone, Richard G., *Education in the United States; its history from the earliest settlements.* New York, 1889 (1893).

Bossu, M., *Nouveaux Voyages aux Indes Occidentales: contenant une rélation des différens peuples qui habitent les environs du grande fleuve Saint-Louis, appellé vulgairement le Mississippi,* etc. Three volumes. Paris, 1768.

Bossu, M., *Nouveaux Voyages dans l'Amérique Septentrionale, contenant une collection de lettres écrites sur les lieux par l'auteur, à son ami M. Douin. . . .* Nouvelle édition. Amsterdam and Paris, 1778.

Botsford, Jay Barrett, *English Society in the Eighteenth Century as Influenced from Oversea.* New York, 1924.

Bourne, E. G., "The Travels of Jonathan Carver," *American Historical Review,* XI, pp. 287-302.

Bourne, E. G., "The Use of History Made by the Framers of the Constitution," *Annual Report of the American Historical Society for 1896,* I, pp. 221-241.

Bourne, Henry E., "American Constitutional Precedents in the French Assembly," *American Historical Review,* VIII, pp. 466-486.

Bowers, Claude G., *Jefferson and Hamilton: The Struggle for Democracy in America.* Boston and New York, 1926.

Bradsher, Earl L., *Mathew Carey. Editor, Author and Publisher. A Study in American Literary Development.* New York, 1912.

Brandon, Edgar A., "A French Colony in Michigan," *Modern Language Notes,* XIII, April, 1898, pp. 242-247.

Branner, John C., "Some Old French Place Names in the State of Arkansas," *Modern Language Notes,* XIV, February, 1899, pp. 64-79.

Breaux, Joseph A., "Some Early Colleges and Schools of Louisiana," *Publications of the Louisiana Historical Society,* VII, 1913-1914, pp. 136-142.

Breck, Samuel. See Scudder, H. E.

Breckenridge, Robert J., D.D., *Memoranda of Foreign Travel (Harper Library Series).* Two volumes. Baltimore, 1845.

Bremer, Fredrika, *The Homes of the New World; Impressions of America.* Translated by Mary Howitt. Two volumes. New York, 1853.

Brillat-Savarin, *Physiologie du gout,* etc. Nouvelle édition. (Classiques Garnier). Paris, n. d.

Brissot de Warville, J. P., *New Travels in the United States of America, performed in M.DCC.LXXXVIII*. Second edition, corrected. London, 1794.
(Volume II) *New Travels in the United States of America: including the Commerce of America with Europe; particularly with France and Great Britain*. Two volumes. Volume II. n.d.

Bristed, John, *The Resources of the United States of America; or, a view of the agricultural, commercial, manufacturing, financial, political, literary, moral and religious capacity and character of the American people*. New York, 1818.

de Broglie, Prince de. See Balch, E. W.

Brooks, Van Wyck, *America's Coming of Age*. New York, 1915.

Brooks, Van Wyck, *The Ordeal of Mark Twain*. New York, 1920.

Brown, Samuel Gilman, *The Life of Rufus Choate*. Fifth edition. Boston, 1885.

Brown, T. Allston, *A History of the New York Stage from the first performance in 1732 to 1900*. Three volumes. New York, 1902.

Brownson, Henry F. (editor), *The Works of Orestes A. Brownson, collected and arranged*. Twenty volumes. Detroit, 1898-1908.

Bruce, Philip Alexander, *Economic History of Virginia in the Seventeenth Century*. Two volumes. New York, 1896.

Bruce, Philip Alexander, *Institutional History of Virginia in the Seventeenth Century*. Two volumes. New York, 1910.

Bruce, Philip Alexander, *Social Life of Virginia in the Seventeenth Century*. Richmond, 1907.

Bryce, James, *The American Commonwealth*. Second edition, revised. Two volumes. London and New York, 1891.

Buckingham, J. S., *America, Historical, Statistic, and Descriptive*. Three volumes. London and Paris, (1841).

Buckingham, J. S., *The Eastern and Western States of America*. Three volumes. London and Paris, (1841?).

Buckley, J. M., *A History of the Methodists in the United States. (American Church History Series)*. New York, 1896.

Burnaby, Andrew, *Travels through the Middle Settlements in North America in the years 1759 and 1760. With observations upon the state of the colonies*. Second edition. London, 1775.

Burr, Clinton Stoddard, *America's Race Heritage*. New York, 1922.

Butler, Pierce, *Judah P. Benjamin (American Crisis Biographies)*. Philadelphia, 1906.

Cable, George W., *The Creoles of Louisiana*. New York, 1884.

Caffin, Charles H., *The Story of American Painting; the evolution of painting in America from colonial times to the present*. New York, 1907.

Cairns, William B., *A History of American Literature*. New York, 1912.

Cairns, William B., "British Criticisms of American Writings, 1783-1815," *University of Wisconsin Studies*, 1918.

Cairns, William B., "British Criticisms of American Writings, 1815-1833," *University of Wisconsin Studies*, 1922.

Caldwell, Charles. See *Autobiography of Charles Caldwell*.

Cambridge History of American Literature. Four volumes. New York, 1917-1921.

(Candler, Isaac), *A Summary View of America: comprising a description of the face of the country, and of several of the principal cities; and remarks on the social, moral, and political character of the people: being the result of observations and enquiries during a journey in the United States by an Englishman.* London, 1824.

Carr, John, Esqu., *The Stranger in France; or a tour from Devonshire to Paris.* First published in London, 1803. Brattleboro; printed for Isaiah Thomas, Jun. Worcester. William Fessenden, printer. 1806.

Carré, Henri, "Les émigrés français en Amérique, 1789-1793," *La Revue de Paris,* 5e. année, numéro 10, May, 1898, pp. 311-340.

Carroll, H. K., *The Religious Forces of the United States (American Church History Series).* New York, 1893.

Carroll, R. R. (editor), *Historical Collections of South Carolina,* etc., II. New York, 1836.

Carter, N. H., *Letters from Europe.* Two volumes, second edition. New York, 1825.

Casson, Henry, *A Gospel Alarm to Christendom: which exhibits vital truth and reprobates all her most lauded notions of religion, both natural and revealed.* Philadelphia, 1794.

Catalogue of Books belonging to the Dialectic Society at Chapel Hill, May, 1835. Raleigh, North Carolina, 1835.

Catalogue of the Library of the United States. To which is annexed, a copious index, alphabetically arranged. Washington, 1815. (This is a catalogue of Jefferson's library as sold to the United States.)

Century of Population Growth, A, from the First Census of the United States to the Twelfth, 1790-1900. Washington, 1909.

Chambers, Henry E., "Early Commercial Prestige of New Orleans," *Louisiana Historical Quarterly,* V, number 4, pp. 451-61.

Channing, W. E., *Works (People's Edition).* Two volumes. London, 1851.

Chaptal, M., *A Treatise upon Wines.* Translated by John H. Sargent. Charleston, South Carolina, 1811.

Chastellux, Marquis de, *Voyages dans l'Amérique septentrionale dans les années 1780, 1781 & 1782.* Two volumes, Seconde édition. Paris, vol. I, 1788; vol. II, 1791.

Chateaubriand, Viscount de, *Travels in America and Italy.* (Translated). Two volumes. London, 1828.

Chevalier, Michael, *Society, Manners and Politics in the United States: being a series of letters on North America.* Translated from the third Paris edition. Boston, 1839.

Chinard, Gilbert, *L'Amérique et le rêve exotique.* Paris, 1913.

Chinard, Gilbert, *Les amitiés américaines de Madame d'Houdetot d'après sa correspondance inédite avec Benjamin Franklin et Thomas Jefferson (Bibliothèque de la revue de la littérature comparée,* tome VIII). Paris, 1924.

Chinard, Gilbert, "La correspondance de Madame de Staël avec Jefferson," *Revue de la littérature comparée,* II, 1922, pp. 621-640.

Chinard, Gilbert, *L'exotisme américain dans la littérature française au xvie. siècle.* Paris, 1911.

Chinard, Gilbert, "Notes sur la voyage de Chateaubriand en Amérique," *University of California Publications in Modern Philology,* IV, number 2, pp. 269-349.

Chinard, Gilbert, *Les réfugiés huguenots en Amérique avec une introduction sur le mirage américain.* Paris, 1925.

Chinard, Gilbert, "Volney et l'Amérique d'après des documents inédits et sa correspondance avec Jefferson," *The Johns Hopkins Studies in Romance Literatures and Languages,* I. Baltimore, 1923.

Chotteau, Léon, *La guerre de l'indépendance (1775-1783): les Français en Amérique.* Avec une préface par M. Édouard Laboulaye. Paris, 1876.

Cline, Isaac Monroe, *Art and Artists in New Orleans during the last half century.* Reprinted from the Biennial Report of the Louisiana State Museum, 1922.

(Cluny, Alexandre), *Le Voyageur Américain ou observations sur l'état actuel, la culture, les commerces des colonies Britanniques en Amérique. . . .* Traduit de l'Anglois. Amsterdam, 1782.

Cobbett, William, *A Year's Residence in the United States of America.* In three parts. London, 1818, 1819, 1819.

Coke, E. T., *A Subaltern's Furlough: description of scenes in various parts of the United States, upper and lower Canada, New Brunswick, and Nova Scotia, during the summer and autumn of 1832.* Two volumes. New York, 1833.

Coker, W. C., "The Garden of André Michaux," *Journal of the Elisha Mitchell Scientific Society,* XXVII, 65-72.

Cole, G. D. H., *The Life of William Cobbett.* New York, 1924.

Coleman, Mrs. Chapman (editor), *The Life of John J. Crittenden, with selections from his correspondence and speeches.* Two volumes. Philadelphia, 1871.

Coleman, Henry, *European Life and Manners.* Two volumes. Boston and London, 1849.

Coleman, John O., *Old New Orleans Houses* (clippings and pictures in the Howard Memorial Library, originally published in the *New Orleans States* in 1922-23).

Collections of the Virginia Historical Society.

Collot, Victor, *A Journey in North America (Reprints of Rare Americana,* number 4). Two volumes. Florence (Italy), 1924.

(Colton, Calvin), *A Voice from America to England.* By an American gentleman. London, 1839.

Combe, George, *Notes on the United States of North America during a phrenological visit in 1838-39-40.* Three volumes. Edinburgh, 1841.

Commemoration of the Founding of the House of Chickering & Sons upon the Eightieth Anniversary of the Event, The. Boston, 1904.

Condon, Peter, article on Knownothingism in *The Catholic Encyclopedia,* VIII.

Conway, Moncure Daniel, *Autobiography: Memories and Experience.* Two volumes. Boston, 1904.

Cook, Elizabeth Christine, *Literary Influences in Colonial Newspapers, 1704-1750.* New York, 1912.

Cooke, G. W., *Unitarianism in America.* New York, 1902.

Cooper, James Fenimore (editor), *Correspondence of James Fenimore-Cooper.* Two volumes, New Haven, 1922.

Corley, Viola F., *American Periodical Criticism of French Fiction from 1800 to 1860.* MS. thesis in the Library of the University of Texas.

Corwin, E. S., "The French Objective in the American Revolution," *American Historical Review,* XXI, pp. 33-61.

de Courcy, Henry, and Shea, John Gilmary, *History of the Catholic Church in the United States,* etc. New York, 1879.

Crèvecoeur, J. Hector St. John, *Letters from an American Farmer, reprinted from the original edition, with a prefatory note by W. P. Trent and an introduction by Ludwig Lewisohn.* New York, 1904.

Cross, Arthur Lyon, *The Anglican Episcopate and the American Colonies. (Harvard Historical Studies),* New York, 1902.

Cross, Arthur Lyon, "Schemes for Episcopal Control in the Colonies," *Annual Report of the American Historical Association for 1896.* I, pp. 233-241.

Cruzat, A., "General Collot's Arrest in New Orleans," *Louisiana Historical Quarterly,* I, pp. 303-20.

Cubberley, Ellwood P., *Public Education in the United States.* Boston and New York, 1919.

Curtis, George Ticknor, *Life of James Buchanan, Fifteenth President of the United States.* Two volumes. New York, 1883.

Curtis, N. C., "The Creole Architecture of Old New Orleans," *The Architectural Record,* XLIII, May, 1918, pp. 435-446.

Dall, William Healey, *Spencer Fullerton Baird: a biography including selections from his correspondence with Audubon, Agassiz, Dana, and others.* Philadelphia and London, 1915.

Dallas, Susan (editor), *Diary of George Mifflin Dallas while United States Minister to Russia 1837 to 1839, and to England 1856 to 1861.* Philadelphia, 1892.

(Darusmont, Frances), *Views of Society and Manners in America; in a series of letters from that country to a friend in England, during the years 1818, 1819, and 1820.* By an Englishwoman. London, 1821.

Davis, John, *Travels of Four Years and a Half in the United States of America; during 1798, 1799, 1800, 1801, and 1802.* Dedicated by permission to Thomas Jefferson, Esq., President of the United States. London, 1803.

Davis, Matthew L. (editor), *The Private Journal of Aaron Burr, during his residence of four years in Europe; with selections from his correspondence.* Two volumes. New York, 1838.

(Davis, Mrs. Varina Howell), *Jefferson Davis, Ex-President of the Confederate States of America. A Memoir.* Two volumes. New York, 1890.

Dawes, E. C., "The Scioto Purchase of 1787," *Magazine of American History,* XXII, pp. 470-82.

Dewey, Rev. Orville, *The Old World and the New.* Two volumes. Revised edition. New York, 1836.

Dexter, Edwin Grant, *A History of Education in the United States.* New York, 1904.

Dexter, Franklin B., "Early Private Libraries in New England," *Proceedings of the American Antiquarian Society,* new series, XVIII, pp. 135-147.

Dexter, Franklin B., "Elder Brewster's Library," *Proceedings of the Massachusetts Historical Society,* second series, V, pp. 37-85.

Dexter, Franklin B., "Estimates of Population in the American Colonies," *Proceedings of the American Antiquarian Society,* V, October, 1887, pp. 22-50.

Dexter, Franklin B. (editor), *The Literary Diary of Ezra Stiles, LL.D.* Two volumes. New York, 1901.

(Dickson, William), *Sermons by J. B. Massillon, Bishop of Clermont, to which is prefixed, the Life of the Author. Selected and Translated by William Dickson.* Second American edition, revised and materially corrected. Two volumes. Philadelphia, 1818.

Didier, Eugene L., *The Life and Letters of Madame Bonaparte (Elizabeth Patterson Bonaparte).* New York, 1879.

Dodd, William E., *The Cotton Kingdom (Chronicles of America Series).* New Haven, 1919.

Dowling, Rev. John, A.M., *The History of Romanism from the earliest corruptions of Christianity to the Present Time,* etc. Twelfth edition. New York, 1846.

(Doysié, Abel), "Journal of a French Traveller in the Colonies, 1765," *American Historical Review,* XXVI, pp. 726-747; XXVII, pp. 70-90.

Drew, Samuel, *The Life of the Rev. Thomas Coke, LL.D.* New York, 1818.

Duane, William (translator), *The Journal of Claude Blanchard, Commissary of the French Auxiliary Army sent to the United States during the American Revolution, 1780-83.* Translated from a French manuscript, and edited by Thomas Balch. Albany, 1876.

Dunbar, Louise B., "A Study of 'monarchical' tendencies in the United States, from 1776 to 1801," *University of Illinois Studies in the Social Sciences,* X, pp. 1-164.

(Duncan, Mary Graham), *America as I Found It.* By the mother of Mary Lundie Duncan. New York, 1852.

Duniway, Clyde August, "French Influence on the Adoption of the Federal Constitution," *American Historical Review,* IX, pp. 403-9.

Dunlap, William, *A History of the Rise & Progress of the Arts of Design in the United States.* A new edition, edited by F. W. Bagley and C. E. Goodspeed. Three volumes. Boston, 1918.

Dwight, Timothy, *Theology Explained and Defended in a series of Sermons . . . with a memoir of the life of the author.* Five volumes. London, 1824.

Dwight, Timothy, *Travels; in New-England and New-York.* Four volumes. New Haven, 1821.

Earle, Alice Morse, *Home Life in Colonial Days.* New York and London, 1898.

Eberlein, Harold Donaldson, *The Architecture of Colonial America.* Boston, 1924.

Edwards, Bryan, *The History, civil and commercial, of the British Colonies in the West Indies,* etc. Four volumes. Charleston, 1810.

Eliot, Thomas D., "The Relations between Adam Smith and Benjamin Franklin before 1776," *Political Science Quarterly,* XXXIX, March, 1924, pp. 67-96.

Ellis, Harold Milton, *Joseph Dennie and His Circle.* Austin, Texas, 1915.

Elson, Louis C., *The History of American Music.* Revised edition. New York, 1915.

Embury, Aymar, "Old New Orleans: the picturesque buildings of the French and Spanish Regime," *The Architectural Record,* III, July, 1911, pp. 85-98.

Emerson, Edward Waldo, and Forbes, Waldo Emerson (editors), *Journals of Ralph Waldo Emerson.* Ten volumes. Boston and New York, 1909-1910.

"Emigration Conditions in Europe." Report of the Immigration Commission. *Senate Document,* No. 748, 61st. Congress, Third Session. Washington, 1911.

Evans, Charles, *American Bibliography (1637-1820).* Volumes I-IX Chicago, 1903-1925.

Eyre, John, *The Christian Spectator: being a journey from England to Ohio, two years in that state, travels in America, etc.* Albany, 1838.

Farmer, John, *A Genealogical Register of the First Settlers of New-England, etc.* Lancaster, Massachusetts, 1829.

Farnham, Luther, *A Glance at Private Libraries.* Boston, 1855.

Faust, Albert B., "Swiss Emigration to the American Colonies in the Eighteenth Century," *American Historical Review,* XXII, pp. 21-44, 98-132.

Faux, W., *Memorable Days in America: being a Journal of a tour to the United States, principally undertaken to ascertain, by positive evidence, the condition and probable prospects of British emigrants; including accounts of Mr. Birkbeck's settlement in the Illinois, etc.* London, 1823.

Faÿ, Bernard, *Bibliographie Critique des ouvrages français relatifs aux états-unis (1770-1800).* Paris, 1925.

Faÿ, Bernard, *L'ésprit révolutionnaire en France et aux états-unis à la fin du xviiie. siècle.* Paris, 1925.

Fearon, Henry Bradshaw, *Sketches of America. A narrative of a journey of five thousand miles through the eastern and western states of America.* Second edition. London, 1818.

Feipel, Louis N., "American Place-Names," *American Speech,* I, November, 1925, pp. 78-91.

(Fessenden, Thomas Green), *Democracy Unveiled, or, Tyranny Stripped of the Garb of Patriotism.* By Christopher Caustic, L.L. D. [*sic*]. Two volumes, third edition, with large additions. New York, 1806.

(Fessenden, Thomas Green), *The Modern Philosopher.* By Christopher Caustic, L.L. D. London, 1806.

Fessenden, Thomas Green, *The Ladies Monitor, A poem.* Bellows Falls, Vermont, 1818.

Fessenden, Thomas Green, *Original Poems.* Philadelphia, 1806.

(Fessenden, Thomas Green), *Pills, Poetical, Political, and Philosophical, etc.* By Peter Pepper-Box, Poet and Physician. Philadelphia, 1809.

Fidler, Isaac, Rev., *Observations on Professions, Literature, Manners, and Emigration in the United States and Canada, made during a residence there in 1832.* New York, 1833.

Field, Flo, "Ironwork of old New Orleans Balconies," *The Times-Picayune,* March 12, 1916.

Field, Thomas Meagher (editor), *Unpublished Letters of Charles Carroll of Carrollton, and of his father, Charles Carroll of Doughoregan.* New York, 1902.

Fischer, David Barrow, "The Story of New Orleans's Rise as a Musical Center," *Musical America,* March 14, 1914, pp. 3-5.

Fiske, A. R., "Profligacy in Fiction," *North American Review,* CXXXI, July, 1880.

Fitzpatrick, Edward A., *The Educational Views and Influence of De Witt Clinton. Teachers College, Columbia University, Contributions to Education,* 44. New York, 1911.

Flagg, Ernest, "The Influence of the French School on Architecture in the United States," *The Architectural Record,* IV, October-December, 1894, pp. 211-228.

Flagg, Jared B., *The Life and Letters of Washington Allston.* New York, 1892.

Fludd, Eliza C. K., *Biographical Sketches of the Huguenot, Solomon Legare.* Charleston, South Carolina, 1886.

Foerster, Norman, "New Viewpoints in American Literature," *The Saturday Review of Literature,* April 3, 1926.

Ford, Paul Leicester, *Checklist of American Magazines printed in the Eighteenth Century.* Brooklyn, 1889.

Ford, Worthington Chauncey, *The Boston Book Market, 1679-1700.* Boston, 1917.

Ford, Worthington Chauncey, *Writings of George Washington.* Vols. I-XIV. New York, 1889-1893.

Forester, Frank, *The Horse of America.* Two volumes. New York, 1857.

Forman, Samuel E., *The Life and Writings of Thomas Jefferson, including all of his important utterances on public questions, compiled from state papers and from his private correspondence.* Indianapolis, 1900.

Forman, Samuel E., "The Political Activities of Philip Freneau," *The Johns Hopkins University Studies,* XX, nos. 9-10, September-October, 1902.

Fortier, Alcée, "The Acadians of Louisiana and their Dialect," *Publications of the Modern Language Association,* VI, pp. 64-94.

Fortier, Alcée, "Bits of Louisiana Folk-Lore," *Transactions and Proceedings of the Modern Language Association,* III, 1887, pp. 100-168.

Fortier, Alcée, "The French Language in Louisiana and the Negro-French Dialect," *Transactions and Proceedings of the Modern Language Association,* I, pp. 40-44.

Fortier, Alcée, "Literature in Louisiana," *Transactions and Proceedings of the Modern Language Association,* II, 1886, pp. 31-60.

Fortier, Alcée, "The French Literature of Louisiana in 1887 and 1888," *Modern Language Notes,* IV, 1889, pp. 97-101, 228-233.

Fortier, Alcée, "The French Literature of Louisiana in 1889 and 1890," *Modern Language Notes,* V, 1890, pp. 165-9, 349-52.

Fortier, Alcée, *A History of Louisiana.* Four volumes. Paris and New York, 1904.

Fosdick, Lucian J., *The French Blood in America.* New York, 1906.

Fox, Dixon Ryan, "The Decline of Aristocracy in the Politics of New York," *Columbia University Studies in History, Economics and Public Law,* LXXXVI, New York, 1919.

Fraser, Charles, *Reminiscences of Charleston.* Charleston, South Carolina, 1854.

Frazee, L. J., *The Medical Student in Europe.* Maysville, Kentucky, 1849.

"French Protestants, The, of the Abbeville District, South Carolina, 1761-1765," *Collections of the South-Carolina Historical Society,* II, pp. 75-103. Charleston, 1858.

Fries, Adelaide L., *The Moravians in Georgia, 1735-1740.* Raleigh, North Carolina, 1905.

Fries, Adelaide L., *Records of the Moravians in North Carolina.* Raleigh, North Carolina, 1922.

Frothingham, Octavius B., *Transcendentalism in New England, a History.* Boston, 1876.

Gaines, Richard Heyward, "Richmond's First Academy, projected by M. Quesnay de Beaurepaire in 1786," *Proceedings (Collections) of the Virginia Historical Society,* XI, new series, pp. 167-175.

Gall, Ludwig, *Meine Auswanderung nach den Vereinigten-Staaten in Nord-Amerika, im Frühjahr 1819 and meine Rückkehr nach der Heimath im Winter 1820.* Erster Theil. Zweiter Theil. Two volumes. Trier, 1822.

Gallier, James, *Autobiography of James Gallier.* Paris, 1864.

Gannett, Henry, "The Origin of Certain Place Names in the United States." Second Edition. Department of the Interior, *United States Geological Survey,* Bulletin no. 258, series F, Geography, 45. Washington, 1905.

Garden, Alexander, *Anecdotes of the American Revolution,* etc. Second series. Charleston, South Carolina, 1828.

Gardiner, H. Norman (editor), *Jonathan Edwards, a restrospect.* Boston and New York, 1901.

Gay, Sydney Howard, *James Madison (American Statesmen Series).* Boston, 1884 (1895).

Gibbon, J. Murray, *Canadian Folk Songs (Old and New), Selected and Translated, Harmonizations by Geoffrey O'Hara and Oscar O'Brien.* New York, 1927.

Gibson, William, M.D., *Rambles in Europe in 1839.* Philadelphia, 1841.

Gilman, Caroline, *The Poetry of Travelling in the United States, with additional sketches by a few friends; and a week among autographs, by Rev. S. Gilman.* New York, 1838.

Girard, William, "Du Transcendantalisme considéré essentiellement dans sa définition et ses origines françaises," *University of California Publications in Modern Philology,* IV, no. 3, October 18, 1916.

Goddard, Harold Clarke, *Studies in New England Transcendentalism.* New York, 1908.

Godley, John Robert, *Letters from America.* Two volumes in one. London, 1844.

Godwin, Parke, *A Biography of William Cullen Bryant, with extracts from his private correspondence.* Two volumes. New York, 1883.

Goldstein, "The Architecture of Old New Orleans," *Architecture and Allied Arts,* I, no. 9.

Goodnight, Scott Holland, *German Literature in American Magazines Prior to 1846.* Madison, Wisconsin, 1907.

(Goodrich, S. G.), *Tales about the United States of America, geographical, political, and historical; with comparative views of other countries.* By Peter Parley. Third edition. London, 1838.

(Grant, Mrs. Anne), *Memoirs of an American Lady: with sketches of manners and scenery in America, as they existed previous to the revolution.* Two volumes. London, 1808.

Greer, George Cabell, *Early Virginia Immigrants, 1623-1666.* Richmond, 1912.

Grima, Edgar, "Municipal Support of Theatres and Operas in New Orleans," *Publications of the Louisiana Historical Society,* IX, pp. 43-45, 1916.

Griscom, John, *A Year in Europe . . . in 1818 and 1819.* Two volumes. New York, 1823.

Griswold, Rufus Wilmot, *The Republican Court, or American society in the days of Washington.* New York, 1855.

Grizzell, Emit Duncan, *Origin and Development of the high school in New England before 1865.* Philadelphia, 1922.

Grund, Francis J., *The Americans in their moral, social, and political relations.* Two volumes. London, 1837.

Grund, Francis J., *The Americans in their moral, social, and political relations.* Two volumes in one. Boston, 1837.

Guilday, Peter, *English Catholic Refugees on the Continent.* London, 1914.

Guilday, Peter, *The Life and Times of John Carroll, Archbishop of Baltimore, (1735-1815).* New York, 1922.

Guizot, M., and Madame Guizot de Witt, *The History of France from The Earliest times to 1848.* Translated by Robert Black. Volume VIII. New York, 1884.

Hageman, John Frelinghuysen, *History of Princeton and Its Institutions.* Two volumes. Philadalphia, 1879.

Haines, Charles G., "Ministerial Responsibility versus the Separation of Powers," *American Political Science Review,* XVI, no. 2, May, 1922.

Haines, Hiram C. E., *The State of Alabama,* etc. Paris, 1867.

Hale, Edward Everett, and Hale, E. E., Jr., *Franklin in France.* Two volumes. Boston, 1888.

Hall, Captain Basil, *Travels in North America, in the Years 1827 and 1828.* Three volumes. Edinburgh, 1829.

Hall, Francis, *Travels in Canada, and the United States, in 1816 and 1817.* Boston, 1818.

Halsey, R. T. H., and Cornelius, Charles O., *A Handbook of the American Wing* [of the Metropolitan Museum of Art]. Third edition. New York, 1926.

(Hamilton, Thomas), *Men and Manners in America.* By the author of Cyril Thornton, etc. Two volumes. Edinburgh and London, 1833.

Handschin, Charles Hart, *The Teaching of Modern Languages in the United States. United States Bureau of Education. Bulletin,* 1913, no. 3, whole number 510. Washington, 1913.

Harper's Bazaar, October 15, 1887. (Picture of the first parish church in New Orleans.)

Harrison, James A. (editor), *The Complete Works of Edgar Allan Poe.* Seventeen volumes. New York, 1902.

Hart, Albert Bushnell, *Slavery and Abolition (American Nation Series).* New York, 1906.

"Harvard College Library Duplicates, 1682," *Publications of the Colonial Society of Massachusetts,* XVIII, Transactions, 1915-1916, pp. 407-417.

Hays, I. Minis (editor), *Calendar of the Papers of Benjamin Franklin in the Library of the American Philosophical Society.* Five volumes. Philadelphia, 1908.

Hazard, Lucy Lockwood, *The Frontier in American Literature*. New York, 1927.

Hazard, Samuel, *Santo Domingo, Past and Present; with a glance at Hayti*. New York, 1873.

Hazen, C. D., "The French Revolution as seen by the Americans of the Eighteenth Century," *Annual Report of the American Historical Association for 1895*, pp. 455-466.

Henkle, Rev. M. M., *The Life of Henry Bidleman Bascom, D.D., LL.D., Late Bishop of the Methodist Episcopal Church, South*. Nashville, Tennessee, 1855.

Herrick, C. H., "The Early New-Englanders: What Did They Read?" *The Library*, IX, 1918, pp. 1-17.

Herrick, Francis Hobart, *Audubon the Naturalist*. Two volumes. New York and London, 1917.

Heywood, William S. (editor), *Autobiography of Adin Ballou, 1803-1890 . . . completed and edited by his son-in-law*. Lowell, Massachusetts, 1896.

Hicks, Frederick Charles (editor), *Thomas Hutchins: a topographical description of Virginia, Pennsylvania, Maryland, and North Carolina*. Reprinted from the original edition of 1778. Cleveland, 1904.

Higgins, Don H., "New Orleans Has a Romantic Opera History," *The Item-Tribune*, Dec. 20, 1925.

Higginson, Thomas Wentworth, *Henry Wadsworth Longfellow (American Men of Letters Series)*. Cambridge, 1902.

Hildeburn, Charles R., *Sketches of Printers and Printing in Colonial New York*. New York, 1895.

Hill, David J., "A Missing Chapter of Franco-American History," *American Historical Review*, XXI, pp. 709-719.

Hinsdale, B. A., "Notes on the history of foreign influences upon education in the United States," chapter XIII of the *Report of the Commissioner of Education for the year 1897-98*, volume I. Washington, 1899.

Historical Sketch Book and Guide to New Orleans and Environs . . . edited and compiled by several leading writers of the New Orleans press. New York, 1885.

History, The, of North America, containing an exact account of their first settlements, etc. London, 1776.

History of the Island of St. Domingo from its First Discovery by Columbus to the Present Period. London, 1818; New York, reprinted, 1824.

Hodgson, Adam, *Letters from North America, written during a tour in the United States and Canada*. Two volumes. London, 1824.

Holmes, Oliver Wendell, *The Autocrat of the Breakfast Table*. Boston, 1866.

Hopkins, Thomas F., D.D., "The First Catholic Church in Charleston," *Yearbook of the City of Charleston*, 1897.

Hornblow, Arthur, *A History of the Theater in America from its beginnings to the present time*. Two volumes. Philadelphia and London, 1919.

Hosmer, James K., *Samuel Adams (American Statesmen Series)*. Revised edition. Boston and New York, 1898.

"How Savarin Described Life in Early America," *New York Times*, February 14, 1926.

Howe, Daniel Wait, *The Puritan Republic of the Massachusetts Bay in New England.* Indianapolis, 1899.

Howitt, E., *Selections from Letters written during a tour through the United States in the summer and autumn of 1819,* etc. Nottingham, n.d.

Hull, A. L., *A Historical Sketch of the University of Georgia.* Atlanta, 1894.

Humphrey, Edward Frank, *Nationalism and Religion in America, 1774-1789.* Boston, 1924.

Imlay, Gilbert, *A Topographical Description of the western territory of North America,* etc. Third edition. London, 1797.

Ingram, John Van Ness, *A Check List of American Eighteenth Century Newspapers in the Library of Congress.* Washington, 1912.

James, Bartlett B., "The Labadist Colony in Maryland." *Johns Hopkins University Studies in Historical and Political Sciences,* series XVII, no. 6. Baltimore, 1899.

James, J. A., "French Diplomacy and American Politics, 1794-5," *Annual Report of the American Historical Association,* I, 1911, pp. 151-164.

Jefferson, Thomas. See Washington, H. A.

Jewett, Charles C. See "Appendix" to the *Report . . . of the Smithsonian Institution.*

Jewett, Isaac Appleton, *Passages in Foreign Travel.* Two volumes. Boston, 1838.

Johnson, Emory R., and others, *History of Domestic and Foreign Commerce of the United States.* Two volumes. Washington, 1915.

Johnston, Alexander, *American Political History, 1763-1876,* edited and supplemented by James Albert Woodburn. Two volumes. New York, 1905.

Johnston, Margaret Avery (editor), *In Acadia: the Acadians in Story and Song.* New Orleans, 1893.

Jones, Adams Leroy, *Early American Philosophers.* New York, 1898.

Journal of a French Traveller. See Doysié, Abel.

Kalm, Peter, *Travels into North America,* etc. Translated by John Reinhold Forster. Second edition. Two volumes. London, 1772.

Kellogg, Thelma Louise, "The Life and Works of John Davis, 1774-1853," *University of Maine Studies,* second series, no. 1. Orono, Maine, 1924.

Kendall, John Smith, *History of New Orleans.* Three volumes. Chicago and New York, 1922.

Kimball, Fiske, *Domestic Architecture of the American Colonies and of the early Republic.* New York, 1922.

Kimball, Fiske, *Thomas Jefferson: Architect.* Boston (privately printed), 1916.

King, Grace, *Creole Families of New Orleans.* New York, 1921.

Kirkland, Mrs. *Holidays Abroad.* Two volumes. New York, 1849.

Kite, Elizabeth S., *Beaumarchais and the War of American Independence.* Two volumes. Boston, 1918.

Küchler, Walter, "Eine Amerikanische Übersetzung Boileauscher Satiren," *Studien zur vergleichenden Literaturgeschichte,* V, pp. 385-391.

Kuhns, Levi O., *German and Swiss Settlements of Colonial Pennsylvania.* New York, 1901.

Laborde, M., *History of the South Carolina College, from its incorporation, December 19, 1801, to November 25, 1857,* etc. Columbia, South Carolina, 1859.

Lafayette, *Mémoires, correspondance et manuscrits du Général Lafayette,* publiés par sa famille. Volumes I to III. Brussells, 1837.

Lahee, Henry C., *Annals of Music in America.* Boston, 1922.

Lamb, Mrs. Martha J., *History of the City of New York; its origin, rise, and progress.* Two volumes. New York and Chicago, 1877-1880.

Lamprey, L., "French Exiles in New York," *Americana,* V, pp. 701-704.

Lanson, Gustave, *Histoire illustrée de la littérature française.* Two volumes. Paris and London, n.d.

La Rochefoucauld-Liancourt, *Voyage dans les états-unis d'Amérique, fait en 1795, 1796 et 1797.* Eight volumes. Paris, L'An VII de la République.

Latrobe, Charles Joseph, *The Rambler in North America: MDCCC-XXXII-MDCCCXXXIII.* Two volumes. Second edition. London, 1836.

Latrobe, J. H. B., *The Journal of Latrobe, being the notes and sketches of an architect, naturalist, and traveler in the United States from 1796 to 1820.* By Benjamin Henry Latrobe. New York, 1905.

Lauzun, Duc de, *Mémoires,* edited by Vitroc and Galopin (Moderne Collection Historique & Anecdotique). Paris, n.d.

Lawson, John, (Gentleman), *History of North Carolina, being a reprint of the copy now in the North Carolina State Library, Raleigh, presented by President James Madison, in the year 1831.* Charlotte, North Carolina, 1903.

Lee, Francis Bozley, "Residence of Joseph Bonaparte in New Jersey," *American Historical Magazine,* I, pp. 178-188.

Lefevre, Ralph, *History of New Paltz, New York, and its Old Families,* etc. Albany, 1903.

Leighton, Walter L., *French Philosophers and New-England Transcendentalism.* University of Virginia Thesis. Charlottesville, Virginia, 1908.

Levasseur, A., *Lafayette in America, in 1824 and 1825; or, journal of travels in the United States.* Two volumes. Translated from the French. New York, 1829.

Lieber, Francis, *The Stranger in America: comprising sketches of the manners, society, and national peculiarities of the United States, in a series of letters to a friend in Europe.* Two volumes. London, 1835.

List, A, of Serials in Public Libraries of Chicago and Evanston, corrected to January, 1901. Compiled by the Chicago Library Club. Chicago, 1901.

Lockitt, C. H., *The Relations of French and English Society (1763-1793).* London, 1920.

Lodge, Henry Cabot, "The Distribution of Ability in the United States," *Century Magazine,* XLII, September, 1891, pp. 687-694.

Lodge, Henry Cabot, *Life of Alexander Hamilton (American Statesmen Series).* Boston, 1882.

Lodge, Henry Cabot, *George Washington (American Statesmen Series).* Two volumes. Boston and New York, 1889.

Loeb, Harry Brunswick, *The Opera in New Orleans.* Baton Rouge, 1917.

Loeb, Harry Brunswick, "What New Orleans has done for French Opera," *Musical Courier,* December 16, 1915.

de Loménie, L., *Beaumarchais et son Temps.* Paris, 1855.

Longfellow, Samuel, *Life of Henry Wadsworth Longfellow.* Two volumes. Boston, 1886.

Louisiana Historical Society. See *Publications* of.

Lounsbury, Thomas R., *James Fenimore Cooper (American Men of Letters Series).* Boston, 1882.

Lowell, Amy, *Tendencies in Modern American Poetry.* New York, 1917.

Lyell, Sir Charles, *A Second Visit to the United States of North America.* Two volumes. New York, 1849.

Lyell, Charles, *Travels in North America; with geological observations on the United States, Canada, and Novia Scotia.* Two volumes. London, 1845.

M. N., *Voyages intéressans dans différentes colonies françaises, espagnoles, anglaises,* etc., *le tout rédigé et mis au jour d'après un grand nombre de manuscrits, par M. N.* A Londres: et se trouve à Paris, chez Jean-François Bastien. M DCC LXXXVIII.

Macdonald, J. R. Moreton, *A History of France in Three Volumes.* Volume III. New York, 1915.

Mackay, Alexander, *The Western World; or travels in the United States in 1846-47,* etc. Three volumes. Third edition. London, 1850.

Mackenzie, Alexander Slidell, *Life of Stephen Decatur.* Boston, 1846.

McLaughlin, Andrew C., *Lewis Cass (American Statesmen Series).* Boston and New York, 1891.

McLaughlin, Andrew C., "Social Compact and Constitutional Construction," *American Historical Review,* V, pp. 470-490.

Maclean, John, *History of the College of New Jersey, from its origin in 1746 to the commencement of 1854.* Two volumes. Philadelphia, 1877.

McMaster, John, *A History of the People of the United States from the Revolution to the Civil War.* Seven volumes. New York, 1885-1910.

Macy, John, *The Spirit of American Literature.* New York, 1913.

Magruder, Allan B., *John Marshall (American Statesmen Series).* Revised edition. Boston and New York, 1898.

Mahan, A. T., *Admiral Farragut.* New York, 1892.

Mandrillon, Jh., *Le Spectateur Américain, ou remarques générales sur l'Amérique Septentrionale, et sur la République des Treize-États-Unis; suivi de recherches philosophiques sur la découverte du Nouveau-Monde.* Séconde édition. Amsterdam, 1785.

Marcou, Jules, *Life, Letters and Works of Louis Agassiz.* Two volumes. New York and London, 1896.

Marryat, Captain, *A Diary in America, with remarks on its institutions.* Three volumes. London, 1839.

Marsden, R. G., "A Virginian Minister's Library, 1635," *American Historical Review,* XI, pp. 328-332.

Martineau, Harriet, *Society in America.* Two volumes. New York, 1837.

Marvel, Ik, (D. G. Mitchell), *Fresh Gleanings; or, a new sheaf from old fields of continental Europe.* New York, 1847.

(Mason, Rev. Jonathan), *Extracts from a diary kept by the Rev.*

Jonathan Mason of a journey from Boston to Savannah in the Year 1804. Cambridge (England), 1885.

(Mason, Richard Lee), *Narrative of Richard Lee Mason in the Pioneer West 1819.* New York, privately printed, n.d.

Mattfeld, Julius, *A Hundred Years of Grand Opera in New York, 1825-1925.* New York, 1927.

(Matthews, Brander, and others), *A History of Columbia University, 1754-1904.* Published in commemoration of the one-hundred-fiftieth anniversary of the founding of King's College. New York, 1904.

Maxwell, Lieut-Col. A. M., K. H., *A Run through the United States, during the autumn of 1840.* Two volumes. London, 1841.

Meade, William Edward, *The Grand Tour in the Eighteenth Century.* Boston and New York, 1914.

Melish, John, *Travels through the United States of America in the years 1806 and 1807, and 1809, 1810 and 1811,* etc. Philadelphia; printed for the author; London and Dublin, 1818.

Mencken, H. L., *A Book of Prefaces.* Fourth edition. New York, 1922.

Mencken, H. L., *The American Language; an inquiry into the development of English in the United States.* Third edition, revised and enlarged. New York, 1923.

de Menil, Alexandre Nicolas, *The Literature of the Louisiana Territory.* St. Louis, 1904.

Mereness, Newton D., (editor), *Travels in the American Colonies.* Edited under the auspices of the Colonial Dames of America. New York, 1916.

Merlant, Joachim, *Soldiers and Sailors of France in the American War for Independence.* New York, 1920.

Merriam, C. E., *A History of American Political Theories.* New York, 1903.

Mesick, Jane Louise, *The English Traveller in America, 1785-1835.* New York, 1922.

Michaud, Régis, "Le Transcendantalisme d'après l'Histoire," *Modern Philology,* XVI, December, 1918. pp. 393-412 (57-76).

Michaux, André, "Journal de André Michaux," *Proceedings of the American Philosophical Society,* XXVI, October 19, 1888, pp. 8-145. (Edited by C. S. Sargent.)

Michaux, F. A., M. D., *Travels to the Westward of the Allegany Mountains in the states of the Ohio, Kentucky, and Tennessee, and return to Charlestown through the upper Carolinas,* etc., *undertaken in the year X, 1802, under the auspices of his Excellency, M. Chaptal, Minister of the Interior. . . . Faithfully translated from the original French by B. Lambert.* London, 1805.

Mills, W. Jay (editor), *Glimpses of colonial society and the life at Princeton College 1766-1773 by one of the class of 1763* (William Patterson). Philadelphia and London, 1903.

Minnigerode, Meade, *The Fabulous Forties: 1840-1850. A presentation of private life.* New York and London, 1924.

Minnigerode, Meade, *Some American Ladies,* New York, 1926.

Mitchell, Julia Post, *St. Jean de Crèvecoeur.* New York, 1916.

Mode, Peter G., *The Frontier Spirit in American Christianity.* New York, 1923.

Montulé, E., *A voyage to North America and the West Indies, in 1817.* London, 1821.

Moré, Comte de, *Mémoires du Comte de Moré,* publiés pour la société d'histoire contemporaine par M. Geoffroy de Grandmaison et le Comte de Pontgibaud. Paris, 1898.

Morse, John T., Jr., *Benjamin Franklin (American Statesmen Series).* Boston and New York, 1889.

Morse, John T., Jr., *John Adams (American Statesmen Series).* Boston and New York, 1884.

Morse, John T., Jr., *John Quincy Adams (American Statesmen Series).* Boston and New York, 1882.

Morse, John T., Jr., *Thomas Jefferson (American Statesmen Series).* Boston and New York, 1898.

Mowatt, Anna Cora, *Autobiography of an Actress; or, eight years on the stage.* Boston, 1854.

Mumford, Lewis, *Sticks and Stones; a study of American architecture and civilization.* New York, 1924.

Mumford, Lewis, *The Golden Age.* New York, 1926.

Munroe, William Bennett, *Crusaders of New France. (Chronicles of America Series).* New Haven, 1918.

Murat, Achille, *A moral and political sketch of the United States of North America,* etc. London, 1833.

Murdock, Kenneth Ballard, *Increase Mather; the foremost American puritan.* Cambridge, Massachusetts, 1925.

Myers, Gustavus, *The History of American Idealism.* New York, 1925.

Neal, Daniel, *The History of New-England, containing an Impartial Account of the Civil and Ecclesiastical Affairs of the Country, to the Year of our Lord, 1700,* etc. Two volumes. London, 1747.

Nevins, Allan, *American Social History as recorded by British travellers.* New York, 1923.

Newman, A. H., *A History of the Baptist Churches in the United States (American Church History Series).* New York, 1894.

Nichols, Dr. Thomas L., *Forty Years of American Life.* Two volumes. London, 1864.

Nitze, William A., and Dargan, E. Preston, *A History of French Literature from the earliest times to the Great War.* New York, 1922.

North, S. N. D., *History and Present Condition of the Newspaper and Periodical Press of the United States.* Census Office Report. Washington, 1884.

Oberholtzer, Ellis Paxson, *Jay Cooke, Financier of the Civil War.* Two volumes, Philadelphia, 1907.

O'Connor, *Fire Department of New Orleans.* (In Howard Memorial Library).

"Olmutz", Statement of the attempted rescue of General Lafayette from Olmutz, (based on conversations with Col. Francis K. Huger). Charleston, South Carolina, n.d.

Orth, S. P., *Our Foreigners (Chronicles of America Series).* New Haven, 1920.

Ouseley, William G., *Remarks on the Statistics and Political Institutions of the United States,* etc. Philadelphia, 1832.

Page. See Quesnay de Beaurepaire.

Parkman, Francis, *Montcalm and Wolfe.* Three volumes. (Frontenac Edition). Boston, 1907.

Parrington, Vernon Louis, (editor), *The Connecticut Wits. (American Authors Series).* New York, 1926.

Pattee, Fred Lewis, *A History of American Literature Since 1870.* New York, 1915.

Pattee, Fred Lewis, "James Fenimore Cooper," *The American Mercury,* March, 1925, pp. 289-297.

Patton, John S., *Jefferson, Cabell, and the University of Virginia.* New York and Washington, 1906.

Pavie, Théodore, *Souvenirs Atlantiques. Voyage aux États-Unis et au Canada.* Two volumes. Paris, 1833.

Paxson, Frederic L., *History of the American Frontier, 1763-1893.* Boston and New York, 1924.

Pellew, George, *John Jay (American Statesmen Series).* Revised edition. Boston and New York, 1898.

Penniman, James Hosmer, *George Washington as a Man of Letters,* n.p., 1918.

Perez, L. M., "French Refugees to New Orleans in 1809, with documents," *Publications of the Southern History Association,* IX, number 5, September, 1905, pp. 293-310.

Perkins, James Breck, *France in the American Revolution.* Boston and New York, 1911.

Philips, Édith, *Les Réfugiés Bonapartistes en Amérique (1815-1830).* Paris, n.d.

Phillips, Henry, Jr., (editor), "Early Proceedings of the American Philosophical Society for the Promotion of Useful Knowledge, compiled by one of the Secretaries, from the manuscript minutes of its meetings from 1744 to 1838," *Proceedings of the American Philosophical Society,* XXII, part II. Philadelphia, 1884.

Phillips, Mary E., *James Fenimore Cooper.* New York, 1912.

Pickett, James, *History of Alabama . . . from the earliest period.* (Webb Book Company), 1900.

Poe, Edgar Allan. See Harrison, James A.

Poole, Reginald Lane, *A History of the Huguenots of the Dispersion at the recall of the Edict of Nantes.* London, 1880.

Potter, Alfred C., (editor), "Catalogue of John Harvard's Library," *Publications of the Colonial Society of Massachusetts,* XXI, Transactions, 1919, pp. 190-230.

Potter, Rev. Eliphalet Nott, *Washington as a Model in his Library and Life.* New York, 1895.

Power, Tyrone, Esq., *Impressions of America, during the years 1833, 1834, and 1835.* Two volumes. London, 1836.

(Pray, Isaac Clark), *Memoirs of James Gordon Bennett and his Times.* By a journalist. New York, 1855.

Price, Nellie Warner, "Le Spectacle de la Rue St. Pierre," *Louisiana Historical Quarterly,* I, pp. 215-23.

Priest, William, *Travels in the United States of America; commencing in the year 1793 and ending in 1797, with the author's journals of his two voyages across the Atlantic.* London, 1802.

Primer, Sylvester, "The Huguenot Element in Charleston's Pronunciation," *Publications of the Modern Language Association of America,* IV, old series, pp. 214-244.

Prudhommeaux, Jules, *Icarie et son Fondateur, Étienne Cabet. Contribution à l'étude du socialisme expérimentale.* Paris, 1907.

Publications of the Louisiana Historical Society, 1895/96——.

Quesnay de Beaurepaire, *Memoir concerning the Academy of the Arts and Sciences for the United States of America.* Translated by Rosewell Page. Richmond, 1922. (Published as part of the report of the Virginia State Library for 1920-1921.)

Quincy, Josiah, *Figures of the Past from the Leaves of Old Journals.* Boston, 1883.

Quincy, Josiah, *The History of Harvard University* (to 1840). Two volumes. Cambridge, Massachusetts, 1840.

Ramon de la Sagra, D., *Cinco Meses en los Estados-Unidos de la América del Norte desde el 20 de Abril al 23 de Setiembre de 1835.* Paris, 1836.

Ramsay, David, M.D., *The History of South Carolina from its first settlement in 1670, to the year 1808.* Two volumes. Charleston, South Carolina, 1809.

Ravenel, Henry E., *Ravenel Records.* Atlanta, 1898.

Ravenel, Mrs. St. Julien, *Charleston: the place and the people.* New York, 1906.

Raynal, G.-T., *Histoire philosophique et politique des établissemens et du commerce des Européens dans les deux Indes, par G.-T. Raynal.* Nouvelle édition. Twelve volumes. Paris, 1820.

Réau, Louis, *L'art français aux États-unis.* Paris, 1926.

Reeves, J. S., "Napoleonic Exiles in America, 1815-1819," *Johns Hopkins University Studies in Historical and Political Science,* XXIII, nos. 9-10. Baltimore, 1905.

Reisner, Edward H., *Nationalism and Education since 1789,* New York, 1922.

Rich, Wesley Everett, *The History of the United States Post Office to the Year 1829 (Harvard Economic Studies).* Cambridge, Massachusetts, 1924.

Rightor, Henry (editor), *Standard History of New Orleans, Louisiana.* Chicago, 1900.

Riley, I. Woodbridge, *American Philosophy; the Early Schools.* New York, 1907.

Riley, Woodbridge, *American Thought from Puritanism to Pragmatism.* New York, 1915.

Riley, Woodbridge, *American Thought from Puritanism to Pragmatism and Beyond.* New York, 1923.

Rivers, John, *Figaro: the Life of Beaumarchais.* New York (1922).

Rivers. William J., *A Chapter in the early history of South Carolina.* Charleston, South Carolina, 1874.

Robin, M. L'Abbé, *Nouveau voyage dans l'Amérique Septentrionale, en l'anné 1781; et campagne de l'armée de M. le Comte de Rochambeau.* A Philadelphie et se trouve à Paris. . . . MDCCLXXXII.

Roosevelt, Theodore, *Gouverneur Morris (American Statesmen Series).* Boston and New York, 1888.

Roosevelt, Theodore, *Life of Thomas Hart Benton (American Statesmen Series).* Boston and New York, 1886.

Roosevelt, Theodore, *The Winning of the West (Statesman Edition).* Four volumes. New York and London, 1889-1896.

Rosengarten, J. G., *French Colonists and Exiles in the United States.* Philadelphia and London, 1907.

Rosenthal, Lewis. "Rousseau at Philadelphia," *Magazine of American History,* XII, pp. 46-55.

Rowland, Kate Mason, *The Life of Charles Carroll of Carrollton,*

1737-1832, with his correspondence and public papers. Two volumes. New York and London, 1898.

Royall, Mrs. Anne, *The Black Book, or a continuation of travel in the United States.* Three volumes. Washington, 1828, 1828, 1829.

(Royall, Mrs. Anne), *Sketches of History, Life and Manners in the United States. By a Traveller.* New Haven, 1826.

Rupp, I. Daniel, *A Collection of Upwards of Thirty Thousand Names of German, Swiss, Dutch, French, and other immigrants to Pennsylvania from 1727 to 1776,* etc. Revised and enlarged edition. Philadelphia, 1876.

Rusk, Ralph Leslie, *The Literature of the Middle Western Frontier.* Two volumes. New York, 1925.

Russo, Joseph Louis, *Lorenzo da Ponte, Poet and Adventurer.* New York, 1922.

Saint-Méry, Moreau de, *Voyages aux États-Unis de l'Amérique, 1793-1798.* Edited with an introduction and notes by Stewart L. Mims. New Haven, 1913.

St. Pierre, Louis de, *On the Art of Planting and Cultivating the Vine; as also, of making, fining, and preserving wines, &c, according to the most approved methods in the most celebrated wine counties in France,* etc. London, 1772.

Sale, Edith Tunis, *Old Time Belles and Cavaliers.* Philadelphia and London, 1912.

Salley, Alexander S. (editor), *Narratives of Early Carolina, 1650-1708. (Original Narratives of Early American History.)* New York, 1911.

Samuels, Marguerite, "Art in the Iron Verandas of New Orleans," *The Times-Picayune,* June 6, 1920.

Scharf, J. Thomas, and Westcott, Thompson, *History of Philadelphia, 1609-1884.* Three volumes. Philadelphia, 1884.

Schinz, Albert, "Un 'Rousseauiste' en Amérique (L'Abeille Française de Joseph Nancrède)," *Modern Language Notes,* XXXV, January, 1920, pp. 10-18.

Schlesinger, Arthur Meier, "The Colonial Merchants and the American Revolution, 1763-1776," *Columbia University Studies in History, Economics and Public Law,* LXXVIII. New York, 1918.

Schoenberger, Harold William, *American Adaptations of French Plays on the New York and Philadelphia Stages from 1790 to 1833.* Philadelphia, 1924.

Schoepf, Johann David, *Reise durch einige der mittlern und südlichen vereinigten nordamerikanischen Staaten nach Ost-Florida und den Bahama-Inseln.* Erster Theil. Zweyter Theil. Erlangen, 1788.

Schoepf, Johann David, *Travels in the Confederation (1783-1784).* Translated and edited by Alfred J. Morrison. Two volumes. Philadelphia, 1911.

Schouler, James, *Americans of 1776.* New York, 1906.

Schouler, James, *History of the United States of America under the Constitution.* Revised edition. Volumes I-V. New York, 1904.

Schultz, Christian, Jun., Esq., *Travels on an Inland Voyage through the states of New York, Pennsylvania, Virginia, Ohio, Kentucky and Tennessee, and through the territories of Indiana, Louisiana, Mississippi and New-Orleans; performed in the years 1807 and 1808; including a tour of near six thousand miles.* Two volumes bound as one. New York, 1810.

Schuyler, Montgomery, "Architecture of American Colleges. VIII: The Southern Colleges," *The Architectural Record*, XXX, July, 1911, pp. 57-84.

Scudder, H. E. (editor), *Recollections of Samuel Breck with passages from his note-books (1771-1862)*. Philadelphia, 1877.

Sedgwick, Miss C. M., *Letters from Abroad to Kindred at Home*. Two volumes. New York, 1841.

Seitz, Don, "Our Presidents," *The Forum*, LXXIII, February, 1925, pp. 239-248.

Shea, John Gilmary, *History of the Catholic Church in the United States, 1763-1815*, volume II. Akron, Ohio, New York, and Chicago, 1888.

Sheldon, Edward S., "Some Specimens of a Canadian French Dialect spoken in Maine," *Publications of the Modern Language Association*, IV, old series, 1887, pp. 210-218.

Sherburn, George, "(Review of) Girard, Du Transcendantalisme considéré essentiellement dans sa définition et ses origines françaises," *Modern Philology*, XV, September, 1917, pp. 317-320 (125-128).

Sherrill, Charles H., *French Memories of Eighteenth Century America*. New York, 1915.

Shirreff, Patrick, *A Tour through North America; together with a comprehensive view of the Canadas and United States as adapted for agricultural emigration*. Edinburgh, 1835.

Shoberl, F., *The Beauties of Christianity*. Translated from Chateaubriand. Philadelphia, 1815.

Simons, A. M., *Social Forces in American History*. New York, 1911.

Singleton, Arthur, *Letters from the South and West. . . .* Boston, 1824.

Smith, Baxter Perry, *The History of Dartmouth College*. Boston, 1878.

Smith, Helen Evertson, *Colonial Days & Ways as gathered from family papers*. New York, 1900.

Smith, Henry A. M., "The Orange Quarter and the first French settlers in South Carolina," *South-Carolina Historical and Genealogical Magazine*, XVIII, no. 3.

Smith, Egbert C., "French-Canadians in New England," *Proceedings of the American Antiquarian Society*, VII, new series, pp. 316-336.

Smyth, Albert H., *The Philadelphia Magazines and their Contributors, 1741-1850*. Philadelphia, 1892.

Smyth, Albert Henry, (editor), *The Writings of Benjamin Franklin*. Ten volumes. New York, 1907.

Smyth, Egbert C., "The New Philosophy against which students at Yale College were warned in 1714," *Proceedings of the American Antiquarian Society*, XI, new series, pp. 251 ff.

Smyth, J. F. D., *A Tour in the United States of America, etc.* Two volumes. London, 1784.

Snowden, Yates, "Acadians in South Carolina," *The Carolinian*. XVIII, no. 2, December, 1905, pp. 74-81.

Sonneck, Oscar G., *Early Opera in America*, New York, 1915.

Sonneck, Oscar G., *Miscellaneous Studies in the History of Music*. New York, 1921.

Sonneck, Oscar G., *Suum Cuique; Essays in Music*. New York, 1916.

Spiller, Robert E., *The American in England during the First Half-Century of Independence*. New York, 1926.

Stapleton, Rev. A(mmon), *Memorials of the Huguenots in America, with special reference to their emigration to Pennsylvania.* Carlisle, Pennsylvania, 1901.

Stauffer, Vernon, "New England and the Bavarian Illuminati," *Columbia Studies in History, Economics and Public Law,* LXXXII, no. 1. New York, 1918.

Stedman, Edmund Clarence and Hutchinson, Ellen Mackay (editors), *A Library of American Literature from the earliest settlement to the present time.* Eleven volumes. New York, 1892.

Steiner, B. C., "Rev. Thomas Bray and his American Libraries," *American Historical Review,* II, pp. 59-75.

Stephenson, George M., "Nativism in the Forties and Fifties, with special reference to the Mississippi Valley," *The Mississippi Valley Historical Review,* IX, December, 1922, pp. 185-202.

Steven, B. F. (editor), *Facsimiles of Manuscripts in European Archives relating to America.* Twenty-five volumes. London, 1889-1898.

Stevens, John Austin, *Life of Albert Gallatin (American Statesmen Series).* Boston, 1883 (1896).

Stiles, Ezra, *Diary.* See Dexter, Franklin B.

Straus, S. N., "Interesting History of New Orleans Theatres," *The Times-Picayune,* May 9, 1920.

Strickland, W. P., *The Pioneer Bishop: or, the life and times of Francis Asbury.* New York, 1858.

Stuart, James, *Three Years in North America.* Two volumes, Edinburgh, 1833.

Sturge, Joseph, *A Visit to the United States in 1841.* Boston, 1842.

Sumner, William Graham, *Andrew Jackson as a Public Man. What he was, what chances he had, and what he did with them (American Statesmen Series).* Boston, 1882 (1896).

Surrey, N. M. Miller, "The Commerce of Louisiana during the French régime, 1699-1763," *Columbia University Studies in History, Economics and Public Law,* LXXI, no. 1. New York, 1916.

Talleyrand, Prince de, *Memoirs of the Prince de Talleyrand,* edited . . . by the duc de Broglie . . . translated by Raphael Ledos de Beaufort. Five volumes. New York and London, 1891.

Tandy, Jennette, *Crackerbox Philosophers in American Humor and Satire.* New York, 1925.

Taylor, Henry Osborne, *Thought and Expression in the Sixteenth Century.* Two volumes. New York, 1920.

Thomas, Isaiah, *The History of Printing in America,* etc. Second edition. Two volumes. Published under the supervision of a special committee of the American Antiquarian Society. Albany, 1874.

Thompson, Edward, *Sailor's Letters written to his select friends in England, during his voyages and travels in Europe, Asia, Africa, and America. From the year 1754 to 1759.* Two volumes bound as one. London, MDCCLXVI.

Thompson, Robert Ellis, *A History of the Presbyterian Churches in the United States (American Church History Series).* Third edition. New York, 1902.

de Tocqueville, Alexis, *Democracy in America.* Translated by Henry Reeve, with a critical and biographical introduction by John Bigelow (*Landmarks of Civilization Series*). Two volumes. New York, 1904.

Toner, J. D., "Some account of George Washington's Library," etc., *Annual Report of the American Historical Association for 1892*, pp. 71-170.

Transactions of the Huguenot Society of South Carolina, 1889 ——.

Trent, William P., "English Culture in Virginia: a study of the Gilmer letters, and an account of the English professors obtained by Jefferson for the University of Virginia." *Johns Hopkins University Studies in Historical and Political Science*, seventh series, V-VI. Baltimore, 1889.

Trevezant, John Timothée, *The Trevezant Family in the United States.* Columbia, South Carolina, 1914.

Trollope, Frances M., *The Domestic Manners of the Americans.* (Originally published in 1832.) New York, 1904.

Tudor, Henry, *Narrative of a Tour in North America*, etc. Two volumes. London, 1834.

Turner, Frederick Jackson, *The Frontier in American History.* New York, 1920.

Turner, Frederick Jackson, "The Policy of France toward the Mississippi Valley in the period of Washington and Adams," *American Historical Review*, X, pp. 249-279.

Tuttle, Julius J., "The Libraries of the Mathers," *Proceedings of the American Antiquarian Society*, XX, new series, pp. 269-356.

Twining, Thomas, *Travels in America 100 Years Ago (Notes and Reminiscences).* New York and London, 1893.

Tyler, Moses Coit, *A History of American Literature during the Colonial Period, 1607-1765.* Two volumes. New York and London, 1878.

Tyler, Moses Coit, *The Literary History of the American Revolution. 1763-1783.* Two volumes. New York and London, 1897.

Tyler, Moses Coit, *Patrick Henry (American Statesmen Series).* Boston and New York, 1887.

Tyler, William S., *A History of Amherst College during the administrations of its first five presidents from 1821 to 1891.* New York, 1894.

Uncle Sam's Peculiarities. By Uncle Sam. Two volumes. London, n.d.

Untermeyer, Louis, *The New Era in American Poetry.* New York, 1919.

Upham, Alfred H., *The French Influence on English Literature from the accession of Queen Elizabeth to the Restoration.* New York, 1908.

van Tyne, C. H., "Influence of the Clergy, and of religious and sectarian forces, on the American Revolution," *American Historical Review*, XIX, pp. 44-64.

van Tyne, C. H., "Influences which determined the French government to make the treaty with America, 1778," *American Historical Review*, XXI, pp. 528-541.

Venable, W. H., *Beginnings of Literary Culture in the Ohio Valley.* Cincinnati, 1891.

The Virginia Magazine of History and Biography. 1893——.

Volney, C. F., *A View of the Soil and Climate of the United States of America; with supplementary remarks*, etc. Translated, with occasional remarks, by C. B. Brown. Philadelphia, 1804.

von Holst, Dr. H., *John C. Calhoun (American Statesmen Series).* Boston, 1882 (1895).

Vreeland, Helen Kearny. See Austin, Mary S.

Wade, John Donald, *Augustus Baldwin Longstreet; a study of the development of culture in the South.* New York, 1924.

Wakefield, Priscilla, *Excursions in North America, described in letters from a gentleman and his young companion, to their friends in England.* The third edition, improved. London, 1819.

Wakeley, Rev. Joseph B. (editor), *Reminiscences, Historical and Biographical, of Sixty-Four Years in the Ministry.* By Rev. Henry Boehm, Bishop Asbury's Traveling Companion, and Executor of his Last Will and Testament. New York, 1865.

Waldron, William Watson, *Huguenots of Westchester and the Parish of Fordham.* New York, 1864.

Waln, Robert, J., *Life of the Marquis de Lafayette; major general in the service of the United States of America, in the War of the Revolution.* Third edition. Philadelphia, 1826.

Wandell, Samuel H., and Minnigerode, Meade, *Aaron Burr.* Two volumes. New York, 1925.

Washington, H. A. (editor), *The Writings of Thomas Jefferson.* Nine volumes. New York, 1853-54.

Waterman, William Randall, *Frances Wright.* New York, 1924.

Watson, Winslow C. (editor), *Men and Times of the Revolution; or, Memoirs of Elkanah Watson.* . . . Second edition. New York, 1856.

Waylen, Rev. Edward, *Ecclesiastical Reminiscences of the United States.* New York, 1846.

Weeden, William B., *Economic and Social History of New England, 1620-1789.* Two volumes. Boston and New York, 1891.

Weeden, William B., "Ideal Newport in the Eighteenth Century," *Proceedings of the American Antiquarian Society,* XVIII, new series, pp. 106-117.

Weeks, Stephen B., "Libraries and Literature in North Carolina in the Eighteenth Century," *Annual Report of the American Historical Association for 1895.*

Weiss, Charles, *History of the French Protestant Refugees.* Translated by Frederick Hardman. Two volumes. New York, 1854.

Weld, Isaac, Jr., *Travels through the states of North America, and the provinces of Upper and Lower Canada, during the years 1795, 1796, and 1797.* Fourth edition. London, 1800.

Wendell, Barrett, *A Literary History of America.* Fourth edition. New York, 1905.

Werlein, Mrs. Philip, *The Wrought Iron Railings of Le Vieux Carré,* New Orleans, n.d. (in Howard Memorial Library).

Wertenbaker, Thomas J., *Patrician and Plebian in Virginia, or the Origin and Development of the Social Classes of the Old Dominion.* Charlottesville, Virginia, 1910.

Wertenbaker, Thomas J., *Virginia under the Stuarts, 1607-1688.* Princeton, New Jersey, 1914.

Weston, James A., *Historic Doubts as to the Execution of Marshal Ney with numerous Illustrations.* New York, 1895.

Wharton, Anne Hollingsworth, *Salons Colonial and Republican.* Philadelphia, 1900.

Whitehead, Russell F., "The Old and the New South; a consideration of Architecture in the Southern States," *The Architectural Record,* XXX, July, 1911, pp. 1-56.

Whitford, R. C., "Madame de Staël's Literary Reputation in America," *Modern Language Notes,* XXXIII, 1918, pp. 476-80.
Wied-Neuwied, Le Prince Maximilien de, *Voyage dans l'intérieur de l'Amérique du Nord.* Three volumes. Paris, 1840.
Wightman, William M., *Life of William Capers, D.D., one of the bishops of the Methodist Episcopal Church, South; including an autobiography.* Nashville, Tennessee, 1858.
The William and Mary Quarterly Historical Magazine, 1892——.
Williamson, Hugh, *The History of North Carolina.* Two volumes. Philadelphia, 1812.
Willis, Eola, *The Charleston Stage in the XVIII Century with social settings of the time.* Columbia, 1924.
Willis, N. P., *Famous Persons and Places.* New York, 1854.
Willis, N. P., *Hurry-graphs; or, sketches of scenery, celebrities and society, taken from life.* New York, 1851.
Willis, N. P., *Life, Here and There; or sketches of society and adventure at far-apart times and places.* Auburn and Rochester, 1853.
Willis, N. P., *Pencillings by the Way; written during some years of residence and travel in Europe.* Auburn and Rochester, 1854.
Willis, N. P., *People I Have Met; or, pictures of society and people of mark, drawn under a thin veil of fiction.* New York, 1850.
Willis, N. P., *The Rag-Bag, a collection of ephemera.* New York, 1855.
Williston, Walker, *A History of the Congregational Churches in the United States (American Church History Series).* New York, 1894.
Winsor, Justin (editor), *Narrative and Critical History of America,* Volume V. Boston and New York, 1887.
(Winsor, Justin, editor), *The Prince Library, A catalogue of the collection of books and manuscripts which formerly belonged to the Reverend Thomas Prince . . . now deposited in the Public Library of the City of Boston.* Boston, 1870.
Woodberry, George Edward, *Ralph Waldo Emerson (English Men of Letters Series).* New York, 1907.
Woolley, Mary E., "The Development of the Love of Romantic Scenery in America," *American Historical Review,* III, pp. 56-66.
Wright, Thomas Goddard, *Literary Culture in Early New-England, 1620-1730.* Edited by his wife. New York, 1920.
Young, Edward, *Special Report on the Customs-Tariff Legislation of the United States, with appendixes.* Washington, 1874.

PERIODICALS

The American Annual Register; from the years 1825-26—1832-33, or the 50th-57th years of American Independence.
The American Eclectic. 1841-42.
The American Magazine. 1787-1788.
The American Monthly Magazine, new series. 1836-1838.
The American Monthly Magazine and Critical Review. 1817-1819.
The American Monthly Review. 1832-1833.
The American Museum. 1787-1792.
The American Museum, or, Annual Register of Fugitive Pieces, Ancient and Modern. 1798.
The American Pioneer. 1842-3.

The American Protestant Magazine. 1845-47.
The American Quarterly Observer. 1833-1834.
The American Quarterly Register. 1829-1842.
The American Quarterly Register and Magazine. 1848.
The American Quarterly Review. 1827-1837.
The American Register, or, General Repository of History, Politics, and Science. 1806-1810.
The American Register, or, Summary Review of History, Politics and Literature. 1817.
The American Review and Literary Journal. 1801-02.
The American Review: a Whig Journal, devoted to Politics and Literature. 1845-48.
The American Review of History and Politics, and General Repository of Literature and State Papers. 1811-12.
L'Ami des Lois & Journal du Soir. 1810-1819.
Analectic Magazine. 1813-1819.
Analectic Magazine, new series. 1820.
The Arminian Magazine; consisting of Extracts and Original Treatises on General Redemption. 1790.
Arthur's Ladies Magazine of Literature, Fashion and the Fine Arts. 1844.
The Balance and Columbian Repository, 1802-1807.
Baltimore Weekly Magazine. 1800-1801.
The Boston Miscellany of Literature and Fashion. 1842.
The Boston News-Letter (title varies). 1704-1735.
The Boston Quarterly Review. 1838-1842.
The Boston Weekly Messenger, a Journal of Politics, Agriculture, Literature and Miscellaneous Intelligence. 1816-1818.
The Broadway Journal. 1845.
Brother Jonathan. 1842.
Brownson's Quarterly Review. 1844-1848.
Campbell's Foreign Monthly Magazine; or, Select Miscellany of the Periodical Literature of Great Britain. 1842-43.
The Casket and Philadelphia Monthly Magazine. 1827.
(Atkinson's) *Casket or Gems of Literature, Wit and Sentiment.* 1838.
The Christian Disciple and Theological Review. 1819-1823.
The Christian Examiner and Theological Review. 1824-48.
The Christian Review. 1836-48.
The Christian Spectator, conducted by an Association of Gentlemen. 1819-28.
La Chronique. Journal Politique et Littéraire. 1847-48.
The Church Review and Ecclesiastical Register. 1848.
The Columbian Lady's and Gentleman's Magazine, embracing Literature in every department, etc. 1844-48.
The Columbian Magazine or Monthly Miscellany. 1786-1790.
The Columbian Phenix, and Boston Review. 1800.
The Critic. A Weekly Review of Literature, Fine Arts and the Drama. 1828-29.
The Daguerreotype. 1847-1848.
(De Bow's) *Commercial Review.* 1846-48.
The Democratic Expositor and United States Journal from the Country. 1845-46.
Democratic Review. See *The United States Magazine.*

The Dial: a Magazine for Literature, Philosophy and Religion. 1840-44.
The Diamond. 1840-42.
Dollar Magazine. See Holden's Dollar Magazine.
The Eclectic Magazine of Foreign Literature, Science and Art. 1844-48.
The Edenton Intelligencer. 1788.
The Emporium of Arts and Sciences. 1812-13.
The Episcopal Watchman. 1827-31.
The Evergreen, or Church-Offering for all Seasons; a Repository of Religious, Literary and Entertaining Knowledge of the Christian Family. 1844-48.
The Examiner; containing Political Essays on the Most Important Events of the Time; Public Laws and Official Documents. 1813-14.
The Fayetteville Gazette. 1792-93.
The General Repository and Review. 1812-13.
The Gentleman's Magazine. 1837-40.
The Guardian: a Family Magazine devoted to the Course of Female Education on Christian principles. 1848.
Hall's Wilmington Gazette. 1797-99.
The Harbinger, devoted to social and political progress. 1845-47.
The Hesperian, or, Western Monthly Magazine, 1838-39.
Holden's Dollar Magazine. 1848.
The Knickerbocker; or, New York Monthly Magazine. 1833-48.
The Ladies' Companion, a Monthly Magazine embracing every department of literature. 1838-43.
The Ladies' Repository, and Gatherings of the West. A monthly periodical devoted to literature and religion. 1841-44.
The Literary and Scientific Repository and Critical Review. 1820-1821.
(Brown's) Literary Magazine and American Register. 1803-7.
The Literary World. A Gazette for Authors, Readers and Publishers. 1847-48.
Littel's Living Age. 1844-1848.
The Magnolia, or, Southern Appalachian. A Literary Magazine and Monthly Review. 1842-1843.
The Massachusetts Quarterly Review. 1848.
The Monthly Anthology and Boston Review, containing sketches and reports of Philosophy, Religion, Arts, and Manners. 1803-6.
The Monthly Rose, a periodical conducted by the present and former members of the Albany Female Academy. 1845.
The National Magazine, or, Ladies' Companion, 1830-31.
The National Register, a Weekly Paper. 1818-1820.
The New England Magazine. 1843-48.
The New Mirror of Literature, Amusement, and Intelligence. 1843-44.
The New World. A Weekly Family Journal of Popular Literature, Science, Art, and News. 1847-48.
The New York Mirror. A Weekly Journal devoted to Literature and the Fine Arts. 1834-5; 1837-42.
The New York Review and Atheneum Magazine. 1825.
The New York Review and Quarterly Church Journal. 1837-1842.
The Newbern Gazette. 1798-1800.
The North American Magazine. 1833.
The North American Review. 1815-1848.
The North Carolina Chronicle, or Fayetteville Gazette. 1790-91.

(Martin's) *North Carolina Gazette.* 1753-1775, 1787-97.
The North Carolina Journal. 1792-94, 1799-1802.
The Parterre. A Weekly Magazine. 1817.
The Patriot. 1826.
The Philadelphia Register and National Recorder. 1819-20.
The Philadelphia Repository and Weekly Register. 1800.
The Polyanthus. 1805-07, 1812.
The Portfolio. 1801-27.
The Portico: a Repository of Science and Literature. 1816; 1817.
The Quarterly Christian Spectator. 1829-38.
Revue Louisianaise. 1846-47.
The Select Journal of Foreign Periodical Literature. 1833-4.
The Southern Lady's Companion, a monthly periodical devoted to literature and religion. 1848.
The Southern Literary Journal and Monthly Magazine. 1835-6.
The Southern Literary Messenger. 1834-48.
The Southern Quarterly Review. 1842-48.
The Southern Review. 1828-32.
The Southern Rose. 1836-7.
The Southwestern Journal. 1837.
The State Gazette of North-Carolina. 1789.
The United States Magazine and Democratic Review (referred to as *The Democratic Review*). 1837-48.
The Virginia Gazette. 1738.
The Western Friend, devoted to religion, morality, literature, general news, and markets. 1847-8.
The Western Monthly Review. 1827-30.
The Wilmington Chronicle; and North Carolina Weekly Advertiser. 1795-96.

NOTE ON MAGAZINES

The years given with each entry are the years within which I have been able to consult, or to have consulted, copies of the publication in question, and are not necessarily the years during which the magazine was published. To attempt an accurate statement of the publication dates of American magazines is well-nigh impossible. It is also to be noted that the title of any particular periodical will vary, sometimes from volume to volume and occasionally from issue to issue. I have selected what seems to be the most characteristic title in each instance. I have not indicated where particular numbers of a given periodical are missing from files consulted by me, or by others for me, in the above list, for I do not see that these minor bibliographical details are necessary for the happiness of the reader.

Index

(Only the more important proper names and references are listed.)